Zagorje
p68
Zagreb
p38
Slavonia
p81
Kvarner
p131
Istria
p95
Northern Dalmatia
p167
Split & Central Dalmatia
p196
Dubrovnik & Southern Dalmatia
p242

VITAL PRACTICAL INFORMATION TO HELP YOU HAVE A SMOOTH TRIP

THIS EDITION WRITTEN AND RESEARCHED BY

Anja Mutić and Vesna Maric

Croatia's Brand of Tourism

Despite its reputation as Europe's vacation hot spot, Croatia hasn't given in to mass tourism. The 'Mediterranean As It Once Was' motto of Croatia's tourist board may be overblown in popular destinations where development has taken a firm hold, but pockets of authentic culture can be found and there's still plenty to discover off the grid. This country in transition, on the brink between Mitteleuropa and Mediterranean, offers good news for visitors on all budgets: Croatia is as diverse as its landscapes. Some of the more popular Adriatic locales come with hefty price tags in the summer months, while continental Croatia costs a fraction of what you'll pay on the coast. The chic and trendy outposts may make you forget that a civil war raged through Croatia in the 1990s. The way in which the country has bounced back is a sign of its people's resilience – people who are remarkable hosts once you cross the tourist–local barrier.

Coastal Croatia

There's a buzz and an undeniable star appeal to Croatia's coast. You'll get glitz and glamour in Dubrovnik and Hvar, where night action and celebrity-spotting, designer cocktail in hand, is de rigueur, and fancy yachts dock in droves. For those wanting peace and quiet, hideaways aplenty wait to

Croatia's rare blend of glamour and authenticity make it Europe's 'it' destination, where beaches vie for attention with cultural treasures, ancient architecture and time-tested folk traditions.

(left) Hvar (p230)
(below) Dubrovnik (p242)

be discovered, including remote lighthouse islets, fetching fishing villages, secluded coves and Robinson-Crusoe-style atolls. Families flock to the string of safe beaches, and there are activities galore for all ages.

Beauty on the Inside: Continental Croatia

Everyone visits the nearly 2000km-long coastline, with over 1000 islands, but most people skip the unsung beauties of inland Croatia. Enjoy a slice of pristine farmland in one of the rural hotels or 'agro-tourisms', roam rugged wilderness or get active – hike, bike, paraglide, sail, raft and canoe. Zagreb may play second fiddle to nearby Vienna, but this pocket-sized capital has an attractive cafe life, a new contemporary art museum, ancient attractions and a jam-packed roster of festivals and events.

Foodie-Friendly Croatia

Croatia has been slowly crawling its way up to the top of Europe's culinary rankings. Its chief assets are locally sourced, prime-quality ingredients from the land and sea, creatively prepared by celeb chefs or cooked up home-style in family-run taverns. Some of these gastronomic havens require a trek, but the minute you taste the food you'll realise the effort was worth it. The wine regions of Croatia are as burgeoning as the country itself, and its olive oils (particularly those of Istria) are getting top awards.

› Croatia

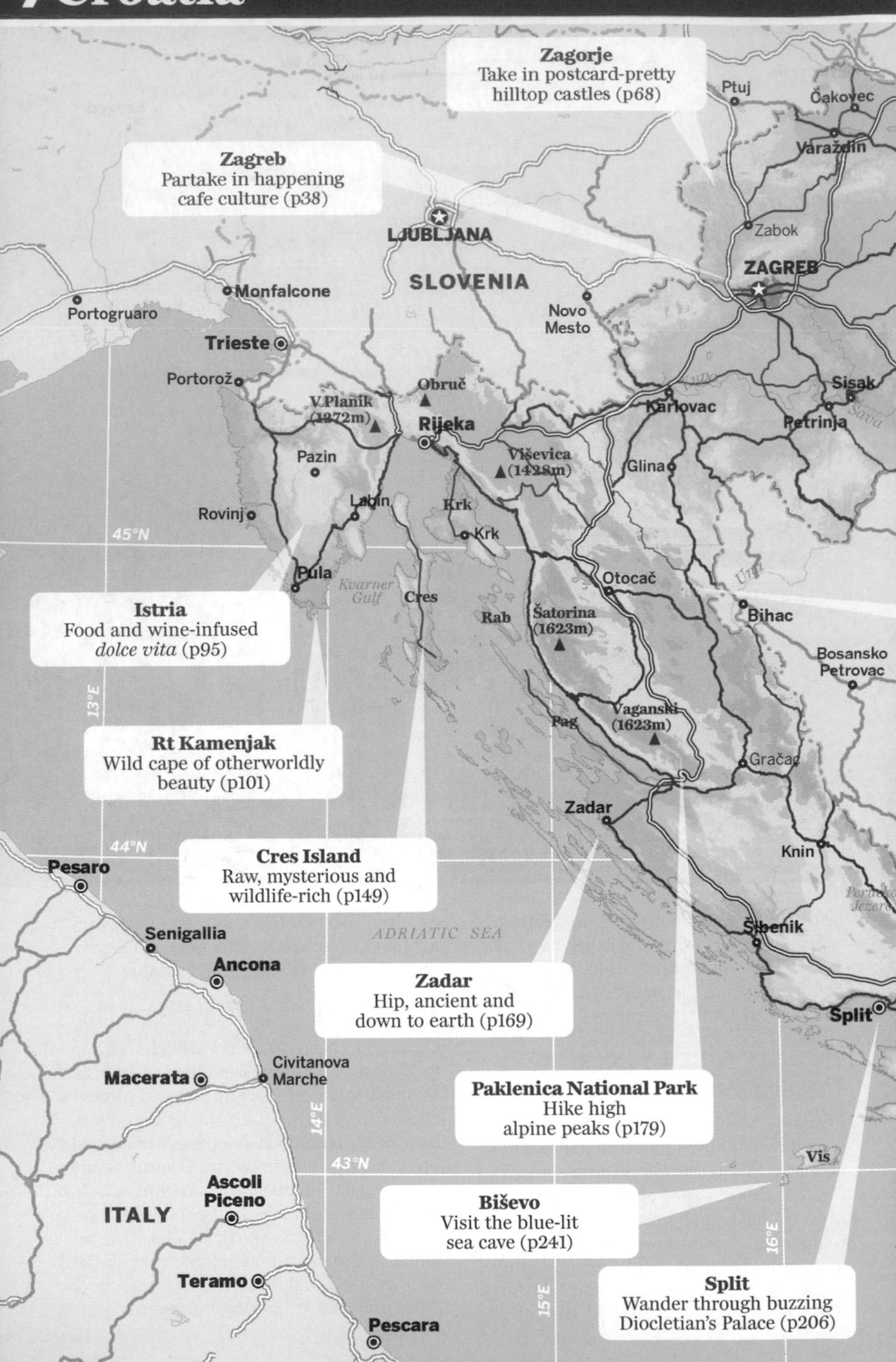

Zagorje
Take in postcard-pretty hilltop castles (p68)
Zagreb
Partake in happening cafe culture (p38)
Istria
Food and wine-infused *dolce vita* (p95)
Rt Kamenjak
Wild cape of otherworldly beauty (p101)
Cres Island
Raw, mysterious and wildlife-rich (p149)
Zadar
Hip, ancient and down to earth (p169)
Paklenica National Park
Hike high alpine peaks (p179)
Biševo
Visit the blue-lit sea cave (p241)
Split
Wander through buzzing Diocletian's Palace (p206)
Ptuj
Čakovec
Varaždin
Zabok
ZAGREB
LJUBLJANA
SLOVENIA
Monfalcone
Portogruaro
Trieste
Portorož
Novo Mesto
Obruč
V.Planik (1272m)
Rijeka
Karlovac
Sisak
Petrinja
Sava
Pazin
Višević (1428m)
Glina
Labin
Krk
Krk
Rovinj
45°N
Pula
Kvarner Gulf
Cres
Otočac
Rab
Šatorina (1623m)
Bihac
Bosansko Petrovac
13°E
Pag
Vaganski (1623m)
Gračac
Zadar
44°N
Pesaro
Knin
Šibenik
Senigallia
ADRIATIC SEA
Ancona
Split
Civitanova Marche
Macerata
14°E
43°N
Vis
Ascoli Piceno
ITALY
16°E
Teramo
15°E
Pescara

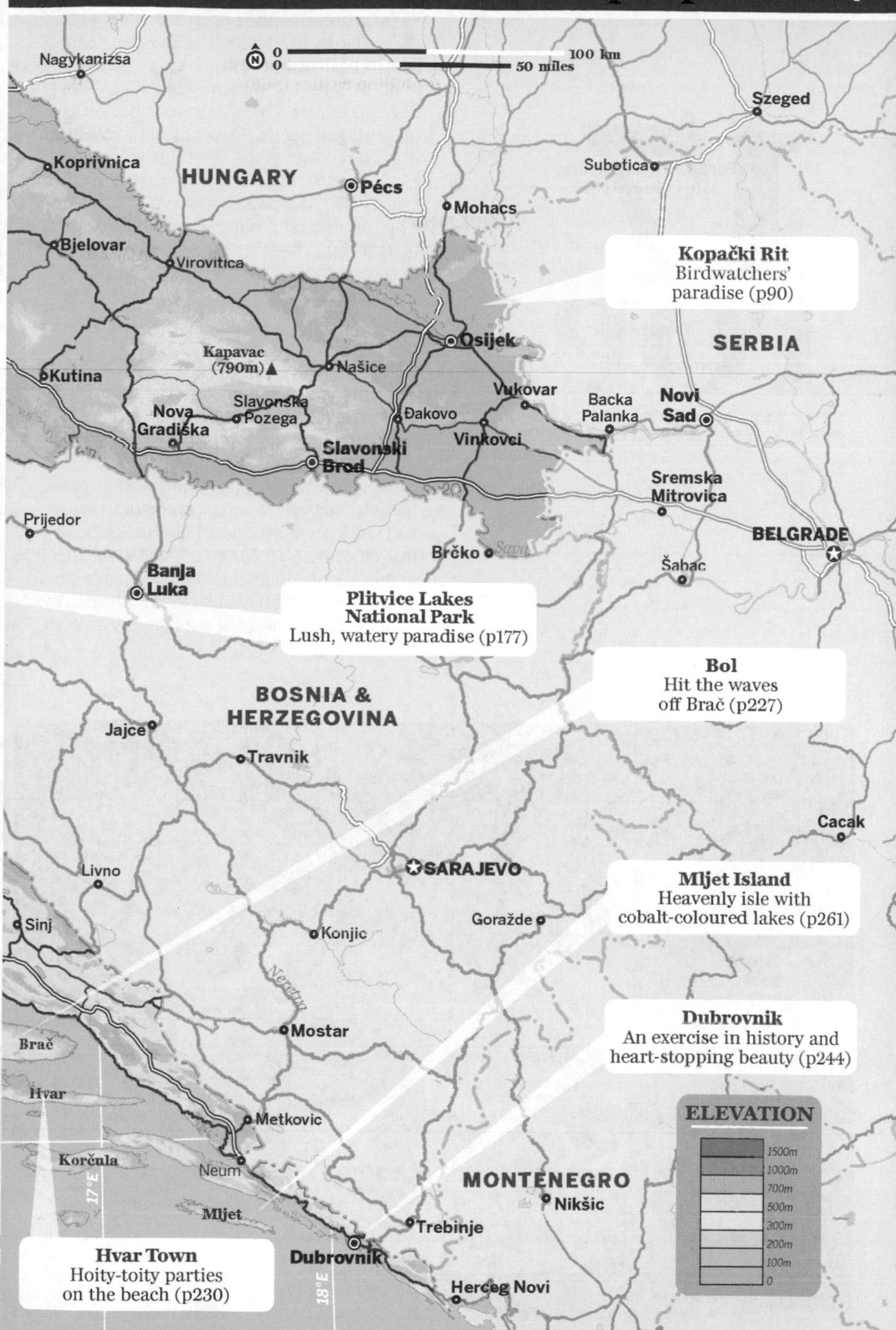
0 100 km
0 50 miles
Nagykanizsa
Szeged
Koprivnica
HUNGARY
Pécs
Subotica
Mohacs
Bjelovar
Virovitica
Kopački Rit
Birdwatchers' paradise (p90)
Osijek
SERBIA
Kapavac (790m)
Našice
Kutina
Vukovar
Backa Palanka
Novi Sad
Nova Gradiška
Slavonska Pozega
Đakovo
Vinkovci
Slavonski Brod
Sremska Mitrovica
Prijedor
BELGRADE
Brčko
Sava
Šabac
Banja Luka
Plitvice Lakes National Park
Lush, watery paradise (p177)
Bol
Hit the waves off Brač (p227)
BOSNIA & HERZEGOVINA
Jajce
Travnik
Cacak
Livno
SARAJEVO
Mljet Island
Heavenly isle with cobalt-coloured lakes (p261)
Sinj
Goražde
Konjic
Neretva
Mostar
Dubrovnik
An exercise in history and heart-stopping beauty (p244)
Brač
Hvar
ELEVATION
Metkovic
1500m
1000m
700m
500m
300m
200m
100m
0
Korčula
Neum
MONTENEGRO
17°E
Nikšic
Mljet
Trebinje
Hvar Town
Hoity-toity parties on the beach (p230)
Dubrovnik
18°E
Herceg Novi

17 TOP EXPERIENCES

Plitvice Paradise

1 A turquoise ribbon of crystal water and gushing waterfalls in the forested heart of continental Croatia, Plitvice Lakes National Park (p177) is an awesome sight. There are dozens of lakes – from 4km-long Kozjak to reed-fringed ponds – all in an incredible hue that's a product of the karst terrain. Travertine expanses covered with mossy plants divide the lakes, while boardwalks allow you to step right over this exquisite water world. Follow hiking trails through beech, spruce, fir and pine trees to escape the crowds on the lake shore.

All That Is Dubrovnik

2 Croatia's most popular attraction, Dubrovnik (p244) is a Unesco World Heritage Site for good reason. This immense walled city was relentlessly shelled during Croatia's 1990s Homeland War. Now, its mighty walls, monasteries, medieval churches, graceful squares and fascinating residential quarters all look magnificent again. For an unrivalled perspective of this Adriatic pearl, first take the cable car up to Mount Srđ, then get up close to the city by walking Dubrovnik's walls, as history unfolds from the battlements.

1

2

JEAN-PIERRE LESCOURRET / GETTY IMAGES ©

Coffee Fix in Zagreb

3 Elevated to the status of ritual, having coffee in one of Zagreb's outdoor cafes (p58) is a must, involving hours of people-watching, gossiping and soul-searching, unhurried by waiters. To experience the truly European and vibrant cafe culture, grab a table along the pedestrian cobbled Tkalčićeva, with its endless street-side cafes, or one of the pavement tables on Trg Petra Preradovića or Bogovićeva. Don't miss the Saturday morning *špica*, the coffee-drinking and people-watching ritual in the city centre that forms the peak of Zagreb's weekly social calendar.

Marvel at Mljet

4 Cloaked in dense pine forests, pristine Mljet (p261) is an island paradise. Legend has it that Odysseus was marooned here for seven years, and it's easy to appreciate why he'd take his time leaving. The entire western section is a national park, where you'll find two sublime, cobalt-coloured lakes, an island monastery and the sleepy little port of Pomena, which is as pretty as a picture. Don't neglect eastern Mljet, home to great cove beaches and the gastronomic heaven that is Stermasi restaurant.

3

RICHARD I'ANSON / GETTY IMAGES ©

4

MARIANNA SULIC / GETTY IMAGES ©

RACHEL LEWIS / GETTY IMAGES ©

ANDREW BURKE / GETTY IMAGES ©

RUDOLF ABRAHAM / ALAMY ©

Hit the Waves in Bol

5 Bol (p227), on the southern coast of Brač Island, is home to the illustrious Zlatni Rat beach, with its tongue-like shape and golden pebbles. The town is a favourite among windsurfers: the channel between the islands of Brač and Hvar provides ideal wind conditions, thanks to the westerly *maestral* that typically blows between May and late September. The wind picks up slowly in the morning, an excellent time for beginners to hit the waves. By afternoon, the winds are very strong, perfect for those looking to get a real-deal adrenalin kick.

Zlatni Rat beach (p227)

Party-Happy Hvar

6 Come high summer, there's no better place to get your groove on than Hvar Town (p230). Gorgeous tanned people descend from their yachts in droves for round-the-clock fun on this glam isle. With beach parties as the sun drops below the horizon far out in the Adriatic, designer cocktails sipped seaside to fresh house tunes spun by DJs, and full-moon beach parties, Hvar caters to a well-dressed, party-happy crowd. Plus there's Hvar beyond the party scene, with its gorgeous interior largely uncharted by tourist crowds.

Carpe Diem nightclub, Hvar (p234)

Wine & Dine in Istria

7 *La dolce vita* reigns supreme in Istria (p95), Croatia's top foodie destination. The seafood, truffles, wild asparagus and a rare breed of Istrian beef called *boškarin* all stand out, as do myriad regional specialities and award-winning olive oils and wines by local small producers. Slow food is a hit here: you can sample the ritual in upmarket restaurants in seafront towns, in traditional family-run taverns in medieval hilltop villages, and in converted olive mills high up in the hills of the peninsula's verdant interior.

Istrian *pršut* (prosciutto) and cheeses

LONELY PLANET / GETTY IMAGES ©

MARTIN MOOS / GETTY IMAGES ©

BORUT FURLAN / GETTY IMAGES ©

Pastries & Ice Cream

8 Croatia is a superior spot to indulge your sweet tooth. You absolutely must not miss the *slastičarna*s (pastry shops) found in towns and villages across the country. Indulge in the Austrian-style creamy cakes, the very local *kremšnites* (custard pies) and home-made strudels. In the summertime, head straight for the ice-cream counters, which typically showcase 10 to 20 flavours of fresh ice cream made right on the premises. Croatian *sladoled* (ice cream) gives Italian gelato a run for its money.

Hike & Climb Paklenica

9 It's some sight. The extraordinary Paklenica National Park (p179) is best viewed from the northern coast of Pag Island, giving you an appreciation of how steeply the Velebit mountains rear up from the shore. Two great canyons cut into these majestic mountains, forming a natural trail for hikers up to the high alpine peaks of Vaganski vrh (1757m) and Babin vrh (1741m). For those craving more adventure, Paklenica is also Croatia's premier rock-climbing centre, with hundreds of spectacular routes criss-crossing the park.

Blue Magic on Biševo

10 Of the numerous caves around the remote limestone island of Biševo (p241), the Blue Grotto (Modra Špilja) is the most spectacular. The light show produced by this rare natural phenomenon will amaze you. On a clear morning, the sun's rays penetrate through an underwater hole in this coastal cave, bathing the interior in a mesmerising silvery-blue light. Beneath the turquoise water, rocks glimmer silver and pink, creating an unearthly effect. Swimming inside is a surreal must-have experience – worth a trip to this far-out island.

The Soul of Split

11 Experience life as it's been lived for thousands of years in Diocletian's Palace (p197), one of the world's most imposing Roman ruins. The maze-like streets of this buzzing quarter, the living heart and soul of Split, are chock-full of bars, shops and restaurants. Getting lost in the labyrinth of narrow streets, passageways and courtyards is one of Croatia's most enchanting experiences – and you'll always find your way out easily. Escape the palace walls for a drink on the marble-paved, palm-fringed Riva along the water's edge. Cathedral of St Domnius (p201), Diocletian's Palace

Ferry Fun in the Adriatic

12 From short jaunts between nearby islands to overnight rides along the length of the Croatian coast, sea travel (p328) is a great and inexpensive way to see the Croatian side of the Adriatic. Take in the stunning coastline as you whiz past some of the country's 1244 islands, including the popular Hvar and Brač and more offbeat options such as Vis. If you have cash to splash, see the islands in style by chartering a sailboat, propelled by winds and sea currents.

11

RICHARD NEŠESKY / GETTY IMAGES ©

12

TIM HUGHES / GETTY IMAGES ©

De-stress in Cres

13 The Tramuntana region in northern Cres has a wild, raw beauty that's intoxicating. Visit the griffon vulture centre in Beli (p152) and learn all about these endangered raptors. Then explore the labyrinth of eco-trails that take you through virgin old-growth forests and abandoned villages, where you almost expect an elf to jump out from behind one of the giant oak trees. Back in Beli, head to Pansion Tramontana (p153) for a robust, hearty dinner of local lamb and delicious leafy salad, washed down with a glass of Dalmatian wine. Beli (p152), Cres Island

Story-Book Castles of Zagorje

14 Don't miss the postcard-perfect medieval castles of Zagorje. Although it dates to 1334, Trakošćan Castle (p76) was restored in the neo-Gothic style. Learn about Croatian aristocracy in its museum and wander the 215-acre castle grounds landscaped into a romantic English-style park with exotic trees and an artificial lake. The hilltop castle of Veliki Tabor (p79) is worth it for its atmospheric interiors that now house a museum, the pentagonal exterior of its towers and turrets, and the bucolic landscapes that surround it. Veliki Tabor Castle (p79)

13

14

EMANUELE CICCOMARTINO / GETTY IMAGES ©

ALEN GUROVIC / ALAMY ©

ERIN BABNIK / ALAMY ©

Discover Zadar

15 Fast becoming one of Croatia's top destinations, the city of Zadar (p169) boasts history and culture in spades yet retains a down-to-earth ambience. Its must-see sights include two extraordinary artistic installations created by architect Nikola Bašić: the mesmerising Sea Organ and the astonishing Sun Salutation. Zadar's musical festivals are equally compelling. Held on the nearby island of Murter, the Garden Festival offers a great opportunity to catch some of the globe's most creative electronic talent. Sun Salutation (p169), Zadar

Kopački Rit – A Wetland Wonder

16 A flood plain of the Danube and Drava Rivers, Kopački Rit (p90) – part of a brand-new Unesco biosphere reserve – offers breathtaking scenery and some of Europe's best birdwatching. Join a boat trip and keep your eyes peeled for white-tailed and imperial eagles, black storks, purple herons and woodpeckers – just some of the nearly 300 species recorded here. Mammals such as red deer and wild boar are common, too. Explore a flooded forest by canoe, hike the nature trails or saddle up and ride a horse.

Go Wild in Kamenjak

17 The wild rugged beauty and end-of-the-world vibe of this small peninsula just south of Pula have earned it cult status among Croatian beach-goers. An undeveloped protected nature reserve, Kamenjak (p101), showcases a carpet of heath plants, shrubs and wildflowers, criss-crossed by a maze of dirt tracks. It's fringed by a string of pebble bays and secluded rocky beaches, surrounded by crystalline blue-green sea. It gets busy in summer, but there's always an empty beach to escape to, plus a fun beach bar for socialising.

need to know

Currency
» Kuna (KN)

Language
» Croatian

When to Go?

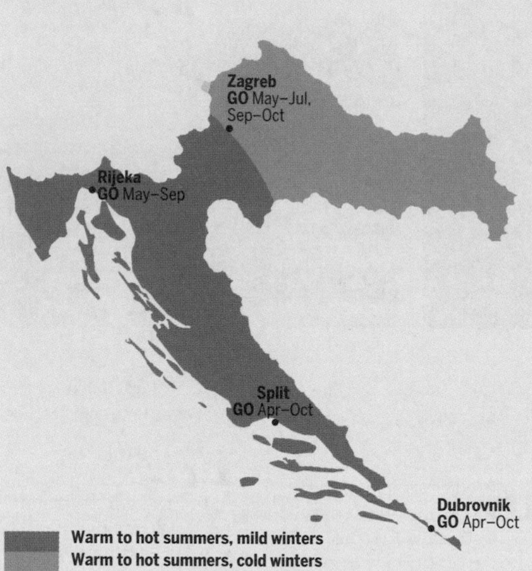

High Season
(Jul & Aug)

» Peak season brings the best weather. Hvar Island gets the most sun, followed by Split, Korčula Island and Dubrovnik.

» Prices are at their highest and coastal destinations at their busiest.

Shoulder
(May–Jun & Sep)

» The coast is gorgeous, the Adriatic is warm enough for swimming, the crowds are sparse and prices are lower.

» In spring and early summer, the steady *maestral* wind makes sailing great.

Low Season
(Oct–Apr)

» Winters in continental Croatia are cold and prices are low.

» Southeasterly winds produce heavy cloud cover; northeasterlies bring powerful gusts of dry air and blow away clouds.

Your Daily Budget

Budget less than
450KN

» Private accommodation; dorm beds around 150KN

» Plenty of markets for self-caterers

» Cheap taverns, pizza and ice-cream

» Lots of free activities

Midrange
450–900KN

» Double room in a midrange hotel

» Meals in decent restaurants and drinks at night

» A tour or two, plus activities

Top end over
900KN

» Small boutique hotels and four-star properties

» Meals in top-tier restaurants

» Spa treatments

» Tours, trips and car rental

Money

» ATMs widely available. Credit cards accepted in most hotels and restaurants. Smaller restaurants, shops and private accommodation owners only take cash.

Visas

» Generally not required for stays of up to 90 days. Some nationalities, such as South Africans, do need them.

Mobile Phones

» Users with unlocked phones can buy a local SIM card, which are easy to find. Otherwise, you'll be roaming.

Driving

» Drive on the right; steering wheel is on the left side of the car.

Websites

» **Croatian National Tourist Board** (www.croatia.hr) The best starting point to plan your holiday.

» **Adriatica.net** (www.adriatica.net) Books rooms, apartments, hotels and lighthouses all along the coast.

» **Like Croatia** (www.likecroatia.hr) An information-packed online guide to Croatia.

» **Taste of Croatia** (www.tasteofcroatia.org) Excellent, informative website.

» **Lonely Planet.com** (www.lonelyplanet.com/croatia) Destination information, hotel bookings, traveller forum and more.

Exchange Rates

Australia	A$1	6.02KN
Canada	CA$1	5.83KN
Europe	€1	7.54KN
Japan	100Y	0.07KN
New Zealand	NZ$1	4.74KN
UK	UK£	9.23KN
US	A$1	5.78KN

For current exchange rates, see www.xe.com.

Important Numbers

To call from outside Croatia, dial your international access code, then the Croatian country code, the area code (without the initial zero) and the local number.

Roadside assistance	☎1987
Country code	☎385
International access code	☎00
International directory assistance	☎11802
Local directory assistance	☎11880
General information	☎18981

Arriving in Croatia

Zagreb Airport

» **Buses to the centre** Timed around plane arrivals, from 5am till 8pm

» **Taxis to the centre** 110KN to 300KN; around 20 minutes to the city

Split Airport

» **Buses to the centre** Timed around plane arrivals

» **Taxis to the centre** 250KN to 290KN; around 30 minutes to the city

Private Accommodation in Croatia

Croatia's hotels are typically overpriced, especially in the high summer season along the coastline. Staying in private accommodation is the best way to save considerable cash and also have a glimpse at Croatia's own brand of hospitality. Many of the owners treat their guests like long-lost friends. Some offer the option of eating with them, which is a great way to get to know the culture.

Finding the right private room or apartment takes a little effort, though. It's best to research your options online or by word of mouth before going. If you prefer on-the-fly travel, once you've arrived in your destination, visit a handful of properties through a travel agency before booking.

Note that in high season many private accommodation owners impose a surcharge for stays of under three or four nights.

what's new

For this new edition of Croatia, our authors have hunted down the fresh, the transformed, the hot and the happening. These are some of our favourites. For up-to-the-minute recommendations, see lonelyplanet.com/croatia.

Museum of Broken Relationships, Zagreb

1 Pine over poignant, often funny remains of failed relationships at Zagreb's quirkiest museum, with exhibits on display donated from all corners of the globe (p39).

Lauba, Zagreb

2 Since it opened inside a former warehouse, this edgy gallery quickly became a creative hub of Croatia's capital, showcasing contemporary art and various events (p48).

Hotel Lone, Rovinj

3 Croatia's first design hotel is a dazzling beauty that looms above Lone bay, a stroll from Rovinj's old town, with gorgeous interiors done up by Croatia's starchitects, 3LHD (p109).

Vela Vrata, Buzet

4 Base yourself in this brand-new boutique hideaway on the hilltop of Buzet's old town, and use it as a jump-off point for forays into Istria's pretty interior (p126).

Art Hotel Kalelarga, Zadar

5 A beautiful designer hotel in the middle of ancient Zadar, with an emphasis on the elegant, minimal and extra classy. A wonderful new place to live it up (p173).

Tisno, Northern Dalmatia

6 The new location for the famous and fantastic Garden Festival (p173), with a private beach, luxury camping and fab apartments, and so many partying options you won't know which to choose.

Terraneo, Šibenik

7 This brand-new festival features top international and local artists and promises to become *the* music event in Croatia. Located in a disused military barracks, and close to the beach, it's a must-do (p190).

Goli + Bosi, Split

8 Split's new design hostel offers lodging that's just the right fit for flashpackers, at the heart of town and a stroll from the seafront (p208).

Oyster & Sushi Bar Bota Šare, Dubrovnik

9 A shot in the arm of Dubrovnik's Old Town dining scene, this is a top-quality yet affordable place to try out something truly new – Japanese cuisine with Croatian ingredients (p256).

Homeland War Museum, Dubrovnik

10 Set inside a Napoleonic fort that overlooks Dubrovnik from the top of a hill, this museum is the place to learn more about Dubrovnik's 1990s wartime hardship (p249).

if you like...

Islands

Croatia's coast is speckled with a multitude of magnificent islands that range from tiny, verdant and unpopulated to massive, arid and buzzing.

Hvar Croatia's most popular island gets the most sun – and the most tourists, thanks to gorgeous glam hub Hvar Town, where people come to party (p230)

Vis Remote, mysterious, off the main trail and off-limits to foreigners for around four decades, Vis has great beaches, adorable seaside towns and top food (p237)

Mljet Long, slender and utterly beguiling, Mljet has a lagoon-like sea lake, an island monastery and superb scenery. It can be covered as a day trip from Dubrovnik (p261)

Cres Blessed with awe-inspiring landscapes, medieval villages and a pretty port capital, Cres is one of Croatia's least touristy islands (p149)

Brač The biggest of the Adriatic islands, Brač sports Croatia's most famous beach, the alluring Zlatni Rat in the pretty town of Bol (p224)

Outdoor Activities

There's plenty for active types to do in Croatia. Start with swimming in the Adriatic and progress to mountain biking, windsurfing, kayaking, climbing, river rafting and more.

Sailing Glide between beautiful Croatian islands on a sailboat (p213), docking at popular destinations like Hvar and exploring remote islands such as Kornati and Vis

Hiking The numerous national parks – including Plitvice (p177), Paklenica (p179) and Krka (p194) – are fantastic for hikers, as is the countryside around Zagreb

Diving The islands are prime spots to plunge in and discover marine beauties off Hvar (p230), Brač (p224), Krk (p143) and Kornati (p194), to name a few. Most coastal towns have diving opportunities, too

Cycling Ride through the flat countryside of Baranja (p90), along the Parenzana route (p120) in Istria, or on the Adriatic islands

Naturism Croatia has been a prime spot for going starkers since 1936, when Edward VIII and Wallis Simpson went skinny-dipping along the Rab coast (p97)

Architecture

Croatia has it all – from Roman, baroque, Renaissance and Romanesque to Venetian, Gothic and contemporary architecture.

Dubrovnik Jutting into the big blue of the Adriatic, Dubrovnik is one of Europe's most visually arresting cities, ringed by monumental defensive walls (p242)

Trogir This pocket-sized seaside town is full of well-preserved Romanesque and Renaissance buildings, and has one of the loveliest cathedrals on the coast (p216)

Zadar Compact, relaxed Zadar (p169) hosts an array of architectural styles, from Roman ruins through to contemporary masterpieces the Sea Organ and the Sun Salutation

Diocletian's Palace One of the world's most impressive Roman ruins, these Unesco-protected remains still function today as the living heart of the city: life continues inside this ancient quarter, Split's heart and soul (p197)

Varaždin A showcase of scrupulously restored baroque architecture, Croatia's former capital is awaiting the coveted World Heritage status for its extraordinarily refined old town (p69)

STUART BLACK / GETTY IMAGES ©

» Lubenice (p154)

Beaches

Get your kit off or don the latest designer swimsuit on one of the mwany gorgeous beaches that dot Croatia's coastline and islands.

Pakleni Islands Pine-shaded beaches for naturists and swimsuit wearers alike (p232)

Bačvice Active, fun and bursting at the seams with local life (p205)

Zrće Croatia's summer clubbing capital (p187)

Lubenice Small, secluded, sensational and difficult to reach (p154)

Zlatni Rat A tongue-shaped stretch of golden pebbles packed with beach bodies and activities galore (p227)

Lokrum A rocky beach with crystalline waters, it is heaven for nudies, and always peaceful (p260)

Paradise Beach A sandy stunner with shallow waters and the shade of pine trees (p166)

Stiniva A spectacular and secluded cove of pebble stones flanked by high rocks (p238)

Brela A string of palm-fringed coves with supersoft pebbles (p224)

Rt Kamenjak Thirty virgin kilometres of inlets, coves, pebbles and rocks (p101)

National Parks

Croatia's appeal is grounded in nature – its waterfalls, forests, mountains and the dazzling Adriatic coast. Luckily, much of it is protected – Croatia has eight national parks covering 961 sq km.

Plitvice Lakes This startling natural phenomenon contains sublime waterfalls, turquoise pools and forests (p177)

Krka Explore stupendous waterfalls and visit a remote monastery (p193)

Paklenica Experience nature on a big scale, a couple of canyons and excellent hiking and climbing (p179)

Risnjak It has shady trails through dense forests and meadows rich in wildflowers (p144)

Kornati Islands The isles' stark otherworldly beauty is the ultimate resort-free Adriatic escape (p194)

Mljet Find Mediterranean paradise on this serene, peaceful and unspoilt island (p261)

Brijuni This archipelago off the coast of Istria is the most cultivated of Croatia's national parks (p105)

Food & Drink

Gastronomic culture is on the rise in Croatia. You'll find top-quality homegrown ingredients such as olive oil, truffles, seafood and smoked ham – plus a burgeoning wine scene.

Slow food Check out Croatia's slow-food movement, which is all about promoting local, fresh and seasonal ingredients, and enjoying the ritual of eating (p299)

Olive oil Istria leads the way on the path to Croatia's olive oil perfection. Follow the marked olive oil routes to visit local producers and taste their oils (p301)

Wine Go to Istria for its excellent white *malvazija*, red *teran* and sweet *muškat*. *Dingač* and *postup* from the Pelješac Peninsula are some of Croatia's best. Don't miss the wine roads of Slavonia and Međimurje (p303)

Truffles Be sure to sample the prized fungus that grows in the forests of Istria, where you can even go truffle-hunting during autumn (p126)

month by month

Top Events

1 **Rijeka Carnival** February

2 **Cest is D'Best** June

3 **Motovun Film Festival** July

4 **Garden Festival** July

5 **Terraneo** August

January

As the country goes back to work after the holidays, snow makes roads difficult to tackle on the continent while strong winds on the coast and islands limit the ferry schedule.

Skiing on Sljeme

Hit the downhill slopes right outside Zagreb at Sljeme (p51), the main peak of Mt Medvednica, complete with ski runs, lifts and even a triple chairlift. Skiing is a popular pastime for sporty Croats.

Beat the Crowds on the Coast

If you want to explore Croatia's coastal cities, this is the prime time to save some cash. Many hotels offer discounts of up to 50% at this time.

February

Enjoy scenic snowy hikes on the continent, but still be mindful on the roads. Bura winds blow along the Adriatic, ferries run infrequently and many hotels in coastal towns shut down.

Carnival

For colourful costumes, plenty of dancing and the nonstop revelry of this pre-Lent celebration, head to Rijeka, where Carnival (p136) is the pinnacle of the year's calendar. Zadar and Samobor host colourful Carnival celebrations, too.

Feast of St Blaise, Dubrovnik

On 3 February each year, the streets of Dubrovnik perk up with folk dancing, concerts, food, processions and lots of street action, all happening in honour of the city's patron saint, St Blaise (p252).

March

Days start to get longer and temperatures begin to rise, especially on the seaside. As winter ice melts, it's a great time to catch the waterfalls in Plitvice and Krka. Most action is still indoors.

Zagrebdox

Catch documentary films from around the globe during this annual festival in Zagreb, the international Zagrebdox (p51). Starting in late February and continuing into March, it draws a small crowd of avid doco lovers.

April

Soak up some sunshine and enjoy the solitude on southern islands and the coastline. Continental Croatia is still chilly but trees start to blossom and, as rivers swell with water, rafting and kayaking are tops.

Music Biennale Zagreb

Held in the capital city each April during odd-numbered years since the 1960s, this is Croatia's most high-profile contemporary music event (p52). By 'contemporary', do not read 'pop' – this prestigious fest celebrates modern-day classical music.

Wild Asparagus Harvest, Istria

During early spring, the fields and meadows of inland Istria become dotted with wild asparagus. Do like the locals do and head out to pick some, and then cook up a mean asparagus *fritaja* (omelette).

May

It's sunny and warm on the coast, and you can take a dip in the sea. Hotels are cheaper, too, and crowds have yet to come. Cafe life in Zagreb and Split kicks into full gear.

Subversive Festival

Mingle with Europe's activists and revolutionaries who storm Zagreb for this two-week festival each May (p52). The first week hosts a series of film screenings, while the second week's program includes lectures as well as panels by left-leaning movers and shakers.

Ljeto na Strossu, Zagreb

Kicking off in late May is this ultra-fun summer-long event (p53) that features free outdoor film screenings, concerts by local bands, artsy workshops, best-in-show mongrel dog competitions and other quirky happenings, all along the leafy Strossmayer Promenade.

Open Wine Cellar Day, Istria

On the last Sunday in May each year, renowned winemakers and winegrowers of Istria open the doors to their wine cellars for free tastings and wine-fuelled merrymaking.

June

Swim in the Adriatic, take in great festivals across the country and enjoy outdoor activities galore. Ferries start their summer schedule, high-season prices haven't kicked in and hotels are still not packed.

INmusic Festival, Zagreb

Get your groove on during this three-day music extravaganza (p52), which takes over leafy Jarun Lake with multiple stages and spots for camping. This is Zagreb's highest-profile music festival; New Order and Franz Ferdinand fronted the 2012 line-up.

Cest is D'Best, Zagreb

For several days in early June, Zagreb's streets come alive with music, dance, theatre, art, sports and other fun events. This street festival (p53) is a much-loved affair, with several stages around the city centre and around 200 international performers.

Eurokaz, Zagreb

Innovative troupes and cutting-edge performers from across the globe bring their acts to Zagreb in the second half of June for the International Festival of New Theatre (p53), which has been showcasing experimental theatre since 1987.

Hartera Festival, Rijeka

To hear some of Croatia's best young rock bands and top indie acts from around Europe, head to this three-day underground fest (p136) in an abandoned paper factory in Rijeka – it's become the highlight of the year for music fans.

July

Tourist season is in full swing: hotels along the coast get booked and beaches are full. Ferries run on their maximum schedule and there are festivals aplenty. A good time to explore Croatia's crowd-free continent.

Garden Festival, Zadar

Party people from around the world have been flocking to the Zadar region for live tunes by big-name electronic music artists at this giant beach party (p173) in Tisno on Murter, kick-started by British producer Nick Colgan and UB40 drummer James Brown, the masterminds behind the Garden bar in Zadar.

Dubrovnik Summer Festival

Kicking off in the middle of July and lasting into late August, this festival (p252) has been taking place in Dubrovnik since the 1950s. It features classical music, theatre and dance at different venues around town, including the Lovrijenac fortress.

Dance & Nonverbal Theatre Festival, Svetvinčenat

The otherwise sleepy Istrian town of Svetvinčenat comes alive during this mid-July fest (p122), which showcases contemporary dance pieces, street theatre, circus and mime acts, and other nonverbal forms of expression.

Motovun Film Festival, Istria

This film festival (p128), Croatia's most fun and glamorous, presents a roster of independent and avant-garde films in late July each year. Nonstop outdoor and indoor screenings, concerts and parties take over the medieval streets of this hilltop town.

August

Tourist season peaks in the Adriatic, with the hottest days and sea temperatures, swarming beaches and highest prices. Zagreb is hot but empty, as people escape to the coast.

Terraneo, Šibenik

Croatia's newest festival has quickly become the highlight of the summer. This big five-day dance party (p190), located in an old army barracks, draws in Croatian hipsters for its amazing line-up of international and local performers and DJs.

Špancirfest, Varaždin

In late August this eclectic festival (p72) enlivens the parks and squares of Varaždin with a rich repertoire of events that range from world music (Afro-Cuban, gypsy, tango and more) to acrobats, theatre, traditional crafts and illusionists.

Vukovar Film Festival, Slavonia

The annual Vukovar Film Festival (p93) in late August shows features, documentaries and shorts, mainly from Danubian countries. Visiting is a great way to support this city, as it is still recovering from the war.

September

The summer rush is over, but sunshine is still plentiful, the sea is warm and the crowds have largely gone – it's a great time to visit Croatia. Zagreb comes alive again, after the summer exodus to the coast.

World Theatre Festival, Zagreb

High-quality contemporary theatre (p53) comes to Zagreb for a couple of weeks each year, often extending into early October and delighting the country's diehard theatre buffs.

Varaždin Baroque Evenings

Baroque music takes over the baroque city of Varaždin for two to three weeks each September. Local and international orchestras play in the cathedral, churches and theatres around town.

October

Children are back in school, parents are at work and the country sways to its regular rhythms. Ferries change to their winter schedule, but the weather is still pretty mild.

Zagreb Film Festival

Don't miss this major cultural event (p53) that takes place in mid-October each year, with film screenings, accompanying parties and international film directors competing for the coveted Golden Pram award.

Truffle Hunting, Istria

Go hunting for the prized white and black truffles (p126) that grow in the forests around Motovun and Buzet in Istria's interior. Then cook up the smelly fungus and eat it in risotto, pasta and omelettes.

November

The continent chills but the seaside can still be sunny, albeit not warm. A number of the hotels along the coast shut their doors for the season, as do many restaurants.

Feast of St Martin

Martinje (St Martin's Day) is celebrated in all the wine-producing regions across Croatia on 11 November. There are wine celebrations and lots of feasting and sampling of new wines.

Itineraries

Essential Croatia

Two Weeks

Take in the heavyweights of Croatia in this two-week journey from the continent to the coast, including the capital city, a pair of national parks and the gems of the Dalmatian coast.

IAN SHIVE / GETTY IMAGES ©

» Start in the capital, **Zagreb** (p38), and take a long weekend to delve into its simmering nightlife, fine restaurants and choice museums.

» Head south to the World-Heritage-listed **Plitvice Lakes National Park** (p177) and spend the day exploring its verdant maze of turquoise lakes and cascading waterfalls.

» Go down to **Zadar** (p169), one of Croatia's most underrated cities. It's a real find: historic, modern, active and packed with attractions.

» Take a day trip to **Pag Island** (p184) and try some of that famous cheese. If it's the height of summer, go partying on one of its beaches.

» Swim under the stupendous falls at **Krka National Park** (p193) or chill out at the gorgeous **Kornati Islands** (p194).

» Stroll through the pretty streets of postcard-perfect **Trogir** (p216).

» Meander around the Roman ruins of **Solin** (p216).

» Prepare yourself for one of the region's best sights: Diocletian's Palace in **Split** (p197) is a living part of this exuberant seafront city.

» Next, take it easy down the winding coastal road to **Dubrovnik** (p242), a magnificent city whose beauty is bound to blow you away.

Clockwise from top left

1 Dalmatian architecture, Trogir (p216) **2** Church of St Donat, Zadar (p169) **3** Skradinski Buk, Krka National Park (p193)

2

EMANUELE CICCOMARTINO / GETTY IMAGES ©

3

HIROSHI HIGUCHI / GETTY IMAGES ©

Cream of the Coast

Two Weeks

Discover the stunners of Croatia's coast in two weeks – from Istria's favourite getaways to the jewels of Kvarner and all the way south to Dalmatia's greatest hits, both on the mainland and the islands.

CESAR LUCAS ABREU / GETTY IMAGES ©

» Start your journey in the town of **Poreč** (p113), admiring the World-Heritage-listed Euphrasian Basilica.

» Head south for the Venetian-inspired architecture and cobblestone streets of **Rovinj** (p106).

» Move on to **Pula** (p98) to tour the evocative Roman ruins and amphitheatre, and enjoy some beachside R&R.

» Go north, making a pit stop in the old Austrian resort of **Opatija** (p139) for a stroll along the seaside promenade and killer views of the Kvarner coast.

» From nearby **Rijeka** (p133), Kvarner's capital, you can take a catamaran to pretty **Rab Town** (p161) on Rab Island. After wandering the ancient town, relax on the aptly named Paradise Beach at **Lopar** (p166).

» Next, visit historic **Zadar** (p169) for its wealth of museums, churches, cafes and bars.

» Travel south to **Split** (p197), a buzzing city and a great base to explore the beaches of **Brela** (p224) and the nearby islands.

» On Brač, visit pretty **Bol** (p227).

» Hop over to chic **Hvar Island** (p230) and the **Pakleni Islands** (p232) for some clothing-optional sunbathing.

» For a few days of real rest, great food and plenty of diving, **Vis** (p237) is your island.

» From Split, drive down to **Dubrovnik** (p242) to explore the city's gleaming marble streets, vibrant street life and fine architecture.

» Don't miss a hop to the gorgeous island of **Mljet** (p261), where the verdancy, salt lakes and tranquillity heal the soul.

Clockwise from top left

1 Old Town, Split (p197) **2** Diving at Vis Island (p238) **3** Opatija (p139) **4** Euphrasian Basilica (p114), Poreč

2

FRANCO BANFI / GETTY IMAGES ©

3

STUART BLACK / GETTY IMAGES ©

City & Country: Zagreb & Around

One Week

Soak up the delights of the pocket-size capital of Zagreb and then head off for green pastures, old towns and fairy-tale castles.

» Start off in Croatia's dynamic capital, **Zagreb** (p38), to enjoy its museums, art and nightlife.

» Head to charming little **Samobor** (p66) for top-class cakes and countryside treks.

» Go forth and explore where not many tourists have gone before in **Zagorje** (p68), a bucolic landscape of forests, pastures and farms. Start with **Klanjec** (p80) and discover the art of Antun Augustinčić in the town museum.

» Don't miss the birthplace of Croatia's most famous son – Josip Broz Tito – at **Kumrovec** (p80). It's not a communist site but a fascinating examination of traditional village life.

» To get acquainted with your Neanderthal ancestors, visit the swanky Museum of the Krapina Neanderthal in **Krapina** (p77).

» If you have a thing for the mystery of times past, you'll revel in **Trakošćan Castle** (p76) and its verdant grounds.

» For more history, head to the beautifully restored castle-fortress at **Varaždin** (p69). Immerse yourself in the town's baroque architecture for an afternoon.

» On the way south, stop at the pilgrimage site of **Marija Bistrica** (p80) for heady views of the surrounding region.

Clockwise from top left
1 Samobor (p66) **2** Zagorje (p68) **3** Dining in Zagreb (p55) **4** Trakošćan Castle (p76)

2

KEN GILLHAM / GETTY IMAGES ©

3

TRISH PUNCH / GETTY IMAGES ©

East to West: Slavonia & Istria

10 Days

Explore the bucolic region of Slavonia in Croatia's east, then head southwest to the Istrian peninsula for hilltop medieval towns, top food and rural hotels.

ADAM JONES / GETTY IMAGES ©

MARTIN CHILD / GETTY IMAGES ©

» Start your trip in Slavonia, on the eastern edge of Croatia. Explore the Hungarian-influenced town of **Osijek** (p84) on the Drava River.

» Move on to **Kopački Rit Nature Park** (p90), with its profusion of birdlife and lush waterways.

» Next, spend a day in the ethno-village of **Karanac** (p91), enjoying local food specialities and traditions.

» Head southwest towards **Istria** (p95). The Istrian peninsula carries the foodie crown for its delicate truffles, air-dried ham, yummy olives and excellent wines. Stop for a meal and a wander around the world's smallest town, **Hum** (p127).

» Explore the truffle epicentre of **Buzet** (p125) and its scenic surroundings.

» Head towards **Pazin** (p123) to walk through its famous chasm, which inspired Jules Verne.

» Drive on to the gorgeous hilltop settlements of **Motovun** (p128) and **Grožnjan** (p130).

» On the way south, stroll through scenic **Svetvinčenat** (p122), which has a Renaissance-era main square with a castle.

» Unwind in captivating **Bale** (p113).

Clockwise from top left

1 Bale (p113) **2** Motovun (p128) **3** Croatian olive oil and preserves

2

Travel with Children

Best Regions for Kids

Dubrovnik & Southern Dalmatia

This region offers lots of beach action, fun museums and unique experiences. The pedestrian old town of Dubrovnik is a treat for little ones.

Split & Central Dalmatia

In Split, wander around the maze that is Diocletian's Palace and run around the marble-paved Riva. Makarska Riviera has great beaches and fun recreational options.

Northern Dalmatia

Zadar offers the fantastic light show of the Sun Salutation and the hypnotic sounds of the Sea Organ. Šibenik has a great children's festival and lovely islands nearby.

Istria

Poreč and Rovinj are great bases for exploring nearby caves, dinosaur parks, fjords and beaches, all while enjoying plenty of delicious *sladoled* (ice cream).

Zagreb

Ride the funicular, check out the many fun museums, get active at Jarun and Bundek and hike up to the mountain peak of Sljeme.

Zagorje

Savour a slice of Croatian country life at Vuglec Breg and Grešna Gorica, tour the interactive museum in Krapina and visit medieval castles.

Croatia for Kids

Featuring sheltered pebble beaches for swimming in the Adriatic Sea, a clutch of fun interactive museums to while away a rainy day, and easy hikes in the many national parks and labyrinthine streets through ancient cities and towns, Croatia offers entertainment aplenty for those with the little ones in tow.

Kids get lots of smiles and compliments, so you won't be made to feel like an annoyance when you're travelling in a pack. Croats are very proud of their children and friendly towards other people's kids – it should be easy for your offspring to make some local friends, too! Come armed with a positive attitude, be ready to improvise and your family will have a blast.

Children's Highlights

Beaches

» Baška, Krk Island: A 2km-long crescent of beach backed by barren mountains.

» Mljet: Any of the three salt lakes; the small lake is warm and perfect for babies.

» Punta Rata, Makarska Riviera: A gorgeous pine-tree-lined stretch of pebbles.

» Lapad, Dubrovnik: Sea slides, sun loungers and parasols steps from the old town.

» Crveni Otok, Rovinj: Two connected islets awash with pebble beaches.

» Lopar, Rab Island: Sandy beaches, shallow seas and facilities aplenty.

Day Trips

» Krka National Park: Have a dip in a cool lake underneath cascading waterfalls.

» Plitvice Lakes National Park: Take in the turquoise lakes, towering waterfalls and dense forests.

» Lokrum: Escape to this lush island with a botanic garden and a medieval monastery.

» Medvednica Nature Park: Explore the verdant footpaths of Zagreb's favourite mountain.

» Dubrovnik Cable Car: Slightly pricey, but kids will love going up and seeing the views, and running around on Srđ mountain.

Museums & Sights

» Technical Museum, Zagreb: A quirky museum with a planetarium and a replica mine.

» Museum of the Krapina Neanderthal, Krapina: Get up close and personal with our cousins.

» Batana House, Rovinj: Multimedia interactive displays illustrate Rovinj's fishing history.

» Staro Selo Museum, Kumrovec: An entertaining slice of Croatia's traditional village life.

» Sun Salutation, Zadar: Come sunset, local and visitor tots have a ball with this marvellous light display, for hours on end.

Planning

Croats are well disposed when it comes to the little ones and will always jump in to help.

Kids love the beach but choose your sites carefully – many 'beaches' are rocky with steep drop-offs that can lead to injuries. The good news is that there are plenty of beaches to choose from along the coast and the islands. Pebble or sand ones are ideal.

Children's discounts are widely available for everything from museum admissions to hotel accommodation. The cut-off age is often nine. Many attractions don't charge admission fees for the little ones.

Accommodation

Most properties in Croatia are family-friendly but few are family specialists. Of those, the best are the Falkensteiner-run Family Hotel Diadora near Zadar and Hotel Vespera in Mali Lošinj.

Hotels may have children's cots, but numbers are usually limited and sometimes there's a surcharge. For greater comfort, look into renting a private apartment for the same price as a hotel room. Make sure you ask for specifics about the facilities – whether there's air-conditioning, a private terrace and how far the beach is, for example.

Kids under three often stay for free, while those under nine get a considerable discount.

When to Go

The last week of June and the first week of July is a great time for families to be in Croatia. The coastal city of Šibenik hosts a renowned International Children's Festival with craft workshops, music, dance, children's film and theatre, puppets and parades.

Go to Croatia in July and August for the most action and activity. If you are looking for fewer people and lower prices, June and September are the best times, as the sea is warm enough for swimming and the days are sunny.

What to Pack

If you plan to go to the islands, especially the more remote ones, it's wise to bring a medical kit, as medical facilities are not always readily available.

Come with plenty of sunscreen and hats, as the sun in the Adriatic can be deceptively strong.

Be mindful of the numerous sea urchins in the shallows, particularly where the beach is rocky; invest in some plastic sandals for safer playing in the water.

Before You Go

No vaccinations are required for Croatia. For those spending a lot of time in nature during spring, summer or early autumn, make sure you check the kids for ticks. There has been a rise in tick-borne diseases in recent years so if you do find one, go to the doctor immediately.

Babies

Breastfeeding in public is uncommon, but is generally accepted if done discreetly. Specific child-friendly facilities are still thin on the ground, although that is slowly changing.

Baby food and powdered baby formulas are easily found at most supermarkets and pharmacies, and are sold according to age group.

Disposable nappies are easy to find, particularly American Pampers and German Linostar. Look for supermarkets such as Konzum and the pharmacy DM.

Very few restaurants or public restrooms have nappy-changing facilities.

Electric sterilisers are expensive and hard to find.

Toddlers

Croatia has a lot of open spaces, playgrounds aplenty and pedestrian zones where there's no danger of traffic. Most seaside towns have a riva (seafront promenade) away from the water's edge that's perfect for strolling and letting the children run around.

Kids

Most destinations on the coast and the islands have trampolines and bungee jumping set up seasonally – these are extremely popular and often involve queuing up.

Teens

Keep in mind that some of Croatia's seaside towns can be too quiet for fun-seeking teenagers. They (and you in turn) will be a lot happier in the more happening coastal destinations with cafe and beachside action.

Eating with Kids

The generally relaxed dining scene means that you can take the children almost everywhere. Even the more upmarket restaurants will have a kid-friendly pasta, pizza or rice dish on the menu. Children's portions are easily arranged. However, you won't often find high chairs for the tinier tots.

Locals are quite happy to take their children out for dinner to restaurants, and you'll often see kids running around on the local square while the adults are eating, drinking and chatting. Children eat mostly the same as the adults, and everyone tucks into an ice cream at the end of the meal.

Transport

Car hire is the best way to go in Croatia if you have a family. Car seats, however, are not always available, so make sure you are very clear about your needs with the hire company before you turn up. It is not obligatory to use a car seat.

Buses and trains are good for older children and for shorter journeys.

The coastal roads are winding, so take precautions if your child is sensitive to motion sickness.

regions at a glance

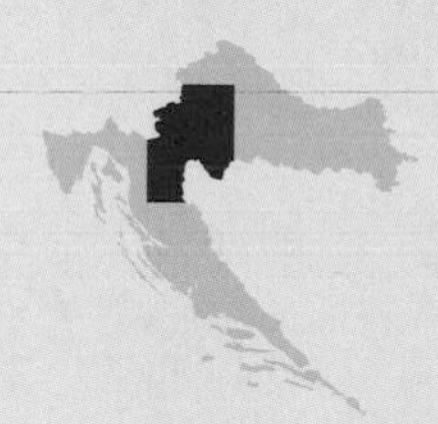

Zagreb

Cafe Culture ✓✓✓
Museums & Galleries ✓
Food ✓

Cafe Culture

A bastion of Europe's famed cafe culture, Zagreb's sidewalk cafes are perennially packed (except in winter), offering strong coffee that packs a punch, and the chance to lazily linger over a cup for hours on end. The prime time to experience this is during the coffee-sipping and people-watching ritual known as *špica,* which happens on warm-weather Saturday mornings, when everyone and their mother comes out to show off their latest outfits.

Museums & Galleries

Zagreb's cultural flagship, the swish Museum of Contemporary Art, has brought an artistic flavour to the city's streetscapes, while the new quirky Museum of Broken Relationships has quickly become a favourite. Then there are the old-timers, such as the Mimara Museum, with a massive collection of painting and sculpture, and the delightful Croatian Museum of Naïve Art. To tap into the contemporary art beat pulsating through the city, don't miss the independent gallery spaces.

Food

On the food front, there is plenty to explore in Croatia's capital, which has become a foodie destination in recent years. A handful of destination restaurants showcase innovative culinary specialities prepared with high-quality ingredients from around the country, while inexpensive taverns serve no-frills but real-deal traditional fare to acquaint you with Croatia's own style of cooking.

p38

Zagorje

Medieval Castles ✓✓
Architecture ✓
Countryside ✓

Medieval Castles

Postcard-perfect fairy-tale castles dot the wooded hills of this bucolic region. The neo-Gothic Trakošćan offers an intimate insight into the life of former Croatian nobility, while the formidable Veliki Tabor, complete with towers, turrets and other castle trimmings, looks down from a verdant hilltop.

Architecture

Soak up the baroque architecture of Varaždin. Its 18th-century buildings shine bright in their fully restored glory, with facades freshly painted in the original pastels: ochres, pinks, pale blues and creams.

Countryside

The pretty pastoral panoramas of Zagorje's vineyard-covered hills, cornfields, dense forests and gingerbread cottages are the stuff of storybooks. Savour traditional Croatian farm life as it unfolds away from the tourist hullabaloo down south.

p68

Slavonia

Birdwatching ✓✓✓
Culture ✓✓
History ✓✓

Birdwatching

One of Europe's most important wetlands, Kopački Rit Nature Park occupies the floodplain where the Danube meets the Drava. Internationally famed for its diverse birdlife, the park is best visited during the spring or autumn migrations.

Culture

Slavonia's capital, Osijek, is one of the greenest cities in Croatia, with a picturesque riverside promenade and many leafy parks. It's also one of the most culturally rich areas, with a fascinating Habsburg quarter bursting with authentic restaurants ideal for trying the local paprika-rich food, including *fiš paprikaš*.

History

Eastern Slavonia suffered terribly during Croatia's Homeland War, when the region was pummelled by heavy artillery. In Vukovar you can visit stirring reminders of the war.

p81

Istria

Food ✓✓✓
Architecture ✓✓
Beaches ✓

Food

Indulge in *la dolce vita* Istrian-style, feasting on superfine meals prepared in creative ways. From white truffles and wild asparagus to award-winning olive oils and wines, dining and wining is a highlight of any stay in Istria, Croatia's most foodie-friendly place.

Architecture

Istria's hotchpotch of architecture includes Roman-era amphitheatres, Byzantine basilicas, Venetian-style townhouses and medieval hilltop towns, all packed tightly and prettily into one small peninsula.

Beaches

From pine-fringed, activity-packed pebble beaches a hop and a skip from Pula, Rovinj and Poreč, to the wild landscapes of Rt Kamenjak and its string of secluded coves, Istria has a beach for every taste (except for diehard fans of sand).

p95

Kvarner

Food ✓✓
Wildlife ✓
Architecture ✓

Food

The tiny cove of Volosko is a gastronomic hotbed of authentic Croatian cooking, with a clutch of high-quality, atmospheric *konobas* (simple family-run establishments) and restaurants.

Wildlife

The connected islands of Lošinj and Cres each boast excellent wildlife projects: in tiny Veli Lošinj you'll find a fascinating Adriatic dolphin research centre, while up in Cres there's a project devoted to griffon vultures.

Architecture

Krk Town has a medieval core. Small but perfectly formed Rab Town has a string of historic churches and belltowers. The townhouses in Cres Town, Veli Lošinj and Mali Lošinj all show strong Venetian influences.

p131

Northern Dalmatia

Nature ✓✓✓
Cities ✓
Landscapes ✓✓

Nature
Most visitors come here for the coast, but this region has inland appeal in abundance. Krka and Plitvice have lovely lakes and exquisite waterfalls. Head to Paklenica for soaring mountains and great hiking.

Cities
Northern Dalmatia's two cities both offer culture and history while being far from touristy. Šibenik arguably has Croatia's most elegant cathedral and a remarkable old quarter, while Zadar has intriguing sights, hip bars and restaurants.

Landscapes
Long, slim and packed with interest, Pag Island has stark, sun-blasted hills that fade to the palest shade of green. The entire coast of the mainland is equally astonishing, with the azure Adriatic on one side and a mountain barrier to the east.

p167

Split & Central Dalmatia

Beaches ✓✓✓
Architecture ✓✓
Activities ✓

Beaches
From fun-filled Bačvice, Split's adored city beach, to the round pebbles of pine-fringed Brela and the tongue-shaped Zlatni Rat on Brač Island, Central Dalmatia has some of Croatia's best beaches – both popular and off the well-worn trail.

Architecture
Two Unesco World Heritage Sites sit a quick drive from one another in Central Dalmatia: the buzzing Roman-era quarter that is Diocletian's Palace in Split, and the architectural medley of Trogir's compact old town.

Activities
Be it sailing, mountain biking, sea kayaking, diving, hiking, river rafting or windsurfing, active travellers will find it all in Central Dalmatia's varied landscapes.

p196

Dubrovnik & Southern Dalmatia

History ✓✓✓
Islands ✓✓
Wine ✓

History
One of the world's most evocatively situated and historic cities, Dubrovnik is a dream to look at, a delight to explore and a wrench to leave. The much smaller but gorgeous Korčula Town offers a similar experience.

Islands
The thinly populated, pine-forested islands of Mljet and Korčula are rightfully acclaimed for their natural beauty and cove beaches. But don't neglect little Lokrum and the lovely Elafitis.

Wine
The unspoilt Pelješac Peninsula is one of Croatia's emerging wine districts. Try rich, vibrant local reds like *postup* and *dingač* on a tour of its vineyards. Neighbouring Korčula is renowned for its white wines from the *grk* grape.

p242

› **Every listing is recommended by our authors, and their favourite places are listed first**

› **Look out for these icons:**

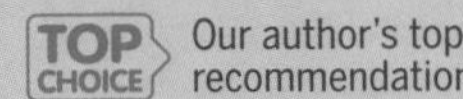

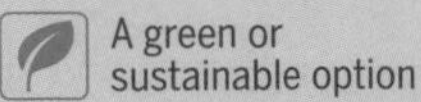

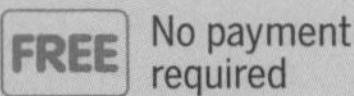

See the Index for a full list of destinations covered in this book.

On the Road

Zagreb

☎01 / POP 792,875

Includes »

Best Places to Eat

» Vinodol (p56)
» Lari & Penati (p56)
» Didov San (p56)
» Karijola (p56)

Best Places to Stay

» Studio Kairos (p54)
» Esplanade Zagreb Hotel (p54)
» Hobo Bear Hostel (p54)
» Hotel Dubrovnik (p54)

Why Go?

Everyone knows about Croatia's coast and islands, but a mention of the country's capital still draws the confused question: 'Is it worth visiting?' Here is the answer: Zagreb is a great destination, with lots of culture, arts, music, architecture, gastronomy and all the other things that make a quality capital.

Visually, Zagreb is a mixture of strait-laced Austro-Hungarian architecture and rough-around-the-edges socialist structures, its character a sometimes uneasy combination of the two elements. This mini metropolis is made for strolling the streets, drinking coffee in the permanently full cafes, popping into museums and galleries, and enjoying the theatres, concerts and cinema. It's a year-round outdoor city: in spring and summer everyone scurries to Jarun Lake in the southwest to swim, boat or dance the night away at lakeside discos, while in autumn and winter Zagrebians go skiing at Mt Medvednica, only a tram ride away, or hiking in nearby Samobor.

When to Go

Zagreb

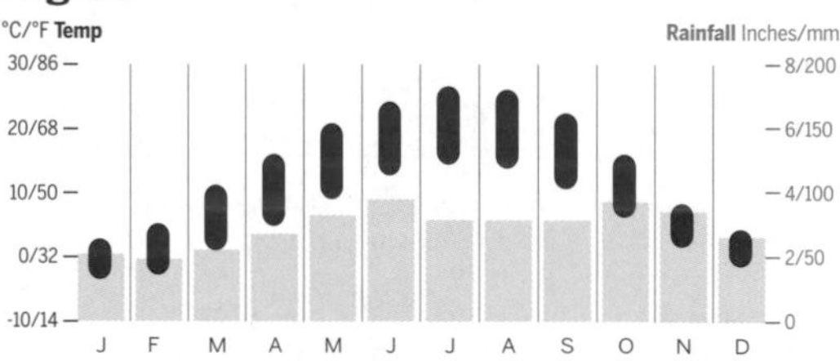

Apr & May The city takes off its winter coat and pavement cafes become a beehive of activity.

Jun Some of Zagreb's best festivals liven up its streetscapes and provide plenty of cultural fodder.

Sep & Oct People return from holidays and the city buzzes with summer energy.

History

Zagreb's known history begins in medieval times with two hills: Kaptol, now the site of Zagreb's cathedral, and Gradec. When the two settlements merged in 1850, Zagreb was officially born.

The space now known as Trg Josipa Jelačića became the site of Zagreb's lucrative trade fairs, spurring construction around its edges. In the 19th century the economy expanded with the development of a prosperous clothing trade and a rail link connecting Zagreb with Vienna and Budapest. The city's cultural life blossomed, too.

Zagreb also became the centre for the Illyrian movement. Count Janko Drašković, lord of Trakošćan Castle, published a manifesto in Illyrian in 1832 and his call for a national revival resounded throughout Croatia. Drašković's dream came to fruition when Croatia and its capital joined the Kingdom of Serbs, Croats and Slovenes after WWI.

Between the two world wars, working-class neighbourhoods emerged in Zagreb between the railway and the Sava River, and new residential quarters were built on the southern slopes of Mt Medvednica. In April 1941 the Germans invaded Yugoslavia and entered Zagreb without resistance. Ante Pavelić and the Ustaše moved quickly to proclaim the establishment of the Independent State of Croatia (Nezavisna Država Hrvatska), with Zagreb as its capital. Although Pavelić ran his fascist state from Zagreb until 1944, he never enjoyed a great deal of support within the capital, which maintained support for Tito's Partisans.

In postwar Yugoslavia, Zagreb (to its chagrin) took second place to Belgrade but continued to expand. Zagreb was made the capital of Croatia in 1991, the same year that the country became independent.

Sights

As the oldest part of Zagreb, the Upper Town (Gornji Grad), which includes the neighbourhoods of Gradec and Kaptol, has landmark buildings and churches from the earlier centuries of Zagreb's history. The Lower Town (Donji Grad), which runs between the Upper Town and the train station, has the city's most interesting art museums and fine examples of 19th- and 20th-century architecture.

UPPER TOWN

Museum of Broken Relationships MUSEUM
(http://brokenships.com; Ćirilometodska 2; adult/concession 25/20KN; ⏲9am-10.30pm Jun–mid-Oct, 9am-9pm mid-Oct–May) Explore mementos that remain after a relationship ends at Zagreb's quirkiest museum. The innovative exhibit toured the world until it settled in its permanent Zagreb home. On display are donations from around the globe, in a string of all-white rooms with vaulted ceilings and epoxy-resin floors. Exhibits hit on a range of

ZAGREB IN...

Two Days

Start your day with a stroll through Strossmayerov trg, Zagreb's oasis of greenery. Take a look at the **Strossmayer Gallery of Old Masters** and then walk to **Trg Josipa Jelačića**, the city's centre.

Head up to **Kaptol Square** for a look at the **cathedral**, the centre of Zagreb's religious life. While in the Upper Town, pick up some fruit at the **Dolac Market** or have lunch at **Amfora**. Then get to know the work of Croatia's best sculptor at **Meštrović Atelier** and see its naive art legacy at the **Croatian Museum of Naïve Art**, followed by a visit to the quirky **Museum of Broken Relationships**. See the lay of the city from the top of **Lotrščak Tower**, then spend the evening bar-crawling along **Tkalčićeva**.

On the second day, tour the Lower Town museums, reserving an hour for the **Museum Mimara** and just as long for the **Museum of Contemporary Art**. Lunch at **Vinodol** and digest in the **Botanical Garden**. Early evening is best at **Preradovićev trg** before dining and sampling some of Zagreb's **nightlife**.

Four Days

Your third day should take in the lovely **Mirogoj cemetery**, with a stop at **Medvedgrad** or **Maksimir Park**.

On day four, take a trip out to **Samobor** for a big dose of small-town charm.

Zagreb Highlights

1 Sip coffee and cocktails alfresco along **Tkalčićeva**

2 Gape at the remains of failed romances at the **Museum of Broken Relationships** (p39)

3 Stroll along the winding streets of the ancient **Upper Town** (p39)

4 Tap into Croatia's current art beat in Zagreb's **Museum of Contemporary Art** (p49)

5 Picnic and stroll in rambling **Maksimir Park** (p50)

6 Contemplate mortality amid the trees and tombs in **Mirogoj** (p49)

7 After a day's hiking, gorge on delicious *kremšnite* (custard pies) in **Samobor** (p66)

8 Trek the trails of **Medvednica Nature Park** (p65), visiting mountain huts en route

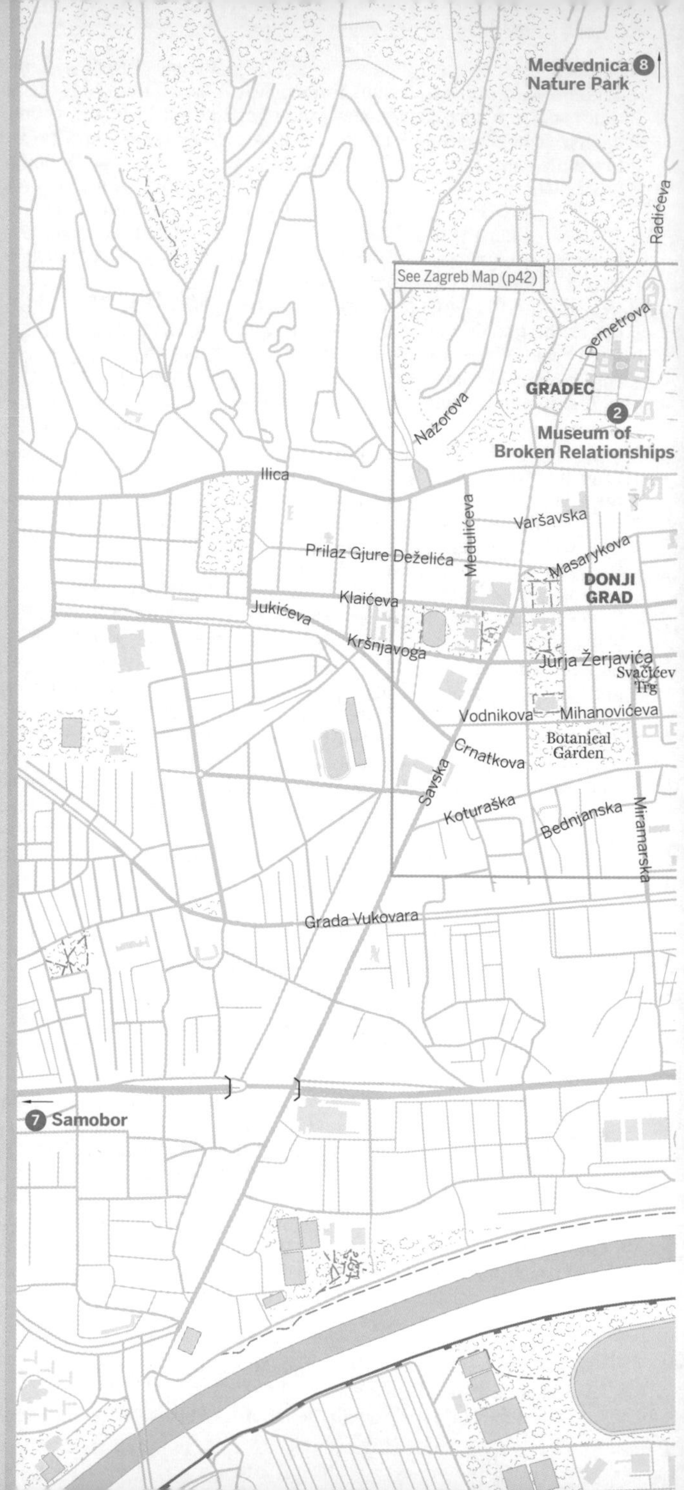

3 Upper Town
6 Mirogoj
Maksimir Park 5
0 1 km
0 0.5 miles
Vončinina
Kaptol
Ribnjak
Tkalčićeva
Kaptol Square
ŠALATA
1 Tkalčićeva
Vlaška
Cesarćeva
Jurišićeva
Račkoga
Praška
Amruševa
Gajeva
Draškovićeva
Trg Žrtava Fašizma
LOWER TOWN
Trg Kralja Petra Krešimira IV
Baruna Trenka
Širolina
Trg Kralja Tomislava
Branimirova
Branimirova
Grgurova
Zagreb Train Station
Radnička
Supilova
Avenija M Držića
Trnjanska
Trg Stjepana Radića
Grada Vukovara
Sava
4 Museum of Contemporary Art
NOVI ZAGREB

Zagreb

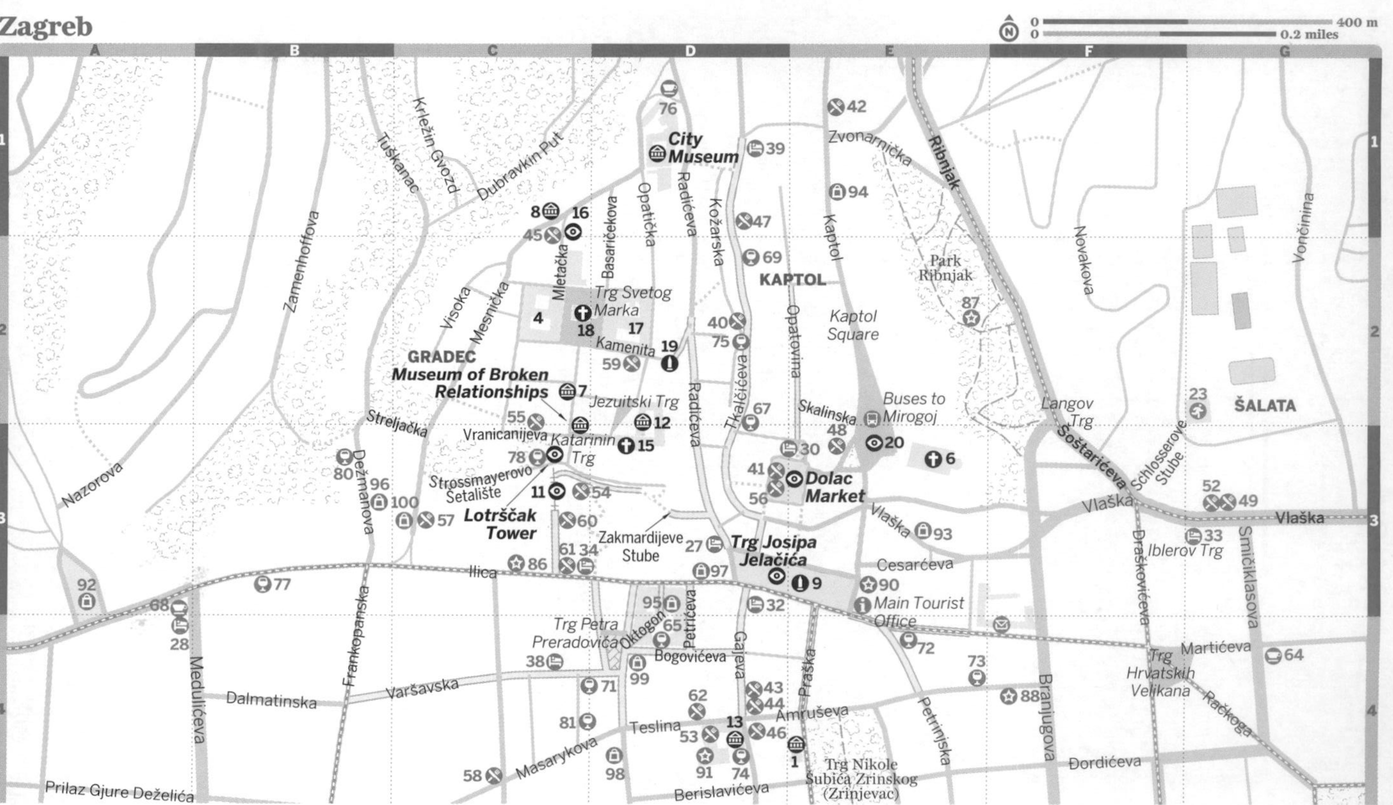

0 400 m
0 0.2 miles
ŠALATA
KAPTOL
GRADEC
City Museum
Museum of Broken Relationships
Lotrščak Tower
Dolac Market
Trg Josipa Jelačića
Kaptol Square
Park Ribnjak
Buses to Mirogoj
Main Tourist Office
Trg Svetog Marka
Jezuitski Trg
Katarinin Trg
Strossmayerovo Šetalište
Zakmardijeve Stube
Trg Petra Preradovića
Trg Nikole Šubića Zrinskog (Zrinjevac)
Trg Hrvatskih Velikana
Iblerov Trg
Langov Trg
Schlosserove Stube
Vončinina
Novakova
Ribnjak
Zvonarnička
Kaptol
Opatovina
Skalinska
Tkalčićeva
Kožarska
Radićeva
Opatička
Basaričekova
Mletačka
Kamenita
Mesnička
Visoka
Dubravkin Put
Krležin Gvozd
Tuškanac
Streljačka
Vranicanijeva
Dežmanova
Zamenhoffova
Nazorova
Ilica
Frankopanska
Medulićeva
Dalmatinska
Varšavska
Masarykova
Teslina
Bogovićeva
Petrićeva
Oktogon
Gajeva
Berislavićeva
Amruševa
Praška
Cesarčeva
Vlaška
Petrinjska
Branjugova
Đorđićeva
Draškovićeva
Martićeva
Račkoga
Smičiklasova
Šoštarićeva
Prilaz Gjure Deželića

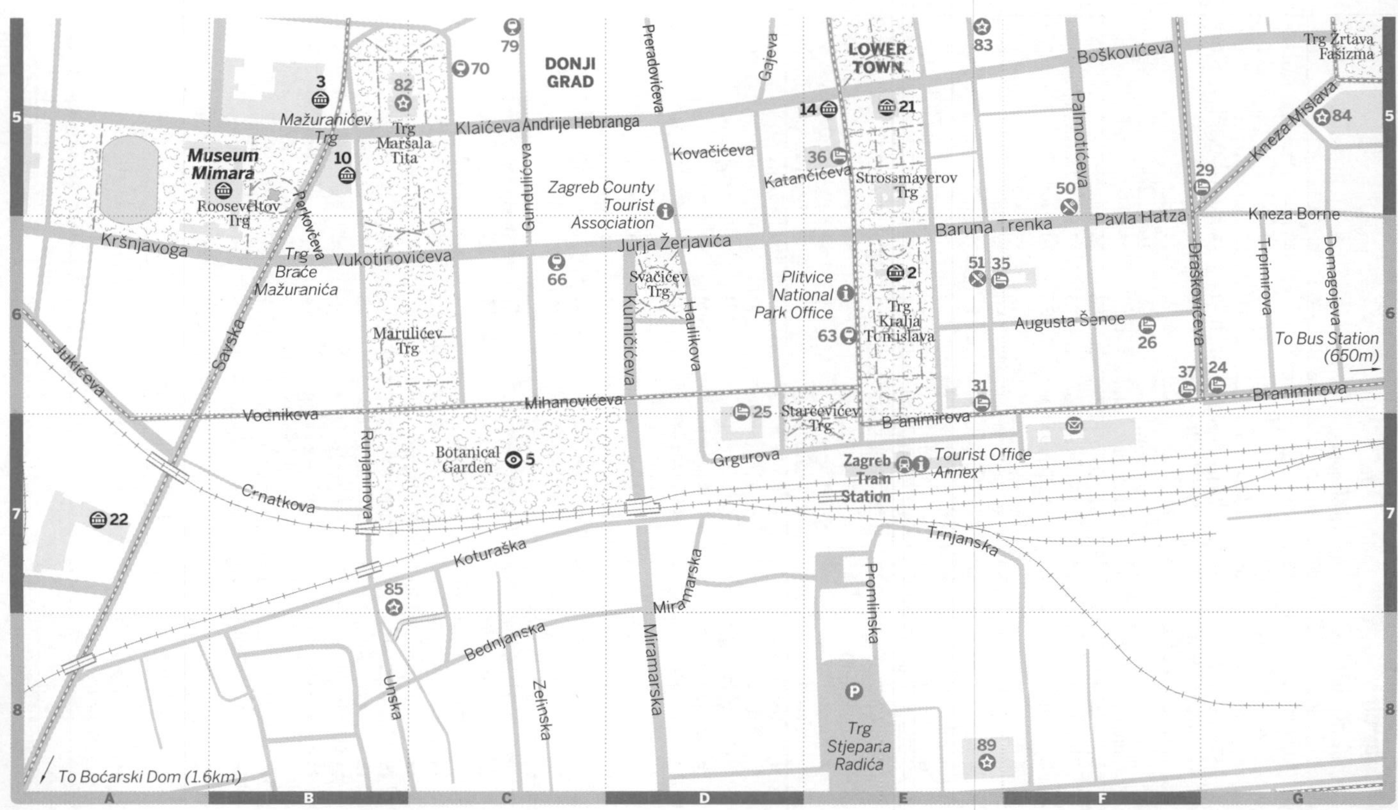
LOWER TOWN
DONJI GRAD
Trg Žrtava Fašizma
Boškovićeva
Kneza Mislava
Kneza Borne
Trpimirova
Domagojeva
To Bus Station (650m)
Branimirova
Draškovićeva
Pavla Hatza
Palmotićeva
Augusta Šenoe
Baruna Trenka
Strossmayerov Trg
Trg Kralja Tomislava
Tourist Office Annex
Zagreb Train Station
Trnjanska
Promlinska
Trg Stjepana Radića
Katančićeva
Plitvice National Park Office
Starčevićev Trg
Gajeva
Kovačićeva
Grgurova
Haulikova
Preradovićeva
Svačićev Trg
Kumičićeva
Jurja Žerjavića
Miramarska
Mira
Klaićeva
Andrije Hebranga
Zagreb County Tourist Association
Mihanovićeva
Gundulićeva
Botanical Garden
Zelinska
Koturaška
Bednjanska
Trg Maršala Tita
Vukotinovićeva
Marulićev Trg
Unska
Runjaninova
Mažuranićev Trg
Perkovčeva
Trg Braće Mažuranića
Savska
Vodnikova
Crnatkova
Museum Mimara
Rooseveltov Trg
Kršnjavoga
Jukićeva
To Bočarski Dom (1.6km)
A
B
C
D
E
F
G
5
6
7
8
2
3
5
10
14
21
22
24
25
26
29
31
35
36
37
50
51
63
66
70
79
82
83
84
85
89

Zagreb

Top Sights

City Museum D1
Dolac Market E3
Lotrščak Tower C3
Museum Mimara B5
Museum of Broken Relationships C3
Trg Josipa Jelačića D3

Sights

1 Archaeological Museum E4
2 Art Pavilion E6
3 Arts & Crafts Museum B5
4 Banski Dvori C2
5 Botanical Garden C7
6 Cathedral of the Assumption of the Blessed Virgin Mary E3
7 Croatian Museum of Naïve Art C2
8 Croatian Natural History Museum C1
9 Equestrian Statue E3
10 Ethnographic Museum B5
11 Funicular Railway C3
12 Galerija Klovićevi Dvori D2
13 Galerija Nova D4
14 Gallery of Modern Art E5
15 Jesuit Church of St Catherine D3
16 Meštrović Atelier C1
17 Sabor D2
18 St Mark's Church C2
19 Statue of Dora D2
20 Stone Gate E3
21 Strossmayer Gallery of Old Masters E5
22 Technical Museum A7

Activities, Courses & Tours

23 Sports & Recreational Centre Šalata G2

Sleeping

24 Arcotel Allegra G6
25 Esplanade Zagreb Hotel D6
26 Evistas F6
27 Fulir Hostel D3
28 Hobo Bear Hostel A4
29 Hostel Day and Night G5
30 Hostel Nokturno E3
31 Hotel Central E6
32 Hotel Dubrovnik D3
33 Hotel Jadran G3
34 Hotel Jägerhorn C3
35 Omladinski Hostel E6
36 Palace Hotel E5
37 Palmers Lodge Hostel Zagreb F6
38 Shappy Hostel C4
39 Taban Hostel D1

Eating

40 Agava D2
41 Amfora D3
42 Baltazar E1
43 Boban D4
44 Čušpajz D4
45 Didov San C1
46 Dinara D4
47 Ivica i Marica D1
48 Kaptolska Klet E3
49 Karijola G3
50 Konoba Čiho F5
51 Lari & Penati E6
52 Mali Bar G3
Nokturno .... (see 30)
53 Pingvin D4
54 Pod Gričkim Topom C3
55 Prasac C2
56 Rubelj D3
57 Stari Fijaker 900 .... C3
58 Tip Top C4
59 Trilogija D2
60 Vallis Aurea C3
61 Vincek C3
62 Vinodol D4
Zinfandel's .... (see 25)

Drinking

63 Bacchus E6
64 Booksa G4
65 Bulldog D4
66 Cafe u Dvorištu C6
67 Cica D2
68 Eli's Cafe A3
69 Funk D2
70 Hemingway C5
71 Kino Europa D4
72 Klub Kino Grič E4
73 Kolaž E4
74 Lemon D4
75 Melin D2
76 Palainovka D1
77 Pivnica Medvedgrad B3
78 Stross C3
79 Tri Praščića C5
80 Velvet B3
81 Vimpi C4

Entertainment

82 Croatian National Theatre B5
83 Hotpot E5
84 Koncertna Direkcija Zagreb G5
85 KSET B7
86 Pepermint C3
87 Purgeraj E2
88 Rush Club F4
89 Vatroslav Lisinski Concert Hall E8
90 Vip Club E3
91 Zagrebačko Kazalište Mladih D4

Shopping

92 Antiques Market A3
93 Aromatica E3
94 Bornstein E1
95 Croata D3
96 I-GLE B3
97 Nama D3
98 Natura Croatica D4
99 Profil Megastore D4
100 Prostor C3

emotions, from a can of love incense from Indiana that 'doesn't work' to an iron from Norway once used to straighten a wedding suit. Check out the lovely adjacent store – the 'bad memories eraser' is a bestseller – and the cosy cafe with sidewalk tables.

Dolac Market MARKET

(⏲7am-3pm Mon-Fri, to 2pm Sat, to 1pm Sun) Zagreb's colourful fruit and vegetable market is just north of Trg Josipa Jelačića. Traders from all over Croatia come to sell their products at this buzzing centre of activity. Dolac has been heaving since the 1930s when the city authorities set up a market space on the 'border' between the Upper and Lower Towns. The main part is on an elevated square; the street level has indoor stalls selling meat and dairy products and, a little further towards the square, flowers. The stalls at the northern end of the market are packed with locally produced honey, handmade ornaments and cheap food.

Cathedral of the Assumption of the Blessed Virgin Mary CATHEDRAL

(Katedrala Marijina Uznešenja; Kaptol; ⏲10am-5pm Mon-Sat, 1-5pm Sun) Kaptol Square is dominated by this cathedral, formerly known as St Stephen's. Its twin spires – seemingly permanently under repair – soar over the city. Although the cathedral's original Gothic structure has been transformed many times over, the sacristy still contains a cycle of **frescos** dating from the 13th century. An earthquake in 1880 badly damaged the cathedral and reconstruction in a neo-Gothic style began around the turn of the 20th century. Inside, don't miss the baroque marble altars, statues and pulpit; and the **tomb of Cardinal Alojzije Stepinac** by Ivan Meštrović.

Stone Gate CITY GATE

Make sure you take a peek at the **Stone Gate**, the eastern gate to medieval Gradec Town, now a shrine. According to legend, a great fire in 1731 destroyed every part of the wooden gate except for the painting of the Virgin and Child by an unknown 17th-century artist. People believe that the painting possesses magical powers and come regularly to pray before it, light candles and leave flowers. Square stone slabs are engraved with thanks and praise to the Virgin.

On the western facade of the Stone Gate you'll see a **statue of Dora**, the hero of an 18th-century historical novel, who lived with her father next to the Stone Gate.

Lotrščak Tower TOWER

(Kula Lotrščak; Strossmayerovo Šetalište 9; adult/concession 10/5KN; ⏲9am-9pm) The tower was built in the middle of the 13th century in order to protect the southern city gate. For the last hundred years a cannon has been fired every day at noon, commemorating the following historical event. According to legend, a cannon was fired at noon one day at the Turks who camped across the Sava River. On its way, the cannonball happened to hit a rooster. The rooster was blown to bits and, the story goes, that's why the Turks became so demoralised and failed to attack the city. A less fanciful explanation is that the cannon shot allows churches to synchronise their clocks.

The tower may be climbed for a sweeping 360-degree view of the city. Near the tower is a **funicular railway** (5KN), which was constructed in 1888 and connects the Lower and Upper Towns.

St Mark's Church CHURCH

(Crkva Svetog Marka; Trg Svetog Marka 5; ⏲7.30am-6.30pm) This 13th-century church is one of Zagreb's most emblematic buildings. Its colourful tiled roof, constructed in 1880, has the medieval coat of arms of Croatia, Dalmatia and Slavonia on the left side, and the emblem of Zagreb on the right. The Gothic portal composed of 15 figures in shallow niches was sculpted in the 14th century. The interior contains sculptures by Meštrović. You can only enter the anteroom during opening hours. The church itself is open only at Mass time.

From late April to October there is a guard-changing ceremony outside the church every Saturday and Sunday at noon.

Croatian Museum of Naïve Art MUSEUM

(Hrvatski Muzej Naivne Umjetnosti; www.hmnu.org; Ćirilometodska 3; adult/concession 20/10KN; ⏲10am-6pm Tue-Fri, to 1pm Sat & Sun) If you like Croatia's naive art, a form that was highly fashionable locally and worldwide during the 1960s and 1970s but has declined somewhat since, this small museum will be a feast. It houses over 1000 paintings, drawings and some sculptures by the discipline's most important artists, such as Generalić, Mraz, Virius and Smaljić.

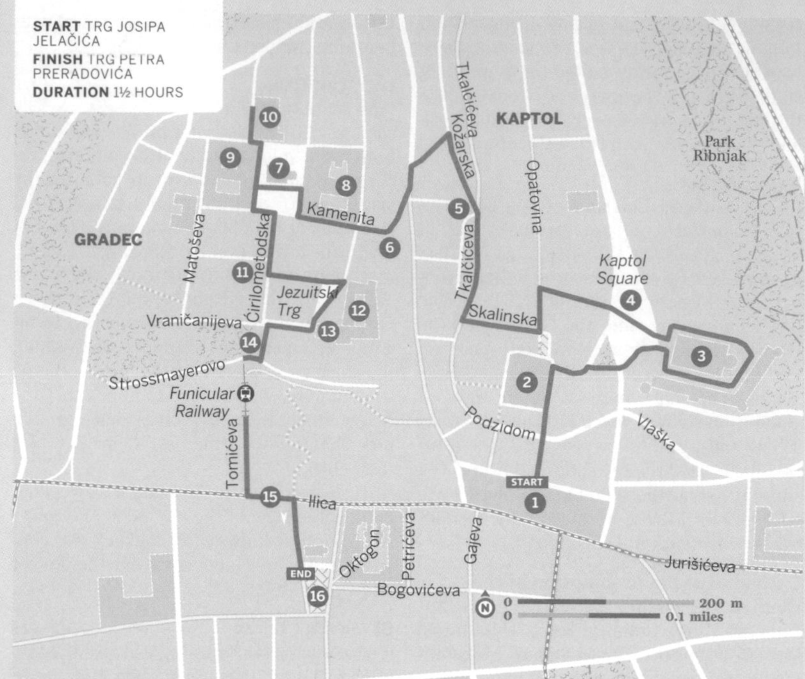

Walking Tour

Architecture, Art & Street Life

You can pick up a copy of *Step by Step* free from any tourist office. It suggests two walking tours around the town centre exploring both the Upper Town and Lower Town.

The natural starting point of any walk in Zagreb is the buzzing 1 **Trg Josipa Jelačića**. Climb the steps up to 2 **Dolac Market** and pick up some fruit or a quick snack before heading for the 3 **neo-Gothic cathedral**. Cross 4 **Kaptol Square**, lined with 17th-century buildings, walk down Skalinska and come out at Tkalčićeva. Wander up the street and climb the stairs next to the terraced 5 **Melin bar**, which will take you up to 6 **Stone Gate**, a fascinating shrine. Next, go up Kamenita and you'll come out at Markov trg, the site of 7 **St Mark's Church**, one of Zagreb's most emblematic buildings; the 8 **Sabor**, the country's parliament; and 9 **Banski Dvori**, the presidential palace. Wander about the winding streets of the Upper Town, and take in different aspects of Croatia's art world in 10 **Meštrović Atelier**. Walk back across Markov trg and down Ćirilometodska, stepping into one of the country's most particular museums, the 11 **Croatian Museum of Naïve Art**. Cross Jezuitski trg and enter 12 **Galerija Klovićevi Dvori**, where local and international contemporary art exhibitions await. When you're finished with art, gaze up at the gorgeous 13 **Jesuit Church of St Catherine**, before finally emerging at 14 **Lotrščak Tower**. Take in the cityscape and, if you fancy, go down in the funicular. Otherwise descend the verdant stairway – both will leave you on the side of 15 **Ilica**, Zagreb's commercial artery.

Cross Ilica and walk to 16 **Trg Petra Preradovića**, where you can take a break at one of the many alfresco cafes.

Meštrović Atelier ART COLLECTION

(Mletačka 8; adult/concession 30/15KN; ⊙10am-6pm Tue-Fri, to 1pm Sat & Sun) Croatia's most recognised artist is Ivan Meštrović. His former home is this 17th-century building where he worked and lived from 1922 to 1942. The excellent collection has some 100 sculptures, drawings, lithographs and pieces of furniture from the first four decades of his artistic life. Meštrović, who also worked as an architect, designed many parts of the house.

City Museum MUSEUM

(Muzej Grada Zagreba; www.mgz.hr; Opatička 20; adult/concession 30/20KN; ⊙10am-6pm Tue-Fri, 11am-7pm Sat, 10am-2pm Sun) The City Museum sits in the 17th-century Convent of St Clair. Since 1907 the convent has housed this historical museum, which presents the history of Zagreb through documents, artwork and crafts, plus interactive exhibits that fascinate kids. Notice the scale model of old Gradec. Summaries of the exhibits are posted in English in each room.

Galerija Klovićevi Dvori ART GALLERY

(www.galerijaklovic.hr; Jezuitski trg 4; adult/concession 30/20KN; ⊙11am-7pm Tue-Sun) Housed in a former Jesuit monastery, the gallery is among city's most prestigious spaces for exhibiting modern Croatian and international art. Exhibitions have included Picasso and Chagall, as well as collections of Croatia's prominent fine artists. The gallery's gift shop has arty souvenirs, and a nice cafe attached to it.

Note that the gallery closes in summer months, typically in August and part of September.

Jesuit Church of St Catherine CHURCH

(Crkva Svete Katarine; Katarinin trg bb; ⊙for Mass 6pm Mon-Fri, 11am Sun) This fine baroque church was built between 1620 and 1632. Although battered by fire and earthquake, the facade still gleams and the interior contains a fine altar dating from 1762. The interior stucco work dates from 1720 and there are 18th-century medallions depicting the life of St Catherine on the ceiling of the nave.

Croatian Natural History Museum MUSEUM

(Hrvatski Prirodoslovni Muzej; Demetrova 1; adult/concession 20/15KN; ⊙10am-5pm Tue-Fri, to 1pm Sat & Sun) This museum houses a collection of prehistoric tools and bones excavated from the Krapina cave as well as exhibits showing the evolution of animal and plant life in Croatia. Temporary shows often focus on specific regions.

During the summer the museum closes at 8pm on Thursdays and 7pm on Saturdays.

Sabor HISTORICAL BUILDING

(Trg Svetog Marka 6) The eastern side of Markov trg is taken up by the Croatian *sabor* (parliament), built in 1910 on the site of baroque 17th- and 18th-century town houses. Its neoclassical style is quite incongruous on the square, but the historical importance of this building is undeniable – Croatia's secession from the Austro-Hungarian Empire was proclaimed from its balcony in 1918.

Banski Dvori HISTORICAL BUILDING

(Ban's Palace; Trg Svetog Marka 2) Once the seat of Croatian viceroys, the presidential palace – composed of two baroque mansions – today houses courts, archives and other government offices. In October 1991 the palace was bombed by the federal army in an assassination attempt (some believe) on President Franjo Tuđman.

LOWER TOWN

Trg Josipa Jelačića CITY SQUARE

Zagreb's main orientation point and the geographic heart of the city is Trg Josipa Jelačića. It's where most people arrange to meet up and, if you want quality people-watching, you can sit in one of the cafes and watch the tramloads of people getting out, greeting each other and dispersing among the newspaper and flower sellers.

The square's name comes from Ban Jelačić, the 19th-century *ban* (viceroy or governor) who led Croatian troops into an unsuccessful battle with Hungary in the hope of winning more autonomy for his people. The **equestrian statue** of Jelačić stood in the square from 1866 until 1947, when Tito ordered its removal because it was too closely linked with Croatian nationalism. Franjo Tuđman's government dug it up out of storage in 1990 and returned it to the square.

Museum Mimara MUSEUM

(Muzej Mimara; www.mimara.hr; Rooseveltov trg 5; adult/concession 40/30KN; ⊙10am-7pm Tue-Fri, to 5pm Sat, to 2pm Sun Jul-Sep, 10am-5pm Tue-Wed & Fri-Sat, to 7pm Thu, to 2pm Sun Oct-Jun) This is the diverse private art collection – Zagreb's best – of Ante Topić Mimara, who donated over 3750 priceless objects to his native Zagreb, even though he spent much of his life in Salzburg, Austria.

ZAGREB'S CONTEMPORARY ART GALLERIES

Zagreb's palpable creative energy is driven by a host of young ambitious artists and curators who think outside the box. Here are some of the places where you can catch home-grown art, much of it dealing with Croatia's society in transition.

Lauba (www.lauba.hr; Baruna Filipovića 23a; adult/concession 25/10KN; ⌚3-11pm Mon-Fri & Sun, 11am-11pm Sat) This private art collection in a former textile weaving mill in an industrial area of western Zagreb provides an insight into Croatian contemporary art from the 1950s to today. Works on display change frequently, and there's a cool bistro (food served between noon and 4pm daily, except Sunday) on site and an exciting roster of events.

Galerija Greta (www.greta.hr; Ilica 92; ⌚2-9pm Mon-Sat) The latest opening in the art scene, this storefront gallery in an old textile shop hosts fun Monday night openings, showcasing different art forms: fine arts, video, sound installations, sculptures, projections and performances.

Galerija Nova (www.whw.hr/galerija-nova; Teslina 7; admission free; ⌚noon-8pm Tue-Fri, 11am-2pm Sat) This independent art space is run by the WHW (Što, Kako i za Koga?) curatorial collective, known for probing politically and socially sensitive topics. The small space has a lively line-up of exhibits, performances, happenings and talks.

Galerija Studentski Centar (www.galerija.sczg.hr; Savska 25; admission free; ⌚noon-8pm Mon-Fri, 10am-1pm Sat) You'll see works by some of Croatia's youngest artists at this space, just southwest of the centre. With a focus on conceptual art, it puts on installations, site-specific works, performances and interactive projects, as well as theatre pieces, concerts and festivals.

Galerija Galženica (www.galerijagalzenica.info; Trg Stjepana Radića 5, Velika Gorica; admission free; ⌚10am-7pm Mon-Fri) This cutting-edge gallery in the nearby town of Velika Gorica is worth the trek. Emphasis is placed on art that has arisen out of the social, political and cultural changes that Croatia has experienced in the past 15 years. Check whether there's an exhibit before you head there.

Galerija Miroslav Kraljević (www.g-mk.hr; Šubićeva 29; admission free; ⌚noon-7pm Tue-Fri, 11am-1pm Sat mid-Sep–mid-Jul) Founded in 1986, this contemporary art space, east of the city centre, dedicates itself to visual art. It has a dynamic repertoire of exhibitions, lectures, presentations and residency programs. Closed during summer.

Housed in a neo-Renaissance former school building (1883), the collection spans a wide range of periods and regions. There is an archaeological section with 200 items; exhibits of ancient Far Eastern artworks; a glass, textile and furniture collection that spans centuries; and 1000 European art objects.

In the painting collection, check out works by Raphael, Caravaggio, Rembrandt, Bosch, Velázquez, Goya, Manet, Renoir and Degas.

Strossmayer Gallery of Old Masters MUSEUM

(Strossmayerova Galerija Starih Majstora; Trg Nikole Šubića Zrinskog 11; adult/concession 30/10KN; ⌚10am-7pm Tue, to 4pm Wed-Fri, to 1pm Sat & Sun) This museum is housed in the 19th-century neo-Renaissance Croatian Academy of Arts and Sciences. The lovely building showcases the impressive fine-art collection donated to the city by Bishop Strossmayer in 1884.

It includes Italian masters from the 14th to 19th centuries, such as Tintoretto, Veronese and Tiepolo; Dutch and Flemish painters such as J Brueghel the Younger; French and Spanish artists Proudhon and El Greco; and the classic Croatian artists Medulić and Benković.

The interior courtyard contains the **Baška Slab** (Bašćanska Ploča), a stone tablet from the island of Krk, which features the oldest example of Glagolitic script, dating from 1102. There is also a **statue of Bishop Strossmayer** by Ivan Meštrović.

Archaeological Museum MUSEUM

(Arheološki Muzej; www.amz.hr; Trg Nikole Šubića Zrinskog 19; adult/concession 20/10KN; ⌚10am-6pm Tue, Wed & Fri, to 8pm Thu, to 6pm Sat, to 1pm

Sun) The artefacts housed here stem from prehistoric times onwards. Among the most interesting are the **Vučedolska golubica** (Vučedol Dove), a 4000-year-old ceramic censer found near the town of Vukovar. The 'bird' has since become a symbol of Vukovar and peace. Also fascinating are the **Egyptian mummies**, with ambient sounds and light designed to provoke pondering. The **coin collection** is one of the most important in Europe, containing some 260,000 coins, medals and medallions.

The courtyard, with a collection of **Roman monuments** dating from the 5th to 4th centuries BC, functions as an open-air cafe in summer.

Ethnographic Museum MUSEUM

(Etnografski Muzej; www.emz.hr; Mažuranićev trg 14; adult/concession 15/10KN, Thu free; ⏲10am-6pm Tue-Thu, to 1pm Fri-Sun) The ethnographic heritage of Croatia is catalogued in this museum inside a domed 1903 building. Out of 70,000 items, about 2750 are on display, including ceramics, jewellery, musical instruments, tools, weapons and Croatian folk costumes, including gold-embroidered scarves from Slavonia and lace from the island of Pag. Thanks to donations from the Croatian explorers Mirko and Stevo Seljan, there are also artefacts from South America, Ethiopia, China, Japan, New Guinea and Australia. Temporary exhibitions are often held on the 2nd floor.

Arts & Crafts Museum MUSEUM

(Muzej za Umjetnost i Obrt; www.muo.hr; Trg Maršala Tita 10; adult/concession 30/20KN; ⏲11am-7pm Tue-Fri, to 2pm Sat & Sun) Built between 1882 and 1892, this museum exhibits furniture, textiles, metal, ceramic and glass dating from the Middle Ages to today. You can see Gothic and baroque sculptures from northern Croatia, as well as paintings, prints, bells, stoves, rings, clocks, bound books, toys, photos and industrial designs. The museum hosts frequent temporary exhibitions.

Art Pavilion ART GALLERY

(Umjetnički Paviljon; www.umjetnicki-paviljon.hr; Trg Kralja Tomislava 22; adult/concession 30/15KN; ⏲11am-7pm Tue-Sat, 10am-1pm Sun) The yellow Art Pavilion presents changing exhibitions of contemporary art. Constructed in 1897 in stunning art-nouveau style, the pavilion is the only space in Zagreb that was specifically designed to host large exhibitions. The gallery shuts its doors from mid-July through August.

Gallery of Modern Art ART GALLERY

(Moderna Galerija; www.moderna-galerija.hr; Andrije Hebranga 1; adult/concession 40/20KN; ⏲11am-6pm Tue-Fri, to 1pm Sat & Sun) Take in this glorious display of Croatian artists of the last 200 years, including such 19th- and 20th-century masters as Bukovac, Mihanović and Račić. It's a fine overview of the vibrant arts scene.

Botanical Garden BOTANICAL GARDEN

(Botanički Vrt; Mihanovićeva bb; ⏲9am-2.30pm Mon & Tue, 9am-7pm Wed-Sun Apr-Oct) If you need a change from museums, galleries and schlepping, take a break in this lovely verdant retreat. Laid out in 1890, the garden has 10,000 species of plants and plenty of restful corners and paths.

NOVI ZAGREB

Museum of Contemporary Art MUSEUM

(Muzej Suvremene Umjetnosti; www.msu.hr; Avenija Dubrovnik 17; adult/concession 30/15KN, 1st Wed of month free; ⏲11am-6pm Tue-Fri & Sun, to 8pm Sat) Housed in a stunning new city icon designed by local star architect Igor Franić, this swanky museum puts on solo and thematic group shows by Croatian and international artists in its 17,000 sq metres. The permanent display, called *Collection in Motion,* showcases 620 edgy works by 240 artists, roughly half of whom are Croatian. Note the fun interactive *Double Slide* piece by Belgian artist Carsten Holler, and the stirring *Ženska Kuća* installation by Croatia's foremost artist Sanja Iveković, dealing with the theme of violence against women. The media facade overlooking the busy avenue is the largest in Central Europe. There is a packed schedule of film, theatre, concerts and performance art year-round.

NORTH OF THE CENTRE

Mirogoj CEMETERY

(⏲6am-8pm Apr-Sep, 7am-6pm Oct-Mar) A 10-minute ride north of the city centre on bus 106 from the cathedral (or a 30-minute walk through leafy streets) takes you to one of the most beautiful cemeteries in Europe, at the base of Mt Medvednica. It was designed in 1876 by Austrian-born architect Herman Bollé, who created numerous buildings around Zagreb. The majestic arcade topped by a string of cupolas looks like a fortress from the outside but feels calm and graceful on the inside. The cemetery is lush, and is criss-crossed by paths and dotted with sculptures and artfully designed tombs. Highlights include the grave of poet Petar Preradović and the bust of Vladimir Becić by Ivan Meštrović. The newest addition is a **memorial cross** in honour of the fallen soldiers in Croatia's Homeland War.

Medvedgrad FORTRESS
(admission 15KN; ⌚11am-7pm Tue-Sun) The medieval fortress of Medvedgrad, on the southern side of Mt Medvednica just above the city, is Zagreb's most important medieval monument. Built from 1249 to 1254, it was erected to protect the city from Tartar invasions. Owned by a succession of aristocratic families, it fell into ruin as a result of neglect and an earthquake. Restoration began in 1979, but was pursued with greater enthusiasm in 1994 when the country was looking to honour monuments from its past. Today you can see the rebuilt thick walls and towers, a small **chapel** with frescos and the **Shrine of the Homeland**, which pays homage to those who have died for a free Croatia. On a clear day, it offers a beautiful view of Zagreb and surrounds.

EAST OF THE CENTRE

Maksimir Park PARK
(www.park-maksimir.hr; Maksimirska bb; ⌚park 9am-dusk, info centre 10am-4pm Tue-Fri, to 6pm Sat & Sun mid-Apr–mid-Oct, 10am-4pm Tue-Fri, 8am-4pm Sat & Sun mid-Oct–mid-Apr) The park, a peaceful wooded enclave covering 18 hectares, is easily accessible by trams 11 and 12 from Jelačić square. Opened to the public in 1794, it was the first public promenade in southeastern Europe. It is landscaped like an English garden-style park, with alleys, lawns and artificial lakes. The most photographed structure in the park is the exquisite **Bellevue Pavilion**, which was constructed in 1843. There is also the **Echo Pavilion** and a house built to resemble a rustic Swiss cottage. The **zoo** (www.zoo.hr; adult/child 30/20KN; ⌚9am-8pm) has a modest collection of the world's fauna and daily feeding times of seals, sea lions, otters and piranhas.

Activities

Sports Park Mladost SPORT
(Jarunska 5, Jarun; day ticket adult/child/family 30/25/100KN; ⌚noon-7pm Mon-Fri, 10am-7pm Sat & Sun) By the Sava River, the park has outdoor and indoor Olympic-size swimming pools, as well as smaller pools for children, a gym and tennis courts. To get to Jarun, take tram 5 or 17.

ART VERSUS HISTORY

The **Croatian Association of Artists** (Hrvatsko Društvo Likovnih Umjetnika; www.hdlu.hr; Trg Žrtava Fašizma bb; adult/concession 20/10KN; ⌚11am-7pm Tue-Fri, 10am-2pm Sat & Sun), east of the centre, is one of the few architectural works by Ivan Meštrović and is a building that's had several fascinating incarnations, reflecting the region's history in a nutshell.

Originally designed by Meštrović in 1938 as an exhibition pavilion, the structure honoured King Petar Karađorđević – the ruler of the Kingdom of Serbs, Croats and Slovenes – which grated against the sensibilities of Croatia's nationalists. With the onset of Croatia's fascist government, the building was renamed the Zagreb Artists' Centre in May 1941, until several months later when Ante Pavelić, Croatia's fascist leader, gave orders for the building to be evacuated of all artwork and turned into a mosque. This was, according to him, so that the local Muslim population would feel at home in Croatia. There were murmurs of disapproval from the artists, but the building was significantly restructured and eventually surrounded by three minarets.

With the establishment of Socialist Yugoslavia, however, the mosque was promptly closed and the building's original purpose restored, although the government renamed it the Museum of the People's Liberation. A permanent exhibition was set up and, in 1949, the government had the minarets knocked down. In 1951 an architect called V Richter set about returning the building to its original state according to Meštrović's design. The building has remained an exhibition space ever since, with a non-profit association of Croatian artists making use of it. Despite being renamed the Croatian Association of Artists in 1991 by the country's new government, everyone in Zagreb still knows it as 'the old mosque'.

LOCAL KNOWLEDGE

IVANA VUKŠIĆ: FOUNDER & DIRECTOR OF ZAGREB'S STREET ART MUSEUM

Founded in spring 2010, Zagreb's **Street Art Museum** (www.muu.com.hr) doesn't have a fixed physical home, opening hours, curators or pompous openings – rather, it was conceived as a series of projects. At least, that is how the museum's director Ivana Vukšić describes the initiative. The first project was successfully completed when over 80 artists were given 450m of the wall that lines Branimirova street and separates it from train tracks. The latest projects beautified the otherwise drab Dugave and Siget neighbourhoods in Novi Zagreb with colourful street art.

Here Ivana lets us in on the latest happenings in the art and culture scene of Zagreb.

Top Art Galleries

The most interesting galleries for discovering new art trends in Croatia are Galerija Studentski Centar (p48), Galerija Nova (p48), Lauba (p48) and the Croatian Association of Artists (p50). The programs at these spaces always surprise with their fresh concepts and quality work presented in unpretentious environments.

Top Cultural Events

For film buffs, three must-see events are the Zagreb Film Festival (p53), **Zagrebdox** (www.zagrebdox.net) and 25 FPS – International Experimental Film and Video Festival (p53).

The delightful festival of street performance Cest is D'Best (p53) wakes Zagreb each summer, transforming it into a circus that doesn't stop. For site-specific and conceptual works, don't miss the Urban Festival (p52).

Also be sure to check out the program of **Pogon Jedinstvo** (www.upogoni.org) for interesting events and browse the website of **Kontejner** (www.kontejner.org), another collective worth following for their art productions.

Sports & Recreational Centre Šalata SPORT

(Schlosserove Stube 2; day tickets on weekends adult/child/family 30/20/60KN; ⌚1.30-5.30pm Mon-Fri, 11am-7pm Sat & Sun) This centre offers outdoor and indoor tennis courts, a gym, a winter ice-skating rink and two outdoor swimming pools. There's also an indoor ice-skating rink that rents out skates.

Sljeme SKIING, HIKING

(www.sljeme.hr) Although Zagreb is not normally associated with winter sports, you can ski right outside town at Sljeme, the main peak of Mt Medvednica, if the snow lasts long enough. It has four ski runs, three ski lifts and a triple chairlift; call the **ski centre** (☎45 53 382) or check the website for information on snow conditions.

Jarun Lake WATER SPORT

Jarun Lake in south Zagreb is a popular getaway for residents at any time of the year, but especially in summer when the clear waters are ideal for swimming. Although part of the lake is marked off for boating competitions, there is plenty of space to enjoy a leisurely swim. Take tram 5 or 17 to Jarun and follow signs to the *jezero* (lake). When you come to the lake you can head left to Malo Jezero for **swimming** and **canoe** or **pedal-boat** rental, or right to Veliko Jezero, where there's a **pebble beach** and **windsurfing**.

Tours

There's a variety of tours to choose from in Zagreb. For more options than we've listed, browse the Zagreb City Tours section on the tourism board website (www.zagreb-touristinfo.hr).

ZET BUS

(www.zet.hr) Zagreb's public transportat network operates **open-deck tour buses** (adult/child 70KN/free) on a hop-on/hop-off basis from April to September. Buses depart from Kaptol Square and take in the old town (marked red) and the outlying parks and Novi Zagreb (marked green).

Funky Zagreb GUIDED TOURS

(www.funky-zagreb.com) Personalised tours that range in theme from wine tasting (200KN

ZAGREB FOR CHILDREN

Zagreb has some wonderful attractions for kids, but getting around with small children can be a challenge. Between the tram tracks, high curbs and cars, manoeuvring a stroller on the streets isn't easy. Buses and trams are usually too crowded to accommodate strollers, even though buses have a designated stroller spot. Up to the age of seven, children travel free on public transport. If you choose taxis, make sure they have working seat belts for junior.

Kids will be fascinated by the insect collection at the Croatian Natural History Museum (p47). The **Technical Museum** (Tehnički Muzej; www.mdc.hr/tehnicki; Savska 18; planetarium 15KN, collections adult/child under 7 15KN/free; ⌚9am-5pm Tue-Fri, to 1pm Sat & Sun) has a planetarium and collections including steam-engine locomotives, scale models of satellites and space ships, and a replica of a mine within the building; the planetarium might not appeal to very young kids. The little ones love the slide at the Museum of Contemporary Art (p49), though, and the interactive exhibits at the City Museum (p47).

For open-air activity, the best place for tots to work off some steam is **Boćarski Dom** (Prisavlje 2). The park has the best in playground equipment, playing fields and a rollerblading ramp. There's also a relaxing path along the Sava River for parents to enjoy. To get there, take tram 17 west to the Prisavlje stop.

Another good spot is **Bundek Lake** in Novi Zagreb, with water fit for swimming in summer and two playgrounds, one for children up to seven years and another for seven plus. To get there, take tram 14 from Jelačić square.

For active fun, head out to **Karting Arena Zagreb** (www.karting-arena.com), located on Velesajam (Zagreb Fair) in Novi Zagreb. Kids' karting is on every weekend from 10am till 1pm. Tram 14 from Trg Josipa Jelačića will get you there.

There are two playgrounds and a zoo inside Maksimir Park (p50), which are all great for little ones. Aquatically minded kids will like the pools in the Sports Park Mladost (p50) and Šalata (p51). Head to Jarun Lake (p51) for other recreational options, such as cycling, rollerblading and kids' parks.

for three hours) to hiking in Zagreb's surroundings (from 635KN per person for a day trip).

Blue Bike Tours BIKE

(www.zagrebbybike.com) To experience Zagreb on a bike, book one of the tours – choose between Lower Town, Upper Town or Novi Zagreb – departing daily at 10am; both last around two hours and cost 170KN. In July and August they have more departures.

Zagreb Talks WALKING

(www.zagrebtalks.com) Tours include 'Do You Speak Croatian?' at 10.30am on Saturdays, which teaches you basic language skills. The price is 95KN for adults (75KN for students). From May to September only; otherwise by appointment.

Festivals & Events

For a complete listing of Zagreb events, see www.zagreb-touristinfo.hr. Croatia's largest international fairs are the Zagreb spring (mid-April) and autumn (mid-September) grand trade fairs.

Music Biennale Zagreb MUSIC

(www.mbz.hr) Croatia's most important contemporary music event is held in April during odd-numbered years.

Urban Festival ARTS

(www.urbanfestival.hr) A contemporary-art festival centred around a yearly theme, Urban Festival places art in public spaces; typically held in spring or autumn.

Subversive Festival CULTURAL

(www.subversivefestival.com) Europe's activists and philosophers descend on Zagreb in droves for film screenings and lectures over two weeks in May.

INmusic Festival MUSIC

(www.inmusicfestival.com) A three-day extravaganza every June, this is Zagreb's highest-profile music festival. Previous years have seen Massive Attack, Iggy Pop and Morrissey take to the Jarun Lake main stage.

World Festival of Animated Film FILM

(www.animafest.hr) Held in June, this prestigious festival has taken place in Zagreb since

1972 – odd-numbered years are devoted to feature films and even-numbered ones to short films.

Cest is D'Best CULTURAL
(www.cestisdbest.com) This street festival delights Zagreb citizens for a few days in early June each year with five stages around the city centre, around 200 international performers, and acts that include music, dance, theatre, art and sport.

Ljeto na Strossu CULTURAL
(www.ljetonastrosu.com) From late May through to late September, this quirky annual event stages free outdoor film screenings, concerts, art workshops and best-in-show mongrel dog competitions, all along the leafy Strossmayer Šetalište.

Eurokaz THEATRE
(www.eurokaz.hr) Since 1987, the International Festival of New Theatre has been showcasing innovative theatre troupes and cutting-edge performances from all over the world in late June/early July.

International Folklore Festival FOLKLORE
(www.msf.hr) Taking place in Zagreb since 1966, for a few days in July, it features folk dancers and singers from Croatia and other countries dressed in traditional costumes. There are free workshops designed to introduce you to Croatian folk culture.

Zagreb Summer Evenings MUSIC
This festival presents a cycle of concerts in the Upper Town each July. The atrium of Galerija Klovićevi Dvori (p47) on Jezuitski trg and the Gradec stage are used for performances of classic music, jazz, blues and world tunes.

International Puppet Theatre Festival PUPPETRY
(http://public.carnet.hr/pif-festival) Typically taking place during the last week of August or first week of September, this prominent puppetry festival, around since 1968, showcases star ensembles, workshops on puppet making and puppetry exhibits.

World Theatre Festival THEATRE
(www.zagrebtheatrefestival.hr) High-quality contemporary theatre comes to Zagreb for a couple of weeks each September, often extending into early October.

25 FPS – International Experimental Film and Video Festival FILM
(www.25fps.hr) Now in its ninth year, this offbeat festival presents alternative visual expressions during one week of screenings, typically in late September.

Zagreb Film Festival FILM
(www.zagrebfilmfestival.com) If you're in Zagreb in mid-October, don't miss this major cultural event, with film screenings and accompanying parties. Directors compete for the Golden Pram award.

Sleeping

Zagreb's accommodation scene has been undergoing a noticeable change with the arrival of some of Europe's budget airlines. The budget end of the market has picked up greatly and various hostel options now abound – from cheap backpacker digs to more stylish hideaways. In addition to those we've included, the following hostels are worth checking out: **Fulir Hostel** (☎48 30 882; www.fulir-hostel.com; ❄@📶), **Hostel Day and Night** (www.hosteldayandnight.com), **Buzz**

A ZAGREB HOME OF YOUR OWN

If you intend staying in a private house or apartment, try not to arrive on Sunday because most of the agencies will be closed, unless you've made prior arrangements. Prices for doubles run from about 300KN and studio apartments start at 400KN per night. There's usually a surcharge for staying only one night.

Evistas (☎48 39 554; www.evistas.hr; Augusta Šenoe 28; s/d/apt from 240/290/340KN) This agency is recommended by the tourist office; it's closest to the train station and finds private accommodation.

InZagreb (☎65 23 201; www.inzagreb.com; Remetinečka 13; apt 490-665KN) Great apartments, centrally located, with wireless internet but a minimum three-night stay. The price includes bike rental and pick-up/drop-off from the railway or bus station. Book through the website or by phone.

Never Stop (Nemoj Stati; ☎091 637 8111; www.nest.hr; Trevoj 65; apt 450-500KN) Great apartments in the centre of town. Check the website for details and contact for prices.

Hostel (☎23 20 267; www.buzzbackpackers.com; ❄@📶) and **Taban Hostel** (www.tabanzagreb.com). Several of the hostels join in together to organise a pub crawl three nights per week, with free entrance to clubs and shots to boot; ask at your hostel.

For those wanting more privacy and a homely feel, there are private rooms and apartments, arranged through agencies. The city's business and high-end hotels are in full flow, thanks to Zagreb's role as an international conference hot spot. At the time of writing, a DoubleTree by Hilton had just opened in Zagreb's business district.

Prices usually stay the same in all seasons, but be prepared for a 20% surcharge if you arrive during a festival or major event, in particular the autumn fair.

TOP CHOICE Studio Kairos B&B €€
(☎46 40 680; www.studio-kairos.com; Vlaška 92; s 380-440KN, d 560-660KN; ❄📶) This adorable new B&B, Zagreb's first, has four well-appointed rooms in a street-level apartment. Rooms are decked out by theme – Writers', Crafts, Music and Granny's – and there's a cosy common space where delicious breakfast is served. The main square (Trg Josipa Jelačića) is a 15-minute stroll away, a five-minute tram ride (take 11 or 12) or a five-minute bike ride (bikes are available for rent). The interior design is gorgeous and the friendly owners a fountain of info.

TOP CHOICE Funk Lounge Hostel HOSTEL €
(☎55 52 707; www.funkhostel.hr; Rendićeva 28b; dm 135-165KN, d 420KN; @📶) Located steps from Maksimir Park, this new outpost of the original Funk Hostel (southwest of the centre) has friendly staff, neat rooms and a range of freebies, including breakfast, a shot of *rakija*, toiletries and lockers. On site is a restaurant and bar, and a full kitchen.

Esplanade Zagreb Hotel HISTORIC HOTEL €€€
(☎45 66 666; www.esplanade.hr; Mihanovićeva 1; s/d 1385/1500KN; P❄@📶) Drenched in history, this six-storey hotel was built next to the train station in 1924 to welcome the *Orient Express* crowd in grand style. It has hosted kings, artists, journalists and politicians ever since. The art-deco masterpiece is replete with walls of swirling marble, immense staircases and wood-panelled lifts. Take a peek at the magnificent Emerald Ballroom and have a meal at superb Zinfandel's restaurant (p57).

Arcotel Allegra DESIGN HOTEL €€€
(☎46 96 000; www.arcotel.at/allegra; Branimirova 29; s/d from 730/840KN; P❄@📶) Zagreb's first designer hotel has 151 airy rooms and a marble-and-exotic-fish reception. The bed throws are printed with faces of Kafka, Kahlo, Freud and other iconic personalities. The top-floor Orlando Fitness & Spa has great city views. The on-site restaurant, Radicchio, is good and Joe's Bar is hot on Latin music. In summer, specials start from 450KN.

Palace Hotel HISTORIC HOTEL €€€
(☎48 99 600; www.palace.hr; Strossmayerov trg 10; s/d from 779/890KN; P❄@📶) This classy hotel, the oldest in Zagreb, oozes European charm. The grand Secessionist mansion, built in 1891, is aristocratic and its 118 elegant rooms and suites are outfitted with the latest modern comforts. Try to get a front room for fantastic views over the park. Look for the frescos in the back of the ground-floor cafe, with its unique Austro-Hungarian finesse.

Hotel Dubrovnik HOTEL €€€
(☎48 63 555; www.hotel-dubrovnik.hr; Gajeva 1; s/d from 740/885KN; P❄📶) Smack on the main square, this glass New York wannabe is a city landmark. It buzzes with business travellers, who love being at the centre of the action. The 245 elegant and well-appointed units have old-school classic style. Try to get a view of Jelačića square and watch Zagreb pass by under your window. Check out the hotel's great packages and specials.

Hobo Bear Hostel HOSTEL €
(☎48 46 636; www.hobobearhostel.com; Medulićeva 4; dm 135-175KN, d from 400KN; ❄@📶) Inside a duplex apartment, this sparkling five-dorm hostel has exposed brick walls, hardwood floors, free lockers, a kitchen with free tea and coffee, a common room, book exchange and friendly service. Take tram 1, 6 or 11 from Trg Josipa Jelačića. The three doubles are across the street.

Hotel Jägerhorn HOTEL €€
(☎48 33 877; www.jaegerhorn.hr; Ilica 14; s/d/apt 598/749/1052KN; P❄@📶) A charming little hotel that sits right underneath Lotrščak Tower (p45), the 'Hunter's Horn' has friendly service and 18 spacious, classic rooms with good views (you can gaze over leafy Gradec from the top-floor attic rooms).

Shappy Hostel HOSTEL €
(☎48 30 179; www.hostel-shappy.com; Varšavska 8; dm 128-170, d from 420KN; P❄@📶) This new six-room hostel is a peaceful oasis tucked away in a courtyard. Rooms range in size and theme – from the Romantic for Two to a six-bed Happy Room. On site is a bar with a terrace, where you can order breakfast.

Palmers Lodge Hostel Zagreb HOSTEL €
(☎88 92 686; www.palmerslodge.com.hr; Branimirova 25; dm 120-150KN; @📶) Convenient for late arrivals, this new hostel – part of the namesake British hostel chain – sits steps from the train station. The dorms aren't spectacular, but each comes with its own bathroom, plus there's a common space, a shared kitchen and excursions.

Hotel Jadran HOTEL €€
(☎45 53 777; www.hoteljadran.com.hr; Vlaška 50; s/d 440/560KN; P📶) This recently renovated six-storey hotel has a superb location only minutes from Jelačić square. The 49 rooms are laid out in a cheery style and the service is friendly. Rates are negotiable depending on availability.

Chillout Hostel Zagreb Downtown HOSTEL €
(☎48 49 605; www.chillout-hostel-zagreb.com; Kačićeva 3b; dm 135-180KN; ❄@📶) Another newbie on Zagreb's hostel scene, this cheerful spot has no less than 100 beds in two buildings hidden away in a courtyard a tram ride from Trg Josipa Jelačića. The trimmings are plentiful – from free lockers to a 24/7 bar. Take tram 1, 6 or 11 to Britanski trg.

Hotel Central HOTEL €€
(☎48 41 122; www.hotel-central.hr; Branimirova 3; s/d 600/700KN; ❄@📶) The best mid-priced place to stay if you have a train to catch, the Hotel Central is in a square concrete building with 76 comfy, if a little pokey, rooms. The larger top-floor rooms face the leafy courtyard.

Ravnice Hostel HOSTEL €
(☎23 32 325; www.ravnice-youth-hostel.hr; Ravnice 38d; dm/d 125/288KN; P@📶) A hike of 45 minutes or a 20-minute tram ride from the centre, this place has clean rooms, a rambling garden and freebies such as lockers, breakfast and evening soup. Musicians and performers get a free night's stay in exchange for an hour's performance for fellow guests.

Omladinski Hostel HOSTEL €
(☎48 41 261; www.hfhs.hr; Petrinjska 77; dm 124-134KN, s/d 209/294KN) Although spruced up not too long ago, this socialist-era spot still maintains a bit of its old gloomy feel. The rooms are sparse and clean, and dorm rooms have three or six beds. It's central and has many rooms, so is a good back-up if you can't find a bed elsewhere.

Eating

You'll have to love Croatian and Italian food to enjoy Zagreb's restaurants, but new places are branching out to include Japanese and other world cuisines. The biggest move is towards elegantly presented haute cuisine at *haute* prices.

SWEET HOME IN THE HILLS

For a taste of Croatian countryside a stone's throw from Zagreb, head to **Kućica** (☎091 549 8118; www.kuchica.com; weekdays/weekends 450/750KN), a lovely traditional cottage made of 120-year-old oak wood. Only 30 minutes from the city, this *Hansel and Gretel*–style retreat in the hills feels worlds away. Outside: orchards, vineyards, an organic garden, a hammock underneath a chestnut tree, bird song... Inside: restored antique furniture, a wood oven and colourful rustic decor...

A dream project by Vanja and Iva, two young marketing professionals from Zagreb, this adorable hideaway can be rented for a day, a week, or as long as you wish (discounts available for longer stays). While the area doesn't offer much in terms of attractions, there are some nice hikes and a charming village with a church, a shop and two cafe-bars. A long wooden table outside and a barbecue make 'the little house' a hit with families and groups of friends. There are occasional yoga retreats, photographers' workshops and other fun events.

It's doable as an easy day trip if you have your own wheels. Otherwise, for 365KN, the owners will pick you up in Zagreb, take you to a local market en route to stock up on food, and drop you off at the house. If you ask, they can even leave you with some homemade pies, breads, cakes, grappa and veggies from their garden.

The city centre's main streets, including Ilica, Teslina, Gajeva and Preradovićeva, are lined with fast-food joints and inexpensive snack bars.

Note that many restaurants close in August for their summer holiday, which typically lasts anywhere from two weeks to a month.

TOP CHOICE Vinodol CROATIAN €€
(Teslina 10; mains from 57KN) Well-prepared Central European fare is much-loved by both local and overseas patrons. On warm days, eat on the covered patio entered through an ivy-clad passageway off Teslina; the cold-weather alternative is the massive dining hall with vaulted stone ceilings. Highlights include the succulent lamb or veal and potatoes cooked under a *peka* (domed baking lid), as well as local mushrooms called *bukovače*.

TOP CHOICE Karijola PIZZERIA €
(Vlaška 63; pizzas from 42KN; ⏲Mon-Sat) Locals swear by the crispy thin-crust pizza churned out of a clay oven at this new location of Zagreb's best pizza joint. Pizzas come with high-quality ingredients, such as smoked ham, olive oil, rich mozzarella, cherry tomatoes, rocket and shiitake mushrooms.

Lari & Penati MODERN CROATIAN €
(Petrinjska 42a; mains from 40KN; ⏲closed Sun, dinner Sat) Small stylish bistro that serves up innovative lunch and dinner specials that change daily according to what's market-fresh. The food is fab, the music cool and the few sidewalk tables lovely in warm weather. Closed for two weeks in August.

Tip Top SEAFOOD €
(Gundulićeva 18; mains from 55KN; ⏲Mon-Sat) How we love Tip Top and its wait staff, who still sport old socialist uniforms and scowling faces that eventually turn to smiles. But we mostly love the excellent Dalmatian food. Every day has a different set menu.

Mali Bar TAPAS €€
(☎55 31 014; Vlaška 63; mains from 60KN; ⏲closed Sun) This new spot by star chef Ana Ugarkovič shares the terraced space with Karijola (p56), hidden away in a *veža* (Zagreb alleyway). The interior is cosy and earth-tone colourful and the food focused on globally inspired tapas-style dishes. Remember to book ahead.

Didov San DALMATIAN €€
(☎48 51 154; Mletačka 11; mains from 60KN) This Upper Town tavern features a rustic wooden interior with ceiling beams and a few tables on the deck. The food is based on traditional cuisine from the Neretva River delta in Dalmatia's hinterland, such as grilled frogs wrapped in proscuitto. Book ahead.

Amfora SEAFOOD €
(Dolac 2; mains from 40KN; ⏲lunch) This locals' lunch favourite serves fresh seafood straight from the market next door, paired with off-the-stalls vegies. This hole in the wall has a few tables outside and an upstairs gallery with a nice market view.

Trilogija MEDITERRANEAN €€
(Kamenita 5; mains from 70KN; ⏲Mon-Sat) Right by the Stone Gate, in a location that has seen many a restaurant open and close, this one seems to be here to stay. The secret lies in the quality of its fresh Croatian-Mediterranean food, friendly staff and friendly prices.

Mano INTERNATIONAL €€
(Medvedgradska 2; mains from 100KN; ⏲Mon-Sat) This swish steakhouse is in a beautiful brick building steps from the Kaptol Centar, with an airy interior featuring exposed stone walls, steel pillars and a glass-enclosed kitchen. The lighting is moody and the mains innovative. Think wild-boar polenta with gorgonzola.

Prasac MEDITERRANEAN €€
(☎48 51 411; Vranicanijeva 6; mains from 87KN; ⏲Mon-Sat) Creative Mediterranean fare is conjured up by the Croatian-Sicilian chef at this intimate place with wooden beamed ceilings and a few alfresco tables. The market-fresh food is superb, but the service is slow and the portions small. Reserve ahead. Perfect for a romantic meal.

Stari Fijaker 900 TRADITIONAL CROATIAN €
(Mesnička 6; mains from 50KN) This restaurant and beer hall was once the height of dining out in Zagreb, and its decor of banquettes and white linen still has a staid sobriety. Tradition reigns in the kitchen, so try the homemade sausages, bean stews and *štrukli* (dumplings filled with cottage cheese), or one of the cheaper daily dishes.

Pod Gričkim Topom CROATIAN €€
(Zakmardijeve Stube 5; mains from 90KN; ⏲Mon-Sat) Tucked away by a leafy path below the

Upper Town, this charming restaurant has an outdoor terrace and serves good Croatian meat-based specialties. It's a great place to hole up on a snowy winter evening or dine under the stars in summer.

Ivica i Marica TRADITIONAL CROATIAN €€
(Tkalčićeva 70; mains from 70KN) Based on the Brothers Grimm story *Hansel and Gretel,* this little restaurant and cake shop is made to look like the gingerbread house from the tale, with waiters clad in traditional costumes. It has vegie and fish dishes plus meatier fare. The ice creams, cakes and *štrukli* are great.

Kaptolska Klet TRADITIONAL CROATIAN €
(Kaptol 5; mains from 50KN) This friendly restaurant has a huge outdoor terrace and a brightly lit beer-hall-style interior. Although famous for its Zagreb specialties, such as grilled meats, lamb and veal under *peka,* and homemade sausages, it also turns out a nice vegetable loaf.

Konoba Čiho SEAFOOD €€
(Pavla Hatza 15; mains from 80KN) An old-school Dalmatian *konoba* (simple family-run establishment), where, downstairs, you can get fish (by the kilo) and seafood grilled or stewed just the way the regulars like it. Try the wide range of *rakija* (grape brandy).

Vallis Aurea TRADITIONAL CROATIAN €
(Tomićeva 4; mains from 37KN; Mon-Sat) This true local eatery has some of the best home cooking you'll find in town, so it's no wonder that it's chock-a-block at lunchtime for its *gableci* (traditional lunches). Right by the lower end of the funicular.

Žlica & Vilica CROATIAN €
(Kneza Mislava 13; mains from 35KN; closed Sun, dinner Sat) Located slightly out of the centre, this bistro serves homemade Croatian fare in a dining room with a chic green-themed atmosphere and on sidewalk tables. There are five dishes to choose from, and breakfast is served. Closed for three weeks in August.

Boban ITALIAN €€
(Gajeva 9; mains from 70KN) Italian is the name of the game in this cellar restaurant that's owned by the Croatian football star Zvonimir Boban. The menu features a robust range of pasta, risotto, gnocchi and meat dishes. Next door is a great quick bite alternative, **Čušpajz** (mains from 38KN; lunch Mon-Sat), which does delicious lunchtime stews.

Nokturno ITALIAN €
(Skalinska 4; mains from 40KN) Right on the sloping street underneath the cathedral, this place has good Italian mainstays and a lively outdoor terrace. There are all the usual pizzas (20KN to 35KN) and huge servings of risotto, good to order if you're starving. **Hostel Nokturno** (www.hostel.nokturno.hr; dm/s 130/200KN; @) is adjacent.

Baltazar CROATIAN €€
(Nova Ves 4; mains from 90KN; closed dinner Sun) Meat – duck, lamb, pork, beef and turkey – is grilled and prepared the Zagorje and Slavonian way in this upmarket old-timer. There's a good choice of Mediterranean dishes and local wines. The summer terrace is a great place to dine under the stars.

Agava INTERNATIONAL €€
(Tkalčićeva 39; mains from 80KN) The best thing about this smart spot on the main strip is its terrace. Food ranges from starters such as swordfish carpaccio to mains of steak and truffle. The wine list features plenty of Istrian and Slavonian choices.

Zinfandel's INTERNATIONAL €€€
(Mihanovićeva 1; mains from 170KN) The tastiest, most creative dishes in town are served with flair in the dining room of the Esplanade Zagreb Hotel (p54). For a simpler but still delicious dining experience, head to French-flavoured **Le Bistro**, also in the hotel, and don't miss its famous *štrukli.*

Rubelj QUICK BITE €
(Dolac 2; mains from 25KN) One of the many Rubeljs across town, this Dolac branch is a great place for a quick portion of *ćevapčići* (small spicy sausage of minced beef, lamb or pork). They come pretty close to those in Bosnia and Hercegovina (the spiritual home of the *ćevapčići*).

Pingvin SANDWICH SHOP €
(Teslina 7; 9am-4am Mon-Sat, 6pm-2am Sun) This quick-bite institution, around since 1987, offers tasty designer sandwiches and salads, which locals savour from a couple of bar stools.

Vincek PASTRIES & CAKES €
(Ilica 18) This institution of a *slastičarna* (pastry shop) serves some of Zagreb's creamiest cakes. They recently got some serious competition, however, with **Torte i To** (Nova Ves 11, Kaptol Centar) on the 2nd floor of Kaptol Centar.

Dinara BAKERY €

(Gajeva 8) The best bakery in town churns out an impressive variety of baked goodies. Try the *bučnica* (filo pie with pumpkin). Also has branches at Ilica 71 and Preradovićeva 1.

Drinking

In the Upper Town, the chic Tkalčićeva is throbbing with bars and cafes. In the Lower Town, there's bar-lined Bogovićeva, just south of Trg Josipa Jelačića, which turns into prime meet-and-greet territory on spring and summer days and balmy nights. Trg Petra Preradovića (known locally as Cvjetni trg) is the most popular spot in the Lower Town for street performers and occasional bands. With half a dozen bars and sidewalk cafes between Trg Preradovića and Bogovićeva, the scene on some summer nights resembles a vast outdoor party. Things wind down by midnight, though, and get quieter from mid-July to late August, when half of Zagreb storms the coast.

TOP CHOICE **Cica** BAR

(Tkalčićeva 18) This tiny storefront bar is as underground as it gets on Tkalčićeva. The funky interior has cutting-edge work by local artists and cool flea-market finds. Sample one or – if you dare – all of the 25 kinds of *rakija* that the place is famous for. Herbal, nutty, fruity: you think it, they've got it.

Booksa CAFE

(www.booksa.hr; Martićeva 14d; ⌚11am-8pm Tue-Sun, closes for 3 weeks from late Jul) Bookworms and poets, writers and performers, oddballs and artists, basically anyone creative in Zagreb comes to chat and drink coffee, browse the library, surf with free wireless and hear readings at this lovely book-themed cafe. There are English-language readings here, too; check the website. Closes for three weeks from late July.

Stross OUTDOOR BAR

(Strossmayerovo Šetalište; ⌚Jun-Sep) From June to September, a makeshift bar is set up at the Strossmayer promenade in the Upper Town, with cheap drinks and live music most nights, starting around 9.30pm. The mixed-bag crowd, great city views and leafy ambience make it a great spot to while away your evenings.

Bacchus BAR

(Trg Kralja Tomislava 16; ⌚closed Sun) You'll be lucky if you score a table at Zagreb's funkiest courtyard garden, lush and hidden in a passageway. After 10pm the action moves inside the artsy subterranean space, which hosts poetry readings and old classic music nights. Things get quiet in the summer.

Kino Europa CAFE-BAR

(www.kinoeuropa.hr; Varšavska 3; ⌚Mon-Sat) Zagreb's oldest cinema, from the 1920s, now houses a splendid cafe, wine bar and *grapperia*. At this glass-enclosed space with an outdoor terrace, enjoy great coffee, over 30 types of grappa and free wireless. The cinema hosts daily film screenings and occasional dance parties.

Funk CAFE-BAR

(Tkalčićeva 52) Sip coffee and watch people during the day, and at night go down the spiral staircase and you'll see why this cult spot has locals at its beck and call. In a small basement with stone vaulted ceilings, DJs spin house, jazz, funk and broken beats to a boogie-happy crowd (unless it's summer).

Pivnica Medvedgrad BREWERY

(www.pivnica-medvedgrad.hr; Ilica 49) Sip on one of five house-brewed beers at this beer hall that offers reliably cheap and tasty grub and a bustling atmosphere. It's accessed through a shopping passageway off Ilica, with a large chestnut-tree-shaded courtyard and happy hour from 5pm to 7pm.

Cafe u Dvorištu CAFE-BAR

(Jurja Žerjavića 7/2; ⌚Mon-Sat) Sweet little cafe-bar tucked away inside a courtyard, serving excellent organic and fair-trade coffee and tea. There are occasional live music performances and art exhibitions. Particularly popular is the Saturday afternoon milonga (tango dancing).

Limb BAR

(Plitvička 16; ⌚Mon-Sat) A secret spot only the locals know about, and probably the most understatedly hip little bar in town, right by KSET (p60). A slightly older boho crowd packs the two small colourful rooms and the glassed-in terrace with a tree in the middle.

Klub Kino Grič CAFE-BAR

(Jurišićeva 6) This old-school cinema was recently revamped into a colourful two-floor bar and a small basement club (weekends only). It has since become a locals' favourite, with art exhibits and film screenings in the cosy projection room.

Sedmica BAR

(Kačićeva 7a) This low-key bar is hidden in an alleyway off Kačićeva, with just a big Guinness sign marking the entrance. A gathering point of Zagreb's boho-intellectual crowd, it has a pokey interior with a mezzanine and an outside patio that buzzes in warmer months.

Velvet CAFE-BAR

(Dežmanova 9; ⌚8am-10pm Mon-Fri, to 3pm Sat, to 2pm Sun) Stylish spot for a good but pricey cup of java and a quick bite amid the minimalist chic interior decked out by owner Saša Šekoranja, Zagreb's hippest florist. Velvet Gallery next door, known as 'Black Velvet', stays open till 11pm (except Sunday).

Melin CAFE-BAR

(Tkalčićeva 47) This is rock 'n' roll as it used to be, with grotty seats, graffiti-splashed walls and ear-busting music. A corner of scruffy old Zagreb on a fast-gentrifying street, it has lots of character and a terrace for alfresco drinking.

Lemon CAFE-BAR

(www.lemon.hr; Gajeva 10) Great spot for summer cocktails on the terrace of the Archaeological Museum (p48), surrounded by ancient slabs of stone. During autumn and winter, boogie in the club downstairs.

Eli's Cafe CAFE

(Ilica 63; ⌚8am-7pm Mon-Fri, to 4pm Sat, 9am-2pm Sun mid-Aug–mid-Jul, 8am-2pm daily mid-Jul–mid-Aug) The award-winning coffee from 100% arabica beans here is tops. Try the smooth cappuccino and the breakfast pastries for dipping.

Bulldog PUB

(Bogovićeva 6) Its sidewalk tables are prime for people-watching on this busy pedestrian street. At night, it's a good place to meet for drinks, with live music in the downstairs club on weekends.

Palainovka CAFE

(Ilirski trg 1) Claiming to be the oldest cafe in Zagreb (dating from 1846), this Viennese-style place serves delicious coffee, tea and cakes under pretty frescoed ceilings.

Tri Praščića WINE BAR

(Gundulićeva 20; ⌚closed evening Sun) The excellent choice of top Croatian wines, paired with tapas that should you get peckish, is poured to a 40-something artsy crowd in a stylish small space.

COFFEE BREAK

Recent rumours of Croatia's first Starbucks died a quick death. That's because Starbucks would never stand a chance competing with *špica*, the very local Zagreb tradition of sipping coffee in the town centre between 11am and 2pm on Saturday, before or after the run at the Dolac market. This showdown of latest fashions, mobile phones and gossip has people rushing for prime sidewalk tables along Bogovićeva, Preradovićeva and Tkalčićeva. It's a great way to experience Zagreb in its liveliest incarnation.

Hemingway LOUNGE BAR

(Trg Maršala Tita 1) The main accoutrements you'll need at this upmarket cocktail bar are black sunglasses and an iPhone. Come to see and be seen.

☆ Entertainment

Admittedly, Zagreb doesn't register highly on a nightlife Richter scale, but it does have an ever-developing art and music scene, and a growing influx of fun-seeking travellers. Zagreb's theatres and concert halls present a great variety of programs throughout the year. Many are listed in the monthly brochure *Zagreb Events & Performances,* which is available from the main tourist office. The back pages of daily newspapers *Jutarnji List* and *Večernji List* show the current offerings on the art and culture circuit.

Many open-air events in the city are free, but admission is usually charged for indoor concerts. Prices depend upon the concert, but tickets for most musical events can be purchased from **Koncertna Direkcija Zagreb** (☎45 01 200; www.kdz.hr; Kneza Mislava 18; ⌚9am-6pm Mon-Fri) and in several music shops around town.

Nightclubs

Nightclub entry ranges from 20KN to 100KN, depending on the evening and the event. Clubs open around 10pm but most people show up around midnight. Many clubs only open from Thursday to Saturday.

Vip Club NIGHTCLUB

(www.vip-club.hr; Trg Josipa Jelačića 9) This newcomer on the nightlife scene quickly became

GAY & LESBIAN VENUES

The gay and lesbian scene in Zagreb is finally becoming more open than it had previously been, although free-wheeling it isn't.

For more information, browse www.zagrebgayguide.com. Also, look out for performances by **Le Zbor** (www.lezbor.com), Croatia's lesbian and feminist female choir with an activist edge.

Kolaž (Amruševa 11) This basement speakeasy-style bar behind an unmarked door caters to a primarily gay crowd.

Rush Club (Amruševa 10) A younger gay and lesbian crowd mixes at this fun club in the city centre, with themed nights such as karaoke.

Hotpot (Petrinjska 31) This new club in town has quickly become one of the favourites.

Vimpi (Miškecov Prolaz 3) Gathering spot for Zagreb's lady-loving ladies.

a favourite. A swank basement place on the main square, it offers a varied program, from jazz to Balkan beats. It closes in summer months.

Tvornica LIVE MUSIC
(www.tvornicakulture.com; Šubićeva 2) Excellent multimedia venue 20 minutes to the east of Trg Josipa Jelačića, showcasing a variety of live music performances, from Bosnian *sevdah* to alternative punk rock. Check out the website to see what's on.

Aquarius NIGHTCLUB
(www.aquarius.hr; Jarun Lake) Past its heyday but still fun, this lakside club has a series of rooms that open on to a huge terrace. House and techno are the standard fare but there are also hip hop and R&B nights. During summer, Aquarius sets up shop at Zrće (p187) on Pag.

Pepermint NIGHTCLUB
(www.pepermint-zagreb.com; Ilica 24) Small and chic city centre club clad in white wood, with two levels and a well-to-do older crowd. Programs change weekly but the vintage rockabilly, twist and swing night on Wednesdays is a definite hit.

Močvara NIGHTCLUB
(www.mochvara.hr; Trnjanski Nasip bb) In a former factory on the banks of the Sava River, 'Swamp' is one of Zagreb's best venues for the cream of alternative music and attractively dingy charm. Live acts range from dub and dancehall to world music and heavy metal.

KSET NIGHTCLUB
(www.kset.org; Unska 3) Zagreb's top music venue, with everyone who's anyone performing here, from ethno to hip-hop sounds. Saturday nights are dedicated to DJ music, when youngsters dance till late. You'll find gigs and events to suit most tastes.

Jabuka NIGHTCLUB
(Jabukovac 28) 'Apple' is an old-time fave, with 1980s hits played to a 30-something crowd that reminisces about the good old days when they were young and alternative. It's a taxi ride or a walk through the woods, tucked away in a posh area.

Medika NIGHTCLUB
(www.pierottijeva11.org; Pierottijeva 11) This artsy venue in an old pharmaceutical factory calls itself an 'autonomous cultural centre'. It's the city's first legalised squat with a program of concerts, art exhibits and parties fuelled by cheap beer and *rakija*.

Purgeraj NIGHTCLUB
(www.purgeraj.hr; Park Ribnjak 1) Live rock, blues and avant-garde jazz are on the music menu at this funky space that attracts a fairly young crowd. Programs feature a fusion of disco, house, breakbeat, pop and '80s music. The new **Park** recently merged with Purgeraj and started drawing in big-name bands.

Sirup NIGHTCLUB
(www.sirupclub.com; Donje Svetice 40) A serious party crowd (of mostly men) frequents this large club outside the city centre for its glittery design and hotshot local and international DJs who churn out techno.

Theatre

Theatre tickets are usually available last minute, even for the most in-demand shows.

Zagrebačko Kazalište Mladih THEATRE
(☎48 72 554; www.zekaem.hr; Teslina 7) Zagreb Youth Theatre, better known as ZKM, is considered the cradle of Croatia's contemporary theatre. It hosts several festivals and lots of visiting troupes from around the world.

Croatian National Theatre THEATRE
(☎48 88 418; www.hnk.hr; Trg Maršala Tita 15) This neobaroque theatre, established in 1895, stages opera and ballet performances. Check out Ivan Meštrović's sculpture *The Well of Life* (1905) standing out the front.

Vatroslav Lisinski Concert Hall CONCERT HALL
(☎61 21 166; www.lisinski.hr; Trg Stjepana Radića 4) This is the city's most prestigious venue in which to hear symphony concerts, jazz and world-music performances, as well as attend theatrical productions.

Sport

Jarun Lake hosts competitions in rowing, kayaking and canoeing in summer; call ☎30 31 888 for details. For information on sporting events dial ☎18 841.

Dražen Petrović Memorial Museum MUSEUM
(☎48 43 146; Savska 30; tickets 100-200KN) Basketball is popular in Zagreb, which is home to the Cibona basketball team. Pay homage to the team's most famous player at the Dražen Petrović Memorial Museum, next to the Technical Museum. Games take place frequently at the Cibona Tower nearby; tickets (30KN to 100KN) can be purchased at the door or online at www.cibona.com.

Stadion Maksimir SPORT
(☎23 86 111; Maksimirska 128; tickets 1-200KN) Dinamo is Zagreb's most popular football team and it plays matches at Stadion Maksimir, on the eastern side of Zagreb. Take trams 4, 7, 11 or 12 to Maksimirska. For more information, check out www.gnkdinamo.hr.

Shopping

Ilica is Zagreb's main shopping street with fashionable international brands peeking out from the staid buildings. Most stores are closed on Sunday.

Prostor FASHION
(www.multiracionalnakompanija.com; Mesnička 5; ⌚noon-8pm Mon-Fri, 10am-3pm Sat) A fantastic little art gallery and clothes shop, featuring some of the city's best independent artists and young designers. Check out the website for exhibition openings, when you can go and hang out with Zagreb's arty crowd. In a courtyard off Mesnička.

Natura Croatica FOOD
(www.naturacroatica.com; Preradovićeva 8) Over 300 Croatian products and souvenirs are sold at this shop, from *rakija,* wines and chocolates to jams, spices and truffle spreads. A perfect pit stop for gifts.

Profil Megastore BOOKSTORE
(Bogovićeva 7) Inside an entryway, this most atmospheric of Zagreb bookstores has a great selection of books (including a whole section of titles in English) and a nice cafe on the gallery.

Aromatica COSMETICS
(www.aromatica.hr; Vlaška 7) Flagship store of a small chain showcasing all-natural skincare products, from handcrafted soaps to fragrant oils, with a focus on local herbs. Great gift baskets, too.

Bornstein WINE
(www.bornstein.hr; Kaptol 19) If Croatia's wine and spirits have gone to your head, get your

MARKET DAYS

Zagreb doesn't have many markets but those it does have are stellar. The Sunday **antiques market** (⌚9am-2pm Sun) on Britanski trg is one of central Zagreb's joys. But to see a flea market that's unmatched in the whole of Croatia, you have to make it to **Hrelić** (⌚7am-3pm Wed & Sun). It's a huge space packed with everything from car parts and antique furniture to clothes, records, kitchenware – you name it. All goods are, of course, secondhand, and bargaining is the norm. Apart from the shopping, it's a great experience in itself and is a side of Zagreb you probably won't see anywhere else – expect lots of Roma people, music, general liveliness and grilled meat smoking in the food section. If you're going in the summer months, take a hat and put on some sunscreen, as there's no shade. Take bus 295 (15KN, 20 minutes, on Sunday only) to Sajam Jakuševac from behind the railway station. By tram, take number 6 in the direction of Sopot, get off near the bridge and walk 15 minutes along the Sava to get to Hrelić; or take tram 14, get off at the last stop in Zapruđe and do the 15-minute walk from there.

ZAGREB CARD

If you're in Zagreb for a day or three, getting the Zagreb Card is a pretty good way to save money. You can choose either 24 or 72 hours (60 or 90KN) and you get free travel on all public transport, a 50% discount on museum and gallery entries, and discounts in some bars and restaurants, on car rental and so forth. A booklet is available listing all the places that offer discounts, or check out www.zagrebcard.fivestars.hr for more details. The card is sold at the main tourist office and in many hostels, hotels, bars and shops.

fix here. Stocks an astonishing collection of brandy, wine and gourmet products.

I-GLE FASHION
(www.i-gle.com; Dežmanova 4) Get one of the almost sculptural yet wearable creations by Nataša Mihaljčišin and Martina Vrdoljak-Ranilović, the movers and shakers of Croatia's fashion industry since the 1990s.

Croata TAILOR
(www.croata.hr; Oktogon Passage, Ilica 5) Since the necktie originated in Croatia, nothing could make a more authentic gift – this is the place to get one. The locally made silk neckties are priced from 249KN to 2000KN.

Nama DEPARTMENT STORE
(Ilica 4) Zagreb's immortal department store.

Information

Emergency
Police Station (☎45 63 311; Petrinjska 30)

Internet Access
There are a number of smaller internet cafes along Preradovićeva.

Sublink (☎48 19 993; www.sublink.hr; Teslina 12; per hr 15KN; ⏰9am-10pm Mon-Sat, 3-10pm Sun) The city's first cybercafe, still going strong.

Laundry
If you're staying in private accommodation, you can usually ask the owner to do your laundry, which would be cheaper than a public laundry.

Petecin (Kaptol 11; ⏰Mon-Sat) Charges 60KN for 5kg of laundry.

Medical Services
Dental Emergency (☎48 28 488; Perkovčeva 3; ⏰10pm-6am)

KBC Rebro (☎23 88 888; Kišpatićeva 12; ⏰24hr) East of the city, provides emergency aid.

Pharmacy (☎48 16 198; Trg Josipa Jelačića 3; ⏰24hr)

Money
There are ATMs at the bus and train stations, the airport, and at numerous locations around town. Some banks in the train and bus stations accept travellers cheques. Exchange offices can be found in the Importanne Centar on Starčevićev trg, as well as in other locations around town.

Post
Post Office (☎66 26 453; Jurišićeva 13; ⏰7am-8pm Mon-Fri, to 1pm Sat) Has a telephone centre.

Main Post Office (☎49 81 300; Branimirova 4; ⏰24hr) Holds poste restante mail. Right by the train station.

Tourist Information
Main Tourist Office (☎info line 800 53 53, office 48 14 051; www.zagreb-touristinfo.hr; Trg Josipa Jelačića 11; ⏰8.30am-9pm Mon-Fri, 9am-6pm Sat & Sun Jun-Sep, 8.30am-8pm Mon-Fri, 9am-6pm Sat, 10am-4pm Sun Oct-May) Distributes free city maps and leaflets, and sells the Zagreb Card.

Plitvice National Park Office (☎46 13 586; Trg Kralja Tomislava 19; ⏰8am-4pm Mon-Fri) Has details and brochures mainly on Plitvice Lakes and Velebit but also on Croatia's other national parks.

Tourist Office Airport (☎62 65 091; ⏰8.30am-9pm Mon-Fri, 9am-6pm Sat & Sun Jun-Sep, 9am-9pm Mon-Fri, 10am-5pm Sat & Sun Oct-May) Handy for airport arrivals.

Tourist Office Annex (train station; ⏰8.30am-9pm Mon-Fri, 9am-6pm Sat & Sun Jun-Sep, 8.30am-8pm Mon-Fri, 12.30-6.30pm Sat & Sun Oct-May) Has the same services as the main tourist office.

Zagreb County Tourist Association (☎48 73 665; www.tzzz.hr; Preradovićeva 42; ⏰8am-4pm Mon-Fri) Has information and materials about attractions in Zagreb's surroundings, including wine roads and bike trails.

Travel Agencies
Atlas Travel Agency (☎48 07 300; www.atlas-croatia.com; Zrinjevac 17) Tours around Croatia.

Croatia Express (☎49 22 237; Trg Kralja Tomislava 17) Train reservations, car rental, air and ferry tickets, hotels around the country and a daily trip to the beach from June to September (90KN round trip to Crikvenica).

CYHA Travel Section (☎48 47 474; www.hfhs.hr; Grada Mainza 6; ⏰8.30am-4.30pm Mon-

Fri) The travel branch of the Croatian YHA can provide information on HI hostels throughout Croatia and make advance bookings.

Zdenac Života (☎48 16 200; www.zdenac-zivota.hr; 2nd fl, Vlaška 40) In addition to thematic sightseeing tours of Zagreb, this small local agency does active day trips from the capital and multi-day adventures around Croatia.

Getting There & Away

Air

Croatia Airlines (☎66 76 555; www.croatiaairlines.hr; Zrinjevac 17) The country's national carrier operates international and domestic flights to and from Zagreb.

Zagreb Airport (☎45 62 222; www.zagreb-airport.hr) Located 17km southeast of Zagreb, this is Croatia's major airport, offering a range of international and domestic services.

Bus

Zagreb's **bus station** (☎060 313 333; www.akz.hr; Avenija M Držića 4) is 1km east of the train station. If you need to store bags, there's a **garderoba** (1st 4hr 20KN, then per hr 2.50KN; ⌚24hr). Trams 2 and 6 run from the bus station to the train station. Tram 6 goes to Trg Josipa Jelačića.

Before buying your ticket, ask about the arrival time – some of the buses take local roads and stop in every town en route.

Note that listed schedules are somewhat reduced outside high season.

Train

The **train station** (☎060 333 444; www.hznet.hr) is in the southern part of the city centre. As you come out of it, you'll see a series of parks and pavilions directly in front of you, which lead into the town centre. It's advisable to book train tickets in advance because of limited seating. The station also has a **garderoba** (lockers per 24hr 15KN; ⌚24hr) if you need to store bags.

BUSES FROM ZAGREB

DOMESTIC DESTINATION	COST (KN)	DURATION	DAILY SERVICES
Dubrovnik	205-250	9½-11hr	9-12
Korčula	264	11hr	1
Krk	113-219	3-4½hr	8-10
Makarska	175-230	6½hr	12-15
Mali Lošinj	287-312	5-6hr	3
Osijek	131-144	4hr	10
Plitvice	92-106	2-3hr	11-15
Poreč	156-232	4-4½hr	11
Pula	105-196	3½-5½hr	17-20
Rab	207-219	4-5hr	5
Rijeka	91-155	2½-4hr	20-25
Rovinj	150-195	4-6hr	9-11
Šibenik	151-165	4½-7hr	20-22
Split	115-205	5-8½hr	32-34
Varaždin	65-87	1-2hr	19-23
Zadar	105-139	3½-5hr	31

INTERNATIONAL DESTINATION	COST (KN)	DURATION	SERVICES
Belgrade	220	6hr	5 daily
Florence	481	10½hr	1 weekly
Munich	375	9½hr	2 daily
Paris	798	10hr	1-2 weekly
Sarajevo	160-210	7-8hr	4-5 daily
Vienna	225-247	5-6hr	3 daily

TRAINS FROM ZAGREB

DOMESTIC DESTINATION	COST (KN)	DURATION	DAILY SERVICES
Osijek	115-137	5-6hr	6-7
Ploče	320	13½hr	1
Rijeka	97	4-6hr	6
Šibenik	156	8hr	1
Split	179-189	5-7hr	3
Varaždin	57	2-3hr	11

INTERNATIONAL DESTINATION	COST (KN)	DURATION	DAILY SERVICES
Banja Luka	105	4½-5hr	2
Belgrade	169	6½hr	4
Budapest	230	6-7hr	2
Ljubljana	130	2½hr	6
Mostar	292	11½hr	1
Munich	726	7-8½hr	2
Sarajevo	231	8-9½hr	2
Venice	450	11½hr	2
Vienna	465	6-7hr	2

Getting Around

To/From the Airport

BUS The Croatia Airlines bus to the airport (30KN) leaves from the bus station every half-hour or hour from about 5am to 8pm, and returns from the airport on the same schedule.

TAXI Costs between 110KN and 300KN.

Car

Zagreb is a fairly easy city to navigate by car (boulevards are wide and parking in the city centre, although scarce, costs 10KN per hour). Watch out for trams buzzing around.

A number of international car-hire companies are represented in Zagreb. Bear in mind that local companies will usually have lower rates.

Avis-Budget (☎46 73 603; www.budget.hr; Oreškovićeva 27) Also at airport.

H&M (☎37 04 535; www.hm-rentacar.hr; Grahorova 11) Local car-rental company; also at airport.

Hertz (☎48 46 777; www.hertz.hr; Vukotinovićeva 4)

Hrvatski Autoklub (HAK, Croatian Auto Club; ☎46 40 800; www.hak.hr; Avenija Dubrovnik 44) Motorists can call ☎987 for help on the road.

Oryx (☎61 15 800; www.oryx-rent.hr; Grada Vukovara 74) Local car-rental company; also at airport.

Taxi

Until recently, Zagreb had only one taxi company, which charged astronomical fees for even the shortest ride. That changed when two other companies joined the fray; all have meters now and competitive rates. **Radio Taxi** (☎060 800 800, 1777) charges 10KN for a start and 5KN per kilometre; waiting time is 40KN per hour. **Eko-taxi** (☎060 77 77, 1414) charges similar rates.

You'll have no trouble finding idle taxis, usually at blue-marked taxi signs; note that these are Radio Taxi stands.

For short city rides, **Taxi Cammeo** (☎060 71 00, 1212) is typically the cheapest, as the 15KN start fare includes the first two kilometres (it's 6KN for every subsequent kilometre).

Tram

Public transport (www.zet.hr) is based on an efficient network of trams, although the city centre is compact enough to make them almost unnecessary. Tram maps are posted at most stations, making the system easy to navigate.

Buy tickets at newspaper kiosks for 12KN. You can use your ticket for transfers within 90 minutes, but only in one direction.

A *dnevna karta* (day ticket), valid on all public transport until 4am the next morning, is available for 40KN at most newspaper kiosks.

Make sure you validate your ticket when you get on the tram by pressing it on the yellow box.

AROUND ZAGREB

The area around Zagreb is rich with quick getaway options, from picturesque Samobor, with its adorable town centre and great cakes, to the peaceful hillside walks around it.

Medvednica Nature Park

Medvednica Nature Park (www.pp-medvednica.hr) to the north of Zagreb offers excellent **hiking** opportunities. There are several popular and well-marked routes. You can take tram 14 to the last stop and then change to tram 15 and take it to its last stop. Walk straight through the tunnel, which takes you directly to Dolje park entrance, leading to the popular and easy Lojstekova trail that ends at Sljeme, the top of Mt Medvednica. Along the way you can stop at one of Sljeme's oldest huts, **Runolist** (www.runolist-sljeme.com), with beautiful views of the city and traditional food and drink.

Alternatively you can hike in the direction of **Puntijarka** (www.puntijarka.com) and **Hunjka** mountain huts. These are very popular on weekends for their home-cooked traditional Croatian dishes served in a rustic setting. This second Bikčevićeva path starts at the Bliznec entrance to Medvednica Nature Park. Follow the tunnel path but then cross to the left side of the road at the ex-funicular station. This is a shorter but also steeper and more intense path.

Or you can take bus 102 from Britanski trg, west of the centre on Ilica, to the church in Šestine and take the easy hiking route from there. There are two huts along the

LONJSKO POLJE NATURE PARK

Lonjsko Polje is a fascinating mix of several diverse delights. It's packed with 19th-century wooden architecture and birdwatchers (well, stork lovers) can have a field day here, as can those who appreciate all things equestrian. If you're a WWII history buff, the area also holds one of former Yugoslavia's most poignant monuments. Nominated for World Heritage Site status in January 2008, **Lonjsko Polje** (☎044-672 080; www.pp-lonjsko-polje.hr; Čigoć; adult/concession 40/30KN; ⏰8am-4pm) is a 506-sq-km stretch of swampland (*polje* is literally 'field') in the Posavina region, between the Sava River and Mt Moslavačka Gora. Seated along Lonja River, a Sava tributary that gives the park its name, this huge retention basin is famed for the diversity of its flora and fauna.

The area is divided into several villages. **Čigoć** is a world-famous 'stork meeting point'; the storks nest on top of Čigoć's lovely wooden houses. The baby-bringing birds flock here in late March and early April, hanging around and munching on the swampland insects until late August, when they start their two- to three-month flight back towards southern Africa. If you're here during autumn and winter, you might catch sight of a few year-round storks who are content to hang out and be fed by the villagers. Čigoć is home to the park's information point and ticket office, and a small ethnographic collection owned by the Sučić family.

The heritage village of **Krapje** is known for its well-preserved traditional wooden houses and rich fishing and hunting areas. Check out the covered external staircases, porches and pillars, and various farm buildings with their barns, drying sheds, pigsties and hen houses. From April to October an information centre in one of the wooden houses is staffed with a guide happy to enlighten you about the cultural heritage of the area. Look out for the *posavski* horse, a local breed that grazes in the oak forests of Lonjsko Polje. You can go horse riding here – ask at the information office in Čigoć.

Also worth a visit is the village of **Mužilovčica**, known for its swallows. Don't miss a meal at the Ravlić family farm here.

Also in the area is **Jasenovac**, the site of a notorious WWII concentration camp. Run by the Ustaše and Croatia's pro-Nazi WWII government, the estimated number of Serbs, Jews, Roma and antifascist Croats who died here is estimated at 80,000. The **Jasenovac Memorial Museum** (www.jusp-jasenovac.hr; admission free; ⏰9am-5pm Tue-Fri, 10am-4pm Sat & Sun) is a touching reminder of the horrors of war.

Lonjsko Polje is 50km southeast of Zagreb. The best way to visit is with your own transport or on a tour, as public transport is poor and makes moving around the park quite difficult. Private accommodation is available in various wooden houses inside the park.

TAKE A HIKE

Samobor is a good jumping-off point for hikes into the **Samoborsko Gorje**, a mountain system (part of the Žumberak Range) that links the high peaks of the Alps with the karstic caves and abysses of the Dinaric Range. It has also been the cradle of organised mountaineering activity in Croatia since 1875 (see www.plsavez.hr). In 1999 the whole area, covering 333 sq km, was proclaimed a nature park because of its biodiversity, forests, karst caves, river canyons and four waterfalls. Carpeted with meadows and forests, the range is the most popular hiking destination in the region. Most of the hikes are easy and there are several mountain huts that make pleasant rest stops. Many are open weekends only (except in high season).

The range is divided into three sections: the Oštrc group in the centre, the Japetić group to the west and the Plešivica group to the east. Both the Oštrc and Japetić groups are accessible from the Šoićeva Kuća mountain hut and restaurant, 10km west of Samobor, reachable by bus 144. From there it's a rather steep 30-minute climb to the medieval hill fort of Lipovac and an hour's hike to the peak of Oštrc (752m), with another mountain hut.

Another popular hike is the 1½-hour climb from Šoićeva Kuća to Japetić (879m), the highest peak of Samobor Hills and a famous paragliding spot (www.parafreek.hr). You can also follow a path from Oštrc to Japetić (two hours). The Plešivica group has ruins of a medieval fort and a protected park forest area; it's also a famous rock-climbing spot. Access it from the village of Rude (bus 143 services Rude and Braslovje). From Rude, head east to the hunting cabin Srndać on the mountain saddle of Poljanice (12km), from where it's a 40-minute, rather steep hike to the peak of Plešivica (779m). The tourist office in town has maps and information on hikes in the region.

way: **Risnjak** and **Grafičar**. For more info about these, see the park website.

Allow about three hours (return) for any of these hikes and remember that this is a heavily wooded mountain with ample opportunities to get lost. Take warm clothes and water, and make sure to return before sundown. There is also a danger of disease-carrying ticks in spring, so wear trousers and long sleeves, and examine your body after the hike. For more information, contact the Zagreb tourist office (p62).

You can also go skiing at the **Sljeme ski resort** (www.sljeme.hr), where there are five slopes of varying difficulty. The website provides the up-to-date status of each slope.

Samobor

☎01 / POP 19,000

Samobor is where stressed-out city dwellers come to wind down and get their fix of hearty food, creamy cakes and pretty scenery. A shallow stream curves through the town centre, which is composed of trim pastel houses and several old churches.

In keeping with its mission to preserve the past, the main economic activity centres on small family businesses involved in handicrafts, restaurants and the production of mustard and spirits. The town's literary and musical traditions are reflected in a number of annual festivals, most famously the **Fašnik** (Samobor Carnival).

Sights & Activities

Town Museum MUSEUM
(Gradski Muzej; Livadićeva 7; adult/concession 8/5KN; ⏰9am-3pm Tue-Fri, to 1pm Sat, 10am-5pm Sun Jul & Aug, 9am-3pm Tue-Fri Sep-Jun) Housed in a historic mansion, it has two floors of vaguely interesting exhibits on regional culture, including an ethnographic collection.

Museum Marton MUSEUM
(☎33 26 426; Jurjevska 7; 10KN; ⏰10am-1pm Sat & Sun, other days by appointment only) Stop by for a look at this private art collection centring on paintings from the Biedermeier period, as well as porcelain, glass and furniture. Outside weekends, visit is by appointment only.

Sleeping

Most people come to Samobor on a day trip from Zagreb, but there are a couple of sleeping options.

Hotel Livadić HOTEL €€
(☎33 65 850; www.hotel-livadic.hr; Trg Kralja Tomislava 1; s/d/ste 360/465/700KN; P❄📶) This atmospheric family-run place decorated in 19th-century style has spacious, comfortable rooms set around a flower-laden patio. Since cuisine is a major draw for Samobor, you can count on the quality of the restaurant and cafe, which serves great cakes.

Hostel Samobor HOSTEL €
(☎33 74 107; www.hostel-samobor.hr; Obrtnička 34; per person 127KN; P@) This 82-bed hostel has clean, bright box-style rooms, a photo exhibit in the dining hall and along hallways, and friendly service. The owner offers guided motorbike tours around Žumberak and other parts of continental Croatia.

Eating

TOP CHOICE **U Prolazu** PASTRIES & CAKES
(Trg Kralja Tomislava 5) The best *kremšnite* (custard pie) in town.

Gabreku 1929 RESTAURANT €
(Starogradska 46; mains from 55KN) This classic restaurant a short walk from the town centre has been run by the same family since the 1920s. It's known for its 35 types of sweet and savoury *palačinke* (crêpes).

Pri Staroj Vuri RESTAURANT €
(Giznik 2; mains from 55KN) Traditional dishes are served in this cosy cottage about 50m uphill from Trg Kralja Tomislava. Try the *pisanica* (beef steak in a spicy mushroom, onion, tomato and red-wine sauce).

Information

Tourist Office (☎33 60 044; www.tz-samobor.hr; Trg Kralja Tomislava 5; ⊙8am-5pm Mon-Fri, 9am-5pm Sat, 10am-5pm Sun) In the town centre, it has plentiful brochures and maps of Samobor, as well as Samoborsko Gorje and Žumberačko Gorje.

Getting There & Away

The bus station (no left-luggage office) is on Ulica 151 Samoborske Brigade HV 1, about 20 minutes on foot from the main square. Samobor is easy to reach by public transport. Get a Samoborček bus from the main bus station in Zagreb (28KN, 30 minutes, half-hourly).

Zagorje

Includes »

Best Places to Eat

- » Vuglec Breg (p78)
- » Grešna Gorica (p79)
- » Verglec (p74)
- » Zlatne Gorice (p75)

Best Places to Stay

- » Vuglec Breg (p78)
- » Villa Magdalena (p79)
- » Spa & Sport Resort Sveti Martin (p76)
- » Hotel Well (p79)

Why Go?

Despite its proximity to Zagreb, the bucolic region of Zagorje in the country's north receives few tourists, even at the height of summer. This is especially surprising given that delightful villages, medieval castles, endless vineyards and thermal springs speckle its rolling hills. These leafy landscapes with Austrian-influenced food and architecture (and the same prices year-round) present a nice alternative to the busy Mediterranean south, offering a good escape from the summer heat. It is blissfully crowd-free, although slightly less so on weekends, when day-tripping families from Zagreb storm the area.

The Zagorje region begins north of Mt Medvednica, near Zagreb, and extends west to the Slovenian border, and as far north as Varaždin, a showcase of baroque architecture. Whether you want to feast on hearty cuisine at rustic restaurants, dip into the hot springs, get a taster of village life or tour ancient castles, you're in for an offbeat treat.

When to Go

Varaždin

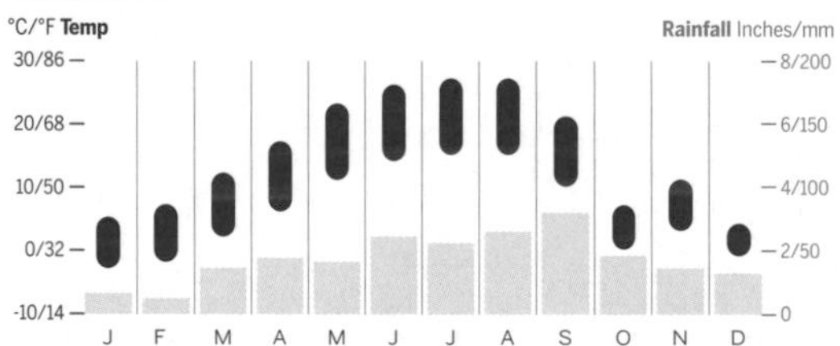

Jun Summer weather kicks in, perfect for touring the hills, castles and thermal spas.

Aug Špancirfest arrives in Varaždin with world music, theatre and other fun performances.

Sep Get a dose of folklore and traditional food at Krapina's Festival of Kajkavian Songs.

Getting There & Around

Although the cities and attractions of Zagorje are linked to Zagreb by bus and train, the connections are sporadic so it helps to have your own wheels to fully appreciate the area. Renting a car for a day or two and setting off along Zagorje's twisting country roads is the best way to take in its rustic charms. Otherwise, you can book excursions with **Viatica Travel** (www.viatica-travel.hr), an online travel agency that specialises in cultural, spa and adventure tourism in Zagorje. Trips include romantic weekends as well as guided visits to castles, wineries, rural taverns and archaeological sites. Several agencies, such as Funky Zagreb (p51) and Zdenac Života (p63) in Zagreb, also organise day trips.

Language

Many of the region's inhabitants speak a local dialect called Kajkavski, named after *kaj?*, their word for 'what?' After Croatian or Kajkavski, the second language is likely to be German. Few people speeak English and those who do will mostly be from younger generations.

Varaždin

☎042 / POP 47,055

Varaždin, 81km north of Zagreb, is a largely overlooked destination that's often used as a mere transit point on the way to or from Hungary. Yet the town is worth a visit in its own right – its centre is a showcase of scrupulously restored baroque architecture and well-tended gardens and parks. It was once Croatia's capital and its most prosperous city, which explains the extraordinary refinement of its buildings. Topping off the symphony is the gleaming white, turreted Stari Grad (old city), which contains a city museum.

The pedestrian zone of attractive 18th-century buildings centres on Trg Kralja Tomislava, with old streets radiating from this square.

History

The town of Garestin (now Varaždin) played an important role in Croatia's history. It first became a local administrative centre in 1181 under King Bela III, and in 1209 it was raised to the status of a free royal borough by King Andrew II, receiving its own seal and coat of arms.

When Croatia was under siege by the Turks, Varaždin was the most powerful stronghold and the residence of choice for generals. Once the Ottoman threat receded, Varaždin prospered as the cultural, political and commercial centre of Croatia. Its proximity to northern Europe facilitated the boom of baroque architecture, which flourished in Europe during this period. Top artisans and builders flocked to Varaždin, designing mansions, churches and public buildings.

The town was made the capital of Croatia in 1767, a position it held until a disastrous fire in 1776, when the Croatian *ban* (viceroy) packed up and moved his administration to Zagreb. The still-thriving town was quickly rebuilt in the baroque style, which is still visible today.

The town is a centre for textiles, shoes, furniture and agricultural products. It's also an increasingly popular day-trip destination, with a recently spruced-up historic core.

Sights

Varaždin's town centre offers a fine ensemble of baroque buildings, a number of which have been turned into museums. Many of its aristocratic mansions and elegant churches are being restored as part of the town's bid to be included in Unesco's list of World Heritage Sites. Conveniently, most buildings have plaques with architectural and historical explanations in English, German and Croatian.

Town Museum MUSEUM

(Gradski Muzej; www.gmv.hr; Strossmayerovo Šetalište 7; adult/concession 25/15KN; ⏰9am-5pm Tue-Fri, to 1pm Sat & Sun) This whitewashed fortress, a gem of medieval defensive architecture housed inside the Stari Grad, is surrounded by a lovingly manicured park. Construction began in the 14th century, with the present Gothic-Renaissance structure dating back to the 16th century, when it was the regional fortification against the Turks. The building was in private hands until 1925; today it's a museum that houses furniture, paintings, watches, ceramics, decorative objects, insignia and weapons amassed over centuries and now divided into 30 exhibition rooms. Far more interesting than the historic collections is the architecture: enter via a drawbridge and wander around to view the archways, courtyards and chapels of this sprawling castle-fortress.

Varaždin Cemetery CEMETERY

(Hallerova Aleja; ⏰7am-9pm May-Sep, to 8pm Mar-Apr, to 5pm Jan-Feb & Nov-Dec) A 10-minute stroll west of the old town takes you to the

Zagorje Highlights

1. Admire the immaculately preserved baroque architecture of **Varaždin** (p69)
2. Experience the life of Croatian nobility at **Trakošćan Castle** (p76)
3. Get an insight into traditional village life at **Staro Selo Museum** (p80) in Kumrovec
4. Sample Croatian culinary specialties at **Vuglec Breg** (p78), near Krapinske Toplice
5. Learn about our Neanderthal cousins at the **Museum of the Krapina Neanderthal** (p77) in Krapina
6. Catch **Špancirfest** (p72), an event that rocks the streets of Varaždin
7. Tour the wine roads of the **Međimurje** region (p76), which stretches northeast of Varaždin

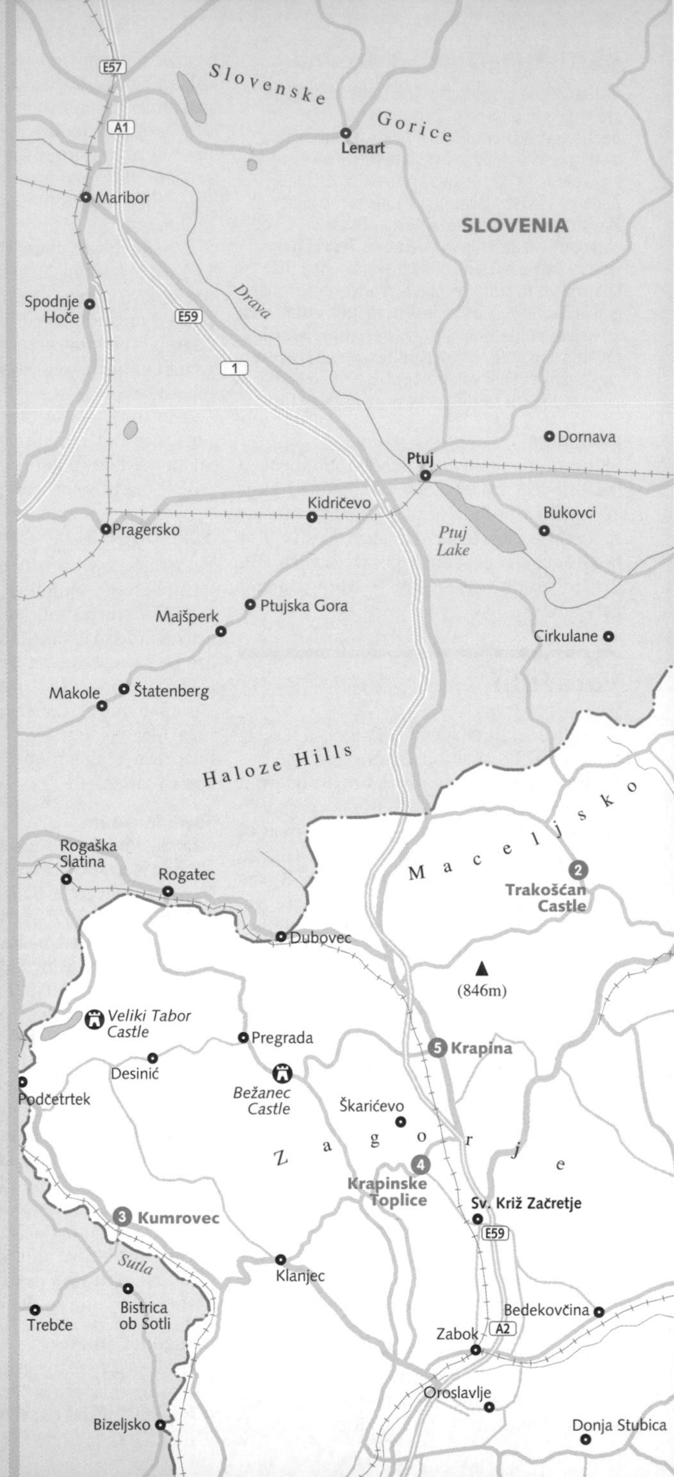

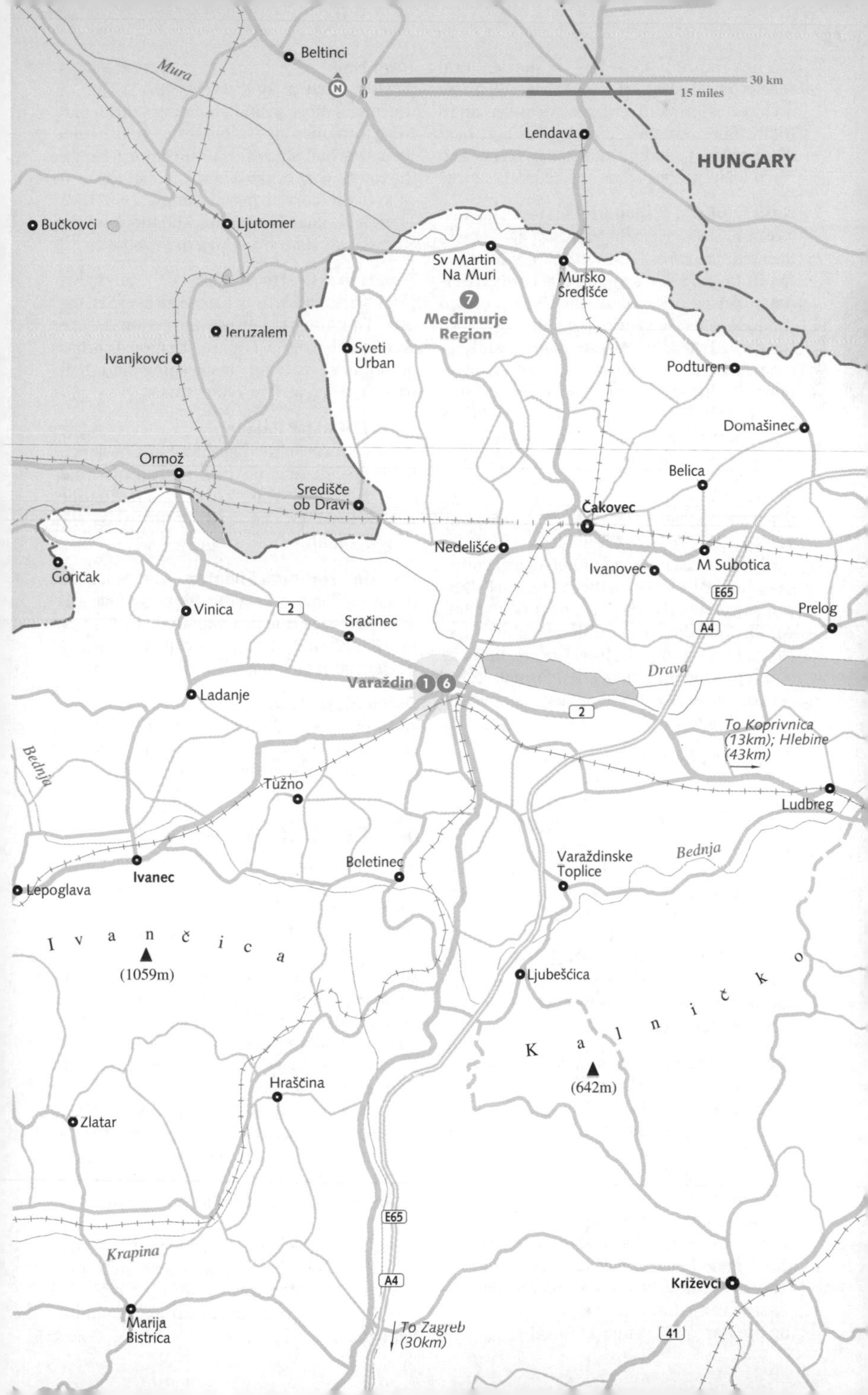

Beltinci
0
0
30 km
15 miles
Mura
Lendava
HUNGARY
Bučkovci
Ljutomer
Sv Martin
Na Muri
Mursko
Središće
7
Međimurje
Region
Jeruzalem
Ivanjkovci
Sveti
Urban
Podturen
Domašinec
Ormož
Središče
ob Dravi
Belica
Čakovec
Nedelišće
Ivanovec
M Subotica
Goričak
E65
Vinica
2
Sračinec
A4
Prelog
Varaždin
1
6
Drava
Ladanje
2
To Koprivnica
(13km); Hlebine
(43km)
Bednja
Tužno
Ludbreg
Beletinec
Varaždinske
Toplice
Bednja
Ivanec
Lepoglava
I v a n č i c a
(1059m)
Ljubešćica
K a l n i č k o
(642m)
Hraščina
Zlatar
E65
Krapina
A4
Križevci
Marija
Bistrica
To Zagreb
(30km)
41

serene Varaždin Cemetery, a horticultural masterpiece designed in 1905 by Viennese architect Hermann Helmer. Meander amid tombstones, avenues, promenades and over 7000 trees, including magnolia, beech and birch to appreciate some superb landscaping.

Gallery of Old & Modern Masters MUSEUM
(Galerija Starih i Novih Majstora; Trg Miljenka Stančića 3; adult/concession 25/15KN; ⌚9am-5pm Tue-Fri, to 1pm Sat & Sun) The rococo-style Sermage Palace that houses the Gallery of Old & Modern Masters was built in 1759. Note the carved medallions on the facade and pay a quick visit to the museum, which displays portraits and landscapes from Croatian, Italian, Dutch, German and Flemish schools. The permanent exhibition occasionally shuts down in favour of temporary shows.

World of Insects MUSEUM
(Entomološka Zbirka; Franjevački trg 6; adult/concession 25/15KN; ⌚9am-5pm Tue-Fri, to 1pm Sat & Sun) This fascinating entomological collection, housed in the classicist Hercer Palace, comprises nearly 4500 exhibits of the bug world, including 1000 different insect species. The examples of insect nests, habitats and reproductive habits are informative and well displayed, with interactive stations and free audioguides.

Franciscan Church & Monastery of St John the Baptist CHURCH
(Crkva Svetog Ivana Krstitelja; Franjevački trg 8; ⌚6.30am-noon & 5.30-7.30pm) Built in 1650 in baroque style on the site of an earlier structure, this church contains the town's tallest tower (54.5m). It also houses an ancient pharmacy ornamented with 18th-century ceiling frescos. Next door is a copy of the bronze **statue of Bishop Grgur Ninski** that Ivan Meštrović created for Split. Touch the statue's big toe and good luck will come your way, the story goes.

Cathedral of the Assumption CATHEDRAL
(Katedrala Uznesenja Marijina; Pavlinska 5; ⌚7am-12.30pm & 3.30-7.30pm) This former Jesuit church, located just south of Trg Kralja Tomislava, was built in 1646. The facade is distinguished by an early baroque portal bearing the coat of arms of the noble Drašković family. Occupying the central nave is the altar, which has elaborate engravings and a gilded painting of the Assumption of the Virgin Mary. Famous for its great acoustics, the cathedral is the site of concerts during the Baroque Evenings festival.

Town Hall HISTORIC BUILDING
(Gradska Vijećnica; Trg Kralja Tomislava 1) Onc of the town's most striking buildings, this handsome Romanesque-Gothic structure has been the town hall since the 16th century. Notice the town's coat of arms at the foot of the tower and the carved portal dating from 1792. There's a guard-changing ceremony every Saturday at 11am from May to September.

Traditional Crafts Square CITY SQUARE
(Trg Tradicijskih Obrta; ⌚10am-6pm Mon-Sat Apr-Oct) The town's newest attraction is the Traditional Crafts Square. Demonstrations of pottery, weaving, beekeeping and hat-making re-create the olden times.

Patačić-Puttar Palace PALACE
(Palača Patačić-Puttar; Zagrebačka 2) Check out this eye-catching mixture of baroque and classical styles. The richly decorated stone portal features the coat of arms of the Patačić family.

Croatian National Theatre HISTORIC BUILDING
(Hrvatsko Narodno Kazalište; Augusta Cesarca 1) This stunning theatre was built in 1873 in neo-Renaissance style, following the designs of Hermann Helmer.

Drava River Waterfront WATERFRONT
A 15-minute walk northeast of the town centre takes you to this verdant, tranquil riverfront bordered by footpaths and several outdoor cafes in which to kick back.

Festivals & Events

Varaždin is famous for its baroque music festival, **Varaždin Baroque Evenings** (www.vbv.hr), which takes place over two weeks each September. Local and international orchestras play in the cathedral, churches and theatres around town. Tickets range from 75KN to 250KN, depending on the event, and become available one hour before the concert at travel agencies or the **Varaždin Concert Bureau** (☎212 907; Augusta Cesarca 1, Croatian National Theatre).

In late August, the eclectic **Špancirfest** (www.spancirfest.com) enlivens the town's parks, streets and squares with world music, street performances, theatre, creative workshops, traditional crafts and contemporary arts.

A more offbeat event is the annual **Trash Film Fest** (www.trash.hr), an extravaganza of low-budget action flicks that takes place in **MMC Kult** (Anina 2) over two days in mid-September.

Varaždin

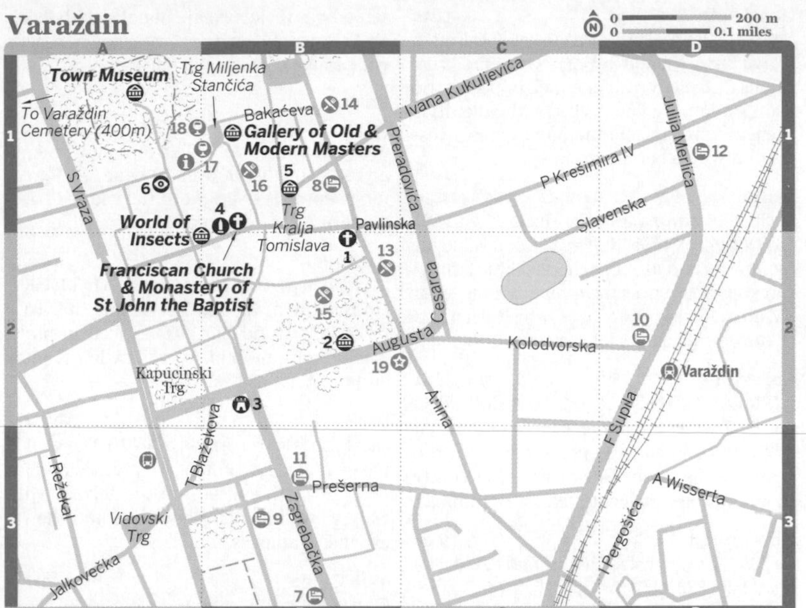

Varaždin

Top Sights

Franciscan Church & Monastery of St John the Baptist B1
Gallery of Old & Modern Masters B1
Town Museum A1
World of Insects B2

Sights

1 Cathedral of the Assumption B2
2 Croatian National Theatre B2
3 Patačić-Puttar Palace B2
4 Statue of Bishop Grgur Ninski B1
5 Town Hall B1
6 Traditional Crafts Square A1

Sleeping

7 Garestin B3
8 Hotel Istra B1
9 Hotel Turist B3
10 Hotel Varaždin D2
11 Maltar B3
12 Studentski Centar Varaždin D1

Eating

13 Angelus B2
14 Market B1
15 Park B2
16 Verglec B1

Drinking

17 Mea Culpa B1
18 Soho A1

Entertainment

19 MMC Kult B2

Information

Varaždin Concert Bureau ..... (see 2)

Sleeping

Generally less expensive than in Zagreb, most hotels in Varaždin are clean, well maintained and offer decent value for money. The clientele consists mostly of visiting businesspeople from Zagreb and neighbouring countries, which means hotels are likely to be busy on weekdays and empty on weekends.

If you're looking for private accommodation turn to the tourist office, which has listings of single/double rooms from about 180/260KN. There is generally no additional charge for a single night's stay and prices remain the same year-round.

Hotel Varaždin HOTEL €€
(☎290 720; www.hotelvarazdin.com; Kolodvorska 19; s/d 388/576KN; P❄@☎) Contemporary rooms at the city's nicest hotel, opposite the train station, are jam-packed with amenities such as minibars. On the premises is a restaurant with a bar and terrace.

Maltar GUESTHOUSE €
(☎311 100; www.maltar.hr; Prešernova 1; s/d 248/488KN, ste 465KN-595KN; P❄@) Good value for money can be had at this cheerful little family-run guesthouse near the centre. Rooms, with TV, are well kept. Four suites (which sleep two or three people) have kitchenettes.

Garestin PANSION €€
(☎214 314; Zagrebačka 34; s/d 300/460KN; P❄) Locals frequent the popular restaurant of this establishment a stone's throw from the centre, while visitors kick back in 13 comfy rooms upstairs, each outfitted with a minibar.

Hotel Turist HOTEL €€
(☎395 395; www.hotel-turist.hr; Kralja Zvonimira 1; s/d from 380/580KN; P@) Lack of character is balanced by solid facilities and nearly four decades of service. Pricier 'business class' rooms come with minibars and air-conditioning.

Hotel Istra HOTEL €€€
(☎659 659; www.istra-hotel.hr; Ivana Kukuljevića 6; s/d from 460/720KN; P❄@☎) The expected facilities, an unbeatable location and in-room perks are all in place at this 11-room property, Varaždin's only four-star. But wowed you won't be.

Studentski Centar Varaždin HOSTEL €
(☎332 910; www.hostel.hr; Julija Merlića bb; s/d 199/298KN; @) This student hall and hostel has recently renovated rooms, each equipped with a TV, cable internet and a fridge. There's laundry service, too, and breakfast (25KN).

Eating & Drinking

While it doesn't stand out as a gourmet destination, Varaždin offers plentiful opportunities to try Croatia's continental cuisine, suitable for all budgets. There is a daily **market** (Augusta Šenoe 12), open until 2pm. Many bakeries sell Varaždin's savoury finger-shaped bread, *klipić*.

Verglec TRADITIONAL CROATIAN €
(Kranjčevića 12; mains from 35KN) No-frills but great-value *gableci* (cheap filling lunches, served on weekdays) are popular with locals at this town-centre eatery known for its wide range of traditional dishes.

Palatin CROATIAN
(Braće Radića 1; mains from 35KN) The newest restaurant in town has an ambitious menu, a great wine list of over 50 wines and great lunch specials daily. Sit in the vaulted basement or on the covered terrace outside.

Angelus ITALIAN €
(Alojzija Stepinca 3; pizzas/mains from 30/45KN) Housed in a vaulted basement, this cosy pizzeria-trattoria churns out excellent pizza, pasta (from gnocchi to tagliatelle), risottos and meat mainstays.

Park CROATIAN €
(Jurja Habdelića 6; mains from 48KN) The grilled meats and salad buffets are pretty standard here – what's special are the terrace with leafy views, the old-school vibe and the inexpensive lunches.

Mea Culpa LOUNGE BAR
(Ivana Padovca 1) Get your caffeine or cocktail fix at this swanky lounge bar with two floors inside and, on sunny days, tables extending out on Trg Miljenka Stančića.

Soho CAFE-BAR
(Trg Miljenka Stančića 1) Just like Mea Culpa, this cafe-bar has tables on the square but its interior is more intimate and toned down.

Information

Internet Access

The entire city centre has free wi-fi.

Caffe Bar Aquamarin (Gajeva 1; ⏰7am-midnight Mon-Thu, to 2am Fri & Sat, to 1am Sun) Free access to the computer terminal with purchase of a drink.

Tourist Information

Tourist Office (☎210 987; www.tourism-varazdin.hr; Ivana Padovca 3; ⏰8am-6pm Mon-Thu, to 7pm Fri, 10am-5pm Sat Jun-Sep; 8am-4pm Mon-Fri, 10am-1pm Sat Oct-May) A wealth of information and plenty of colourful brochures are available here.

Travel Agencies

Horizont Travel (☎395 111; www.horizont-travel.hr; Kralja Zvonimira 1) Located right next to Hotel Turist, this agency offers tours around the city and Zagorje region.

BUSES FROM VARAŽDIN

DESTINATION	COST (KN)	DURATION	SERVICES
Berlin (Germany)	851	15hr	2 weekly
Munich (Germany)	380	8hr	1 daily
Trakošćan Castle	36	1¾hr	9 daily
Varaždinske Toplice	21	30min	hourly
Vienna (Austria)	219	5hr	1 daily
Zagreb	81	1¾hr	hourly

Getting There & Away

The **bus station** (Zrinskih i Frankopana bb) lies just to the southwest of the town centre. The **train station** (Kolodvorska 17) is to the east, at the opposite end of town. About 1km apart, the stations are linked by a minibus (5KN to 15KN) that serves the town and nearby villages (not on Sundays). Both offer left luggage services; at the bus station you can leave your bags at the **garderoba** (per bag 7KN; ⌚4.30am-8.30pm); at the train station there's also a **garderoba** (per day 15KN; ⌚5am-8.20pm).

Varaždin is a major transport hub in north Croatia, with bus and train lines running in all directions. Remember that northbound buses originate in Zagreb, stop at Varaždin and cost the same whether you buy the ticket in Zagreb or Varaždin.

Most buses to the coast go through Zagreb. Note that service to Trakošćan and Varaždinske Toplice is greatly reduced on weekends.

There are 14 daily trains to Zagreb (57KN, 2½ hours); connect in Zagreb for trains to the coast. Two trains daily run to Budapest, Hungary (251KN, six to eight hours), with a change in Koprivnica.

Varaždinske Toplice

☎042 / POP 6973

Sulphurous thermal springs at a steaming temperature of 58°C (136°F) have attracted weary visitors to Varaždinske Toplice since the Romans first established a health settlement here in the 1st century AD. Gentle, wooded hills surround this appealing spa town, which has an assortment of churches and historic buildings, including the baroque castle of **Stari Grad**. Behind its neo-Gothic facade hides the **tourist office** (☎633 133; www.toplice-vz.hr; Trg Slobode 16; ⌚7.30am-3.30pm Mon-Fri), which distributes brochures and info about relaxing health therapies, and can help you find private accommodation.

Adjacent is the **city museum** (Trg Slobode 16; adult/concesssion 20/15KN; ⌚9am-1pm Mon, Wed & Fri, 9am-1pm & 3-5pm Tue & Thu, 9am-2pm Sat), which showcases a sculpture of Minerva from the 3rd century AD. History buffs should take a stroll around **Aqua Iasae**, the remains of the Roman spa built between the 1st and 4th centuries AD. It is located just a quick stroll up from Stari Grad.

The spa is 12km southeast of Varaždin and 69km northeast of Zagreb. There are numerous buses from Varaždin.

Sleeping & Eating

Hotel Minerva HOTEL €€
(☎630 831; www.minerva.hr; Trg Slobode 1; s 340-440KN, d 420-720KN; P ≋) This hotel is built around the thermal pools, which are said to have curative powers, especially for rheumatic ailments. The unsightly concrete building features rooms with balconies, indoor and outdoor pools, an aqua park and a fitness room. Guests have free access to the pools; day visitors pay 35KN on weekdays and 40KN on weekends. There is also a sauna (45KN per hour), massages (from 90KN) and various antistress programs.

Ozis GUESTHOUSE €
(☎250 130; www.ozis.hr; Zagrebačka 7; s/d 180/300KN; P @) This charming family-run guesthouse at the town entrance has 10 spick-and-span rooms and three suites, plus a lovely courtyard.

Zlatne Gorice CENTRAL EUROPEAN €€
(www.zlatne-gorice.com; Banjščina 104, Gornji Kneginec; mains from 42KN) If you have your own wheels, stop for lunch at this sparkling restored mansion 3km from Toplice along

EN ROUTE TO HUNGARY: MEĐIMURJE

The undulating landscapes of Međimurje stretch northeast of Varaždin towards the borders with Hungary and Slovenia. Fertile, scenic and packed with vineyards, orchards, wheat fields and gardens, this area sees few tourists. That is slowly changing, however, as its attractions, such as up-and-coming wine cellars and the spa village of Sveti Martin, are discovered.

To sample the region's top wines in an authentic family environment, head to **Lovrec vineyard** (☎040 830 171; www.vino-lovrec.hr; Sveti Urban 133, Štrigova; ⊙by appointment) in the village of Sveti Urban, 20km northwest of Čakovec, the region's capital. The guided tour (available in English, French and German) of this country estate tells you about the boutique wine production and its fascinating history, which spans six generations of winemakers. You'll peek into the 300-year-old wine cellar with ancient wine presses and barrels, rest in the shade of two towering plane trees, take in the vistas of the 6-hectare vineyards, and top it off with tasting about 10 wine varieties, from chardonnay to local *graševina*. The whole experience lasts up to two hours and costs 80KN (20KN extra for tasty snacks of cheese, salami and bread), with a bottle of wine to take home. You're encouraged to buy another bottle.

A few kilometres away along verdant hilly roads, the pleasant village of Sveti Martin Na Muri showcases a recently renovated four-star property, **Spa & Sport Resort Sveti Martin** (☎040 371 111; www.spa-sport.hr; Grkavešćak bb; s/d 413/826KN). It has a series of outdoor, indoor and thermal pools, a water park, tennis courts, forest trails, shops, restaurants and a golf course. Adjacent to the resort are swanky apartment-style units, each with a living room, a kitchen and a balcony (from 400KN). For nonguests, day tickets to the pools start at 50KN (60KN on weekends); the price drops by 10KN after 1pm. Other facilities include a fitness room (25KN per day), a sauna complex (105KN for three hours) and various body therapies, including mud wraps (320KN per hour) and chocolate massages (300KN for 45 minutes).

At **Goričanec farm** (☎040 868 288; Dunajska 26), about 4km from the village, you can try horse riding, fishing or hunting. **Potrti Kotač** (☎040 868 318; Jurovčak 79; mains from 50KN), 1km uphill from the spa, serves good local food and has an apartment for rent (250KN).

the old road to Varaždin. Surrounded by vineyards, it serves Central European fare (think schnitzels, stews and veal medallions) in the four interior salons or on a terrace with pastoral views. There's a wine trail, a garden labyrinth, wine tastings and three cosy doubles (300KN) upstairs.

Trakošćan Castle

Among continental Croatia's most impressive castles, **Trakošćan Castle** (☎796 281; www.trakoscan.hr; adult/concession 30/15KN; ⊙9am-6pm Apr-Oct, to 4pm Nov-Mar), 80km northwest of Zagreb, is worth a visit for its well-presented museum and attractive grounds. The exact origin of its construction is unknown but the first official mention dates to 1334. Not many of the castle's original Romanesque features were retained when it was restored in neo-Gothic style in the mid-19th century and the 215-acre castle grounds were landscaped into a romantic English-style park with exotic trees and an artificial lake.

Occupied by the aristocratic Drašković family until 1944, the castle features three floors of exhibits that display the family's original furniture and a plethora of portraits. The series of rooms range in style from neo-Renaissance to Gothic and baroque. There's also an armaments collection of swords and firearms, and a period kitchen in the basement.

After soaking up the history, wander along the verdant paths down to the wooden jetty at the lake, where you can rent a two-person paddleboat (50KN per hour) in warm weather.

No buses operate between Zagreb and Trakošćan but there are weekday connections from Varaždin, making a day trip possible.

Krapina

☎049 / POP 12,950

Krapina is a busy provincial town at the heart of a pretty rural region. The main reason to visit is one of Europe's largest Neanderthal excavation sites, now a museum that recently reopened in its swanky new incarnation. In 1899 an archaeological dig on the Hušnjakovo hill unearthed findings of human and animal bones from a Neanderthal tribe that lived in the cave from 100,000 BC to 35,000 BC. Alongside stone tools and weapons from the Palaeolithic Age, the remains of 876 humans were found, including 196 single teeth belonging to several dozen individuals. These findings are the focus of the museum.

Once you've connected with our long-gone cousins and briefly meandered around town, Krapina offers little to keep you entertained.

The main road that runs through town is Zagrebačka Ulica, which becomes Ljudevita Gaja in the centre and Magistratska at the northern end. The town centre is Trg Stjepana Radića, between Zagrebačka and Ljudevita Gaja.

Sights

Museum of the Krapina Neanderthal MUSEUM
(Šetalište Vilibalda Sluge bb; adult/concession 50/25KN; ⌚9am-7pm Apr-Sep, 9am-5pm Nov-Feb, 9am-6pm Mar & Oct) Krapina's highlight is this newly built museum just west of the centre. Built into a vertical rock and fronted with a glass wall, this cavernous two-floor space has high-tech exhibits tracing the history and geology of the region, with trilingual signage. After an introductory video in the main hall, the walk through the museum is designed to emulate a journey of discovery back to the site's origins, with subterranean chambers, hyper-realistic dioramas of Neanderthals and lots of interactive games. Don't miss the entrance to the 2nd floor, through a dark passageway with funky lights.

The outdoor part of the museum, the leafy hill where the remains were found, contains a display of sculpted life-sized models of Neanderthals engaged in everyday activities such as wielding clubs and throwing stones.

Note that the doors shut one hour before the official closing time.

Franciscan Monastery MONASTERY
Peek into this baroque monastery, which once housed a philosophy and theology school. The adjoining church has evocative frescos by Pauline monk Ivan Ranger in the sacristy.

FREE **City Art Gallery** ART GALLERY
(Magistratska 25; ⌚10am-3pm Mon-Fri, to 6pm Sat, 11am-6pm Sun) Features rotating exhibits of Croatian artists.

CROATIAN NAIVE ART

Croatia is the birthplace of its own version of naive art, a distinct style of 20th-century painting that features fantastical and colourful depictions of rural life.

It was the painter Krsto Hegedušić (1901–75) who founded the Hlebine School in the village of the same name in the Podravina region, 13km east of the provincial centre of Koprivnica. Upon his return from studying in Paris in the 1930s, he gathered a group of self-taught artists and gave them a chance to shine. This first generation of Croatian naive painters included Ivan Generalić (1914–92), now the most internationally acclaimed, Franjo Mraz (1910–81) and Mirko Virius (1889–1943). All were amateur artists portraying vibrantly coloured and vividly narrated scenes of village life.

Today, a clutch of painters and sculptors still work in Hlebine. Their work can be seen on display in **Hlebine Gallery** (Trg Ivana Generalića 15, Hlebine; adult/concession 10/5KN; ⌚10am-4pm Tue-Fri, to 2pm Sat & Sun). Also in Hlebine is **Galerija Josip Generalić** (☎048 836 430; Gajeva 75; adult/concession 10/5KN; ⌚10am-5pm Mon-Fri); named after the son of the famous Ivan, also a renowned painter, it is located in the Generalić family home. It's best to call ahead to check that it's open.

Other places to see naive art in Croatia are the Croatian Museum of Naïve Art (p45) in Zagreb and the **Koprivnica Gallery** (Zrinski trg 9, Koprivnica; ⌚8am-6pm Tue-Sat), which has a small applied arts section.

TOP RURAL INNS & FARMSTAYS

Rural inns and farmstays have been mushrooming all around Zagorje in the last few years. Weekends at these hideaways are typically packed with Zagreb day-trippers but come on a weekday and you'll have them practically to yourself. In addition to food and wines, all of the following offer accommodation and are best reached with your own wheels.

Vuglec Breg (☎345 015; www.vuglec-breg.hr; Škarićevo 151; s/d 390/550KN, mains from 75KN; P@) is a delightful rural inn with a scenic location in the village of Škarićevo, 4km from Krapinske Toplice. The four traditional cottages (with seven rooms and three suites) sit amid hills, vineyards and forests. The restaurant serves fantastic Zagorje specialties from the bread oven, such as *purica s mlincima* (slow-roasted turkey with baked noodles) and *štrukli*, on a terrace with panoramic vistas. The grounds feature tennis courts, hiking trails and a wine cellar. Mountain bikes are available for rent, plus there's a playground, a badminton court and pony riding to keep the little ones busy.

For tastings of award-winning wines, head to **Bolfan Vinski Vrh** (www.bolfanvinskivrh.hr) in the village of Hraščina, near the town of Zlatar. Inside this beautiful hilltop *klet* (typical Zagorje cottage), with vineyards sloping down and some of Zagorje's best views, is a great restaurant (open Wednesdays to Sundays) and a handful of rustic rooms. If you want to try one of their specialties, like veal baked under *peka*, you must order a day ahead. Otherwise, you can always do cheeses, cold cuts and wine. Look out for their fun blues evenings, advertised on the website.

Also worth a trip is **Klet Kozjak** (www.klet-kozjak.hr) in Sveti Križ Začretje, southeast of Krapina. The adorable little cottage serves traditional food from the region – such as homemade nettle pasta with cheese and vegetable sauce and *štrukle* soup – and pairs it with sweeping views of the hills and valleys from the terrace. Run by a local family that has been in the goat breeding business for generations, it is known for its excellent goat cheese and oven-baked kid goat.

Another sweet place is **Majsecov Mlin** (www.majsecov-mlin.com) near the village of Donja Stubica. Housed in two traditional cottages, it serves up local mainstays, seasonally inspired and cooked up by one of Zagorje's best chefs. Try the delicious steak with nettle chips and Zagorje-style pesto. On site is an old mill which to this day grinds maize for use in corn flour. In summer months, small producers sell their edible wares at the small market here.

Festivals & Events

At the beginning of September, the annual **Festival of Kajkavian Songs** (Festival Kajkavske Popevke) features folkloric performances, poetry readings and traditional Zagorje food.

Sleeping

Pod Starim Krovovima PANSION €

(Trg Ljudevita Gaja 15; s/d 205/326KN) This pleasant *pansion* in the town centre has eight plain but clean en suite units. On weekdays, cheap and tasty *gablec* (lunch) can be had at the downstairs restaurant for 25KN.

Eating & Drinking

Neandertal Pub BARBECUE €

(Šetalište Vilibalda Sluge bb; mains from 50KN) This Neanderthal-themed cafe-restaurant at the entrance to the museum claims to dish out barbecue from a recipe that's 130,000 years old.

Ilir CAFE-BAR

(Trg Ljudevita Gaja 3) For a coffee break in the sun, grab an outside table at this loungey spot or soak up the old-fashioned vibe inside.

Information

Tourist Office (☎371 330; www.tz-zagorje.hr; Magistratska 28; ⌚8am-3pm Mon-Fri, 8am-noon Sat) Not particularly helpful but does offer some brochures and scant information.

Getting There & Away

One early morning bus runs Monday to Saturday from Zagreb to Krapina (45KN, one hour) but none on Sunday. There are up to 11 trains on weekdays from Zagreb (35KN, 1½ hours); of those only two are direct, the rest have to change at Zabok. Trains run less frequently on weekends.

The train station is about 300m to the south. The bus terminal is another 600m away along the same street, at Frana Galovića 15.

Veliki Tabor Castle

As you approach the hilltop castle of Veliki Tabor, 57km northwest of Zagreb, what unfolds is a pleasing panorama of hills, corn fields, vineyards and forests. The rural vistas alone make a visit worthwhile, as does good traditional dining nearby.

The Croatian aristocracy began building fortified castles in the region at the end of the 16th century to stave off the Turkish threat. The pentagonal **Veliki Tabor Castle** (www.velikitabor.com; Košnički Hum 1, Desinić; adult/concession 20/10KN; ⌚9am-5pm Tue-Fri, to 7pm Sat & Sun Apr-Sep, 9am-4pm Tue-Fri, to 5pm Sat & Sun Oct & Mar, 9am-4pm Tue-Fri Nov-Feb), which was recently renovated and now houses a museum, was built on the grounds of an earlier medieval structure in the early 16th century, with the four semicircular towers added later. Strategically perched on top of a hill, the golden-yellow castle-fortress has everything a medieval master could want: towers, turrets and holes in the walls for pouring tar and hot oil on the enemy. It even houses the skull of Veronika Desinić, a poor village girl who, according to local lore, was punished for her romance with the castle owner's son and bricked up in the walls.

The castle hosts the **Tabor Film Festival** (www.taborfilmfestival.com) in July, an extravaganza of international short films with screenings in the castle as well as several locations in nearby Kumrovec. Another event to catch is the **medieval fair** in September, a one-day celebration featuring sword battles, falcon-hunting tournaments and Renaissance dancing.

To admire the castle from a distance, grab an alfresco table at **Grešna Gorica** (www.gresna-gorica.com; Taborgradska Klet 3, Desinić; mains from 50KN), a rustic eatery often overtaken by day-tripping families from Zagreb on weekends. The place is a

WORTH A TRIP

SWEET SPA SPOTS IN THE HILLS

While lots of Zagorje's spas cater to an ageing clientele with time-induced ailments, they are worth an outing if you want to spend a day steaming the travel stress away and/or you want to see these remnants of the socialist era. In most of these spa towns, the discovery of thermal waters with purportedly healing properties spurred often unseemly development. But there is charm to these spots regardless and if you like to soak and be pampered, they provide a welcome outing.

As the spa closest to Zagreb, **Stubičke Toplice** (www.stubicketoplice.net) caters to the geriatric crowd as well as a devoted band of Zagreb habitués who frequent this old-timer. The hot spring water (69°C) rising from the subterranean rock layers has spurred tourism since the 18th century. The pools – eight outdoor and one indoor – have a temperature of between 32°C and 36°C, and are used to treat a variety of muscular and rheumatic conditions.

Krapinske Toplice (www.krapinsketoplice.com), about 17km southwest of Krapina, is a spa town set amid the rolling hills of the Zagorje countryside. The showpieces are the four thermal springs, rich in magnesium and calcium and never below 39°C. Soon to be unveiled is the new spa centre (currently under construction), which will feature indoor pools, saunas and various other fitness and wellness facilities. In the meantime, you can stay at the recently opened **Villa Magdalena** (☎233 333; www.villa-magdalena.net; Mirna Ulica 1; s/d 690/960KN; P ❄ @ ☜) guesthouse, a pink-themed lap of luxury with its swank and spacious suites with jacuzzis and balconies, a la carte restaurant and an outdoor pool.

Tuheljske Toplice (www.tuheljsketoplice.com), a short drive from Zagreb in the pretty village of Tuhelj, en route to Kumrovec, has been a longstanding favourite for urbanites. It recently got another boost with an unveiling of the four-star **Hotel Well** (www.terme-tuhelj.hr), with a series of swimming pools, a swank wellness centre and an adventure park.

Another worthwhile spa destination is **Hotel Terme Jezerčica** (www.terme-jezercica.hr) in the village of Donja Stubica, which has a new swimming pool complex.

tad gimmicky but great for kids, with farm animals roaming around, a playground and lots of open space. Adults will appreciate the countryside views and the well-prepared Zagorje staples, such as *štrukli* (dumplings with cottage cheese) and *srneći gulaš* (venison goulash). The restaurant can be found about 2km east of Veliki Tabor; a marked trail leads from the back of the castle to the restaurant (40 minutes on foot).

There are several daily buses from Zagreb to Desinić (62KN, 1½ to two hours) from Monday to Saturday and four on Sunday. You will have to walk 3km northwest to Veliki Tabor.

Kumrovec

049 / POP 1854

The Zagorje region was the birthplace of several celebrated Croats, most notably Tito, who was born as Josip Broz in Kumrovec. Nestled in the Sutla River valley near the Slovenian border, this pretty village has been thoughtfully transformed into an open-air ethnographic museum. A re-creation of a 19th-century village, the **Staro Selo Museum** (www.mdc.hr/kumrovec; Kumrovec bb; adult/concession 20/10KN; 9am-7pm Apr-Sep; 9am-4pm Mon-Fri, to 6pm Oct & Mar; 9am-4pm Nov-Feb), features 40 restored houses and barns made of pressed earth and wood. These *hiže* (Zagorje huts) are now filled with furniture, mannequins, toys, wine presses and baker's tools (all accompanied by English captions) in order to evoke the region's traditional arts, crafts and customs.

With a stream bubbling through the idyllic setting, the museum presents a vivid glimpse of peasant traditions and village life. Note the life-sized bronze sculpture of Marshal Tito outside his humble place of birth, with the original furniture, letters from foreign leaders and random memorabilia inside. On some weekends from April to September, the museum hosts demonstrations of blacksmithing, candlemaking, pottery making and flax weaving.

There are two daily buses between Zagreb and Kumrovec (52KN, 1¼ hours) on weekdays, one on Saturday and none on Sunday.

Klanjec

049 / POP 3234

Another notable Croat from Zagorje was sculptor Antun Augustinčić (1900–1979), who created the *Monument to Peace* in front of the UN building in New York. Klanjec, his pleasant home town, has the **Antun Augustinčić Gallery** (www.mdc.hr/augustincic; Trg Antuna Mihanovića 10; adult/concession 20/10KN; 9am-5pm Apr-Sep, to 3pm Tue-Sun Oct-Mar) devoted to his opus, plus lots of headless bronze torsos and a huge replica of the *Peace* statue. There's a small sculpture garden outside and the sculptor's memorial to fallen Partisans nearby.

Once you've seen the gallery, you'll be strapped for more sightseeing, but do stroll around the charming town to see the 17th-century **baroque church** and the **Franciscan monastery** opposite the gallery, and to take in the views of surrounding hills.

The two daily buses running from Zagreb to Kumrovec stop in Klanjec (51KN, one to 1½ hours). Note that there's only one on Saturday and none on Sunday.

Marija Bistrica

049 / POP 6612

Croatia's largest pilgrimage centre is in Zagorje at Marija Bistrica, a village 37km north of Zagreb on the slopes of Mt Medvednica. What steals the show here is the **Marija Bistrica Church** (Hodočasnička Crkva Marije Bistričke), which contains a wooden Gothic statue of the Black Madonna created in the 15th century. The statue's alleged miraculous power dates back to the 16th-century Turkish invasions, when it was saved from destruction. It was further proven when a disastrous 1880 fire destroyed everything but the statue.

Behind the church is the **Way of the Cross**, a path leading up Calvary Hill, with 14 stations marked with works by Croatian sculptors and paired with excellent vistas. To witness a display of serious religious devotion, visit on 15 August for the most popular pilgrimage of **Velika Gospa** (Assumption of the Virgin Mary).

There are up to 20 buses a day from Zagreb to Marija Bistrica (36KN to 44KN, 40 minutes to one hour) on weekdays, fewer on weekends.

Slavonia

Includes »

Best Places to Eat

» Kod Ruže (p88)
» Baranjska Kuća (p92)
» Josić (p92)
» Zelena Žaba (p91)

Best Places to Stay

» Maksimilian (p87)
» Zdjelarević (p85)
» Ivica Marica (p92)
» Stari Podrum (p94)

Why Go?

Pancake-flat, river-rich Slavonia is all but untouched by tourism, with unique natural wonders and delicious regional cuisine. The wetlands of Kopački Rit are one of Europe's finest ornithological reserves, perfect for boat tours, biking and hiking. Osijek, Slavonia's largest town, has a lovely riverfront setting and fortress quarter while the Baranja region is renowned for its wineries.

The impact of the war hit hardest in southeast Slavonia, where historic Vukovar is slowly regaining its role as an important regional city; and Ilok, on the Serbian border, is again attracting visitors to its fine wine cellars and historic old town.

Bordered by three major rivers (Sava, Drava and Danube), this fascinating region has long held strong connections with Hungary, Serbia and Germany. Here lies Slavonia's key appeal, in this culturally intriguing mix that makes it closer to Central Europe than coastal Croatia.

When to Go

Osijek

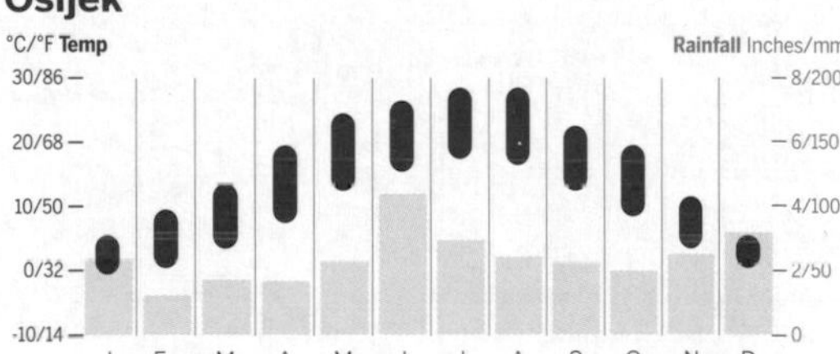

Apr–May Spring in Slavonia is a delight with mild temperatures and almost no mosquitoes.

Jun–Sep Catch any number of festivals, from urban music to sculpture.

Oct–Mar The short days are an ideal time to savour paprika-rich Slavonian stews and game.

Slavonia Highlights

1. Explore **Kopački Rit Nature Park** (p90), one of Europe's largest wetlands and a birdwatchers' paradise
2. Feast on Slavonian specialties in Osijek's fortress quarter **Tvrđa** (p85)
3. Visit the haunting war memorials in **Vukovar** (p92)
4. Travel the wine roads of **Baranja** (p90)
5. Spend a day taking in the impressive cultural sights of **Osijek** (p84)
6. Enjoy an outstanding museum then sample local fare in pretty **Ilok** (p93)
7. Get to savour village life in **Karanac ethno-village** (p91)
8. View the Danube from the imposing war memorial of **Batina** (p92)

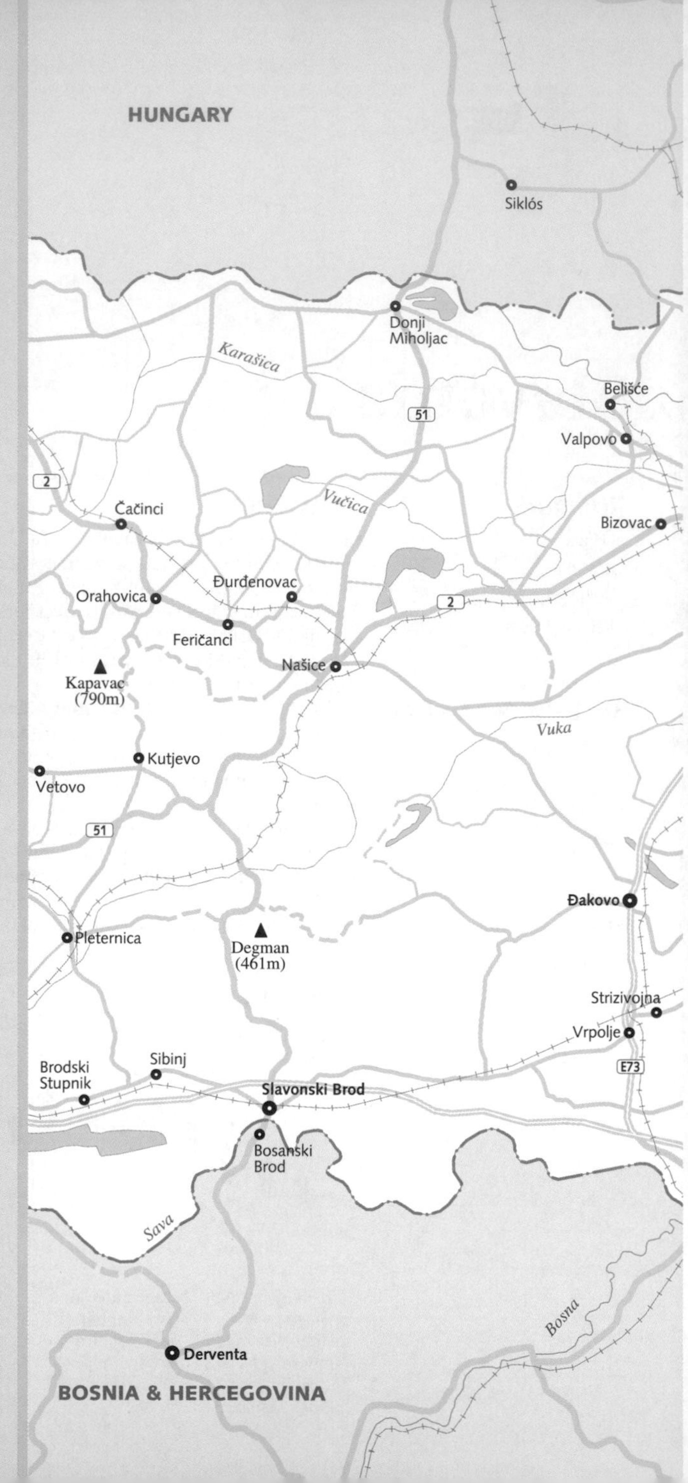

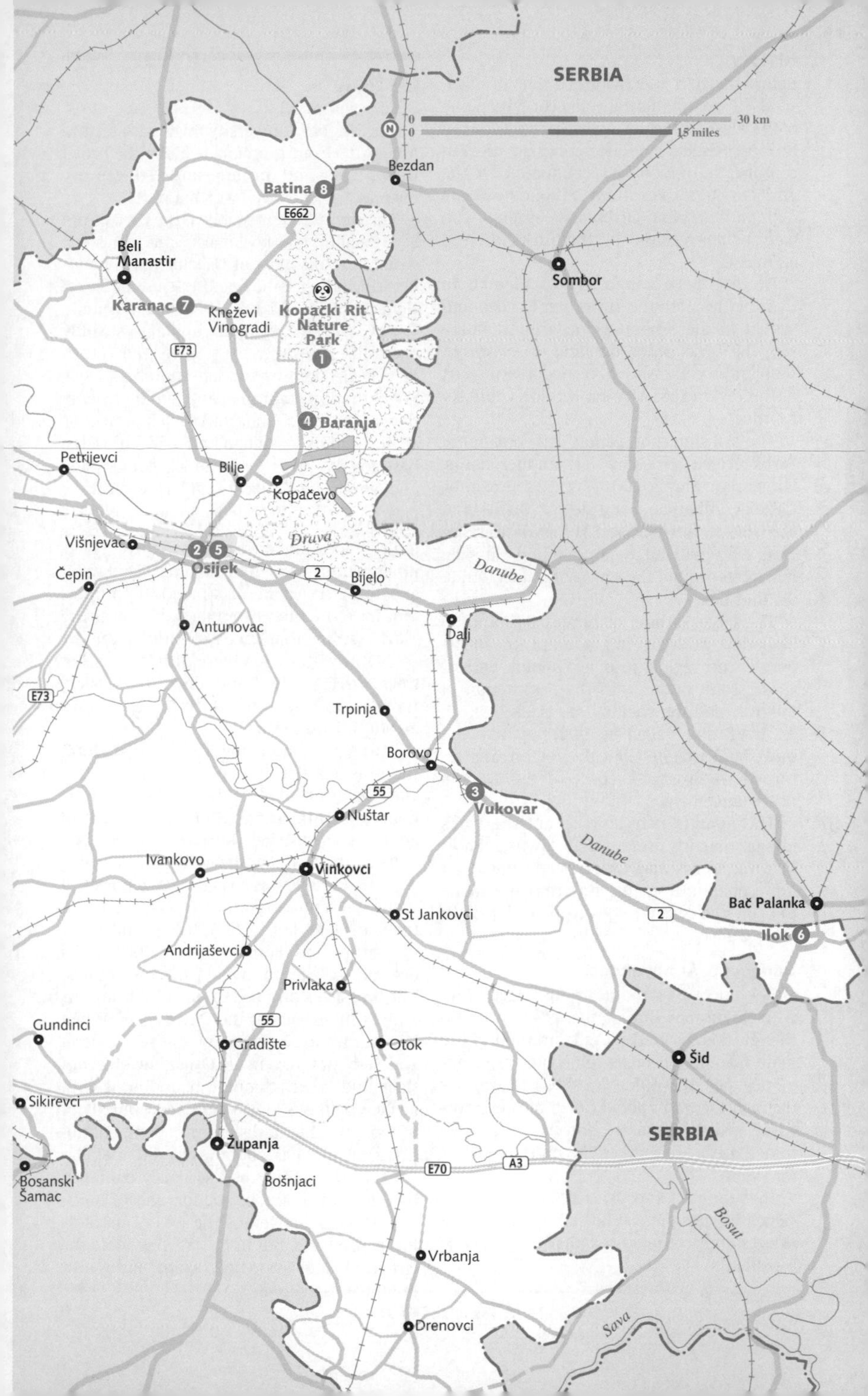

SERBIA
0
30 km
0
15 miles
Bezdan
Batina 8
E662
Beli Manastir
Sombor
Karanac 7
Kneževi Vinogradi
Kopački Rit Nature Park 1
F73
4 Baranja
Petrijevci
Bilje
Kopačevo
Višnjevac
Druva
2 5 Osijek
Čepin
2
Bijelo
Danube
Antunovac
Dalj
E73
Trpinja
Borovo
55
3 Vukovar
Nuštar
Danube
Ivankovo
Vinkovci
St Jankovci
2
Bač Palanka
Ilok 6
Andrijaševci
Privlaka
55
Gundinci
Gradište
Otok
Šid
Sikirevci
SERBIA
Županja
E70
A3
Bošnjaci
Bosanski Šamac
Bosut
Vrbanja
Drenovci
Sava

History

Before the 1991 war displaced tens of thousands of inhabitants, Slavonia contained one of the most ethnically diverse populations in Europe. Settled by Slavic tribes in the 7th century, the region was conquered by the Turks in the 16th century. Catholic residents fled and Serbian Orthodox settlers, who were better received by the Turks, arrived en masse.

In 1690 Serb supporters of Vienna, in their battles with the Turks, left Kosovo and settled in the Srijem region around Vukovar. The Turks ceded the land to Austria in 1699 and the Habsburgs turned a large part of the region into a Vojna Krajina (military frontier).

The Muslim population left but more Serbs arrived, joined by German merchants, Hungarian, Slovak and Ukrainian peasants, Catholic Albanians and Jews. Much land was sold to German and Hungarian aristocrats who built huge baroque and classical mansions around the towns of Osijek, Vukovar and Ilok.

The large Serbian community prompted Slobodan Milošević to attempt to incorporate the region into a 'Greater Serbia'. This assault began with the destruction of Vukovar and the shelling of Osijek in 1991. A ceasefire prevailed in 1992, but it wasn't until January 1998 that the region was returned to Croatia as part of the Dayton peace agreement.

The fighting may be over but the war's impact remains profound. In towns such as Vukovar, Serbs and Croats lead almost totally separate lives. Efforts are being made to bring the communities together but with limited success.

Dangers & Annoyances

Osijek and its surrounds were heavily laid with landmines during the 1990s war. Although the city and its outskirts along the main road have been de-mined and are completely safe, it would be unwise to wander through the swampland north of the Drava River, which leads to Kopački Rit. Most mined areas are marked; be on the lookout for signs.

In summer, Kopački Rit is simply besieged by mosquitoes. Be sure to wear long sleeves and trousers or slather on plenty of repellent.

Osijek

031 / POP 107,784

A historic, leafy university town with a stunning waterfront promenade along the broad Drava River and an imposing 18th-century fortress, Osijek is well worth a visit.

The city suffered terribly in the 1990s from Serb shelling and pockmarks still scar some structures, but most of Osijek's grand buildings (including some fine 19th-century Secessionist mansions) have now been renovated.

This elegant regional capital is steadily regaining its poise, boosted by the return of exiles, booming student numbers, new hotels and restaurants and an increasing flow of tourists. You'll find Osijek perfect as an intriguing, cosmopolitan and enjoyable base for day trips to Slavonia's countryside and wonderful Kopački Rit Nature Park.

History

Osijek's location on the Drava River, near its junction with the Danube (Dunav in Croatian), has made it strategically important for more than two millennia. It was the Slavic settlers that gave Osijek its name; by the 12th century it was a thriving market town. In 1526 the Turks destroyed Osijek, rebuilt it in Ottoman style and made it into an administrative centre.

Austrians chased the Turks out in 1687, the Muslims fled into Bosnia, and the city was repopulated with Serbs, Croats, Germans and Hungarians. Still wary of Turkish attacks, the Austrians built the fortress that still stands, Tvrđa, in the early 18th century.

Until the 1990s war, Osijek was a powerful industrial centre of former Yugoslavia. When the war broke out in 1991, the federal Yugoslav army and Serbian paramilitary units overran the Baranja region north of Osijek. The first shells dropped in July 1991 from Serbian positions across the Drava River. When Vukovar fell in November of that year, federal and Serbian forces made Osijek the object of their undivided attention, pounding it with artillery as thousands of residents poured out of the city. This devastating shelling continued until May 1992, but the city did not fall.

Osijek's economy was seriously damaged by the costs of reconstruction and of housing refugees, as well as the loss of markets for its products. But in the last few years the city has begun to prosper again, and a new optimism is evident.

Sights

TVRĐA

Built under Habsburg rule as a defence against Turkish attacks, the 18th-century citadel was relatively undamaged during the recent war. This baroque complex of cobblestone streets, spacious squares and stately mansions reveals a remarkable architectural unity, lending it an open-air museum feel.

The main square, Trg Svetog Trojstva, is marked by the elaborate **Holy Trinity Monument**, a baroque pillar erected in 1729 to commemorate the victims of the 18th-century plague that swept the city.

Gloria Maris Museum MUSEUM
(www.gloria-maris.hr; Svodovi bb; adult/concession 20/15KN; 10am-4pm Tue, Wed & Fri, to 8pm Thu, to 1pm Sat & Sun) Housed inside vaults of the old citadel, this extraordinary museum is dedicated to seashells and marine life. It's the labour of love of Vladimir Filipović, who has amassed around one million shells in his 48 years of collecting, from all corners of the globe. Check out the most poisonous creature in the ocean (the remains of an octopus from the Philippines), fossils from 650 million years ago, a megalodon tooth and the shells – from giant clam to tiny specimens.

There's not much information available in English so call in advance to request an English translator. Enter through the street to the right side of the church.

Museum of Slavonia MUSEUM
(Muzej Slavonije Osijek; www.mso.hr; Trg Svetog Trojstva 6; adult/concession 15/10KN, free Sundays; 9am-7pm Tue-Fri, 5-9pm Sat, 10am-2pm

WINE TASTING IN SLAVONIA

Vines have been cultivated in Slavonia for millennia – it's thought the name Baranja is derived from the Hungarian for 'wine mother' – and after a period of stagnation the region is undergoing a serious renaissance. White wines with local grapes including *graševina* are justifiably renowned, and earthy reds are also produced, primarily from *frankovka* (*blaufränkisch*), merlot and cabernet sauvignon. You should call ahead at all these cellars to make sure somebody is there to receive you and show you around.

Kutjevo (800 600 006; www.kutjevo.com; Kralja Tomislava 1, Kutjevo; by appointment), in the town of the same name, is home to a medieval wine cellar dating from 1232, formerly of the Cistercian Abbey. You can visit on a guided tour (20KN) and sample their award-winning De Gotho line-up (including reds).

Nearby are two of Slavonia's top wineries: **Krauthaker** (034-315 000; www.krauthaker.hr; Ivana Jambrovića 6, Kutjevo; tasting & tour 40KN), whose *graševina* and sweet wines regularly win top awards, and **Enjingi** (034-267 200; www.enjingi.hr; Hrnjevac 87, Vetovo; tasting & tour 50KN), one of Croatia's leading ecological producers, with winemaking experience dating back to 1890; try his award-winning Venje white blend. The winery also offers accommodation overlooking the vineyards. For a complete selection of Kutjevo's wines, visit the new **Kolijevka Graševine** (098 363 312), a wine shop and tasting room in the town centre.

In Baranja, grape cultivation has been revived on the gentle hills around Kneževi Vinogradi. Up-and-coming winegrowers, mainly in the villages of Zmajevac and Suza, work along well-marked wine trails. Traditionalist in its approach to winemaking, **Gerštmajer** (031-735 276; Šandora 31, Zmajevac) offers tasting tours of its 11 hectares of vineyard and the cellar. Just down the hill is the area's biggest producer, **Josić** (098 252 657; www.josic.hr; Planina 194, Zmajevac), which also has a fine restaurant. **Kolar** (031-733 184; Maršala Tita 141; 9am-5pm) offers a restaurant, shop and wine tastings in its 100-year-old cellar located on the main road in nearby Suza.

Slavonia also boasts the ancient cellars in Ilok as well as Croatia's first wine hotel, **Zdjelarević** (035-427 775; www.zdjelarevic.hr), located in Brodski Stupnik near Slavonski Brod, set among beautiful rolling hills and fish ponds. The hotel has marked bicycle and educational paths through the vineyards, which you can visit with an agronomist who will teach you about pedology (soils) and the differences between grape varieties. There's a terrace restaurant serving haute cuisine paired with local wines and vineyard views, nicely appointed rooms and guided cellar tours. For a more down-home experience, visit **Sobe Tonkić** (035-273 408; www.sobe-tonkic.hr), a rustic family-run guesthouse and restaurant featuring home-cooked local specialties and family wines.

Osijek

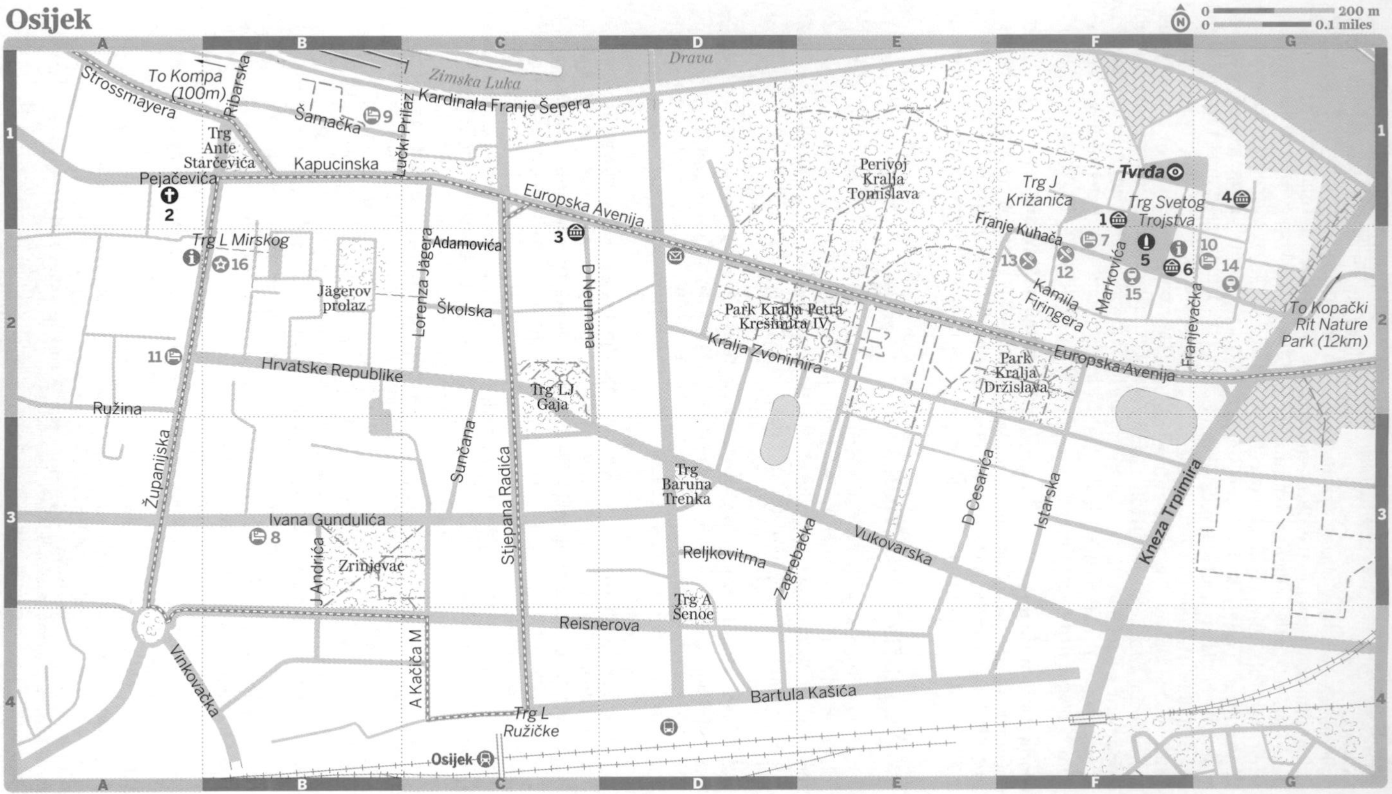

0 200 m
0 0.1 miles
Drava
Zimska Luka
To Kompa (100m)
Strossmayera
Ribarska
Šamačka
9
Lučki Prilaz
Kardinala Franje Šepera
Trg Ante Starčevića
Kapucinska
Pejačevića
2
Europska Avenija
Perivoj Kralja Tomislava
Tvrđa
Trg J Križanića
Trg Svetog Trojstva
4
1
Franje Kuhača
7
5
6
10
14
13
12
15
Markovića
Kamila Firingera
Franjevačka
To Kopački Rit Nature Park (12km)
Trg L Mirskog
16
Adamovića
3
Jägerov prolaz
Lorenza Jägera
Školska
D Neumana
Park Kralja Petra Krešimira IV
Kralja Zvonimira
Park Kralja Držislava
11
Hrvatske Republike
Trg LJ Gaja
Ružina
Županijska
Sunčana
Stjepana Radića
Trg Baruna Trenka
D Cesarića
Istarska
Kneza Trpimira
Ivana Gundulića
8
Zrinjevac
J Andrića
Reljkovitma
Zagrebačka
Vukovarska
Trg A Šenoe
Reisnerova
A Kačića M
Vinkovačka
Bartula Kašića
Trg L Ružičke
Osijek

Osijek

Top Sights
Tvrđa ... F1

Sights
1 Archaeological Museum of Osijek ... F1
2 Church of St Peter & Paul ... A1
3 Gallery of Fine Arts ... C2
4 Gloria Maris Museum ... G1
5 Holy Trinity Monument ... F2
6 Museum of Slavonia ... F2

Sleeping
7 Hostel Tufna ... F2
8 Hotel Drava ... B3
9 Hotel Osijek ... B1
10 Maksimilian ... G2
11 Waldinger ... A2

Eating
Kavana Waldinger ... (see 11)
12 Kod Ruže ... F2
13 Slavonska Kuća ... F2

Drinking
14 Old Bridge Pub ... G2
15 St Patrick's Pub ... F2

Entertainment
16 Croatian National Theatre ... B2
Tufna ... (see 7)

Sun) Houses a huge collection of treasures and artefacts relating to Slavonian history, including Bronze Age implements, Roman finds from the colony of Mursa, beautiful textiles and weavings, jewellery and fine furniture. Exhibits rotate every few months. From June to September the museum is open late on Thursday nights.

Archaeological Museum of Osijek MUSEUM
(Arheološki Muzej Osijek; Trg Svetog Trojstva 2; adult/concession 10/5KN; 9am-7pm Tue-Fri, 5-9pm Sat, 10am-2pm Sun) The building itself (a renovated city guard structure) is stunning, with a lovely oak-block floor and glass dome over an arcaded patio. Showcases finds from Roman stones to Celtic helmets, with explanations also in English. Open late on Thursdays from June to September.

A joint ticket for Museum of Slavonia, Archaeological Museum and the Gallery of Fine Arts costs 25KN.

UPPER TOWN

Church of St Peter & Paul CHURCH
(8am-noon & 3-6pm Mon-Fri, to noon Sat Sep-Jun, 8am-noon & 4-6pm Mon-Fri, 11am-noon Sat Jul & Aug) The Church of St Peter & Paul looms over Trg Ante Starčevića – its 90m-high tower is surpassed in height only by the cathedral in Zagreb. Built in the 1890s, this red-brick neo-Gothic structure features an interior with 40 elaborate stained-glass windows in Viennese style, and vividly coloured frescos by Croatian painter Mirko Rački.

Gallery of Fine Arts ART GALLERY
(Galerija Likovnih Umjetnosti; www.gluo.hr; Europska Avenija 9; adult/concession 10/5KN, free on Thu & Sun; 10am-6pm Tue, Wed & Fri, to 8pm Thu, to 1pm Sat & Sun) Housed in an elegant neoclassical mansion, the Gallery of Fine Arts contains a collection of paintings and sculptures by Slavonian artists from the 18th century onwards.

BEYOND THE CENTRE

Zoo Osijek ZOO
(www.zoo-osijek.hr; Sjevernodravska Obala 1; adult/concession 20/10KN; 9am-7pm Mar-Aug, to 5pm Sep-Feb) As an escape from museums and churches, take a free ride on the emblematic *kompa* (a wooden pedestrian ferry propelled by the water current) from the shore of Gornji Grad to Zoo Osijek on the other side of the Drava. Croatia's largest zoo spreads over 11 verdant riverside hectares, with 80 animal species and a reptile-filled aquarium.

The *kompa* operates from 9am to 7pm April to October.

Festivals & Events

Urban Fest Osijek MUSIC
(www.ufo.com.hr) June music event showcasing hip hop, rock and electronic artists.

Pannonian Challenge SPORT
(www.pannonian.org) Extreme sports as well as a music festival in August.

Sleeping

Osijek has a slim selection of hotels; for private rooms ask at the tourist office or OK Tours.

TOP CHOICE **Maksimilian** GUESTHOUSE €
(497 567; www.maksimilian.hr; Franjevačka 12; s/d from 220/320KN;) In the heart of

the old town, this superb guest house is run by a hospitable English-speaking team. All nine spacious rooms in the historic 1860 building come with satellite TV, high ceilings and good fittings (most have air-con). There's a kitchen, free coffee and tea, generous breakfast (included) and bike rental. The huge deluxe rooms with leafy views are worth the higher rate.

Waldinger HISTORIC HOTEL €€€
(☎250 450; www.waldinger.hr; Županijska 8; pansion s/d 340/440KN, hotel s/d 650/950KN; P❄@📶) This is a grand little hotel of two halves. The bedrooms in the main building offer lashings of old-school charm, with plush furnishings and thick carpets. The pansion in the back is a humbler abode, with functional rooms. A fine breakfast is served in the stately dining room and there's a top-floor fitness area with a sauna, an upscale restaurant and an atmospheric cafe. The hotel offers hefty discounts for midsummer stays.

Hotel Osijek HOTEL €€€
(☎230 333; www.hotelosijek.hr; Šamačka 4; s/d 840/910KN; P❄@📶) Right on the river, this towering concrete landmark is the town's most luxurious hotel, drawing business travellers in droves. The 147 rooms and suites are city-slicker smart, with a nod to modernist style; most have spectacular views. The wellness centre on the 14th floor has a Turkish bath, jacuzzi and sauna. Reserve by phone and get a 10% discount.

Hostel Tufna HOSTEL €
(☎215 020; www.tufna.com.hr; Franje Kuhača 10; dm per person 100KN; @📶) Osijek's only backpacker joint, this quirky hostel has two 10-bed cramped dorms and a guests' lounge and kitchen with mismatched '70s decor. It's directly above a club-bar, so pack those earplugs on weekends. Ring the number at the door if nobody answers the buzzer.

Hotel Drava HOTEL €€
(☎250 500; www.hotel-drava.com; Ivana Gundulića 25a; s/d 421/622KN; P❄@📶) Inviting hotel close to the train and bus stations with 11 colourful well-appointed rooms with a little kitsch thrown in. There are discounts for weekend stays and if you pay in cash.

Eating

Osijek is the place to sample hearty and spicy Slavonian cuisine. The local food is strongly influenced by neighbouring Hungary, with paprika sprinkled on almost every dish, and meat and freshwater fish featuring strongly. *Fiš paprikaš* (fish stewed in a paprika sauce, served with noodles) is the signature regional meal.

Check out the cheap weekday lunches at the Old Bridge Pub.

TOP CHOICE **Kod Ruže** SLAVONIAN €
(Kuhačeva 25a; mains from 50KN; ⏰closed dinner Sun) The rustic paraphernalia is laid on pretty thick here (think taxidermy galore) but this is certainly a highly atmospheric place for a Slavonian meal, especially at weekends when a live band plays gypsy music. Try the *čobanac* meat stew or one of the substantial salads, such as the *alas salata* with river fish.

Slavonska Kuća SLAVONIAN €
(Kamila Firingera 26a; mains from 45KN; ⏰closed Sun) This is a great choice for authentic Slavonian food, with lots of *pečena riba* (baked fish), including delicious catfish. Prices are moderate and portions hearty. Wash your meal down with *graševina,* a fruity white wine.

Kompa SLAVONIAN €
(Splavarska 1; mains from 40KN) A locals' favourite, this joint on the riverfront, across from the zoo, is a no-frills spot with a tiny interior and tables right on the river. Good for mainstays and low prices, although there's no menu in English nor English spoken.

Galija INTERNATIONAL €
(Gornjodravska Obala bb; mains from 40KN) The best of Osijek's boat restaurants, a little away from the hubbub that surrounds Hotel Osijek. A range of international and regional dishes is paired with river views, particularly pretty at sunset. It shuts down from October to early spring.

Kavana Waldinger CAFE €
(Županijska 8; cakes from 10KN) Dignified cafe that attracts local notables with its proper service and range of cakes that are worth every calorie.

Drinking & Entertainment

The outdoor cafe-bars that line the riverfront around Hotel Osijek are popular when the weather permits. Otherwise your best bet for bar action is the Tvrđa area, where you'll find everything from British-style pubs to raucous turbo folk joints.

Old Bridge Pub PUB
(www.oldbridgepub.com; Franje Kuhača 4) A dead ringer for a London boozer, the Old Bridge has three levels and a slim outdoor terrace – the top floor is a classy space with elegant Chesterfield sofas. There's a live band on weekend nights (till 4am) and good-value weekday lunches.

St Patrick's Pub PUB
(Franje Kuhača 15) Your best bet to start the evening, this sociable, welcoming pub has an intimate interior of dark wood and neon, and a huge terrace on the main square.

Tufna NIGHTCLUB
(www.tufna.com.hr; Franje Kuhača 10) A small club with an underground vibe. DJs play eclectic electronic sounds – anything from house anthems to drum 'n' bass.

Croatian National Theatre THEATRE
(Hrvatsko Narodno Kazalište; 220 700; www.hnk-osijek.hr; Županijska 9) Grand theatre that features a regular program of drama, ballet and opera performances from September to June.

Information

There's free wi-fi around both the Gornji Grad and the Tvrđa.

Hospital (511 511; Josipa Huttlera 4)

OK Tours (212 815; www.ok-tours.hr; Trg Slobode 7) Tours, information and some private accommodation.

Panturist (214 388; www.panturist.hr; Kapucinska 19) Slavonia's largest travel agency. Runs buses to the coast as well as to international destinations.

Post Office (Kardinala Alojzija Stepinca 17; 7am-8pm Mon-Sat) Phone calls and cash advances on MasterCard.

Press Cafe (Lorenza Jägera 24; internet access per hr 15KN; 7am-11pm Mon-Sat, 8am-11pm Sun) Surf the net inside a bar.

Privredna Banka (Stjepana Radića 19) Has an ATM.

Tourist Information Centre (210 120; www.tzosijek.hr; Trg Svetog Trojstva 5; 10am-4pm Mon-Fri, 9am-1pm Sat) Friendly info point, in the same building as Museum of Slavonia.

Tourist Office (203 755; www.tzosijek.hr; Županijska 2; 8am-8pm Mon-Fri, to noon Sat mid-Jun–mid-Sep; 8am-4pm Mon-Fri, to noon Sat rest of the year) A well-briefed office with plentiful brochures, booklets and maps.

Zlatna Greda (091 421 1424; www.zlatna-greda.org) An excellent environmental agency, which organises canoe trips along the Danube and into Kopački Rit, hikes, bird-watching expeditions, city tours by boat, photo safaris, horseback riding jaunts and bike tours.

Getting There & Away

Osijek is a major transport hub with buses and trains arriving and departing in all directions.

Air

Klisa Airport (514 400; www.osijek-airport.hr) is 20km from Osijek on the road to Vukovar. Klisa is a very minor airport with only a few Croatia Airlines flights, to Dubrovnik and Zagreb.

Bus

A full list of international buses can be found at the station.

Train

There's one train a day in each direction between Pećs and Osijek (54KN, two hours). The train from Osijek connects to Budapest (115KN, five hours). There is a daily train to Sarajevo (164KN, 6½ hours).

Getting Around

A shuttle bus meets arrivals at the airport and heads to the city centre for 25KN. It also departs from the bus station 2½ hours before each flight with international connections and 1½ hours before domestic flights.

There's an excellent, very affordable taxi service in the city. **Cammeo** (205 205) has modern cars with meters; most rides in town cost just 20KN.

Osijek has two tram lines. The fare is 10KN, payable to the driver.

For visitors, the most useful tram lines are 2, which connects the train and bus station with Trg Ante Starčevića in the centre, and 1, which goes to Tvrđa.

TRAINS FROM OSIJEK

DESTINATION	COST (KN)	DURATION	DAILY SERVICES
Rijeka	200	9-10hr	1
Zagreb	120	4½hr	5

BUSES FROM OSIJEK

DOMESTIC DESTINATIONS	COST (KN)	DURATION	DAILY SERVICES
Đakovo	33	45min	26
Dubrovnik	350	14hr	1
Ilok	61	2hr	5
Rijeka	265	7hr	1
Split	290	11hr	1
Toplice	48	1hr	6
Vukovar	34	45min	12
Zagreb	138	4hr	8

INTERNATIONAL DESTINATIONS	COST (KN)	DURATION	SERVICES
Belgrade	122	3½hr	4 daily
Vienna	295	9hr	1 daily
Zürich	882	19½hr	1 weekly

Buses connect Osijek to nearby Bilje; take Panturist bus from the bus station, heading to Beli Manastir, and ask to get off in Bilje (15min, 16KN).

Baranja

☎031

A small triangle in the far northeast of Croatia at the confluence of the Drava and Danube Rivers, Baranja stretches east of Osijek towards Serbia, north towards the town of Beli Manastir and southwest towards Đakovo. The Hungarian influence is strongly felt in this largely agricultural area; all the towns have bilingual names and some villagers can't speak much Croatian.

In the last few years this scenic area of swamps, vineyards, orchards and wheat fields has been on the rise as eastern Croatia's most interesting tourist destination. That's thanks in part to its star attraction, the bird sanctuary of Kopački Rit, but also to a clutch of authentic farmstays, regional restaurants and up-and-coming wineries.

KOPAČKI RIT NATURE PARK

Only 12km northeast of Osijek, **Kopački Rit Nature Park** (Park Prirode Kopački Rit; www.kopacki-rit.com; adult 10KN, children under 2yr free) is one of the largest wetlands in Europe: 293 bird species have been recorded here. Formed by the meeting of the Drava and Danube rivers, this vast flood plain has two main lakes, Sakadaško and Kopačevo, surrounded by a rather remarkable variety of vegetation that ranges from aquatic and grassland flora to willow, poplar as well as oak forests. Depending on the season, you can find water lilies, sedges, water ferns, duckweeds, reeds and ryegrass. The Drava and Danube rivers, together with Mura River, were pronounced a biosphere reserve by Unesco in July 2012.

Beneath the waters lie 44 species of fish, including carp, bream, pike, catfish and perch. Above the water buzz 21 kinds of mosquito (bring a tonne of repellent!) and roam red deer, wild boar, beaver, pine marten and foxes. But it's really about the birds here – look for the rare black storks, white-tailed eagles, great crested grebes, purple herons, spoonbills and wild geese. The best time to come is during the spring and autumn migrations.

The park was heavily mined during the war and closed for many years as a result. Most mines have now been cleared: safe trails have been marked. The park has a modern **visitor centre** (☎752 320; www.kopacki-rit.com; ⊙9am-5pm) located at the main entrance along the Bilje-Kopačevo road. You can walk the two educational trails nearby, or there are various **guided tours** offered. A tour of the zoological reserve by boat, taking in a castle complex and farm, costs 70KN for adults/50KN for children and students; a wildlife tour in a small boat is 100KN per hour (maximum four people). Tours depart from an embarkation point about 1km from the visitor centre. Book in advance, especially during spring and autumn.

At the northern end of the park, 12km from the visitor centre, is an Austro-Hungarian castle complex and bio-ecological research station, **Dvorac Tikveš** (☎752 320; www.kopacki-rit.com; per person 160KN), where the seven pleasant en suite rooms have leafy views. Once used by Tito as a hunting lodge, the castle was occupied by Serbs during the 1990s, and forests around the complex are still mined, so don't wander off. Best lunch to be had is on the very edge of the park, at **Kormoran** (Podunavlje bb, Podunavlje; Mains from 50KN), which serves the full roster of local dishes.

There's no public transport to the park, but you can take a local Osijek bus to Bilje and walk the remaining 3km. Alternatively you can rent a bike in Osijek at **Šport za Sve** (☎208 135; Istarska 1d; ⏲9am-1pm Mon-Fri) or at the park entrance for 25KN per day.

Zlatna Greda (☎091 42 11 424; www.zlatna-greda.org) also runs superb tours of Kopački Rit and has its own new ecocentre in a deserted village – now a protected cultural heritage sight – on the border of the park, 28km north of Osijek. Hikes, birdwatching trips, horseback riding and canoe adventures begin here. It's a work-in-progress but Zlatna Greda plans to open a campsite, a cafe and an adrenaline-fuelled fun park.

AROUND KOPAČKI RIT

Bilje, 5km north of Osijek, is a dormitory suburb with lots of cheap accommodation. It makes an alternative base for Kopački Rit. **Bilje Plus** (☎750 264; www.biljeplus.hr) is an association of three B&Bs that rents out rooms and bikes (70KN per day). Also, family-run **Mazur** (☎750 294; www.mazur.hr; Kneza Branimira 2; s/d 176/312KN; P❄📶) is a good bet with four neat rooms with private bathrooms and filling breakfasts.

A cycle path connects Bilje with Osijek. Biking is an increasingly popular activity in the region. The Pannonian Peace Route is an 80km ride from Osijek to the Serbian city of Sombor, along the Danube and through Kopački Rit. For more info and a map, browse www.zeleni-osijek.hr, a local association for environmental protection. Also popular is the 138km Danube Route, which traces easternmost Croatia along the borders with Hungary and Serbia.

The quiet village of Kopačevo on the edge of Kopački Rit is home to an outstanding regional restaurant, **Zelena Žaba** (Ribarska 3; mains from 40KN), or 'green frog', after the thousands of squatters bellowing in the backyard swamp. You have to try the house specialty, *fiš perkelt,* a fish stew with homemade noodles, soft cheese and bacon.

KARANAC & AROUND

Located in the far north of Baranja, 8km east of Beli Manastir, the ethno-village and farming community of Karanac provides an authentic slice of Slavonian village life and is well set up to welcome visitors. Lined with cherry trees and lovingly tended gardens, it is home to three churches (Reformist, Catholic and Orthodox) and some well-preserved Pannonian architecture.

Several accommodation options are available in Karanac, including the atmospheric **Sklepić** (☎720 271; www.sklepic.hr; Kolodvorska 58; s/d 225/370KN; P📶) with lovely little

ĐAKOVO CATHEDRAL & HORSES

The peaceful provincial town of Đakovo is just 35km to the south of Osijek and makes an easy day trip. There are three major reasons to visit: its impressive cathedral, the Lipizzaner horses and a wonderful folk festival every summer.

The town's pride and glory is the red-brick **cathedral** (Strossmayerov trg bb; ⏲6.30am-noon & 3-7.30pm), which dominates the town centre with its two 84m-high belfries. Commissioned by Bishop Strossmayer in 1862, this neo-Romanesque structure features a three-nave interior colourfully painted with biblical scenes.

Đakovo is famous for its Lipizzaner horses, a noble pure breed with a lineage that can be traced to the 16th century. They are bred on a farm outside town and trained at **Ergela** (www.ergela-djakovo.hr; Augusta Šenoe 45; adult/concession 20/10KN; ⏲7am-5pm Mon-Fri, by appointment Sat & Sun), a short walk from the cathedral. About 50 horses undergo daily training for their eventual work as high-class carriage horses.

Đakovački Vezovi (Đakovo Embroidery) features a display by the Lipizzaner horses and a folklore show on the first weekend in July each year, complete with folkloric dancing and traditional songs.

rustic en-suite rooms. **Ivica Marica** (☎091 13 73 793; www.ivica-marica.com; Ivo Lola Ribara 8a; s/d 350/450KN; P📶) is another excellent choice on the edge of the village, an upmarket working farm run by a young couple with delightful pine-trimmed rooms and suites, bike rental (100KN per day) plus good kids' facilities and fun such as horse-drawn carriage rides (350KN per hour).

Sklepić also has an **ethno-museum** (15KN; by appointment only), in an 1897 rural estate at the end of the village with 2000 traditional objects, workshops, a wine cellar and stables.

You'll find several excellent restaurants and wineries in this part of Baranja. **Baranjska Kuća** (☎720 180; www.baranjska-kuca.com; Kolodvorska 99; mains from 45KN; ⊙closed dinner Sun) is one of these, with many traditional dishes, such as fish stews; there's a chestnut-tree-shaded backyard with barn and a blacksmith's workshop. **Josić** (☎99 736 59 45; www.josic.hr; Planina 194, Zmajevac; mains from 45KN; ⊙closed Mon), in the nearby village of Zmajevac, is an upmarket alternative, with tables set in vaulted cellars; meat is the strong suit here. Try the duck *perkelt* stew and be sure to visit the wine cellar for tastings of local *graševina*. Book ahead in Sept and Oct.

Also nearby, in the small village of Suza, the Hungarian-run **Kovač Čarda** (Maršala Tita 215, Suza; mains from 45KN) is a no-frills roadside eatery, at the far end of the village, known to make the best *fiš paprikaš* in Baranja. They make it spicy so ask for paprika on the side.

Right on the tripartite border where Croatia touches Serbia and Hungary, **Batina** is a striking memorial from the communist era, commemorating a key victory of Soviet-lead forces over the Nazis in WWII. A colossal female statue sits on high ground, and there are spectacular views over the Danube.

Vukovar

☎032 / POP 28,016

When you visit Vukovar today, it's a challenge to visualise this town as it was before the war. A pretty place on the Danube, with roots that stretch back to the 10th century and a series of elegant baroque mansions, it once bustled with art galleries and museums. All that changed with the siege of 1991 that destroyed its economy, culture, physical infrastructure, civic harmony and soul.

Since the return of Vukovar to Croatia in 1998, there has been much progress in repairing the damage. In the centre, there are new buildings, but many pock-marked and blasted facades remain. The former water tower on the road to Ilok has been left as a testament to destruction.

Less progress has been made in restoring civic harmony. Serbs and Croats live in

THE SIEGE OF VUKOVAR

Before the war, Vukovar had a multi-ethnic population of about 44,000, of which Croats constituted 44% and Serbs 37%. As Croatia edged away from former Yugoslavia in early 1991, tensions mounted between the two groups. In August 1991 the federal Yugoslav force launched a full-scale artillery and infantry assault in an attempt to seize the town.

By the end of August all but 15,000 of Vukovar's original inhabitants had fled. Those who remained cowered in bomb-proof cellars, living on tinned food and rationed water while bodies piled up in the streets above them. For several months of the siege, the city held out as its pitifully outnumbered defenders warded off the attacks.

After weeks of hand-to-hand fighting, Vukovar surrendered on 18 November. On 20 November Serb-Yugoslav soldiers entered Vukovar's hospital and removed 400 patients, staff and their families, 194 of whom were massacred near the village of Ovčara, their bodies dumped in a mass grave nearby. In 2007 at the War Tribunal in The Hague, two Yugoslav army officers, Mile Mrkšić and Veselin Šljivančanin, were sentenced to 20 and five years in prison respectively for their role in this massacre. Mrkšić's sentence was upheld in a 2009 appeal, while Šljivančanin's was increased to 17 years for aiding and abetting the murders.

It's estimated that 2000 people – including 1100 civilians – were killed in the defence of Vukovar. There were 4000 wounded, several thousand who disappeared, presumably into mass graves, and 22,000 who were forced into exile.

parallel and hostile universes, socialising in separate spheres. Children attend separate schools and their parents drink in either Serb or Croat cafes. International organisations are trying to encourage harmony and integration, but forgiveness comes hard to those who have lost family members and livelihoods.

Inevitably, many of Vukovar's sights deal with the war and visiting them is an emotionally wrenching experience.

Sights

Place of Memory: Vukovar Hospital MUSEUM
(Županijska 37; adult/concession 15/7KN; by appointment only) This multimedia museum recounts the tragic events that took place in the hospital during the 1991 siege. The stirring tour takes you through a series of sandbag-protected corridors with video projections of war footage, bomb holes and the claustrophobic atomic shelter where newborn babies and the nurses' children were kept. There are small cubicles where you can listen to interviews and speeches by the victims and survivors. Drop-ins are not recommended as nobody at the hospital speaks English. Best to make an appointment through the tourism office.

Ovčara Memorial MEMORIAL
(10am-5pm) Around 6km out of town en route to Ilok there's a turn-off to the Ovčara Memorial, which is another 4km down the road. This is the hangar where the 200 victims from the hospital were beaten and tortured. Inside the dark room are projections of the victims' photos, with a single candle burning in the middle. The victims met their death in a cornfield another 1.5km down the road, now marked with a black marble gravestone, covered with candles and flowers.

Ada BEACH
Head out to the sand island in the Danube, where on a summer weekend you'll find lots of locals swimming, lounging on the beaches and hanging out at the cafe. Boats depart from Vrška restaurant and charge 35KN for a seasonal ticket (unlimited rides).

Festivals & Events

The annual **Vukovar Film Festival** (www.vukovarfilmfestival.com) in late August shows features, documentaries and shorts, mainly from Danubian countries.

Sleeping & Eating

Hotel Lav HOTEL €€€
(445 100; www.hotel-lav.hr; JJ Strossmayera 18; s/d 597/914KN; P@) A modern, well-run four-star hotel with spacious, well-equipped rooms, many with lovely river views. There's a good bar, a coffee room, a restaurant, a small fitness room and a terrace.

Vila Rosa GUESTHOUSE €
(091 520 40 36; vilarosavukovar@gmail.com; Josipa Rukavine 2b; s/d 200/300KN;) This new guesthouse is run by a pair of kooky but friendly owners. The five en-suite rooms have hardwood floors and modern trimmings, there's a shared kitchen where breakfast is served (25KN) and you have the Danube right across the road.

Dunavska Golubica SLAVONIAN €
(Lenjinovo Šetalište 1; mains from 35KN) Pleasant restaurant by the riverside, which has an excellent reputation for Slavonian specialties and live music on weekends.

Information

There are banks with ATMs at several locations along Strossmayera, the main drag. The young enthusiastic staff at the **tourist office** (442 889; www.turizamvukovar.hr; J J Strossmayera 15; 7am-3pm Mon-Fri, 8am-1pm Sat) do their best to help visitors. **Danubium Tours** (445 455; www.danubiumtours.hr; Franje Tuđmana 19) offers biking trips, kayaking on the Danube and various activities in and around Vukovar.

Getting There & Away

The town has good bus connections to Osijek (35KN, 50 minutes, nine daily), Ilok (35KN, 50 minutes, nine daily) and Zagreb (166KN, five hours, four daily). There are also regular services to Belgrade (96KN, three hours, four daily) in Serbia. Vukovar has one daily direct train to Zagreb (121KN, 4½ hours).

Ilok

032 / POP 6000

The easternmost town in Croatia, 37km from Vukovar, Ilok sits perched on a hill overlooking the Danube and the Serbian region of Vojvodina across the river. Surrounded by the wine-growing hills of Fruška Gora, famous for viniculture since Roman times, this well-preserved medieval town has a landmark castle that's now one of Slavonia's best museums.

Occupied by Serbia in the early 1990s, Ilok was reintegrated into Croatia in 1998. Wine production has since been revived – the area now has 17 wineries you can tour – and the fortified town centre is being renovated following recent archaeological excavations.

Sights & Activities

The **medieval town** is a leafy place surrounded by the remains of huge city walls. It has two rare specimens of Ottoman heritage: a 16th-century **hammam** and a **turbe**, the grave of a Turkish nobleman.

City Museum MUSEUM
(Muzej Grada Iloka; Šetalište Oca Mladena Barbarića bb; adult/concession 20/10KN; ⏲9am-3pm Tue-Thu, to 6pm Fri, 11am-6pm Sat) Ilok's principal attraction is this excellent municipal museum located in the Odescalchi palace high above the Danube, with spectacular river views. The castle was built on the foundations of a 15th-century structure, which the Italian family Odescalchi later rebuilt in today's baroque-classicist style.

The museum's displays are very well presented, with illustrated information panels in English and Croatian. Sabres and muskets represent the town's Turkish period, there's fine 19th-century furniture and art, and a tombstone and tapestry from an ancient synagogue.

Iločki Podrumi WINE TASTING
(☎590 003; www.ilocki-podrumi.hr; Šetalište O M Barbarića 4; tours 10KN; ⏲8am-10pm) The old wine cellars adjacent to the castle are well worth a look. Be sure to taste the *traminac,* a dry white wine served at the coronation of Queen Elizabeth II. A 20-minute tour takes you to the atmospheric underground cellar with its oak barrels. There's a terrific wine store. Tours in English need to be arranged in advance.

Sleeping & Eating

Stari Podrum HOTEL €€
(☎590 088; www.ilocki-podrumi.hr; s/d 350/500KN; P❄@📶) The motel-style accommodation block at the back has 18 large, modern rooms, all with Danube views and plush decor. Located inside the castle's old wine cellars are banqueting rooms lined with wood panelling and giant oak barrels, a splendid setting for a hearty meal of Ilok pork sausages and shepherd's stew with dumplings (mains from 50KN). The wine list is, of course, superb.

Hotel Dunav HOTEL €€
(☎596 500; www.hoteldunavilok.com; Julija Benešića 62; s/d 300/500KN; P@📶) Right on the Danube, this fine hotel has 16 attractive rooms with verdant views, some with balconies overlooking the river, and a lovely cafe terrace on the riverfront.

Old Town Hostel HOSTEL €
(☎591 159; www.cinema.com.hr; Julija Benešića 42; dm/s/d 100/250/400KN; ❄@📶) Inside a restored old cinema, this new hostel just below the old town has four colourful dorms upstairs, a funky bar with vinyl-plastered walls, a disco on weekend nights and a pizzeria (closed Mondays).

Information

Tourist Office (☎590 020; www.turizamilok.hr; Trg Nikole Iločkog 2; ⏲9am-5pm Mon-Fri) Can recommend rural hotels, walking routes around Ilok and has a lot of local information. Call ahead as its hours are sporadic.

Getting There & Away

The bus stops in the town centre just steps from the medieval town. Ilok is connected to Osijek by six daily buses (60KN, 1¾ hours), all passing through Vukovar.

Istria

☎052

Includes »

Best Places to Eat

» Konoba Batelina (p103)
» Monte (p111)
» Toklarija (p128)
» Damir & Ornella (p120)

Best Places to Stay

» Hotel Lone (p109)
» Monte Mulini (p110)
» Hotel Kaštel (p128)
» Vela Vrata (p126)

Why Go?

Continental Croatia meets the Adriatic in Istria (Istra to Croats), the heart-shaped, 3600-sq-km peninsula just south of Trieste in Italy. The bucolic interior of rolling hills and fertile plains attracts artsy visitors to Istria's hilltop villages, rural hotels and farmhouse restaurants, while the verdant indented coastline is enormously popular with the sun-and-sea set. While vast hotel complexes line much of the coast and the rocky beaches are not Croatia's best, facilities are wide ranging, the sea is clean and secluded spots are still plentiful.

The coast, or 'Blue Istria', as the tourist board calls it, is flooded with tourists in summer, but you can still feel alone and undisturbed in 'Green Istria' (the interior), even in mid-August. Add acclaimed gastronomy (starring fresh seafood, prime white truffles, wild asparagus, top-rated olive oils and award-winning wines), sprinkle it with historical charm and you have a little slice of heaven.

When to Go

Pula

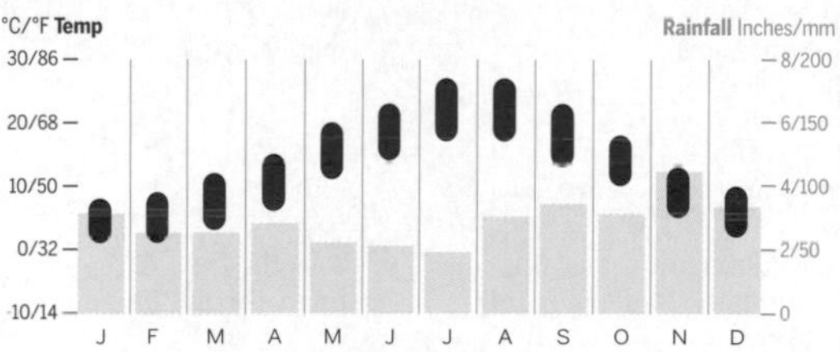

Apr Celebrate spring by heading out to the fields to pick wild asparagus.

Jul–Aug A festival roster of classical music, jazz, films and art sets Istrian towns alight.

Sep The white-truffle season kicks off with the Festival of Subotina in Buzet.

Istria Highlights

1 Admire the mosaics at **Euphrasian Basilica** (p114) in Poreč

2 Go truffle hunting in the forests around **Buzet** (p125)

3 Take in Rovinj's fishing history at **Batana House** (p108)

4 Walk the trails of the legendary **Pazin Chasm** (p123)

5 Catch al fresco screenings during the summer film festival of **Motovun** (p128)

6 Soak up the communist chic at Tito's playground of **Brijuni** (p105)

7 Explore the wild landscapes of **Rt Kamenjak cape** (p101) near Pula

History

Towards the end of the 2nd millennium BC, the Illyrian Histrian tribe settled the region and built fortified villages on top of the coastal and interior hills. The Romans swept into Istria in the 3rd century BC and began building roads and more hill forts as strategic strongholds.

From AD 539 to 751, Istria was under Byzantine rule, the most impressive remnant of which is the Euphrasian Basilica in Poreč. In the period that followed, power switched between Slavic tribes, the Franks and German rulers until an increasingly powerful Venice wrested control of the Istrian coast in the early 13th century.

With the fall of Venice in 1797, Istria came under Austrian rule, followed by the French (1809–13) and then the Austrians again. During the 19th and early 20th centuries, most of Istria was little more than a neglected outpost of the Austro-Hungarian Empire.

When the empire disintegrated at the end of WWI, Italy moved quickly to secure Istria. Italian troops occupied Pula in November 1918 and, in the 1920 Treaty of Rapallo, the Kingdom of Serbs, Croats and Slovenes ceded Istria along with Zadar and several islands to Italy, as a reward for joining the Allied powers in WWI.

A massive population shift followed as 30,000 to 40,000 Italians arrived from Mussolini's Italy and many Croats left, fearing fascism. Their fears were not misplaced, as Istria's Italian masters attempted to consolidate their hold by banning Slavic speech, education and cultural activities.

Italy retained the region until its defeat in WWII when Istria became part of Yugoslavia, causing another mass exodus, as Italians and many Croats fled Tito's communists. Trieste and the peninsula's northwestern tip were points of contention between Italy and Yugoslavia until 1954, when the region was finally awarded to Italy. As a result of Tito's reorganisation of Yugoslavia, the northern part of the peninsula was incorporated into Slovenia, where it remains.

THE ISTRIAN COAST

At the tip of the Istrian peninsula is Pula, the coast's largest city. The Brijuni Islands, Tito's former playground, are an easy day trip from here. The east coast of Istria centres

TAKING IT OFF IN ISTRIA

Naturism in Croatia enjoys a long and venerable history that began on Rab Island around the turn of the 20th century. It quickly became a fad among Austrians influenced by the growing German Freikörperkultur movement, which loosely translates as 'free body culture'. Later, Austrian Richard Ehrmann opened the first naturist camp on Paradise Beach in Lopar (on Rab), but the real founders of Adriatic naturism were Edward VIII and Wallis Simpson, who popularised it by going skinny-dipping along the Rab coast in 1936.

The coast of Istria now has many of Croatia's largest and most well-developed naturist resorts. Naturist campgrounds are marked as FKK, an abbreviation of Freikörperkultur.

Start in the north at **Camp Kanegra** (www.istracamping.com), north of Umag, a relatively small site on a long pebbly beach. Continuing south along the coast, you'll come to **Naturist Centre Ulika** (www.plavalaguna.hr) in Červar, just outside Poreč, which has 559 pitches, as well as caravans and mobile homes available for rent. For those who prefer to stay in an apartment, **Naturist Resort Solaris** (www.valamar.hr) is the ideal choice. Only 12km north of Poreč, on the wooded Lanterna Peninsula, the complex also includes a naturist campground. South of Poreč, next to the fishing village of Funtana, is the larger **Naturist Camping Istra** (www.valamar.hr), which sleeps up to 3000 people. Continue south past Vrsar and you come to the mother ship of naturist resorts, **Koversada** (www.campingrovinjvrsar.com). In 1961 Koversada islet went totally nude and the colony soon spread to the nearby coast. Now this behemoth can accommodate up to 8000 people in campsites, villas and apartments. If that seems a little overwhelming, keep going south to **Valalta Naturist Camp** (www.valalta.hr), on the other side of the Lim Channel north of Rovinj. It has a manageable number of apartments, bungalows, caravans, mobile homes and campsites. If you prefer to be within easy reach of Pula, travel down the coast to Medulin and **Camp Kažela** (www.arenacamps.com), which has mobile homes for rent, plus campsites right by the sea.

on the modern seaside resort of Rabac, just below the ancient hilltop town of Labin. The west coast is the tourist showcase. Rovinj is the most enchanting town and Poreč the easiest – and cheaper – holiday choice, with lodging and entertainment options aplenty. Just across the water is Italy, and the pervasive Italian influence makes it seem even closer. Italian is a second language in Istria, many Istrians have Italian passports and each town name has an Italian counterpart.

Pula

POP 57,765

The wealth of Roman architecture makes otherwise workaday Pula (ancient Polensium) a standout among Croatia's larger cities. The star of the show is the remarkably well-preserved Roman amphitheatre, smack in the heart of the city, which dominates the streetscape and doubles as a venue for summer concerts and festivals.

Historical attractions aside, Pula is a busy commercial city on the sea that has managed to retain a friendly small-town appeal. Just a short bus ride away, a series of beaches awaits at the resorts that occupy the Verudela Peninsula to the south. Although marred with residential and holiday developments, the coast is dotted with fragrant pine groves, seaside cafes and a clutch of fantastic restaurants. Further south along the indented shoreline, the Premantura Peninsula hides a spectacular nature park, the protected cape of Kamenjak.

History

In 1853, during Austro-Hungarian rule, the monarchy chose Pula as the empire's main naval centre. The construction of the port and the opening of its large shipyard in 1886 unleashed a demographic and economic expansion that transformed Pula into a military and industrial powerhouse.

The city fell into decline once again under Italian fascist rule, which lasted from 1918 to 1943, when the city was occupied by the Germans. At the end of WWII, Pula was administered by Anglo-American forces until it became part of postwar Yugoslavia in 1947. Pula's industrial base weathered the 1990s war relatively well and the city remains an important centre for shipbuilding, textiles, metals and glass.

Sights

The oldest part of the city follows the ancient Roman plan of streets circling the central citadel, while the city's newer portions follow a rectangular grid pattern. Most shops, agencies and businesses are clustered in and around the old town as well as on Giardini, Carrarina, Istarska and Riva, which runs along the harbour. The new Riva is currently under construction, which makes the harbourfront one big construction site; the work is expected to finish in late 2013. With the exception of a few hotels and restaurants in the old town, most others, as well as the beaches, are 4km to the southwest on the Verudela Peninsula; these can be reached by

Pula

Top Sights

Archaeological Museum ... C4
Roman Amphitheatre ... D3
Temple of Augustus ... A4
Zerostrasse ... C5

Sights

1 Cathedral ... B4
2 Museum of Contemporary Art of Istria ... B3
3 Museum of History ... B4
4 Roman Floor Mosaic ... A5
5 Triumphal Arch of Sergius ... C5

Sleeping

6 Hostel Pipištrelo ... A5
7 Hotel Amfiteatar ... C3
8 Hotel Galija ... C5
9 Hotel Omir ... C5
10 Hotel Scaletta ... D2
11 Riviera Guest House ... C2

Eating

12 Garfield ... C6
13 Jupiter ... C4
14 Kantina ... D6
15 Markat ... C6

Drinking

16 Cvajner ... A4
17 Pietas Julia ... C2
18 Scandal Express ... C6
19 Uliks ... B5

Entertainment

20 Club Uljanik ... B6

walking south on Arsenalska, which turns into Tomasinijeva and then Veruda.

Roman Amphitheatre AMPHITHEATRE

(Arena; Flavijevska bb; adult/concession 40/20KN; ⌚8am-midnight Jul & Aug, 8am-9.30pm Jun, 8am-9pm Sep, 9am-7pm Oct, 9am-5pm Nov-Mar, 8am-8pm Apr, 8am-9pm May) Pula's most famous and imposing sight is this 1st-century amphitheatre, overlooking the harbour northeast of the old town. Built entirely from local limestone, the amphitheatre, known locally as the Arena, was designed to host gladiatorial contests, with seating for up to 20,000

Pula

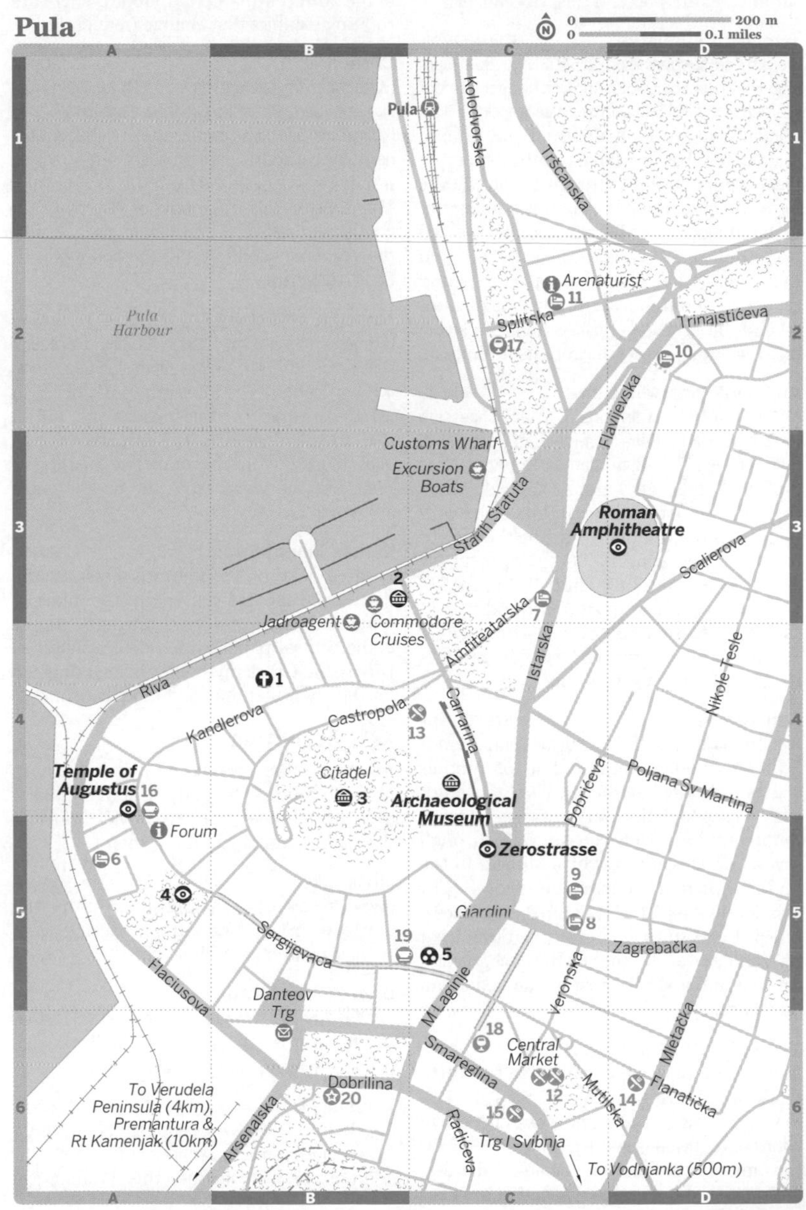

spectators. On the top of the walls is a gutter that collected rainwater. You can still see the slabs used to secure the fabric canopy, which protected spectators from the sun. In the chambers downstairs is a small **museum** with a display of ancient olive-oil equipment. **Pula Film Festival** is held here every summer, as are pop and classical concerts.

Temple of Augustus ROMAN TEMPLE

(Forum; adult/concession 20/10KN; ⏲9am-8pm Mon-Fri, to 3pm Sat & Sun Apr-Oct, by appointment via Archaeological Museum at other times) This is the only visible remnant from the Roman era on the Forum, Pula's central meeting place from antiquity through to the Middle Ages. It used to contain temples and public buildings, but today this temple, erected from 2 BC to AD 14, is the showcase. When the Romans left, it became a church and then a grain warehouse. Reconstructed after a bomb hit it in 1944, it now houses a small historical museum with captions in English.

Archaeological Museum MUSEUM

(Arheološki Muzej; Carrarina 3; adult/concession 20/10KN; ⏲8am-8pm Mon-Fri, 9am-3pm Sat & Sun May-Sep, 9am-2pm Mon-Fri Oct-Apr) This museum presents archaeological finds from all over Istria. The exhibits cover prehistory to the Middle Ages, but the accent is on the 2nd century BC to 6th century AD. Even if you don't enter the museum, visit the **sculpture garden** around it, and the **Roman theatre** behind. The garden, entered through 2nd-century twin gates, is the site of concerts in summer.

Zerostrasse HISTORICAL SITE

(adult/concession 15/5KN; ⏲10am-10pm Jun–mid-Sep) This underground system of tunnels was built before and during WWI to shelter the city's population and serve as storage for ammunition. Now you can walk through several of its sections, which all lead to the middle, where a photo exhibit shows early aviation in Pula. There are three entrances – one by the Forum (in a tiny unmarked street off Kandlerova), another by the Archaeological Museum and the third by the taxi stand on Giardini.

Triumphal Arch of Sergius RUINS

Along Carrarina are Roman walls, which mark the eastern boundary of old Pula. Follow these walls south and continue down Giardini to this majestic arch erected in 27 BC to commemorate three members of the Sergius family who achieved distinction in Pula.

Museum of Contemporary Art of Istria MUSEUM

(Ivana 1; admission 10KN; ⏲11am-2pm & 5-9pm Tue-Sun summer, 11am-7pm Tue-Sun winter) Pop in to Pula's new contemporary-art museum, inside the old printing house off the harbour, for a look at Istria's art from the second half of the 20th century up until today. There are rotating exhibits that change frequently.

Cathedral CATHEDRAL

(Katedrala; Trg Svetog Tome 2; ⏲10am-5pm mid-Jun–mid-Sep, Mass in Croatian 8am daily & in Italian 9am Sun) The main altar of Pula's 5th-century cathedral is a Roman sarcophagus holding relics of saints from the 3rd century. The floor reveals fragments of 5th- and 6th-century mosaics. Stones from the amphitheatre were used to build the bell tower in the 17th century.

Museum of History MUSEUM

(Povijesni Muzej Istre; Uspon Gradini 14; adult/concession 10/7KN; ⏲9am-9pm Jun-Sep, 9am-4.30pm Oct-May) The Museum of History is in a 17th-century Venetian fortress on a hill in the old town's centre. The meagre exhibits deal mostly with the maritime history of Pula, but the views from the citadel walls are worth a stop.

Roman Floor Mosaic MOSAIC

Located just off Sergijevaca, this mosaic dates from the 3rd century. In the midst of remarkably well-preserved geometric motifs is the central panel, which depicts bad girl Dirce from Greek mythology being punished for the attempted murder of her cousin.

Activities

An easy 41km cycling trail from Pula to Medulin follows the path of Roman gladiators. The tourist centre can provide information on the trail, including a map.

Istria Bike CYCLING

(www.istria-bike.com) A website run by the tourist board, outlining trails, packages and agencies that offer cycling trips.

Orca Diving Center DIVING

(☎098 409 850; www.orcadiving.hr; Hotel Histria) At this centre on the Verudela Peninsula, you can arrange boat and wreck dives.

Windsurf Bar WINDSURFING

(☎091 512 3646; www.windsurfing.hr; windsurfing equipment/courses per hr from 70/200KN) In addition to windsurfing, this Premantura

BEACHES

Pula is surrounded by a half-circle of rocky beaches, each one with its own fan club. Like bars or nightclubs, beaches go in and out of style. The most tourist-packed are undoubtedly those surrounding the hotel complex on the **Verudela Peninsula**, although some locals will dare to be seen at the small turquoise-coloured **Hawaii Beach** near the Hotel Park.

For seclusion, head out to the wild **Rt Kamenjak** (www.kamenjak.hr; pedestrians & cyclists free, per car/scooter 25/20KN; ⌚7am-10pm) on the Premantura Peninsula, 10km south of Pula. Istria's southernmost point, this gorgeous, entirely uninhabited cape has lovely rolling hills, wild flowers (including 30 species of orchid), low Mediterranean shrubs, fruit trees and medicinal herbs, and around 30km of virgin beaches and coves. It's criss-crossed with a maze of gravel roads and paths, making it nice and easy to get around. The views to the island of Cres and the peaks of Velebit are extraordinary. Leave no trace – be sure to use the plastic bag and the eco-ashtray you get at the entrance for all your rubbish. Watch out for strong currents if swimming off the southern cape.

Stop by the visitor centre in the old school building in the centre of Premantura, which has an informative bilingual display about the park's ecosystems. Nearby Windsurf Bar rents out bikes and windsurfing equipment. It also offers trial windsurfing courses.

Kolombarica Beach, on the southern end of the peninsula, is popular with daring young men who dive from the high cliffs and swim through the shallow caves at the water's edge. Just above it is a delightful beach bar, Safari, half-hidden in the bushes near the beach, about 3.5km from the entrance to the park. A shady place with lush alcoves, lots of driftwood, found objects and a bar that serves tasty snacks, it's a great place to while away an afternoon. For the wildest and least-discovered stretch of the cape, head to Gornji Kamenjak, which lies between the village of Volme and Premantura.

Getting to Rt Kamenjak by car is the easiest option, but drive slowly in order not to generate too much dust, which is detrimental to the environment. A more ecofriendly option is taking city bus 26 from Pula to Premantura (15KN), then renting a bike to get inside the park. On full-moon nights in summer, an organised 10km bike ride, adapted to all ages, leaves from Premantura.

outfit offers cycling (250KN) and kayaking (300KN) excursions.

Tours

Most travel agencies in Pula offer trips to Brijuni, Limska Draga, Rovinj and inner Istria, but it's often cheaper to book with one of the boats at the harbour. These run regularly and offer fishing picnics (220KN), two-hour 'panorama' excursions to Brijuni (150KN) and a jaunt to Rovinj, Limska Draga and Crveni Otok (300KN).

Two ships go to Brijuni and actually stop and tour: Martinabela and Fissa Brijuni.

Martinabela BOAT
(www.martinabela.hr; 280KN) Twice daily in summer.

Fissa Brijuni BOAT
(www.fissa-brijuni.hr; 280KN) From Monday to Saturday in summer.

Festivals & Events

Pula Film Festival FILM
(www.pulafilmfestival.hr) Now in its 60th year, this July film festival is the town's most important event, with screenings of mainly Croatian and some international films in the Roman Amphitheatre and other locations around town.

Seasplash Festival MUSIC
(www.seasplash.net) Each July, this hopping music fest, featuring wide-ranging live performances – from reggae and ska to dancehall and hip hop – lights up Punta Christo Fort.

Outlook Festival MUSIC
(www.outlookfestival.com) Europe's largest bass music and sound system culture festival takes place in early September in Punta Christo Fort in Štinjan, just outside Pula.

Jazzbina MUSIC

(www.jazzbina.net) A year-long program of jazz concerts, many featuring world-renowned musicians, is held on Portarata square during summer and in theatres and clubs other times of year.

Sleeping

Pula's peak tourist season runs from the second week of July to late August. During this period it's wise to make advance reservations. The tip of the Verudela Peninsula, 4km southwest of the city centre, has been turned into a vast tourist complex replete with hotels and apartments. It's not especially attractive, except for the shady pine forests that cover it, but there are beaches, restaurants, tennis courts and water sports. Any travel agency can give you information and book you in to one of the hotels, or you can contact **Arenaturist** (529 400; www.arenaturist.hr; Splitska 1a).

The travel agencies in Pula can find you private accommodation, but there is little available in the town centre. Count on paying from 250KN to 490KN for a double room and from 300KN to 535KN for a two-person apartment. You can also browse the list of private accommodation at www.pulainfo.hr.

Hotel Amfiteatar HOTEL €€

(375 600; www.hotelamfiteatar.com; Amfiteatarska 6; s/d 475/658KN;) The swankiest spot in town, right by the amphitheatre, this new hotel has contemporary rooms with upscale trimmings such as minibars and flat-screen TVs. Rooms range in size and view. The restaurant is one of Pula's best. There's a surcharge for stays of one night.

Hostel Pipištrelo HOSTEL €

(393 568; www.hostel-pipistrelo.com; Flaciusova 6; dm/s/d 124/148/296KN;) With its colourful facade, this recent addition to Pula's hostel scene sits right across the harbour. Its quirky thematic rooms were done up by young Pula designers. It is cash only and closed Sundays, so call ahead. The shipyard across the way makes it a bit noisy.

Hotel Scaletta HOTEL €€

(541 025; www.hotel-scaletta.com; Flavijevska 26; s/d 505/732KN;) There's a friendly family vibe at this cosy hotel. The rooms have tasteful decor and a bagful of trimmings (such as minibars). Plus it's just a hop and a skip from town, and a short walk from the amphitheatre and the waterfront.

Hotel Galija HOTEL €€

(383 802; www.hotelgalija.hr; Epulonova 3; s/d 505/725KN;) This two-part hotel sits a stone's throw from the central market. Standard rooms are in the building above the restaurant, while the newer, more modern rooms (for 100KN extra) are in the building that houses the reception.

Park Plaza Histria Pula HOTEL €€€

(525 400; www.arenaturist.hr; Verudella 17; s 750-950KN, d 1200-1400KN;) Extensive four-star facilities, newly renovated rooms with balconies and easy beach access make up for the lack of character at this concrete behemoth. There are indoor and outdoor swimming pools and a spa. Reserve online for the best prices.

Hotel Omir HOTEL €€

(213 944; www.hotel-omir.com; Dobrićeva 6; s/d 450/600KN;) The best budget option smack in the heart of town, Hotel Omir has modest but clean and quiet rooms with TVs. Rooms on the 2nd and 3rd floors are more spacious; some have air-conditioning. There's no elevator.

Riviera Guest House HOTEL €€

(525 400; www.arenaturist.hr; Splitska 1; s/d 360/590KN;) This once-grand property in a neobaroque 19th-century building is in dire need of a thorough overhaul. The saving grace: it's in the centre of town and the front rooms have water views.

Youth Hostel HOSTEL €

(391 133; www.hfhs.hr; Valsaline 4; dm 126KN, caravan 146KN, campsite per person/tent 73/15KN;) This hostel overlooks a beach in Valsaline Bay, 3km south of central Pula. There are dorms, caravans split into two tiny four-bed units and campsites. To get here, take bus 2A or 3A to the 'Piramida' stop, walk back towards the city to the first street, then turn left and look for the hostel sign.

Camping Stoja CAMPGROUND €

(387 144; www.arenacamps.com; Stoja 37; per person/tent 58/37KN; Apr-Oct) The closest campground to Pula, 3km southwest of the centre. It has lots of space on the shady promontory, with a restaurant, a diving centre and swimming off the rocks. Take bus 1 to Stoja.

Eating

The centre of Pula is full of tourist traps, so for the best food and good value you'll have to head out of town. For cheap bites, browse around the central market, where you'll find excellent sandwiches at **Garfield** (Narodni trg 9; sandwiches from 25KN; ⏲9am-3pm Mon-Fri, to 2pm Sat) on the 1st floor. For a reliably good meal, head to the al fresco restaurant of Hotel Amfiteatar.

CITY CENTRE

Vodnjanka ISTRIAN €
(Vitezića 4; mains from 40KN; ⏲closed Sat dinner & winter Sun) Locals swear by the real-deal home cooking at this no-frills spot. It's cheap, casual and cash-only, and there's a small menu that concentrates on simple Istrian dishes. To get here, walk south on Radićeva to Vitezića.

Fish-Food More SEAFOOD €
(Rizzijeva 47; mains from 40KN; ⏲Mon-Sat) A simple seafood joint in a residential area some 15 minutes' walk from the central market (part of it uphill). It buzzes with locals at lunchtime, who come for fresh fish dishes. The marinated sardines are to die for.

Kantina INTERNATIONAL €€
(Flanatička 16; mains from 70KN; ⏲Mon-Sat) The beamed stone cellar of this Habsburg building has been redone in a modern style. The ownership and culinary helm changed recently so the food quality is hit and miss, but the location is central and the ambience pleasant.

Jupiter PIZZERIA €
(Castropola 42; pizzas 30-96KN) Good thin-crust pizzas and decent pasta dishes. There's a terrace upstairs and a 20% discount on Wednesday.

Markat CANTEEN €
(Trg I Svibnja 5; mains from 20KN; ⏲8am-9pm Mon-Fri, to 3pm Sat & Sun) This self-service local canteen opposite the central market is worth a stop for decent cheap grub. Pick what you want and pay at the end of the line.

SOUTH & EAST OF THE CITY

TOP CHOICE **Konoba Batelina** SEAFOOD €€
(☎573 767; Čimulje 25, Banjole; mains from 85KN; ⏲dinner only) The superb food that awaits at this family-run tavern is worth a trek to Banjole village, 3km southeast of Pula. The owner, fisherman and chef David Skoko, dishes out seafood that's some of the best, most creative and lovingly prepared you'll find in Istria. Reserve ahead.

Gina ISTRIAN €€
(Stoja 23; mains from 60KN) This low-key eatery near Stoja campground draws in a local crowd for its well-prepared Istrian mainstays, cosy decor and lovely sea views. Try the cream fish soup with *malvazija* (local wine) and the lavender semifreddo with a hot sauce of figs and pine nuts.

Farabuto MEDITERRANEAN €€
(Sisplac 15; mains from 70KN; ⏲closed Sun lunch) It's worth a trek to this nondescript residential area southwest of the centre for stylish decor but, more importantly, stellar Mediterranean fare with a creative touch. There are daily specials and a good wine list; try the house wine from Piquentum winery.

Milan MEDITERRANEAN €€
(www.milanpula.com; Stoja 4; mains from 85KN) An exclusive vibe, seasonal specialities, four sommeliers and an olive-oil expert on staff all create one of the city's best dining experiences. The five-course fish menu is well worth it. There's also a 12-room upscale **hotel** (single/double 590/850KN) out the back.

Drinking & Entertainment

You should definitely try to catch a concert in the spectacular amphitheatre – the tourist office has schedules and there are posters around Pula advertising live performances.

Most of the nightlife is out of the town centre, but in mild weather the cafes on the Forum and along the pedestrian streets Kandlerova, Flanatička and Sergijevaca are lively people-watching spots. To mix with Pula's young crowd, grab some beers and head to the Lungomare coastal strip, where music blasts out of parked cars.

For beach bar action, head to Verudela or Medulin.

TOP CHOICE **Cabahia** BAR
(Širolina 4) This artsy hideaway in Veruda has a cosy wood-beamed interior, eclectic decor of old objects, dim lighting, South American flair and a great garden terrace out the back. It hosts concerts and gets packed on weekends. If it's too full, try the more laid-back **Bass** (Širolina 3), just across the street.

Rojc CULTURAL CENTRE
(www.rojcnet.pula.org; Gajeva 3) For an arty underground experience, check out Rojc, a converted army barracks that now houses a multimedia art centre and studios with

occasional concerts, exhibitions and other events.

Cvajner CAFE

(Forum 2) Snag a prime al fresco table at this artsy cafe right on the buzzing Forum and check out rotating exhibits in the funky interior, which showcases works by up-and-coming local artists.

Pietas Julia CAFE-BAR

(Riva 20; 📶) At this trendy bar right on the harbour, things don't start to get happening until late on weekends, as it stays open till 4am. During the day, there are breakfasts and snacks. Wi-fi is free. Great spot for a sundowner.

Scandal Express CAFE-BAR

(Ciscuttijeva 15) Mingle with a mixed-bag crowd of locals at this popular gathering spot with a cool train-carriage vibe and lots of posters. Try *pašareta,* a local Istrian soft drink. Smoking is allowed.

Uliks CAFE

(Trg Portarata 1) James Joyce once taught in this apartment building, where you can now linger over a drink at the ground-floor cafe, pondering *Ulysses* or Pula's pebble beaches.

Zeppelin BEACH BAR

(Saccorgiana Bay) Après-beach fun is on the menu at this new beach bar in Saccorgiana bay on Verudela, but it also does night parties ranging in theme from vodka to reggae and karaoke to martini.

Club Uljanik NIGHTCLUB

(www.clubuljanik.hr; Dobrilina 2) Going strong since the 1960s, the legendary Pula club today caters to a young party crowd who come for its themed weekend parties.

Aruba NIGHTCLUB

(Šijanska 1a) On the road to the airport, this cafe-bar and club is a relaxing hang-out during the day and a hopping venue for live music and parties at night. The outdoor terrace gets crowded.

Information

Internet Access

MMC Luka (Istarska 30; per hr 25KN; ⌚8am-midnight Mon-Fri, to 3pm Sat) There's also free wi-fi all around town; enquire with the tourist office about specific locations.

Laundry

Mika (Trinajstićeva 16; ⌚8am-2pm Mon-Fri, to noon Sat)

Medical Services

Hospital (☎376 548; Zagrebačka 34)

Tourist Ambulance (Flanatička 27; ⌚8am-9.30pm Mon-Fri Jul & Aug)

Post

Main Post Office (Danteov trg 4; ⌚7am-8pm Mon-Fri, to 1pm Sat) You can make long-distance calls here. Check out the cool staircase inside.

Tourist Information

Tourist Information Centre (☎212 987; www.pulainfo.hr; Forum 3; ⌚8am-9pm Mon-Fri, 9am-9pm Sat & Sun summer, 8am-7pm Mon-Fri, 9am-7pm Sat, 10am-4pm Sun rest of year) Knowledgeable and friendly staff provide maps, brochures and schedules of events in Pula and around Istria. Pick up two useful booklets: *Domus Bonus,* which lists the best-quality private accommodation in Istria; and *Istra Gourmet,* with a list of all restaurants.

Travel Agencies

Active Travel Istra (☎215 497; www.activa-istra.com; Scalierova 1) Excursions around Istria, adventure trips and concert tickets.

Arenaturist (☎529 400; www.arenaturist.hr; Riviera Guest House, Splitska 1a) Books rooms in the network of hotels it manages and offers guide services and excursions.

IstrAction (☎383 369; www.istraction.com; Prilaz Monte Cappelletta 3) Offers fun half-day tours to Kamenjak and around Pula's fortifications, as well as medieval-themed full-day excursions around Istria.

Maremonti Travel Agency (☎384 000; www.maremonti-istra.hr; Flavijevska 8) Books accommodation and rents cars and scooters (from 150KN to 250KN per day).

Getting There & Away

Air

Pula Airport (☎530 105; www.airport-pula.hr) is located 6km northeast of town. There is one daily flight to Zagreb (40 minutes). In summer, there are low-cost and charter flights from major European cities, such as with Ryanair and easyJet. **Croatia Airlines** (☎218 909; www.croatiaairlines.hr; Valtursko polje 210) has an office at the airport.

Boat

Pula's harbour is located west of the bus station.

Jadroagent (☎210 431; www.jadroagent.hr; Riva 14; ⌚7am-3pm Mon-Fri) has schedules and tickets for boats connecting Istria with the islands and south of Croatia. It also represents Jadrolinija.

Commodore Cruises (☎211 631; www.commodore-travel.hr; Riva 14) Commodore Cruises sells tickets for a catamaran between Pula and Zadar (100KN, five hours), which runs

BUSES FROM PULA

DOMESTIC DESTINATION	COST (KN)	DURATION	DAILY SERVICES
Dubrovnik	580	15hr	1
Labin	42	45min	10
Poreč	72	1hr	5
Rovinj	38	45min	12
Split	392	10hr	2
Zadar	255	7hr	3
Zagreb	190	4hr	12

INTERNATIONAL DESTINATION	COST (KN)	DURATION	SERVICES
Milan	420	9hr	1 weekly
Padua	235	6hr	1 daily (none Sun)
Trieste	110	3hr	4 daily
Venice	170	5hr	1 daily (none Sun)

five times weekly from July through to early September and twice weekly in June and the rest of September. It also offers a Wednesday boat service to Venice (430KN, 3½ hours) between June and September.

Bus

The Pula **bus station** (☎060 304 091; Šijanska 4) is 500m northeast of the town centre, and has a **garderoba** (per hr 2.50KN; ⏰24hr) for those who need to store bags. Buses head from the bus station to Rijeka (97KN, 1½ hours) almost hourly. In summer, reserve a seat a day in advance and be sure to sit on the right-hand side of the bus for a stunning view of the Kvarner Gulf.

Train

Less than 1km north of town, the train station is near the sea along Kolodvorska. There is one direct train daily to Ljubljana (144KN, 4½ hours) and three to Zagreb (140KN, nine hours), but you must board a bus for part of the trip, from Lupoglav to Rijeka. There are four daily trains to Buzet (50KN, two hours).

ℹ Getting Around

An airport bus (15KN) departs from the bus station several times weekly, coinciding with Ryanair flights; check at the bus station. Taxis cost about 50KN to 80KN.

The city buses of use to visitors are 1, which runs to Camping Stoja, and 2A and 3A to Verudela. The frequency varies from every 15 minutes to every half hour (from 5am to 11.30pm). Tickets are sold at *tisak* (news-stands) for 6KN, or from the driver for 11KN.

Brijuni Islands

The Brijuni (Brioni in Italian) archipelago consists of two main pine-covered islands and 12 islets off the coast of Istria, just northwest of Pula across the 3km-wide Fažana Channel. Only the two larger islands, Veli Brijun and Mali Brijun, can be visited. Covered by meadows, parks and oak and laurel forests – and some rare plants such as wild cucumber and marine poppy – the islands were pronounced a national park in 1983.

Even though traces of habitation go back more than 2000 years, the islands really owe their fame to Tito, the extravagant Yugoslav leader who turned them into his private retreat.

Each year from 1947 until just before his death in 1980, Tito spent six months in Brijuni at his hideaway. To create a lush comfort zone, he introduced subtropical plant species and created a safari park to house the exotic animals gifted to him by world leaders. The Somali sheep you'll see roaming around came from Ethiopia, while a Zambian leader gave a gift of waterbuck.

At his summer playground, Tito received 90 heads of state and a bevy of movie stars in lavish style. Bijela Vila on Veli Brijun was Tito's 'White House': the place for issuing edicts and declarations as well as entertaining. The islands are still used for official state visits, but are increasingly a favourite on the international yachting circuit, and a holiday spot of choice for royalty from obscure kingdoms and random billionaires who love its bygone aura of glamour.

Every summer, theatre aficionados make their way across the channel to the Minor Fort on Mali Brijun for performances by **Ulysses Theatre** (www.ulysses.hr).

Sights

As you arrive on Veli Brijun, after a 15-minute boat ride from Fažana, you'll dock in front of the Hotel Istra-Neptun, where Tito's illustrious guests once stayed. A guide will take you on a four-hour island tour on a miniature tourist train, beginning with a visit to the 9-hectare **safari park**. Other stops on the tour include the ruins of a **Roman country house**, dating from the 1st century BC, an **archaeological museum** inside a 16th-century citadel, and **St Germain Church**, now a gallery displaying copies of medieval frescos in Istrian churches.

Most interesting is the **Tito on Brijuni exhibit** in a building behind Hotel Karmen. A collection of stuffed animals occupies the ground floor. Upstairs are photos of Tito with film stars such as Josephine Baker, Sophia Loren, Elizabeth Taylor and Richard Burton, and world leaders including Indira Gandhi and Fidel Castro. Outside is a 1953 Cadillac that Tito used to show the island to his eminent guests. These days, you can pay 55KN for a photo op inside or rent it for a measly 2750KN for 30 minutes. Bikes (35KN per hour) and electric carts (300KN per hour) are a cheaper option, and a great way to explore the island.

Sleeping & Eating

There is no private accommodation on Veli Brijun but there are three luxurious villas available for rent through the national park office. Boat transport to and from the mainland is included in the following hotel prices; both are on Veli Brijun. There are no sleeping options on Mali Brijun. Veli Brijun's hotel restaurants are the only places to eat.

Hotel Neptun-Istra HOTEL €€€
(☎525 807; www.brijuni.hr; s/d 840/1430KN; @ wifi) This is the ultimate in communist chic. Even though it's spruced up and comfy, rooms retain their plain utilitarian look. Each comes with a balcony; some have forest views, too. You can just imagine Tito's famous guests lounging here.

Hotel Karmen HOTEL €€€
(☎525 807; www.brijuni.hr; s/d 705/1160KN; @) Designers and architects from Zagreb flock to this spot on the harbour for its authentic communist design – it's trashy, real and feels as if it's still in the 1950s. Let's just hope they don't renovate.

Getting There & Away

A number of excursion boats leave from the Pula waterfront for the islands. Instead of booking an excursion with one of the travel agencies in Pula, Rovinj or Poreč, you could take public bus 21 from Pula to Fažana (15KN), 8km away, then sign up for a tour at the **national park office** (☎525 888; www.brijuni.hr; tours 125-210KN), near the wharf. In July and August, tours cost 210KN per person (children 110KN). It's best to book in advance, especially in summer, and request an English-speaking tour guide. In summer, picnic and swimming excursions to Mali Brijun are also offered.

Check along the Pula waterfront for excursion boats to Brijuni. Note that many of the two-hour 'panorama' trips from Pula to Brijuni (150KN) don't actually stop at the islands; *Martinabela* (280KN) does.

Rovinj

POP 14,367

Rovinj (Rovigno in Italian) is coastal Istria's star attraction. While it can get overrun with tourists in summer, and residents have developed a sharp eye for maximising profits by upgrading hotels and restaurants to four-star status, it remains one of the last true Mediterranean fishing ports. Fishers haul their catch into the harbour in the early morning, followed by a horde of squawking gulls, and mend their nets before lunch. Prayers for a good catch are sent forth at the massive Church of St Euphemia, which has a 60m bell tower that punctuates the peninsula. Wooded hills and low-rise hotels surround the old town, which is webbed with steep cobbled streets and piazzas. The 14 green islands of the Rovinj archipelago make for a pleasant afternoon away; the most popular islands are Crveni Otok (Red Island), Sveta Katarina and Sveti Andrija.

The old town is contained within an egg-shaped peninsula. About 1.5km south is the Punta Corrente Forest Park and the wooded cape of Zlatni Rt (Golden Cape), with its age-old oak and pine trees and several large hotels. There are two harbours: the northern

Rovinj

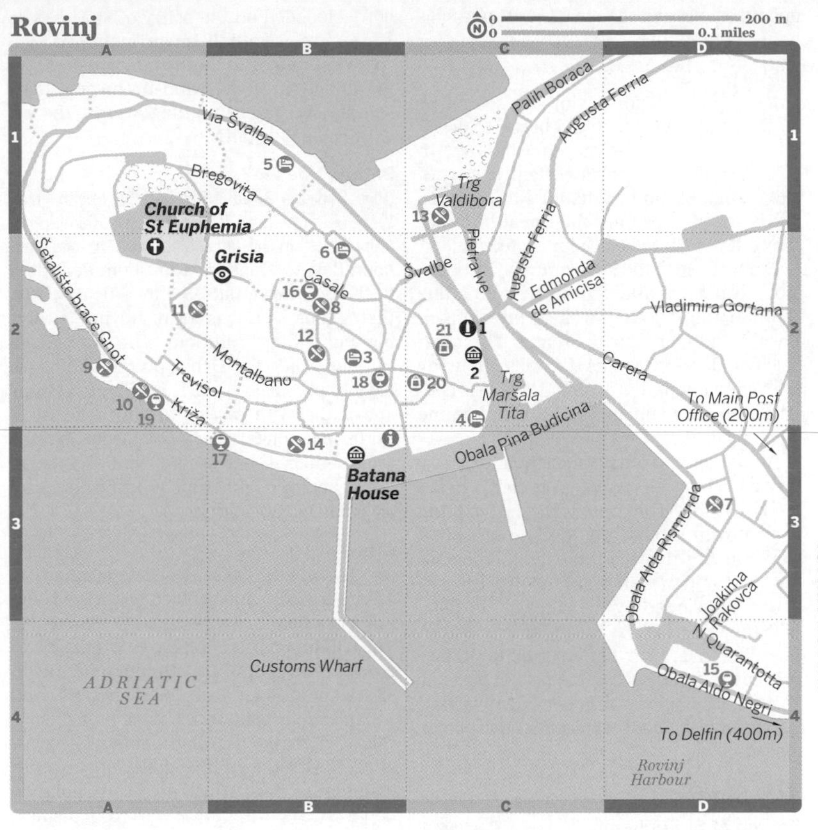

Rovinj

Top Sights

- Batana House ... B3
- Church of St Euphemia ... A2
- Grisia ... B2

Sights

- 1 Balbi Arch ... C2
- 2 Heritage Museum ... C2

Sleeping

- 3 Casa Garzotto ... B2
- 4 Hotel Adriatic ... C2
- 5 Angelo D'Oro ... B1
- 6 Villa Valdibora ... B2

Eating

- 7 Kantinon ... D3
- 8 Da Sergio ... B2
- 9 Puntulina ... A2
- 10 Male Madlene ... A2
- 11 Monte ... A2
- 12 Ulika ... B2
- 13 Vegetable Market ... C1
- 14 Veli Jože ... B3

Drinking

- 15 Havana ... D4
- 16 Limbo ... B2
- 17 Monte Carlo ... B3
- 18 Piassa Granda ... B2
- 19 Valentino ... A2

Shopping

- 20 Galerija Brek ... C2
- 21 Zdenac 13 ... C2

open harbour and the small, protected harbour to the south.

History

Originally an island, Rovinj was settled by Slavs in the 7th century and began to develop a strong fishing and maritime industry. In 1199 Rovinj signed an important pact with Dubrovnik to protect its maritime trade, but in the 13th century the threat of piracy forced it to turn to Venice for protection.

From the 16th to 18th centuries, its population expanded dramatically with an influx of immigrants fleeing Turkish invasions of Bosnia and continental Croatia. The town began to develop outside the walls put up by the Venetians, and in 1763 the islet was connected to the mainland and Rovinj became a peninsula.

Although the town's maritime industry thrived in the 17th century, Austria's 1719 decision to make Trieste and Rijeka free ports dealt Rovinj a blow. The decline of sailing ships further damaged its shipbuilding industry, and in the middle of the 19th century it was supplanted by the shipyard in Pula. Like the rest of Istria, Rovinj bounced from Austrian to French to Austrian to Italian rule before finally becoming part of postwar Yugoslavia. There's still a considerable Italian community here, who speak a particular dialect.

Sights

Church of St Euphemia CHURCH
(Sveta Eufemija; Petra Stankovića; 10am-6pm Jun-Sep, 10am-4pm May, 10am-2pm Apr, by appointment Oct-Mar) The town's showcase is this imposing church, which dominates the old town from its hilltop location in the middle of the peninsula. Built in 1736 it's the largest baroque building in Istria, reflecting the period during the 18th century when Rovinj was its most populous town.

Inside, look for the marble **tomb of St Euphemia** behind the right-hand altar. Rovinj's patron saint was tortured for her Christian faith by Emperor Diocletian before being thrown to the lions in AD 304. According to legend, the body disappeared one dark, stormy night only to appear off the coast of Rovinj in a spectral boat. The townspeople were unable to budge the heavy sarcophagus until a small boy appeared with two calves and moved it to the top of the hill, where it still stands in the present-day church. On the anniversary of her martyrdom (16 September), devotees congregate here. Modelled on the belfry of St Mark's in Venice, the 60m **bell tower** is topped by a copper statue of St Euphemia, which shows the direction of the wind by turning on a spindle. You can climb the tower (to the left of the altar) for 15KN.

Batana House MUSEUM
(Pina Budicina 2; adult/child 10/5KN, with guide 15KN; 10am-2pm & 7-11pm Jun-Sep, 10am-2pm & 4-6pm Tue-Sun Oct-Jan & Mar-May) On the harbour, Batana House is a museum dedicated to the *batana,* a flat-bottomed fishing boat that stands as a symbol of Rovinj's seafaring and fishing traditions. The multimedia exhibits inside the 17th-century town house have interactive displays, excellent captions and audio with *bitinada,* which are typical fishers' songs. Check out the *spacio,* the ground-floor cellar where wine was kept, tasted and sold amid much socialising (open on Tuesday and Thursday).

Grisia STREET
Lined with galleries where local artists sell their work, this cobbled street leads uphill from behind the arch to St Euphemia. The winding narrow backstreets that spread around Grisia are an attraction in themselves. Windows, balconies, portals and squares are a pleasant confusion of styles – Gothic, Renaissance, baroque and neoclassical. Notice the unique *fumaioli* (exterior chimneys), built during the population boom when entire families lived in a single room with a fireplace.

Punta Corrente Forest Park PARK
Follow the waterfront on foot or by bike past Hotel Park to this verdant area, locally known as Zlatni Rat, about 1.5km south. Covered in oak and pine groves and boasting 10 species of cypress, the park was established in 1890 by Baron Hütterott, an Austrian admiral who kept a villa on Crveni Otok. You can swim off the rocks or just sit and admire the offshore islands.

Heritage Museum MUSEUM
(www.muzej-rovinj.com; Trg Maršala Tita 11; adult/concession 15/10KN; 10am-2pm & 6-10pm Tue-Fri, 10am-2pm & 7-10pm Sat & Sun Jun-Sep, 10am-1pm Tue-Sat Oct-May) This museum in a baroque palace contains a collection of contemporary art and old masters from Rovinj and elsewhere in Croatia, plus archaeological finds, a maritime section and occasional special exhibits (such as a recent one on medieval torture).

Balbi Arch MONUMENT

The elaborate Balbi Arch was built in 1679 on the location of the former town gate. The top of the arch is ornamented with a Turkish head on the outside and a Venetian head on the inside.

Activities

Most people hop aboard a boat for **swimming**, **snorkelling** and **sunbathing**. A trip to Crveni Otok or Sveta Katarina is easily arranged. **Nadi Scuba Diving Centar** (☎813 290; www.scuba.hr) and **Petra** (☎812 880; www.divingpetra.hr) offer daily boat dives. The main attraction is the **Baron Gautsch wreck**, an Austrian passenger steamer sunk in 1914 by a sea mine in 40m of water.

There are 80 **rock-climbing routes** in a former Venetian stone quarry at Zlatni Rt, many suitable for beginners. Birdwatchers can bike to the **ornithological reserve** at Palud Marsh, 8km southwest of Rovinj.

Cycling around Rovinj and the Punta Corrente Forest Park is a superb way to spend an afternoon.

Tours

Most travel agencies in Rovinj sell day trips to Venice (390KN to 520KN), Plitvice (500KN to 600KN) and Brijuni (380KN to 470KN). There are also **fish picnics** (250KN), **panoramic cruises** (100KN) and boat outings to **Limska Draga Fjord** (150KN). These can be slightly cheaper if booked through one of the independent operators that line the waterfront; **Delfin** (☎848 265) is reliable.

There are more exciting options, such as **kayaking**; book a trip through **Adistra** (☎095 838 3797; Carera 69). Nine-kilometre jaunts around the Rovinj archipelago cost 270KN; a 14km outing to the Lim fjord is 290KN. Both include picnic lunch and snorkelling gear. Adistra also offers a sunset paddle (190KN) wine, cheese and olives.

Festivals & Events

The city's annual events include various regattas from late April through to August. The **Rovinj Summer Festival** is a series of classical concerts that takes place in the Church of St Euphemia and the Franciscan monastery.

The second Sunday in August sees the town's most renowned event, when narrow Grisia becomes an open-air **art exhibition**. Anyone from children to professional painters display their work in churches, studios and on the street.

From late June to mid-September, on Tuesdays and Thursdays, there's a **procession of batanas** with lanterns. It departs at 8.30pm and costs 50KN, or 200KN for procession and dinner at a traditional tavern. Reserve a couple of days ahead at Batana House Museum. On Sundays and Wednesdays in summer there's a traditional fish festival outside the museum, with *bitinada* music and cheap seafood snacks.

The **Avantgarde Jazz Festival** (www.avantgardejazzfestival.com) brings in big-name jazz performers to Maistra hotels, from May through to July.

Sleeping

Rovinj has become Istria's destination of choice for hordes of summertime tourists, so reserving in advance is strongly recommended. Prices have been rising steadily and probably will continue to do so, as the city gears up to reach elite status.

If you want to stay in private accommodation, there is little available in the old town, where there's also no free parking and accommodation costs are higher. Double rooms start at 220KN in the high season, with a small discount for single occupancy; two-person apartments start at 330KN. Out of season, prices go down considerably.

The surcharge for a stay of less than three nights is up to 50%, and guests who stay only one night are sometimes punished with a 100% surcharge. Outside summer months, you should be able to bargain the surcharge away. You can book through one of the travel agencies.

Except for a few private options, most hotels and campgrounds in the area are managed by **Maistra** (www.maistra.com).

TOP CHOICE **Hotel Lone** DESIGN HOTEL €€€

(☎632 000; www.lonehotel.com; Luje Adamovića 31; s/d 1478/1847KN; P ❄ @ ⓦ) Croatia's first design hotel, this 248-room powerhouse of style is a creation of Croatia's starchitects 3LHD. It rises over Lone bay, next door to Monte Mulini, like a ship dropped in the forest. Light-flooded rooms come with private terraces and five-star trimmings. Facilities include a restaurant, an extensive spa and a cool store with Croatian design items. Guests can use the pools at Monte Mulini.

Monte Mulini HOTEL €€€
(☎636 000; www.montemulinihotel.com; A Smareglia bb; s/d 2960/3695KN; P❄@📶≋) This swanky hotel slopes down towards the peaceful Lone bay, a 10-minute stroll from the old town along the Lungomare. Balconied rooms all have sea views and upscale trimmings. The spa is tops, as is the renowned Wine Vault restaurant. There are three outdoor pools and the overall design is bold and bright.

Angelo D'Oro BOUTIQUE HOTEL €€€
(☎840 502; www.rovinj.at; Via Švalba 38-42; s/d 1028/1666KN; P❄📶) In a renovated Venetian town house, the 23 plush rooms and (pricier) suites of this boutique hotel have lots of antiques, plus mod cons aplenty. There are massages (400KN per hour), sauna and jacuzzi, bikes for rent (60KN per day) and two terraces – a lush interior terrace amid ancient stone and a tiny top-floor one with sea views.

Villa Valdibora HOTEL €€€
(☎845 040; www.valdibora.com; Silvano Chiurco 8; s/d 1080/1440KN; ❄📶) The 11 rooms, suites and apartments in this historic building come with cool stone floors and upscale trimmings such as hydromassage sauna showers. There's a fitness room (60KN), massages (150KN to 450KN) and bikes for rent (80KN per day).

Villa Baron Gautsch PANSION €€
(☎840 538; www.baron-gautsch.com; IM Ronjgova 7; s/d 293/586KN; ❄📶) This German-owned *pansion* (guesthouse), up the leafy street leading up from Hotel Park, has 17 spick-and-span rooms, some with terraces (40KN per person extra) and lovely views of the sea and the old town. Breakfast is served on the small terrace out the back. It's cash (kuna) only.

Casa Garzotto GUESTHOUSE €€€
(☎811 884; www.casa-garzotto.com; Via Garzotto 8; s/d 790/1050KN; P❄@📶) Rooms and apartments in this historic town house have original details such as fireplaces and wooden beams, an antique touch and up-to-the-minute amenities. Bikes and breakfast are complimentary. The complex has three other buildings nearby, one with more basic rooms (830KN).

Hotel Istra HOTEL €€€
(☎800 250; www.maistra.com; Otok Sveti Andrija; s/d 1183/1480KN; P❄@≋) The renowned wellness centre and spa and good facilities for children are chief assets of this four-star complex, a 10-minute boat ride away on Sveti Andrija Island. There's a restaurant in an old castle on site.

Hotel Adriatic HOTEL €€€
(☎800 250; www.maistra.com; Pina Budicina bb; s/d 747/933KN; P❄📶) The location right on the harbour is excellent and the rooms well equipped, albeit in need of renovation and on the kitschy side. The pricier (by 120KN per person) sea-view rooms have more space and newer fittings. There's an extra charge for wi-fi and parking.

Hotel Park HOTEL €€€
(☎800 250; www.maistra.com; IM Ronjgova bb; s/d 747/933KN; P❄@📶≋) It's conveniently close to the ferry dock for Crveni Otok and has crowd-pleasing amenities such as two outdoor pools, a fitness room with a range of classes, and a sauna. Most rooms have balconies.

Porton Biondi CAMPGROUND €
(☎813 557; www.portonbiondi.hr; Aleja Porton Biondi 1; per person/tent 42/26KN; ⏰mid-Mar–Oct) This beachside campground, which sleeps 1200, is about 700m from the old town.

Polari Camping CAMPGROUND €
(☎801 501; www.campingrovinjvrsar.com; Polari bb; per person/tent 71/82KN; ⏰Apr-Sep; @📶≋) On the beach about 3km southeast of town, it features swimming pools, restaurants and playgrounds.

Eating

Picnickers can get supplies at the supermarket next to the bus station or at one of the Konzum stores around town. For a cheap bite, pick up a *burek* (heavy pastry stuffed with meat or cheese) from one of the kiosks near the **vegetable market**.

Most of the restaurants that line the harbour offer the standard fish and meat mainstays at similar prices. For a more gourmet experience, you'll need to bypass the water vistas. Note that many restaurants shut their doors between lunch and dinner.

TOP CHOICE **Male Madlene** TAPAS €
(Križa 28; snacks from 30KN; ⏰11am-2pm & 7-11pm May-Sep) Adorable spot in the owner's tiny living room hanging over the sea, where she serves up creative tapas with market-fresh ingredients, based on old Italian recipes.

Think tuna-filled zucchini, goat-cheese-stuffed peppers and bite-size savoury pies and cakes. A 12-snack plate for two is 100KN. Great Istrian wines by the glass.

Monte MEDITERRANEAN €€€
(☎830 203; Montalbano 75; mains from 190KN) Rovinj's top restaurant, right below St Euphemia Church, is worth the hefty cost. Enjoy beautifully presented dishes on the elegant glassed-in terrace. Don't want to splurge? Have a pasta or risotto (from 124KN). Try the fennel ice cream. Reserve ahead in high season.

Da Sergio PIZZERIA €
(Grisia 11; pizzas 28-71KN) It's worth waiting in line to get a table at this old-fashioned two-floor pizzeria that dishes out Rovinj's best thin-crust pizza, which locals swear by. The best is Gogo, with fresh tomato and arugula (rocket) and prosciutto.

Maestral MEDITERRANEAN €
(Vladimira Nazora bb; mains from 45KN) Grab an al fresco table at this tavern on the sea edge for great views of the old town and well-prepared simple food that's priced just right. Its *ribarska pogača* (pizza-like pie with salted fish and veggies) is delicious. It's in an old stone house away from the tourist buzz.

Kantinon SEAFOOD €
(Alda Rismonda 18; mains from 30KN) A fishing theme runs through this high-ceilinged canteen, which specialises in fresh seafood at low prices. The Batana fish plate for two is great value, as are the set menus (starting at 35KN).

Ulika MEDITERRANEAN €€
(Porečka 6; mains from 100KN) Tucked away in an alleyway, this small pretty tavern with streetside seating excludes staples of Adriatic food kitsch (pizza, calamari, *čevapčići*) and instead features well-prepared if pricey Mediterranean fare.

Puntulina MEDITERRANEAN €€€
(☎813 186; Svetog Križa 38; mains from 100KN) Sample creative Med cuisine on one of the three al fresco terraces. Pasta dishes are more affordable (from 70KN). At night grab a cushion and sip a cocktail on the rocks below this converted town house. Reservations recommended.

Veli Jože FISH €
(Križa 3; mains from 50KN) Graze on good Istrian standards, either in the eclectic interior crammed with knick-knacks or at the clutch of outdoor tables with water views.

Drinking

Limbo CAFE-BAR
(Casale 22b; 📶) A cosy cafe-bar with small candlelit tables and cushions laid out on the stairs leading to the old town's hilltop. It serves tasty snacks and good prosecco.

Piassa Granda WINE BAR
(Veli trg 1) This stylish little wine bar with red walls and wood-beamed ceilings has 150 wine labels, mainly Istrian, 20 *rakija* (Croatian grappa) varieties and delicious snacks.

Valentino COCKTAIL BAR
(Križa 28) Premium cocktail prices at this high-end spot include fantastic sunset views from cushions scattered on the water's edge.

Havana COCKTAIL BAR
(Aldo Negri bb) Tropical cocktails, Cuban cigars, straw parasols and the shade of tall pine trees make this open-air bar a popular spot.

Monte Carlo COCKTAIL BAR
(Križa 21) More quiet and down to earth than its showy neighbour Valentino, this low-key cafe-bar has great views of the sea and Sveta Katarina across the way.

Shopping

Rovinj is jam-packed with galleries, many touting overpriced souvenirs. A few stand out, including **Galerija Brek** (Fontica 2), which sells diverse works by local artists; and **Zdenac 13** (Zdenac 13), which has beautiful ceramic pieces on the ground floor of a gorgeous old town house.

Information

Internet Access

A-mar (☎841 211; Carera 26; per 10min 6KN; ⏰9am-10pm Jul & Aug, shorter hr Sep-Jun) Conveniently located. There's also free wi-fi in the town centre.

Laundry

Galax (Istarska bb; per 5kg 70KN; ⏰7am-8pm)

Medical Services

Medical Centre (☎813 004; Istarska bb)

Money

There are banks with ATMs all around town. Most travel agencies and many hotels will change money.

BUSES FROM ROVINJ

DESTINATION	COST (KN)	DURATION	DAILY SERVICES
Dubrovnik	628	16hr	1
Labin	80	2hr	2
Poreč	35-50	50min	15
Pula	35-45	50min	20
Rijeka	93-127	1½-3hr	5
Split	444	11hr	1
Trieste (Italy)	100-120	1½hr	2
Zagreb	150-200	4-6hr	10

Post

Main Post Office (Matteo Benussi 4; ⌚8am-9pm Mon-Sat summer, 8am-7pm Mon-Fri, to 1pm Sat winter) You can make phone calls here.

Tourist Information

Tourist Office (☎811 566; www.tzgrovinj.hr; Pina Budicina 12; ⌚8am-10pm Jun-Sep, 8am-3pm Mon-Fri, to 1pm Sat Oct-May) Has plenty of brochures and maps. Just off Trg Maršala Tita.

Travel Agencies

Globtour (☎814 130; www.globtour-turizam.hr; Alda Rismonda 2) Excursions and private accommodation.

Kompas (☎813 211; www.kompas-travel.com; Trg Maršala Tita 5) Daily excursions.

Planet (☎840 494; www.planetrovinj.com; Križa 1) Good bargains on private accommodation. Doubles as an internet cafe (6KN per 10 minutes) and has a printer.

Getting There & Away

The bus station is just to the southeast of the old town, and offers a **garderoba** (per day 10KN; ⌚6.30am-8pm). The closest train station is at Kanfanar, 20km away on the Pula–Divača line; buses connect Kanfanar and Rovinj.

Getting Around

You can rent bicycles at many agencies around town for around 20KN per hour or 70KN per day. Scooters are also available from around 240KN per day.

Around Rovinj

A popular day trip from Rovinj is a boat ride to lovely **Crveni Otok** (Red Island). Only 1.9km long, the island includes two islets, Sveti Andrija and Maškin, connected by a causeway. In the 19th century, Sveti Andrija became the property of Baron Hütterott, who transformed it into a luxuriantly wooded park. The Hotel Istra complex now dominates **Sveti Andrija**, where a playground and small gravel beaches make it popular with families. **Maškin** is quieter, more wooded and has plenty of secluded coves. Bring a mask for snorkelling around the rocks.

Right across the peninsula is **Sveta Katarina**, a small island forested by a Polish count in 1905 and now home to **Hotel Katarina** (☎800 250; www.maistra.com; Otok Sveta Katarina; s/d 770/962KN; P 📶 ❄).

In summer, there are hourly boats from 5.30am till midnight to Sveta Katarina (return 30KN, 10 minutes) and to Crveni Otok (return 40KN, 15 minutes). They leave from just opposite Hotel Adriatic and also from the Delfin ferry dock near Hotel Park.

About 10km long, 600m wide and with steep valley walls that rise to a height of 100m, the **Limska Draga Fjord** (Limski Kanal) is the most dramatic sight in Istria. The inlet was formed when the Istrian coastline sank during the last Ice Age, allowing the sea to rush in and fill the Draga Valley. The deep-green bay has a hillside cave on the southern side where the 11th-century hermit priest Romualdo lived and held ceremonies. Fishing, oyster and mussel farming and excursion boating are the only activities found here.

At the fjord you'll find souvenir stands and two waterside restaurants that serve up superbly fresh shells, right from the source. Of the two, **Viking** (Limski Kanal 1; mains from 55KN) is the better option. Enjoy oysters (11KN per piece), great scallops (22KN per piece) and mussels, or fish (priced by the kilogram) on a terrace overlooking the fjord.

WORTH A TRIP

MEDIEVAL BALE

In the southwestern section of Istria, between Rovinj and Vodnjan, the medieval town of **Bale** is one of Istria's best-kept secrets. Only 7km from the sea, it features a maze of narrow cobblestone streets and ancient town houses that developed around the recently restored Gothic-Renaissance castle of the Bembo family. Dominated by the 36m-high belfry of the baroque St Julian church, it also has several old churches and a town hall with a 14th-century loggia. The 9km stretch of shoreline nearby is the most pristine in Istria, with delightful beaches and shallow water.

Bale draws a spiritually minded and bohemian crowd for its apparently very powerful energy – a fact you won't find in the tourist brochures. Come here to meet kindred spirits and spend endless hours talking, drinking, dreaming and scribbling.

Head to **Kamene Priče** (Stone Tales; www.kameneprice.com; Castel 57; meals from 100KN), an artsy oasis amid the ancient stone. There's no real menu as such at this restaurant-bar-performance space; the food depends on the season and the chef's mood. The whimsical decor, a plethora of bizarre objects and two terraces out the back, make this the perfect place for whiling the day away.

The small but excellent **Last Minute Open Jazz Festival** takes place in early August. Other times you may find poetry readings, theatre performances, comedy, workshops in lucid dreaming...there's always something happening at Kamene Priče. Tomo, the owner, is a great source of info about 'the other side of Bale'. There are four apartments upstairs for those who want to stay (525KN per night, 675KN during the festival).

The new boutique **La Grisa Hotel** (☎824 501; www.la-grisa.com; La Grisa 23; s/d 390/675KN; P ❄ ☎) has 22 tasteful rooms and suites in eight interconnected buildings on the edge of the old town. It also has an ambitious restaurant – try the dishes with *boškarin* (Istrian ox) – and a spa with a sauna, jacuzzi and massages (from 150KN).

There's also a picnic area, a waterside cafe with wooden tables and chairs and a swimming cove behind the other restaurant (named Fjord).

Small excursion boats will take you on a one-hour boat ride for 75KN per person (negotiable); these run frequently in July and August, and sporadically in June and September. To get to the fjord, you can take an excursion from Rovinj, Pula or Poreč, or follow the signs to Limski Kanal past the village of Sveti Lovreč.

Poreč

POP 20,559

The ancient Roman town of Poreč (Parenzo in Italian; Parentium in Roman times) and the surrounding region are entirely devoted to summer tourism. Poreč is the centrepiece of a vast system of tourist resorts that stretches north and south along the west coast of Istria. The largest is Zelena Laguna, with a full range of facilities and accommodation.

These holiday villages and tourist camps offer a rather industrialised package-type experience, with too much concrete and plastic and too many tour buses for some tastes. The hotels, restaurants, tourist offices and travel agencies, however, are almost universally staffed with multilingual people who make an effort to welcome visitors.

While this is not the place for a quiet getaway (except out of season), there's a World Heritage–listed basilica, a medley of Gothic, Romanesque and baroque buildings and a well-developed tourist infrastructure, and the pristine Istrian interior is within easy reach. It has also become the party hub of Istria, drawing in young party goers from all corners of Europe and beyond.

History

The coast of Poreč measures 37km, islands included, but the ancient town is confined to a peninsula 400m long and 200m wide. The Romans conquered the region in the 2nd century BC and made Poreč an important administrative centre, from which they were able to control a sweep of land from the Limska Draga Fjord to the Mirna River. Poreč's street plan was laid out by the Romans, who divided the town into rectangular parcels marked by the longitudinal Decumanus and the latitudinal Cardo.

Poreč

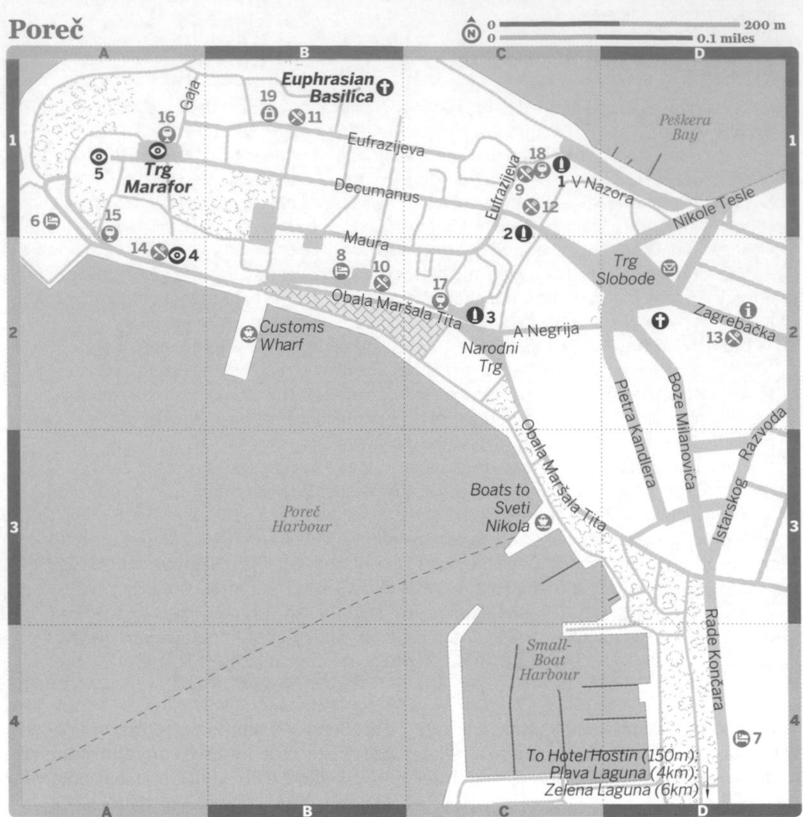

With the collapse of the Western Roman Empire, Poreč came under Byzantine rule between the 6th to 8th centuries. It was during this time that the Euphrasian Basilica, with its magnificent frescos, was erected. In 1267 Poreč was forced to submit to Venetian rule.

With the decline of Venice, the town oscillated between Austrian and French dominance before the Italian occupation that lasted from 1918 to 1943. Upon the capitulation of Italy, Poreč was occupied by the Germans and damaged by Allied bombing in 1944 before becoming part of postwar Yugoslavia and, more recently, Croatia.

Sights

The compact old town is squeezed onto the peninsula and packed with hundreds of shops and agencies. The ancient Roman Decumanus, with its polished stones, is still the main street running through the peninsula's middle. Hotels, travel agencies and excursion boats are on the quayside Maršala Tita, which runs from the small-boat harbour to the tip of the peninsula.

Euphrasian Basilica BASILICA
(Eufrazijeva bb; adult/concession 30/15KN; 9am-6pm Mon-Sat, 2-6pm Sun Apr-Sep) The main reason to visit Poreč is to see the 6th-century Euphrasian Basilica, a World Heritage Site and one of Europe's finest intact examples of Byzantine art. Built on the site of a 4th-century oratory, the sacral complex includes a church, an atrium and a baptistery. What packs in the crowds are the glittering wall **mosaics** in the apse. These 6th-century masterpieces feature biblical scenes, arch-angels and Istrian martyrs. Notice the group to the left, which shows Bishop Euphrasius, who commissioned the basilica, with a model of the church in his hand. The **belfry**, accessed through the octagonal baptistery, affords an invigorating view of the old town. Make sure to pop into the adjacent **Bishop's Palace**,

Poreč

Top Sights

	Euphrasian Basilica	B1
	Trg Marafor	A1

Sights

1	Northern Tower	C1
2	Pentagonal Tower	C1
3	Round Tower	C2
4	Sveti Nikola	A2
5	Temple of Neptune	A1

Sleeping

6	Hotel Palazzo	A1
7	Hotel Poreč	D4
8	Valamar Riviera Hotel	B2

Eating

9	Buffet Horizont	C1
10	Dva Ferala	B2
11	Gourmet	B1
12	Konoba Ulixes	C1
13	Nono	D2
	Peterokutna Kula	(see 2)
14	Sv. Nikola	A2

Drinking

15	Epoca	A1
16	Rakijarnica	A1
17	Saint & Sinner	C2
	Torre Rotonda	(see 3)
18	Vinoteka Bacchus	C1

Shopping

19	Koza	B1

which contains a display of ancient stone sculptures, religious paintings and 4th-century mosaics from the original oratory.

Trg Marafor SQUARE

The Roman Forum, where public gatherings took place, once stood on the site of the present-day Trg Marafor. The original pavement has been preserved along the northern row of houses on the square. West of this rectangular square, inside a small park, are the ruins of the 2nd-century **Temple of Neptune**, dedicated to the god of the sea.

Venetian Towers RUINS

The town has three 15th-century towers that date from the Venetian rule and once formed the city walls: the gothic **Pentagonal Tower** at the beginning of Decumanus; the **Round Tower** on Narodni trg; and the **Northern Tower** on Peškera Bay.

Sveti Nikola ISLAND

There are pebble and concrete beaches to choose from, as well as rocky breakwaters, shady pine forests and great views of the town across the way. From May to October there are **passenger boats** (adult/concession 20/10KN) travelling to Sveti Nikola, the small island that lies opposite Poreč harbour. They depart every 30 minutes (from 6.45am to 1am) from the wharf on Maršala Tita.

Activities

Nearly every activity you might want to enjoy is on offer outside the town in either Plava Laguna or Zelena Laguna. Most of the sports and recreational centres (there are 20) are affiliated with hotels and have tennis, basketball and volleyball courts, windsurfing, rowing, bungee jumping, paintball, golf, water-skiing, parasailing, boat rentals, go-karting and canoeing. If the weather turns bad, you can always work out in a fitness centre or get a massage at one of the spas. For details pick up the annual *Poreč Info & Events* booklet, which lists all the recreational facilities in the area, from the tourist office.

The gentle rolling hills of the interior and the well-marked paths make **cycling** and **hiking** prime ways to explore the region. The tourist office issues a free map of roads and trails stemming from Poreč, along with suggested routes. You can rent a bike at many agencies around town.

There is good **diving** in and around shoals and sandbanks in the area, and at the nearby *Coriolanus,* a British Royal Navy warship that sank in 1945. At **Diving Center Poreč** (☎433 606; www.divingcenter-porec.com), boat dives start at 135KN (more for caves or wrecks); 355KN with full equipment rental.

Festivals & Events

During July and August there's **Poreč Annale**, one of the oldest Croatian contemporary art exhibitions, curated around a single theme. The **Street Art Festival**, held for a week in August, attracts international artists performing anything from acrobatics to theatre and music in the old town squares and streets. **Classical music concerts** (www.concertsinbazilika.com) take place at the basilica several times a week during summer; tickets can be purchased one hour before the concert at the venue. There are **jazz concerts** (www.jazzinlap.com) between late June and late August, held once a week in the courtyard of the regional museum, beside the Lapidarium. Free concerts take place on Trg Slobode, part of **Poreč Summer**. **Valamar Jazz Festival** (www.valamarjazz.com) brings big-name musicians for a series of concerts each June, with various locations in and around town.

The tourist office publishes a free *Poreč Info & Events* booklet that lists seasonal events.

Sleeping

Accommodation in Poreč is plentiful but gets booked ahead of time, so advance reservations are essential if you come in July or August.

The old town has a handful of hotels, though most of the campgrounds, hotels, apartment complexes and resorts spread along the coast north and south of Poreč. The major tourist complexes are in Brulo, 2km south of town, Plava Laguna, 4km south of the old town, and Zelena Laguna, 2km further south. North of Poreč are the tourist settlements of Borik and Špadići. Some 20 hotels and a dozen apartment complexes are planted in these wooded areas. Most hotels are managed by **Valamar Hotels & Resorts** (☎465 000; www.valamar.com) or **Laguna Poreč** (☎410 101; www.lagunaporec.com). All hotels are open from April to October; several remain open all year. For stays shorter than three nights, some impose a 20% surcharge.

Many travel agencies can help you find private accommodation. Expect to pay between 200KN and 250KN for a double room with private bathroom in the high season, plus a 30% surcharge for stays shorter than three nights. There is a limited number of rooms available in the old town, which has no parking. Look for the *Domus Bonus* certificate of quality in private accommodation.

Valamar Riviera Hotel HOTEL €€€
(☎400 800; www.valamar.com; Maršala Tita 15; s/d 1230/1455KN; P❄@🛜) A rather swanky four-star incarnation right on the harbourfront. The rooms with seafront balconies are lovely but considerably more expensive. There's a private beach on Sveti Nikola that you can reach by boat (free) every 30 minutes. Down the seafront promenade is the recently renovated **Villa Parentino** (☎400 800; Maršala Tita 15; ste 2707KN; P❄), which has eight luxury suites.

Hotel Palazzo HOTEL €€€
(☎858 800; www.hotel-palazzo.hr; Maršala Tita 24; s/d 1320/1650KN; P❄@🛜≋) Housed in a 1910 building on the seafront, this recent addition to Poreč's hotel scene has 70 rooms and four suites plus a spa, restaurants and bars. The style is elegant historic, blending modern design with classical beauty. Rooms 120 to 126 have open sea and lighthouse views – and higher prices.

Hotel Hostin HOTEL €€
(☎408 800; www.hostin.hr; Rade Končara 4; s/d 634/964KN; P❄@🛜≋) This unassuming hideaway in verdant parkland just steps from the bus station has 39 well-equipped rooms, each with a balcony. An indoor swimming pool, a fitness room, a Turkish bath and a sauna are nice perks, as is the pebble beach only 70m away.

Hotel Poreč HOTEL €€
(☎451 811; www.hotelporec.com; Rade Končara 1; s/d 496/760KN; P❄🛜) While the rooms inside this concrete box have uninspiring views over the bus station and the construction site for the shopping centre opposite, they're acceptable, with balconies and an easy walk from the old town.

Camping Zelena Laguna CAMPGROUND €
(☎410 102; www.lagunaporec.com; Zelena Laguna; per adult/site 62/117KN; ⊙mid-Apr–Sep; ❄@🛜≋) Well equipped for sports, this campground 5km from the old town can house up to 2700 people. It has access to many beaches, including a naturist one.

Camping Bijela Uvala CAMPGROUND €
(☎410 102; www.lagunaporec.com; Zelena Laguna; per adult/site 62/117KN; ⊙mid-Apr–Sep; @🛜≋) This campground can be crowded, as it houses up to 6000 people, but there are two outdoor pools and the facilities of Zelena Laguna are a stone's throw away.

Eating

TOP CHOICE **Konoba Daniela** ISTRIAN €€
(☎460 519; Veleniki; mains from 65KN) In the sweet little village of Veleniki, 4.5km northeast of town, is this family-run tavern in an 1880s house with rustic decor and a big terrace. It is known for its steak tartare and seasonal Istrian mainstays. Taxis charge 80KN to 100KN one way.

Gourmet ITALIAN €€
(Eufrazijeva 26; mains from 60KN) Comforting Italian concoctions come in all shapes and forms here – penne, tagliatelle, fusilli, gnocchi and so on. There are also pizzas from a wood-fired oven as well as meat and seafood dishes. Tables spill out on the square.

Peterokutna Kula INTERNATIONAL €€
(Decumanus 1; mains from 60KN) Inside the medieval Pentagonal Tower, this upmarket restaurant has two al fresco patios in a stone vault, and a roof terrace with great vistas. It serves a full spectrum of fish and meat dishes, although the service is spotty and the food hit and miss.

Dvi Murve ISTRIAN €€
(Grožnjanska 17; mains from 70KN) This restaurant, 2km northeast of the town centre, is where locals go for a good meal. You'll find a big terrace, two mulberry trees in front and Istrian specialities such as *boškarin* (a rare breed of Istrian beef) carpaccio. A taxi here costs about 70KN.

Konoba Ulixes MEDITERRANEAN €€
(Decumanus 2; mains from 75KN) The fish and shellfish are excellent at this tavern just off Decumanus. Try the salt-encrusted fish baked in the oven, which first gets deboned right in front of you. There's a good selection of Istrian wines.

Sv. Nikola MODERN CROATIAN €€
(Maršala Tita 23; mains from 70KN) Culinary innovation is part of the deal at this elegant waterfront restaurant. You can't go wrong with the set menus for lunch (99KN) and dinner (meat 139KN, fish 149KN).

Dva Ferala ISTRIAN €
(Maršala Tita 13a; mains from 60KN) Savour well-prepared Istrian specialities, such as *istarski tris* (a copious trio of homemade pastas) for two, on the terrace of this pleasant *konoba* (tavern).

Buffet Horizont QUICK BITE €
(Eufrazijeva 8; mains from 30KN) For cheap and tasty seafood snacks such as sardines, shrimp and calamari, look out for this yellow house with wooden benches outside.

Nono PIZZERIA €
(Zagrebačka 4; pizzas from 30KN) Nono serves the best pizza in town, with puffy crusts and toppings such as truffles. Other dishes are also tasty.

Drinking & Entertainment

In the last couple of years, Poreč has turned into Istria's party capital, with nightlife hawks coming from all parts of Europe to let loose in its late-night clubs.

Byblos NIGHTCLUB
(www.byblos.hr; Zelena Laguna 1) On weekends, celeb guest DJs such as David Morales crank out electro house tunes at this humongous open-air club, one of Croatia's hottest places to party.

Rakijarnica BAR
(Trg Marafor 10) Funky new bar that specialises in *rakija*, serving up no less than 50 varieties. The vibe is boho and there are occasional live bands and DJs.

Vinoteka Bacchus WINE BAR
(Eufrazijeva 10) Sweet little wine shop with a clutch of tables outside, where you can try local wines on tap from 9KN per glass. Try the *malvazija* and the *refošk*.

Saint & Sinner CAFE-BAR
(Maršala Tita 12) A black-and-white plastic theme runs throughout this waterfront hangout, where the young ones sip chococcinos during the day and strawberry *caipiroskas* late into the night.

Epoca CAFE-BAR
(Maršala Tita 24) Kick back by the water and watch the sun go down, grab a quickie espresso or have a leisurely nightcap cocktail at this low-key cafe-bar.

Torre Rotonda CAFE-BAR
(Narodni trg 3a) Take the steep stairs to the top of the historic Round Tower and grab a table at the open-air cafe to watch the action on the quays.

Shopping

Don't miss the great leather items designed and handmade by a brother-and-sister team at **Koza** (Eufrazijeva 28), a tiny storefront with cool bags, flip-flops, briefcases and wallets.

Information

Internet Access

Cold Fusion (K Huguesa 2; per hr 30KN; 9am-10pm) A computer centre at the bus station. Note that there's free wi-fi on Trg Slobode and along the seafront.

Medical Services

Poreč Medical Centre (426 400; Maura Gioseffija 2)

BUSES FROM POREČ

DESTINATION	COST (KN)	DURATION	DAILY SERVICES
Pula	63	1-1½hr	5
Rijeka	89	1½hr	7
Rovinj	42	45min	5
Zagreb	226	4½hr	5

Money

You can exchange currency at any of the many travel agencies or banks. There are ATMs all around town.

Post

Main Post Office (Trg Slobode 14; ⌚8am-8pm Mon-Sat) Has a telephone centre.

Tourist Information

Tourist Office (☎451 293; www.to-porec.com; Zagrebačka 9; ⌚8am-9pm Mon-Sat, 9am-1pm & 5-9pm Sun Jun-Sep, 8am-4pm Mon-Fri, 9am-1pm Sat Oct-Mar, 8am-5pm Mon-Fri, 9am-1pm Sat Apr, 8am-8pm Mon-Sat, 9am-1pm Sun May) Gives out lots of brochures and useful info.

Travel Agencies

Fiore Tours (☎431 397; www.fiore.hr; Mate Vlašića 6) Handles private accommodation and adventure travel.

Sunny Way (☎452 021; sunnyway@pu.t-com.hr; Negrija 1) Specialises in boat tickets and excursions to Italy and around Croatia.

Getting There & Away

Ustica Line (www.usticalines.it) runs catamarans to Trieste every Saturday during the high season (210KN, 1½ hours). There are four fast catamarans to Venice daily in high season (one way 250KN to 440KN, return 390KN to 880KN, two hours), operated by **Venezia Lines** (www.venezialines.com) and **Commodore Cruises** (www.commodore-cruises.hr).

The **bus station** (☎060 333 111; K Huguesa 2) is just outside the old town, behind Rade Končara. The station's **garderoba** (per hr 10KN; ⌚6am-9pm) will store your bags.

Between Poreč and Rovinj the bus runs along the Limska Draga Fjord. To see it clearly, sit on the right-hand side if you're travelling south, or on the left if you're northbound.

Getting Around

You can rent bikes for about 80KN per day. From April to October, a tourist train operates regularly from Šetalište Antona Štifanića, by the marina, to Brulo (10KN), Plava Laguna (20KN) and Zelena Laguna (20KN). There's a passenger boat (15KN) that makes the same run from the ferry landing every hour from 9am till just before midnight. The frequent buses to Vrsar stop at Plava Laguna, Zelena Laguna and the other resorts south of the city.

THE ISTRIAN INTERIOR

Head inland from the Istrian coast and you'll notice that crowds dissipate, hotel complexes disappear and what emerges is an unspoiled countryside of medieval hilltop towns, pine forests, fertile valleys and vineyard-dotted hills. The pace slows down considerably, defined less by the needs of tourists and more by the demands of harvesting grapes, hunting for truffles, picking wild asparagus and cultivating olive groves. Farmhouses are opening their doors to visitors looking for an authentic holiday experience, rustic taverns in the middle of nowhere serve up slow-food delights and Croatia's top winemakers provide tastings in their cellars. Remote hilltop villages that once seemed doomed to ruin are attracting colonies of artists and artisans as well as well-heeled foreigners. While many compare the region to Tuscany – and the Italian influence can't be denied – it's a world all its own: unique, magnetic and wholesome.

You'll need a car to explore this area, as the bus and train connections are sporadic. Good news – you're never far from the sea!

Labin

POP 12,426

Perched on a hilltop just above the coast, Labin is the undisputed highlight of eastern Istria, as well as its historical and administrative centre. The showcase here is the old town, a beguiling potpourri of steep streets, cobbled alleys and pastel houses festooned with stone ornamentation.

Surrounding it below is a grubby new town that has sprouted as a result of the coal-mining industry. Labin was the mining capital of Istria until the 1970s, its hill mined so extensively that the town began to collapse. Mining stopped in 1999, the necessary repairs were undertaken and the town surfaced with a new sense of itself as a tourist destination.

Labin has plenty to offer for a day-long visit. The labyrinth of its old town hides an unusual museum in a baroque palace, a wealth of Venetian-inspired churches and palaces, and a sprinkling of craft shops and galleries. The coastal resort of Rabac, 5km southwest of Labin, is overdeveloped with tightly packed holiday houses, hotels and apartment blocks, but its beaches are decent and it can be a nice place to spend an afternoon.

Sights

Wandering the medieval streets of Labin is the highlight of any visit. Labin is divided into two parts: the hilltop old town with most of the sights and attractions; and Podlabin, a much newer section below the hill, with most of the town's shops and services.

Town Museum MUSEUM
(Gradski Muzej; 1 Maja 6; adult/concession 15/10KN; ⏲10am-1pm & 6-10pm Mon-Sat Jun-Aug, 10am-1pm & 6-8pm Sep, 10am-2pm Mon-Sat Apr & May) The ground floor of this museum, housed in the baroque 18th-century Battiala-Lazzarini Palace, is devoted to archaeological finds. Upstairs is a collection of musical instruments with some fun interactive features, and the top floor has a contemporary art gallery. The museum is over a coal pit that has been turned into a realistic re-creation of an actual coal mine.

Fortress FORTRESS
(Forica) This fortress at the western edge of town is the highest point in Labin. To get there, either walk along Ulica 1 Maja or take the long way around by following Šetalište San Marco along the town walls. What unfolds below you is a sweeping view of the coast, the Učka mountain range and Cres island.

Loggia HISTORIC BUILDING
(Titov Trg) This 1550 loggia served as the community centre of Labin in the 16th century. News and court verdicts were announced here, fairs were held and waywards were punished on the pillar of shame.

Festivals & Events

Labin Art Republic ARTS
(Labin Art Republika) Every July and August Labin Art Republic takes over this artsy town – there are more than 30 artists living and working here. During the festival, the town comes alive with street theatre, concerts, plays, clown performances and open studios.

Sleeping

There are no hotels in Labin itself, but choices abound just below in Rabac. Most of the lodging is of the large hotel-resort kind, with a few smaller properties. **Valamar** (www.valamar.com) manages nine properties here, including two deluxe options (Valamar Sanfior Hotel & Casa and Valamar Bellevue Hotel & Residence), three three-star properties, a tourist village, an apartment complex and a villa complex. Peak season (August) prices range greatly, from 740KN to 1130KN at a two-star hotel to 1460KN to 1950KN in a double room at a four-star hotel (half board). Two-person studios and apartments are also available in two-star, three-star and deluxe-villa properties.

Two independent hotels with more character are **Hotel Amfora** (☎872 202; www.hotel-amfora.com; Rabac bb; s/d 300/860KN; P❄@≋) in town, and the posh **Villa Annette** (☎884 222; www.villaannette.hr; Raška 24; s/d 1117/1397KN; P❄@≋) up on a hill slope; the latter has an outdoor pool overlooking the bay.

Sidro (☎881 010; www.sidro-istra.hr; Aldo Negri 20) travel agency finds double rooms (225KN) and apartments (320KN) in the old town of Labin. Note there's a 30% surcharge at all of the above accommodation for stays of fewer than three nights. Gostiona Kvarner has several simple rooms to rent for 545KN.

Eating

Labin is known for its truffles cooked with pasta or eggs, which are generally well priced. Rabac has plenty of restaurants serving seafood standards, but most cater to the unfussy tourist crowds.

Gostiona Kvarner ISTRIAN €
(Šetalište San Marco bb; mains from 50KN) Steps from Titov trg, this restaurant has a terrace overlooking the sea, good food and a loyal local following. The lasagne with truffles costs a measly 80KN, which is a bargain considering the expense of truffle hunting.

ISTRIA'S DIVERSE HIDEAWAYS

Istria has many more highlights for those willing to explore. Here's a rundown.

Novigrad is an attractive old town crammed onto a peninsula, only 20 minutes (11 miles) north of Poreč. It has one of Istria's best restaurants, **Damir & Ornella** (☎758 134; www.damirornella.com; Zidine 5), a 28-seat tavern famous for its raw-fish specialities. The Mediterranean-style sashimi are to die for; reserve ahead.

The fishing village of **Savudrija** is Croatia's westernmost point and home to Istria's oldest **lighthouse** (www.lighthouses-croatia.com), built in 1818. The lighthouse is now available for weekly rental (8200KN per week for four people).

Vrsar, located between Rovinj and Poreč, is a delightful fishing town rising on a hilltop in a jumble of medieval buildings. It's quieter than its neighbours and has an outdoor sculpture park featuring the work of renowned Croatian sculptor Dušan Džamonja. The story goes that Casanova frequented Vrsar back in the day, which the town today celebrates each June during Casanovafest (www.casanovafest.com), the Love & Erotic Festival.

In the interior, art aficionados should head to **Beram**, near Pazin, to take in the amazing 15th-century frescos in the Church of St Mary of Škriljine; the Pazin tourist office has details. The village *konoba* (tavern) is called **Vela Vrata** (mains from 40KN; ⌚Tue-Sun) and serves great homemade pastas, good meat and mean crêpes with *skuta* (ricotta) and honey, paired with leafy views.

Within easy reach of Poreč is the **Baredine Cave** (www.baredine.com; adult/concession/child 6-12 yr 60/45/35KN; ⌚9.30am-6pm Jul & Aug, 10am-5pm May, Jun & Sep, 10am-4pm Oct & Apr), whose subterranean chambers are replete with stalagmites and stalactites; various agencies offer excursions.

Near Labin is Istria's youngest town, **Raša**, a showcase of modernist functionalist architecture that sprang up under Mussolini's rule in the 1930s. Nearby, in the fishing village of Trget, wrapped around a small bay, is one of Istria's best seafood restaurants, **Martin Pescador** (Trget 11/A; mains from 45KN). This Istrian *konoba* is right on the water, with a boat-shaped bar inside and a lovely terrace right on the sea. It serves a mean fish soup and excellent seafood.

On a hilltop north of Motovun is **Oprtalj**, less developed than its neighbour, with cypress trees and fantastic views of the surrounding scenery. Four kilometres to the southeast, amid scenic hills, is the gorgeous **Ipša Estate** (☎664 010; www.ipsa-maslinovaulja.hr), worth a visit for the taste of its award-winning olive oils; call ahead.

Don't miss the abandoned ancient village of **Kotli**, located 2.5km from the main road between Hum and Roč, on the Mirna River. This protected rural complex has preserved courtyards, outer staircases, arched passages and picturesque chimneys.

For a fine gastronomic experience, head to **Konoba Morgan** (www.konoba-morgan.eu; Bracanija 1; mains from 60KN; ⌚Wed-Mon), 2km northeast of Brtonigla on the road to Buje. It has a lovely terrace on a hill, with sweeping views of the countryside. The menu, which changes daily, focuses on game meat and seasonal ingredients such as truffles and asparagus.

Cyclists shouldn't miss the **Parenzana bike trail** (www.istria-bike.com), which runs along a defunct gauge railway that operated from 1902 to 1935 between Trieste and Poreč. Today, it traverses three countries: Italy, Slovenia and Croatia (the Croatian stretch is 78km).

Also worth a trip is the **Višnjan Observatory** (☎449 212; www.astro.hr; ⌚by appointment only) in the interior of western Istria, 13km from Poreč. Active since the 1970s, it stands third in the world for the number of asteroids it has discovered. Even though the centre is geared towards educational purposes, it's a lovely place to visit. The observatory recently moved into its new premises in a gorgeous hilltop park, with a 'cyber-romantic building' housing the telescope, fragrant pine forests and incredible views that on a clear day show the curvature of the Earth. Call ahead to book a free tour (donations encouraged) or visit during the two-day AstroFest that starts on 21 June (summer solstice), with New Age music, drumming and plenty of stargazing.

Information

Tourist Office (☎852 399; www.rabac-labin.com; Titov trg 2/1; ⊙8am-9pm Mon-Fri, 10am-2pm & 6-9pm Sat & Sun May-Oct, 8am-3pm Mon-Fri Nov-Apr) At the entrance to the old town.

Getting There & Away

Labin is well connected by bus with Pula (42KN, one hour, 14 daily). In summer, the bus to Rabac (12KN), via the old town, leaves every hour between 6am and midnight.

Getting Around

Buses stop at Trg 2 Marta in Podlabin, from where you can catch a local bus to the old town. This bus continues on to Rabac in the peak season.

Vodnjan

POP 3500

Connoisseurs of the macabre can't miss Vodnjan (Dignano in Italian), located 10km north of Pula. Lying inside a sober church in this sleepy town are the mummies that constitute Vodnjan's primary tourist attraction. These desiccated remains of centuries-old saints, whose bodies mysteriously failed to decompose, are considered to have magical powers.

There's not much going on in the rest of the town. The centre is Narodni trg, composed of several neo-Gothic palaces in varying stages of decay and restoration. Vodnjan also has Istria's largest Roma population.

Sights

St Blaise's Church CHURCH

(Crkva Svetog Blaža; Župni trg bb; Collection of Sacral Art admission incl mummies 55KN, mummies only 35KM, Collection of Sacral Art only 35KN; ⊙9am-7pm Jun-Sep) A few steps from Narodni trg, this handsome neobaroque church was built at the turn of the 19th century, when Venice was the style setter for the Istrian coast. With its 63m-high **bell tower** as high as St Mark's in Venice, it's the largest parish church in Istria, and worth a visit for its magnificent altars alone. The **mummies** are in a curtained-off area behind the **main altar**. In the dim lighting, the complete bodies of Nikolosa Bursa, Giovanni Olini and Leon Bembo resemble wooden dolls in their glass cases. Assorted body parts of three other saints complete the display. As you examine the skin, hair and fingernails of these long-dead people, a tape in English narrates their life stories. Considered to be Europe's best-preserved mummy, the body of St Nikolosa is said to emit a 32m bioenergy circle that has caused 50 miraculous healings.

If the mummies have whet your appetite for saintly relics, head to the **Collection of Sacral Art** (Zbirka Sakralne Umjetnosti) in the sacristy. Here there are hundreds of **relics** belonging to 150 different saints, including the casket with St Mary of Egypt's tongue. Less grisly exhibits include a masterful 14th-century polyptych of St Leon Bembo by Paolo Veneziano. Make sure you cover up as the eccentric parish priest is known for turning away 'inappropriately dressed' people.

Eating

Vodnjanka ISTRIAN €

(Istarska bb; mains from 60KN; ⊙Mon-Sat) This excellent regional restaurant has several rustic rooms, lots of style and personal service. The specialities include *fuži* (home-made egg pasta twisted into a unique shape) topped with truffles, *maneštra* (vegetable and bean soup similar to minestrone), various kinds of *fritaja* (omelette often served with seasonal vegies) and prosciutto. The terrace has pretty views of the old town rooftops and the church spire.

Entertainment

Lighthouse Music Club NIGHTCLUB

(www.lighthouseclub.com; Krnjaloža 1) On the road between Bale and Vodnjan, this new club has quickly become one of Istria's best places to party, with big-name DJs and jazz concerts.

Information

The **tourist office** (☎511 700; www.istra.hr/vodnjan; Narodni trg 3; ⊙8am-3pm & 7-9pm Mon-Sat, 9am-1pm Sun Jun–mid-Sep, 8am-3pm Mon-Fri mid-Sep–May) is located in the main square.

Getting There & Away

Vodnjan is well connected with Pula by bus (15KN, 30 minutes, 10 daily).

ISTRIA'S TOP RURAL RETREATS

Agritourism is an increasingly popular accommodation option in Istria's interior. Some of these residences are working farms engaged in producing wine, vegetables and poultry; some are upmarket country houses with rustic rooms to let; while others are plush modern villas with swimming pools. Whatever you choose, the highlights are wholesome food, and hiking and cycling opportunities.

The Istrian tourist office has issued a brochure with photos and information about rural holidays throughout Istria. You'll need your own car to reach most of these lodgings, as many are located in the middle of nowhere. There's often a supplement for stays of fewer than three nights.

At leafy **Agroturizam Ograde** (☎693 035; www.agroturizam-ograde.hr; Katun Lindarski 60; per person incl breakfast 250KN; P 📶 🏊), in the village of Katun Lindarski, 10km south of Pazin, you'll hang out with horses, sheep, chickens, pigs and geese. The food, served in a dark and cool *konoba* (tavern), is a real-deal affair: vegies from the garden, home-cured meats and wine from the cellar. Accommodation is in two separate houses, one with a pool.

Agroturizam San Mauro (☎779 033; www.sinkovic.hr; San Mauro 157; per person 176KN with breakfast), near the hilltop town of Momjan, 5km from Buje, specialises in tastings of its award-winning wines (40KN), truffle dishes (the sweet *tartufone* cake is a delight) and homemade jams, honeys and juices that you get to sample for breakfast. Some of the apartments, each with a kitchenette, have terraces and sea vistas. There's a small surcharge for one-night stays, and payments are cash only.

At the higher end of the scale sits **San Rocco** (☎725 000; www.san-rocco.hr; Srednja Ulica 2; d from 1380KN; P ❄ @ 📶 🏊), a family-run boutique inn in the village of Brtonigla, near Buje. This rural hideaway has 14 stylish rooms – no two are alike, but all are equipped with modern conveniences and graced with original detail. There's an outdoor swimming pool, a top-rated restaurant and a small spa.

La Parenzana (☎777 460; www.parenzana.com.hr; Volpia 3; s/d 290/580KN; P @ 📶) is another notable rural inn, 3km from Buje in the village of Volpia. It features 16 rooms with rustic wood-and-stone decor, and a *konoba* popular for its Istrian food, such as *čripnja* (roast meat or fish cooked with potatoes in a cast-iron pot over an open fire). There's bike rental (70KN per day) and tours on request.

Stancija 1904, near Svetvinčenat, also fits the bill as a top rural retreat.

Svetvinčenat

POP 180

Lying halfway between Pazin and Pula in southern Istria, Svetvinčenat (also known as Savičenta) is an endearing little town. First settled by Benedictines, it centres on a Renaissance town square. With its surrounding cypress trees, harmoniously positioned buildings and laid-back ambience, it's a delightful place for a wander.

Sights

Grimani Castle CASTLE

The northern part of the main square is occupied by this beautifully preserved 13th-century palace. A Venetian makeover in the 16th century added towers that served as a residence and a prison. The site held feasts, parades, fairs and witch burnings (Marija Radoslović was allegedly tortured and burnt at the stake here on charges of sorcery, but was in fact killed for having an improper love affair with one of the Grimanis). The castle is also home to a seasonal tourist office.

Church of Mary's Annunciation CHURCH

This parish church on the east side of the square has a trefoil Renaissance facade made of local cut stone, and five elaborate Venetian marble altars inside.

Festivals & Events

The time to be in Svetvinčenat is mid-July, during the annual **Dance & Nonverbal Theatre Festival** (www.svetvincenatfestival.com). The festival features contemporary dance pieces, street theatre, circus and mime acts, and various other nonverbal forms of expression. This international event hosts performers from Croatia and Europe, its acts ranging from Finnish hip hop to Brazilian capoeira.

Sleeping & Eating

Stancija 1904 RURAL INN €€€

(☎560 022; www.stancija.com; Smoljanci 2-3; s/d 625/840KN; P) In the village of Smoljanci, just 3km from Svetvinčenat on the road to Bale, this traditional stone Istrian house has been stylishly converted by a Swiss-Croatian family. Surrounded by fragrant herb gardens and shaded by tall old-growth trees, it offers elaborate breakfasts (100KN) served till noon. There's a surcharge of 30% for one-night stays.

Kod Kaštela ISTRIAN €

(Savičenta 53; mains from 50KN) Right at the heart of town, with great views of the castle and the square, this regional restaurant serves homemade pastas and tasty *pršut* (prosciutto).

Information

The **tourist office** (☎560 349; www.tz-svetvincenat.hr; Svetvinčenat 20; ⏲7am-7pm Mon-Fri, 11am-7pm Sat & Sun Jun-Sep, 7am-3pm Mon-Fri Oct-May), opposite the main square that fronts the castle, has information about private accommodation in and around town (from 150KN per person), brochures and a map of a bike path that takes you on a 35km circuit from Svetvinčenat to Sveti Petar, with information boards explaining the local history, flora and fauna in English.

There is also a seasonal **tourist info point** (⏲10am-7pm Mon-Fri, 11am-7pm Sat & Sun Jul & Aug) inside the castle.

Pazin

POP 4500

Most famous for the gaping chasm that inspired Jules Verne, and for its medieval castle, Pazin is a workaday provincial town in central Istria. It deserves a stop mainly for the chasm and the castle, but part of the appeal is its small-town feel and the lack of fashionable foreigners stomping its streets. Most of the town centre is given over to pedestrian-only areas, while rolling Istrian countryside surrounds the rather unsightly outskirts.

Lying at the geographic heart of Istria, Pazin is the county's administrative seat and is excellently connected by road and rail to virtually every other destination in the region. The hotel and restaurant pickings in town are skimpy – you're better off visiting on a day trip since you're within an hour of most other Istrian towns. However, the countryside around Pazin offers plentiful activities, such as hiking, free climbing, ziplining, cycling and visiting local honey makers.

Sights

Pazin Chasm CAVE

(www.pazinska-jama.com; adult/concession 30/15KN; ⏲10am-7pm Jun-Aug, 10am-6pm May & Sep) Pazin's most renowned site is undoubtedly this deep abyss of about 100m, through which the Pazinčica River sinks into subterranean passages forming three underground lakes. Its shadowy depths inspired the imagination of Jules Verne, as well as numerous Croatian writers. Visitors can walk the 1.3km **marked path** inside the natural canyon, which takes about 45 minutes

MATHIAS SANDORF & THE PAZIN CHASM

The writer best known for going around the world in 80 days, into the centre of the earth and 20,000 leagues under the sea found inspiration in the centre of Istria. The French futurist-fantasist Jules Verne (1828–1905) set *Mathias Sandorf* (1885), one of his 27 books in the series Voyages Extraordinaires, in the castle and chasm of Pazin.

In the novel, later made into a movie, Count Mathias Sandorf and two cohorts are arrested by Austrian police for revolutionary activity and imprisoned in Pazin's castle. Sandorf escapes by climbing down a lightning rod but, struck by lightning, he tumbles down into the roaring Pazinčica River. He's carried along into the murky depths of the chasm, but our plucky hero holds on fast to a tree trunk and (phew!) six hours later the churning river deposits him at the tranquil entrance to the Limska Draga Fjord. He walks to Rovinj and is last seen jumping from a cliff into the sea amid a hail of bullets.

Verne never actually visited Pazin – he spun Sandorf's adventure from photos and travellers' accounts – but that hasn't stopped Pazin from celebrating it at every opportunity. There's a street named after Jules Verne as well as special Jules Verne days.

and involves a gentle winding climb. There are two entrances, one by Hotel Lovac and one by the footbridge that spans the abyss 100m from the castle. You can enter the cave with an expert speleologist (100KN) if arranged in advance through the tourist office, and even zipline across it. If the trip into the abyss doesn't appeal, there's a **viewing point** just outside the castle.

Castle CASTLE

(Trg Istarskog Razvoda 1) Looming over the chasm, Pazin's castle is the largest and best-preserved medieval structure in all of Istria. First mentioned in AD 983, it's a medley of Romanesque, Gothic and Renaissance architecture. Within the castle, there are two museums; the price of admission is for both. The **town museum** (Trg Istarskog Razvoda 1; adult/concession 25/18KN; ⊙10am-6pm daily Jul & Aug, 10am-6pm Tue-Sun mid-Apr–Jun & Sep–mid-Oct, 10am-3pm Tue-Thu, 11am-4pm Fri, 10am-4pm Sat & Sun mid-Oct–mid-Apr) has a collection of medieval Istrian church bells, an exhibition about slave revolts, and torture instruments in the dungeon. The **Ethnographic Museum** (www.emi.hr; ⊙10am-6pm daily Jul & Aug, 10am-6pm Tue-Sun mid-Apr–Jun & Sep–mid-Oct, 10am-3pm Tue-Thu, 11am-4pm Fri, 10am-4pm Sat & Sun mid-Oct–mid-Apr) has about 4200 artefacts portraying traditional Istrian village life, which includes garments, tools and pottery.

Festivals & Events

The first Tuesday of the month is **Pazin Fair**, featuring products from all over Istria. The **Days of Jules Verne** (www.julesvernedays.com), in the last week of June, is Pazin's way of honouring the writer who put the town on the cultural map. There are races, re-enactments from the novel and journeys retracing the footsteps of Verne's hero Mathias Sandorf.

Sleeping & Eating

The tourist office helps to arrange private accommodation, which is generally reasonably priced. Count on spending from 100KN per person for a room.

Hotel Lovac HOTEL €€

(☎624 324; Šime Kurelića 4; s/d 268/550KN; P) The late-1960s architecture of Pazin's only hotel could be a hit, if only the rooms were done up right. Request one of the spruced-up rooms with a chasm view. The hotel restaurant serves acceptable food, especially given that there are no notable restaurants in Pazin itself. On the western edge of town.

TRANSPORT FROM PAZIN

Bus Services

DESTINATION	COST (KN)	DURATION	DAILY SERVICES
Motovun	28	30min	2 daily Mon-Fri
Osijek	275	8hr	1 daily
Poreč	37	45min	5 daily
Pula	45	50min	2 daily
Rijeka	46-57	1hr	5 daily
Rovinj	36-41	40min	5 daily
Trieste (Italy)	60-70	2hr	1 daily Mon-Sat
Zagreb	173-197	3-4hr	10 daily

Train Services

DESTINATION	COST (KN)	DURATION	DAILY SERVICES
Buzet	22	50min	6
Ljubljana	116	3½-4½hr	2, with a transfer in Buzet or Divača
Pula	32	1hr	7-9
Zagreb	118	5-8½hr	4

Information

The best source of information about Pazin is the **tourist office** (☎622 460; www.sredisnja-istra.hr; Franine i Jurine 14; ⏰9am-7pm Mon-Fri, 10am-1pm Sat Jul & Aug, 9am-4pm Mon-Fri, 10am-1pm Sat Sep-Jun), which also manages the entire central Istrian region. It distributes a map of hiking trails and honey spots (you can visit beekeepers and taste their delicious acacia honey), and a brochure about wine cellars around Pazin. It can also hook you up with ziplining over the Pazin Chasm (100KN) and horse riding near town.

Getting There & Away

Bus Station (☎060 306 040; Miroslava Bulešića 2) Services are reduced on weekends.
Train Station (☎624 310; Stareh Kostanji 1) Services are reduced on weekends.

Getting Around

The town is relatively compact, stretching little more than 1km from the train station on the eastern end to the castle on the western end. The bus station is 200m west of the train station and the old part of town comprises the 200m leading up to the castle.

Gračišće

Gračišće is a sleepy medieval town, just 7km southeast of Pazin, surrounded by rolling hills and one of Istria's well-kept secrets. Its collection of ancient buildings includes the 15th-century Venetian-Gothic **Salamon Palace**, the Romanesque **Church of St Euphemia**, and the **Church of St Mary** from 1425.

Most of these buildings are unrestored (although some work is being done). You won't need more than 30 minutes to circle the tiny town, but the ambience is truly lovely. There's an 11.5km circular **hiking trail** that leads from here, which is well marked with signs.

Istrian specialties are served at **Konoba Marino** (Gračišće 75; mains from 35KN; ⏰closed Wed), a cosy tavern that dishes out copious portions of *fuži* with game as well as *ombolo* (boneless pork loin) with cabbage. The same owners run a restored town house just steps away with four charming rustic rooms (150KN per person, including breakfast).

Buzet

POP 6059

It may not be Istria's most fascinating town, but sleepy Buzet, 39km northeast of Poreč over the Mirna River, offers a sense of the timeless grace of old Istria. First settled by the Romans, Buzet achieved real prominence under the Venetians, who endowed it with walls, gates and several churches. With its grey-stone buildings in various stages of decay and restoration, and the cobblestone streets nearly deserted (most of Buzet's residents resettled at the foot of the hill in the unbecoming new part of town long ago), the old town is a quiet but charming place.

Enjoy a wander around the maze of Buzet's narrow streets and squares, its sights all well marked with English plaques. The other reason to come here is the glorious truffle. Self-dubbed the city of truffles, Buzet takes its title seriously. Lying at the epicentre of the truffle-growing region, it offers a variety of ways to celebrate the smelly fungus, from sampling it at the old town's restaurant to various truffle-related activities. The best event is the **Festival of Subotina** on the second Saturday in September, marking the start of the white-truffle season (which lasts through to December). The pinnacle of this event is the preparation of a giant truffle omelette – with more than 2000 eggs and 10kg of truffles – in a 1000kg pan.

Sights & Activities

Most commerce is in the new Fontana section of town at the foot of the hilltop old town. If you have wheels, you must park your car by the cemetery on the hill and make the five-minute walk up to the old town.

Regional Museum MUSEUM
(Zavičajni Muzej Buzet; Ulica Rašporskih Kapetana 5; adult/concession 15/10KN; ⏰9am-3pm Mon-Fri, by appointment through tourist office Sat & Sun) You'll find Buzet's main sight housed inside a 17th-century palace. The museum displays a collection of prehistoric and Roman artefacts as well as some ethnological items such as field tools and folk costumes.

MAGIC MUSHROOMS?

The truffle trade is less like a business than a highly profitable cult. It revolves around an expensive, malodorous, subterranean fungus allegedly endowed with semimagical powers, which is picked in dark woods and then sent across borders to be sold for a small fortune. Devotees claim that once you've tasted this small, nut-shaped delicacy, all other flavours seem insipid.

There are 70 sorts of truffle in the world, of which 34 come from Europe. The traditional truffle-producing countries are Italy, France and Spain, but Istrian forests boast three sorts of black truffles as well as the big white truffle – one of the most prized in the world, at 34,000KN per kilogram. Croatia's largest exporter of Istrian truffles is Zigante Tartufi, with its share of the overall Croatian export market being about 90%. In 1999 the company's owner, Giancarlo Zigante, along with his dog Diana, found the world's largest truffle in Istria, weighing 1.31kg and making it into *Guinness World Records*.

The Istrian truffle business is relatively young. In 1932, when Istria was occupied by Italy, an Italian soldier from the truffle capital of Alba allegedly noticed similarities in vegetation between his region and Istria. He returned after his military service with specially trained dogs, which, after plenty of sniffing and digging, eventually uncovered the precious commodity.

Because no sign of the truffle appears above ground, no human can spot it, so dogs (or, traditionally, pigs) are the key to a successful truffle hunt. Istrian *breks* (truffle-hunting dogs) may be mongrels, but they are highly trained. Puppies begin their training at two months, but only about 20% of them go on to have fully fledged careers as truffle trackers.

The truffle-hunting season starts in early October and continues for three months, during which time at least 3000 people and 9000 to 12,000 dogs wander around the damp Motovun forests. The epicentre of the truffle-growing region is the town of Buzet.

Some people believe truffles are an aphrodisiac, though scientific research has failed to prove this. Conduct your own experiment!

Baroque Well LANDMARK
On a square a few metres north of the museum is this exquisite well, which was restored in 1789 and sports a Venetian lion relief.

Tours

Truffle Hunting CULINARY
(☎667 304; www.karlictartufi.hr; Paladini 14; tour 260-965KN per person, depending on number of participants) If you want to experience truffle hunting, contact the friendly Karlić family, who live in the village of Paladini, 12km from Buzet; request a tour in English ahead of time. The tour includes cheese and truffle tasting, a story about truffles and a hunt in the forest that lasts up to two hours.

Sleeping & Eating

A number of farmhouses in the surrounding area have rooms and apartments to rent (from 100KN to 150KN per person). The tourist office has details and contact information.

Vela Vrata BOUTIQUE HOTEL €€€
(☎494 750; www.velavrata.net; Šetalište Vladimira Gortana 7; s/d 555/810KN; ❄📶) This lovely new boutique hotel on the edge of the old town, with panoramic views of the surrounding hills, has revitalised Buzet's hilltop. Twenty rooms in five interconnected buildings are tasteful and well-equipped. Room 11 has a gorgeous vista from its balcony. There's a restaurant and a cafe on site, a small spa, bikes for rent and talk of an outdoor swimming pool down the line.

Stara Oštarija ISTRIAN €€
(Petra Flega 5; mains from 70KN; ⏱closed Sun dinner and some Tue out of season) This is the place to try truffles in the old town. The restaurant even serves pannacotta with truffle honey. For a splurge, order a slow-food truffle menu of six courses (690KN for two) and enjoy views of the valley below.

Shopping

Zigante Tartufi FOOD
(www.zigantetartufi.com; Trg Fontana) Stock up on truffles in various shapes and forms – whole, hand-sliced, puréed, and with olives or mushrooms. Zigante stores are ubiquitous in Istria.

Information

The **tourist office** (☎662 343; www.tz-buzet.hr; Šetalište Vladimira Gortana 9; ⏰8am-3pm Mon-Fri, 9am-2pm Sat Apr-Oct, 8am-3pm Mon-Fri Nov-Mar), in a swanky new space next to Vela Vrata, has info about accommodation and plentiful maps and brochures about wine, olive oil and truffle roads throughout the region, as well as various activities such as hiking, cycling (there are 14 trails around town), free climbing, hot-air ballooning and paragliding.

Istriana Travel (☎667 022; www.istrianatravel.hr; Vrh 28) offers truffle-hunting excursions, a fresco workshop, wine and olive-oil tours, bike jaunts, hiking, caving, paragliding and more.

Getting There & Away

Buzet is connected by bus with Poreč (50KN, 1½ hours, two daily), Rijeka (49KN to 59KN, one hour, four daily) and Pula (60KN, 1½ hours, one daily except Sunday). The **bus station** (☎663 285; Riječka bb) is in the new part of town.

Around Buzet

The rolling hills, woods, pastures and vineyards around Buzet make for a memorably scenic drive. You really need your own wheels to explore this region.

ROČ

Small and sleepy Roč, 8km southeast of Buzet, is snug within its 15th-century walls. A meander will reveal the Romanesque **Church of St Anthony**, a 15th-century **Renaissance house** in the square next to the church, and a **Roman lapidarium** within the town gate. The **tourist office** (⏰9am-8pm Jun-Aug, 10am-5pm Sat & Sun Mar-May & Sep-Oct) has keys to all the town's churches, so ask here if you want to see the interiors, and a replica of the Gutenberg press. It also has information about the fresco workshop that's on offer in town.

Roč slumbers most of the year, roused only by the annual **Accordion Festival** on the second Sunday in May, which gathers accordion players from Croatia, Italy and Slovenia.

One of the town's stone buildings houses a regional restaurant, **Ročka Konoba** (mains from 30KN; ⏰Tue-Sun), which has outdoor tables and a fireplace indoors. Discover Istrian specialities such as *fuži,* homemade sausages and *maneštra.* At the new **Biskoteka** (Roč 14) shop you can try about 30 *rakija* varieties, including seven brands of *biska.*

There are private rooms in town for about 100KN per night; the tourist office has details.

HUM

Outside Roč is **Glagolitic Alley**, a series of 11 outdoor sculptures placed along the road commemorating the area's importance as a centre of the Glagolitic alphabet. There's horse riding at an equestrian club near here; the tourist office in Buzet has details.

Running for 7km to the southwest, the road ends in **Hum**, a beautifully preserved place that bills itself as the world's smallest town, with a permanent population of 24. Legend has it that the giants who built Istria had only a few stones left over and they used them to build Hum.

In summer, this tiny and adorable town gets a steady stream of visitors who come to meander around the narrow lanes and to visit **Aura** (admission free; ⏰10am-7pm), which displays some old village tools but serves mostly as a souvenir shop. It takes just 30 minutes to see the town on a self-guided tour, as each church and building is marked with informative multilingual plaques. Don't miss the 12th-century frescos in the Romanesque **Chapel of St Jerome** (Crkvica Svetog Jerolima), which depict the life of Jesus in unusually vivid colours. The chapel, by the cemetery outside the town gates, is locked, but you can get the key at the town inn.

That very inn is reason enough to come to Hum. **Humska Konoba** (www.hum.hr; Hum 2; mains from 30KN; ⏰closed Mon mid-Mar–mid-May & mid-Oct–mid-Nov) not only serves first-rate Istrian mainstays, but also has a lovely outdoor terrace offering panoramic views. Start with a shot of sweet *biska* (white mistletoe grappa made according to an ancient Celtic recipe), then go on to *maneštra s kukuruzom* (bean and fresh maize soup), continue with truffle-topped *fuži* and end with *kroštuli* (fried crispy dough covered in sugar). If you like *biska*, stock up at the **Imela shop**, which is run by the restaurant owners and has olive oils, truffles, jams, wines, honey and souvenirs. It lies where the village ends.

On the last Sunday of October, about 4000 visitors pour into Hum for **Dan Rakije** (Day of Grappa). During this very fun event, you will get a tasting glass and sip on different-flavoured grappas produced in the area – until they run out.

SOVINJSKO POLJE

The sleepy hamlet of Sovinjsko Polje is up in the hills off the road from Buzet to Istarske Toplice (follow the signs for about 4km along a narrow curvy road).

The reason to come to this tiny hamlet is **Toklarija** (☎091 926 6769; Sovinjsko Polje 11; 6-course meal incl wine 400-500KN; ⊙closed Tue), which offers one of Istria's finest dining experiences. At this beautifully converted 600-year-old olive mill, bought by his grandfather in the 1950s, eccentric owner Nevio Sirotić serves delectable, homemade Istrian slow food. A meal can take up to four hours in a well-timed string of delicate courses. The menu changes daily and features dried Istrian ham, porcini mushrooms, asparagus salad, truffles and juicy meats. Ninety per cent of the food is local, all fruit and vegetables come from the family's gardens, and even the bread and pasta are homemade. It's all paired with local wines such as *teran* and *malvazija*. Reserve ahead.

Motovun

POP 480

Motovun is a captivating little town perched on a 277m hill in the Mirna River Valley, about 25km northeast of Poreč. It was the Venetians who decided to fortify the town in the 14th century, building two sets of thick walls.

There are a number of galleries and shops before you enter the old town and between the town gates, including a wine-tasting shop and a Zigante food store. Within the walls, an atmospheric cluster of Romanesque and Gothic buildings houses a smattering of artist studios. Newer houses have sprung up on the slopes leading to the old town, where the popular film festival takes place every summer – the very film fest that has, in recent years, made Motovun the most touristy of Istria's hilltop towns.

A Venetian lion scowls down from the outer gate, beyond which sprawls a terrace with a baroque loggia and a cafe's outside tables, perfect for watching the sun go down below the valley. A cheerier lion adorns the inner gate, which holds a long-running restaurant. Inside is a tree-shaded square with the town's hotel, an old well and the Church of St Stephen.

Sights & Activities

Church of St Stephen CHURCH

(Svetog Stjepana; Trg Andrea Antico) The town highlight is the Renaissance Church of St Stephen. Designed by Venetian artist Andrea Palladio, the interior is currently under renovation and opening hours are sporadic. Along the inner wall that encloses the old town rises a 16th-century **bell tower**.

Ramparts CITY WALLS

Be sure to walk on the outer walls of the ramparts for memorable vistas over vineyards, fields and oak woods below.

Paragliding PARAGLIDING

(☎098 922 8081; www.istraparagliding.com; per person 550KN) Jump off Motovun's hilltop for a tandem glide (with an instructor) with stunning vistas over Istria's hills. Book ahead.

Festivals & Events

The **Motovun Film Festival** (www.motovunfilmfestival.com) presents a roster of independent and avant-garde films in late July. Since its inception in 1999, this small event has grown pretty popular and now attracts quite a crowd, with nonstop outdoor and indoor screenings, concerts and parties.

Sleeping

House of Gold B&B €€

(☎681 816; www.motovunaccommodation.com; Gradiziol 46; s 260-408KN, d 483-557KN;) Motovun's cosiest choice, this three-room B&B in a renovated town house sits at the entrance to town, lovingly run by its live-in owners. The interiors feature hardwood floors and simple but stylish decor. The priciest room, Kučar, has its own terrace with two hammocks; the room called Kortel has sweeping valley views. There's a shared kitchen and living room where you help yourself to breakfast. Book ahead for high season, when there's a two-night minimum.

Hotel Kaštel HOTEL €€

(☎681 607; www.hotel-kastel-motovun.hr; Trg Andrea Antico 7; s/d 423/722KN; P@) The town's only hotel is an utterly charming little place in a restored 17th-century palazzo, with 33 simply furnished rooms. For 1098KN get one of three rooms with balconies overlooking the leafy square. There's a good restaurant offering truffles and Istrian wines, and a wellness centre.

Motovun Camping CAMPGROUND €
(☎681 557; www.motovun-camping.com; 2-person site for 1 night 180KN, subsequent nights 108KN) Small campground with 12 pitches right below town, run by Hotel Kaštel. Campers get free use of the hotel's swimming pool and a 10% discount at the restaurant.

Eating & Drinking

Mondo ISTRIAN €€
(Barbacan 1; mains from 75KN; ⊙closed Tue in low season) Just before the outer town gate, this little tavern with a small side terrace serves up well-prepared Istrian mainstays, many featuring truffles. Wash down your meal with wines from Tomaz winery.

Pod Voltom ISTRIAN €
(Trg Josefa Ressela 6; mains from 60KN; ⊙closed Wed Oct-Jul) In a vaulted space within the town gates, just below the hotel, this wood-beamed place serves simple down-home Istrian cuisine and pricier truffle dishes. From June to September, grab a seat in the loggia with great valley views.

Konoba Dolina ISTRIAN €
(Gradinje 59/1; mains from 38KN; ⊙Wed-Mon) If you have wheels, this low-key locals' favourite is worth the drive for its unassuming vibe and honest simple fare featuring Istrian dishes, many with truffles. Pair your meal with Favorit beer. Coming down from Motovun, make a right towards Buzet and continue till the left turnoff for Gradinje; it's 2.5km from here. It closes for summer holidays for three weeks in late June each year.

Restaurant Zigante GASTRONOMIC €€€
(☎664 302; www.zigantetartufi.com; Livade 7, Livade; mains from 185KN) Gourmets from afar come to this destination restaurant a few kilometres below Motovun in the village of Livade. Expect five-star fancy dining, with truffles as the showcase – goose liver with banana potato and black truffle, fresh sea bass carpaccio with black truffles, even black-truffle ice cream… A five-course set menu ranges from 590KN to 635KN. The complex also has three luxury apartments (including truffle breakfast 1168KN), and a shop next door.

Rakijarnica BAR
(Pietra Kandlera 2) Just below the tower off the main square, this buzzy bar specialises in *rakija*, Croatia's *l'eau de vie*. Try one of 30-plus flavours, all by small family producers, and sip it under starry skies.

Information

The town's **tourist office** (☎681 726; www.tz-motovun.hr; Trg Andrea Antico 1; ⊙10am-5pm daily Jun-Aug, 10am-4pm May, Sep & Oct) is located on the main town square, right below Hotel Kaštel. There's an ATM just past the town entrance, on the right.

Montona Tours (☎681 970; www.montonatours.com; Kanal 10) is another great source of info; it can help with accommodation in central Istria, rural stays and private apartments.

Getting There & Away

It's not easy to visit Motovun without your own car. There are bus connections from Pazin (35KN, 40 minutes, two daily) and Poreč (35KN, 45 minutes, one daily), but on weekdays only during the school year.

Getting Around

There are three parking areas in town. The first is at the foot of the village, from where it's a steep 2km hike up to the city gates. Another is 300m below the old town. The last one is for residents and hotel guests. Unless you're staying at the hotel, there's a 15KN charge per day from April to October at the other two parking lots.

Istarske Toplice

Dating from the Roman era, **Istarske Toplice** (www.istarske-toplice.hr) is one of Croatia's oldest and most scenic thermal spas. Beneath an 85m-high cliff and surrounded by greenery, the complex features a concrete-box-style hotel, a wellness centre and, like most spa spots in Croatia, a slightly geriatric vibe. The rotten-egg smell is due to the high sulphur content of the large outdoor pool, where temperatures reach 34°C. The thermal waters are said to help rheumatism, skin diseases and respiratory tract disorders.

It's not worth spending the night – unless you love spas – but come for a few hours to indulge in a choice of treatments. The menu is wide and varied, and includes anything from hot stone (350KN for 1¼ hours) and Mediterranean (300KN per hour) massage to signature body treatments with wine, honey and lavender (350KN each). Or simply spend time paddling around in the thermal pool (35KN for three hours) or sweating it all away in the sauna (100KN for three hours).

There's no public transport, but the spa is easily accessible by road, only 10km north of Motovun and 11km south of Buzet on the main road that connects the two towns.

Grožnjan

POP 100

Until the mid-1960s, Grožnjan, 27km northeast of Poreč, was slipping towards oblivion. First mentioned in 1102, this hilltop town was a strategically important fortress for the 14th-century Venetians. They created a system of ramparts and gates, and built a loggia, a granary and several fine churches. With the collapse of the Venetian empire in the 18th century, Grožnjan suffered a decline in its importance and population.

In 1965 sculptor Aleksandar Rukavina and a small group of other artists 'discovered' the crumbling medieval appeal of Grožnjan and began setting up studios in the abandoned buildings. As the town crawled back to life, it attracted the attention of Jeunesses Musicales International, an international training program for young musicians. In 1969 a summer school for musicians, Jeunesses Musicales Croatia, was established in Grožnjan and it has been going strong ever since. Each year there are music, orchestra and ballet courses and recitals. Throughout the summer, concerts and musical events are held almost daily. You can hear the musicians practising while you browse the many craft shops and galleries of this tiny town, comprised of a jumble of crooked lanes and leafy squares.

Sights & Activities

All the town's sights are marked with plaques that have English explanations. The Renaissance **loggia** is immediately to the right of the town gate by the tourist office. Keep going and on your right you'll see the baroque **Spinotti Morteani Palace**, its patio overtaken by the outdoor tables of the **Zigante Tartufi** (www.zigantetartufi.com; Umberta Gorjana 5) shop. Next on the right comes the **Kaštel** (castle), where many concerts are held.

The town is dominated by the yellow sandstone bell tower of the **Church of St Vitus, St Modest & St Crescentia**, which was built in the 14th century and renovated in baroque style in 1770.

There are more than 30 galleries and studios scattered around town; most are open daily from May to September. **Fonticus Gallery** (Gradska Galerija Fonticus; Trg Lođe 3; ⏲10am-1pm & 5-8pm Tue-Sun) promotes recent work of mainly Croatian artists. It doesn't have a permanent collection but does host a small display of heraldic paraphernalia that includes helmets, insignia and escutcheon.

Festivals & Events

Summer music concerts are organised by the **International Cultural Centre of Jeunesses Musicales Croatia** (www.hgm.hr). The concerts are free; no reservations necessary. They are usually held in the church, the main square, the loggia or the Kaštel.

Sleeping & Eating

There are no hotels in Grožnjan, but the staff at the **tourist office** (☎776 131; Umberta Gorjana 3; ⏲8am-3pm Mon-Fri) can put you in touch with private room owners. About 175KN per person.

Bastia ISTRIAN €€

(1 Svibnja 1; mains from 60KN) The town's oldest restaurant sits on the verdant main square. The decor is bright and cheerful, and the menu extensive and heavy on truffles.

Konoba Pintur ISTRIAN €

(1 Svibnja bb; mains from 40KN) This cheaper option on the main square has tables outside and acceptable food. It also rents rooms upstairs (300KN).

Drinking

Kaya Energy Bar & Design CAFE-BAR

(Vincenta iz Kastva 2; ⏲closed Jan & Feb) This spot at the entrance to town has many faces: cafe, bar, shop, showroom and gallery. The family-run hideaway has a stylish stone interior, tables outside on the square and a lovely terrace with fantastic valley views. It serves fresh-squeezed juices, smoothies, breakfasts, all-day snacks and really good local *malvazija* wine. The showroom concept means that everything inside is on sale, from small bags of organic lavender to more expensive handcrafted jewellery.

Cafe Vero CAFE-BAR

(Trg Cornera 3) The marvellous valley views below are the main draw of this cafe-bar at the end of the village, with wooden tables gracing its terrace.

Getting There & Away

You will have to rely on private transport to get to Grožnjan, as there are no buses. If you're driving from Motovun, do not take the first marked turn-off for Grožnjan as it's unsealed and takes a lot longer. Continue along the road for another kilometre or so until you get to another sign for Grožnjan – this is a far better approach.

Kvarner

☎051

Includes »

Best Places to Eat

» Bora Bar Trattoria/Tartufferia (p159)
» Na Kantunu (p137)
» Tramerka (p142)
» Konoba Bukaleta (p151)
» Skalinada (p143)
» Restaurant Nada (p148)

Best Places to Stay

» Hotel Marina (p146)
» Hotel Ambasador (p140)
» Hotel Arbiana (p164)

Why Go?

Sheltered by soaring mountains, the Kvarner Gulf has long been loved by visitors attracted by the mild climate and cobalt waters, and those in search for more than just beach appeal. From the gateway city of Rijeka you can easily connect to the foodie enclave of Volosko and the hiking trails inside the national parks of Učka and Risnjak. The islands of Krk, Rab, Lošinj and Cres all have highly atmospheric old ports, and stretches of pristine coastline dotted with remote coves for superb swimming. And dramatic wildlife puts in an appearance too: Cres has an important griffon-vulture project and Lošinj a marine centre that monitors Adriatic dolphins.

The region's historical connections to Austria and Hungary have bestowed the coastline with stately architecture: Opatija's Habsburg mansions and the Venetian-style houses of the islands. Links to central Europe and Italy remain strong today, with visitors filling the resorts in high season.

When to Go

Rijeka

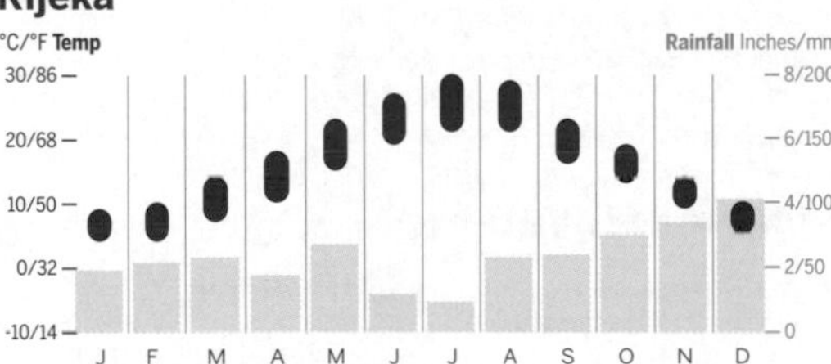

Jan–Mar Rijeka becomes Rio-in-Europe during two weeks of carnival action.

May–Jun Dolphins are regularly spotted off the coast of Lošinj.

Jul–Aug Rab Island lets its hair down with a fashion week and DJ festival.

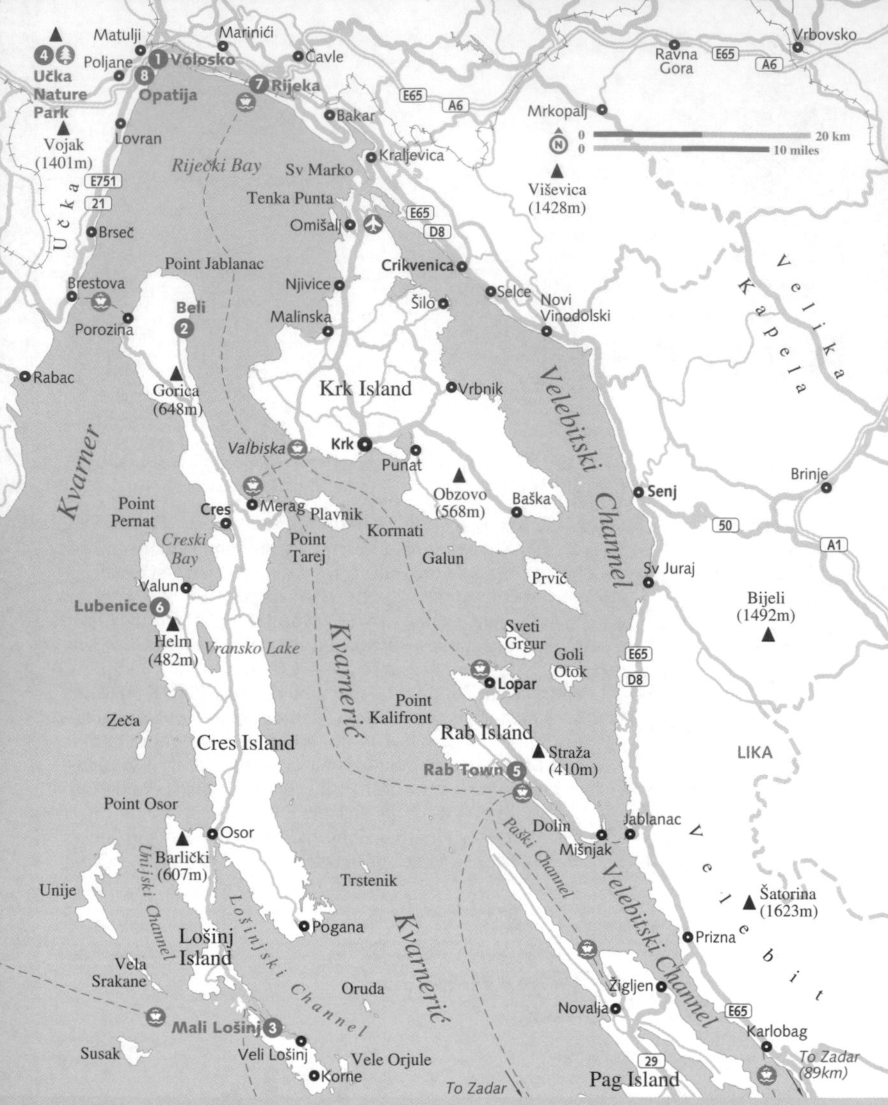

Kvarner Highlights

1 Sample Croatian specialties in **Volosko** (p142), a diner's delight

2 Learn all about griffon vultures and trek their domain at **Beli** (p152) on the island of Cres

3 Swim the numerous pristine **remote coves** (p157) south of Mali Lošinj

4 Hike, bike or even just drive through breathtaking **Učka Nature Park** (p142)

5 Wander the cobbled streets of majestic, medieval **Rab Town** (p161)

6 Look isolation in the eye at **Lubenice** (p154) and wonder at its beauty and hardship

7 Take in the panoramic views from Rijeka's **Trsat Castle** (p133)

8 Walk past grandiose Habsburg mansions along the promenade in **Opatija** (p139)

KVARNER COAST

Rijeka

POP 128,735

Rijeka, Croatia's third-largest city, is an intriguing blend of gritty port and Habsburg grandeur. Most people rush through en route to the islands or Dalmatia, but those who pause will discover charm and culture. Blend in with the coffee-sipping locals on the bustling Korzo pedestrian strip, take in the city museums and visit the imposing hilltop fortress of Trsat. Rijeka also boasts a good nightlife, intriguing festivals and Croatia's most colourful carnival.

Despite some regrettable architectural ventures in the outskirts of the city, much of the centre is replete with ornate Austro-Hungarian-style buildings. It is a surprisingly verdant city once you've left its concrete core, which contains Croatia's largest port, with ships, cargo and cranes lining the waterfront.

Rijeka is a vital transport hub, but as there's no real beach in the city (and hotel options are few) most people base themselves in nearby Opatija.

History

Following their successful conquest of the indigenous Illyrian Liburnians, the Romans established a port here called Tarsaticae. Slavic tribes migrated to the region in the 7th century and built a new settlement within the old Roman town.

The town changed feudal masters – from German nobility to the Frankopan dukes of Krk – before becoming part of the Austrian empire in the late 15th century. Rijeka was an important outlet to the sea for the Austrians and a new road was built in 1725 connecting Vienna with the Kvarner coast. This spurred economic development, especially shipbuilding, the industry that has remained the centrepiece of Rijeka's economy ever since.

With the birth of the Austro-Hungarian Dual Monarchy in 1867, Rijeka was given over to the jurisdiction of the Hungarian government. Imposing municipal buildings were constructed and a new railway linked the city to Zagreb, Budapest and Vienna, bringing the first tourists to the Kvarner Gulf.

Between 1918, when Italian troops seized Rijeka and Istria, and 1942, when Rijeka became part of postwar Yugoslavia, it changed hands several times, with sporadic periods as a free city. In 1991 Rijeka became part of independent Croatia but still retains a sizeable Italian minority who have their own newspaper, *La Voce del Popolo*.

Sights

Korzo, the main pedestrian promenade, was built as a commercial avenue on the site of the demolished town walls.

The maze of streets and squares in the ancient core of Rijeka is excellently marked with multilingual plaques explaining the history of each sight. Pick up a map of this **walking route**, called Turistička Magistrala, from the tourist office.

Trsat Castle CASTLE

(adult/concession 15/5KN; ⌚9am-8pm May-Oct, to 5pm Nov-Apr) High on a hill above the city is this semiruined 13th-century fortress. Vistas from its bastions and ramparts are magnificent, looking down the Rječina river valley to the docks, Adriatic and

CYCLING THE KVARNER

Kvarner offers a variety of options for biking enthusiasts, from gentle rides to heart-pumping climbs on steep island roads. There are several trails around Opatija; two easier paths depart from Mt Kastav (360m), while a challenging 4½-hour adventure goes from Lovran to Učka Nature Park. Lošinj offers a moderately difficult 2½-hour route that starts and ends in Mali Lošinj. On Krk, a leisurely two-hour ride from Krk Town shows you meadows, fields and hamlets of the little-visited island's interior. A biking route from Rab Town explores the virgin forests of the Kalifront Peninsula. On Cres, a 50km trail takes you from the marina at Cres Town past the medieval hilltop village of Lubenice and the seaside gem of Valun.

For details on these itineraries, ask at any tourist office for the *Kvarner by Bicycle* brochure, which outlines 19 routes across the region. The websites www.kvarner.hr and www.pedala.hr both have details of rides in this region.

Rijeka

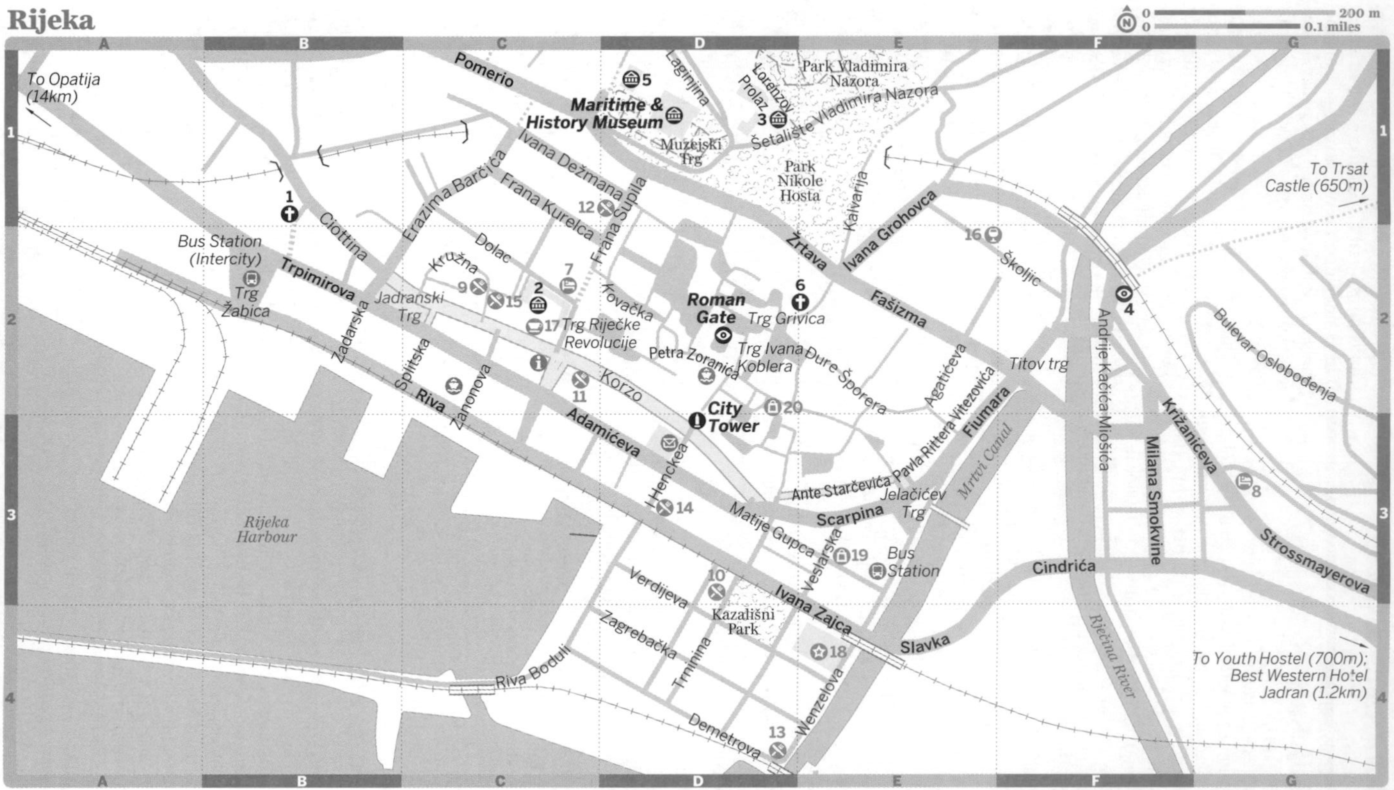

0 — 200 m
0 — 0.1 miles

To Opatija (14km)
Pomerio
Maritime & History Museum
Laginjina
Lorenzov Prolaz
Park Vladimira Nazora
Šetalište Vladimira Nazora
Muzejski Trg
Park Nikole Hosta
Kalvarija
To Trsat Castle (650m)
Ivana Dežmana
Erazima Barčića
Frana Kurelca
Frana Supila
Ciottina
Bus Station (Intercity)
Trg Žabica
Trpimirova
Dolac
Kružna
Jadranski Trg
Zadarska
Splitska
Zanonova
Riva
Trg Riječke Revolucije
Kovačka
Roman Gate
Trg Grivica
Trg Ivana Koblera
Petra Zoranića
Korzo
City Tower
Adamićeva
Žrtava Fašizma
Ivana Grohovca
Školjic
Titov trg
Đure Šporera
Agatićeva
Pavla Rittera Vitezovića
Fiumara
Mrtvi Canal
Ante Starčevića
Jelačićev Trg
Scarpina
Henckea
Matije Gupca
Vestarska
Bus Station
Verdijeva
Kazališni Park
Ivana Zajca
Slavka
Zagrebačka
Trninina
Wenzelova
Demetrova
Riva Boduli
Rijeka Harbour
Andrije Kačića Miošića
Milana Smokvine
Križanićeva
Bulevar Oslobođenja
Strossmayerova
Cindrića
Rječina River
To Youth Hostel (700m); Best Western Hotel Jadran (1.2km)

1, 2, 3, 4, 5, 6, 7, 8, 9, 10, 11, 12, 13, 14, 15, 16, 17, 18, 19, 20

A B C D E F G
1 2 3 4

Rijeka

Top Sights
City Tower ... D3
Maritime & History Museum ... D1
Roman Gate ... D2

Sights
1 Capuchin Church of Our Lady of Lourdes ... B1
2 Museum of Modern & Contemporary Art ... C2
3 Natural History Museum ... D1
4 Petar Kružić Stairway ... F2
5 Rijeka City Museum ... D1
6 St Vitus Cathedral ... E2

Sleeping
7 Grand Hotel Bonavia ... C2
8 Hotel Neboder ... G3

Eating
9 Bracera ... C2
10 City Market ... D3
11 Food City ... C2
12 Mlinar ... D1
13 Na Kantunu ... D4
14 Restaurant Spagho ... D3
15 Zlatna Školjka ... C2

Drinking
16 Caffe Jazz Tunel ... E2
17 Filodrammatica Bookshop Cafe ... C2

Entertainment
18 Croatian National Theatre Ivan Zajc ... E4

Shopping
19 Happy Hobby ... E3
20 Mala Galerija ... D2

distant island of Krk. The present structure was built by the Frankopan dukes of Krk, but the latest facelift was done in 1824 when Irish-born count Laval Nugent, a commander in the Austrian army, bought the castle and had it restored in a romantic Classicist-Biedermeier design. The ancient Greek–style Nugent family mausoleum houses a gallery, while underground a former dungeon hosts occasional exhibits. During summer, the fortress features concerts, theatre performances and fashion shows. The open-air cafe (open until midnight in summer) is a wonderful spot to take in the views.

Church of Our Lady of Trsat CHURCH
(Crkva Gospe Trsatske; Frankopanski trg; 8am-5pm) This church is a centuries-old magnet for believers. According to legend, the angels carrying the house of the Virgin Mary from Nazareth rested here in the late 13th century before moving it to Loreto in Italy. Pilgrims started trickling into the chapel erected on the site, and then pouring in when the pope donated an icon of Mary in 1367. The famous painting is on the main altar behind a magnificent wrought-iron gate. Check out the offerings of votive gifts across the baroque cloister and make an appointment to see the valuable sacral-art collection in the treasury, where you can view a 15-minute film about the church. To follow in the pilgrims' steps, climb the **Petar Kružić Stairway** from Titov trg, built in 1531 for the faithful on their way to Our Lady of Trsat. The steep stairs are lined with chapels dedicated to saints, once used as rest stops for the pilgrims. For an easier way up, take a quick ride on city bus 2 to Trsat Castle.

City Monuments MONUMENTS
(Trg Ivana Koblera) One of the few buildings to have survived the earthquake, the distinctive yellow **City Tower** (Gradski Torani; Korzo) was originally a gate from the seafront to the city. The Habsburgs added the baroque decorations after the disaster, including the portal with coats-of-arms and busts of emperors. The still-functioning clock was mounted in 1873.

Pass under the City Tower to the **Roman Gate** (Stara Vrata). This plain archway marks the former entrance to Praetorium, an ancient military complex, the remains of which you can see in a small excavation area.

Maritime & History Museum MUSEUM
(Pomorski i Povijesni Muzej Hrvatskog Primorja; www.ppmhp.hr; Muzejski trg 1; adult/concession 10/5KN; 9am-4pm Tue-Fri, 9am-1pm Sat) Housed in the Governor's Palace, this is a splendid showcase of Hungarian architecture. Pick up the small leaflet in English for a vivid picture of life among seafarers, with model ships, sea charts, navigation instruments and portraits of captains. Longer opening hours during summer.

Astronomical Centre OBSERVATORY
(Astronomski Centar; www.rijekasport.hr; Sveti Križ 33; 8am-11pm Tue-Sat) High on a hill in the east of the city, Croatia's first astronomical centre is a striking modern complex encompassing an observatory, planetarium

and study centre. There's a planetarium program at 9pm (10pm on Wednesday for English, French and Italian speakers). The observatory is open to the public on Thursday and Saturday evenings (weather permitting). To get here, catch bus 7A from the centre.

Natural History Museum NATURAL HISTORY MUSEUM
(Prirodoslovni Muzej; www.prirodoslovni.com; Lorenzov Prolaz 1; adult/concession 10/5KN; ⌚9am-7pm Mon-Sat, to 3pm Sun) This museum, in a very grand 19th-century villa, is devoted to the geology, botany and sealife of the Adriatic area. There's a small aquarium, exhibits on sharks and rays, and lots of bugs. Don't miss the delightful adjacent botanical garden with over 2000 native plant species.

Museum of Modern & Contemporary Art ART GALLERY
(Muzej Moderne i Suvremene Umjetnosti; www.mmsu.hr; Dolac 1; adult/concession 10/5KN; ⌚10am-1pm & 6-9pm Mon-Fri, to 1pm Sat) On the 2nd floor of the university library, this small museum puts on high-quality rotating shows, from street photography to contemporary Croatian artists.

St Vitus Cathedral CATHEDRAL
(Katedrala Svetog Vida; Trg Grivica 11; ⌚7am-noon & 4.30-7pm Mon-Sat, to noon Sun Jun-Aug, 6.30am-noon Sep-May) North of the Roman Gate is the cathedral, built by the Jesuit order in 1638 on the site of an older church and dedicated to Rijeka's patron saint. Massive marble pillars support the central dome, under which are housed baroque altars and a 13th-century Gothic crucifix.

Rijeka City Museum MUSEUM
(Muzej Grada Rijeke; Muzejski Trg 1/1; adult/concession 10/5KN, Mon admission free; ⌚10am-1pm & 5-8pm Mon-Fri, to 1pm Sat) Housed in a 1970s cubist structure, this modest museum has a small permanent eclectic collection of exhibits that have a connection to the city (including a couple of torpedoes, which were invented here). Also hosts temporary events.

Capuchin Church of Our Lady of Lourdes CHURCH
(Crkva Gospe Lurdske; Kapucinske Stube 5; ⌚8am-noon & 4-6pm) This church, with its ornate neo-Gothic facade, dates from 1904 and stands above an elaborate Italianate double staircase. It's right by the bus station.

Festivals & Events

Rijeka Carnival CARNIVAL
(www.ri-karneval.com.hr) The largest carnival in Croatia, Rikeja Carnival has two weeks of partying that involves pageants, street dances, concerts, masked balls, exhibitions and a parade. Check out the *zvončari,* masked men clad in animal skins who dance and ring loud bells to frighten off evil spirits. Festivities are between late January and early March, depending on when Easter falls.

Hartera MUSIC
(www.hartera.com) A cool, annual electronic music festival with DJs and artists from across Europe. It's held in a former paper factory on the banks of the Rječina River over three days in mid-June.

Rijeka Summer Nights THEATRE
(Riječke Ljetne Noći) Concerts are held at the Croatian National Theatre in June and July.

Sleeping

Prices in Rijeka hotels are generally consistent year-round except at Carnival time, when you can expect to pay a surcharge; book well in advance at this time. There are few private rooms in Rijeka itself; the tourist office lists these on its website. Nearby Opatija has a lot more accommodation.

Grand Hotel Bonavia HOTEL €€€
(☎357 100; www.bonavia.hr; Dolac 4; s/d from 800/977KN; P❄@☜) Right in the heart of town, this striking glass-fronted modernist building is Rijeka's top hotel. The rooms are well equipped and comfort levels are high (though perhaps their design is slightly too non-specific and streamlined). There's a well-regarded restaurant, a spa and a stylish pavement cafe.

Best Western Hotel Jadran HOTEL €€€
(☎216 600; www.jadran-hoteli.hr; Šetalište XIII Divizije 46; s/d from 706/833KN; P❄@☜) Located 2km east of the centre, this is an attractive four-star hotel: book a seaview room and revel in the tremendous Adriatic vistas from your balcony right above the water. An excellent breakfast and wi-fi access are included in the rate; there's a tiny beach below, too.

Hotel Neboder HOTEL €€
(☎373 538; www.jadran-hoteli.hr; Strossmayerova 1; s/d from 462/578KN; P❄@) An iconic design, this modernist tower block might appeal to architecture students, for it was way

ahead of its time when it opened in 1939. Offers small, neat and modish rooms, most with balconies and amazing views; only the superior rooms have air-conditioning.

Youth Hostel HOSTEL €
(☎406 420; www.hfhs.hr; Šetalište XIII Divizije 23; dm/s/d 130/236/314KN; @☎) In the leafy residential area of Pečine, 2km east of the centre, this renovated 19th-century villa has clean, spacious (if plain) rooms and a communal TV area. It can get block-booked by school groups so reserve ahead. Skip the breakfast.

Eating

There's very little choice on Sundays, when most places are closed. Many cafes on Korzo serve light meals. Foodies should consider heading to nearby Volosko where there's a strip of high-quality restaurants.

TOP CHOICE **Na Kantunu** SEAFOOD €€
(Demetrova 2; mains from 45KN) Ignore the grimy location alongside the port – the food here is excellent. It's all about fresh fish and seafood: choose the daily catch of your choice or let the staff prepare it house style. You can also choose the excellent octopus *brodet* (stew) with some chilled Croatian white, and end with a plate of crispy fruit pastry. The little terrace by the water is quiet and relaxed.

Kukuriku CROATIAN €€€
(☎691 519; www.kukuriku.hr; Trg Matka Laginje 1a, Kastav; 6-course meals 380-550KN; ⊙closed Mon Nov-Easter) This opulent yet modern hotel-restaurant is owned by slow-food pioneer Nenad Kukurin, who has a reputation for his innovative take on traditional Croatian recipes. Located in historic Kastav, Rijeka's hilltop suburb, it's worth the splurge. Bus 18 from Rijeka (and 33 and 37 from Opatija) will get you here.

Restaurant Spagho ITALIAN €
(Ivana Zajca 24a; mains from 40KN) A stylish, modern Italian place with exposed brickwork, art and hip seating that offers delicious and filling portions of pasta, pizza, salads, and meat and fish dishes. You can sample some good Croatian wine and olive oil here, too.

Zlatna Školjka SEAFOOD €€
(Kružna 12; mains from 65KN) Savour the superbly prepared seafood and choice Croatian wines at this formal maritime-themed restaurant. Daily specials such as *pečena hobotnica* (roast octopus) are chalked up on a blackboard.

Bracera PIZZERIA €€
(Kružna 12; mains from 60KN) Adjacent to Zlatna Školjka and run by the same owners, Bracera serves crusty pizza daily.

City Market MARKET €
(between Vatroslava Lisinskog & Trninina; ⊙7.30am-2pm Mon-Sat, to noon Sun) Excellent for seasonal fruit and vegetables.

Mlinar BAKERY €
(Frana Supila; items from 13KN; ⊙6am-8pm Mon-Fri, 6.30am-3pm Sat, 7am-1pm Sun) The best bakery in town, with delicious filled baguettes, wholemeal bread, croissants and *burek* (pastry stuffed with meat, spinach or cheese). There are several branches around.

Food City TAKEAWAY €
(Korzo; items from 12KN; ⊙24hr) Good for a quick bite.

MADE IN RIJEKA

Croatian design has really taken a turn in the past few years – there are quirky fashion and quality craft and design pieces to be had, at good prices. Look for the traditional Rijeka design known as *morčići*, a ceramic jewellery piece of a Moor wearing a turban. You can pick one up at **Mala Galerija** (www.mala-galerija.hr; Užarska 25).

One of the coolest places around is the charming Rijeka shop **Happy Hobby** (☎301 094; Matije Gupca 8; ⊙9am-7pm, Mon-Sat). The Rijeka-born designers whose work is sold here are Luka Jelušić, who makes the heart-stealing eco-friendly toys and olive wood lamps; Andrej Urem, who produces unusual palmtree candles; and Dejan Stanić, the creator of quirky lamps and lampshades. At the helm of the whole operation is the friendly Amna Šehović, who has a small fashion line in store. You can get bags, jewellery and even notebooks made out of recycled materials, or snap up one of the best-selling T-shirts and wooden badges printed with local sayings. If you want to bring back a memory of Croatia with a difference, this is the place.

Drinking

The main drags of Riva and Korzo are the best bet for a drink, with everything from lounge bars to no-nonsense pubs.

TOP CHOICE **Gradena** CAFE
(www.bascinskiglasi.hr; Trsat; 📶) Set in the grounds of the hilltop castle, this happening cafe-bar with chillout music and friendly service would rate anywhere. Chuck in *those* views and no wonder everyone lingers for hours longer than they'd intended.

Filodrammatica Bookshop Cafe CAFE
(☎498 141; www.vbz.hr; Korzo 28) A cafe and bar with a luxurious decor and a VBZ (Croatia's biggest publisher) bookshop at the back, Filodrammatica also prides itself on specialist coffees and fresh, single-source beans. Get a book, a coffee and sit back on one of the comfy sofas.

Caffe Jazz Tunel BAR
(☎327 116; www.jazztunel.com; Školjić 12; ⏰9am-2am Mon-Fri, 5pm-2am Sat) One of the city's most popular bars, this place is crowded all week long, but full to bursting on Friday and Saturday nights when you can find live music or DJs rocking the night away.

Entertainment

Croatian National Theatre Ivan Zajc THEATRE
(☎355 900; www.hnk-zajc.hr; Verdieva 5a) In 1885 the inaugural performance at this imposing theatre was lit by the city's first lightbulb. Today you can catch dramas in Croatian and Italian, as well as opera and ballet. Gustav Klimt painted some of the ceiling frescos.

Terminal BAR, NIGHTCLUB
(Lukobran bb) This is Rijeka's most glamorous club, replete with giant globe lights, bubblegum-coloured seating and stupendous harbour views. It draws a young, fashionable crowd who rave into the early hours.

Nina 2 NIGHTCLUB
(www.nina2.com; Adamićev Gat) This boat moored on the harbourfront offers daytime drinking and lots of night-time action, including house DJs and live bands.

Information

There are ATMs and exchange offices along Korzo and at the train station.

Hospital (☎658 111; Krešimirova 42)

Main Post Office (Korzo 13; ⏰7am-8pm Mon-Fri, to 2pm Sat) Has a telephone centre and an exchange office.

Tourist Information Centre (☎335 882; www.tz-rijeka.hr; Korzo 33a; ⏰8am-8pm Mon-Sat Apr-Sep, to 8pm Mon-Fri, to 2pm Sat Oct-Mar) Has good colour city maps, lots of brochures and private accommodation lists, though the staff can be aloof.

Getting There & Away

Air

Rijeka airport is mainly served by charter airlines.

Air Berlin (www.airberlin.com) Flies to German cities including Hamburg and Berlin, and Vienna.

Croatia Airlines (☎330 207; www.croatiaairlines.hr; Jelačićev Trg 5) Book international and domestic flights here, though there are currently no flights from Rijeka airport.

Ryanair (www.ryanair.com) The Irish budget airline flies to Rijeka from July to October every year.

Boat

Jadroagent (☎211 626; www.jadroagent.hr; Trg Ivana Koblera 2) Has information on all boats around Croatia.

Jadrolinija (☎211 444; www.jadrolinija.hr; Riječki Lukobran bb; ⏰8am-8pm Mon-Fri, 9am-5pm Sat & Sun) Sells tickets for the large coastal ferries that run all year between Rijeka and Dubrovnik on their way to Bari in Italy, via Split, Hvar, Korčula and Mljet. Other ferry routes include Rijeka–Cres–Mali–Lošinj and Rijeka–Rab–Pag. Check Jadrolinija's website for up-to-date schedules and prices. All ferries depart from the new ferry terminal at Riva 1.

Bus

If you fly into Zagreb, there is a Croatia Airlines van that goes directly from Zagreb airport to Rijeka daily (160KN, two hours, 3.30pm). It goes back to Zagreb from Rijeka at 5am. There are three daily buses to Trieste (60KN, 2½ hours) and one daily bus to Ljubljana (175KN, five hours). To get to Plitvice (142KN, four hours), you have to change in Otočac.

The **intercity bus station** (Trg Žabica) is in the town centre. For those who wish to store bags, there's a **garderoba** (Intercity Bus Station; left luggage per day 15KN; ⏰5.30am-10.30pm).

Car

AMC (☎338 800; www.amcrentacar.hr; Lukobran 4), based in the new ferry terminal building, has cars starting from 250KN per day. **Dollar & Thrifty Rental Car** (☎325 900; www.subrosa.hr), with a booth inside the intercity bus station, is also competitive.

BUSES FROM RIJEKA

DESTINATION	COST (KN)	DURATION	DAILY SERVICES
Baška	80	2¼hr	4-8
Dubrovnik	362-503	12-13hr	3-4
Krk	59	1-2hr	14
Pula	97	2¼hr	8
Rab	135	3hr	2-3
Rovinj	90	1-2hr	4
Split	253-330	8hr	6-7
Zadar	161-210	4-5hr	6-7
Zagreb	137-160	2¼-3hr	13-15

Train

The **train station** (☎213 333; Krešimirova 5) is about a 10-minute walk east of the city centre. Seven daily trains run to Zagreb (100KN, four to five hours). Heading south, there's one daily connection to Split (170KN, eight hours), though it does leave at 5.45am and involves a change at Ogulin. Two direct daily services head to Ljubljana (98KN, three hours) and one daily train goes to Vienna (319KN to 525KN, nine hours). At the station, you can store your bags at the **garderoba** (left luggage per day 15KN; ⏲4.30am-10.30pm).

Getting Around

To/From the Airport

Rijeka Airport (☎842 040; www.rijeka-airport.hr) is on Krk Island, 30km from town. An airport bus meets all flights for the 40-minute ride to Jelačićev trg; it leaves from this same square for the airport two hours and 20 minutes before flight times. You can buy the ticket (28KN) on the bus. Taxis from the airport charge up to 300KN to the centre.

Bus

Rijeka has an extensive network of city buses that run from the **central bus station** (Jelačićev trg). Buy two-trip tickets for 18KN from any *tisak* (news-stand). A single ticket from the driver costs 12KN.

Rijeka also has a hop-on hop-off sightseeing bus (one day 80KN) that runs between major sights in Rijeka, Trsat and Opatija. For tickets and detailed schedules, visit the tourist office.

Taxi

Taxis are very reasonable in Rijeka (if you use the right firm). **Cammeo** (☎313 313) cabs are modern, inexpensive, have meters and are highly recommended; a ride in the central area costs 20KN.

Opatija

POP 7872

Just 15km west of Rijeka, Opatija is a genteel resort in a spectacular setting. The breathtaking location and the agreeable year-round climate made Opatija the most fashionable seaside resort for the Viennese elite during the Austro-Hungarian Empire. Between the world wars and during the Yugoslav period, however, the belle époque villas went into decline and Opatija lost its former lustre.

The grand residences of the wealthy have since been revamped and turned into upmarket hotels, with a particular accent on spa and health holidays. Foodies should flock to the clutch of fantastic restaurants in nearby Volosko. Forested hills slope down to the sparkling Adriatic, and the whole coastline is connected by a delightful waterfront promenade that stretches between pretty Volosko and Lovran. Don't expect great beaches (there aren't any), but there's still excellent swimming in the sheltered bays.

History

Until the 1840s Opatija was a minuscule fishing village with 35 houses and a church, but the arrival of wealthy Iginio Scarpa from Rijeka turned things around. He built Villa Angiolina (named after his wife) and surrounded it with species of exotic subtropical plants. The villa hosted European aristocrats aplenty (including the Austrian queen Maria Anna, wife of Ferdinand) and Opatija's classy reputation was sealed.

Opatija's development was also assisted by the completion of a rail link on the Vienna-Trieste line in 1873. Construction of

Opatija's first hotel, the Quarnero (today the Hotel Kvarner), began and wealthy visitors arrived en masse. It seemed everyone who was anyone was compelled to visit Opatija, including kings from Romania and Sweden, Russian tsars and the celebrities of the day.

Today Opatija remains a refined (some would say conservative) resort, very popular with German and Austrian senior citizens. It's not the place for wild nights or round-the-clock clubbing, and that's just how the regulars like it.

Sights & Activities

Lungomare PROMENADE

Lined with majestic villas and ample gardens, this wonderful promenade is a voyeur's dream and a walker's delight. It winds along the coast, past villa after villa, for 12km from Volosko to Lovran via the villages of Ičići and Ika. Along the way you can peer into the homes of the wealthy and marvel at their seafront palaces. The path weaves through exotic bushes, thickets of bamboo, a marina and rocky bays where you can throw down a towel and jump into the sea – a better option than Opatija's concrete beach.

Villa Angiolina HISTORICAL BUILDING

(Park Angiolina 1; 9am-1pm & 4.30-9.30pm Tue-Sun summer, shorter hr rest of year) The restored Villa Angiolina gives you the chance to view the interior of one of Opatija's grandest structures – a marvel of trompe l'œil frescos, Corinthian capitals, gilded mirrors and geometric floor mosaics – though the addition of plastic windows is unforgivable. The villa now houses the **Croatian Museum of Tourism**, a grand title for a modest collection of old photographs, postcards, brochures and posters tracing the history of travel, but there's always a well-presented exhibition that has a travel or tourism theme too. Don't miss a stroll around the verdant gardens that surround the villa, replete with gingko trees, sequoias, holm oaks, Japanese camellia (Opatija's symbol) and even a little open-air theatre where there are costumed recitals.

Sleeping

There are no real budget hotels in Opatija, but there's plenty of value in the midrange and top end. **Liburnia Hotels** (710 444; www.liburnia.hr) manages 15 hotels in the area and is a good bet for getting a room. Opatija gets booked up over the Christmas holidays, so reserve ahead for this time.

Private rooms are abundant but a little more expensive than in other areas; expect to pay around 170 to 240KN per person. The travel agencies listed all find private accommodation.

There are a few camping grounds.

TOP CHOICE **Hotel Ambasador** HOTEL €€€

(710 444; www.liburnia.hr; Feliksa Perišića 1; s/d 915/1350KN; P ❄ 📶) Opatija's five-star wonderchild is the result of a recent refurbishment that makes it rank among the world's top-class establishments. Choose from the twelve uberplush doubles or eight apartments on the executive 10th floor – the beds are firm and grand, the balconies sunny and large, and the pool area (downstairs) sleek and perfect for a cocktail-in-hand look. It's a splash-out to remember.

Villa Ariston HISTORIC HOTEL €€

(271 379; www.villa-ariston.com; Ulica Maršala Tita 179; s/d 600/800KN; P ❄ @ 📶) With a gorgeous location beside a rocky cove this historic hotel has celeb cachet in spades (Coco Chanel and the Kennedys are former guests). The interior remains grand and impressive, with a sweeping staircase, chandeliers and plenty of period charm, and you can gaze out to the gulf from the restaurant terrace.

Hotel Mozart HOTEL €€€

(718 260; www.hotel-mozart.hr; Obala Maršala Tita 138; r from 800KN; P ❄ 📶) The beautifully decorated classic rooms harmonise perfectly with the Secession-style halls, dining room and rosy facade. It's in the centre of town and provides a high standard of comfort. Rates are the same all year.

Design Hotel Astoria HOTEL €€

(706 350; www.hotel-astoria.hr; Ulica Maršala Tita 174; r from 800KN; P ❄ @ 📶) Bored with all that antiquated Habsburg style? Then the sleek, understated rooms here should fit the bill nicely: check out the subtle colour schemes and balconies with magnificent views of the Kvarner coast.

Hotel Opatija HOTEL €€

(271 388; www.hotel-opatija.hr; Trg Vladimira Gortana 2/1; r from 486KN; P ❄ @ 🏊) The setting in a Habsburg-era mansion is the high point at this large hilltop three-star with comfortable rooms, an amazing terrace, a small indoor seawater pool and lovely gardens (it even has its own maze!).

Hotel Kvarner Amalia HISTORIC HOTEL €€€
(☎271 233; www.liburnia.hr; Pave Tomašića 1-4; s/d 578/1039KN; P ❄ @ ≋) Opatija's oldest hotel offers a whiff of jet-set charm with indoor and outdoor pools, fabulous grounds and ornate reception areas (but the bedrooms are less grand). The Amalia annexe has moderate rates for such an upmarket address.

Medveja CAMPGROUND €
(☎291 191; medveja@liburnia.hr; per adult/tent 44/32KN; ⊙Easter–mid-Oct) On a pretty pebble cove 10km south of Opatija; has apartments and mobile homes for rent too.

Autocamp Opatija CAMPGROUND €
(☎704 836; Liburnijska 46, Ičići; adult/tent 39/29KN; ⊙Apr-Oct) Enjoys a nice pine forest location close to Ičići beach.

Eating

Maršala Tita is lined with serviceable restaurants that offer pizza, grilled meat and fish, but don't expect anything outstanding. Head to nearby Volosko for fine dining and regional specialities.

For self-catering there's a **supermarket-deli** (Ulica Maršala Tita 80).

Istranka ISTRIAN €
(Bože Milanovića 2; mains from 55KN) This atmospheric little *konoba* (simple family-run establishment) specialises in Istrian cuisine such as *maneštra* (vegetable and bean soup), and, of course, you'll find plenty of truffle flavour dotted around the menu. There's a shady side terrace (with no view) and live traditional folk music some evenings.

Bevanda INTERNATIONAL €€€
(Zert 8; mains from 180KN) A marble pathway leads to this amazing-looking restaurant, which enjoys a huge ocean-facing terrace complete with Grecian columns and hip monochrome seating (though the bland piped muzak spoils the atmosphere). A short modern menu features terrific fresh fish and meat dishes – try the rolled duckling breast with pistachio and raisin risotto.

Kaneta CROATIAN €
(Nova Cesta 64; mains from 50KN) This unassuming family restaurant specialises in big flavours and generous portions: feast on roast veal shanks (order ahead), steak with gorgonzola, game and risottos. The wine list is well chosen.

Drinking & Entertainment

Opatija is a pretty sedate place, and hotel terraces and Viennese-style coffeehouses are popular with the mature clientele, though there are a few stylish bars too.

Tantra BAR
(Lido) Jutting out into the Gulf of Kvarner, this is the only slightly bohemian joint in town. It's a great place to spend the day, with stylish sun loungers and a manmade beach just below.

Hemingway LOUNGE BAR
(Zert 2) A very sleek bar ideal for a cocktail session with cool seating and distant views of the Rijeka skyline. It's the original venue of what's now a nationwide chain; there's an adjoining restaurant too.

Disco Seven NIGHT CLUB
(www.discoseven.hr; Ulica Maršala Tita 125) Intimate club right on the seafront that features upcoming Croatian DJs. Fairly mainstream dance sounds are the order of the day.

Information

Ulica Maršala Tita has numerous ATMs and travel agencies eager to change money. There's free wi-fi in central Opatija and Volosko.

Da Riva (☎272 990; www.da-riva.hr; Ulica Maršala Tita 170) A good source for private accommodation, and runs excursions around Croatia.

GI Turizam (☎273 030; www.tourgit.com; Ulica Maršala Tita 65) Finds private accommodation, books excursions, rents cars and changes money.

Linea Verde (☎701 107; www.lineaverde-croatia.com; Andrije Štangera 42, Volosko) Specialist agency with trips to Risnjak and Učka Nature Park and gourmet tours around Istria.

Post Office (Eugena Kumičića 4; ⊙7am-8pm Mon-Fri, to 2pm Sat) Behind the market.

Tourist Office (☎271 310; www.opatija-tourism.hr; Ulica Maršala Tita 128; ⊙8am-10pm Mon-Sat, 5-9pm Sun Jul & Aug, 8am-7pm Mon-Sat Apr-Jun & Sep, to 4pm Mon-Sat Oct-Mar) This office has knowledgeable staff, lots of maps, leaflets and brochures.

Getting There & Away

Bus 32 runs through the centre of Rijeka along Adamićeva to the Opatija Riviera (20KN, 15km) as far as Lovran every 20 minutes daily until late in the evening.

UČKA NATURE PARK

One of Croatia's best-kept natural secrets, this 160-sq-km park lies just 30 minutes from the Opatija Riviera. Comprised of the Učka mountain massif and the adjacent Ćićarija plateau, it's officially split between Kvarner and Istria. Vojak (1401m), its highest peak, affords sublime views of the Italian Alps and the Bay of Trieste on clear days.

Much of the area is covered by beech forests, but there are also sweet chestnut trees, oaks and hornbeam. Sheep graze the alpine meadows, golden eagles fly overhead, brown bears roam and endemic bellflowers blossom.

Well-informed staff at the **park office** (☎293 753; www.pp-ucka.hr; Liganj 42; ⏲8am-4.30pm Mon-Fri) in Lovran will help plan a trip. There are also two seasonal info points: one at **Poklon** (⏲9am-6pm mid-Jun–mid-Sep) and another at **Vojak** (⏲9am-6pm mid-Jun–mid-Sep).

The spectacular canyon of **Vela Draga** on the eastern side of the park is an astounding sight, its valley floor scattered with limestone pillars or 'fairy chimneys'. Raptors, including kestrels and peregrine falcons, can be seen cruising the thermals here, and eagle owls and wallcreepers are also present. From the highway, it's a lovely 15-minute descent along an interpretive trail to a viewpoint over the canyon.

Mala Učka, a half-abandoned village at over 995m above sea level, is highly intriguing. A few shepherds live here from May to October and you can buy delicious sheep's cheese from the house with green windows by the stream at the village's end. Just ask for *sir* (cheese).

Organised activities in the park include **mountain biking** and **trekking** on 150km of trails. Pick up a map (55KN) from the park office or the tourist office in Opatija. There's also **free-climbing** in the Vela Draga canyon, **horse riding** (80KN per hr) and **birdwatching**. **Paragliding** and **hang-gliding** can be organised through **Homo Volans Free Flying Club** (www.homo-volans.hr) in Opatija.

The park has several sleeping options including **Učka Lodge** (☎091 76 22 027; www.uckalodge.com; r from 800KN), an eco B&B deep in the woods, run by an English couple. The accommodation is in renovated traditional stone houses, with individual cabins made by local tradesmen. The cabins range from standard to deluxe, and some even have their own spa. Food is fresh and local (jam from forest fruits and sheep's cheese from the neighbours), and trips and tours can be arranged.

For country cooking, **Dopolavoro** (☎299 641; www.dopolavoro.hr; Učka 9; mains from 50KN; ⏲Tue-Sun) offers excellent game: deer steak with blueberries, wild boar with forest mushrooms as well as, er, bear. Bikes are available for rent beside the restaurant (25/95KN per hour/day).

Volosko

Volosko, 2km east of Opatija, is one of the prettiest places on this coastline, a fishing village that has also become something of a restaurant mecca in recent years. It's very scenic indeed – men repair fishing nets in the tiny harbour, while stone houses with flower-laden balconies rise up from the coast via a warren of narrow alleyways. This is not a tourist resort, and whether you're passing through for a drink or having a gourmet meal you'll enjoy the local ambience and wonderful setting.

Rijeka and Volosko are connected by bus, or you can walk along the coastal promenade from Opatija, a 30-minute stroll past bay trees, palms, figs and oaks and magnificent villas.

Sleeping

Apartments Komel APARTMENTS €

(☎701 007; www.apartmani-komel-opatija.hr; Put Uz Dol 8; apt 370-570KN; P❄) Seven apartments above the main coastal road, a five-minute walk from the shore. A bit garish, they're certainly not going to win any awards for decor or design, but they represent fair value and some are family-sized.

Eating & Drinking

TOP CHOICE **Tramerka** CROATIAN €€

(Andrije Mohorovičića 15; mains from 65KN; ⏲Tue-Sun) It doesn't have sea views, but this wonderful place scores on every other level. Actually, the setting is tremendous, a cave-like restaurant that occupies the cool, crepuscular interior of an ancient town house. Chef-patron Andrej Barbieri will expertly guide you through the short menu, chosen from the freshest available seafood (the *gregada* fish stew is just stupendous) and locally sourced meats.

TOP CHOICE Skalinada CROATIAN €€
(www.skalinada.org; Put Uz Dol 17; meals from 80KN) An intimate, highly atmospheric little bistro-style place with sensitive lighting, exposed stone walls and a creative menu of Croatian food (small dishes or mains) using seasonal and local ingredients. Many local wines are available by the glass. It's at the north end of the village high street.

Le Mandrać MEDITERRANEAN €€€
(Supilova Obala 10; dishes from 60KN) Innovative Mediterranean food, of quality – such as sea bass with Istrian olive oil – and accomplishment; try *limun buzara* (shellfish in lemon-foam sauce with a little local ham and parsley). The premises, including a glass box extension, are perhaps a tad flash for low-key Volosko but there's plenty of substance to the style.

Konoba Ribarnica Volosko FISH €
(Štangerova 5; mains from 45KN; ⊙closed dinner Sun) No cash to splash? This tiny shopfront has Volosko's cheapest fresh fish. Point to your desired sea creature – whatever is in season – and eat the well-prepared dish in a small downstairs dining room around the corner. Located on the main village road up from the harbour.

Caffe Bar Surf BAR
(Supilova Obala bb) Prefer somewhere very down to earth? This scruffy but very friendly little waterfront bar has a shady sea-facing terrace and a good mix of Rijeka trendies and fishing folk.

KRK ISLAND

Croatia's largest island, connected to the mainland by a bridge, Krk (Veglia in Italian) is also one of the busiest – in summer, Germans and Austrians stream over to its holiday houses, campsites and hotels. It's not the lushest or most beautiful island (in fact, it's overdeveloped), though its landscape is quiet varied, and you'll discover some wonderful and verdant landscapes in the south. You'll find Krk an easy place to visit, with good transport connections and infrastructure.

The northwestern coast of the island is rocky and steep with few settlements because of the fierce *bura* that whips the coast in winter. The climate is milder in the south, with more vegetation and beaches, coves and inlets. The major towns – Krk, Punat and Baška – are found on the forested southwestern coast.

Centrally located Krk Town makes a good base. Nearby Punat is the gateway for Košljun Island and monastery. Baška, on a wide pebble bay at the foot of a scenic mountain range, is a popular beach destination. On the east coast and off the beaten trail, Vrbnik is a cliff-top medieval village known for its *žlahtina* wine.

History

The oldest-known inhabitants of Krk were the Illyrian Liburnian tribe, followed by the Romans who settled on the northern coast. Krk was later incorporated into the Byzantine Empire, then passed between Venice and the Croatian-Hungarian kings.

In the 11th century Krk became the centre of the Glagolitic language. The oldest preserved example of the script was found in a former Benedictine abbey in Krk Town. Glagolitic was used here until the 19th century.

In 1358 Venice granted rule over the island to the Dukes of Krk, later known as the Frankopans, who became one of the richest and most powerful families in Croatia. Although vassals of Venice, they ruled with a measure of independence until 1480, when the last member of the line put the island under the protection of Venice.

Although tourism is the dominant activity on the island, there are two small shipyards in Punat and Krk, and some agriculture and fishing.

Getting There & Away

Krk is home to Rijeka Airport, the main hub for flights to the Kvarner, though it's relatively underused – a few low-cost and charter airlines fly here during the summer months. The Krk toll bridge links the northern part of the island with the mainland.

Twelve daily Jadrolinija car ferries link Valbiska with Merag (passenger/car 18/115KN, 30 minutes) on Cres in summer; during winter

WORTH A TRIP

ADVENTURE IN LIKA & GORSKI KOTAR

Having been heavily affected by the 1990s war, the regions of Lika and Karlovac – located between Zagreb and the coast – have resurfaced as one of Croatia's top adventure sports areas. Rushing rivers, high peaks and thick forests stretch from Karlovac and come up against the soaring Velebit mountain range where wolves and bears still run wild. Hiking is a huge attraction here, and hundreds of kilometres of trails cover the region, but you can also pop on a mountain bike and huff up the hills that way (check www.takeadventure.com). At **Linden Tree Retreat & Ranch** (☎053-685 616; www.lindenretreat.com; Velika Plan, Velebit Nature Park; tipi 672KN for four, lodges 1120KN for six) in Velebit Nature Park, a half-hour ride from Gospić, you can stay in tipis or one of two lodges. The highlights here are horseback rides (335KN for a two-hour jaunt, 970KN for a day trip), but you can also do guided hikes to nearby caves, mountain biking and mountain climbing. The food served in the restored 1924 log house on site uses delightful local foodstuffs such as wild edibles and *skripavac* cheese from the village. The region also has two incredible caves: the **Grabovača cave** (www.pp-grabovaca.hr) is so big that music concerts are held in its main hall; 75km south of Karlovac is the **Barać cave** (www.baraceve-spilje.hr), a smaller but no less fascinating space. Don't miss the watersports – Mrežnica river is fantastic for rafting with **Kanuking Avantura** (www.kanuking-avantura.hr), and Gacka river has great canoeing and wildlife spotting. Contact the local **tourist office** (www.tz-otocac.hr) for details of trips.

Another relatively isolated and rarely visited delight is **Risnjak National Park** (adult/concession 30/15KN), only 35km northeast of Rijeka. Part of the wooded Gorski Kotar region, it covers an area of 63 sq km and rises up to 1528m at its highest peak, Veliki Risnjak. The landscape is thickly forested with beech and pine trees, and carpeted with meadows and wildflowers. The bracing alpine breezes make it the perfect hideaway when the coastal heat and crowds become overpowering. Wildlife includes brown bears, lynx (*ris* in Croatian, after which the park is named), wolves, wild cats, wild boar, deer, chamois and 500 species of butterfly. Most of the park is unspoiled virgin forest, with only a few settlements. The **park information office** (☎836 133; ⏰9am-4pm Mon-Fri, to 6pm Sat & Sun) is just west of the village of Crni Lug. You'll find the region's best base, **Hotel Risnjak** (☎508 160; www.hotel-risnjak.hr; Lujzinska 36; s/d from 350/580KN; P 📶), is a great place with good rooms, a restaurant, and fitness and spa facilities, 14km west of the entrance in Delnice village. Many activities, including mountain biking, rafting, archery and even paragliding can be set up here. The best way to discover the park is to hike the Leska Path, a delightful 4.5km trail that begins at the park's entrance. It's an easy and shady walk punctuated by several dozen explanatory panels (in English) telling you all about the park's history, topography, geology, flora and fauna. You'll pass crystal-clear streams, forests of tall fir trees, bizarre rock formations, a feeding station for the deer, and a mountain hut with a picnic table. There's no public transport to the park. To get there by car, exit the main Zagreb–Rijeka motorway at Delnice and follow the signs.

And finally, the area hides a museum dedicated to one of Croatia's most interesting personalities, the scientist Nikola Tesla. The little village of Smiljan, Tesla's birthplace, sits beneath Velebit Mountain, off the A1 highway between Zagreb and Split, and holds the **Nikola Tesla Memorial Centre** (☎053 746 530; www.mcnikolatesla.hr; Smiljan; adult/concession 50/30KN; ⏰9am-8pm Tue-Sun, March-Nov), a multimedia centre and a platform for demonstrations, as well as his birthhouse and other biographical sights. The most fascinating are the replicas of his four most significant inventions: the electric motor, the 'Egg of Columbus,' the Tesla transformer, and the Tesla turbine, all of which have shaped the way we live in the modern world.

services are reduced but still regular. Split Tours operates a ferry link between Valbiska and Lopar (37KN/225, 1½ hours) on Rab four times daily in summer and twice daily the rest of the year when prices are reduced.

Rijeka and Krk Town are connected by nine to 13 daily bus services (56KN, one to two hours), some via Punat. Two daily buses continue on to Vrbnik (25KN, 35 minutes) from Monday to Friday. There are nine daily buses to Baška from

Krk Town (29KN, 45 minutes). All services are reduced, if running at all, on weekends.

There are six daily buses from Zagreb to Krk Town (179KN to 194KN, three to four hours). Note that some bus lines are more direct than some, which stop in every village en route. **Autotrans** (www.autotrans.hr) has two quick daily buses. Out of the summer season, all services are reduced.

To go from Krk to Cres and Lošinj on the bus, change at Malinska for the Lošinj-bound bus that comes from Rijeka or Zagreb, but check the departure and arrival times carefully on the website as the connection only works well at certain times of day.

Getting Around

Bus connections between towns are frequent because the many buses to and from Rijeka pick up passengers in all the island's main towns.

Krk Town

POP 3373

On the island's southwestern coast, Krk Town clusters around a medieval walled centre and, spreading out into the surrounding coves and hills, a modern development that includes a port, beaches, camping grounds and hotels. The seafront promenade can get seriously crowded in summer with tourists and weekending Croats, who spill into the narrow cobbled streets that make up the pretty old quarter.

Minus the crowds, this stone labyrinth is the highlight of Krk Town. The former Roman settlement still retains sections of the ancient city walls and gates, as well as the Romanesque cathedral and a 12th-century Frankopan castle.

You won't need more than a couple of hours to see these sights, but from a base in Krk Town it's easy to explore the rest of the island.

Sights

Cathedral of the Assumption CATHEDRAL
(Katedrala Uznešenja; Trg Svetog Kvirina; ⊗morning & evening Mass) On the site of a Roman baths and an early basilica, this imposing Romanesque structure dates from the 12th century. Note the rare early Christian carving of two birds eating a fish on the first column next to the apse. The left nave features a Gothic chapel from the 15th century, with the coats-of-arms of the Frankopan princes who used it as a place of worship.

St Quirinus CHURCH
(Trg Svetog Kvirina; admission 7KN; ⊗9am-1pm Mon-Sat) The cathedral's 18th-century campanile topped with an angel statue is shared with the adjoining St Quirinus, an early Romanesque church built of white stone and dedicated to the town's patron saint. The **church museum** is a treasury of sacral art, with a silver altarpiece of the Virgin Mary from 1477 and a polyptych by Paolo Veneziano.

Kaštel FORTRESS
(Trg Kamplin) This crumbling old seafront fortress once guarded the old town from pirate attacks. There's also a 12th-century tower that was used as a Frankopan courtroom and another round defence tower built by Venetians. The castle is now an open-air venue for summer concerts and plays.

Activities

Pick up an island map from the tourist office and get out and explore the lanes around Krk Town by bike: **Speed** (☎221 587; S Nikolića 48) and **Losko** (☎091 91 50 264), based at the bus station, both have bikes to rent from 80KN a day.

Dive schools including **Diving Centre Krk** (☎222 563; www.fun-diving.com; Braće Juras 3) and **Adria Krk** (☎604 248; Creska 12) offer courses and dives around the island. Some of the best dive sites are *Peltastis*, the wreck of a 60m Greek cargo ship, and the Punta Silo and Kamenjak reefs, which are rich with sealife including sea snails and octopi, as well as a variety of underwater caves.

Krk's excellent **Wakeboard Club Krk** (☎091 27 27 302; www.wakeboarder.hr; 5 rounds 50KN; ⊗Apr-Sep) is a 650m-long cableway for wakeboarding and waterskiing, running at a speed of 32km/h. Don't be intimidated: most of its clients are absolute beginners. Or if you're more experienced, wakeboards, wakeskates and wetsuits can be hired here too. It's located between Krk Town and Punat.

Festivals & Events

Every July and August the **Krk Summer Festival** hosts concerts, plays and dances in an ancient Franciscan monastery (located 500m north of the harbour) and on the squares of the old town. The tourist office has schedules. The **Krk Fair** is a Venetian-inspired event that takes over the town for three days in mid-August with concerts, people dressed in medieval costumes, and stalls selling traditional food.

Sleeping

The old town only has one hotel; all the others are located in a large complex east of the centre and are very family orientated. Consult travel agencies for private accommodation. Note that the only hostel in town is pretty rundown.

TOP CHOICE **Hotel Marina** BOUTIQUE HOTEL €€€
(☎221 357; www.hotelikrk.hr; Obala Hrvatske Mornarice 6; s/d 590/1460KN; P ❄ @ ☎) This is the only hotel in the old town, and it's a good one. It enjoys a prime waterfront location and you can gaze out over the harbour and yachts from the balcony of some of the 10 deluxe units (book a room with a terrace for the best views). All boast stylish contemporary decor and hip bathrooms.

Bor HOTEL €€
(☎220 200; www.hotelbor.hr; Šetalište Dražica 5; s/d from 480/960KN; ⊙Apr-Oct; P ☎) Very close to a little beach and attractive rocky shoreline, this small hotel has 22 modest rooms, some with balconies and a lovely front terrace. It's surrounded by mature pines and only a 10-minute walk from the centre. Rates do drop markedly in the low season.

Autocamp Ježevac CAMPGROUND €
(☎221 081; camping@valamar.com; Plavnička bb; per adult/site 50/62KN; ⊙mid-Apr–mid-Oct) Beachfront campground with shady pitches located on old farming terraces; good swimming and barbecue sites. It's a 10-minute walk southwest of town.

Politin FKK CAMPGROUND €
(☎221 351; www.camping-adriatic.com; per adult/site 48/58KN; ⊙mid-Apr–Sep; ☎) Attractive naturist camp on the wooded Prniba Peninsula, a short distance from town, with views of Plavnik and Cres islands. There's free wireless internet and good, renovated shower blocks.

Camping Bor CAMPGROUND €
(☎221 581; www.camp-bor.hr; Crikvenička 10; per adult/site 57/34KN; ⊙Apr-Oct) On a hill of olive groves and pine forests, this campground has well-kept shower blocks and a restaurant. It's a 10-minute walk west of the seafront.

Eating

Konoba Nono CROATIAN €
(Krčkih Iseljenika 8; mains from 40KN) A rustic-style place that's renowned for its Krk cooking, try the signature dish *šurlice sa junećim* (pasta topped with goulash). Nono even has its own olive-oil press, and the owners will encourage you to sample their home brew.

Galija PIZZERIA €
(www.galija-krk.com; Frankopanska 38; mains from 45KN) Set well back from the seafront in the narrow lanes of the old town, this atmospheric, convivial old stone building is part *konoba*, part pizzeria. Munch your margarita or *vagabondo* pizza, pasta, risotto, grilled meat or fresh fish under beamed ceilings.

Konoba Šime CROATIAN €
(Antuna Mahnića 1; mains from 45KN) You can't beat the setting on the harbourfront, and the cooking at this popular place is probably the best on this busy strip: pasta, *ćevapčići* (small spicy sausages of minced beef, lamb or pork) and fresh Adriatic squid.

There's a well-stocked Konzum supermarket on Stjepana Radića for self-catering.

Drinking & Entertainment

Casa dei Frangipane CAFE-BAR
(Šetalište Svetog Bernardina bb) This stylish place has a wonderful seafront location and its cafe terrace offers a fine coffee selection (plus a full cocktail list). Check out the cakes, including fresh baklava. Doubles as a night-time venue: the clubby interior hosts DJ and dance action.

Caffettaria XVIII CAFE
(Vela Placa 1; ☎) Right on the main square, this is the perfect place for people-watching and a delicious coffee in the shade. There is also good wi-fi and nice sofas to lounge on.

Volsonis BAR, NIGHTCLUB
(Vela Placa) Cocktails and lounge music is the scene at this slick place that has an outdoor terrace and cave-like interior (there's even a collection of archaeological relics). Live DJs do their thing on weekend nights.

Information

Aurea (☎221 777; www.aurea-krk.hr; Vršanska 26l; ⊙8am-2pm & 3-8pm) Offers island excursions by boat and bus. Can book private accommodation.

Autotrans (☎222 661; www.autotrans-turizam.com; Šetalište Svetog Bernardina 3) Based in the bus station, this agency finds private accommodation and sells bus tickets.

Erste Banka (Trg Bana Josipa Jelačića 4) Changes money and has an ATM.

Hospital (☎221 224; Vinogradska bb)

Krk Sistemi (☎222 999; Šetalište Svetog Bernardina 3; internet access per 20min 10KN; ⏰9am-2pm & 5-10pm Mon-Sat, 10am-9pm Sun) Sells wireless internet vouchers and has terminals for surfing.

Post Office (Bodulska bb; ⏰7.30am-9pm Mon-Fri, to 2pm Sat) You can get cash advances on your credit cards here.

Main Tourist Office (☎220 226; Vela Placa 1; ⏰8am-3pm Mon-Fri)

Seasonal Tourist Office (☎220 226; www.tz-krk.hr; Obala Hrvatske Mornarice bb; ⏰8am-8pm Mon-Sat, 8am-2pm Sun Jun-Oct & Easter-May) This seasonal tourist office distributes brochures and materials, including a map of hiking paths. Out of season, go to the main tourist office nearby.

WORTH A TRIP

BEACH PEACE

Many of Krk's best beaches are heavily developed and crowded in summer. For more tranquillity, head south of Punat on the lonely road that heads to Stara Baška (not southeast to Baška). It's a superlative drive, through steep parched hills and lunar scenery. Stara Baška itself is a run-of-the-mill tourist sprawl of holiday homes and caravan parks, but if you pull up 500m before the first campsite there is a series of gorgeous pebble-and-sand coves with wonderful swimming. You'll have to park on the road, and then walk down one of the rocky paths for five minutes to get to the coast.

Punat

POP 1789

Eight kilometres southeast of Krk is the small town of Punat, frequented by yachties for its marina. The main attraction here is the islet of **Košljun**, only a 10-minute boat ride away. The tiny island contains a 16th-century **Franciscan monastery** (admission 20N; ⏰9.30am-6pm Mon-Sat, 10.30am-12.30pm Sun) built on the site of a 12th-century Benedictine abbey. Highlights include a large, appropriately chilling *Last Judgment*, painted in 1653 and housed in the monastery church, and the small museum with a display of other religious paintings, an ethnographic collection and a rare copy of Ptolemy's *Atlas* printed in Venice in the late 16th century. Take a little extra time to stroll around the forested island with 400 plant species.

It's easy to get to Košljun via buses from Krk Town. Taxi boats shuttle you across from the harbourside (30KN return). In summer there'll be plenty of interested parties with whom you can share a boat.

With an attractive promenade lined with *gelaterias* and decent beaches on its outskirts, Punat could also serve as an alternative place to stay, though it is very staid. Better to head along the coast where there are two camping grounds. The very large **Campsite Pila** (☎854 020; www.hoteli-punat.hr; Šetalište Ivana Brusića 2; per adult/site 45/132KN; ⏰Apr–mid-Oct; @), just south of the town centre, suits organised types who like a range of facilities – you'll find an internet cafe and very smart washrooms here, and it's run ecologically (including solar power). Alternatively, the naturist **FKK Konobe** (☎854 049; www.hoteli-punat.hr; Obala 94; per adult/site 53/102KN; ⏰mid-Apr–Sep; wi-fi), about 3km south, has a less developed feel and enjoys a fine location next to a blue-flag beach.

Vrbnik

POP 947

Perched on a 48m cliff overlooking the sea, Vrbnik is a beguiling medieval village of steep, arched streets. It's not a real secret (tour groups pass through from time to time), but most of the year it's a peaceful, unhurried place.

Vrbnik was once the centre of the Glagolitic language and repository for many Glagolitic manuscripts. The language was kept alive by priests, who were always plentiful in the town since many young men entered the priesthood to avoid serving on Venetian galleys.

Now the town is a terrific place to soak up the vistas and sample the *žlahtina* white wine produced in the surrounding region. After wandering the tightly packed cobbled alleyways, descend to the town beach for some swimming.

The small **tourist office** (☎857 479; Placa Vrbničkog Statuta 4; ⏰8am-3pm Mon-Fri, 9am-1pm Sat & Sun Jul & Aug) has limited info. **Mare Tours** (☎604 400; www.mare-vrbnik.com;

Pojana 4) is an alternative source of information, and offers guided tours of the village and region, as well as private rooms.

Restaurant Nada (www.nada-vrbnik.hr; Glavača 22; mains from 55KN) is the most famous eatery on this side of the Krk, and justifiably so. The covered terrace upstairs is a good place to sample Krk lamb, *šurlice* (noodles) topped with meat goulash, scampi risotto or salted fish. Or descend to the cellar (March to November only) where you can snack on sheep's cheese, wine, prosciutto and olive oil surrounded by wine barrels. The Nada's owners also rent classy stone houses in town and just outside.

Four daily weekday buses travel from Krk Town to Vrbnik (30KN, 20 to 35 minutes), some via Punat, and back. There are no weekend services.

Baška

POP 904

The drive to the southern end of Krk Island is stunning, passing through a fertile valley that's bordered by eroded mountains. Eventually the road peters out at Baška, one of Krk's main resorts where there's a fine crescent beach set below barren hills. And with the dramatic peaks of the mainland directly opposite you're effectively enveloped by soaring highlands.

However, and this is a considerable caveat, in summer tourists are spread towel-to-towel, and what's otherwise a pretty, if slimline, pebble beach turns into a fight for your place under the sun. Baška's promenade is also lined with a tatty excess of souvenir stalls.

The small 16th-century core of Venetian town houses is pleasant enough, but what surrounds it is a bland tourist development of modern apartment blocks and generic restaurants. Facilities are plentiful, however, and there are nice hiking trails into the surrounding mountains, and more secluded beaches to the east of town, reachable on foot or by water taxi.

Sights & Activities

One of the hiking trails leads to the Romanesque **St Lucija Church** (Sveta Lucija; admission 10KN; 8am-noon & 2-8pm) in the village of Jurandvor, 2km away; this is where the 11th-century Baška tablet was found. What's inside is a replica, as the original is now in the Archaeological Museum in Zagreb.

Several popular trails begin around Camping Zablaće, including a stunning 8km walk to Stara Baška, a bay surrounded by stark, salt-washed limestone hills.

There are also two **rock-climbing** sites in the area; the tourist office has maps and information.

Sleeping

Contact the agencies **PDM Guliver** (www.pdm-guliver.hr; Zvonimirova 98) or **Primaturist** (856 132; www.primaturist.hr; Zvonimirova 98) next door for private accommodation. There's usually a four-night minimum stay in summer (or a hefty surcharge) and rooms fill up quick. Many hotels and the town's two camping grounds are managed by the **Hoteli Baška** (656 111; www.hotelibaska.hr) group.

Hotel Tamaris HOTEL €€€
(864 200; www.baska-tamaris.com; r from 899KN; P) This small three-star hotel has decent, if smallish, carpeted rooms that are in good shape - most have recently upgraded bathrooms and cable TV. It's right on the beach on the west side of the resort and the cafe-restaurant is a great spot to gaze over the bay.

Atrium Residence Baška HOTEL €€€
(656 111; www.hotelibaska.hr; r from 900KN; P) Atrium Residence Baška looks the part, with sleek and modern rooms and apartments, many with lovely sea vistas. But note that the hotel group's main base is 1km inland, so you'll have to leg it to the indoor–outdoor pool and wellness centre.

FKK Camp Bunculuka CAMPGROUND €
(856 806; www.bunculuka.info; per adult/site 48/109-149KN; Apr-Oct) This shady naturist camp is a 15-minute walk over the hill east of the harbour on a lovely beach. It's equipped with good facilities for kids, including minigolf and table tennis as well as a restaurant, a fruit-and-veg market and a bakery.

Camping Zablaće CAMPGROUND €
(856 909; www.campzablace.info; per adult/site 47/108KN; Apr–mid-Oct) Spreads along a long pebble beach and has good showers and laundry facilities.

Eating

Standard-issue tourist fodder is the name of the game, with a few exceptions.

There are simply tons of minimarts for self-caterers.

Cicibela INTERNATIONAL €€
(Emila Geistlicha bb; mains from 60KN) This is the resort's top cat, with stylish seating and a tempting menu of fish, seafood and meat dishes. It's at the eastern end of the beach promenade.

Bistro Forza INTERNATIONAL €
(Zvonimirova 98; mains from 40KN) A good cheap-bite option, this place dishes out pizza and the usual grilled meat, pasta and salad options.

Information

Just down the street from the bus station, between the beach and the harbour, is the **tourist office** (856 817; www.tz-baska.hr; Zvonimirova 114; 7am-9pm Mon-Sat, 8am-1pm Sun Jun–mid-Sep, to 2pm Mon-Fri mid-Sep–May). Walkers should definitely head here to pick up their hiking-paths map. Staff are multilingual.

CRES & LOŠINJ ISLANDS

Separated by an 11m-wide canal, these two sparsely populated and highly scenic islands in the Kvarner archipelago are often treated as a single entity. Although their topography is different, the islands' identities are blurred by a shared history. On Lošinj the pretty ports of Mali Lošinj and Veli Lošinj attract plenty of tourists in summer. Wilder, more barren Cres has remote camping grounds and pristine beaches, especially outside Cres Town, and a handful of medieval hilltop villages. Both islands are criss-crossed by hiking and biking trails, and nature lovers will be in heaven here.

History

Excavations indicate that a prehistoric culture spread out over both islands from the Stone Age to the Bronze Age. The ancient Greeks called the islands the Apsyrtides, which were in turn conquered by the Romans, then put under Byzantine rule and settled by Slavic tribes in the 6th and 7th centuries.

The islands subsequently came under Venetian rule, followed by that of the Croatian-Hungarian kings, then back to the Venetians. By the time Venice fell in 1797, Veli Lošinj and Mali Lošinj had become important maritime centres, while Cres devoted itself to wine and olive production. During the 19th century shipbuilding flourished in Lošinj, but with the advent of steamships it was replaced by health tourism as a major industry. Meanwhile, Cres had its own problems in the form of a phylloxera epidemic that wiped out its vineyards. Both islands were poor when they were annexed to Italy as part of the 1920 Treaty of Rapallo. They became part of Yugoslavia in 1945 and, most recently, Croatia in 1991.

Today, apart from a small shipyard in Nerezine in north Lošinj, and some olive cultivation, sheep farming and fishing on Cres, the main source of income on both islands is tourism.

Getting There & Away

BOAT The main maritime port of entry for the islands is Mali Lošinj, which is connected to Rijeka, Pula, Zadar, Venice and Koper in the summer. **Jadrolinija** (231 765; www.jadrolinija.hr; Riva Lošinjskih Kapetana 22) runs a daily ferry between Zadar and Mali Lošinj (50KN, seven hours) from June through September. In July and August it also runs a daily catamaran from Mali Lošinj to Cres (35KN, 2½ hours) and Rijeka (49KN, four hours). You'll also find a regular Jadrolinija car ferry from Brestova in Istria to Porozina at the tip of Cres (passenger/car 23/120KN, 20 minutes).

Split Tours (www.splittours.hr) runs a catamaran service from Zadar to Pula via Mali Lošinj five times weekly during July and August (55KN, two hours); in June and September, the service is reduced to twice weekly. In July and August **Venezia Lines** (www.venezialines.com) runs catamarans from Venice to Mali Lošinj via Pula twice weekly (€149, five hours).

BUS Most buses in the islands begin (or end) in Veli Lošinj and stop in Mali Lošinj and Cres; some continue on to the mainland. There are six to nine daily buses from Veli Lošinj to Cres Town (59KN, 1½ hours); four daily to Merag (70KN, two hours) and Valbiska on Krk (110KN, 2½ hours); three per day to Porozina on Cres (89KN, 2½ hours); two daily to Brestova in Istria (123KN, three hours); four daily buses to Rijeka (158KN, 4¼ hours); and three to four daily to Zagreb (267KN to 295KN, 5½ to six hours). There's also one daily to Ljubljana (315KN, 6¼ hours) in Slovenia between June and early September.

Cres Island

Cres has a wild, natural allure that's intoxicating and inspiring. Sparsely populated, it's covered in dense primeval forests, and boasts a craggy coastline of soaring cliffs, hidden coves and ancient hilltop towns. Big skies and huge vistas are very much on the agenda in Cres, and it seems every road and

THE HUNTERS & THE HUNTED

Cres' indigenous Tramuntana sheep is unique to the island and is perfectly adapted to karst pastures that were first developed by the Illyrians over 1000 years ago. But now the island's culture of free-range sheep farming is on the slide. A couple of decades ago Cres had 100,000 Tramuntana sheep, but now it's around 15,000. One of the main factors in this decline has been the introduction of wild boar by Croatia's powerful hunting lobby. Boar numbers have grown exponentially (they have even spread as far as the campsites in Mali Lošinj). Wild boar prey on sheep and lambs – in the winter of 2006 Beli's Eco-Centre Caput Insulae documented 2500 lamb kills due to boar attacks, though the actual figure is thought to be much higher.

Declining sheep numbers have an impact on the environment in many ways. Griffon vultures now don't have enough sheep carrion to survive upon, and have to be fed at feeding sites by volunteers. As pastureland has dwindled, juniper and thornbush have replaced native grasses and wildflowers, with a resulting drop in plant biodiversity. Low stone walls used by sheep farmers called *gromače* used to criss-cross Cres, acting as windbreaks and preventing soil erosion, but these are no longer maintained and many are crumbling away.

pathway offers scenery on a very grand scale indeed – this is some island.

The northern half of Cres, known as Tramuntana, is covered with dense oak, hornbeam, elk and chestnut forests. It's prime cruising terrain for the protected griffon vulture, and you'll see these giant birds at an excellent visitor centre in Beli, on the eastern coast.

Until very recently one of Cres' main income sources was rearing sheep (the island's lamb is famed for its flavour) but the introduction of wild boar has upset Cres' unique environment and an age-old culture is now waning.

The main seaside settlements lie on the western shore of Cres. Southwest of Valun there are highlands that include the astounding medieval town of Lubenice.

Locally the island is pronounced 'Tres'.

CRES TOWN

POP 2340

Pastel-coloured terrace houses and Venetian mansions hug the medieval harbour of Cres Town, a beautiful sheltered bay that's encircled by vivid green hills of pine trees and Adriatic scrubs. As you stroll along the seaside promenade and the atmospheric maze of old town streets, you'll notice reminders of Italian rule, including coats-of-arms of powerful Venetian families and Renaissance loggias.

The town's strong Italian influence dates back to the 15th century when Venetians relocated here after Osor fell victim to plague and pestilence. Public buildings and patricians' palaces were built along the harbour; a town wall was added in the 16th century.

Sights

Trg Frane Petrića CITY SQUARE

At the end of Riva Creskih Kapetana is Trg Frane Petrića with the graceful 16th-century **municipal loggia**, which was the scene of public announcements, financial transactions and festivals under Venetian rule. Today it is the site of a morning fruit-and-vegetable market.

St Mary of the Snow Church CHURCH

(Sv Marije Snježne; Pod Urom; ⌚Mass only) Behind the loggia is the 16th-century gate that leads to St Mary of the Snow Church. The facade is notable for the Renaissance portal with a relief of the Virgin and Child. It's worth checking out the serene interior before or after Mass for the carved wooden pietà from the 15th century (now under protective glass) at the left altar.

Ruta CRAFT CENTRE

(☎571 835; Zazid 4; ⌚sporadic or by appointment) This fascinating local collective promotes the island's cultural tradition of wool weaving and felting. Using the discarded wool of indigenous Cres sheep, the craftspeople make wonderful slippers, hats, handbags and clothes. You can see the workshop, learn about felting or even try it yourself (three-hour classes are available for 150KN).

Activities

There's an attractive promenade on the west side of the bay with sunbathing zones and good swimming, and good beaches around Hotel Kimen. **Diving Cres** (571 706; www.divingcres.de) in Autocamp Kovačine offers courses and fun dives. **Cres-Insula Activa** (091 73 89 490; www.cres-activa.hr) can organise windsurfing, biking and climbing trips. Drop by the tourist office for a map of footpaths and trails around Cres.

Sleeping

For the cheapest accommodation contact travel agencies for private room rentals. Single rooms in Cres Town start at around 150KN per person, doubles cost from 220KN.

Autocamp Kovačine CAMPGROUND €
(573 150; www.camp-kovacine.com; adult/child/tent 81/31/73KN; Easter–mid-Oct) This campsite has a fine location on the tip of a little wooded peninsula, so there are sea views aplenty and the beach is a step or two away. You'll find beachside bathing platforms, solar-powered bath facilities, a restaurant and activities galore, including basketball, volleyball and diving. A quarter of the campsite is reserved for naturists and there's an FKK beach. It's about 1km southwest of town.

Tamaris RENTAL ROOMS €€
(573 150; www.camp-kovacine.com; Melin 1/20; s/d 323/646KN;) Part of Autocamp Kovačine, this small building has 13 modern en-suite rooms with phone and satellite TV; some have seaview balconies.

Hotel Kimen RESORT €€
(573 305; www.hotel-kimen.com; Melin 1/16; s/d 405/810KN;) This is a large resort-style hotel with a beachside location and grounds shaded by pine forests. The recently renovated rooms are fresh and have balconies; there's a wellness centre and (free) wi-fi. Most guests here are German, Italian and Croatian families.

Eating & Drinking

The **supermarket** (Trg Frane Petrića) can be found right across from the loggia.

TOP CHOICE **Konoba Bukaleta** GRILL €€
(571 606; Loznati; Apr-Oct) Cres lamb is the top billing at this lovely village restaurant, which has been run by the same family for 30 years. Lamb (from 85KN) is either breaded, grilled or roasted on the spit; gnocchi and pasta are available for noncarnivores. It's a down-to-earth place with wooden benches, gingham tablecloths and homemade *rakija* (brandy). Love it so much you don't want to leave? You don't have to; there are inexpensive rooms for rent on the premises (from 250KN). Bukaleta is in Loznati, 5km south of Cres Town, and signposted from the highway.

Busola MEDITERRANEAN €€
(Kopača 2; mains from 60KN) Directly behind the church this little *konoba* has an atmospheric setting with tables beneath an ancient archway and a beamed dining room with exposed stone walls. It's renowned for its fresh fish – just pick yours from the glistening iced display.

Restaurant Riva SEAFOOD €€
(Riva Creskih Kapetana 13; mains from 50KN) This well-established place has a lovely terrace on the harbour and is many locals' choice for fish and seafood: scampi, Adriatic squid and prawns.

Santa Lucia SEAFOOD
(Lungomare Sveti Mikule 4; mains from 45KN) Fish baked in salt is the speciality at this restaurant on the coastal promenade.

Information

Autotrans (572 050; www.autotrans-turizam.com; Zazid 4) Efficient agency that arranges private accommodation, bike rental (25KN per hour), excursions and bus tickets.

Cresanka (750 600; www.cresanka.hr; Varozina 25) Contact these guys for private accommodation, excursions or money exchange.

Erste Banka (Cons 8) With ATM.

Post Office (Cons 3; 7.30am-7pm Mon-Fri, to 1pm Sat)

Tourist Agency Croatia (573 053; www.cres-travel.com; Melin 2/33) Arranges private accommodation, has internet access (1KN per minute) and hires bikes and scooters.

Tourist Office (571 535; www.tzg-cres.hr; Cons 10; 8am-8pm Mon-Sat, 9am-1pm Sun Jul & Aug, 8am-2pm Mon-Fri Sep-Jun) Well stocked with maps and brochures, including accommodation listings with photographs.

Getting There & Away

Two daily buses run to Opatija (92KN, two hours) and four to Rijeka (115KN, 2¼ hours). Two daily buses go to Brestova in Istria (with ferry ticket 75KN, 1½ hours).

Buses also run between Cres and Mali and Veli Lošinj.

Getting Around

Gonzo Bikes (571 000) Rents out good-quality bikes (24 hours 90KN).

BELI

POP 30

Lying at the heart of the Tramuntana region on the island's northern tip, with ancient virgin forests, abandoned villages, lone chapels and myths of good elves, Beli is one of the island's oldest settlements, clinging to a 130m hill above a lovely pebble beach. Its 4000-year history can still be felt in its twisting lanes and austere stone town houses overgrown with plants. You can walk a loop around this evocative but diminutive settlement in five minutes or so, stopping at a viewpoint to take in stunning vistas over the Adriatic to the mainland mountains. Note that the road leading to Beli is narrow and winding (but ultimately worth it).

Sights & Activities

Eco-Centre Caput Insulae NATURE RESERVE
(☎840 525; www.supovi.hr; Beli 4; adult/concession 50/25KN; ⏲9am-8pm, closed Nov-Mar) Part nature park, part sanctuary for the endangered Eurasian griffon, this eco-centre, set up in 1994, is devoted to caring for and maintaining the habitat of these majestic birds. It works with farmers to ensure a supply of sheep needed for the griffons' survival and with local boat captains to rescue drowning vultures. Around a dozen young griffons are saved each summer. Griffon vultures are severely threatened by the decline of sheep farming in Cres due to the importation of game (particularly wild boar) for hunting.

A visit to the centre, inside an old schoolhouse, starts with exhibits explaining the biology and habits of the vulture, but the highlight is the vultures themselves. There are usually about 15 birds in residence flapping around in a large netted enclosure behind the centre. There's also one African red-necked vulture (found on a beach in

THE THREATENED GRIFFON VULTURE

With a wingspan of almost 3m, measuring about 1m from end to end, and weighing 7kg to 9kg, the Eurasian griffon vulture looks big enough to take on passengers. It cruises comfortably at 40km/h to 50km/h, reaching speeds of up to 120km/h. The vulture's powerful beak and long neck are ideally suited to rummaging around the entrails of its prey, which is most likely to be a dead sheep.

Finding precious sheep carcasses is a team effort for griffon vultures. Usually a colony of birds will set out and fly in a comb formation of up to a kilometre apart. When one of the vultures spots a carcass, it circles as a signal for its neighbours to join in the feast. Shepherds don't mind griffons, reasoning that the birds prevent whatever disease or infection killed the sheep from spreading to other livestock.

The total known number of griffon vultures in Croatia is around 230, more than half of them living on the coastal cliffs of Cres, the others in small colonies on Krk and Prvić islands. The birds' dietary preferences mean that griffons tend to follow sheep, although they will eat other dead mammals, to their peril: the last remaining birds in Paklenica National Park died after eating poisoned foxes, and in 2005 20 Cres vultures died after eating poisoned meat.

The griffon population now enjoys legal protection as an endangered species in Croatia. Killing a bird or disturbing it while nesting carries a €5000 fine. Intentional killing is rare, but because the young birds cannot fly more than 500m on a windless day, tourists on speedboats who provoke them into flight often end up threatening their lives. The exhausted birds drop into the water and drown (the lucky ones are scooped up and taken to the Eco-Centre Caput Insulae in Beli).

Breeding habits discourage a large population, as a pair of griffons only produces one fledgling a year and it takes five years for the young bird to reach maturity. During that time the growing griffons travel widely: one tagged in Paklenica National Park was found in Chad, 4000km away. When they're about five, the vultures head home to Cres (sometimes to the same rock where they were born) to find a mate, who will be a partner for life.

It's thought vultures can live for up to 60 years, but 35 years is more normal – the (premature) mortality rate is 90 per cent. The dangers facing young Cres vultures include the guns of Italian hunters, poison and power lines, but by far the biggest issue is the massive decline in sheep farming in Cres, which is reducing the birds' food source day by day. Like some morbid comment on tourism, Cres' vultures now have to be fed at 'restaurants' dotted around the north of the island where staff and volunteers lay out meat for the birds.

Croatia and thought to have been kept as a pet). Keep an eye on the sky and you may spot one of the birds swooping overhead.

The ecocentre has a well-established volunteer program that runs throughout the year, as well as a griffon adoption programme. Check out the herb garden (arranged as a labyrinth) and features designed to amuse and educate children.

Admission to the centre includes access to seven well-marked **ecotrails** (between 1.5km and 20km) that connect the abandoned villages of Tramuntana, past olive, oak, fig and pomegranate trees and ancient dry-stone walls. There are also 20 **stone sculptures** and labyrinths dedicated to ancient Croatian and Slavic gods, designed to connect walkers to nature's spirit. Pick up an informative booklet and maps from the centre, explaining the history, culture, and flora and fauna of the region.

Diving Beli DIVING
(☎840 519; www.diving-beli.com) Offers boat- and beach-based dive trips; nondivers can come along too.

Sleeping & Eating

Down on the beach, about 1km from town, there's a snack bar and the small **Brajdi campsite** (☎840 532, fax 840 532; Beli bb; per person & site 56KN; ⊙May-Sep).

Pansion Tramontana CROATIAN €
(☎840 519; www.beli-tramontana.com; mains from 30KN; P 🛜) Next door to the griffon-vulture centre is this fine rustic restaurant where great chunks of meat are barbecued. Superb organic salads are available too, as is draught Guinness. Upstairs, the rooms (225KN to 300KN per person) are cosy and comfortable.

Getting There & Away

In summer, there are three daily buses from Cres Town to Beli (30KN, 30 minutes), except on Sundays.

OSOR

POP 70

The tiny, historic settlement of Osor is one of the most peaceful places you could imagine, despite its grand (and troubled) past.

The village sits on a narrow channel dividing Cres and Lošinj, which is thought to have been dug by the Romans – because of it, Osor was able to control a key navigational route. In the 6th century a bishopric was established here, with authority over both islands throughout the Middle Ages. Until the 15th century Osor was a strong commercial, religious and political presence in the region, but a combination of plague, malaria and new sea routes devastated the town's economy and it slowly decayed.

Now it's gaining new life as a museum-town of churches, open-air sculptures and lanes that meander off from its 15th-century town centre. Tourist information is available in Mali Lošinj. Osor is still waiting for its own tourist office.

When crossing from Lošinj to Osor, you may have to wait at the drawbridge spanning the Kavuada Canal, as the bridge is raised twice a day (at 9am and 5pm) to allow boats to pass.

Sights

Entering through the gate on the canal, you pass old city walls and the remains of a castle before you hit the centre of town.

Archaeological Museum MUSEUM
(http://www.muzej.losinj.hr; admission 15KN; ⊙10am-1pm & 7-10pm Tue-Sun Jun-Sep, 10am-1pm Tue-Sat Oct-May) On the main square in the 15th-century town hall, this museum contains a collection of stone fragments and reliefs from the Roman and early Christian periods, ceramics and sculptures.

Church of the Assumption CHURCH
(Crkva Uznešenja; ⊙10am-noon & 7-9pm Jun-Sep) Next door to the museum is the Church of the Assumption, built in the late 15th century, with a rich Renaissance portal on its facade. The baroque altar inside has relics of St Gaudencius, Osor's patron saint.

Daleki Akordi MONUMENT
Before leaving the square, check out the Ivan Meštrović statue, *Daleki akordi* (distant chords), one of the town's many modern sculptures on a musical theme.

Festivals & Events

During **Musical Evenings of Osor** (Osorske Glazbene Večeri; www.osorskeveceri.org) from mid-July to late August, high-calibre Croatian artists perform classical music in the cathedral and on the main square. The tourist offices in Mali Lošinj and Cres Town have details.

Sleeping & Eating

Private accommodation is available and there are two camping grounds in the area. The tourist offices in Mali Lošinj and Cres Town have listings of rooms and apartments.

WORTH A TRIP

LUBENICE

Perched on an exposed rocky ridge, 378m above the western shore of the island, this medieval hilltop hamlet is one of the most evocative places in Cres. Semi-abandoned (there's a permanent population of 17), Lubenice's maze of ancient austere stone houses and churches seems fused to the very bedrock of the island itself, giving the village the appearance of a Moorish fortress.

Lubenice sits above one of Kvarner's most remote and beautiful **beaches**, a secluded cove accessible by a steep path through the bush. The 45-minute descent is a breeze, but coming up is more of a challenge (so you could consider taking a taxi boat from Valun or Cres).

Another reason to visit Lubenice is for the annual **Lubeničke Glazbene Večeri** (Lubenice Music Nights), with alfresco classical concerts every Friday night in July and August.

The tourist office in Cres Town has listings of private rooms in Lubenice, although there aren't many to choose from.

You'll find two places get a meal or a drink: **Konoba Hibernicia** (Lubenice 17; mains from 45KN), notable for its lamb dishes and local ham, and **Bufet Loza**, by the entrance to the village, which is great for a beer.

In summer, two daily buses connect Lubenice with Cres Town (33KN, 35 minutes), except on Sunday. If you're driving up, note that the road is narrow and winding.

Osor Pansion HOTEL, RESTAURANT €
(☎237 135; osor.webs.com; Osor bb; r per person 184-221 KN, mains from 40KN; ⊙Mar-Nov; P❄) A gorgeous garden restaurant is the main appeal of this well-run place with tables located under vines and between flowering shrubs. The menu features Cres lamb and Adriatic fish. The seven attractive pine-trimmed rooms above (184KN to 220KN per person) are a good option, too.

Konoba Bonifačić CROATIAN €€
(Osor 64; mains from 50KN) This garden restaurant's menu has a home-cooking flavour about it with dependable risottos, grilled meats and fish. Have a shot of elderflower grappa while you're there.

Bijar CAMPGROUND €
(☎237 027; www.camps-cres-losinj.com; per person 60KN) A location on a lovely pebbly cove with fabulous swimming. Facilities include table tennis, volleyball and basketball. It's 500m from Osor, on the way to Nerezine.

ℹ Getting There & Away

All buses from Cres (39KN, 45 minutes) and Mali Lošinj (32KN, 30 minutes) travel along the island's sole highway, passing through Osor.

VALUN

POP 68

The pretty seaside hamlet of Valun, 14km southwest of Cres Town, is buried at the foot of cliffs and surrounded by shingle beaches. Park and go down steep steps to the old town and cove. Valun bay and its restaurants are rarely crowded, and there's a refreshing lack of souvenir stalls or touristy tack.

The **tourist bureau** (☎525 050; ⊙8am-9pm Jul & Aug), an ATM and a branch of **Cresanka** (www.cresanka.hr) are a few steps up from the harbour. Cresanka can arrange private accommodation and book hotels and ferry tickets. Accommodation is scarce and usually reserved way in advance.

The main sight is the 11th-century **Valun Tablet**, kept in the parish **Church of St Mary** (where the opening hours are sporadic). Inscribed in both Glagolitic and Latin, this tombstone reflects the ethnic composition of the island, which was inhabited by Roman descendants and newcomers who spoke Croatian.

Valun's appeal lies in its tranquillity and cove **beaches**. To the right of the harbour, a path leads to a shingle beach and camping ground. West of the hamlet, about 700m further on, there's another lovely pebble beach bordered by pines.

The idyllic **Zdovice campsite** (per person 101KN; ⊙May-Sep) is a small affair with pitches occupying old terraced fields. It's right on a beach with great swimming, has a volleyball court and is very popular with German and Austrian families. No reservations.

Valun has six restaurants, all but one right by the sea. **Konoba Toš-Juna** (Valun bb;

mains from 40KN) stands out for seafood. It's inside a converted olive mill with exposed stone and a nice terrace on the harbour.

Valun is not well served by public transport. There's only one daily bus from Cres Town (26KN, 20 minutes), and none on Sundays. Return buses leave only twice a week (at 5.31am on Monday and Wednesday).

Lošinj Island

The more populated and touristy of the twin islands, 31km-long Lošinj also has a more indented coastline than Cres, especially in the south where there are some stunning deserted bays. It's a heavily wooded island: the historic towns of Mali Lošinj and Veli Lošinj are ringed by pine forests. Vegetation is lush and varied, with 1100 plant species, 230 medicinal herbs and some atypical growths such as lemon, banana, cedar and eucalyptus brought from exotic lands by sea captains.

Lošinj is known for its dolphin population; in fact, its waters are the first protected marine area for dolphins in the entire Mediterranean. The Blue World NGO, based in Mali Lošinj, has done much to safeguard these graceful sea creatures with an educational research centre.

MALI LOŠINJ

POP 6314

Mali Lošinj is a stunner. It sits at the foot of a protected V-shaped harbour on the southeast coast of Lošinj island, with a string of imposing 19th-century sea captains' houses lining the seafront of the pretty old town. Even with the summer tourist commotion, this ancient quarter still retains charm and atmosphere. All the resort hotels sit out of town, leading up from the harbour to Sunčana Uvala in the south and Čikat in the southwest.

This leafy area started to flourish in the late 19th century, when the wealthy Vienna and Budapest elite, who gravitated to the 'healthy air' of Mali Lošinj, started building villas and luxurious hotels around Čikat. Some of these grand residences remain, but most of the current hotels are modern developments surrounded by pine forests that blanket the coves and its pretty beaches.

Although it's more relaxed visiting in spring and autumn, even in the hectic summer months Mali Lošinj can serve as a good base for excursions around Lošinj and Cres or to the small islands of Susak, Ilovik and Unije nearby.

Sights

The main attraction here is Mali Lošinj's sublime setting: a stunning natural harbour ringed by graceful, gently weathered Mediterranean town houses and the greenery of the surrounding hills.

Art Collections GALLERY
(Umjetničke Zbirke; www.muzej.losinj.hr; Vladimira Gortana 35; adult/concession 10/5KN; ⌚10am-1pm & 7-9pm Tue-Fri, 10am-1pm Sat Easter-Oct, shorter hr rest of year) This grand mansion showcases the art collections of the Mihičić and Piperata families and hosts rotating exhibitions. Browse the modern Croatian works, including bronze statues by Kršinć, as well as the old masters.

Apoksiomen MONUMENT
The exquisite antique statue of Apoksiomen was found on the seabed near Lošinj in 1999. It's scheduled to return to the island, to a museum being built especially for the statue inside the Kvarner Palace, in late 2013, after a tour around Zadar, Zagreb and the Louvre in Paris. This 2000-year-old bronze athlete, possibly a wrestler, has been meticulously restored.

Garden of Fine Scents GARDEN
(Miomirisni Otočki Vrt; www.miomirisni-vrt.hr; Braće Vidulić bb; admission free; ⌚10am-noon & 6-9pm Jul & Aug, 10am-noon Sep-Jun) This fragrant paradise on the southern edge of town has over 250 native plant varieties plus 100 exotic species, all framed with *gromače* (traditional stone fences). Natural fragrances, salts and liquors are sold too.

Church of the Nativity of the Virgin CHURCH
(Župna Crkva Male Gospe) In the town centre, peek into the parish Church of the Nativity of the Virgin either before or after Sunday Mass at 10am. Inside are some notable artworks, including a painting of the Nativity of the Blessed Virgin by an 18th-century Venetian artist, and relics of St Romulus.

Activities

The coves south of Mali Lošinj are highly scenic and surrounded by pine forests, though they can get very busy in high season with holidaying families. **Sunčana Uvala** offers sheltered pebble beaches that are excellent for swimming and safe for children. Neighbouring **Čikat** is *the* spot for windsurfing with its narrow shingle beach and great wind exposure. Take a windsurfing session at **Sunbird** (☎095 837 7142; www.sunbird.de), near Hotel Bellevue, where a beginners' course costs 933KN; it also has boards for hire (as well as mountain bikes and kayaks).

Cycling and **hiking** have become increasingly popular on Lošinj. The tourist board has an excellent brochure, *Promenades & Footpaths,* with maps of 220km of trails and accurate walking times. All five islands of the archipelago (Lošinj, Cres, Ilovik, Susak and Unije) are covered. Climb the highest peak of Televrina (588m) for great views, hike to the remote coves south of Mali Lošinj or access secret coves in Susak.

Lošinj has good **diving** with excellent visibility and good sealife. Who knows, you may uncover the next Apoksiomen! There's a wreck dating from 1917, a large, relatively shallow cave suitable for beginners and the wonderful Margarita Reef off the island of Susak. **Diver Sport Center** (☎233 900; www.diver.hr) on Čikat offers courses (a 'Discovery' course is 410KN, and SSI Open Water is 2539KN) and teach diving to deep Adriatic wrecks like the *Audace* torpedo boat.

Sleeping

Mali Lošinj itself has a slim but characterful range of accommodation options. Most hotels are dotted around the coves and pine forests over in Čikat and Sunčana Uvala, and are geared to package tourism. The majority are pretty bland resorts aimed at holidaying families, fall under the umbrella of **Lošinj Hotels & Villas** (www.losinj-hotels.com), and close between November and Easter.

Travel agencies find rooms and apartments, and the tourist office has a detailed brochure with private accommodation.

IN TOWN

Hotel Apoksiomen HOTEL €€
(☎520 820; www.apoksiomen.com; Riva Lošinjskih Kapetana 1; s/d 700/1000KN; P ❄ @ ≋) A well-run harbourside hotel where the 25 modern rooms all come with sea or park views, plush carpets, modern art, satellite TV, safes and contemporary bathrooms (most with twin sinks). Staff are helpful and you'll find an inviting cafe-restaurant on the ground floor. Book via the website for the best deals.

Alaburić B&B €
(☎233 996; S Radića 17; per person 188KN; P) A welcoming family-run guest house with simple, well-equipped rooms and apartments, all with bathroom – two have distant sea views. It's about a 700m walk down to the harbourfront.

Mare Mare Suites BOUTIQUE HOTEL €€€
(☎232 010; www.mare-mare.com; Riva Lošinjskih Kapetana 36; s/d/ste 900/1050/1350KN; P ❄ @ ≋) Enjoying a prime position towards the northern end of the harbour, this historic townhouse has been converted into rooms and mini-suites: all are immaculately presented and individually styled. Check out the top-floor Captain's Suite complete with telescope and old naval charts. Good, but a little overpriced; consider the cheaper annexe next door.

BEACHSIDE

Villa Favorita HISTORIC HOTEL €€€
(☎520 640; www.villafavorita.hr; Sunčana Uvala; d 1210KN; P ❄ @ ≋) Enveloped by pine forests and just off a small beach, this very attractive Habsburg mansion has loads of character, helpful staff and a great location. Offers eight deluxe rooms, sauna, massage and a seawater pool in a well-kept garden.

Hotel Vespera HOTEL €€
(☎231 304; www.losinj-hotels.com; Sunčana Uvala bb; s/d 462/810KN; P ❄ @ ≋) A huge hotel very much orientated to families, with excellent facilities including tennis courts and an excellent swimming complex with three pools (one is 37m long) and jacuzzi.

Camping Village Poljana CAMPGROUND €
(☎231 726; www.poljana.hr; Poljana bb; per adult/site 88/92KN; ≋) Surrounded by mature trees, this upmarket site has power-fitted pitches and perks such as wireless internet (for a fee), a restaurant and a supermarket, and good, air-conditioned mobile homes. There is also a small pebble beach and a rocky area for FKK (nude) bathers.

Camping Čikat CAMPGROUND €
(☎232 125; www.camps-cres-losinj.com; Dražica 1; per adult/site 60/60KN; ⊙Easter-Oct) More of a canvas and caravan city than a campsite, this huge pine-shaded place has hundreds of pitches, mobile homes for rent and facilities. You'll even find a market, shops and a mobile masseur.

Eating

The harbourside restaurants may have the best views but they tend to serve pretty standard fare (pasta, seafood and grilled meats) aimed at tourists, with little variety in price or quality. Try the streets inland and

WORTH A TRIP

A COVE OF YOUR OWN

South of Mali Lošinj the island forms a glorious, barely inhabited thumb-shaped peninsula that's blessed with exquisite natural bays and is perfect for hiking. Pick up a copy of the tourist office's excellent *Promenades and Footpaths* map for this region. One lonely road snakes down the spine of this hilly, wooded landmass, eventually fizzling out at Mrtvaška, Lošinj's land's end. You can circumnavigate the entire peninsula in a full day by foot, stopping to swim at deserted coves. If you only want to hit one beach, drive 5km to the turn-off for **Krivica**, park, and it's a 30-minute descent to this idyllic, sheltered bay which is ringed by pine trees. The water is emerald-tinged and superb for swimming.

out-of-town restaurants for more inventive cooking.

Self-caterers can head to the large supermarket on Trg Zagazinjine, just north of the harbour's edge.

Corrado SEAFOOD €
(Svete Marije 1; mains from 50KN) Owned by a deep-sea fisher, this is one of Lošinj's premier restaurants, with a lovely walled garden setting. Lamb baked under a *peka* (domed baking lid; book ahead) and lobster *buzzara* are specialities, and it doesn't serve any farmed fish. It's off the main street that leads into town from the car park.

Porto SEAFOOD €€
(Sveti Martin 35) Up over the hill on the east side of town, this fine fish restaurant sits on a pretty cove next to a church. Fish fillet with sea urchins is the signature dish, but all seafood is expertly prepared and presented.

Barakuda SEAFOOD €€
(Priko 31; mains from 70KN) This place is rated highly by locals for the freshness of its fish and skills of the resident chefs. There's a harbour-facing terrace and usually a daily special or two chalked up on the blackboard.

Konoba-Pizzeria Bukaleta PIZZERIA €
(☎098 170 8155; Del Conte Giovanni; pizzas from 50KN) A great place for a casual lunch or dinner of perfect pizza that comes out of the wood-fired oven mozzarella and basil-scented.

Drinking & Entertainment

Mystik LOUNGE BAR
(Braće Ivana i Stjepana Vidulića 40) The HQ for Lošinj's bright young things, with live DJs, sleek decor and lush cocktails. Musically, things are quite innovative at times with a wide range of electronic sounds, not just bangin' dance-floor bombs.

Marina BAR, CLUB
(Velopin bb) Party on the water at this cocktail-bar-cum-club docked on the southwest side of the harbour.

Information

There's no shortage of travel agencies to arrange private accommodation, change money and book excursions.

Cappelli (☎231 582; www.cappelli-tourist.hr; Kadin bb) Books private accommodation on Cres and Lošinj, and offers Adriatic cruises and excursions.

Manora Lošinj (☎520 100; Priko 29) Friendly agency with a full gamut of services.

Erste Banka (Riva Lošinjskih Kapetana 4) With ATM.

Hospital (☎231 824; Dinka Kozulića 1)

Post Office (Vladimira Gortana 4; ⊙8am-9pm Mon-Fri, to noon Sat)

Tourist Office (☎231 884; www.tz-malilosinj.hr; Riva Lošinjskih Kapetana 29; ⊙8am-8pm Mon-Sat, 9am-1pm Sun Jun-Sep, 8am-5pm Mon-Fri, 9am-1pm Sat Oct-May) A very useful office, with knowledgeable staff and tons of (practical and glossy) leaflets and maps, plus a comprehensive accommodation list with owners' emails and websites.

Getting There & Away

There are six to nine buses a day between Mali Lošinj and Veli Lošinj (15KN, 10 minutes). There are also other bus and boat connections. The Jadrolinija office has ferry information and sells tickets.

Getting Around

Between late April and mid-October there's an hourly shuttle bus (10KN) that runs from the town centre to the hotel district in Sunčana Uvala and Čikat, till 11pm. Head to **SanMar** (☎233 571; www.sanmar.hr; Priko 24) to rent mountain bikes (100KN per day) and mopeds (250KN).

Note that you have to pay to enter the centre of Mali Lošinj in a car (two hours, 12KN).

BLUE WORLD

The **Blue World Institute of Marine Research & Conservation** (☎236 406; www.blue-world.org; Kaštel 24) is a Veli Lošinj–based NGO founded in 1999 to promote environmental awareness in the Adriatic. It now has a second office in Vis. Blue World raises public awareness through lectures, media presentations and the organisation of Dolphin Day in Veli Lošinj on the first Saturday in August, which sees photography exhibitions, an ecofair, street performances, water-polo contests, treasure hunts and displays of hundreds of children's drawings and paintings. It's quite an event.

As part of the Adriatic Dolphin Project, Blue World studies bottlenose dolphins that frequent the Lošinj–Cres area. Each dolphin is named and catalogued by photos taken of the natural marks that can be seen on its dorsal fin.

Dolphins were hunted locally in the 1960s and '70s, when each kill was rewarded by the local government – fishermen were paid by the tail. Protection began in 1995, but a steep decline in bottlenose dolphins was recorded between 1995 and 2003. Subsequently, Blue World managed to establish the **Lošinj Dolphin Reserve**. Numbers are now believed to be stable, though still critically endangered, at around 120 individuals. In August 2009 a pod of 60 dolphins was seen near the island of Trstenik, a record sighting. Occasionally other species are seen too, including striped dolphins (as well as basking sharks).

The biggest threat to Lošinj's dolphins is boat traffic, which brings noise and disturbance. During July and August dolphins are never seen close to the shore and avoid their main feeding grounds south and east of Cres where hake are common. Overfishing is another big concern, reducing available prey.

You can get involved by adopting a dolphin (150KN), which supports the Adriatic Dolphin Project, or volunteering: a 10-day programme starts at €675 per person, with discounts available for students.

VELI LOŠINJ

POP 920

Despite the name (in Croatian, *veli* means big and *mali* means small), Veli Lošinj is much smaller, more languid and somewhat less crowded than Mali Lošinj, only 4km to the northwest. This is an exceptionally scenic place, really nothing more than a huddle of pastel-coloured houses, cafes, hotels and stores around a tiny inlet. Dolphins sometimes enter the narrow mouth of the bay in April and May. Don't miss a walk to Rovenska, another idyllic little cove, just a 10-minute stroll along a coastal path to the southeast.

Like its neighbour, Veli Lošinj had its share of rich sea captains who built villas and surrounded them with gardens of exotic plants they brought back from afar. You can glimpse these villas on a walk up the steep streets from the harbour. Sea captains also furnished the churches in town, most notably St Anthony's on the harbour.

Be aware that you will have to park up above the bay and then hoof it down the narrow cobblestone streets in the summer months.

Sights & Activities

Lošinj Marine Education Centre MARINE CENTRE

(www.blue-world.org; Kaštel 24; adult/concession 15/10KN; 9am-1pm & 6-10pm Jul & Aug, 9am-1pm & 6-8pm Jun & Sep, 10am-4pm rest of year) The town's most enlightening attraction is the Lošinj Marine Education Centre, a superb resource that manages to be entertaining and educational – kids will love the AV displays, though some are disappointed there are no dolphins kept here. Exhibits include a vertebra from an 11m fin whale (a baby), an acoustic room where you can hear dolphin click communications, a mural of all 12 of the Mediterranean's whale and dolphin species, and there are souvenirs for sale. The centre is a project of Blue World.

Tower Museum MUSEUM

(adult/concession 10/5KN; 10am-1pm & 4-10pm Tue-Sun mid-Jun to mid-Sep, 10am-1pm Tue-Sat mid-Sep to Oct & Easter to mid-Jun) This striking defence tower, in the maze of streets set back from the harbour, was built by the Venetians in 1455 to defend the town from pirates. It's well worth a visit, and contains a small museum and gallery dedicated to the island's maritime history, explaining events with English captions. Browse the Roman ceramic fragments, Austrian and Turkish sabres, old postcards and a model of an old *bark* (ship) before climbing up to the battlements for unrivalled Veli views.

Church of St Anthony the Hermit CHURCH
Built in baroque style in 1774, this church is elaborately decked out with marble altars, a rich collection of Italian paintings, a pipe organ and relics of St Gregory. It's only open for Sunday Mass, but you can glimpse the interior through its metal gate.

Sleeping

Both Val and Turist travel agencies will find private accommodation.

TOP CHOICE **Youth Hostel** HOSTEL €
(☎236 234; www.hfhs.hr; Kaciol 4; per person 111KN; ⏲Jun-Oct; @) One of Croatia's best youth hostels, this converted town house has a friendly vibe and hospitable management, and feels more like a relaxed backpackers' than a YH institution. Dorms (all with lockers) are spacious, the pine-trimmed private rooms are quite classy and the front terrace is a great place to meet people and have an evening beer (10KN a pop).

Villa Mozart GUESTHOUSE €€
(☎236 262; www.villa-mozart.hr; Kaciol 3; per person 295KN; ❄@) Attractive guesthouse with 18 characterful rooms; all are smallish but have TV and bathroom, and some come with harbour views. The breakfast terrace overlooks the shimmering harbour waters and the church.

Pansion Saturn B&B €€
(☎236 102; www.val-losinj.hr; Obala Maršala Tita 1; s/d 289/678KN) This is a cheap and cheerful little B&B overlooking the central bay, with a slightly old-school feel. The rooms are spacious and bathrooms modern, and there is a terrace bar with lovely views of the bay and the pastel houses.

Eating & Drinking

The cafe-restaurants in the harbour tend to serve inexpensive but not wildly exciting Italian, seafood and meat dishes.

TOP CHOICE **Bora Bar Trattoria/Tartufferia** MEDITERRANEAN €€
(www.borabar.com; Rovenska Bay 3; mains from 70KN; 🛜) Truffle-lover heaven, this casual-chic restaurant is the gastro dream child of Italian-born chef Marco Sasso, who has a passion for the magic fungi. Feast on tuna carpaccio with celery root and truffle, or the wonderful *tagliata* with potatoes baked in

ISLANDS AROUND LOŠINJ

The nearby car-free islands of Susak, Ilovik and Unije are the most popular day trips from Mali Lošinj. Tiny **Susak** (population 183, area 3.8 sq km) is unique for the thick layer of fine sand that blankets the underlying limestone and creates delightful beaches. It's the island's unusual culture that makes it particularly interesting. Islanders speak their own dialect, which is nearly incomprehensible to other Croats. On feast days and at weddings you can see the local women outfitted in traditional multicoloured skirts and red leggings. When you see the old stone houses on the island, consider that each stone had to be brought over from Mali Lošinj and carried by hand to its destination. The island has steadily lost its population in the last few decades (it was over 1600 in 1948), with many of its citizens settling in Hoboken, New Jersey.

In contrast to flat Susak, **Ilovik** (population 145, area 5.8 sq km) is a hilly island known for its profusion of flowers. Overgrowing with oleanders, roses and eucalyptus trees, it's popular with boaters and has some secluded swimming coves.

The largest of the islands in the Lošinj archipelago, **Unije** (population 274, area 18 sq km) has an undulating landscape that abounds with Mediterranean shrubs, pebble beaches and numerous coves and inlets. The island's only settlement is a picturesque fishing village of gabled stone houses.

Travel agencies in Lošinj sell excursions to Susak, Ilovik and Unije, or you can get there on your own. **Jadrolinija** (www.jadrolinija.hr) makes a daily summer circuit from Rijeka to Mali Lošinj: six days a week it travels via Susak, four days a week via Unije and three days a week via Ilovik. The ferry leaves Rijeka at 6am and one returns at 5pm. The website has the latest schedules and prices.

local herbs. Finish with a *panna cotta* with truffle honey. Istrian wines and organic locally sourced vegetables feature strongly. Located on Rovenska Bay, a 10-minute walk from Veli.

Ribarska Koliba CROATIAN €€
(Obala Maršala Tita 1; mains from 55KN) Just past the church, this old stone structure has a nice portside terrace and serves up flavoursome meat dishes (try the suckling pig on a spit) as well as seafood.

Saturn BAR
(Obala Maršala Tita bb) The best bar in town, this atmospheric little place has harbour-facing tables, rattan seats and cushions, and an eclectic playlist of Western and Croatian music. Nine good-value modern rooms lie upstairs too (book through the Val agency).

Information

Erste Banka (Obala Maršala Tita) Has a foreign-exchange counter. There are other ATMs in Veli too.

Palma (236 179; www.losinj.com; Vladimira Nazora 22) Offers tourist information, currency exchange, internet access and private accommodation.

Post Office (Obala Maršala Tita 33; 8am-9pm Mon-Fri, to 1pm Sat)

Turist (236 256; www.island-losinj.com; Obala Maršala Tita 17) Runs excursions to Susak and Ilovik (130KN), finds private accommodation, changes money and rents bikes (85KN per day) and scooters (365KN).

Val (236 352; www.val-losinj.hr; Vladimira Nazora 29) Agency that books private accommodation, runs excursions and offers internet access (30KN per hour).

Getting There & Away

There are seven to nine buses a day between Veli Lošinj and Mali Lošinj (17KN, 10 minutes).

RAB ISLAND

Rab (Arbe in Italian) is the most enticing island in Kvarner when it comes to landscape diversity. The more densely populated southwest is replete with pine forests, beaches and coves, while the northeast coast is a windswept region with few settlements, high cliffs and a barren look. In the interior, fertile land is protected by mountains from cold winds, allowing the cultivation of olives, grapes and vegetables. The island's Lopar Peninsula offers the best sandy beaches.

The cultural and historical highlight of the island is enchanting Rab Town, characterised by four elegant bell towers rising from the ancient stone streets. Even at the peak of the summer season, when the island is overrun with visitors, you still get a sense of discovery wandering its old quarter and escaping to nearly deserted beaches just a quick boat ride away. In spring and autumn, Rab Island is a lovely place to visit, as the climate is famously mild and visitors are scarce.

History

Originally settled by Illyrians, Rab underwent periods of Roman, Byzantine and Croatian rule before being sold to Venice, along with Dalmatia, in 1409. Farming, fishing, vineyards and salt production were the economic mainstays, but most income ended up in Venice. Two plague epidemics in the 15th century nearly wiped out the population and brought the economy to a standstill.

When Venice fell in 1797, there was a short period of Austrian rule until the French arrived in 1805. After the fall of Napoleon in 1813, the power went back to the Austrians who favoured the Italianised elite and it was not until 1897 that Croatian was made an 'official' language. The tourism industry began at the turn of the 20th century. After the fall of Austro-Hungarian Empire in 1918, Rab eventually became part of the Kingdom of Yugoslavia. Occupied by Italian and then German troops in the early 1940s, it was liberated in 1945. During Tito's rule, Goli Otok ('Barren Island'), off the Lopar Peninsula, served as a notorious prison camp for Stalinists, anticommunists and political opponents.

These days, tourism is Rab's bread and butter. Even during the 1990s war, Rab managed to hold onto its German and Austrian tourists.

Getting There & Away

The Split Tours catamaran between Valbiska on Krk and Lopar (passenger/car 40/230KN, 1½ hours) operates twice daily (October to May) and four times daily in high season; prices drop in winter.

A car ferry by Rapska Plovidba shuttles back and forth nonstop in the summer months between Mišnjak on the island's southeastern edge and Jablanac (passenger/car 20/100KN, 20 minutes) on the mainland; even in winter there are a dozen daily boats. A new harbour is being

Rab Island

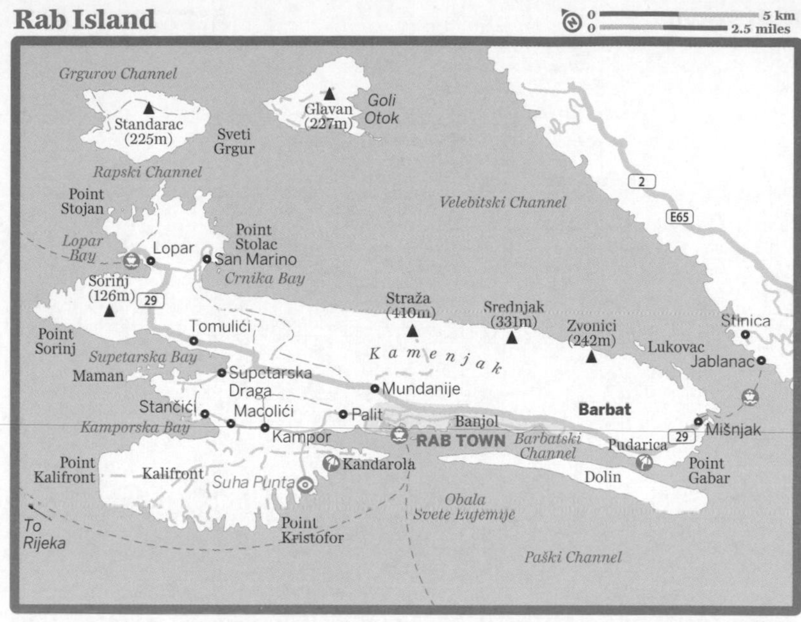

built at Jablanac, which will enable large ferries to sail this notoriously queue-prone route, tripling capacity from 2013.

Between June and September Jadrolinija operates a fast (passenger only) catamaran service between Rijeka and Rab (45KN, two hours); it continues on to Novalja on Pag.

There's no direct bus from Rab to Zadar, but there are several daily buses that connect at Senj with Rijeka buses travelling to Zadar (220KN, five hours). Two daily buses connect Rab and Rijeka (135KN, three hours). In the high season there are three to four direct daily buses from Zagreb to Rab (205KN, four to five hours); book ahead on this busy route. The Rab Town bus station has a **garderoba** (Mali Palit bb; per hr 1KN; ⌚5.30am-8pm) for travellers who need to store bags.

Getting Around

From Rab Town to Lopar (27KN, 15 minutes) there are 11 daily buses (nine on Sundays) in either direction; some are timed to meet the Valbiska–Lopar ferry.

There's a water-taxi service between Rab Town and Suha Punta resort (30KN) that operates four times daily in July and August, leaving from the harbour. Taxi boats will take you to any island beach, including Frkanj and the nudist Kandarola (30KN per person; both almost hourly June to September).

Rab Town

POP 556

Medieval Rab Town is among the northern Adriatic's most spectacular sights. Crowded onto a narrow peninsula, its four instantly recognisable bell towers rise like exclamation points from a red-roofed huddle of stone buildings. A maze of streets leads to the upper town, from where there are ancient churches and dramatic lookout points. It's quite a scene, the glinting azure waters of Rab's pocket-sized harbour set against the island's backbone of hills that shelter the bay from cool *bura* winds. Once you've soaked up the town, there are excursion and taxi boats to whisk you off to lovely cove beaches scattered around the island.

A five-minute walk north of the old town is the ageing, down-at-heel commercial centre, with stores and the bus station.

Sights

It's a pure delight to meander through the narrow old alleys of Rab and explore the harbourfront, upper town and parks.

UPPER TOWN

Rab's principal sights are its historic churches and towers, which are clustered

Rab Town

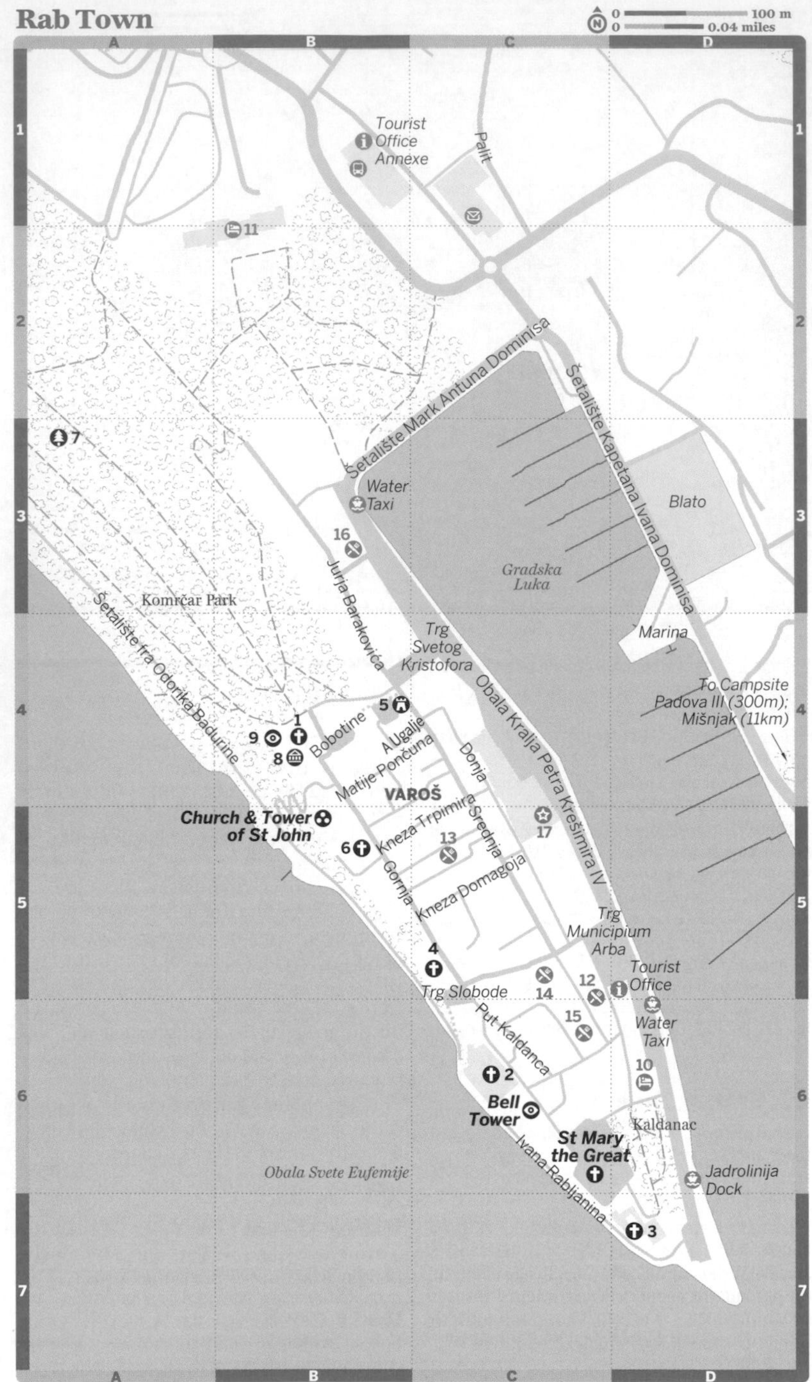

0 100 m
0 0.04 miles
A
B
C
D
1
2
3
4
5
6
7
Tourist Office Annexe
Palit
11
7
Šetalište Mark Antuna Dominisa
Šetalište Kapetana Ivana Dominisa
Water Taxi
16
Blato
Gradska Luka
Komrčar Park
Jurja Barakovića
Trg Svetog Kristofora
Marina
To Campsite Padova III (300m); Mišnjak (11km)
Šetalište fra Odorika Badurine
Obala Kralja Petra Krešimira IV
1
5
9
8
Bobotine
A Ugalje
Matije Pončuna
Donja
VAROŠ
Church & Tower of St John
17
6
Kneza Trpimira
13
Srednja
Gornja
Kneza Domagoja
Trg Municipium Arba
4
Tourist Office
12
14
Trg Slobode
15
Water Taxi
Put Kaldanca
10
2
Bell Tower
Kaldanac
St Mary the Great
Ivana Rabljanina
Obala Svete Eufemije
Jadrolinija Dock
3

Rab Town

Top Sights

	Bell Tower	C6
	Church & Tower of St John	B5
	St Mary the Great	C6

Sights

1	Chapel of St Christopher	B4
2	Church of St Andrew	C6
3	Church of St Anthony	D7
4	Church of St Justine	C5
5	Dominis Palace	B4
6	Holy Cross Church	B5
7	Komrčar Park	A3
8	Lapidarium	B4
9	Viewpoint	B4

Sleeping

10	Hotel Arbiana	D6
11	Hotel Imperial	B2

Eating

12	Astoria	C5
13	Konoba Rab	C5
14	Paradiso	C5
15	Santa Maria	C6
16	Supermarket	B3

Entertainment

17	Dock 69	C5

together on the narrow lane of Gornja Ulica (and its continuation Ivana Rabljanina) in the Upper Town. Most of the churches usually only open for morning and evening Mass, but even when they're closed you can peer through metal railings to view their interiors.

Church & Tower of St John RUINS
(Crkva Svetog Ivana; tower admission 7KN; ⏲10am-1pm) Approaching Gornja from the west, this crumbling church is the first you come to – it's thought to date back as far as the 5th century. The Romanesque basilica lies in atmospheric semiruin today, though some columns and pillars are still standing. Climb the adjacent, restored 12th-century **bell tower** for spectacular sea views.

Holy Cross Church CHURCH
(Crkva Svetog Križa) This 13th-century church has a cross upon which Christ allegedly wept because of the town residents' immoral conduct. Today it's the venue for summer concerts during Rab Musical Evenings.

Church of St Justine CHURCH
(Crkva Svete Justine) This church (currently under renovation) has a bell tower dating from 1572 and a collection of religious artefacts. It's located beside pretty **Trg Slobode**, which has an oak tree and sea vistas.

Church of St Andrew CHURCH
(Crkva Svetog Andrije) This has Rab's oldest bell tower. Peer through the railings and there's a triple nave; some of the plasterwork has been uncovered to reveal the original stonework.

Bell Tower NOTABLE BUILDING
(Zvonik; admission 10KN; ⏲10am-1pm & 7.30-10pm May-Sep) Rab's tallest bell tower, and one of the most beautiful on the entire Croatian coast, dates from the 13th century. This 26m edifice is topped with an octagonal pyramid surrounded by a Romanesque balustrade and features a cross with five small globes and reliquaries of several saints. Climb up the very steep wooden staircase and you emerge right by the chiming mechanism itself along with stunning views of the old town rooftops and the sea.

St Mary the Great CHURCH
(Crkva Svete Marije Velike) Locally called the *katedrala* (cathedral), this is the grandest church in the upper town. Key features include a striking, unadorned facade, 15th-century choir stalls, a long nave and weathered pillars. It's been remodelled a lot over the years, but mosaics found here indicate this has been a Christian place of worship since the 4th or 5th century.

Church of St Anthony CHURCH
(Crkva Svetog Antuna) At the eastern end of the strip, this church has inlaid marble and a carving of a seated St Anthony the Hermit decorating the altar. Next door there's a working convent of Franciscan nuns who tend the garden and make tablecloths out of agave threads.

Just north of the Church of St Anthony, steps lead down to the beautifully landscaped **Komrčar Park**, a great place for a break on a hot summer's day.

OTHER ATTRACTIONS

Chapel of St Christopher CHAPEL
(Kapela Svetog Kristofora; lapidarium admission by donation; ⏲lapidarium 10am-12.30pm & 7.30-9pm Mon-Sat, 7.30-9pm Sun May-Sep) This lovely chapel houses a small collection of ancient

WORTH A TRIP

ST EUPHEMIA

The **Franciscan Monastery of St Euphemia** (Samostan Svete Eufemije; Kampor; admission 10KN; ⏲10am-noon & 4-6pm Mon-Sat) and adjacent baroque church of St Bernardine are well worth the 2.5km walk northwest from Palit to Kampor. Franciscan monks have a small museum here with old parchment books, stones and religious paintings, but it's the peaceful ambience that makes the monastery special. Check out the pleasant cloister and, inside the church, the ethereal painted ceiling, a stark contrast to the agony depicted on the late-Gothic wooden crucifix. Note also the 15th-century polyptych by the Vivarini brothers.

stones inside its **lapidarium**. There's a terrific **viewpoint** here too.

Dominis Palace PALACE
(Srednja) Built at the end of the 15th century for a prominent patrician family who taught the public to read and write here, the facade has Renaissance windows and a striking portal decorated with the family coat-of-arms.

Activities

Rab is criss-crossed with 100km of marked **hiking trails** and 80km of **biking trails**, several of which can be accessed from Rab Town. Pick up the excellent *Biking & Trekking* map from the tourist office. From behind Hotel Istra, there's a trail that leads northeast to the mountain peak of Sveti Ilija. It only takes about 30 minutes on foot and the view is great. Bikes can be rented from several travel agencies.

Diving sites are many and varied: the wreck of the *Rosa* with its red gorgonian forest, conger eels and lobster; submarine caves and tunnels; and a protected amphora field off the cape of Sorinj. **Mirko Diving Centre** (☎721 154; www.mirkodivingcenter.com; Barbat 710), based in nearby Barbat, offers courses (Discover Diving is €30) and fun dives.

A long pebbly beach stretches all around Rab Town, so take a towel and freshen up after sightseeing – just mind those sea urchins!

Tours

Day tours of the island by boat, including swim stops and visits to nearby islands such as Sveti Grgur and the infamous Goli Otok, are offered by many travel agents; prices start at about 125KN. You can also chat to skippers themselves about trips: in the evening the main harbourfront is lined with excursion boats. Trips to Lošinj (170KN) and Krk (170KN), as well as to Plitvice (385KN), are also possible.

Festivals & Events

The whole town goes back to the Middle Ages during **Rab Fair** (Rapska Fjera; ⏲25-27 July), when residents dress in period garb and there are drumming, processions, fireworks, medieval dancing and crossbow competitions.

Rab Musical Evenings take place from June to September and revolve around Thursday-night concerts (9pm) at venues including the Holy Cross Church and St Mary's.

In July Rab hosts a busy **fashion week** and in early August a large **Summer Festival** in the Blato area on the north side of Rab Town. The latter attracts some big trance and house turntablists, and also Croatian pop artists.

Sleeping

Campgrounds and hotels (though few of real quality) are pretty plentiful around Rab Town; many are managed by the **Imperial** (www.imperial.hr) group. Contact travel agencies for private rooms and apartments or sniff one out yourself.

TOP CHOICE **Hotel Arbiana** HISTORIC HOTEL €€€
(☎775 900; www.arbianahotel.com; Obala Kralja Petra Krešimira IV 12; s 876KN, d 1300KN; P❄@☎) The classiest address in Rab, this historic hotel dates back to 1924 and retains plenty of period character and formal elegance. All 28 rooms were recently updated and come with LCD TV, desks and good-quality repro furniture. Most have balconies. There's a great restaurant (Santa Maria; p165) here too.

Pansion Tamaris PANSION €€
(☎724 925; www.tamaris-rab.com; Palit 285; d 760KN; P❄☎) About a 10-minute walk east of town this is a well-run little hotel, with attentive staff and a peaceful location. Rooms are simple but quite stylish with laminate

floors and soft linen, and most have sea views from their balconies.

Hotel Imperial HOTEL €€
(☎724 522; www.imperial.hr; Palit bb; d 960KN; P❄@📶) A little old-fashioned, but enjoys a great location in shady Komrčar Park. The rooms vary in quality and aspect. There are tennis courts, a gym and a spa, and a free boat ride to the beach is included.

Campsite Padova III CAMPGROUND €
(☎724 355; www.rab-camping.com; Banjol bb; per adult/tent 47/32KN; ⊙Apr-Oct) About 2km east of town, it's right on a sandy beach and has extensive facilities and mobile houses for rent too.

Eating

Rab cuisine revolves around fresh fish, seafood and pasta. Quality and prices are fairly uniform, though there are some notable exceptions.

There is a **supermarket** out on the harbourfront.

Astoria MEDITERRANEAN €€
(www.astoria-rab.com; Trg Municipium Arba 7; mains 90-160KN) This refined place has an elevated view of the harbour from the terrace and very accomplished, ambitious cooking. Try the monkfish, or wonderful *scampi municipium arbe* (in white wine and garlic). There are delicious Croatian and Italian wines.

Santa Maria CROATIAN €€
(Dinka Dokule 6; mains from 80KN) The terrace here is one of Rab's most atmospheric and romantic places to eat, with candlelit tables surrounded by the old city walls. The menu is inventive – try the chicken with sage honey and *limetta* sauce, or roasted calamari – and the cooking accomplished.

Paradiso CROATIAN €€
(www.makek-paradiso.hr; Stjepana Radića 1; mains 75-140KN; ⊙8am-midnight May-Oct) Bundle together art, wine and good food, serve it all up in an ancient stone townhouse and you're halfway to paradise. Sample Istrian and Pelješac wines in the *vinoteka* then dine on meat, fish or pasta in the wonderful Venetian loggia, or the rear patio.

Konoba Rab CROATIAN €€
(Kneza Branimira 3; mains from 65KN; ⊙closed lunch Sun) For real country cooking this place excels, though the menu's English is ropy: 'grotto of the island of Rab', anyone? Stick to meat and fish staples or order the lamb baked under a *peka* in advance.

Entertainment

Hardcore clubbers often head to Zrće beach in neighbouring Pag Island, catching the late-afternoon catamaran connection and returning on the 6am boat.

Dock 69 BAR, CLUB
(Obala Kralja Petra Krešimira IV) This slick lounge bar has a harbour-facing terrace and clubby interior where DJs ramp up the volume later on with rhythm and blues, house and chart tunes.

Santos Beach Club CLUB
(www.sanantonio-club.com; Pudarica Beach; ⊙10am-dawn late Jun-early Sep) Summer-only beach club about 10km from Rab Town near Barbat (shuttles run at night). DJs spin to a lively party crowd and there are live concerts and fashion shows. Also doubles as a daytime beach hangout, with loungers and beach volleyball.

Information

There's free wireless internet around the tourist office and Trg Svetog Kristofora.

Digital X (☎777 010; Donja bb; per hr 30KN; ⊙10am-2pm & 6pm-midnight Mon-Sat, 6pm-midnight Sun) Internet access.

Erste Banka (Mali Palit bb) Changes money and has an ATM.

Katurbo (☎724 495; www.katurbo.hr; Šetalište Markantuna Dominisa 5) Private accommodation, money exchange, bike rental (per hour 20KN) and tours to places including Plitvice Lakes National Park.

Numero Uno (☎724 688; www.numero-uno.hr; Šetalište Markantuna Dominisa 5) Books private accommodation, rents bicycles and offers trekking trips, plus boat, kayak (320KN) and bike tours (290KN).

Post Office (Mali Palit 67; ⊙7am-8pm Mon-Fri, to 2pm Sat)

Tourist Office (☎771 111; www.tzg-rab.hr; Trg Municipium Arba 8; ⊙8am-10pm mid-May–Sep, to 8pm Mon-Fri Oct–mid-May) A well-organised office with helpful staff and loads of useful maps, brochures and leaflets. There's another branch, open 8am to 10pm June to September, round the corner from the bus station.

Lopar

POP 1194

The tourist development on Lopar Peninsula occupying the northern tip of Rab Island has little charm, but there is a compelling reason to come – 22 sandy beaches bordered by shady pine groves. Central European families flock here in the summer months, as the sea is very shallow and perfect for small children. This is particularly so on 1500m-long **Paradise Beach** (Rajska Plaža) on Crnika Bay, where you can (almost) wade right across to a little offshore island. Nearby **Livačina Beach** is a quieter option.

If you wish to strip out of your bikini, **Sahara Beach** is a popular nudist spot in a delightful northern cove. It's a 45-minute hike along a marked trail through pine forests; pick up the trail after the San Marino hotel complex.

The town centre has a **tourist office** (☎775 508; www.lopar.hr; Lopar bb; ⌚8am-9pm Jul & Aug, to 8pm Mon-Sat, to 2pm Sun Jun & Sep). **Sahara Tours** (☎775 444; www.sahara-tours.hr; Lopar bb) has dozens of private rooms, houses and apartments on its books and offers boat excursions around the island.

For a meal, **Lukovac** (mains from 35KN), right on Paradise beach, is inexpensive and serves tasty *picarels* (tiny fried fish) and salads. **Fortuna** (Lopar bb; mains from 50KN), slightly out of town, is fancier with a nice shady terrace.

The ferry from Valbiska stops 1km from the town centre; it's served by a small bus-train for foot passengers (adult/child 10/5KN).

Northern Dalmatia

☎022, 023

Includes »

Best Places to Eat

- » Pelegrini (p191)
- » Boškinac (p186)
- » Foša (p175)
- » Taverna-Konoba Marasović (p181)
- » Bistro Na Tale (p185)

Best Places to Stay

- » Boškinac (p186)
- » Hotel Bastion (p173)
- » Art Hotel Kalelarga (p173)
- » Konoba B&B (p190)
- » Pansion Eco-House (p178)

Why Go?

Isolated from Continental Europe by the Velebit mountains, Northern Dalmatia is an incredibly scenic and temperate region. It's prime holiday country and, given the exquisite coastline, historic cities, sublime offshore islands and national parks, it's easy to appreciate why. Yet Northern Dalmatia is far from being overrun: whole stretches are pristine and retain a ravishing natural beauty.

Zadar, the main gateway, is a cultured city rich with museums, Roman ruins, quirky sights, restaurants and music festivals. Nearby Šibenik has an extraordinary medieval quarter. Of the dozens of Adriatic islands, Pag hosts Croatia's premier summer clubbing scene, while Dugi Otok and the Kornati Islands are an escapist's heaven.

Croatia's most impressive national parks are here too: Paklenica offers exceptional hiking and rock climbing, while Krka and Plitvice boast waterfalls and lakes in abundance.

When to Go

Zadar

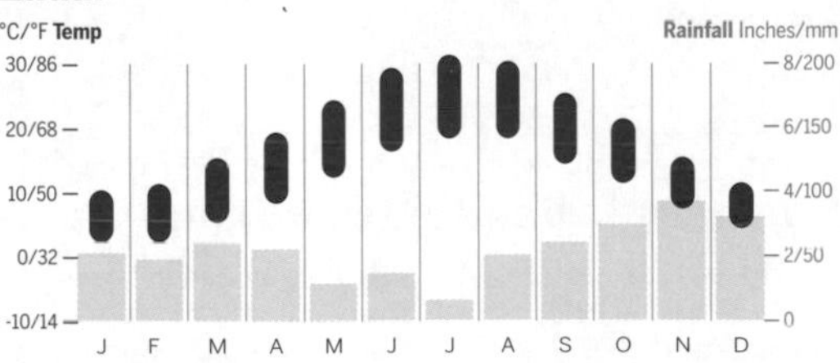

Apr–May Mild temperatures are ideal for hiking Paklenica and Plitvice National Parks.

Jun–Jul Catch Šibenik at its best during the city's famous Children's Festival.

Aug–Sep Tisno hosts a merry bunch of music festivals.

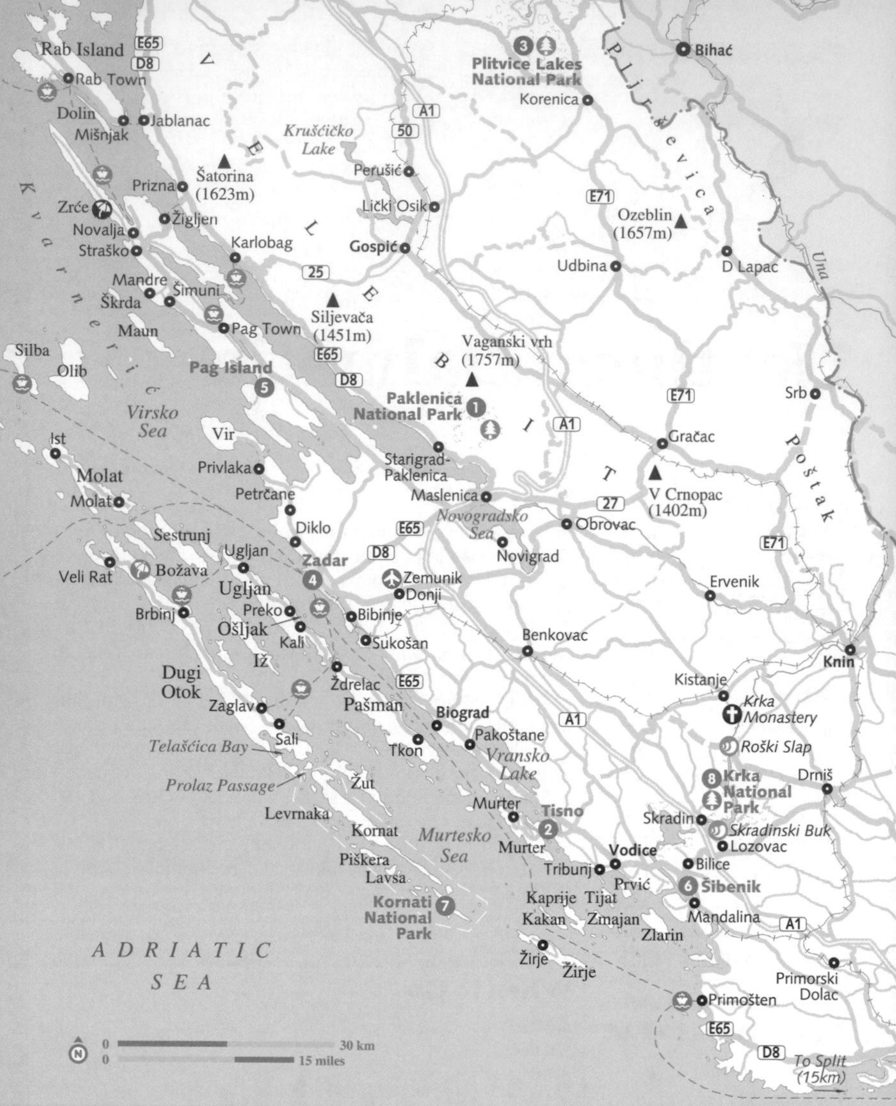

Northern Dalmatia Highlights

1. Hike the incredible canyons and alpine trails at **Paklenica National Park** (p179)
2. Party in **Tisno**, home turf of some of Europe's most innovative music festivals (p173)
3. Marvel at the turquoise lakes and waterfalls in **Plitvice Lakes National Park** (p177)
4. Discover **Zadar**, one of the coast's most underrated towns, and visit its wonderful **Sun Salutation and Sea Organ** (p169)
5. Enjoy the delights of **Pag Island** (p184) – heady nightlife, stunning scenery and exquisite cheese
6. Wander the medieval streets of Šibenik and learn about raptors at the **Sokolarski Centre** (p191)
7. Explore the eerie beauty of the **Kornati National Park** (p192)
8. Swim in the pristine lakes at **Krka National Park** (p193)

ZADAR REGION

This area, loaded with appeal, includes the cosmopolitan town of Zadar and the amazing national parks of Plitvice and Paklenica.

Zadar

023 / POP 73,442

Boasting a historic old town of Roman ruins and medieval churches, cosmopolitan cafes and quality museums, Zadar is an excellent city. It's not too crowded, it's not overrun with tourists and its two unique attractions – the sound-and-light spectacle of the Sea Organ and Sun Salutation – need to be seen and heard to be believed.

It's not a picture-postcard kind of place, but the mix of beautiful Roman architecture, Habsburg elegance, a wonderful seafront and some unsightly ordinary office blocks is what gives Zadar so much character. It's no Dubrovnik, but it's not a museum town either – this is a living, vibrant city, enjoyed by its residents and visitors alike.

The centre of town is not well blessed with hotels, though a few new places spring up each year. Most visitors stay in the leafy resort area of Borik nearby. Zadar is a key transport hub with superb ferry connections to Croatia's Adriatic islands, Kvarner, southern Dalmatia and Italy.

History

Zadar was inhabited by the Illyrian Liburnian tribe as early as the 9th century BC. By the 1st century BC, Zadar had become a minor Roman colony. Slavs settled here in the 6th and 7th centuries AD, and Zadar eventually fell under the authority of Croatian-Hungarian kings.

The rise of Venetian power in the mid-12th century was bitterly contested – there was a succession of citizens' uprisings over the next 200 years, but the city was finally acquired by Venice in 1409, along with the rest of Dalmatia.

Frequent Veneto-Turkish wars resulted in the building of Zadar's famous city walls in the 16th century. With the fall of Venice in 1797, the city passed to Austrian rulers who administered the city with Zadar's Italianised ruling aristocracy. Italian influence endured well into the 20th century, with Zadar remaining an Italian province. When Italy capitulated to the Allies in 1943, the city was occupied by the Germans and then bombed to smithereens by the Allies, with almost 60% of the old town destroyed. The city was rebuilt following the original street plan.

History repeated itself in November 1991 when Yugoslav rockets kept Zadar under siege for three months. No war wounds are visible, however, and Zadar has re-emerged as one of Croatia's most dynamic towns.

Sights

Sea Organ MONUMENT

Zadar's incredible Sea Organ, designed by local architect Nikola Bašić, is unique. Set within the perforated stone stairs that descend into the sea is a system of pipes and whistles that exudes wistful sighs when the movement of the sea pushes air through it. The effect is hypnotic – the mellifluous tones increasing in volume when a boat or ferry passes by. You can swim from the steps off the promenade while listening to the sound of the Sea Organ.

Sun Salutation MONUMENT

Right next to the Sea Organ is the Sun Salutation, another wacky and wonderful creation by local architect Nikola Bašić. It's a 22m-wide circle cut into the pavement, filled with 300 multilayered glass plates that collect the sun's energy during the day and, together with the wave energy that makes the Sea Organ's sound, produce a trippy light show from sunset to sunrise that's meant to simulate the solar system. Thanks to Croatia's climate, the Sun Salutation collects enough energy to power the entire harbourfront lighting system.

The place is packed with tourists, excited children and locals every night, especially at sunset, when the gorgeous sea views and the illuminated floor make for a spectacular sight.

Church of St Donat CHURCH

(Crkva Svetog Donata; Šimuna Kožičića Benje; admission 15KN; 9am-9pm May-Sep, to 4pm Oct-Apr) Dating from the beginning of the 9th century, this church was named after Bishop Donat, who had it built following the style of early Byzantine architecture. The unusual circular ground plan is especially visible on the southern side, while the interior is wonderfully simple and unadorned, and is refreshingly cool on warm days. It's no longer used for services.

The church was built over the **Roman forum**, which was constructed between the 1st century BC and the 3rd century AD. A few architectural fragments are preserved

Zadar

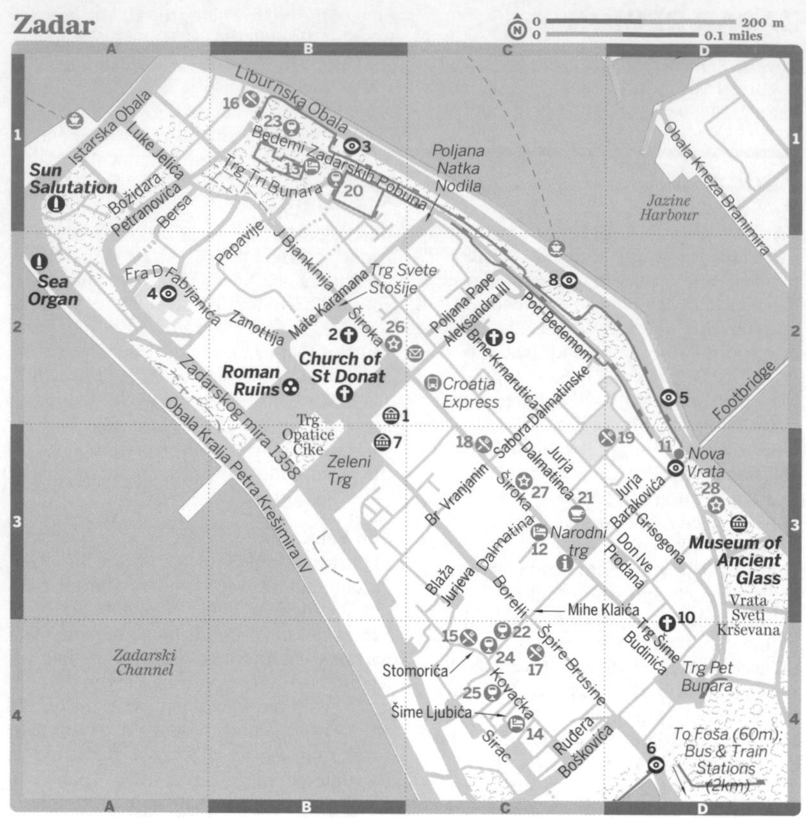

and two complete pillars are built into the church. The original floors have been removed, revealing slabs from the ancient forum. Notice the Latin inscriptions on the remains of the Roman sacrificial altars.

Outside the church on the northwestern side is a pillar from the Roman era that served in the Middle Ages as a **shame post**, where wrongdoers were chained and publicly humiliated. The western side of the church has more **Roman remains**, including pillars with reliefs of the mythical figures Jupiter Ammon and Medusa. Underneath, you can see the remains of the altars used in pagan blood sacrifices. It is believed that this area was a temple dedicated to Jupiter, Juno and Minerva, and dates from the 1st century BC.

City Walls CITY WALLS

A tour of the city walls provides a good insight into Zadar's history. Start with the eastern walls near the footbridge, the only remains of the ancient Roman and early medieval fortifications (most of the walls were built under Venetian rule). Nearby are four old city gates. To the northwest is the **Gate of St Rok**, then the **Port Gate**. The latter was built in 1573 and still sports the Venetian lion and part of a Roman triumphal arch, and has a memorial inscription of the 1571 Battle of Lepanto. A little further west is the **Chain Gate**. In the southeast is the elaborate **Land Gate** (Kopnena Vrata), dating from 1543, which was entirely renovated in 2011. Its Renaissance-style decorations include St Krževan on horseback and the Venetian lion.

Museum of Ancient Glass MUSEUM

(www.mas-zadar.hr; Poljana Zemaljskog Odbora 1; adult/concession 30/10KN; 9am-9pm May-Sep, to 7pm Mon-Sat Oct-Apr) This is an impressive, well-designed museum: its layout is superb, with giant light boxes and ethereal music to make the experience special. The history and invention of glass is explained, with ex-

Zadar

Top Sights

Church of St Donat	B2
Museum of Ancient Glass	D3
Roman Ruins	B2
Sea Organ	A2
Sun Salutation	A1

Sights

1	Archaeological Museum	B2
2	Cathedral of St Anastasia	B2
3	Chain Gate	B1
4	Franciscan Monastery & Church	A2
5	Gate of St Rok	D2
6	Land Gate	D4
7	Museum of Church Art	B3
8	Port Gate	C2
9	St Grisogonus Church	C2
10	St Simeon's Church	D4

Activities, Courses & Tours

11	Aquarius Travel Agency	D3

Sleeping

12	Art Hotel Kalelarga	C3
13	Hotel Bastion	B1
14	Hotel Venera	C4

Eating

15	Do Ortuna	C4
16	Kornat	B1
17	Na po ure	C4
18	Supermarket	C3
19	Market	D3

Drinking

20	Arsenal	B1
21	Caffe Bar Lovre	C3
22	Galerija Đina	C4
23	Garden	B1
24	Kult Caffe	C4
25	Zodiac	C4

Entertainment

26	Callegro	B2
27	National Theatre	C3
28	Satir	D3

amples of tools, blowpipes and early vessels from Egypt and Mesopotamia. Thousands of pieces are on display: goblets, jars and vials; jewellery, including rings and amulets; and many unusual pieces found in the Zadar area, including Roman miniatures used by ladies to store perfume and essential oils.

St Simeon's Church CHURCH

(Crkva Svetog Šime; Trg Šime Budinića; ⌚8am-noon & 6-8pm Jun-Sep) This church was reconstructed in the 16th and 17th centuries on the site of an earlier structure. The sarcophagus of St Simeon is a masterpiece of medieval goldsmith work. Commissioned in 1377, the coffin is made of cedar and covered inside and out with finely executed gold-plated silver reliefs. The middle relief showing the Presentation of Jesus at the Temple is a copy of Giotto's fresco from Cappella dell'Arena in Padua, Italy. Other reliefs depict scenes from the lives of the saints and King Ludovic's visit to Zadar. The lid shows a reclining St Simeon.

Cathedral of St Anastasia CATHEDRAL

(Katedrala Svete Stošije; Trg Svete Stošije; ⌚8am-noon & 5-6.30pm Mon-Fri) The Romanesque Cathedral of St Anastasia was built in the 12th and 13th centuries on the site of an older church. Behind the richly decorated facade is an impressive three-nave interior marked by 13th-century wall paintings in the side apses. On the altar in the left apse is a marble sarcophagus containing the relics of St Anastasia, while the presbytery contains lavishly carved choir stalls. The cathedral was badly bombed during WWII and has since been reconstructed. Climb its **bell tower** (10KN) for stunning old-town views.

Museum of Church Art MUSEUM

(Trg Opatice Čike bb; adult/concession 20/10KN; ⌚10am-12.45pm & 6-8pm Mon-Sat, 10am-noon Sun) This impressive museum in the Benedictine monastery boasts a fine collection of reliquaries and religious paintings. Along with the goldsmiths' works, of note are the 14th-century portrait of the Madonna, marble sculptures and a painting by Paolo Veneziani. On the 2nd floor are 15th- and 16th-century sculptures and embroidery, and six pictures by the 15th-century Venetian painter Vittore Carpaccio.

Archaeological Museum MUSEUM

(Arheološki Muzej; www.amzd.hr; Trg Opatice Čike 1; adult/concession 20/10KN; ⌚9am-10pm daily May-Sep, 9am-3pm Tue-Fri, 10am-1pm Sat & Sun Oct-Apr) The recently renovated Archaeological Museum spreads out over three floors. Its upper floor showcases prehistory, with Illyrian and Liburnian pottery and metalwork. The 2nd floor houses impressive Roman stelae from Asseria, a 2.5m-high marble statue of Augustus from the 1st century AD, and a model of the old Forum, among other Roman pieces. The ground floor is dedicated to the Middle Ages, and you can see some odd local tombstones.

FREE Franciscan Monastery & Church MONASTERY
(Samostan Svetog Frane; Zadarskog mira 1358; ⌚7.30am-noon & 4.30-6pm) The oldest of its kind in Dalmatia, the Gothic church was consecrated in 1280. Its interior has a number of Renaissance features, such as the lovely Chapel of St Anthony. In the sacristy, a memorial tablet commemorates the 1358 treaty under which Venice relinquished its rights to Dalmatia in favour of the Croatian-Hungarian king, Ludovic.

St Grisogonus Church CHURCH
(Crkva Svetog Krševana; Brne Krnarutića; ⌚Mass only) This beautiful structure was formerly part of a 12th-century Benedictine monastery. It's currently closed for renovations but has a fine baroque altar and Byzantine frescos.

Activities

There's a **swimming area** with diving boards, a small park and a cafe on the coastal promenade off Kralja Dmitra Zvonimira, north of the bridge that connects the old town with the new part. Bordered by pine trees and small parks, the promenade takes you to a beach in front of Hotel Kolovare and then winds on for about 1km along the coast.

As an alternative to using the bridge, hop aboard a *barkarioli* (row boat) for a relaxing trip between the old town peninsula and the mainland (5KN).

Acquapura Thalasso WELLNESS CENTRE
(☎206 184; www.borik.falkensteiner.com; Club Fulmination Borik, Majstora Radovana 7, Borik; ⌚8am-10pm) An outstanding wellness centre spread across a huge space, with beautifully renovated premises, sauna and jacuzzi rooms, and all manner of pools and plunge facilities, massages and beauty treatments. You're worth it!

Supernova CYCLING
(☎311 010; Obala Kneza Branimira 2a) Zadar is a great place to explore by bicycle. Supernova has bikes from 90KN per day.

Tours

Travel agencies offer boat cruises to Telašćica Bay and the beautiful Kornati Islands; tours generally include lunch and a swim in the sea or a salt lake. Ask around on Liburnska Obala (where the excursion boats are moored).

Organised trips to the national parks of Paklenica, Krka and Plitvice Lakes are also very popular. They make it easy for visitors to access and enjoy the parks without having to worry about organising transport.

Aquarius Travel Agency TOURS
(☎212 919; www.juresko.hr; Nova Vrata bb) Charges 250KN to 300KN per person for a full-day trip.

Festivals & Events

The Zadar area now has an internationally renowned programme of music festivals.

Musical Evenings MUSIC
Classical music performances featuring prominent artists from across the globe are held in the Church of St Donat and other Zadar venues throughout the year.

CITY SQUARES

Narodni trg was traditionally the centre of public life. The western side of the square is dominated by the late-Renaissance Town Watchtower, dating from 1562. The clock tower was built under the Austrian administration in 1798. Public proclamations and judgments were announced from the loggia opposite, which is now an art-exhibition space. Several hundred metres northwest of Narodni trg is the Orthodox Church, behind which is a small Serbian neighbourhood.

Trg Pet Bunara (Five Wells Sq) was built in 1574 on the site of a former moat and contains a cistern with five wells that supplied Zadar with water until 1838.

Its smaller cousin, **Trg Tri Bunara** (Three Wells Sq), on the other side of town, sports the excellent Arsenal, a former shipping warehouse, now a cultural centre containing a bar, restaurant and several shops. Just off the square is the Garden bar and club, making this area a mini cultural hub.

THE GARDEN IS GROWING

Between July and September the Zadar region is imbued with some of the globe's most celebrated electronic music. Styles are myriad and music is eclectic: cosmic disco, soul and funk, folk-tinged electronica, deep house and jazzy lounge. Full-on trance is not part of the scene, and the crowd is musically knowledgable and mature. The ringmaster for these festivals is the Zadar-based Garden Bar, but the festivals are held in a gorgeous new location, in the small village of Tisno, 45km southeast of Zadar.

The original event, the **Garden Festival** (www.thegardenfestival.eu), has been running since 2006, but by 2010 four other festivals (Soundwave, Suncebeat, Electric Elephant and Stop Making Sense) had joined the party between July and September. By 2012 the old location in the town of Petrčane had become too big for its boots, calling for a new venue.

The new location in Tisno is a grand affair. The club has a private sandy bay beach, 80 renovated apartments and a luxury campsite – with breathable, cotton Indian Shikar 30-sq-metre tents that have electric fans and lighting, real beds and mosquito nets, and even a separate dressing room and porch area. This is all for the revellers to stay in and make as much noise as they like without annoying the local residents. There are shady chill-out zones and three different music areas, including the open-air Barbarella's club, a short bus or water taxi ride away. Chuck in the infamous Argonaughty boat parties (and the sparkling Adriatic sea on tap) and it's quite a scene.

All events feature innovative artists (rather than big names and bangin' DJs), like Jose Padilla, Laura Jones, Maxxi Soundsystem, and Steve Cobby (Fila Brazillia).

Zadar Dreams THEATRE
(Zadar Snova; www.zadarsnova.hr) A theatrical festival that takes over Zadar's parks and squares in early August with contemporary theatre, dance, music and art.

Full Moon Festival CULTURAL
During this festival (held on the night of the full moon in August), Zadar's quays are lit with torches and candles, stalls sell local delicacies and boats lining the quays become floating fish markets.

Choral Festival MUSIC
Choral events featuring some of Europe's best choirs are held in Zadar churches in October.

Sleeping

There's little accommodation in Zadar itself. Most visitors stay in the 'tourist settlement' of Borik, which isn't as bad as it sounds: it has good swimming, a nice promenade and lots of greenery. Most hotels in Borik date from Yugo days (or before) and there's also a hostel, campsite and *sobe* (rooms). Many hotels are managed by the Austria-based **Falkensteiner group** (www.falkensteiner.com).

Contact travel agencies for private accommodation, though very little is available in the old town.

ZADAR

TOP CHOICE **Art Hotel Kalelarga** BOUTIQUE HOTEL €€€
(233 000; www.arthotel-kalelarga.com; Široka 23; s/d/ste 1225/1430/2300KN; P ❄) Right in the heart of Zadar's old town, this 10-room boutique hotel is an understated, luxurious beauty that got its name from the historic street it stands on – Kalelarga is the local name for Široka street. Built and designed under strict conservation rules due to its old-town location, the place blends in elegantly with its surrounds. Walk in through the stylish cafe boasting delicious cakes to discover spacious rooms in hues of sand and stone, with grand beds, elaborate lighting and cool lines. It is designed by Slovenian architect Jani Vozelj, who also worked on Hotel Bastion (which shares an owner with this place). There is also a restaurant, **Gourmet Kalelarga**, which has tables in the lower ground floor and on the main square, outside the Ethnological Museum.

TOP CHOICE **Hotel Bastion** BOUTIQUE HOTEL €€€
(494 950; www.hotel-bastion.hr; Bedemi Zadarskih Pobuna 13; s/d/ste from 905/1140/1290KN; P ❄ @) The older but no less stylish sister to Art Hotel Kalelarga, the Bastion is another luxurious beauty in Zadar's old town.

Built over the remains of a fortress, the Bastion radiates character, with a pleasing art-deco theme throughout. The 28 rooms are very well finished, many with marble trim, while the suite has its own terrace with harbour views. As for location, things couldn't be better: it's right next to the **Garden Bar** and **Arsenal**. Also boasts a top-drawer restaurant and basement spa, though fitness facilities are disappointing. Parking is 70KN per day.

Villa Hrešć HOTEL €€€
(☎337 570; www.villa-hresc.hr; Obala Kneza Trpimira 28; s/d 670/850KN; P❄🛜≋) This condo-style villa has a full-frontal view of the old town from its coastal garden. The good-value rooms and apartments benefit from subtle colours and attractive decor; some have massive terraces. Note that the apartments are not really of the self-catering sort, ie the cooking facilities are mostly for decorative purposes. It's north of the centre, about a 20-minute walk from Zadar's historic sights along the coastal promenade.

Hotel Venera GUESTHOUSE €€
(☎214 098; www.hotel-venera-zd.hr; Šime Ljubića 4a; d 460KN) A modest guesthouse that has two things going for it: a good location on a quiet street in the old town and friendly family owners. The plain rooms are clean, but old fashioned and small, each with twin (single) beds, fan, desk and en-suite shower. There are plans to install air-con and build a restaurant downstairs. No breakfast is included.

BORIK

Hotel Adriana BEACH RESORT €€€
(☎206 636; www.falkensteiner.com; Majstora Radovana 7; s/d 1510/2370KN; ⏱mid-May–Oct; P❄@🛜≋) A very relaxing place to stay, this hotel is centred on a handsome 19th-century villa and has lovely shady grounds that extend down to the Adriatic. The rooms, in a 1960s extension, are finished to a high standard and retain wonderful features of the decade. Many guests opt for half-board as the restaurant is excellent, with tables scattered around an elegant terrace.

Hotel Niko BEACH RESORT €€€
(☎337 888; www.hotel-niko.hr; Obala Kneza Domagoja 9; s/d 752/963KN; P❄@🛜) A small, well-run hotel that enjoys lovely views over the Adriatic towards the old town from its grounds and restaurant terrace, Niko. The spacious rooms are kitted out with thick red carpets and good-quality furniture, and many have balconies with sea views. Staff are efficient and friendly.

Club Funimation Borik BEACH RESORT €€€
(☎206 636; www.falkensteiner.com; Majstora Radovana 7; s/d 1296/1714KN; P❄@🛜≋) Efficiently run family hotel right on the Borik seafront with superb facilities, including a great gym and indoor-outdoor pool complex. Children are well looked after in their own 'Falky Land'. The hotel dates from the 1960s, and the renovated design faithfully reflects the era with zany lighting and a kitsch safari-style bar. Rooms are very spacious and suites are palatial. Funimation's trump card is its outstanding spa.

Pansion Albin GUESTHOUSE €€
(☎331 137; www.albin.hr; Put Dikla 47; s/d 335/447KN; P❄@🛜≋) A good choice, this warmly managed guesthouse has well-presented rooms, some with balconies. The in-house restaurant is good (breakfast is generous) and the location is quiet, with a beach close by.

Zadar Youth Hostel HOSTEL €
(☎331 145; zadar@hfhs.hr; Obala Kneza Trpimira 76; dm 90-127KN; P@) This very large (300-bed capacity) hostel is the cheapest place in town for budget travellers. It has a pretty typical youth-hostel set-up, with plain rooms (11 doubles) and large dorms, close to the Borik coast. It's fine for a night or two, but note that it does get periodically overrun with huge groups of school children.

Autocamp Borik CAMPGROUND €
(☎332 074; per adult 56KN, per site 94-146KN; ⏱May-Oct) A good option for those who want easy access to Zadar, this campground is steps away from the shore at Borik. Pitches are shaded by tall pines and facilities are good.

Eating

Dining options in Zadar are eclectic and generally good value. You'll find elegant restaurants specialising in Dalmatian cuisine (particularly seafood) and no-nonsense canteen-style places offering filling grub.

ZADAR

Zadar's **market** (⏱6am-3pm), off Jurja Barakovica, is one of Croatia's best, with seasonal, local produce at cheap prices: juicy watermelons and oranges, cured ham and Pag cheese (at around 100KN per half kilo).

There's also a **supermarket** (cnr Široka & Sabora Dalmatinske) that keeps long hours.

TOP CHOICE **Foša** MEDITERRANEAN €€

(www.fosa.hr; Kralja Dmitra Zvonimira 2; mains from 85KN) With a gorgeous terrace that juts out into the harbour and a sleek interior that combines ancient stone walls with 21st-century style, Foša is a very classy place. Start by tasting the olive oils, and move on to a grilled Adriatic fish of your choice, tuna or scampi (though red-meat eaters won't be disappointed either). Desserts include yummy Dalmatian almond cake and panna cotta with sour-cherry essence.

Kornat CROATIAN €€

(www.restaurant-kornat.com; Liburnska Obala 6; mains from 70KN) Sitting pretty in a prime harbour-front spot, this elegant place with lots of polished wood and a slim pavement terrace is one of Zadar's best restaurants. The cooking is full of flavour, though quite traditional with lots of rich sauces in evidence – try beef steak with truffle sauce, lamb with rosemary and red wine, or black risotto.

Na po ure DALMATIAN €

(Špire Brusine 8; mains from 40KN) This unpretentious *konoba* (family-run restaurant) is the place to sate that appetite, with from-the-heart Dalmatian cooking: grilled lamb, calf's liver and fresh fish served with potatoes and vegetables.

Zalogajnica Ljepotica DALMATIAN €

(Obala Kneza Branimira 4b; mains from 35KN) The cheapest place in town prepares three to four dishes a day (think risotto, pasta and grilled meat) at knockout prices in a no-frills setting.

Do Ortuna QUICK BITE €

(Stomorića 4; mains 12-30KN) This hole in the wall with two pavement tables serves huge sandwiches, crêpes, *papaline* (tiny fried fish in breadcrumbs) and salads. It does what it does very well indeed.

BORIK

Niko SEAFOOD €€

(www.hotel-niko.hr; Obala Kneza Domagoja 9; mains from 60KN) A wildly popular hotel restaurant that's great for grilled fish and other seafood (though the menu has red meat and vegetarian dishes too). Eat on a large terrace that overlooks the Adriatic.

Drinking

Zadar has pavement cafes, lounge bars, boho bars and everything in between. Head to the district of Varoš on the southwest side of the old town for interesting little dive bars popular with students and arty types.

TOP CHOICE **Garden** BAR, RESTAURANT

(www.thegardenzadar.com; Bedemi Zadarskih Pobuna; late May-Oct) If anywhere can claim to have put Zadar on the map it's this remarkable bar-club-garden-restaurant perched on top of the old city walls with jaw-dropping harbour views. It's very Ibiza-esque with cushion mattresses, secluded alcoves, vast sail-like sunshades, purple and white decor, and contemporary electronic music. Prices are pretty moderate given the surrounds. Everyone stays here longer than they intended – the place has a hypnotic appeal!

Arsenal BAR, RESTAURANT

(www.arsenalzadar.com; Trg Tri Bunara 1) A huge renovated former shipping warehouse that now contains a lounge bar, a restaurant, a gallery and a cultural centre, and has a cool, cultured vibe. It's a fascinating place to spend some time, with zany chill-out alcoves, art to browse, boutiques, musical events, good food and drink, and even a tourist info desk (which may or may not be staffed). Sample the cocktails and relax in the lounge area. It's the perfect place for a drink or three with friends.

Caffe Bar Lovre CAFE

(Narodni trg 1) With a huge terrace on Narodni trg, gorgeous Lovre has plenty of atmosphere thanks to having the remains of the 12th-century Church of St Lovre on the premises (you'll find it at the rear). Good for a light breakfast: munch on a croissant, sip a cappuccino and soak up the heart-of-the-city vibe.

Kult Caffe BAR

(Stomorića 4) The Kult Caffe draws a young fashionable crowd with its stylish interior and contemporary tunes. Its huge terrace is one of the old town's key meeting points.

Zodiac BAR

(Olica Simana Ljubavca bb) Zadar HQ for the city's artists and writers, daydreamers and doers. Its backstreet seats are full of interesting characters.

Galerija Đina BAR
(Varoška 2) A lively hole-in-the-wall bar that spills out into a narrow lane in the heart of the Varoš action. Gets infectiously raucous at weekends.

Entertainment

Satir NIGHTCLUB
(www.satir.hr; Poljana Zemaljskog Odbora 2; ⌚Thu-Sat) An intimate club that features leading house and techno DJs and fetish nights, and hosts bands and fashion shows.

Callegro CINEMA
(www.callegro.com; Široka 18; tickets 20-25KN) Smaller cinema with everything from art-house films to Hollywood blockbusters, screened in their original language.

National Theatre THEATRE
(☎314 552; Široka; ⌚box office 9am-5pm Mon-Fri) Much of Zadar's rich thespian history has played out at the National Theatre.

Information

Geris.net (Federica Grisogona 81; internet access per hr 25KN) The city's best cybercafe.

Hospital (☎315 677; Bože Peričića 5)

Miatours (☎/fax 212 788; www.miatours.hr; Vrata Svetog Krševana) Arranges excursions and accommodation.

Post Office (Poljana Pape Aleksandra III; ⌚7.30am-9pm Mon-Sat, to 2pm Sun) You can make phone calls and it has an ATM.

Tourist Office (☎316 166; www.tzzadar.hr; Mihe Klaića 5; ⌚8am-10pm Mon-Fri, to 9pm Sat & Sun Jun-Sep, to 8pm daily Oct-May) Publishes a good colour map and the free *Zadar City Guide*.

Zagrebačka Banka (Knezova Šubića Bribirskih 4) With ATM and money-changing facilities.

Getting There & Away

Air

Zadar's airport is about 12km east of the town centre. The Croatia Airlines bus (23KN) meets all arrivals and travels to/from the main bus station.

Croatia Airlines (☎250 101; www.croatia airlines.hr; Poljana Natka Nodila 7) Has flights to Zagreb and Pula.

Ryanair (www.ryanair.com) Flies to destinations including London Stansted, Dublin and Stockholm.

Boat

Jadrolinija (☎254 800; www.jadrolinija.hr; Liburnska Obala 7) On the harbour; has tickets for all local ferries.

Jadroagent (☎211 447; jadroagent-zadar@zd.t-com.hr; Poljana Natka Nodila 4) Sells international tickets; just inside the city walls.

Bus

The **bus station** (☎211 035; www.liburnija-zadar.hr) is about 2km east of the old town. Buses run to Zagreb (97KN to 147KN, 3½ to seven hours, every 30 minutes), Rijeka (155KN, five hours, six daily), Split (115KN, three hours, eight daily) and Dubrovnik (180KN to 230KN, eight hours, seven daily).

Croatia Express (☎250 502; www.croatia-express.com; Široka 14) Sells tickets to Zagreb, Split and Trieste (Italy), plus many German cities.

Train

The **train station** (☎212 555; www.hznet.hr; Ante Starčevića 3) is adjacent to the bus station. There are six daily trains to Zagreb, but the journey time is very slow: the fastest trains take over eight hours.

Getting Around

Buses run frequently from the bus station to the harbour and Borik. Buses marked 'Poluotok' run to the harbour and those marked 'Puntamika' (buses 5 and 8) run to Borik every 20 minutes (hourly on Sunday). Tickets cost 10KN – or 15KN for two from a *tisak* (news-stand).

Call the very efficient and cheap **Lulic** (☎494 494) for a taxi. A ride costs just 20KN to 25KN for up to 5km.

Ugljan

POP 7500

The island of Ugljan is easily accessible by boat from Zadar, making it a popular getaway for the locals and a kind of leafy island suburb for people who work in the city. It's densely populated, housing about 7500 people, and it can get crowded on summer weekends. There are few forested areas but many *macchia* (shrubs), some pines and a good deal of farmland with vegetable gardens, olive groves and vineyards. The eastern coast is the most developed part of the island, while the west is relatively deserted.

The port of entry is **Preko**, directly across from Zadar, with two small harbours and a ferry port. Although there's a town beach, the best beach is on the little island of **Galovac**, only 80m from the town centre. Small, pretty and wooded, Galovac has a Franciscan monastery dating from the 15th century. If you have your own car, you could visit **Ugljan village**, positioned on a bay with a

THE NATURE OF PLITVICE LAKES

The Plitvice lake system is divided into upper and lower sections. The upper lakes, lying in a dolomite valley, are surrounded by dense forests and are linked by several gushing waterfalls. The lower lakes are smaller and shallower. Most of the water comes from the Bijela and Crna (White and Black) Rivers, which join south of Prošćansko Lake, but the lakes are also fed by underground springs. In turn, water disappears into the porous limestone at some points only to re-emerge in other places. All the water empties into the Korana River near Sastavci Falls.

The upper lakes are separated by dolomite barriers, which expand with the mosses and algae that absorb calcium carbonate as river water rushes through the karst. The encrusted plants grow on top of each other, forming travertine barriers and creating waterfalls. The lower lakes were formed by cavities created by the water of the upper lakes. They undergo a similar process, as travertine is constantly forming and reforming itself into new combinations so that the landscape is ever changing. This unique interaction of water, rock and plant life has continued more or less undisturbed since the last ice age.

The lakes' colours also change constantly. Most of the time they're a surreal shade of turquoise, but hues shift with the quantity of minerals and organisms in the water, rainfall and the angle of sunlight. On some days the lakes can appear more jade green or steely grey.

The luxuriant vegetation of the national park is another delight. The northeastern section of the park is covered with beech forests while the rest is covered with beech, fir, spruce and white pine, dotted with patches of whitebeam, hornbeam and flowering ash, which change colour in autumn.

The stars of the park are bears and wolves, but there are also deer, boar, rabbits, foxes and badgers. Look out for bird species including hawks, owls, cuckoos, kingfishers, wild ducks and herons, and occasionally black storks and ospreys.

sandy beach; the fishing village of **Kali**; and the nearby islet of **Ošljak**, which is covered with pine and cypress trees.

Jadrolinija runs hourly ferries between 5.30am and 11pm from Zadar to Preko (20KN, 25 minutes) year-round.

Plitvice Lakes National Park

053

Plitvice Lakes National Park lies roughly midway between Zagreb and Zadar. It's magnificently scenic – forested hills enclose gorgeous turquoise lakes, which are linked by a series of waterfalls and cascades. Wooden footbridges and pathways snake around the fringes of the lakes – and under and across the rumbling water – for an exhilaratingly damp 18km. In 1979 Unesco proclaimed the Plitvice Lakes a World Heritage Site.

The extraordinary natural beauty of the park merits visiting for a couple of days, but you can experience a lot simply on a day trip from Zadar or Zagreb. There's no bad time to visit: in the spring the falls are flush with water, in summer the surrounding hills are greener, and in autumn there are fewer visitors and you'll be treated to the changing colours of leaves.

History

A preservation society was founded in 1893 to ensure the protection of the lakes, and the first hotel was built here in 1896. The boundaries of the national park were set in 1951 and the lakes became a major tourism attraction until the civil war (which actually began in Plitvice on 31 March 1991, when rebel Serbs took control of the park headquarters). Croatian police officer Josip Jović became the war's first victim when he was killed here in the park. Rebel Serbs held the area for the war's duration, turning hotels into barracks and plundering park property. The Croatian army retook the park in August 1995, and a long programme to repair facilities began. Today, Plitvice is well and truly back on the map, and you'll encounter groups of tourists from as far away as Korea, South America and Russia as you explore these remarkable lakes and waterfalls.

Sights

If you start at Entrance 2, the southernmost of the two entrances, it's an easy amble down to the shore of **Kozjak Lake** and P1 (a hut and boat stop), where you can rent rowing boats (55KN per hour). (Unfortunately, it's not possible to swim in the lakes.) Kozjak is the largest lake (about 4km in length) in the park and forms a boundary between the upper and lower valleys. Surrounded by steep, forested slopes, Kozjak contains a small oval island, composed of travertine. A good path runs along the lake's eastern shore: follow it to reach the spectacular lower lakes – with forests, grottoes, steep cliffs and waterfalls – or take one of the regular boats (every 20 minutes).

Next up is emerald **Milanovac Lake**, and then the path runs below cliffs beside **Gavanovac Lake**. Above here is the open-topped cavern of **Šupljara**, where there's a lovely viewpoint over Plitvice's lower reaches. A wooden walkway then cuts across to the north bank, around reed-fringed **Kaluđerovac Lake** and past two towering sets of waterfalls. The second, the aptly named **Veliki Slap**, is the tallest in Croatia with a 78m drop.

To explore the upper section of the lakes, return to P1 and then follow the trails to **Gradinsko Lake**, bordered by reeds that often harbour nesting wild ducks. A series of cascades links Gradinsko to beautiful **Galovac Lake**, where an abundance of water has formed a series of ponds and falls. A set of concrete stairs over the falls, constructed long ago, has eventually been covered by travertine, forming even more falls in a spectacular panorama. Several smaller lakes are topped by the larger **Okrugljak Lake**, supplied by two powerful waterfalls. Continuing upwards you'll come to **Ciginovac Lake** and, finally, **Prošćansko Lake**, surrounded by thick forests.

Sleeping

Guesthouses and *sobe* (rooms) are dotted along all access roads to the national park.

Most midrange hotels are clustered in Velika Poljana, close to Entrance 2, overlooking Kozjak Lake. All of these are Yugo-style (lots of browns and beiges and smoked glass), though a couple have been renovated. Book rooms at www.np-plitvicka-jezera.hr.

TOP CHOICE **Pansion Etno House** GUESTHOUSE €€
(☎774 760; www.plitviceetnohouse.com; d 450KN; P 📶 🏊) A genuine mountain lodge, this lovely place has eight pine-trimmed rooms of real character and comfort: all have TV, desk, stripped floorboards, en-suite shower and bright bedspreads. There's also a pool outside, with a little paddling area for children. A little dining room downstairs hosts breakfast and evening meals. The owner's father is building a very similar place next door with eight more rooms. It's 1.5km south of Entrance 2.

Hotel Plitvice HOTEL €€
(☎751 100; s/d 533/710KN; P @) Enjoys a quiet forest location and has three classes of rooms; the smarter ones are quite modern, spacious and attractive.

Hotel Jezero HOTEL €€€
(☎751 400; s/d 614/873KN; P @ 🏊) A dated (or retro?) Yugo hotel, Jezero has plenty of facilities (sauna, pool, bowling alley, gym and tennis courts). With 229 rooms, it gets all the tour groups.

Korana Camping Ground CAMPGROUND €
(☎751 015; per person/tent 51/65KN; ⊙Apr-Oct) An autocamp with a restaurant, cafe-bar and 40 bungalows for rent, it's about 6km north of Entrance 1, on the road to Zagreb.

Eating

Most hotels in the area also have restaurants. There's an inexpensive self-service cafeteria next to the tourist office at Entrance 2.

Lička Kuća TRADITIONAL CROATIAN €
(mains from 55KN) Just across from Entrance 1, this busy place is good for lamb, local sausages and *duveč* (stew of rice, carrots, tomatoes, peppers and onions).

Information

The **tourist office** (☎751 015; www.np-plitvicka-jezera.hr; ⊙7am-8pm) has branches at both Entrance 1 (Plitvička Jezera), which is the main entrance, and Entrance 2 (Velika Poljana), near the hotels. Both entrances have ticket offices and offer brochures and a map to walk you around the lakes. The admission ticket (adult/concession April to October 110/80KN, November to March 80/60KN) includes the boats and bus-trains that get you around the park. You'll find a network of well-marked trails – choose a route lasting from an hour or two to a 10-hour slog. A system of wooden walkways allows you to appreciate the beauty of the landscape without disturbing the environment.

There's an ATM at Hotel Bellevue, which is near the main entrance. Luggage can be left at the tourist information centre at the park's main entrance. Parking is expensive (per hour/day 8/80KN).

Getting There & Away

Buses stop at the camping ground and both entrances. Not all Zagreb–Zadar buses stop at the park as the quicker ones use the freeway, so check before boarding. You can check the schedules at www.akz.hr. The journey takes three hours from Zadar (95KN to 108KN) and 2½ hours from Zagreb (93KN to 106KN), and there are 10 daily services.

Paklenica National Park

023

Rising high above the Adriatic, the stark peaks of the Velebit Massif stretch for 145km and form a dramatic barrier between continental Croatia and the Adriatic coast. Paklenica National Park covers 36 sq km of this mountain chain. For everyone from Sunday strollers to rock climbers, the park offers a wealth of opportunities to explore and get up front and personal with some of the country's finest scenery: trek up gorges, climb walls of stone or meander along shady paths next to a rushing stream.

The national park encompasses two deep gorges, Velika Paklenica (Great Paklenica) and Mala Paklenica (Small Paklenica), which scar the mountain range like giant hatchet marks, with cliffs over 400m high. The dry limestone karst that forms the Velebit Range is highly absorbent, but several springs provide a continuous source of water and nurture lush vegetation. About half the park is covered with forests, mostly beech and pine followed by white oak and varieties of hornbeam. The vegetation changes as you ascend, as does the climate, which progresses from Mediterranean to continental to subalpine. The lower regions, especially those with a southern exposure, can be fiercely hot in the summer, while the *bura* (cold northeasterly wind) that whips through the range in winter brings rain and sudden storms.

Animal life is scarce, but you may see Egyptian vultures, golden eagles, striped eagles and peregrine falcons, which nest on the cliffs of the two gorges. Lynx, bears and wolves live in the park's upper regions, but your chances of seeing any are minuscule.

The best time to visit the park is in April, May, June or September. In late spring the park is at its greenest, the streams become torrents and there are few other visitors. In July and August you'll still find the trails uncrowded, since most people come to the region for the sun and sea, but it can be too hot to hike comfortably.

Activities

Most hikes in the park are one-day affairs from 'base camp' at Starigrad or Seline, or from one of the mountain huts.

Mala Paklenica to Velika Paklenica HIKING

This spectacular eight- to 10-hour hike takes in both Mala Paklenica and Velika Paklenica gorges. Beginning at Mala Paklenica (Entrance 2), the route follows a stunning narrow karst gorge. The initial three hours are quite tough – you have to scramble over colossal boulders (and use ropes at times) – but the route is well marked. The trail can get slippery after rain, and it crosses streams several times. It steadily progresses up Mala Paklenica gorge then zigzags up the west side of a hill to 680m. Eventually it evens out in a lovely high valley and then winds through pastureland and the abandoned hamlet of Jurline (an ideal spot for lunch). You're rewarded with stunning views over canyon-like Velika Paklenica, before the path descends abruptly through forest to the valley floor. The route follows a river for an hour or so, passing grey-stone massifs and **tunnels** (currently being renovated for visitor access) that were a top-secret bunker in Tito's time, until you reach the car park at Velika Paklenica. From here a signposted country lane loops back to Mala Paklenica, which is about an hour away.

Starigrad to Planinarski Dom HIKING

Start this hike at Entrance 1 and head right up into the Velika Paklenica gorge. When you pass a rocky waterfall with a stream on your right, you'll be at **Anića Luka**, a green, semicircular plateau. After another kilometre, a steep trail leads up to the cave of **Manita Peć** (adult/concession 20/10KN; 10am-1pm Jul-Sep, hours vary Oct-Jun). There's a wealth of stalagmites and stalactites enhanced by strategically placed lighting in the main chamber (40m long and 32m high). This cave is about a two-hour walk from the car park and must be visited with a guide (not included with admission; organise at the park entrance).

From the cave you can follow the trail to **Vidakov Kuk**, which takes 1½ hours. The ascent up the 866m peak is fairly rugged but, on a clear day, you'll be rewarded with an unforgettable view over the sea to Pag. You can continue on an easy trail to **Ramići** and then head east to the main trail up to the Planinarski Dom Paklenica shelter.

Another option is to bypass the Manita Peć detour and continue up to the forest cottage of **Lugarnica** (a bit over two hours' walk from the car park), which is open daily from mid-April to late October. Snacks and drinks are sold here. A trail continues on through beech and pine forests to Planinarski Dom Paklenica shelter.

Upper Velebit HIKING

From Planinarski Dom Paklenica you'll easily reach any of the Velebit peaks in a day, but you'd need about a week to explore all of them. The highest point in the Velebit Range is **Vaganski vrh** (1757m). From the flat, grassy top, there's a view of up to 150km inland over the Velebit peaks when visibility is good. It may be a long, hard day (depending on your fitness level), but it can be reached with enough time to return to the shelter by nightfall.

Another popular destination is **Babin vrh** (Grandmother's Peak; 1741m). Follow the trail with the Brezimenjača stream on the left to the pass of Buljma (1394m) and then continue to Marasova gora through deciduous forest. There's a small lake at the foot of Babin vrh that never dries up (but the water has been polluted by sheep).

It's also possible to reach all the peaks along the Velebit ridge from Mala Paklenica, but make sure you have survival equipment, a map and the assurance that both huts are open. Past **Sveti Jakov** in Mala Paklenica take the right path to the Ivine Vodice hut. Marked trails lead past **Sveto brdo** (1751m), **Malovan** (1709m), Vaganski vrh and Babin vrh before descending to the Planinarski Dom Paklenica shelter.

Mosoraški, Velebitaški & Klin ROCK CLIMBING

Paklenica has rock-climbing routes ranging from beginner's level to borderline suicidal. The firm, occasionally sharp limestone offers graded climbs, including 72 short sports routes and 250 longer routes. You'll see the beginner's routes at the entrance to the park with cliffs reaching about 40m, but the best and most advanced climbing is on Anića Kuk, which offers over 100 routes up to a maximum of 350m. Nearly all routes are well equipped with spits and pitons, except for the appropriately named **Psycho Killer**.

The most popular climbs here are Mosoraški (350m), Velebitaški (350m) and Klin (300m). Spring is the best climbing season as summers can be very warm and winters too windy. A rescue service is also available.

Rock-climbing permits cost 60KN to 80KN depending on the season; climbers should talk to guides at the park office for advice. Consult Boris Čulić's Paklenica climber's guide for the complete rundown.

Sleeping

There's some rustic accommodation managed by the park authorities for hikers and climbers.

FREE **Ivine Vodice** MOUNTAIN HUT

(Sklonište; ⏱daily Jun-Sep, Sat & Sun Oct-May) East of Planinarski Dom Paklenica, this hut has no beds or running water but can host 10 people with sleeping bags. It's free and it's not necessary to reserve in advance.

Planinarski Dom Paklenica MOUNTAIN CHALET €

(☎301 636; www.pdpaklenica.hr; dm 65KN; ⏱daily mid-Jun–mid-Sep, Sat & Sun rest of year) There's running water and electricity, and you can reach the highest peaks of Velebit from here. The lodge has 50 beds in four rooms; bring a sleeping bag. There's a kitchen and dining room. Reservations are recommended on summer weekends.

Information

Croatian Mountaineering Association (☎01-48 24 142; www.plsavez.hr; Kozaričeva 22, Zagreb) Has up-to-date information and publishes a useful map of the park.

Paklenica National Park office (☎/fax 369 202; www.paklenica.hr; Dr F Tuđmana 14a; park entry adult/concession Apr-Oct 40/20KN, Nov-Mar 30/20KN; ⏱office 8am-4pm Mon-Fri Apr-Oct, park from 7am year-round) Sells booklets and maps. The *Paklenica National Park* guide gives an excellent overview of the park and details walks.

Getting There & Away

The best way to get to Paklenica (unless you're driving) is to get on one of the Rijeka–Zadar buses (see www.autotrans.hr), all of which stop at Starigrad (30KN, 45 minutes from Zadar, six daily). Get off the bus at Hotel Alan.

Starigrad

☎023 / POP 1103

Starigrad sprawls on either side of the main coastal road from Rijeka to Zadar and is a good base for exploring Paklenica National Park.

Sights

FREE **Ethno-House Marasović** MUSEUM

(1-8pm May-Oct) This centre occupies a small, renovated house in the village of Marasović, 1km inland from Entrance 1 of the Paklenica National Park. There are modest displays of old agricultural tools, photographs of the region and an old textile loom. Maps and postcards are sold, and park rangers are on hand for information.

Sleeping

You won't struggle to find a campground, apartment or a room in the Starigrad area as there are dozens of places strung along (and just off) the highway. Hotels are in shorter supply.

Hotel Alan HOTEL €€€

(209 050; www.bluesunhotels.com; Dr Franje Tuđmana 14; s/d 765/1230KN; mid-Mar–mid-Nov; P ✻ @ 🛜 ≋) Something of a landmark, this mini-tower resort hotel has modern rooms and facilities including tennis courts and a spa (with steam rooms and plenty of treatments available). A lot of entertainment is laid on, mainly evening concerts.

Camping Pinus CAMPGROUND €

(658 652; www.camping-pinus.com; Dr Franje Tuđmana bb; per adult/tent 35/25KN; Apr-Oct) This very relaxing campground is a no-frills scenic place right on the coast, 3km north of town on the road to Rijeka.

Camping Paklenica CAMPGROUND €

(209 062; www.paklenica.hr; Dr Franje Tuđmana bb; per adult 45KN; Apr-Oct) Next to the park office, this small site is right on a pebble beach with good swimming. It's very popular with hikers, though no reservations are accepted.

Hotel Vicko HOTEL €€€

(369 304; www.hotel-vicko.hr; Jose Dokoze bb; s/d 620/823KN; P ✻ @) A well-run modern hotel with 18 bright, light rooms, some with balconies. It has a leafy garden and is only 50m from the beach. There is a three-day minimum stay policy.

Eating

TOP CHOICE **Taverna-Konoba Marasović** DALMATIAN €

(mains from 40KN; May-Oct) A kilometre inland from Entrance 1 of Paklenica National Park, this *konoba* occupies a fantastic old village house with a terrace at the front and chunky tables in the dining room. Dine on Dalmatian ham, squid risotto, calamari, or lamb or pork baked in a *peka* (order in advance). All the food is sourced locally and according to season. It's located below a renovated ethno-house (a new house built in the traditional Croatian style).

Buffet Dinko SEAFOOD €

(mains from 45KN) At the junction of the highway and access road to Entrance 1 of Paklenica National Park, this popular restaurant has a shady terrace and excellent fish and seafood.

Information

The **tourist office** (369 245; www.rivijera-paklenica.hr; 8am-9pm daily Jul & Aug, to 3pm Mon-Sat Sep-Jun) is in the town centre on the main road across from the small harbour. HVB Splitska Banka (between the tourist office and Hotel Alan) has an ATM. Hotel Alan offers internet access (per hour 30KN).

Getting There & Around

Starigrad is about 51km from Zadar and 165km from Rijeka. Six daily buses pass through in either direction; consult www.autotrans.hr for timetables. Buses stop outside Hotel Alan and along the highway.

Annoyingly, there are no taxis at all in Starigrad. Some hotels will drop off and pick up guests at the park's entrance gates.

DUGI OTOK

023 / POP 1800

Dugi Otok is all about natural, unspoilt beauty, so if you're seeking a peaceful, relaxing holiday, you'll find your paradise here. The cluster of small islands on Telašćica Bay Nature Park is a must-see, while the nearby saltwater Lake Mir (Peace), sandy Sakarun Bay and the panoramic drive along the rocky coast are real delights.

The name Dugi Otok means 'long island'. Stretching from northwest to southeast, the island is 43km long and just 4km wide. The southeastern coast is marked by steep hills and cliffs, while the northern half is cultivated with vineyards, orchards and sheep pastures. In between is a series of karstic hills rising to 338m at Vela Straža, the island's highest point.

Most people base themselves in either Sali on the southeastern coast or Božava on the northeastern coast. Sali has more opportunities for private accommodation, while Božava offers more of a resort experience.

There's a brief high season in the first three weeks of August, when Italian vacationers descend en masse.

History

Ruins on the island reveal early settlement by Illyrians, Romans and then early Christians, but the island was first documented in the mid-10th century. It later became the property of the monasteries of Zadar. Settlement expanded with the 16th-century Turkish invasions, which prompted immigration from elsewhere along the coast.

Dugi Otok's fortunes have largely been linked with Zadar as it changed hands between Venetians, Austrians and the French, but when Northern Dalmatia was handed over to Mussolini the island stayed within Croatia. Old-timers still recall the hardships they endured when the nearest medical and administrative centre was Šibenik, a long, hard boat ride along the coast.

Economic development has always been hampered by the lack of any freshwater supply – drinking water must be collected from rainwater or brought over by boat from Zadar. The population has drifted away over the last few decades, leaving a few hardy souls to brave the dry summers and *bura*-chilled winters.

Getting There & Away

Jadrolinija (p176) has daily ferries all year from Zadar to Brbinj (27KN, 1½ hours, two to three daily) and a ferry and catamaran link Zaglav and Sali with Zadar (21KN, 45 minutes to 1½ hours, three daily).

Getting Around

The only bus services in Dugi Otok are timed to coincide with boat connections, running between Božava and Brbinj in the north and from Sali to Zaglav in the south (before and after boats). You can rent scooters in both Sali and Božava.

Sali

POP 1152

As the island's largest town and port, Sali is a positive metropolis when compared with the rest of the towns and villages scattered around Dugi Otok. Named after the salt works that once employed villagers, the town has a rumpled, lived-in look. Its little harbour is a working fishing port, and it's busy with small passenger boats and yachts that dock here during summer on their way to and from Telašćica Bay and the Kornati Islands. Although the town is tantalisingly close to these natural wonders, you'll need to join a tour or rent your own boat to visit them.

Sights & Activities

There's little in the way of sightseeing within the town.

St Mary's Church CHURCH
(Crkva Svete Marije; Svete Marije; Mass only) Built in the 15th century, its wooden altar and several Renaissance paintings are impressive.

Kornati Islands DIVING
The underwater marine park of the Kornati Islands offers exceptional diving in pellucid waters, with steep drop-offs and numerous caves. You'll find two dive schools in the neighbouring bay of Zaglav: **Dive Kroatien** (377 079; www.dive-kroatien.de) and **Kornati Diver** (377 167; www.kornati-diver.com). Note you have to pay a €20 entrance fee to dive inside the Kornati National Park.

Tome BOATING
(377 489; www.tome.hr; boat trips from 350KN) Boat trips, including a leisurely tour of Telašćica Bay and a stop on one of the Kornati Islands, run from Sali harbour. Fishing trips (from 1487KN) are also offered.

Festivals & Events

Saljske Užance Festival CULTURAL
The weekend before the Assumption (15 August), Saljske Užance Festival draws visitors from the entire region with donkey races and a candlelight procession of boats around the harbour. Men and women don traditional costumes, play instruments devised from cow horns and perform traditional village dances.

Sleeping

Private accommodation is reasonably priced in Sali, especially out of season, and the tourist office can connect you with some wonderful, out-of-the-way places, including a house on its own little island. Check out www.sali-dugiotok.com (in Croatian) for apartments.

Room and apartment prices are based on a three-night minimum stay in summer, with a 30% surcharge for fewer nights. As the island is very dry, try to avoid long, luxurious showers.

There are no campgrounds.

Hotel Sali HOTEL €€

(☎377 049; www.hotel-sali.hr; r 571KN; ⊙Apr-Oct; P❄) About 1km inland from the port, this hotel is set above its own rocky cove in grounds shaded by mature pines. Its four separate accommodation blocks are painted white and marine blue and there's a restaurant. Rooms are simply decorated; all have satellite TV, fridge and a balcony (many have sea views). Bikes are available to rent.

Apart Šoštarić HOTEL €

(☎377 050; bsostaric@gmail.com; r/apt 219/366KN; P❄) This dusky-pink block at the northern end of the port is a bit of an eyesore, but it's rarely full so is worth a try at busy times. Offers slightly dated but serviceable accommodation; rooms at the front have fine views.

Eating & Drinking

Half a dozen restaurants are clustered around the harbour and there's a well-stocked supermarket.

Pizza Bruc ITALIAN €

(pizza from 38KN; ⊙Apr-Oct) The friendliest restaurant in town, it has a terrace right by the yachts. Try the *pizza picante*.

Maritimo BAR

The heart and soul of Sali, this bar has a vibrant buzz about it, rain or shine. It's got plenty of character, with a long wooden bar and photographs of yesteryear decorating the walls, plus a popular terrace that's good for a cocktail, coffee or draught beer. Croatia's no-smoking legislation is routinely ignored.

Information

The **tourist office** (☎/fax 377 094; www.dugiotok.hr; ⊙8am-9pm daily Jun-Sep, to 3pm Mon-Fri Oct-May) on the harbour front is very well informed about the island and can provide an excellent hiking and biking colour map with route profiles and other brochures. Private accommodation and excursions are arranged and you can surf the internet (15KN per 30 minutes).

There's no bank but there is an ATM on the harbour and you can change money or get cash on your MasterCard at the **post office** (Obala Petra Lorinija; ⊙8am-2pm Mon-Sat).

Call **Louvre** (☎098 650 026) to hire a scooter.

Telašćica Bay

The southeastern tip of Dugi Otok is split in two by the deeply indented Telašćica Bay, dotted with five small islands and five even tinier islets. With superb sheltered azure waters, it's one of the largest, most beautiful and least spoilt natural harbours in the Adriatic. It's very popular with yachties.

The Kornati Islands extend nearly to the edge of Telašćica Bay and the topography of the two island groups is identical – stark white limestone with patches of brush. The tip of the western side of the island faces the sea where the wind and waves have carved out sheer cliffs dropping 166m. There are no towns, settlements or roads on this part of Dugi Otok, only a couple of restaurants in **Mir Bay** catering to boaters.

Next to Mir Bay is saltwater **Mir Lake**, fed by underground channels that run through limestone to the sea. The lake, which is clear but has a muddy bottom, is surrounded by pine forests and its water is warmer than the sea. Like most mud in unusual places, it's supposed to be very good for your skin.

Božava

POP 111

Božava is a peaceful little place huddled around a lovely natural harbour that's mutated from fishing village to holiday resort in a couple of generations. The village is overgrown with lush, flowering trees and there are lovely shady paths along the coast. Tourism now totally dominates the local economy in the shape of the four hotels of the Božava 'tourist village' and there are a couple of harbourside restaurants.

The **Božava Hotel complex** (☎291 291; www.hoteli-bozava.hr; per person from 600KN; P❄@🛜≋) includes three three-star hotels, of which **Hotel Mirta** stands out. The four-star **Hotel Maxim** (per person 710KN) is more upmarket and has smart rooms and family apartments, all with satellite TV, fridge, internet access and balconies overlooking the sea, plus access to floodlit tennis courts, and fitness and massage services.

The **tourist office** (☎/fax 377 607; turisticko-drustvo-bozava@zd.t-com.hr; ⊙9am-2pm & 6-8pm Mon-Sat, to noon Sun Jun-Sep), just above the tiny harbour, can arrange bike, scooter and car rental, and find private accommodation. Buses run to/from Brbinj for boat connections.

Nearby **Veli Rat** is a pretty village with a marina on a sheltered bay close to the north-western point of the island. Buses run to/from Brbinj, but otherwise it's an extremely isolated place of a few dozen people and a solitary store-cum-bar.

PAG ISLAND

Pag is like something you'd find in a 1950s Italian film, perfect for a broody B&W Antonioni set – it's barren, rocky and sepia coloured, with vast empty landscapes stretching across the horizon. The Adriatic has a steely blue around it and, when the sky is stormy, it's the most dramatic-looking place in the whole of Croatia: its karstic rock forms a moonscape defined by two mountain ridges, patches of shrubs and a dozen or so villages and hamlets.

Technically Pag is no longer an island at all – it's connected to the mainland by a bridge – but in terms of culture and produce it's very independent and distinct. Islanders farm the miserly soil and produce a decent domestic white wine, Šutica. Tough local sheep graze on herbs and salty grasses, lending their milk a distinctive flavour and producing *paški sir* (Pag cheese; soaked in olive oil and aged in stone). Intricate Pag lace is famed and framed on many a Croat's wall.

But Pag has put a twist to its image as a place of centuries-old tradition and culture: the northern port of Novalja is one of Croatia's most carefree and lively resorts, while nearby Zrće beach is a clubbing mecca.

History

The island was inhabited by the Illyrians before falling to Rome in the 1st century BC. The Romans constructed forts and aqueducts. Slavs settled around Novalja in the 7th century AD and began building churches and basilicas. In the 11th century, salt production began to take off, resulting in conflicts with Zadar and Rab over the salt trade. In 1409 Pag was sold to Venice along with Zadar and the rest of Dalmatia. Subsequent squabbles saw the island invaded by Venetians, Austrians, French (and Austrians again) and then a German-Italian occupation during WWII.

Getting There & Away

Boat

A catamaran operated by **Jadrolinija** (www.jadrolinija.hr) connects Rijeka to Novalja (40KN, 2½ hours), passing through Rab. Regular car ferries (12KN) also link Žigljen on Pag's north-east coast to Prizna on the mainland; these run roughly hourly in winter and nonstop from June to September.

Bus

Five daily buses operated by **Antonio Tours** (www.antoniotours.hr) connect Novalja, Pag Town and Zadar in summer. From Pag Town two buses per day go to Rijeka (166KN, 3½ hours) from Monday to Saturday and one on Sunday, passing Novalja on the way; one bus per day goes to Split (158KN, four hours); and there are three daily buses to Zagreb (243KN, six hours).

Getting Around

Six buses per day make the 30-minute trip between Pag Town and Novalja (22KN).

Pag's (fairly) flat profile is ideal for bike riding. **Jadranka** (☎098 306 602) in Pag Town has bikes for 20/100KN per hour/day. There are about 115km of bike paths, taking you all around the island.

Pag Town

☎023 / POP 2709

Historic Pag Town enjoys a spectacular setting, fringing a narrow spit of land between sun-scorched hills, with an azure bay on its eastern flank and shimmering salt pans to its west. It's an intimate collection of narrow lanes and bleak-looking stone houses where life spills out onto the streets – locals make lace on stools, and the lovely white marble square is a socialising hot spot. There are pebble beaches close by.

In the early 15th century the prosperous salt business prompted the construction of Pag Town when adjacent Stari Grad could no longer meet the demands of its burgeoning population. Venetian rulers engaged the finest builder of the time, Juraj Dalmatinac, to design a new city – the first cornerstone was laid in 1443. In accordance with what were then the latest ideas in town planning, the main streets and the cross lanes intersect at right angles and lead to four city gates. In the centre, there's a square with a cathedral, a ducal palace and an unfinished bishop's palace. In 1499 Dalmatinac began working on the city walls, but only the northern corner, with parts of a castle, remains.

Sights

Lace Museum MUSEUM
(Kralja Dmitra Zvonimira, Trg Kralja Krešimira IV; admission 10KN; ⌚10am-noon & 6-10pm Jun-Sep) Now housed in the spectacular, restored Ducal Palace (Kneževa Palača), designed by Juraj Dalmatinac, this excellent museum showcases some remarkably intricate designs. The history of lacemaking in Pag and its importance to the community is skilfully illustrated with dramatic photographs and good information panels. It's open to groups only outside peak season.

St Mary's Church CHURCH
(Crkva Svete Marije; Trg Kralja Krešimira IV; ⌚9am-noon & 5-7pm May-Sep, Mass only Oct-Apr) Dalmatinac's Gothic St Mary's Church sits in perfect harmony with the modest structures surrounding it. The lunette over the portal shows the Virgin with women of Pag in medieval blouses and headdresses, and there are two rows of unfinished sculptures of saints. Completed in the 16th century, the interior was renovated with baroque ceiling decorations in the 18th century.

Museum of Salt MUSEUM
(Stari Grad; admission 10KN; ⌚10am-noon & 8-10pm Jun-Sep) Over the bridge in what remains of ancient Stari Grad – which is very little – this new museum (in a former salt warehouse) documents the production of salt in Pag with photography and exhibits. Open to groups only outside summer.

Festivals & Events

Pag Carnival CULTURAL
The last day of July is the Pag Carnival, a good chance to see the traditional *kolo* (a lively Slavic circle dance) and appreciate the elaborate traditional dress of Pag. The main square fills with dancers and musicians, and a theatre troupe presents the folk play *Paška robinja* (The Slave Girl of Pag).

Sleeping

Most hotels in Pag are scattered around the bay west of town and close between October and May.

Travel agencies will find you private accommodation and women wait at the bus station offering *sobe*. Many rooms and apartments are located across the bridge.

Hotel Pagus HOTEL €€€
(☎611 310; www.hotel-pagus.hr; Starčevića 1; s/d 554/1150KN; P❄@📶🏊) This hotel has a great beach location within walking distance of the old town. Rooms are elegant and stylish, and the wellness centre is a real treat.

Camping Šimuni CAMPGROUND €
(☎697 441; www.camping-simuni.hr; Šimuni; per adult 78KN) On a gorgeous cove with a shingle beach, about halfway between Pag Town and Novalja, near the port of Šimuni. All local buses stop here. The mobile homes (from €30) are smart and an inexpensive option outside high season.

Barcarola RENTAL ROOMS €
(☎611 239; Vladimira Nazora 12; r 300KN; ⌚Apr-Nov) Right next to the bus stop, these modern rooms are above a *konoba*. All are spacious, with wooden floors, and are attractively if simply presented with wardrobe and bathroom.

Meridijan Hotel HOTEL €€
(☎492 200; www.meridijan15.hr; Starčevića bb; r 685KN; P❄@📶🏊) A four-star hotel with commodious rooms, modern furnishings and large bathrooms. Rooms on the upper floor have great island and bay views. The pool is small, though.

Eating

While you're here, it would be rude not to sample a slice of Pag cheese. Self-caterers can pick up fruit, vegetables and local cheese at the daily morning fruit and vegetable market; head to the Konzum supermarket for more elaborate supplies.

TOP CHOICE **Bistro Na Tale** TRADITIONAL CROATIAN €
(Radićeva 2; mains from 40KN) This dependable, casual and highly popular place has a little front terrace facing the salt flats and another with plenty of shade. Pag lamb is a real speciality, or opt for the fresh fish of the day cooked in wine and herbs.

Konoba Bodulo DALMATIAN €
(Vangrada 19; mains from 40KN) Right by the city walls, this attractive traditional place scores for seafood (scampi, mussels or octopus). There's a nice courtyard setting.

Bistro Diogen CROATIAN €
(K Lidija Uhl 9; mains from 50KN) The stand-out option along this strip, with an extensive menu, friendly service and reliable fish and meat dishes – plus superb views.

PAG CHEESE

There's no other cheese quite like the distinctive *paški sir* (Pag cheese). Salty and sharp, its taste easily recalls the island that makes it. As sea winds whip through the low slopes of Pag Island, a thin deposit of salt permeates the ground and the flora it sprouts. The free-range sheep of Pag Island graze freely on the salty herbs and plants, transmitting the flavour to their meat and milk.

The milk for Pag cheese is gathered in May when flavour is at its peak. It's left unpasteurised, which allows a stronger flavour to emerge during the fermentation process. When the cheese finally ferments, it's rubbed with sea salt, coated with olive oil and left to age for anywhere from six months to a year. The result is a tangy, firm cheese that matures into an aromatic, dry, crumbly cheese. As a starter, it's served in thin slices with black olives, but it can also be grated and used as a topping instead of Parmesan.

Look out too for the ricotta-like *skuta*, a subtle-flavoured (though rare) soft cheese found in restaurants including Boškinac, near Novalja.

Drinking & Entertainment

Pag Town is a sleepy place with little bar action or nightlife, though things get a tad more lively during the summer season.

Club Vanga NIGHTCLUB
Just over the bridge, this club is the only dance game in town. Nights rotate; each week there are R&B, house and '70s, '80s and '90s sounds. There's an outside terrace for smokers.

Shopping

Pag offers the most distinctive products in all Croatia. It would be a shame to leave the island without buying **lace**, since the prices are relatively cheap and buying a piece helps keep the tradition alive. A small circle or star about 10cm in diameter costs about 125KN, but takes a good 24 hours to make. If you walk down Kralja Tomislava or Kralja Dmitra Zvonimira you can buy directly from the lace makers, virtually all of whom have fixed prices.

Pag cheese is not as easy to find, although you should be able to get it at the morning market. Otherwise, look out for homemade *'Paški sir'* signs posted outside a house on a remote road somewhere. The asking price for a kilogram is around 130KN.

Information

Erste Banka (Vela 18) Changes money.

Medical Centre (☎611 001; Gradska Plaža bb)

Mediteran (☎/fax 611 238; www.mediteranpag.com; Vladimira Nazora 12) Agency with a very wide selection of private accommodation.

Meridian 15 (☎612 162; www.meridijan15.hr; Ante Starčevića 1) Travel agency that runs island excursions and trips to national parks including Paklenica. Also books accommodation.

Post Office (Antuna Šimića; ⏰8am-8pm Mon-Fri, to 2pm Sat)

Sunturist (☎612 040; www.sunturist-pago.hr; Vladimira Nazora bb) Accommodation and trips.

Tourist Office (☎/fax 611 286; www.pag-tourism.hr; Trg Kralja Krešimira IV 1; ⏰8am-10pm daily May-Oct, to 4pm Mon-Fri Nov-Apr) A very switched-on office, with a decent colour town map that includes local beaches.

Novalja

☎023 / POP 2084

In a nation of sedate resorts, Novalja bucks the trend – with interest – for its bars and clubs offer nightlife as raucous as you'll find in Croatia. Cultural interest is confined to the incendiary club scene based on nearby Zrće's beach; there are no historic sights. That said, the promenade is an appealing place for a stroll, and there are fine beaches close by.

Sleeping & Eating

Contact the tourist office or any travel agency for private accommodation.

TOP CHOICE **Boškinac** RURAL INN €€€
(☎663 500; www.boskinac.com; s/d 1241/1387KN; P❄@🛜≋) About 5km east of Novalja, this is one of Croatia's most enjoyable hotels, with a superb restaurant (mains from 140KN) and winery to boot. The location is rustic bliss, surrounded by vines. The eight

rooms and three suites are elegant, stylish and simply huge, each with a sofa bed and lovely bathroom. Sample the estate wines in the basement *vinoteka*, where there's a little deli with snacks available. The restaurant (tasting menus 220KN to 490KN) is one of Dalmatia's very best, with a wonderful terrace and dining room. The menu features local lamb, cheese (try the *skuta*), olive oil and even Pag snails. A pool, a fitness room and a spa are planned. Check the hotel website for gastronomic packages.

Hotel Loža HOTEL €€
(☎663 381; www.turno.hr; Trg Loža; s/d 356/734KN; P@☎) Right on the prom, this attractive hotel has neat smallish rooms, many with seaview balcony. Wi-fi is free.

Starac i More SEAFOOD €
(Braće Radić; mains from 40KN) Just off the harbour, this seafood restaurant is authentic, unpretentious and renowned for its seafood: try a mixed platter.

ℹ Information

Aurora (☎663 493; Slatinska bb) Well-organised agency with lots of apartments and rooms on its books. Excursions too.

Novalja Tourist Board (☎663 570; www.tz-novalja.hr; Šetalište Hrvatskih Mornara 1; ⊙8am-9pm daily Jun-Sep, to 3pm Mon-Fri Oct-May) Finds private accommodation and has lots of timetables for boats and buses.

ŠIBENIK-KNIN REGION

An underrated part of Croatia, this region is actually loaded with interest. There's the incredible medieval city of Šibenik, pristine Kornati Islands and Krka National Park, which is brimming with swimming and hiking opportunities.

Šibenik

☎022 / POP 37,170

Though still gritty around the edges, Šibenik is seriously up-and-coming. It has exciting sights, new restaurants and bars are opening every year, and the city is abuzz with energy. Šibenik's real appeal, however, has actually not changed for centuries – its magnificent medieval quarter, consisting of a stone labyrinth of steep backstreets and alleys, ancient chapels and a stunning cathedral are a joy to explore.

The city is also an important access point for the national park of Krka, the Kornati Islands and the bird-of-prey centre of Sokolarski.

BEACH CLUBBING

Despite the overwhelming sense of calm on Pag Island, there's a pocket of wild partying every summer. About 3km southeast of Novalja, **Zrće beach** has three major clubs and a scattering of bars. It's a fairly mainstream DJ scene – don't expect too much underground flavour. The clubs are right on the beach (unlike Ibiza, which Zrće is often compared with).

Kalypso is the most sophisticated venue, a beautifully designed place built into a cove at the north end of the beach with myriad bars surrounded by palm trees. During the day you can chill out here on wonderful bed mattresses, while after dark DJs spin deep house mixes to an older crowd. **Aquarius** (www.aquarius.hr) is the flashiest joint, a huge space with stylish alcoves, great views and a glassed-off area. **Papaya** (www.papaya.com.hr) is an attractive club built in terraces, one of which is the main dance floor, which draws a mixed crowd. The music can be a bit hit and miss, though plenty of huge trance DJs, including Tiësto and Paul Van Dyk, have played to the hedonistic regulars. All the clubs open in late June and close by mid-September. Entrance prices very much depend on the event: nights are usually free at the beginning of the season and as much as €35 in mid-August.

The beach itself is a very sheltered bay, a 1km-long treeless crescent of pebbles – rent an umbrella for shade. Swimming is excellent, though you'll have to endure the buzz of jet skis (which are confined to certain sections). Zrće has an attractive aspect, overlooking a parched strip of eastern Pag, with the mountains of the mainland rearing up on the horizon. Parking costs 7KN per hour.

Šibenik

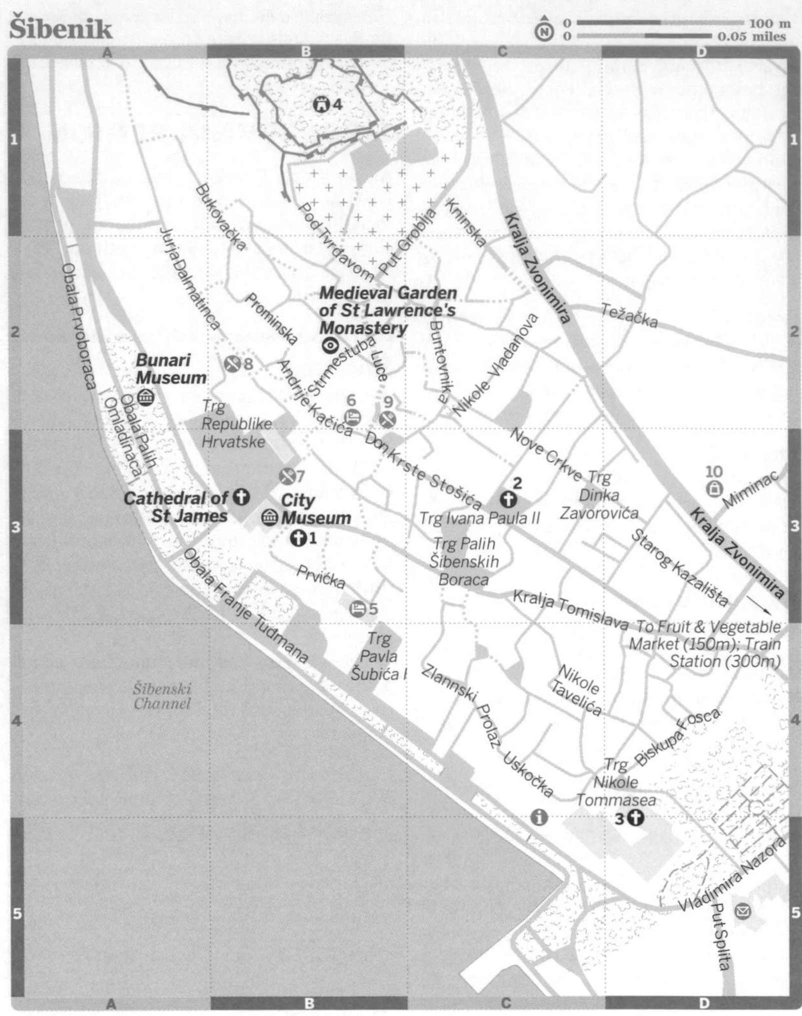

History

Unlike many other Dalmatian coastal communities, Šibenik was first settled by Croat tribes, not Illyrians or Romans.

First mentioned in the history books in the 11th century by the Croatian king Krešimir IV, the city was conquered by Venice in 1116, but was tossed around between Venice, Hungary, Byzantium and the Kingdom of Bosnia until Venice seized control in 1412. Ottomans periodically attacked the town, disrupting trade and agriculture in the 16th and 17th centuries. Venetian control was usurped in 1797 by Austrian rule, which continued until 1918.

Šibenik fell under attack in 1991 from Yugoslav federal forces, and was subject to shelling until its liberation as part of 'Operation Storm' by the Croatian army in 1995. Little physical damage is evident, but the city's aluminium industry was shattered. However Šibenik has started to make a serious comeback in the past few years, and tourism is becoming a vital part of the economy.

Šibenik

Sights

Many of Šibenik's beautiful smaller churches are only open for Mass.

Cathedral of St James CATHEDRAL

(Katedrala Svetog Jakova; Trg Republike Hrvatske; 8am-8pm Jun-Sep, to 7pm Oct-May) The Cathedral of St James is Juraj Dalmatinac's masterpiece. The crowning glory of the Dalmatian coast, the cathedral, a World Heritage Site, is worth a considerable detour to see. Its most unusual feature is the **frieze** of 71 heads on the exterior walls of the apses. These portraits – placid, annoyed, comical, proud and fearful – almost appear like caricatures, but are depictions of ordinary 15th-century citizens. The cathedral cost a great deal of cash to construct, and it's said that the stingier the individual, the grosser the caricature.

Dalmatinac was not the first (nor the last) architect to work on the cathedral. Construction began in 1431 but, after 10 years of toying with various Venetian builders, the city appointed Dalmatinac, a Zadar native, who increased the size and transformed the conception of the church into a transitional Gothic-Renaissance style.

In addition to the exterior frieze, other examples of Dalmatinac's style include the two aisle staircases descending into the sacristy on one side and the exquisite **baptistery** (admission 10KN) on the other, in which three angels support the baptismal font. The latter was carved by Andrija Aleši after Dalmatinac's designs. Other interior artworks worth noting are the **crypt** of Bishop Šižigorić (by Dalmatinac), who supported the building of the cathedral; the altar painting of St Fabijan and St Sebastijan (by Zaniberti); the painting *The Gift of the Wise Men* (by Ricciardi); and, next to it, two marble reliefs of angels (by Firentinac). Note also the **Lion's Portal** on the northern side, created by Dalmatinac and Bonino da Milano, in which two lions support columns containing the figures of Adam and Eve, who appear to be excruciatingly embarrassed by their nakedness.

The cathedral was constructed entirely of stone quarried from the islands of Brač, Korčula, Rab and Krk, and is reputed to be the world's largest church built completely of stone without brick or wood supports. The unusual domed-roof complex was completed after Dalmatinac's death by Nikola Firentinac, who continued the facade in a pure Renaissance style. The cathedral was completed in 1536.

Bunari Museum MUSEUM

(Obala Palih Omladinaca 2; adult/concession 15/10KN; 8am-midnight) Completely renovated and re-opened in summer 2012, this exhibition space is set inside a highly atmospheric old water reservoir complex with a soaring barrel-vaulted roof. It's an interactive museum with lots of informative panels and exhibits about Šibenik's history and culture, and has demonstrations of local skills. You'll encounter plenty of stuff to keep children amused (including a shipwreck pinball machine). It's a great place to see concerts and other live events, so check with the staff if there's anything on when you're there.

City Museum MUSEUM

(Gradski Muzej; www.muzej-sibenik.hr; Gradska Vrata 3; admission 10KN; 10am-1pm & 6-8pm Jun-Sep, 7.30am-3.30pm Oct-May) This museum has a well-designed permanent collection of historical artefacts relating to the Šibenik and Dalmatia region. It also hosts changing exhibitions of art, paintings, photographs and ceramics.

Medieval Garden of St Lawrence's Monastery GARDEN
(Vrt Svetog Lovre; Andrije Kačića bb; adult/concession 15/10KN; ⊙8.30am-7.30pm May-Oct, shorter hours Nov-Apr) Designed and completed by Dragutin Kiš (an award-winning landscape artist), this recreated medieval garden has a formal layout with herbs and medicinal plants in neat borders between pathways. There's a nice cafe (ice cream and drinks only) and a few essential oils for sale.

St Michael Fortress FORTRESS
(Tvrđava Sv Mihovila; admission 20KN; ⊙9am-9pm) This huge medieval fort has magnificent views over Šibenik, the Krk River and the Adriatic from its battlements. Parts of the structure date back to the 13th century, and there are four well-preserved towers and a Gothic-style entrance.

Church of St Ivan CHURCH
(Crkva Svetog Ivana; Trg Ivana Paula II) A fine example of Gothic-Renaissance architecture dating from the end of the 15th century.

Franciscan Church & Monastery CHURCH
(Franjevački Samostan; Ćulinoviča) Dates from the end of the 14th century. Has fine frescos and an array of Venetian baroque paintings.

Museum of Church Art MUSEUM
(Kralja Tomislava; admission 10KN; ⊙9am-1pm Mon-Fri) Housed in the **Church of St Barbara**, the museum exhibits paintings, engravings and sculptures from the 14th to the 18th centuries.

Festivals & Events

Terraneo Festival MUSIC
(www.terraneofestival.com) If you're here in August, don't miss the Terraneo Festival, a great big five-day dance party located in an old army barracks, 4km from the centre of Šibenik and 500 metres from the beach. Past line-ups have included The Roots, The Ting Tings, Thievery Corporation, Groove Armada and Friendly Fires, among many other international and local performers and DJs.

International Children's Festival CHILDREN
Šibenik hosts a renowned international children's festival during the last week of June and the first week of July. There are craft workshops, along with music, dance, children's film and theatre, puppets and parades.

Sleeping

There's very little accommodation actually in Šibenik, which has only one hotel. Primošten, Tribunj and Vodice along the coast are all close. Women offering *sobe* may greet you in high season, or contact the travel agencies for private digs.

TOP CHOICE **Konoba B&B** B&B €€
(☎091 60 19 789; www.bbdalmatia.com; Andrije Kačića 8; studio 486-636KN, apt 711-860KN) Dutch-owned and bang in the medieval quarter, these two gorgeous restored stone houses might just be Šibenik's most charming places

WORTH A TRIP

KNIN & THE INTERIOR

Located on a historical hot seat on the borders of Dalmatia and Bosnia, Knin was an important trading centre in the Middle Ages at the intersection of roads running between Slavonia, Bosnia and the Dalmatian coast. When Croatia was ruled by Croatian kings in the 10th century, Knin was the capital. Realising their vulnerability, they erected the brooding fortress that still looms over the town from steep Spas hill. When the Croatian kings fell, Knin was battered by a series of invaders until the Ottomans snatched it in 1522. Later, Venice swept in followed by Austria, France and then Austria again.

The huge Croatian flag flying from the top of the fortress is more to do with recent events than medieval history, though the town's economy evaporated along with the expelled Serbs in 1995. Climb up the partly restored fortress for mountain views towards Bosnia and Hercegovina; there's a cafe here too.

You'll see the town at its best on 13 June, Knin's patron saint's day, when there are a load of religious, sporting and musical events. For more information about the town drop by the **tourist office** (☎022 664 822; www.tz-knin.hr; Tuđmana 24). **Hotel Mihovil** (☎022 664 444; www.hotelmihovil.com; Ante Anića 3; r 250KN) has friendly owners, simple rooms and good food; it's 3km north of town.

RAPTOR RESCUE

Dedicated to protecting birds of prey in Croatia, the **Sokolarski Centre** (☎022 330 116; www.sokolarskicentar.com; adult/concession 40/30KN; ⏲9am-5pm Apr-Oct) performs a kind of rescue and rehab service for around 150 injured raptors each year. Visitors are treated to an exceptional, highly amusing and educational presentation from centre director Emilo Mendušić, who uses owls, falcons and hawks to demonstrate these birds' agility and skills.

You'll learn how eagle owls hunt (they can pick out one weak pigeon from a large flock), using sight that enables them to see things in slow motion. Their hearing is so acute they can concentrate on a square metre of land, and isolate their ears from peripheral sounds.

Most raptors at the centre have been involved in a collision on Croatian roads. Other threats include illegal poisoning, shooting and the use of pesticides. All birds are free to fly for an hour or so a day, and the vast majority are released back into the wild when healthy.

The Sokolarski Centre is about 7km from Šibenik and is not served by public transport. To get there take the road to Krka National Park, turn east at Bilice and follow the signs.

to stay. One house has a studio and a two-bed apartment with a terrace and great views, and the second house has a larger apartment with a huge rooftop terrace that has sweeping views of the old town and Šibenik bay. All the furnishings are tasteful and elegant, with a touch of Dutch minimalism against the exposed old stone walls.

Camp Solaris CAMPGROUND €
(☎364 450; www.solaris.hr; Solaris; per adult/site 55/143KN; ⏲mid-Mar–Nov; @📶🏊) If you're in the market for a well-equipped camping ground, this must be one of Croatia's best. There's a seawater pool, sports stuff including tennis and minigolf, tons of facilities for kids and a spa. You won't go thirsty – there are 10 bars! It's 6km east of Šibenik town centre.

Hotel Jadran HOTEL €€€
(☎242 000; www.rivijera.hr; Obala Oslobođenja 52; s/d 512/835KN; P@) This dated concrete five-storey hotel at least has a very convenient location right on the harbour front. It's a bit charmless and overpriced, but it's the only big hotel in town. Rooms are equipped with satellite TV and minibar (though there's no air-conditioning, so things get very steamy in summer).

✕ Eating

There's a popular strip of restaurants along the harbour front with great views, but for great dining head into the old town.

Self-caterers can stock up at the **supermarket** (Kralja Zvonimira) or the **fruit & vegetable market** (btwn Ante Starčevića & Stankovačka).

TOP CHOICE **Pelegrini** MODERN MEDITERRANEAN €€
(☎485 055; www.pelegrini.hr; Obala Palih Omladinaca 2; mains from 60KN) Responsible for upping the culinary ante in Šibenik, this restaurant is simply wonderful. The menu raids the globe for flavours, with influences from Japan and France, but at heart it's Mediterranean – try the roasted pork belly with white figs and bacon. Design-wise, Pelegrini manages to mix minimalism with the historic. Staff are well informed and multilingual. Dalmatian wines are very well represented on the list. Call ahead to bag one of the outside tables for unrivalled views over the cathedral.

Restoran Tinel CROATIAN €€
(Trg Puckih Kapetana 1; mains from 75KN; ✎) Stylish and well regarded, this old-town restaurant has a lovely elevated terrace on a little square and dining rooms spread over two floors. You'll find lots of interesting dishes including octopus *à la tinel* (like a goulash), and vegetarian choices including ricotta salad with grilled courgette.

Gradska Vijećnica DALMATIAN €€
(☎213 605; Trg Republike Hrvatske; mains from 70KN) On the ground floor of the town hall and across from the cathedral; the terrace and stunning interior offer a fine setting. There are many Dalmatian dishes on the menu, with lots of seafood stews and grilled fish, and also several vegetarian options, such as peppers stuffed with local cheese. Check out the scrumptious daily-changing offerings.

WORTH A TRIP

EXCURSIONS FROM ŠIBENIK

Šibenik has good ferry connections to several small islands that can be explored on a day trip or overnight. There's also **Primošten**, about 20km south on the mainland, by far the most attractive town within reach of Šibenik. This small village of medieval streets is dominated by a large belfry and is neatly contained within a peninsula. Across the bay is another peninsula, thickly wooded with pines and bordered by pebbly beaches.

Zlarin is only 30 minutes by boat from Šibenik and is known for the coral that used to be abundant before it was torn from the sea and sold for jewellery. Because there are no cars allowed on the island, it makes a tranquil retreat from Šibenik and boasts a sandy beach, pine woods and a spacious port.

Only 15 minutes further on from Zlarin, **Prvić** contains two villages, Prvić Luka and Šepurine (another 10 minutes on the ferry), which retain the flavour of simple fishing settlements.

The island of **Murter** is 29km northwest of Šibenik, separated from the mainland by a narrow channel. Its steep southwestern coast is indented by small coves, most notably **Slanica**, which has great swimming. Contact the **tourist office** (☎434 995; www.tzo-murter.hr; Rudina bb; ⊙7.30am-9.30pm mid-Jun–mid-Sep, 8am-noon mid-Sep–mid-Jun) for further information.

Although Murter village is unremarkable, it is an excellent base from which to explore the Kornati Islands. Booking an excursion to these islands from Murter will allow you to see more of the archipelago in a day than if you were to come from Šibenik or Zadar, since Murter is much closer. **Coronata** (☎435 933; www.coronata.hr; Žrtava Ratova 17) is one of several agencies that run full-day excursions to the Kornati Islands (adult/concession 270/140KN) from Murter.

If you'd like to stay on a Kornati island, **KornatTurist** (☎435 854; www.kornatturist.hr; Hrvatskih Vladara 2, Murter) arranges private accommodation – small cottages start at around 4800KN per week including a boat transfer, a twice-weekly delivery of gas for lighting, and the admission fee for the Kornati National Park. You can also rent a motor boat for 1550KN per week.

Uzorita CROATIAN €€
(Bana Josipa Jelačića 50; mains from 60KN; 📶) The oldest restaurant in Šibenik, dating from 1899. Dine on meat or seafood (try the kebabs) on the vine-shaded terrace or in the atmospheric interior with period fireplace. It's a 20-minute walk northeast of the town centre.

Drinking

Godimento LOUNGE BAR
(Stjepana Radića 1) A great place for drinks and coffee on weekdays, and a vibrant atmosphere on weekends with DJs playing house and R&B. Sample the sizeable range of Croatian *rakijas* (brandys). It's northeast of the historic centre.

Information

Atlas Travel Agency (☎330 232; atlas-sibenik@si.t-com.hr; Kovačića 1a) Changes money and books excursions.

Hospital (☎334 421; Stjepana Radića 83)

NIK Travel Agency (☎338 540; www.nik.hr; Ante Šupuka 5) Large agency offering excursions to Kornati and Krka, private accommodation and international bus and air tickets.

Post Office (Vladimira Nazora 51; ⊙8am-7pm Mon-Fri, 9am-noon Sat) Make phone calls and change money.

Tourist Information Centre (☎214 441; www.sibenik-tourism.hr; Obala Franje Tuđmana 5; ⊙8am-9pm May-Oct, to 4pm Nov-Apr) Offers excellent advice and information in no fewer than 14 languages.

Getting There & Away

Jadrolinija (☎213 468; Obala Franje Tuđmana 8; ⊙9am-6pm Mon-Fri) has tickets for ferry sailings.

Though it's pretty rundown, Šibenik bus station has numerous regular bus services; it's a short walk from the old town.

There's one overnight train (161KN, eight hours) and two daily trains (11 hours) between Zagreb and Šibenik.

BUSES FROM ŠIBENIK

DESTINATION	COST (KN)	DURATION	DAILY SERVICES
Dubrovnik	245	6hr	9
Murter	28	45min	8
Osijek	352	8½hr	1
Primošten	19	30min	7
Pula	240	8hr	3
Rijeka	205	6hr	11
Split	93	1¾hr	22
Zadar	71	1½hr	34
Zagreb	190	6½hr	16

Krka National Park

022

Stretching from the western foot of the Dinaric Range into the sea near Šibenik, the 72.5km Krka River and its wonderful waterfalls define the landscape of the Šibenik-Knin region and are the focus of the Krka National Park. The Krka waterfalls are a karstic phenomenon: over millennia, river water has created a canyon (up to 200m deep) through limestone hills, bringing calcium carbonate with it. Mosses and algae retain the calcium carbonate and encrust it in their roots. The material is called tufa and is formed by billions of plants growing on top of one another. These growths create barriers in the river that produce spectacular waterfalls.

Sights

The landscape of rocks, cliffs, caves and chasms is a remarkable sight, but the national park also contains several important cultural landmarks.

Krka Monastery MONASTERY

Near the park's northernmost point there is the Orthodox monastery sometimes called Aranđelovac (Holy Archangel), or often simply referred to as the Krka Monastery. First mentioned in the history books in 1402 as the endowment of Jelena Šubić, the sister of Emperor Dušan of Serbia, it was built and rebuilt until the end of the 18th century. The monastery has a unique combination of Byzantine and Mediterranean architecture.

Roški Slap VALLEY

Below Krka Monastery, the river becomes a lake created by the Roški Slap barrier downstream and the valley narrows into a 150m gorge. Roški Slap is a 650m-long stretch that begins with shallow steps and continues in a series of branches and islets to become 27m-high cascades. On the eastern side of the falls you can see water mills that used to process wheat.

Lake Visovac LAKE

The first kilometre of the lake is bordered by reeds and bulrushes sheltering marsh birds. Downstream is the **Među Gredama gorge** with 150m-high cliffs cut into a variety of dramatic shapes. The gorge opens out into Lake Visovac, with **Samostan Visovac** its lovely island monastery. In the 14th century hermits built a small monastery and church; Bosnian Franciscans remained here throughout Turkish rule until 1699. The church on the island dates from the end of the 17th century and the bell tower was built in 1728. On the western bank is a forest of holm oaks and on the eastern bank are white oaks.

Skradinski Buk WATERFALL

Six kilometres downstream from Lake Visovac is the park's largest waterfall, Skradinski Buk, with an 800m-long cascade covering 17 steps and rising to almost 46m. Here water mills used to grind wheat, mortars pounded felt and huge baskets held rugs and fabrics. Downstream from Skradinski Buk is less interesting due to the construction of the Jaruga power plant in 1904. It takes about an hour to walk around Skradinski Buk and see the waterfalls. Bring a swimsuit because it is possible to swim in the lower lake, though it gets extremely crowded in summer.

Sleeping & Eating

Restaurants and stores line the harbour. Skradinski Buk has a few snack places and inexpensive restaurants.

Hotel Skradinski Buk HOTEL €€
(771 771; www.skradinskibuk.hr; Burinovac bb, Skradin; s/d 417/652KN; P❄@) A modern hotel with 29 renovated though smallish rooms, all with desk, satellite TV and internet access. There's a good restaurant downstairs with a covered terrace that serves grilled meats and Dalmatian dishes.

Information

Krka National Park Office (217 720; www.npkrka.hr; Trg Ivana Pavla II, Skradin; park entry adult/concession Jul & Aug 95/70KN, Apr-Jun, Sep & Oct 80/60KN, Nov-Mar 30/20KN; 9am-5pm Mon-Fri) Provides good maps and information and can arrange excursions. The park entry ticket includes a boat or bus ride to Skradinski Buk.

Tourist Office (771 306; www.skradin.hr; Trg Male Gospe 3; 8am-9pm Jul & Aug, 9am-1pm & 4-6pm Sep-Jun) Skradin's tourist office is along the harbour and will put you in touch with owners of private accommodation.

Getting There & Around

Several agencies sell excursions to the falls from Šibenik, Zadar and other cities, but it's not hard to visit the falls independently.

Seven (fewer in winter) daily buses from Šibenik make the 30-minute run to Skradin. The bus drops you outside Skradin's old town. You pay the park admission fee here, which allows you to board a boat to Skradinski Buk. If you take one of the five daily buses to Lozovac, you can take a bus to Skradinski Buk (also included in the park admission price), but you miss out on the boat ride through the canyon that you can enjoy from Skradin.

From Skradinski Buk there are three boats daily from March to November going to Visovac (adult/concession 110/60KN) and Roški Slap (140/70KN). From Roški Slap there's a boat to Krka Monastery (110/60KN); these run from April to October.

Organised tour groups and people with their own transport are able to visit the park at other times of the year.

Kornati Islands

022

Composed of 147 mostly uninhabited islands, islets and reefs covering 69 sq km, some of which are a national park, the Kornatis are the largest and densest archipelago in the Adriatic. Typically karst terrain, the islands are riddled with cracks, caves, grottoes and rugged cliffs. Since there are no sources of freshwater on the islands, they are mostly barren, sometimes with a light covering of grass. The evergreens and holm oaks that used to be found here were long ago burned down. Far from stripping the islands of their beauty, the deforestation has highlighted startling rock formations, whose stark whiteness against the deep blue Adriatic is an eerie and wonderful sight.

Sights

The Kornati Islands form four groups running northwest to southeast. The first two groups of islands lie closer to the mainland and are known locally as **Gornji Kornat**. The largest of these islands is **Žut**.

The other two series of islands, facing the open sea, comprise the **Kornati National Park** and have the most dramatically rugged coastline. **Kornat Island** is by far the largest island in the park, extending 25km in length but only 2.5km in width. Both the land and sea are within the protection of the national park. Fishing is strictly limited in order to allow the regeneration of fish shoals. Groper, bass, conger eel, sea bream, pickerel, sea scorpion, cuttlefish, squid, octopus and smelt are some of the sea life trying to make a comeback in the region.

The island of **Piškera**, also within Kornati National Park, was inhabited during the Middle Ages and served as a fishing collection and storage point. Until the 19th century, the islands were owned by the aristocracy of Zadar, but about a hundred years ago peasant ancestors of the present residents of Murter and Dugi Otok bought the islands, built many kilometres of rock walls to divide their properties and used the land to raise sheep.

The islands remain privately owned: 90% belong to Murter residents and the remainder to residents of Dugi Otok. Although there are no longer any permanent inhabitants on the islands, many owners have cottages and fields that they visit from time to time to tend the land, and there are houses to rent. Olive trees account for about 80% of the land under cultivation, followed by vineyards, orchards and vegetable gardens. There are about 300 buildings on the Kornati Islands, mostly clustered on the southwestern coast of Kornat.

 Information

Entrance fees are priced by boat; a small vessel costs 150KN per day if bought in advance. Fishing and scuba-diving permits cost 100KN per person per day.

Kornati National Park office (434 662; www.kornati.hr; Butina 2; 8.30am-5pm Mon-Fri) Located in Murter, the office is well stocked with information.

 Getting There & Away

There is no ferry transport between the Kornatis and other islands or the mainland. Unless you have your own boat, you'll have to book an excursion from Zadar, Sali, Šibenik, Split or another coastal city, or arrange private accommodation from Murter.

The largest marina is on the island of Piškera, on the southern part of the strait between Piškera and Lavsa. There's another large marina on Žut and a number of small coves throughout the islands where boaters can dock.

Split & Central Dalmatia

☎ 021

Includes »

Best Places to Eat

» Pojoda (p239)
» Figa (p209)
» Antika (p236)
» Bako (p241)

Best Places to Stay

» Hotel Vestibul Palace (p208)
» Goli + Bosi (p208)
» Hotel Adriana (p233)

Why Go?

Central Dalmatia is the most action-packed, sight-rich and diverse part of Croatia, with pretty islands, quiet ports, rugged mountains, dozens of castles and an emerging culinary scene, as well as Split's Diocletian's Palace and medieval Trogir (both Unesco World Heritage sites).

Roman ruins, a buzzing Mediterranean-flavoured city, and chic dining, wining and partying on the most glamorous isle in the Adriatic all vie for visitors' attention. Let's not forget the slender and seductive sand beaches, secluded pebble coves on islands near and far, and gorgeous nudie hideaways. Whatever your beat, this part of Croatia, with the rugged 1500m-high Dinaric Range providing a dramatic background to the coastline, will grip even the pickiest of visitors.

Best of all: Dalmatia is always warmer than Istria or the Kvarner Gulf. You can plunge into the crystalline Adriatic from the middle of May right up until the end of September.

When to Go

Split

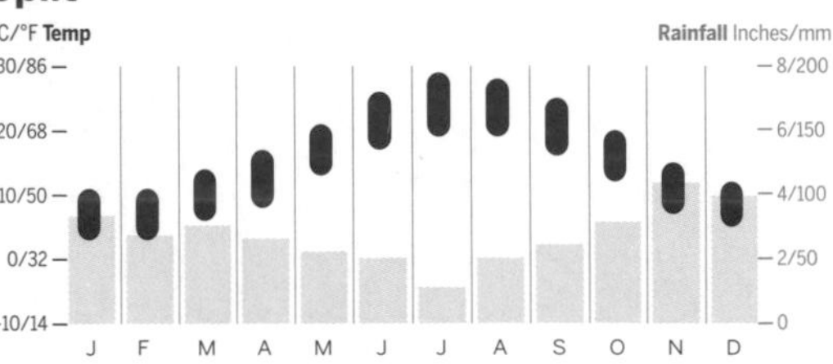

May The sea is already warm enough to swim in, so beat the crowds and enjoy sunshine aplenty.

Jul–Aug A full roster of festivals, lots of action wherever you go and the weather is tops.

Sep Come for warm seas and lower prices after the summer hordes have left.

SPLIT

POP 178,192

The second-largest city in Croatia, Split (Spalato in Italian) is a great place to see Dalmatian life as it's really lived. Always buzzing, this exuberant city has just the right balance of tradition and modernity. Step inside Diocletian's Palace (a Unesco World Heritage site and one of the world's most impressive Roman monuments) and you'll see dozens of bars, restaurants and shops thriving amid the atmospheric old walls where Split life has been going on for thousands of years. To top it off, Split has a unique setting. Its dramatic coastal mountains act as the perfect backdrop to the turquoise waters of the Adriatic. You'll get a chance to appreciate this gorgeous cityscape when making a ferry journey to or from the city.

Split is often seen mainly as a transport hub to the hip nearby islands (which, indeed, it is), but the city has been sprucing itself up and attracting attention by renovating the old Riva (seafront) and replacing the former cement strolling ground with a marble look. Even though the modern transformation hasn't pleased all the locals, the new Riva is a beauty. The growing tourist demand also means that Split's city authorities are under pressure to expand the city's transport resources, and there's talk that in the near future the currently very handy bus station may be moved further out to make way for the harbour expansion and luxury hotels.

History

Split achieved fame when the Roman emperor Diocletian (AD 245–313), noted for his persecution of early Christians, had his retirement palace built here between 295 and 305. After his death the great stone palace continued to be used as a retreat by Roman rulers. When the nearby colony of Salona (now Solin) was abandoned in the 7th century, many of the Romanised inhabitants fled to Split and barricaded themselves behind the high palace walls, where their descendants live to this day.

First the Byzantine Empire and then Croatia controlled the area, but from the 12th to the 14th centuries medieval Split enjoyed a large measure of autonomy, which favoured its development. The western part of the old town around Narodni trg, which dates from this time, became the focus of municipal life, while the area within the palace walls remained the ecclesiastical centre.

In 1420 the Venetians' conquering of Split led to its slow decline. During the 17th century, strong walls were built around the city as a defence against the Ottomans. In 1797 the Austrians arrived; they remained until 1918, with only a brief interruption during the Napoleonic Wars.

Sights

Obala Hrvatskog Narodnog Preporoda – commonly known as the Riva (waterfront promenade) – is your best central reference point in Split. Most of the large hotels and the best restaurants, nightlife and beaches lie east of the harbour along Bačvice, Firule, Zenta and Trstenik bays. The wooded Marjan Hill dominates the western tip of the city and has many beaches at its foothills.

Diocletian's Palace HISTORICAL CENTRE

(Map p202) Facing the harbour, Diocletian's Palace is one of the most imposing Roman ruins in existence and the place you'll spend most of your time while in Split. Don't expect a palace though, nor a museum – this is the living heart of the city, its labyrinthine streets packed with people, bars, shops and restaurants. The narrow streets hide passageways and courtyards, some deserted and eerie, others thumping with music from bars and cafes, while the local residents hang out their washing overhead, kids play football amid the ancient walls, and grannies sit in their windows watching the action below. It's an enchanting place.

Although the original structure was modified in the Middle Ages, the alterations have only served to increase the allure of this fascinating site. The palace was built from lustrous white stone from the island of Brač, and construction lasted 10 years. Diocletian spared no expense, importing marble from Italy and Greece, and columns and sphinxes from Egypt. A military fortress, imperial residence and fortified town, the palace measures 215m from east to west (including the square corner towers) and is 181m wide at the southernmost point. The walls at their highest measure 26m and the entire structure covers 31,000 sq metres.

Each wall has a gate named after a metal: at the northern end is the **Golden Gate**, while the southern end has the **Bronze Gate**. The eastern gate is the **Silver Gate** and to the west is the **Iron Gate**. Between the eastern and western gates there's a straight road (Krešimirova; also known as Decumanus), which separates the imperial residence on

Split & Central Dalmatia Highlights

1. Discover Split's ancient heart in **Diocletian's Palace** (p197), a quarter that buzzes day and night
2. Savour the foodie scene and beautiful beaches of **Vis** (p238), Croatia's most remote island
3. Stretch out on Croatia's sexiest beach, **Zlatni Rat** (p227), in Bol
4. Soak up the glamour and party all out at the seafront bars in **Hvar Town** (p230)
5. Hike up dramatic **Mt Biokovo** (p222) and enjoy views of Italy from the top
6. Take in the remarkably preserved ancient architecture of tiny **Trogir** (p216), the World Heritage star of Central Dalmatia
7. Explore the dreamy interior of **Hvar Island** (p230), with its endless fields of lavender, stretching sea vistas and abandoned hamlets

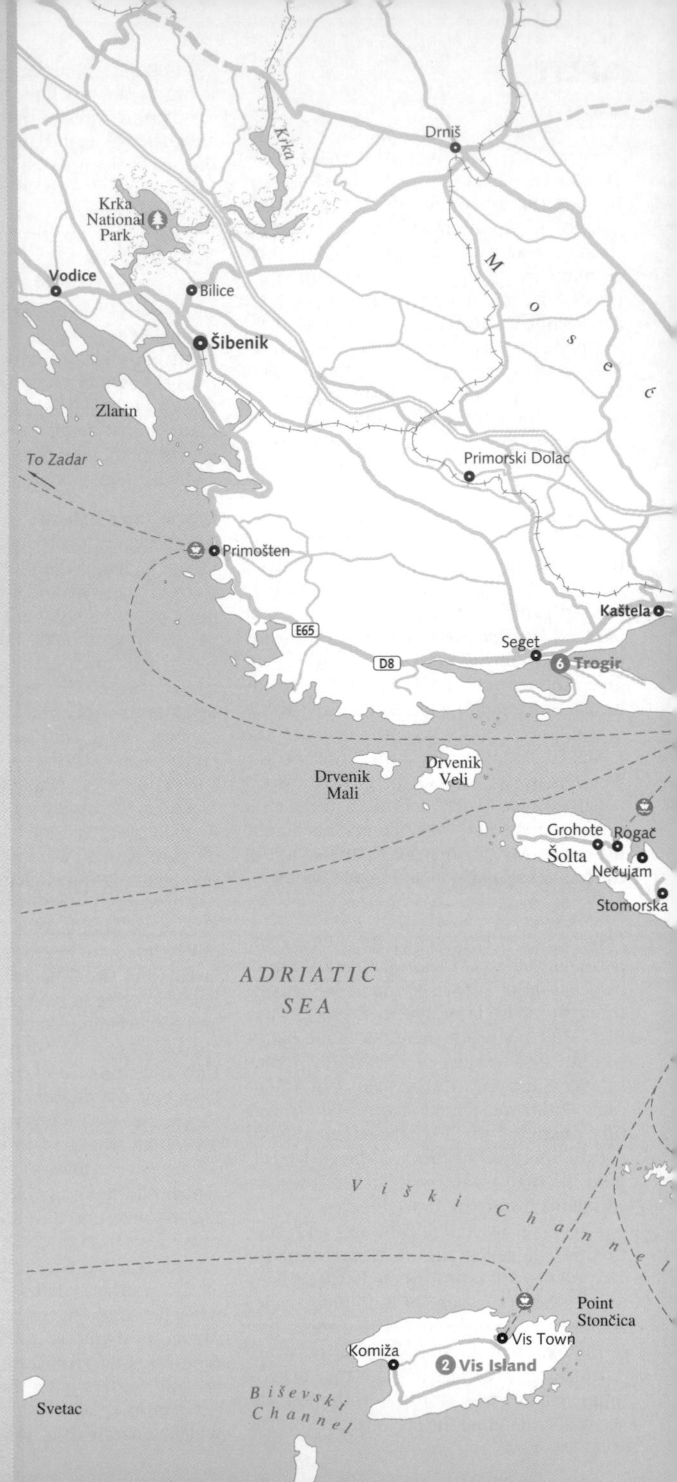

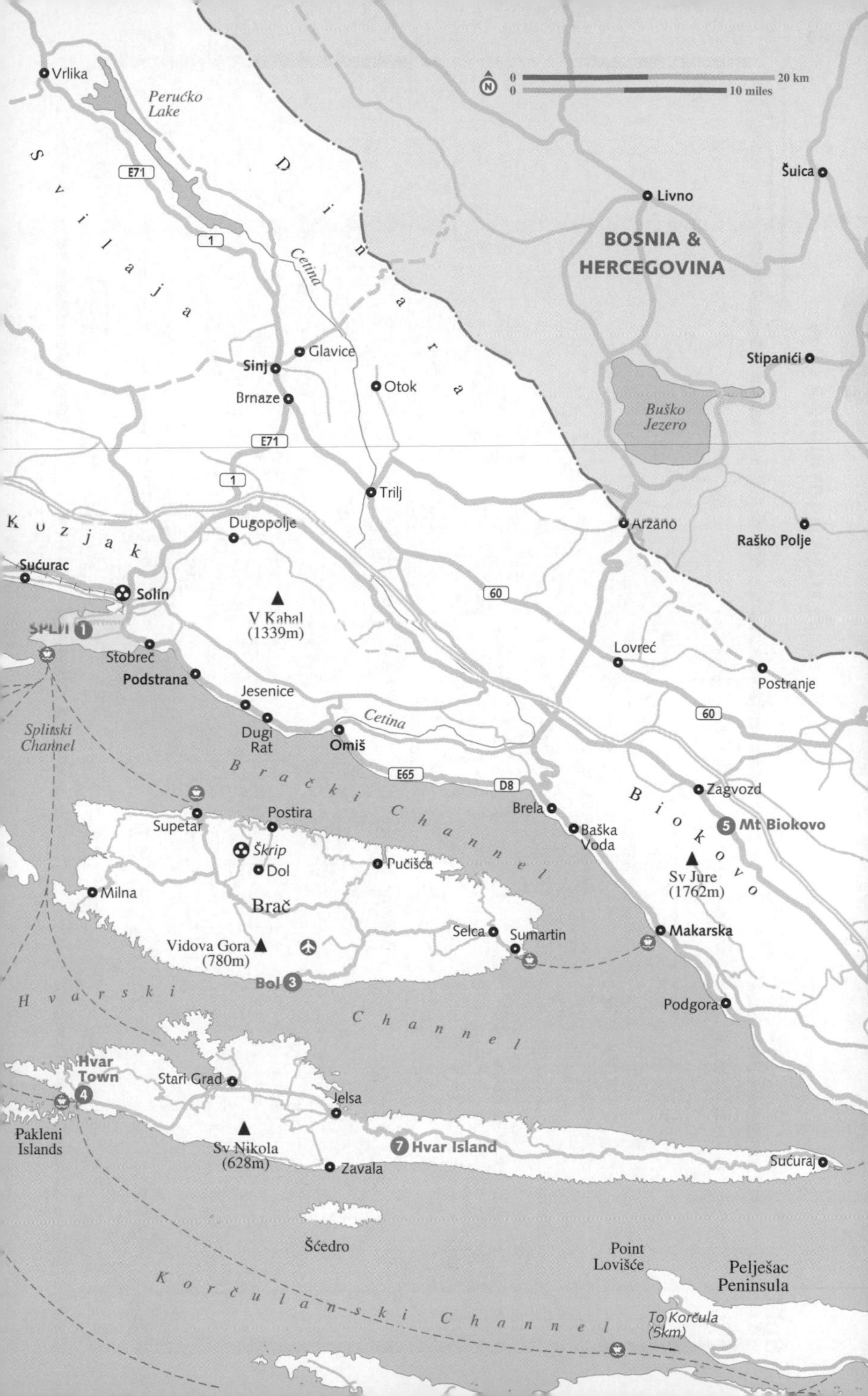

0
20 km
0
10 miles
Vrlika
Perućko Lake
S v i l a j a
D i n a r a
E71
1
Cetina
Šuica
Livno
BOSNIA & HERCEGOVINA
Glavice
Sinj
Otok
Brnaze
Stipanići
Buško Jezero
E71
1
Trilj
Arzano
Raško Polje
K o z j a k
Dugopolje
Sućurac
Solin
V Kabal (1339m)
60
Split 1
Stobreč
Podstrana
Lovreć
Postranje
Jesenice
Cetina
60
Dugi Rat
Omiš
Splitski Channel
B r a č k i C h a n n e l
E65
D8
Zagvozd
Brela
B i o k o v o
Postira
Supetar
Baška Voda
5 Mt Biokovo
Škrip
Dol
Pučišća
Sv Jure (1762m)
Milna
Brač
Selca
Sumartin
Makarska
Vidova Gora (780m)
Bol 3
H v a r s k i C h a n n e l
Podgora
Hvar Town 4
Stari Grad
Jelsa
Pakleni Islands
Sv Nikola (628m)
7 Hvar Island
Sućuraj
Zavala
Šćedro
Point Lovišće
Pelješac Peninsula
K o r č u l a n s k i C h a n n e l
To Korčula (5km)

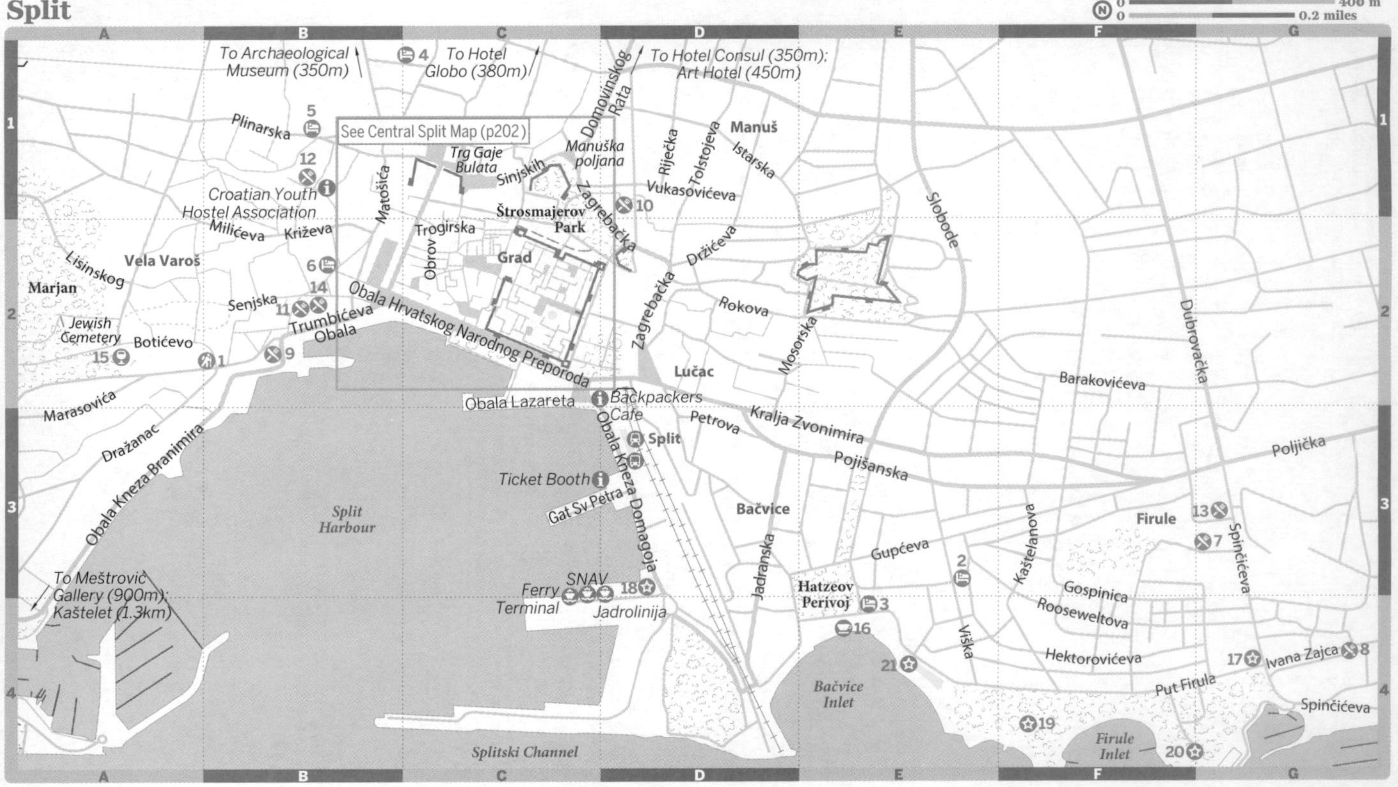
Split
400 m
0.2 miles
To Archaeological Museum (350m)
To Hotel Globo (380m)
To Hotel Consul (350m); Art Hotel (450m)
See Central Split Map (p202)
Plinarska
Trg Gaje Bulata
Manuška poljana
Domovinskog Rata
Manuš
Rijećka
Tolstojeva
Istarska
Croatian Youth Hostel Association
Matošića
Sinjskih
Vukasovićeva
Štrosmajerov Park
Zagrebačka
Milićeva
Križeva
Trogirska
Grad
Obrov
Držićeva
Slobode
Vela Varoš
Lisinskog
Marjan
Senjska
Obala Hrvatskog Narodnog Preporoda
Rokova
Mosorska
Jewish Cemetery
Botićevo
Trumbićeva Obala
Lučac
Dubrovačka
Barakovićeva
Marasovića
Obala Lazareta
Backpackers Cafe
Petrova
Kralja Zvonimira
Dražanac
Split
Obala Kneza Domagoja
Pojišanska
Poljička
Obala Kneza Branimira
Ticket Booth
Gat Sv Petra
Split Harbour
Bačvice
Firule
Spinčićeva
Kaštelanova
Gupćeva
To Meštrović Gallery (900m); Kaštelet (1.3km)
SNAV
Ferry Terminal
Jadrolinija
Jadranska
Hatzeov Perivoj
Gospinica
Rooseweltova
Viška
Hektorovićeva
Ivana Zajca
Put Firula
Bačvice Inlet
Splitski Channel
Firule Inlet

Split

Activities, Courses & Tours

1 Stairway to Marjan Hill ... B2

Sleeping

2 Beach Hostel Split ... E3
3 Hotel Park ... E4
4 Tchaikovsky Hostel ... C1
5 Villa Baguc ... B1
6 Villa Varoš ... B2

Eating

7 Boban ... G3
Bruna ... (see 3)
8 Kadena ... G4
9 Kod Fife ... B2
10 Kod Joze ... D1
11 Konoba Matejuška ... B2
12 Makrovega ... B1
13 Pimpinella ... G3
14 Šperun ... B2

Drinking

15 Vidilica ... A2
16 Žbirac ... E4

Entertainment

Egoist ... (see 17)
17 Hedonist ... G4
18 Imperium ... D3
Kino Bačvice ... (see 21)
19 Mediteranium ... F4
20 O'Hara ... F4
21 Tropic Club ... E4

the southern side, with its state rooms and temples, from the northern side, once used by soldiers and servants. The Bronze Gate, in the southern wall, led from the living quarters to the sea. Two of the gates, the Bronze and the Golden, are fronted by city landmarks: **Meštrović sculptures** of literary scholar Marko Marulić and the medieval bishop Grgur Ninski.

There are 220 buildings within the palace boundaries, home to about 3000 people. Each street has small signs at its beginning and end marking what you'll find upon it: bars, cafes, restaurants, shops, museums. It makes moving around much easier, though one of the best things you can do is get lost in the palace – it's small enough that you'll always find your way out easily. In any case, once you enter the palace, forget about street names.

The best way to see the palace's main sights is to follow our walking tour.

Town Museum

(Map p202; Muzej Grada Splita; www.mgst.net; Papalićeva 1; adult/concession 10/5KN; ⏲9am-9pm Tue-Fri, to 4pm Sat-Mon Jun-Sep, 10am-5pm Tue-Fri, to 1pm Sat-Mon Oct-May) Built by Juraj Dalmatinac for one of the many nobles who lived within the palace in the Middle Ages, **Papalić Palace** is considered a fine example of late Gothic style, with an elaborately carved entrance gate that proclaimed the importance of its original inhabitants. The interior has been thoroughly restored to house this museum. Captions are in Croatian, but wall panels in a variety of languages provide a historical framework for the exhibits. The museum has three floors, with drawings, heraldic coats of arms, 17th-century weaponry, fine furniture, coins and documents from as far back as the 14th century.

Cathedral of St Domnius

(Map p202; Katedrala Svetog Duje; Svetog Duje 5; admission cathedral/treasury/belfry 15/15/10KN; ⏲8am-7pm Mon-Sat, 12.30-6.30pm Sun Jun-Sep, sporadic hours Oct-May) Split's cathedral was originally built as Diocletian's mausoleum, with an octagonal form, encircled by 24 columns, that is almost completely preserved to this day. Its round-domed interior has two rows of Corinthian columns and a frieze showing Emperor Diocletian and his wife, Prisca. The oldest monuments in the cathedral are the scenes from the life of Christ on the wooden entrance doors. Carved by Andrija Buvina in the 13th century, the scenes are presented in 28 squares and recall the fashion of Romanesque miniatures of the time.

Also notice the **right altar** carved by Bonino da Milano in 1427 and the vault above the altar decorated with murals by Dujam Vušković. To the left is the altar of St Anastasius (Sveti Staš; 1448) by Dalmatinac, with a relief of *The Flagellation of Christ*, which is one of the finest sculptural works of its time in Dalmatia.

The **choir** is furnished with 13th-century Romanesque seats that are the oldest in Dalmatia. Cross the altar and follow the signs to the **treasury**, rich in reliquaries, icons, church robes, illuminated manuscripts and documents in Glagolitic script. Part of the same structure, the Romanesque **belfry** was constructed between the 12th and 16th centuries and reconstructed in 1908 after it collapsed. Notice the two lion figures at the foot of the belfry and the Egyptian black-granite sphinx dating from the 15th century BC on the right wall. South of the mausoleum, there are remains of the Roman baths, a Roman building with a mosaic and the remains of the imperial dining hall, in various stages of preservation.

Note that admission to the cathedral also gets you free access to the Temple of Jupiter and its crypt. For 35KN, you can get a ticket that includes access to all these highlights.

Temple of Jupiter
(Map p202; admission temple/crypt 5/5KN; ⏲8am-7pm Mon-Sat, 12.30-6.30pm Sun May-Sep) The headless sphinx in black granite guarding the entrance to the temple was imported from Egypt at the time of the temple's construction in the 5th century. Of the col-

Central Split

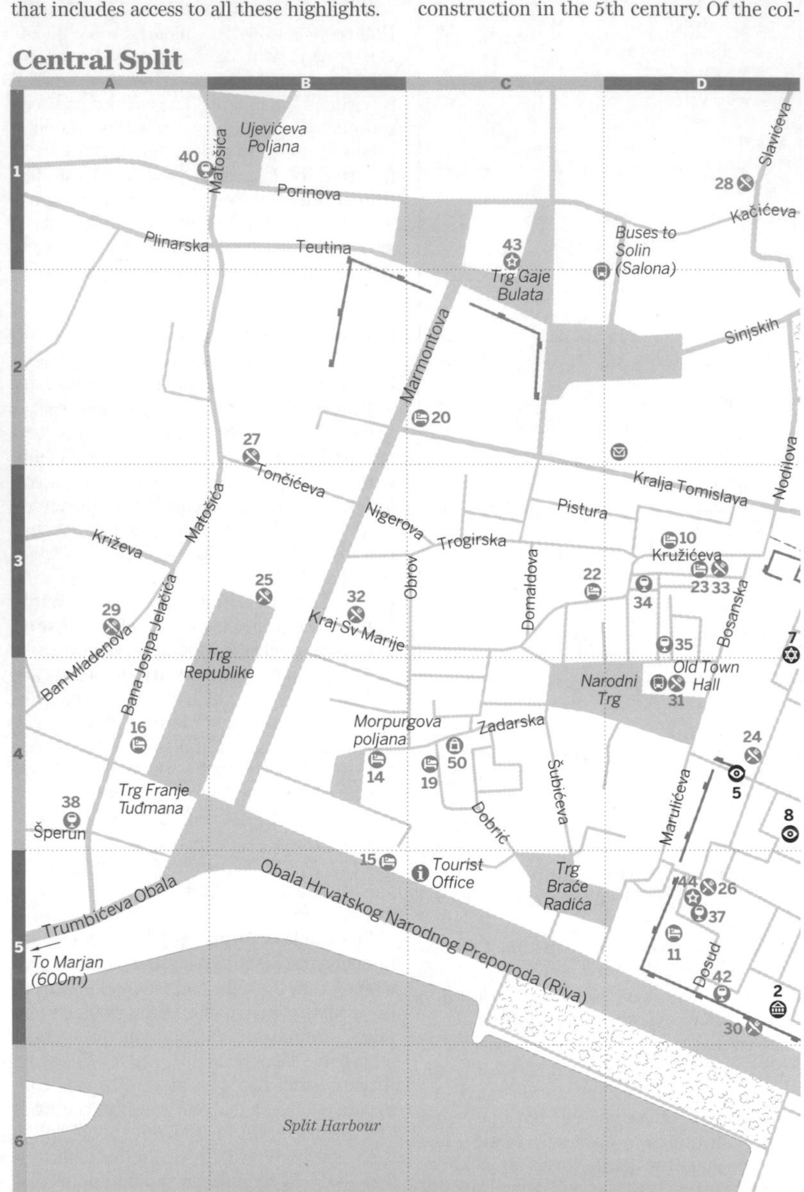

umns that supported a porch the temple once had, only one remains. Take a look at the barrel-vaulted ceiling and a decorative frieze on the walls. You can also pop into the crypt, which was used as a church back in the day.

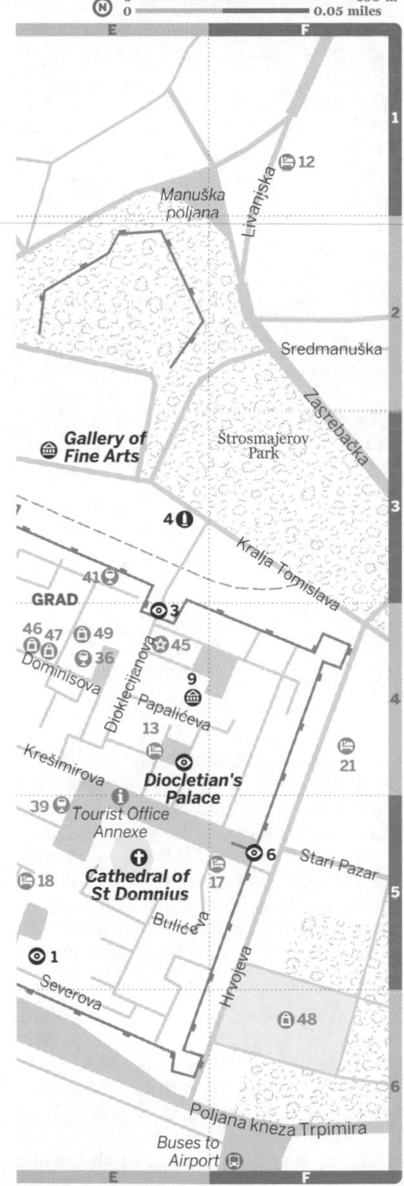

Ethnographic Museum
(Map p202; Etnografski Muzej; www.etnografski-muzej-split.hr; Severova 1; adult/concession 10/5KN; ⏲9am-7pm Mon-Fri, to 1pm Sat Jun-Sep, 9am-4pm Mon-Fri, to 1pm Sat Oct-May) This mildly interesting museum has a collection of photos of old Split, traditional costumes and memorabilia of important citizens, housed on two floors and an attic. The ground floor hosts temporary exhibits. Make sure you wander through this early medieval palace and climb the reconstructed Roman staircase that leads to the Renaissance terrace on the southern edge of the vestibule. The views from up there are reason enough to visit the museum.

Synagogue
(Map p202; www.zost.hr; Židovski prolaz 1) Built into the western wall of the palace, Split's synagogue is the third-oldest synagogue in Europe that's still in use. Created out of two medieval houses in the 16th century, in what was then the Jewish ghetto, it got its current appearance around 1728.

Split's Jewish community today, which can be traced back to the Roman times, has around 100 members. As there is no rabbi, the community is more traditional than religious. Split's first Jewish wedding for 70 years was held at the synagogue in September 2012, the first official ceremony since WWII. The last wedding was in 1943, a year after the synagogue had been pillaged by Italian fascists.

Basement Halls
(Map p202; adult/concession 35/15KN; ⏲9am-9pm Jun-Sep, 9am-8pm Mon-Sat, to 6pm Sun Apr, May & Oct, 9am-6pm Mon-Sat, to 2pm Sun rest of year) Although mostly empty, save an exhibit or two, the rooms and corridors underneath Diocletian's Palace exude a haunting timelessness that is well worth the price of a ticket. The cellars, filled with stands selling souvenirs and handicrafts, open onto the southern gate.

Gregorius of Nin MONUMENT
(Map p202; Grgur Ninski) The 10th-century Croatian bishop Gregorius of Nin fought for the right to use old Croatian in liturgical services. Sculpted by Ivan Meštrović, this powerful work is a defining image of Split. His left big toe has been polished to a shine – it's said that rubbing it brings good luck and guarantees you'll come back to Split.

Archaeological Museum MUSEUM
(Map p200; Arheološki Muzej; www.armus.hr; Zrinsko-Frankopanska 25; adult/concession 20/10KN; ⏲9am-2pm & 4-8pm Mon-Sat Jun-Sep, 9am-2pm & 4-8pm

Central Split

Top Sights
- Cathedral of St Domnius ... E5
- Diocletian's Palace ... E4
- Gallery of Fine Arts ... E3

Sights
- 1 Basement Halls ... E5
- Bronze Gate ... (see 1)
- 2 Ethnographic Museum ... D5
- 3 Golden Gate ... E4
- 4 Gregorius of Nin ... E3
- 5 Iron Gate ... D4
- 6 Silver Gate ... F5
- 7 Synagogue ... D3
- 8 Temple of Jupiter ... D4
- 9 Town Museum ... E4

Sleeping
- 10 Al's Place ... D3
- 11 B&B Villa Kaštel 1700 ... D5
- 12 Dalmatian Villas ... F1
- 13 Diocletian's Rooms ... E4
- 14 Goli + Bosi ... B4
- 15 Hotel Adriana ... B5
- 16 Hotel Bellevue ... A4
- 17 Hotel Peristil ... F5
- 18 Hotel Vestibul Palace ... E5
- 19 Marmont Hotel ... C4
- 20 Silver Central Hostel ... C2
- 21 Silver Gate ... F4
- 22 Split Hostel Booze & Snooze ... C3
- 23 Split Hostel Fiesta Siesta ... D3

Eating
- 24 Bajamont ... D4
- 25 Bajamonti ... B3
- 26 Figa ... D5
- 27 Galija ... B2
- 28 Gušt ... D1
- 29 Konoba Hvaranin ... A3
- 30 Le Maison de Sarah ... D5
- 31 No Stress Cafe & Bistro ... D4
- 32 Noštromo ... B3
- 33 Villa Spiza ... D3

Drinking
- 34 Bifora ... D3
- 35 Gaga ... D3
- 36 Galerija ... E4
- 37 Ghetto Club ... D5
- 38 Libar ... A4
- 39 Luxor ... E5
- Mosquito ... (see 36)
- 40 Paradox ... A1
- Porta ... (see 41)
- 41 Teak ... E3
- 42 Tri Volta ... D5

Entertainment
- 43 Croatian National Theatre ... C1
- 44 Fluid ... D5
- 45 Kinoteka Zlatna Vrata ... E4

Shopping
- 46 Arka ... E4
- 47 Arterija ... E4
- Diocletian's Cellars ... (see 1)
- 48 Food Market ... F6
- 49 GetGetGet ... E4
- 50 Think Pink ... C4

Mon-Fri, to 2pm Sat Oct-May) Just north of the town centre, the Archaeological Museum is worth the leisurely 10-minute walk. The emphasis is on the Roman and early Christian period, with exhibits devoted to burial sculpture and excavations at Solin. The quality of the sculpture is high, and there are interesting reliefs based on Illyrian mythical figures. There are also jewellery, ceramics and coins on display.

Gallery of Fine Arts GALLERY

(Map p202; Galerija Umjetnina Split; www.galum.hr; Kralja Tomislava 15; adult/concession 20/10KN; ⏲11am-4pm Mon, 11am-7pm Tue-Fri, 11am-3pm Sat May-Sep, 9am-2pm Mon, 9am-5pm Tue-Fri, 9am-1pm Sat Oct-Apr) After a very long renovation, this gallery opened in 2009 in the building that once housed the city's first hospital. It exhibits nearly 400 works of art spanning almost 700 years. Upstairs is the permanent collection of mainly paintings and some sculpture, a chronological journey that starts with the old masters and continues with works of modern Croatian art by the likes of Vlaho Bukovac and Ignjat Job. Temporary exhibits downstairs change every few months. The pleasant cafe has a terrace overlooking the palace.

Meštrović Gallery GALLERY

(Map p200; Galerija Meštrović; Šetalište Ivana Meštrovića 46; adult/concession 30/15KN; ⏲9am-7pm Tue-Sun May-Sep, 9am-4pm Tue-Sat, 10am-3pm Sun Oct-Apr) At this stellar art gallery, you'll see a comprehensive, well-arranged collection of works by Ivan Meštrović, Croatia's premier modern sculptor, who built the gallery as a personal residence from 1931 to 1939. Although Meštrović intended to retire here, he emigrated to the USA soon after WWII. Don't miss the nearby **Kaštelet** (Map p200; Šetalište Ivana Meštrovića 39; admission by Meštrović Gallery ticket; ⊙9am-7pm Tue-Sat, 10am-7pm Sun May-Sep, 9am-4pm Tue-Sat, 10am-3pm Sun Oct-Apr), a fortress that Meštrović bought and restored to house his powerful *Life of Christ* wood reliefs.

Activities

Bačvice SWIMMING

(Map p200) A flourishing beach life gives Split its aura of insouciance in summer. Bačvice is the most popular beach, awarded with a Blue Flag eco label. This pebbly beach with good swimming and a lively ambience is where you'll find *picigin* games galore. There are showers and changing rooms at both ends of the beach. Bačvice is also a popular summer bar and club area for Split's younger crowd and for visitors.

Marjan WALKING TRAIL

(Map p200) For an afternoon away from the city buzz, Marjan (178m) is the perfect destination. Considered the lungs of the city, this hilly nature reserve offers **trails** through fragrant pine forests, scenic **lookouts** and ancient **chapels**. There are different ways of reaching Marjan. One is to head up Plinarska street just behind the National Theatre, cross Nazorova street and continue west down Mandalinski Put until you get to the Northern Gate (Spinutska Vrata). Otherwise, you can start the walk closer to the centre, from the stairway (Marjanske Skale) in Varoš, right behind the Church of Sveti Frane. It's a mild incline along old stone stairs and a scenic 10-minute trek to get to Vidilica cafe at the top. From here, right by the old Jewish cemetery, you can follow the marked trail, stopping en route to see the chapels, all the way to **Kašjuni cove**, a quieter beach option than buzzing Bačvice.

Seafront of Marjan WALKING TRAIL

Another lovely walk is along the seafront of Marjan, entering at ACI Marina in the Meje neighbourhood, continuing on to Sustipan peninsula on the southwestern point of Split's harbour, passing by the Jadran swimming-pool complex, then Zvončac Bay and on to Kaštelet. This walk takes about 25 minutes from the Riva. From here, you climb up to Šetalište Ivana Meštrovića, past the Meštrović Gallery, and continue west for another 20 minutes to Kašjuni. Or rent a bike for 15KN per hour by Spinutska Vrata on Marjan.

Tours

Atlas Travel Agency (☎343 055; Trg Braće Radića 6; ⊙9am-6pm Mon-Fri) runs excursions to the waterfalls at Krka National Park (370KN), Hvar (485KN) and Plitvice (610KN). If you're after a party tour, check out Split Hostel Booze & Snooze (p209) for daily **boat cruises** to Brač (280KN). Silver Central Hostel (p208) offers trips to Krka (315KN) and a **4WD safari** to Mosor (555KN).

Secret Dalmatia (www.secretdalmatia.com) is an excellently run outfit that offers customised tours in Split and all around Dalmatia, including sailing trips, cooking classes at a 13th-century palace in Trogir, wine tastings with local experts and unique outings to Dalmatia's uncharted interior.

In town, **Travel 49** (☎572 772; www.travel49.com; Dioklecijanova 5) offers a two-hour Split bike tour that departs daily between May and October and costs 150KN. Its Split walking tour departs from the Peristil three times daily (80KN); it also offers rafting on Cetina

KLAPA YOUR HANDS!

There won't be a visitor to Croatia who hasn't heard the dulcet tones of a *klapa* song. This music involves a bunch of hunky men in a circle, singing tear-jerkers about love, betrayal, patriotism, death, beauty and other life-affirming subjects in honeyed multitonal harmonies.

First tenor Branko Tomić, a man whose high-toned voice complements the basses and baritones that accompany him, says of the music: 'I've sung with the Filip Dević *klapa* for 35 years. It's a passion of mine. I started singing in high school and I loved it. We sing about so many different things: we serenade, we sing traditional songs, sentimental songs about missing your family or your home town. It's a gentler, more companionship-based experience, though the new generations are starting to prefer our covers of pop songs. That's a really big thing in Croatia nowadays.'

To catch a *klapa* doing its thing, head to the Vestibule, where morning performances take place during the high season.

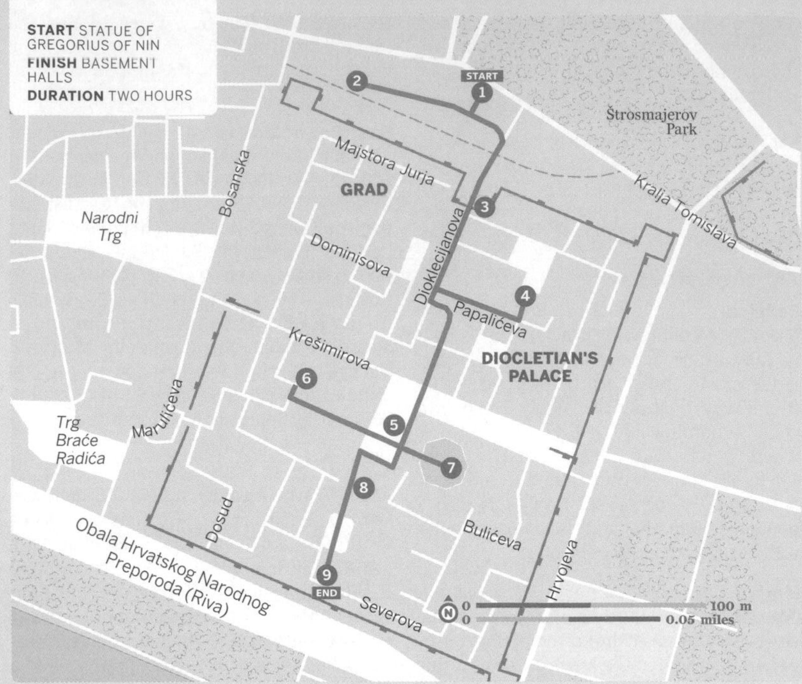

Walking Tour
Diocletian's Palace

Begin just outside the palace at the imposing statue of **1 Gregorius of Nin** (Grgur Ninski), and rub his toe for good luck. Between the statue and the well-preserved corner tower of the palace are the remains of the pre-Romanesque church of St Benedict with the 15th-century **2 Chapel of Arnir**. Through the protective glass you'll see the altar slab and sarcophagus carved by the early Renaissance master Juraj Dalmatinac.

The statue is outside the **3 Golden Gate**, which features fragments of statues, columns and arches. Turn left at Papalićeva and at No 1 is Papalić Palace, housing the worthwhile **4 town museum**.

Return to Dioklecijanova, turn left and look for the Peristil, the ceremonial entrance court, three steps below street level. The longer side is lined with six granite columns, linked by arches and decorated with a stone frieze. The southern side is enclosed by the **5 Protiron**, the entrance to the imperial quarters.

Turn right (west) onto the narrow Sveti Ivana, which leads to the palace's former ceremonial and devotional section. You can still see parts of columns and a few fragments of the two temples that once flanked these streets. At the end of the street is the **6 Temple of Jupiter**, notable for its arched roof.

Returning to the Peristil, go up the eastern stairs to the **7 Cathedral of St Domnius**. Immediately west of the cathedral are massive steps leading down through the Protiron into the well-preserved **8 vestibule**. The circular ground floor has such great acoustics that different *klapas* sing a cappella here in the mornings. To the left is the entrance to the palace's **9 basement halls**. The story goes that Diocletian was so paranoid someone would kill him that he often slept in different rooms. To get to the sleeping quarters you had to pass a circular space with great acoustics so the echo would warn the emperor if anyone was coming. You can still hear the echo when you stand in the basement's circular room.

PICIGIN

For a bit of fun, join the locals at the beach and play the very Dalmatian sport of *picigin*. The rules are simple: stand in the water up to your knees or waist and pass a small ball (the size of a squash ball) to other players at a rather high speed by whacking it with the palm of your hand. The idea is to keep the ball from falling and touching the water's surface. It is imperative that you throw yourself about and into the water as much as possible. It's also advised to splash all the people standing around you and freely display your sporting vigour.

Check out the *picigin* 'headquarters' page at www.picigin.org or the several YouTube videos demonstrating *picigin* techniques (which vary between Split, Krk and other parts of the coast). Have a go at the special New Year's Eve *picigin* game if you think you're tough enough.

(300KN). **Falco Tours** (☎548 646; www.falco-tours.com; Zrnovnicka 11) runs kayaking trips (230KN, four person minimum) departing from Trstenik beach and ending in Stobreč. **Celebrus** (☎098 869 871; www.celebrus-travel.com) offers a boat tour to Šolta (260KN), departing daily from the Riva.

Festivals & Events

Most festivals in Split take place along the Riva. The tourist office can give you more information about all the festivals. From June through to September a variety of evening entertainment is presented in the old town, usually around the Peristil.

Carnival CULTURAL
This traditional February event sees locals dressing up and dancing in the streets for two very fun days.

Feast of St Duje RELIGIOUS
Otherwise known as Split Day, this 7 May feast involves much singing and dancing all around the city.

xSTatic Festival SPORT
(www.festive.hr) Celebration of hip-hop culture and extreme sports each May, in different locations around town.

World Championship in Picigin SPORT
For the last nine years, locals have been showing off their *picigin* skills competitively at this fun early June event in Bačvice.

Mediterranean Film Festival FILM
(www.fmfs.hr) Week-long festival each June screening films from the Mediterranean region, spiced up with exhibitions and parties.

Festival of Pop Music MUSIC
Four days of music held around the end of June or early July.

Split Summer Festival ARTS
(www.splitsko-ljeto.hr) From mid-July to mid-August, it features opera, drama, ballet and concerts on open-air stages.

Split Jazz Festival MUSIC
For about a week in August, Split comes alive with jazz in venues around town.

Split Film Festival FILM
(www.splitfilmfestival.hr) Focuses on new international films and screens lots of art-house movies; held in mid-September.

Sleeping

Good budget accommodation has become more available in Split in the last couple of years but it's mostly comprised of hostels. Private accommodation is a great option and in summer you may be deluged at the bus station by women offering *sobe* (rooms available). Make sure you are clear about the exact location of the room or you may find yourself several bus rides from the town centre. The best thing to do is to book through one of the travel agencies, but there is little available within the heart of the old town.

Expect to pay between 300KN and 500KN for a double room; in the cheaper ones you will probably share the bathroom with the proprietor. If you have your own wheels and don't mind staying out of town, you will find a wealth of *pansions* (guesthouses) along the main Split–Dubrovnik road just south of town.

Also consider **Dalmatian Villas** (Map p202; ☎340 680; www.accommodationinsplit.com; Livanjska 6; d/apt 525/825KN), where you can rent rooms or apartments in renovated stone villas in the old town. It also has cottages (520KN to 635KN) and villas (2230KN to 3715KN) on Brač.

Split has some very swanky hotels popping up. The swish Radisson Blu opened a couple of years ago, with an exclusive spa, and another luxury property is in the works, also on the waterfront. So if you fancy lazing in a jacuzzi or an aromatic wellness centre after you've been relaxing by the Adriatic all day long, Split is the place to be.

TOP CHOICE **Hotel Vestibul Palace** HOTEL €€€
(Map p202; ☎329 329; www.vestibulpalace.com; Iza Vestibula 4; s/d 1380/1670KN; P❄@📶) The poshest in the palace, this award-winning boutique hideaway has seven stylish rooms and suites, all with exposed ancient walls, leather and wood, and the full spectrum of upscale amenities. There's parking for 100KN per day. The hotel's annex, Villa Dobrić, a stone's throw away, has four double rooms (single/double 1050/1250KN).

Goli + Bosi HOSTEL €€€
(Map p202; ☎510 999; www.gollybossy.com; Morpurgova Poljana 2; dm/s/d 245/714/818KN) Split's design hostel is the premier destination for flashpackers, with its sleek futuristic decor, hip vibe and a cool lobby cafe-bar-restaurant. For 1153KN you get the superior double (called Mala Floramy), with breakfast included and gorgeous views.

Hotel Peristil HOTEL €€€
(Map p202; ☎329 070; www.hotelperistil.com; Poljana Kraljice Jelene 5; s/d 1000/1200KN; ❄@📶) This lovely hotel overlooks the Peristil, in the Diocletian's Palace. Service is warm and the 12 rooms are gorgeous, with hardwood floors, antique details and good views but smallish bathrooms. Rooms 204 and 304 have small alcoves with a bit of the palace's ancient wall exposed *and* they overlook the Peristil.

CroParadise Split Hostels HOSTEL €
(☎091 44 44 194; www.croparadise.com; Čulića Dvori 29; dm 180KN, d 400-500KN, apt from 500KN; ❄@📶) A great collection of three hostels – Blue, Green and Pink – inside converted apartments in the neighbourhood of Manuš. The shared bar Underground (open June to September) is a starting point for pub crawls (Monday to Saturday nights). Other facilities include laundry, bike and scooter rental. Five apartments are also available.

Marmont Hotel HOTEL €€€
(Map p202; ☎308 060; www.marmonthotel.com; Zadarska 13; s/d 1500/2100KN; ❄@📶) A boutique hideaway with 21 rooms, this stylish spot features lots of marble, exposed stone, skylights and hardwood floors. The 2nd-floor terrace has great rooftop views. Rooms are spacious and contemporary, with dark walnut furniture, oak flooring and fancy bathrooms. The presidential suite is a steal at 8000KN.

Hotel Park HOTEL €€€
(Map p200; ☎406 400; www.hotelpark-split.hr; Hatzeov Perivoj 3; s/d 950/1440KN; P❄@📶) Split's oldest hotel (since 1921) is much loved for its seafront location (behind Bačvice), gorgeous palm-fringed terrace and amazing buffet breakfasts. Rooms are smallish but comfy, with lovely vistas. The hotel's restaurant, Bruna, is a coveted place to splash out.

Hotel Bellevue HOTEL €€€
(Map p202; ☎345 644; www.hotel-bellevue-split.hr; Bana Josipa Jelačića 2; s/d 620/865KN; P@) This atmospheric old classic with a 2nd-floor reception has sure seen better days, but it remains one of the more dreamy hotels in town, with character aplenty. It's all regal-patterned wallpaper, dark-brown wood, art-deco elements, billowing gauzy curtains and faded but well-kept rooms, some with sea views.

Villa Varoš GUESTHOUSE €€
(Map p200; ☎483 469; www.villavaros.hr; Miljenka Smoje 1; d/ste 600/900KN; ❄📶) Midrangers are getting a better deal in Split nowadays, with places such as Villa Varoš around. Owned by a New Yorker Croat, Villa Varoš is central, the rooms are simple, bright and airy, and the apartment has a jacuzzi and a small terrace.

Villa Baguc GUESTHOUSE €€€
(Map p200; ☎770 456; www.baguc.com; Plinarska 29/2; s/d 860/970KN; ❄📶) Four rooms on four floors of a restored 150-year-old family house in Varoš, with modern fittings combined with original details such as exposed stone walls. The villa is tucked away, yet a five-minute walk to the town centre.

Silver Central Hostel HOSTEL €
(Map p202; ☎490 805; www.silvercentralhostel.com; Kralja Tomislava 1; dm 167-190KN; ❄@📶) In an upstairs apartment, this light-yellow-coloured boutique hostel has four dorm rooms and a pleasant lounge. Plus it runs fun day trips. It has a two-person apartment nearby (300KN to 535KN) and another hostel, **Silver Gate** (☎322 857; www.silvergatehostel.com; Hrvojeva 6; dm per person 167KN), near the food market.

B&B Villa Kaštel 1700 B&B €€
(Map p202; ☎343 912; www.kastelsplit.com; Mihovilova Širina 5; s/d 620/760KN; ❄@📶) Among Split's best value-for-money places, this B&B is in an alleyway within the palace walls. It's near the bars and has small tidy rooms, friendly service

and free wi-fi. Triple rooms are available, as are apartments with small kitchens.

Hotel Adriana HOTEL €€€
(Map p202; ☎340 000; www.hotel-adriana.com; Hrvatskog Narodnog Preporoda 8; s/d 750/1100KN; ❄☎) Good value, excellent location smack in the middle of the Riva. The rooms are not massively exciting, with their navy curtains and beige furniture, but some come complete with lovely sea views.

Tchaikovsky Hostel HOSTEL €
(Map p200; ☎317 124; www.tchaikovskyhostel.com; Petra Ilića Čajkovskog 4; dm 187KN; ❄@☎) Four-dorm hostel in the neighbourhood of Špinut, run by a German-born Croat. Rooms are neat and tidy, with bunks featuring built-in shelves. Freebies include cereal, espresso and tea.

Diocletian's Rooms RENTAL ROOMS €€
(Map p202; ☎099 33 32 207; www.staytosee.com; Poljana Kraljica Jelene 2; r 680KN; ❄@) The views of the palace and the cathedral don't get much better than from these four double rooms with an all-white contemporary Ikea look. It also has a studio apartment nearby for 717KN.

Split Hostel Booze & Snooze HOSTEL €
(Map p202; ☎342 787; www.splithostel.com; Narodni trg 8; dm 200-215KN; ❄@☎) Run by a pair of Aussie-Croat women, this party place at the heart of town has four dorms, a terrace, book swap and boat trips. Its newer outpost, **Split Hostel Fiesta Siesta** (Map p202; Kružićeva 5; dm 200-215KN, d 560KN; ❄@☎), has five sparkling dorms and one double above the popular Charlie's Backpacker Bar.

Beach Hostel Split HOSTEL €
(Map p200; ☎098 94 50 998; Viška 9; dm 200KN; ⊙Apr-Oct; @☎) A hop and a skip from Bačvice beach, this no-frills hostel is managed by a friendly Norwegian called Ladybird, who gives the place soul. There's free coffee and tea, and a terrace with a guitar ready.

Hotel Consul HOTEL €€€
(Map p200; ☎340 130; www.hotel-consul.net; Tršćanska 34; s/d 650/950KN; P❄☎) A good 20-minute walk from the centre, Hotel Consul has spacious carpeted rooms with flat-screen TVs and jacuzzis (in some). It's quiet, with a leafy terrace, and good for travellers with their own wheels.

Le Meridien Grand Hotel Lav HOTEL €€€
(☎500 500; www.lemeridien.com; Grljevačka 2A; s/d 2189/2491KN; P❄@☎≋) The daddy of all Split hotels, this five-star giant sits 8km south of the city, at Podstrana, with 800m of beach, five interlinking buildings, 381 beautifully designed rooms, endless sea views and luscious gardens. Excellent online rates.

Art Hotel HOTEL €€€
(Map p200; ☎302 302; www.arthotel.hr; Slobode 41; s/d 937/1237KN; P❄@☎) This Best Western property sits between boutique and business, with four-star rooms sporting plush beds and minibars, plus a gym and a spa. Ask for a room on the quiet side. The annex out the back has smaller, simpler rooms (single/double 675/900KN).

Hotel Globo HOTEL €€€
(Map p200; ☎481 111; www.hotelglobo.com; Lovretska 18; s/d 1040/1330KN; P❄☎) Geared towards business travellers, this swish four-star hotel has a red-carpeted entrance, a marble reception and 33 elegantly decorated long rooms with high ceilings. It's a 15-minute walk from the centre of town, in a slightly drab area.

Al's Place HOSTEL €
(Map p202; ☎098 91 82 923; www.hostelsplit.com; Kružićeva 10; dm 135KN; ❄@☎) Run by a friendly British owner, Al, this place in a two-floor apartment has basic dorms, a kitchen for guests' use and a low-key quiet vibe. Call ahead if you'll be arriving late at night or between 2pm and 5pm.

Camping Stobreč CAMPGROUND €
(☎325 426; www.campingsplit.com; Lovre 6, Stobreč; sites per adult 59KN, mobile homes for 4 people 807KN; @☎) Roughly halfway between Split and Solin, this well-equipped place has two beaches, three bars, a restaurant, a shop and a gazillion activities on offer nearby. Take bus 25 or 60. Bring your own tent.

Eating

TOP CHOICE **Figa** INTERNATIONAL €
(Map p202; Buvinina 1; mains from 50KN) Split's coolest little restaurant and bar, with a funky interior and tables on the stairs outside, Figa serves nice breakfasts, innovative dishes and a wide range of salads. There's live music some nights and the kitchen stays open late. Service can be slow but comes with smiles and jokes.

TOP CHOICE **Villa Spiza** DALMATIAN €
(Map p202; Kružićeva 3; mains from 40KN; ⊙Mon-Sat) Locals' favourite within the palace walls, this low-key joint offers Dalmatian mainstays that change daily – think calamari, risotto, stuffed peppers – at low prices. It's fresh home cooking served at the bar inside

or at a couple of benches outside. Service is slow but the food is prepared with care.

Šperun SEAFOOD €
(Map p200; Šperun 3; mains from 65KN) A sweet little restaurant decked out with rustic details and exposed stone walls, Šperun is a favourite among foreigners – possibly because the waiters, clad in sailor T-shirts, seem to speak every language under the sun. The food is classic Dalmatian, with a decent *brujet* (seafood stew with wine, onions and herbs, served with polenta), fresh mussels in a tomato and parsley sauce, or grilled tuna with capers. **Šperun Deva**, a corner bistro across the street with a few tables outside, offers breakfasts, lighter summer fare and a great daily menu (from 50KN).

Konoba Matejuška DALMATIAN €
(Map p200; Tomića Stine 3; mains from 50KN) Cosy, rustic tavern in an alleyway minutes from the seafront, it specialises in well-prepared seafood that also happens to be well priced. The waitstaff are friendly. Wash down your meal with a glass of *kujunđuša*, a local white wine from Dalmatia's hinterland.

Bajamonti INTERNATIONAL €€
(Map p202; Trg Republike 1; mains from 75KN) Sleek restaurant and cafe on Prokurative square, right off the Riva, with classic decor and excellent international fare. Try the delicious beef risotto with *plavac mali* wine and Mediterranean herbs. Grab a table on the square or on the mezzanine level inside.

Kod Joze DALMATIAN €
(Map p200; Sredmanuška 4; mains from 60KN) A die-hard faction of locals keeps this *konoba* (tavern) alive. In a dark basement and an upstairs terrace, it's Dalmatian all the way – ham, cheese, cuttlefish risotto, green tagliatelle with seafood – plus great game dishes during the hunting season (October to May).

Konoba Hvaranin DALMATIAN €€
(Map p202; Ban Mladenova 9; mains from 70KN) A mother-father-son business that feeds Split's journalists and writers, this miniscule spot with few tables is a long-standing favourite of the city's creatives. Mum and dad cook great fish and seafood, bake their own bread and stew their own tomato sauce. Note that prices for foreigners sometimes come inflated.

Pimpinella DALMATIAN €
(Map p200; Spinčićeva 2A; mains from 50KN; ⏲Mon-Sat) As local as you'll find in Split, this *konoba* on the ground floor of a family house next door to Boban serves unfussy but tasty food on a small terrace and in a no-frills dining room. Its tuna *pašticada* (stew with wine and spices) on Friday is a hit. Try the squid stuffed with shrimp and Dalmatian ham.

Kod Fife DALMATIAN €
(Map p200; Trumbićeva 11; mains from 40KN) Dragan presides over a motley crew of sailors, artists and misfits who drop in for his simple Dalmatian home cooking (of hit-and-miss quality), especially the *pašticada*, the meat-stuffed courgettes, and his own brand of grumpy, slow hospitality.

Bajamont DALMATIAN €
(Map p202; Bajamontijeva 3; mains from 70KN; ⏲closed Sun dinner in winter) This tiny joint within the palace walls is like a granny's living room, with old-school sewing machines used as tables. There's no sign above the door, and the daily menu is written out in marker pen, often featuring *brujet*.

Galija PIZZERIA €
(Map p202; Tončićeva 12; pizzas from 38KN) The go-to place for pizza for several decades now, Galija is the sort of joint where locals take you for a good, simple meal, where everyone relaxes on the wooden benches with the leftovers of a *quattro stagioni* in front of them. Die-hard pizza fans have recently turned to the new favourite in town, **Gušt** (Slavićeva 1; pizzas from 32KN).

No Stress Cafe & Bistro CROATIAN €€
(Map p202; Iza Lože 9; mains from 80KN) Located next to the town hall on bustling Narodni trg, this chic outdoor bistro serves up contemporary Croatian dishes crafted with premium ingredients. It's a great spot for people-watching, does simple breakfasts and serves good Lavazza coffee.

Makrovega VEGETARIAN €
(Map p200; Leština 2; mains from 50KN; ⏲9am-8pm Mon-Fri, to 5pm Sat) This meat-free haven has a stylish, spacious interior and delicious buffets (60KN to 70KN). À la carte food includes macrobiotic and vegetarian offerings. Think lots of seitan, tofu and tempeh, a great tea selection and excellent cakes.

Noštromo SEAFOOD €€
(Map p202; Svete Marije 10; mains from 80KN) This multilevel place is one of Split's favourite upmarket restaurants. The locals love it because it prepares fish bought daily at the *ribarnica* (fish market) across the street. There are no culinary surprises, just fresh, well-prepared seafood.

Bruna INTERNATIONAL €€
(Map p200; Hatzeov Perivoj 3; mains from 80KN) Hotel Park's restaurant has kept its head chef and excellent reputation for 30 years. It's known for its steak tartare and black (cocoa) crêpes decorated with 24-carat gold.

Boban SEAFOOD €€
(Map p200; Hektorovićeva 49; mains from 80KN) This family-run place has been Split's restaurant of choice for exec types since 1975. You'll know why when you sink your teeth into the juicy fish that's served with imaginative sauces.

Kadena MEDITERRANEAN €€
(Map p200; Ivana Zajca 4; mains from 80KN) A restaurant, wine bar and lounge with a swank all-white contemporary design and an airy terrace overlooking the sea in Zenta. Food can be pretentious and overpriced but its fortes are the views and the superb wine list.

Le Maison de Sarah QUICK BITE €
(Map p202; Hrvatskog Narodnog Preporoda 20) Briocherie counter on the Riva serving great brioches, croissants, pastries, cakes and tarts to take away and sit with at a nearby cafe or on one of the benches that line the seafront.

Drinking

Split is great for nightlife, especially in spring and summer. The palace walls are generally throbbing with loud music on Friday and Saturday nights, and you can spend the night wandering the maze-like streets, discovering new places. Note that palace bars close around 1am (as people live within the palace walls). The entertainment complex of Bačvice has a multitude of open-air bars and clubs that stay open till the wee hours. Daytime coffee sipping is best along the Riva or on one of the squares inside the palace walls.

Žbirac CAFE
(Map p200; Bačvice bb) This beachfront cafe is like the locals' open-air living room, a cult hang-out with great sea views, swimming day and night, *picigin* games and occasional concerts.

Bifora CAFE-BAR
(Map p202; Bernardinova 5) A quirky crowd of locals frequents this artsy spot on a little square, much loved for its intimate, low-key vibe.

Ghetto Club BAR
(Map p202; Dosud 10) Head for Split's most bohemian bar, in an intimate courtyard amid flower beds, a trickling fountain, great music and a friendly atmosphere.

Luxor CAFE-BAR
(Map p202; Sveti Ivana 11) Touristy, yes, but it's great to have coffee and cake in the courtyard of the cathedral: cushions are laid out on the steps so you can watch the locals.

Tri Volta BAR
(Map p202; Dosud 9) A crowd of misfits, fishers and bohos gathers at this legendary hang-out under three ancient vaults, with low-priced drinks and *sir i pršut* (cheese and prosciutto).

Vidilica CAFE-BAR
(Map p200; Nazorov Prilaz 1) It's worth the climb up the stone stairs through the ancient Varoš quarter for a sunset drink at this hilltop cafe with amazing city and harbour views.

Paradox WINE BAR
(Map p202; Poljana Tina Ujevića 2) Stylish new wine bar with cool wine-glass chandeliers inside, al fresco tables and a great selection of well-priced Croatian wines and local cheeses to go with them.

Gaga BAR
(Map p202; Iza Lože 9) Right behind the town hall on Narodni trg, this spot serves coffee during the day and transforms into a buzzy bar at night, with a cocktail station and DJs.

Galerija CAFE-BAR
(Map p202; Vuškovićeva bb) Catch up with friends without blasting music drowning out the conversation. The interior is granny chic, with pretty floral sofas and armchairs, paintings and little lamps everywhere.

Libar CAFE-BAR
(Map p202; Trg Franje Tuđmana 3) This fun, relaxed little spot away from the palace buzz has a lovely upper terrace, great breakfasts and tapas all day plus a big TV for sports.

Mosquito CAFE-BAR
(Map p202; Vuškovićeva 4) Right next door to Galerija. Sit on the big terrace, grab a cocktail, listen to music and hang out with the locals.

Teak CAFE-BAR
(Map p202; Majstora Jurja 11) Located on a busy square, the Teak's terrace is superpopular for coffee and chats during the day, and it gets busy in the evenings, too.

Porta CAFE-BAR
(Map p202; Majstora Jurja 4) Come here for cocktails. On the same square are a couple of other bars, all of which end up merging into one when the night gets busy, so remember your waiter!

☆ Entertainment

Nightclubs

After all the bars go quiet at 1am, head over to Bačvice for some clubbing under the stars. Alternatively, look out for flyers in any of the late-night bars.

Fluid NIGHTCLUB
(Map p202; Dosud 1) This chic little spot is a jazzy party venue, pretty low-key and cool. Great for people-watching.

O'Hara NIGHTCLUB
(Map p200; Uvala Zenta 3) For al fresco clubbing, head to this fun Zenta hang-out with a waterfront terrace. Come to boogie the night away to a mixed bag of music – from Dalmatian and club hits to house and reggae – depending on the night.

Mediteranium NIGHTCLUB
(Map p200; Put Firula 6) Amid pine trees above Ovčice beach, with a large terrace overlooking the Adriatic. This spot, which locals still call Šumica, draws a young moneyed crowd to its purple velvet interior. Try the popular *Sex and the City* party on Saturdays.

Imperium NIGHTCLUB
(Map p200; Gat Sv Duje bb) Split's only megaclub overlooks the harbour from the 1st floor of the ferry terminal, with two large dance floors and an outdoor terrace with a bar. It's quiet on weekdays but fills up with a mixed crowd for concerts and DJ events on weekends.

Tropic Club NIGHTCLUB
(Map p200; Bačvice bb) A beachfront terrace disco with a black-white-and-blue theme; house, pop or Croatian music (depending on the night); and the lapping of the Adriatic.

Quasimodo NIGHTCLUB
(Gundulićeva 26) Splićani have been partying at this 1st-floor miniclub for decades. There's live and DJ-spun alternative music: rock, indie rock, jazz, blues… It shuts down in summer months.

Hedonist NIGHTCLUB
(Map p200; Put Firula bb) The cashed-up crowd – iPhones and designer outfits required – comes out to play at this glitzy little club in Zenta, and its older brother, **Egoist**, right next door.

Cinemas

Kino Bačvice CINEMA
(Map p200; Put Firula 2) Bačvice's entertainment zone makes a perfect venue for the open-air cinema. Runs nightly in summer.

Kinoteka Zlatna Vrata CINEMA
(Map p200; Dioklecijanova 7) Classic films, art flicks and retrospectives are screened at this university-affiliated cinema. It shuts down in July and August.

Theatre

Croatian National Theatre THEATRE
(Map p202; ☎306 908; www.hnk-split.hr; Trg Gaje Bulata 1) Opera, ballet and music performances are presented here year-round. Built in 1891, the theatre was fully restored in 1979; it's worth attending a performance for the architecture alone. Tickets start at 80KN; buy at the box office or online.

Shopping

Shopaholics will find their habit hard to kick in Split – this is the place with the most shoe shops in Croatia. The Diocletian's Palace walls are packed with shops: small boutiques and international chains alike. Marmontova is equally popular among the locals for shopping.

Diocletian's Cellars (Map p202), part of the palace's basement halls, is a market for crafted jewellery, reproductions of Roman busts, silver cigarette cases, candlestick holders, wooden sailing ships, leather goods and other odds and ends. Prices aren't too steep; you might find the perfect lightweight item to fulfil your back-from-a-trip gift-giving obligations.

Check out the little creative corner within the palace walls, where you will find several boutiques selling Croatian design and arts. To name a few: **Arka** (Map p202; Domisinova 14) sells unique handicrafts; **Arterija** (Map p202; Domisinova 9) has Croatian fashion, design and art; **GetGetGet** (Map p202; www.getgetget.com.hr; Vuškovićeva 5) is a concept store touting offbeat Croatian design items; and **Think Pink** (Map p202; www.thinkpink.com.hr; Zadarska 8), just outside the palace walls, has boho women's clothing made by home-grown designers.

There's a **daily market** above Obala Lazareta where you can buy fruit, vegetables, shoes, confectionery, clothing, flowers, souvenirs and other products. If you can't find what you're looking for in this market, the chances are it doesn't exist in Split.

Information

Internet Access

Several spots around town offer free wi-fi access, including Luxor and Twins on the Riva and Bajamonti on Trg Republike. Backpackers

Cafe offers happy hour for internet use between 3pm and 5pm, when it's 15KN per hour instead of 30KN.

Laundry

Modrulj (☎315 888; www.modrulj.com; Šperun 1; ⏰8am-8pm Apr-Oct, 9am-5pm Mon-Sat Nov-Mar) A laundromat with coin-operated washing machines (wash/dry 25/20KN), which also has internet access (5KN per 15 minutes) and bag storage (10KN per day).

Medical Services

KBC Firule (☎556 111; Spinčićeva 1) Split's hospital.

Money

You can change money at travel agencies or at any post office. There are ATMs around the bus and train stations and throughout the city.

Post

Main Post Office (Kralja Tomislava 9; ⏰7.30am-7pm Mon-Fri, to 2.30pm Sat). Also has telephone centres.

Tourist Information

Backpackers Cafe (☎338 548; Kneza Domagoja bb; ⏰7am-9pm) Also sells used books, offers luggage storage and provides information for backpackers.

Croatian Youth Hostel Association (☎396 031; www.hfhs.hr; Domilijina 8; ⏰8am-4pm Mon-Fri) Sells HI cards and has information about youth hostels all over Croatia.

Tourist Office (☎360 066; www.visitsplit.com; Hrvatskog Narodnog Preporoda 9; ⏰8am-9pm Mon-Sat, to 1pm Sun Apr–mid-Oct, 8am-8pm Mon-Fri, to 1pm Sat mid-Oct–Mar) Has info on Split and sells the Split Card (35KN), which offers free and reduced prices to Split attractions and discounts on car rental, restaurants, shops and hotels.

Tourist Office Annexe (Map p202; ☎345 606; www.visitsplit.com; Peristil bb; ⏰9am-4pm Mon-Sat, 8am-1pm Sun Apr–mid-Oct, 9am-4pm Mon-Fri, 8am-1pm Sat mid-Oct–Mar) This tourist office annex on Peristil has shorter hours.

Travel Agencies

Daluma Travel (☎338 424; www.daluma-travel.hr; Kneza Domagoja 1) Arranges private accommodation, excursions and car rental.

Maestral (☎470 944; www.maestral.hr; Boškovića 13/15) Monastery stays, horse-riding excursions, lighthouse holidays, trekking, sea kayaking and more.

Split Tours (☎352 553; www.splittours.hr; Gat Sv Duje bb; ⏰closed Sat & Sun afternoon) In the ferry terminal, it handles tickets to Ancona (Italy) on Blue Line, and finds private accommodation.

Touring (☎338 503; Kneza Domagoja 10) Near the bus station, it represents Deutsche Touring and sells bus tickets to German cities.

Turist Biro (☎347 100, www.turistbiro-split.hr; Hrvatskog Narodnog Preporoda 12) Its forte is private accommodation and excursions.

 Getting There & Away

Air

Split airport (www.split-airport.hr) is 20km west of town, just 6km before Trogir.

Airlines serving Split include the following:

Croatia Airlines (☎362 997; www.croatiaairlines.hr; Hrvatskog Narodnog Preporoda 9; ⏰8am-4pm Mon-Fri) Operates one-hour flights to and from Zagreb several times a day and a weekly flight to Dubrovnik (during summer only).

Easyjet (www.easyjet.com)

Germanwings (www.germanwings.com)

Norwegian (www.norwegian.com)

CHARTERING A YACHT OR BOAT

Yachting enthusiasts may wish to charter their own boat. Experienced sailors can charter a yacht on a 'bareboat' basis, or you can pay for the services of a local captain for a 'skippered' boat. The price depends upon the size of the boat, the number of berths and the season.

Ultra Sailing (www.ultra-sailing.hr) Among the best and most reliable Croatian charters, plus it has a popular sailing school. The base marinas are in Dubrovnik, Kaštela, Split and Trogir.

Cosmos Yachting (www.cosmosyachting.com) This UK company offers charters out of Dubrovnik, Pula, Rovinj, Split, Trogir, Zadar, Lošinj, Punat and other destinations.

Nautilus Yachting (www.nautilus-yachting.com) Another UK outfitter; it offers rentals from Pula, Split, Dubrovnik and the Kornati Islands.

Sunsail (www.sunsail.com) An international operator offering bareboat and skippered charters from Dubrovnik, Pula and Kremik, south of Šibenik.

BUS SERVICES FROM SPLIT

DESTINATION	COST (KN)	DURATION	DAILY SERVICES
Dubrovnik	115-145	4½hr	25
Makarska	52	1½hr	40
Međugorje (Bosnia & Hercegovina)	100	3-4hr	4
Mostar (Bosnia & Hercegovina)	105-128	3½-4½hr	9
Pula	423	10-11hr	3
Rijeka	330	8-8½hr	11
Sarajevo (Bosnia & Hercegovina)	220	6½-8hr	4
Zadar	99-128	3-4hr	27
Zagreb	114-204	5-8hr	40

Boat

Car ferries and passenger lines depart from separate docks; the passenger lines leave from Obala Lazareta and car ferries from Gat Sv Duje. You can buy tickets from either the main Jadrolinija office in the large ferry terminal opposite the bus station, which handles all car ferry services that depart from the docks around the ferry terminal, or at one of the two stalls near the docks. In summer it's usually necessary to reserve at least a day in advance for a car ferry and you are asked to appear several hours before departure. There is rarely a problem obtaining a ticket off-season, but reserve as much in advance as possible in July and August.

Jadrolinija (☎338 333; www.jadrolinija.hr; Gat Sv Duje bb) handles most of the coastal ferry lines and catamarans that operate between Split and the islands. There is also a twice-weekly ferry service between Rijeka and Split (147KN, 7.30pm Thursday and Sunday, arriving at 6am). Three times weekly a car ferry goes from Split to Ancona in Italy (435KN, nine to 11 hours).

Other boat options:

BlueLine (www.blueline-ferries.com) Car ferries to Ancona (Italy), on some days via Hvar Town and Vis (per person/car from 480KN/540KN, 10 to 12 hours).

Krilo (www.krilo.hr) A fast passenger boat that goes to Hvar Town (45KN, one hour) daily and then on to Korčula (65KN, 2¾ hours). Buy tickets through Jadrolinija.

SNAV (☎322 252; www.snav.it) Daily ferries to Ancona (660KN, five hours) from June through to mid-September. In the ferry terminal.

Bus

Bus tickets purchased in advance with seat reservations are recommended. There are buses from the main **bus station** (☎060 327 777; www.ak-split.hr) beside the harbour to a number of destinations. If you need to store bags, there's a **garderoba** (Left Luggage; Bus Station; 1st hr 5KN, then 1.50KN per hr; ⏲6am-10pm).

Bus 37 goes to Split airport and Trogir (21KN, every 20 minutes), also stopping at Solin; it leaves from a local bus station on Domovinskog Rata, 1km northeast of the city centre, but it's faster and more convenient to take an intercity bus heading north to Zadar or Rijeka.

Note that Split–Dubrovnik buses pass briefly through Bosnian territory, so keep your passport handy for border-crossing points.

Car

Dollar Thrifty (☎399 000; www.thrifty.com.hr) Branches at Trumbićeva Obala 5 and Split airport.

Train

There are five daily trains between Split **train station** (☎338 525; www.hznet.hr; Kneza Domagoja 9) and Zagreb (189KN, six to eight hours), two of which are overnight. There are three daily trains between Šibenik and Split (55KN, two hours), with a change in Perković. There are also two trains a day from Split to Zadar (111KN, five hours) via Knin.

If you need to store bags, there's a **garderoba** (Left Luggage; Train Station; per day 15KN; ⏲6am-10pm).

Getting Around

The bus, train and ferry terminals are clustered on the eastern side of the harbour, a short walk from the old town.

You can rent scooters, bikes, speed boats and cars from **Split Rent Agency** (☎091 59 17 111; www.split-rent.com).

To/From the Airport

Bus 37 From the local bus station on Domovinskog Rata (21KN, 50 minutes).

Pleso Prijevoz (www.plesoprijevoz.hr) Buses depart to Split airport (30KN) from Obala Lazareta three to six times daily.

Promet Žele (www.split-airport.com.hr) Buses travel between Obala Lazareta and the airport even more frequently than Pleso Prijevoz.

Taxis Cost between 250KN and 290KN.

Bus

Local buses by Promet Split connect the town centre and the harbour with outlying districts; the city is broken up into four travel zones. A one-zone ticket costs 11KN for one trip in central Split; it's 21KN to the surrounding districts. A two-journey ticket in zone one costs 17KN if bought at a kiosk; it's 34KN for the zone-four two-journey ticket. Buses run about every 15 minutes from 5.30am to 11.30pm.

AROUND SPLIT

Šolta

This lovely, wooded island (just 59 sq km) is a popular getaway for Split inhabitants escaping the sultry summer heat. The island's main entry point is **Rogač**, where ferries from Split tie up in front of the **tourist office** (☎654 491; www.visitsolta.com; ⏲7.30am-9.30pm Wed, & Fri-Mon, 9am-4pm Tue & Thu Jun-Sep) on the edge of a large bay. A shady path leads around the bay to smaller coves with rocky beaches, and a small road leads uphill to the island's administrative centre of **Grohote**, with a market and shops. **Maslinica** is the island's prettiest settlement, with seven islets offshore, a luxury heritage hotel-spa, **Martinis Marchi** (www.martinis-marchi.com), with its own marina, a handful of restaurants (Šismiš and Šešula are the best), and a good choice of private accommodation. Another gorgeous village is **Stomorska,** with its pretty sheltered harbour popular with yachters. The island's interior has several worthwhile family-run farm eateries; Kaštelanac in **Gornje Selo** does tastings of its olive oils, grappas and wines. The tourist offices have details on other inland options.

JADROLINIJA SERVICES FROM SPLIT

Note that the schedules listed for these ferries are for services between June and September. Service is reduced outside these months.

Car Ferries

DESTINATION	COST PER PERSON/CAR (KN)	DURATION	DAILY SERVICES
Šolta	33/160	1hr	6
Supetar (Brač)	33/160	1hr	12-14
Stari Grad (Hvar)	47/318	2hr	6-7
Vis	54/370	2½hr	2-3
Vela Luka (Korčula)	60/530	3hr	2

Catamarans

DESTINATION	COST (KN)	DURATION	DAILY SERVICES
Bol (Brač)	40	1hr	1
Hvar Town	47	1hr	4-5
Jelsa (Hvar)	40	2hr	1
Vela Luka (Korčula)	50	2hr	1
Vis	50	1¼hr	1

There are three ATMs on the island, in Stomorska, Rogač and Grohote, which also has the island's main **tourist office** (☎654 657; www.visitsolta.com; ⏰7am-3pm daily year-round).

In high season, six daily car ferries run between Split and Rogač (33KN, one hour) as well as two catamarans per day (16.50KN).

Solin (Salona)

The ruins of the ancient city of Solin (Roman Salona), among the vineyards at the foot of mountains just northeast of Split, are the most archaeologically important in Croatia.

Today Solin is surrounded by noisy highways and industry. It was first mentioned in 119 BC as the centre of the Illyrian tribe. The Romans seized the site in 78 BC and under the rule of Augustus it became the administrative headquarters of the Roman Dalmatian province.

When Emperor Diocletian built his palace in Split at the end of the 3rd century AD, it was the proximity to Solin that attracted him. Solin was incorporated into the Eastern Roman Empire in the 6th century, but was levelled by the Slavs and Avars in 614. The inhabitants fled to Split and neighbouring islands, leaving Solin to decay.

Sights

A good place to begin your visit to the city is at the main entrance near Caffe Bar Salona, where you'll see an info map of the complex. **Tusculum Museum** (admission 20KN; ⏰7am-7pm Mon-Fri, 8am-7pm Sat, 9am-1pm Sun Apr-Sep, 7am-3pm Mon-Fri, 9am-1pm Sat Oct-Mar) is where you pay admission for the entire archaeological reserve, including the small museum with interesting sculpture embedded in the walls and in the garden. It also serves as an information centre and distributes a brochure about Salona.

Manastirine, the fenced area behind the car park, was a burial place for early Christian martyrs prior to the legalisation of Christianity. The excavated remains of **Kapljuč Basilica** – built on one of the early Christian cemeteries – and the 5th-century **Kapjinc Basilica** that sits inside it are highlights, although this area was outside the ancient city itself.

A path bordered by cypresses runs south to the northern city wall of Solin. Notice the **covered aqueduct** located south of the wall. It was probably built around the 1st century AD and supplied Solin and Diocletian's Palace with water from the Jadro River. The ruins you see in front of you as you stand on the wall were an early Christian site; they include a three-aisled, 5th-century **cathedral** with an octagonal **baptistery**, and the remains of **Bishop Honorius' Basilica** with a ground plan in the form of a Greek cross. **Public baths** adjoin the cathedral on the east.

Southwest of Solin's cathedral is the 1st-century eastern city gate, **Porta Caesarea**, later engulfed by the growth of the city in all directions. Grooves in the stone road left by ancient wheels can still be seen at this gate. South of the city gate was the forum, the centre of town, with temples to Jupiter, Juno and Minerva, none of which are visible today.

At the western end of Solin is the huge 2nd-century **amphitheatre**, destroyed in the 17th century by the Venetians to prevent it from being used as a refuge by Turkish raiders. At one time it could accommodate 18,000 spectators, which gives an idea of the size and importance of this ancient city.

The southeastern corner of the complex contains the **Gradina**, a medieval fortress around the remains of a rectangular early Christian church.

Getting There & Away

The ruins are easily accessible on Split city bus 1 (13KN), which goes all the way to the parking lot for Salona every half-hour from Trg Gaje Bulata.

From Solin you can continue on to Trogir by catching westbound bus 37 (17KN) from the Širine crossroad. Take city bus 1 back to Širine and then walk for five minutes on the same road to get to the stop for bus 37 on the adjacent highway.

TROGIR & AROUND

Trogir

POP 12,995

Gorgeous and tiny Trogir (formerly Trau) is beautifully set within medieval walls, its streets knotted and maze-like. It's fronted by a wide seaside promenade lined with bars and cafes, and yachts in the summer. Trogir is unique among Dalmatian towns for its profuse collection of Romanesque and Renaissance architecture (which flourished under Venetian rule); this, along with its magnificent cathedral, earned it World Heritage status in 1997.

Trogir is an easy day trip from Split and a relaxing place to spend a few days, taking an outing or two to nearby islands.

History

Backed by high hills in the north, the sea to the south and snug in its walls, Trogir (Tragurion to the Romans) proved an attractive place to settlers. The early Croats settled the old Illyrian town by the 7th century. Its defensive position allowed Trogir to maintain its autonomy throughout Croatian and Byzantine rule, while trade and nearby mines ensured its economic viability. In the 13th century sculpture and architecture flourished, reflecting a vibrant, dynamic culture. When Venice bought Dalmatia in 1409, Trogir refused to accept the new ruler and the Venetians were forced to bombard the town into submission. While the rest of Dalmatia stagnated under Venetian rule, Trogir continued to produce great artists who enhanced the beauty of the town.

Sights & Activities

Even though it's a pocket-sized town, Trogir has plenty to see. The town has retained many intact and beautiful buildings from its age of glory between the 13th and 15th centuries. The old town of Trogir occupies a tiny island in the narrow channel between Čiovo Island and the mainland, just off the coastal highway. Most sights can be seen on a 15-minute walk around this island.

Portal travel agency runs a 90-minute walking tour of the old town twice a day (morning and evening) from May to October, departing from outside the agency. It also rents out two-person kayaks for 250KN per day, which you can use to kayak around the island and to Pantan beach.

Cathedral of St Lovro CATHEDRAL
(Katedrala Svetog Lovre; Trg Ivana Pavla II; admission 25KN; ⏲8am-8pm Mon-Sat, 2-6pm Sun Jun-Sep, 8am-6pm Mon-Sat, 2-6pm Sun Apr & May, 8am-6pm Mon-Sat Oct-Mar) The showcase of Trogir is this three-naved Venetian cathedral, one of the finest architectural works in Croatia, built from the 13th to 15th centuries. Note first the **Romanesque portal** (1240) by Master Radovan. The sides of the portal depict lion figures (the symbol of Venice) with Adam and Eve above them, the earliest example of the nude in Dalmatian sculpture. At the end of the portico is another fine piece of sculpture – the **baptistery** sculpted in 1464 by Andrija Aleši.

Enter the building through an obscure back door to see the richly decorated **Renaissance Chapel of St Ivan**, created by the masters Nikola Firentinac and Ivan Duknović from 1461 to 1497. Within the **sacristy** there are paintings of St Jerome and John the Baptist. Be sure to take a look at the **treasury**, which contains an ivory triptych and several medieval illuminated manuscripts. You can even climb the 47m-high cathedral **tower** for a delightful view.

A sign informs that you must be 'decently dressed' to enter the cathedral, which means that men must wear tops (women too, of course) and shorts are a no-no.

Kamerlengo Fortress FORTRESS
(Tvrđava Kamerlengo; admission 20KN; ⏲9am-11pm May-Oct) The fortress, once connected to the city walls, was built around the 15th century. At the furthest end, you'll see an elegant gazebo built by the French Marshal Marmont during the Napoleonic occupation of Dalmatia, where he used to sit and play cards amid the waves. At that time, the western end of the island was a lagoon; the malarial marshes were not drained until the 20th century. The fortress hosts concerts during the Trogir Summer festival.

Town Museum MUSEUM
(Gradski Muzej; Gradska Vrata 4; admission 15KN; ⏲10am-5pm Jun-Sep, 9am-2pm Mon-Fri, to noon Sat Oct-May) Housed in the former Garagnin-Fanfogna palace, the museum has five rooms that exhibit books, documents, drawings and period costumes from Trogir's long history.

Convent of St Nicholas CONVENT
(Samostan Svetog Nikole; admission 25KN; ⏲10am-noon & 4-6pm Jun-Sep) The treasury of this Benedictine convent is home to a dazzling 3rd-century relief of Kairos, the Greek god of opportunity, carved out of orange marble. Access by appointment from October to May.

Town Hall HISTORIC BUILDING
(Gradska Vijecnica) This 15th-century building opposite the cathedral has a Gothic yard decorated with coats of arms and a monumental staircase. Its well features a preserved winged lion of St Mark (the coat of arms of the Venetian Republic).

Grand Cipiko Palace PALACE
(Palaca Cipiko) This palace, originally a set of Romanesque structures and home to a prominent family during the 15th century, has a stunning carved gothic triforium, the work of Andrija Aleši.

Trogir

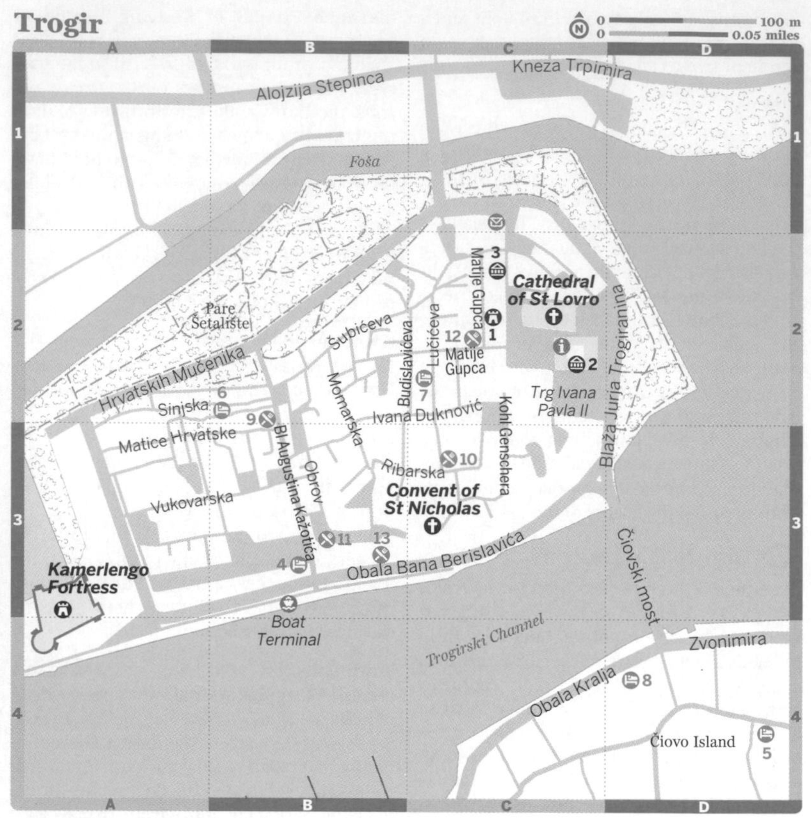

Festivals & Events

Every year from 21 June through early September, the town hosts **Trogir Summer**, a music festival with classical and folk concerts presented in churches, open squares and the fortress. Posters advertising the concerts are all around town.

Sleeping

Atlas (p220) can arrange private rooms from 300KN a double. Portal (p220) also has rooms and apartments, from 300KN for a double and 450KN for a two-person apartment. Also check www.trogir-online.com.

TOP CHOICE Hotel Tragos HOTEL €€
(☎884 729; www.tragos.hr; Budislavićeva 3; s/d 600/800KN; P ❄ @ ☎) This medieval family house has been exquisitely restored, with lots of exposed stone and original details. Its 12 sleek, beautifully decorated rooms come complete with satellite TV and minibars. Even if you don't stay here, come for the wonderful home cooking served in the hotel restaurant (mains from 60KN); try the *trogirska pašticada* (Trogir-style beef stew).

Hotel Pašike HOTEL €€€
(☎885 185; www.hotelpasike.com; Sinjska bb; s/d 650/850KN; ❄ @ ☎) This delightful hotel in a 15th-century house showcases 19th-century furniture, walnut timber and wrought-iron beds. Each of the 14 vividly painted rooms has a separate sitting area and a hydromassage shower. The friendly staff wear traditional outfits, there is a two-table roof terrace and upon arrival you get *rafioli*, a traditional Trogir almond cake.

Vila Sikaa HOTEL €€€
(☎881 223; www.vila-sikaa-r.com; Kralja Zvonimira 13; s/d 896/952KN; P ❄ @ ☎) This hotel on Čiovo has 10 decent rooms with fantastic views of the old town. Some are equipped with saunas, massage showers and jacuzzis.

Trogir

Top Sights

Sights

Sleeping

Eating

Room 14 has a balcony. Note that the rooms in the attic are claustrophobic and service can be sloppy. The reception also offers scooter, boat and car rental.

Villa White GUESTHOUSE €€
(☎091 22 14 473; www.villawhite.net; Kralja Tomislava 22; r 635KN; P ❄ @ ≋) This new 14-room guesthouse is a 10-minute walk from the town centre. With a minimalist theme, it has small but inviting rooms with TVs and showers. Breakfast is included. Open May to October.

Hotel Palace HOTEL €€€
(☎685 555; www.trogir-palace.com; Put Gradine 8; s/d 940/1240KN; P ❄ @ ≋) This recent upscale addition to Trogir's hotel scene sits in a pinkish-white building on Čiovo island, with lots of marble, hardwood floors and a restaurant. The 36 beige-coloured rooms sport tubs and balconies. Room 305 has great old-town views across the way.

Hostel Trogir HOSTEL €
(☎091 57 92 190; www.hosteltrogir.com.hr; Trg Sv Jakova 7; dm 120KN; ❄ @ ≋) Trogir's only hostel is located just across the bridge on Čiovo, so only 200m from the Riva. It has four clean dorms (of six and eight beds) with lockers, a small common room with a kitchenette and a shaded terrace out the front.

Concordia HOTEL €€
(☎885 400; www.concordia-hotel.net; Bana Berislavića 22; s/d 450/730KN; P ❄ ≋) The somewhat faded rooms here are clean but pretty basic, though the service and location (right on the seafront) are lovely. Try to get a recently refurbished room with sea views. Boats to the beaches depart right outside.

Villa Tina HOTEL €€
(☎888 305; www.vila-tina.hr; Cesta Domovinske Zahvalnosti 63, Arbanija; s/d 499KN/670KN; P ❄ @ ≋) Tastefully decorated, with spacious and bright rooms, a jacuzzi and infrared sauna, Villa Tina is excellent for those wanting to relax and swim. It's about 5km east of Trogir, steps from the beach.

Seget CAMPGROUND €
(☎880 394; www.kamp-seget.hr; Hrvatskih Žrtava 121, Seget Donji; per adult/site 54/120KN; ⊙Apr-Oct) Located just 2km from Trogir, this intimate campground has a small shingle beach and a cemented diving point. It is just 2km from Hotel Medena, which offers tennis, cycling, windsurfing and other activities.

Eating

Capo SEAFOOD €
(Ribarska 11; mains from 55KN) Characterful family-run tavern tucked away in an old town alleyway, with an al fresco area and a fishing-themed interior. Dishes focus on fish: specialities include sardines, *gavuni* (smelt fish) and anchovies, all served with vegies. The family also runs a pizzeria on the Riva.

Konoba Trs DALMATIAN €€
(Matije Gupca 14; mains from 75KN) Rustic little tavern with a welcoming courtyard shaded by grapevines. The interior has wooden benches and old stone walls. Its lamb *pašticada* (stew), served with savoury pancakes stuffed with *pršut* (prosciutto) and Swiss chard, is a signature dish.

Fontana SEAFOOD €€
(Obrov 1; mains from 70KN) The large waterfront terrace is the main appeal of this long-standing restaurant. You can get almost anything, from inexpensive risotto and spaghetti to pricier grilled meat, but the speciality is fish (300KN per kilogram).

Alka INTERNATIONAL €€
(Augustina Kažotića 15; mains from 85KN) This restaurant has an outdoor terrace and a huge menu, with lots of meat specialities (such as chicken liver wrapped in bacon) and lobster.

Pizzeria Mirkec PIZZERIA €
(Bana Berislavića 15; pizzas from 35KN) Pizza at this seafront joint comes out of a wood-burning oven and tastes pretty good. It also does breakfasts.

Information

Atlas Trogir (☎881 374; www.atlas-trogir.hr; Kralja Zvonimira 10) This travel agency arranges private accommodation and runs excursions.

Portal Trogir (☎885 016; www.portal-trogir.com; Bana Berislavića 3) Private accommodation; bike, scooter and kayak rental; excursions – from quad safaris and rafting to sea kayaking and canyoning – and an internet corner.

Post Office (Blaža Jurjeva Trogiranina 5; ⏲7.30am-7pm Mon-Fri, to 2.30pm Sat) There's a telephone centre here.

Tourist Office (☎885 628; Trg Ivana Pavla II 1; ⏲8am-9pm Mon-Sat, to 2pm Sun Jun-Aug, shorter hours Sep-May) Hands out basic town maps.

Getting There & Away

Southbound intercity buses from Zadar (130km) and northbound buses from Split (28km) will drop you off in Trogir. Getting buses from Trogir to Zadar can be more difficult, as they often arrive full from Split.

City bus 37 from Split leaves every 20 minutes throughout the day, with a stop at Split airport en route to Trogir. It leaves from the local bus station and takes longer than the intercity bus. You can buy the four-zone ticket (21KN) from the driver in either direction.

There are boats to and from Split four times daily (24KN) from Čiovo (150m to the left of the bridge). A passenger boat also leaves from right in front of Hotel Concordia to Okrug Gornji (20KN) hourly from 8.30am till 11.30pm as well as to Medena (15KN, 10 daily). A ferry goes to Drvenik Veli three times daily (16KN).

Getting Around

The old town is just a few minutes' walk from the bus station, which has a **garderoba** (Left Luggage; per day 15KN; ⏲7am-8pm) for those who need to store bags. After crossing the small bridge near the station, go through the North Gate. Turn left (east) at the end of the square and you'll come to Trogir's main street, Gradska. Trogir's finest sights are around Trg Ivana Pavla II, straight ahead. The seafront, Bana Berislavića, is lined with bars, restaurants and cafes, overlooking Čiovo Island. The old town is connected to Čiovo Island to the south by a drawbridge.

Around Trogir

The area around Trogir is lined with beaches. The nearest is **Pantan**, 1.5km east of the old town, a gravel and sand beach on the estuary of Pantan River, surrounded by a protected nature reserve. To reach the beach, follow the path that leads from the old town to Pantan. The most popular beach, **Okrug Gornji**, lies 5km south of Čiovo. Known as Copacabana, this 2km-long stretch of pebbles is lined with cafe-bars. It can be reached by road or boat. For the most extensive beach facilities, head 4km southwest to **Medena** beach on the Seget Riviera, home to the **Hotel Medena** (www.hotelmedena.com) megaresort.

For more isolation, it is better to head to the beaches on Drvenik Mali and Drvenik Veli islands, an easy boat trip from town. Boats leave from the ferry terminal in front of the Concordia hotel. Both islands are sparsely inhabited and make idyllic getaways.

In addition there is the beautiful Kaštela area, with seven ports and several castles built by the Dalmatian nobility some 500 years ago.

DRVENIK MALI & DRVENIK VELI

Drvenik Mali, the smaller island, has olive trees, a population of 56 and a sandy beach that curves around the cove of Vela Rina. Drvenik Veli has secluded coves and olive trees plus a few cultural highlights to get you off the beach: the **Church of St George** dates from the 16th century and houses baroque furniture and a Venetian altarpiece. Outside Drvenik Veli village is the unfinished 18th-century **Church of St Nicholas**, whose builder never quite got past the monumental front.

To get to the islands from Trogir, take a **Jadrolinija ferry** (www.jadrolinija.hr). Three daily ferries operate from June through September (two on Friday). The return schedule makes it possible to visit Drvenik Veli on a day trip; Drvenik Mali is trickier. The journey to Drvenik Veli (15KN) takes one hour; it's a further 20 minutes to Drvenik Mali.

For those wanting to spend more time on the islands, Portal (p220) agency in Trogir can find private accommodation.

KAŠTELA

If you're looking to snuggle down in safety, you can't do much better than have the mountains behind you and the sea in front of you. At least that's what the Dalmatian nobility thought when they looked at the invading Ottomans in the 15th and 16th centuries. The 20km stretch of coast between

Trogir and Split, backed by long, low Kozjak hill, looked like the perfect place to relax in a well-fortified castle. One after the other, rich families from Split filed down to Kaštela bay to build their mansions. The Turks never reached them and the castles remain today.

Kaštela is the name given to the seven little ports around these coastal fortified castles, and it is a delightful day trip from Split or Trogir. Starting in the west, from Trogir, you'll come first to **Kaštel Štafilić**, a castle on an islet connected to the mainland by a drawbridge. There's also a Renaissance church in town. Next up is **Kaštel Novi**, built in 1512, and then **Kaštel Stari**, built in 1476 and the oldest in the bay. An arcaded cloister stands in the middle. Further on is **Kaštel Lukšić**, the most impressive of all. Built in a transitional Renaissance-baroque style in 1487, it now houses municipal offices, a small museum and the regional tourist office. It's also the site of a rather involved tale of thwarted lovers who were married and buried here. Continue east to **Kaštel Kambelovac**, a cylindrically shaped defense castle built in 1517 by local noblemen and landowners, and then on to **Kaštel Gomilica**, built by Benedictine nuns and surrounded by shallow, sandy beaches. Finish at **Kaštel Sućurac**, then take the path that runs past the cemetery, climbing to the refuge at Putalj (480m), where you can climb to the ridge of Kozjak.

For details on accommodation in Kaštela, contact the **tourist office** (☎227 933; www.dalmacija.net/kastela.htm; Kaštel Lukšić; ⌚8am-2pm & 5-9pm Mon-Fri, 8am-noon & 5-9pm Sat, to noon Sun Jun-Sep, 8am-2pm & 5-8pm Mon-Sat, 8am-noon Sun Oct-May).

To get to Kaštela, take bus 37 from Split to Trogir (21KN, every 20 minutes) – this bus stops in all the towns along the bay. It's best to get off at Kaštel Štafilić and walk eastward along the coastal promenade through the towns, until you've had enough. Then catch a bus back from the main road.

MAKARSKA RIVIERA

The Makarska Riviera is a 58km stretch of coast at the foot of the Biokovo Range, where a series of cliffs and ridges forms a dramatic backdrop to a string of beautiful pebble beaches. The foothills are protected from harsh winds and covered with lush Mediterranean greenery, including pine forests, olive groves and fruit trees. The seaside towns here are orientated towards package tourism; this is one of the most developed stretches of Dalmatian coast. It is a great place for families as facilities are vast, and it offers some active holiday possibilities. Note that in July and especially August the entire Riviera is jam-packed with holidaymakers, and many hotels impose a seven-night minimum stay. To avoid the hubbub, head to Makarska before or after the summer rush.

Makarska

POP 17,000

Makarska is a pretty port town with a limestone centre that turns peachy orange at sunset. It's an active place – there's an abundance of hiking, climbing, paragliding, mountain biking, windsurfing and swimming opportunities – with a spectacular natural setting, backed by the gorgeous Mt Biokovo. It's the locus of Croatia's package tourism, focused on the town's long pebbly beach, which is filled with a feast of activities, from beach volleyball to screaming-children's games.

Makarska is favoured by tourists from neighbouring Bosnia and Hercegovina, who descend in huge numbers during summer. It's also popular with seniors as a 'medical tourism' destination, for the great climate and facilities. The high season is pretty raucous, with many rocking nightlife spots, but also a lot of fun for those with children. If you're interested in hanging around beach bars and clubs, playing beach volleyball and generally lounging about with beach bodies, you'll like Makarska. Outside the high season, things are pretty quiet.

Being the largest town in the region, Makarska has very good transport connections, making it a good base for exploring the coast and neighbouring Bosnia and Hercegovina. Don't miss venturing up Mt Biokovo.

Sights & Activities

Franciscan Monastery MONASTERY
(Franjevački Samostan; Franjevački Put 1; ⌚9am-noon & 5-8pm mid-Jun–mid-Sep) Just east of the centre, the single-nave church of this monastery has a huge contemporary mosaic in its apse and a well-presented **shell museum** (admission 15KN) in the cloister, with reportedly the largest collection of snails and shells in the world.

Beaches BEACH
Makarska is located on a large cove bordered by Cape Osejava in the southeast and

RAFTING ON THE CETINA RIVER

The Cetina is the longest river in central Dalmatia, stretching 105km from the eponymous village. It flows through the Dinara mountains, through the fields around Sinj, and gathers steam until it pours into a power plant around Omiš. It is an extraordinarily scenic journey as the limpid blue river is bordered by high rocky walls, thick with vegetation. Rafting is possible from spring to autumn, but the rapids can become quite fast after heavy rains. Summer is best for inexperienced rafters. It usually takes three to four hours to raft the Cetina. To organise a trip, try Biokovo Active Holidays in Makarska, which organises a day's rafting, canyoning or canoeing on the Cetina for 395KN.

the Sveti Petar peninsula in the northwest. The long pebble **town beach**, lined with hotels, stretches from the Sveti Petar park at the beginning of Kralja Tomislava northwest along the bay. To the southeast are rockier and lovelier beaches, such as **Nugal**, popular with nudists (take the marked trail from the eastern end of the Riva). For a party atmosphere all day long, head to **Buba beach** to the west of Sveti Petar peninsula, near Hotel Rivijera, where music pumps all day during the summer.

Biokovo Botanical Garden BOTANICAL GARDEN
Just up from the village of Kotišina on Biokovo, this once-major regional highlight doesn't offer much to look at except some indigenous flora and stunning views of the islands of Brač and Hvar. The scenic walk is worth it – follow the marked trail northeast of town that passes under a series of towering peaks.

Town Museum MUSEUM
(Gradski Muzej; Kralja Tomislava 17/1; admission 10KN; ⌚9am-1pm & 6-10pm Mon-Fri, 6-10pm Sat Jul-Sep, 9am-1pm Mon-Sat Oct-Jun) On a rainy day when indoors beckons, trace the town's history by checking out this less-than-gripping collection of photos, old stones and nautical relics.

Sleeping

There's an overwhelming blandness to Makarska's hotels. Be prepared for nothing special, though comfortable beds and good views are reliable in the more upmarket spots. Private accommodation is, as always, the best bet for budget lodging.

Biokovo HOTEL €€€
(615 244; www.hotelbiokovo.hr; Kralja Tomislava 14; s/d 605/980KN; P ❄ @) One of the better hotels in Makarska, right on the promenade. Get a sea-view room with balcony for excellent vistas of the town.

Park HOTEL €€€
(608 200; www.parkhotel.hr; Petra Krešimira IV bb; s/d 1500/2026KN; P ❄ @) This sleek spot is a top choice in Makarska, if luxury is

ADVENTURE ON MT BIOKOVO

The limestone massif of Mt Biokovo, which is administered and protected by **Biokovo National Park** (www.biokovo.com; admission 40KN; ⌚8am-4pm Apr–mid-May & Oct–mid-Nov, 7am-8pm mid-May–Sep), offers wonderful hiking opportunities. If you're hiking independently, you have to enter the park at the beginning of 'Biokovo Rd' – basically the only road that runs up the mountain and impossible to miss – and buy an admission ticket there.

Vošac peak (1422m), only 2.5km from Makarska, is the nearest target for hikers. From St Mark's Church on Kačićev trg, you can walk or drive up Put Makra, following signs to the village of Makar, where a trail leads to Vošac. From Vošac a good marked trail leads to **Sveti Jure** (4hr), the highest peak at 1762m, from where you can get spectacular views of the Croatian coast and, on a clear day, the coast of Italy on the other side of the Adriatic. Take plenty of water, sunscreen, a hat and waterproof clothes – the weather on top is always a lot colder than it is by the sea.

Biokovo Active Holidays offers guided walks and drives on Mt Biokovo at all levels of physical exertion. You can go part-way up the mountain by minibus and then take a short hike to Sveti Jure peak, take a 5½-hour trek through black pine forests and lush fields, or enjoy an early drive to watch the sun rise over Makarska.

what you seek. Mingle with Croatian celebs at the pool deck. There's a spa and a full spectrum of facilities.

Meteor HOTEL €€€
(☎602 686; www.hotcli-makarska.hr; Kralja Petra Krešimira IV bb; s/d 810/1456KN; P❄≋) On a pebble beach 400m west of the centre, Meteor has all you'd want from a 277-room behemoth – swimming pools, a shop, tennis courts and a wellness centre.

Hostel Makarska HOSTEL €
(☎091 25 67 212; www.hostelmakarska.com; Prvos vibanjska 15; dm/d 110/250KN; P❄@令) A five-minute walk to the waterfront, this basic spot has doubles and a 10-person dorm plus a shared kitchen and an outdoor area. It's open May through September.

Makarska HOTEL €€
(☎616 622; www.makarska-hotel.com; Potok 17; s/d 410/660KN; P❄@令) About 300m from the beach, it has well-equipped if chintzy rooms and friendly hosts.

Eating & Drinking

Konoba Kalalarga DALMATIAN €
(Kalalarga 40; mains from 45KN) Traditional Dalmatian tavern with dim lighting, dark woods and al fresco bench seating in an alleyway tucked away at the end of Kalalarga street, which leads from the main square. It serves food the way grandma would make it, and dishes out the best *pašticada* in town.

Konoba Ranč DALMATIAN €€
(Kamena 62, Tučepi; mains from 70KN; ⊙dinner May-Sep) This cosy spot away from the tourist buzz is worth the 10-minute drive south at the end of Tučepi; follow the sign left and ascend along winding lanes. Dine on log chairs under olive trees, feasting on meat and fish on grill, *peka* on order, house wine and sporadic *klapa* performances.

Decima DALMATIAN €
(Trg Tina Ujevića bb; mains from 40KN) Well-prepared Dalmatian staples and occasional live *klapa* performances are served up at this family-run *konoba* just behind the Riva promenade.

Riva SEAFOOD €€
(Kralja Tomislava 6; mains from 75KN) Linger in the quiet leafy courtyard of this classy restaurant just off the main drag, feasting on fresh fish and seafood. Good wine list, too.

Yeti CAFE
(Kačićev trg bb) A cosy, much-loved spot for local bohos, misfits and alternative types, right on the main square. It closes for siesta between 3pm and 5pm in summer.

Entertainment

Grota NIGHTCLUB
(Šetalište Svetog Petra bb) On Sveti Petar peninsula, just after the port, this popular disco tucked into a cave welcomes local DJs plus an array of jazz, blues and rock bands.

Deep NIGHTCLUB
(Fra Jure Radića 21) Another club in a cave, at the other end of town on Osejava. This one attracts a supertrendy set who sip cocktails as a DJ spins the latest beats in the background.

Notturno LOUNGE
(Lištun 2) On Makarska's most happening little street, this contemporary cocktail lounge with a terrace showcases the latest house tunes spun by a resident DJ.

Rockatansky BAR
(Fra Filipa Grabovca bb) Makarska's most alternative spot, where a diverse crowd gathers to hear live rock, grunge, metal and jazz on a small stage.

Information

There are many banks and ATMs along Kralja Tomislava and you can change money at the travel agencies on the same street.

Atlas Travel Agency (☎617 038; www.atlas-croatia.com; Kačićev trg 9) At the far end of town; finds private accommodation.

Biokovo Active Holidays (☎679 655; www.biokovo.net; Kralja Petra Krešimira IV 7b) A fount of information on Mt Biokovo, it organises hiking, cycling, rafting and kayaking trips.

Marivaturist (☎616 010; www.marivaturist.hr; Kralja Tomislava 15a) Has money-exchange facilities, and books excursions and private accommodation along the whole Makarska coast.

Tourist Office (☎612 002; www.makarska-info.hr; Kralja Tomislava 16; ⊙8am-9pm Mon-Sat May-Sep, 7am-2pm Mon-Sat rest of yr) Publishes a useful guide to the city with a map; pick it up here or at any of the travel agencies.

Getting There & Away

In July and August there are five ferries daily between Makarska and Sumartin on Brač (33KN, one hour), reduced to four in June and September. The **Jadrolinija stall** (Kralja Tomislava bb) is near the Hotel Biokovo.

From the **bus station** (☎612 333; Ante Starčevića 30), 300m uphill from the centre of the old town, there are 12 buses daily to Dubrovnik (110KN, three hours), 50 to Split (50KN, 1¼ hours), four to Rijeka (313KN to 363KN, seven hours) and six to Zagreb (230KN, six hours). There are also five daily buses to Mostar (100KN, 2¼ hours) and two to Sarajevo (200KN, four hours) in Bosnia and Hercegovina.

Brela

The longest and arguably loveliest coastline in Dalmatia stretches through the tiny town of Brela, which has a more chic flavour than neighbouring Makarska, 14km southeast. Six kilometres of pebble beaches curve around coves thickly forested with pine trees, where you can enjoy beautifully clear seas and fantastic sunsets. A shady promenade lined with bars and cafes winds around the coves, which are on both sides of the town. The best beach is **Dugi Rat**, a gorgeous stretch of pebbles about 300m southwest of the town centre.

Sleeping & Eating

Much of the private accommodation on offer from the tourist office or travel agencies is really small *pansions,* where double rooms start at 300KN in high season.

The four large hotels are managed by **Blue Sun Hotels & Resorts** (www.bluesun-hotels.com). The most secluded of those is **Hotel Berulia** (☎603 599; Frankopanska bb; s/d 960/1620KN; P❄@📶🏊), a four-star giant 300m east of the town centre. **Hotel Marina** (☎608 608; s/d 700/1160KN; P❄📶) is the most affordable of the four properties and the best for families, with a wall of pine trees to separate it from the Brela beach. The most affordable place in town is also its most adorable, the funky **Hostel Casa Vecchia** (☎619 014; www.hostel-casa.com; Breljanska Cesta 40; dm/d 110/300KN; P📶) on the coastal highway (Magistrala), typically open from May through September. The friendly Aussie owner will even let you set up a tent for 37KN if space allows, and there's a restored wooden boat that does daily booze cruises for hostel guests.

For a good meal, head to **Konoba Feral** (Obala Domagoja 30; mains from 60KN), a friendly tavern with wooden tables and well-prepared seafood and fish; try the line-caught squid grilled with garlic and parsley. For the most scenic meal, head up above the coastal highway and follow the signs to **Konoba Galinac** (☎618 251; Sv Jurja 52; mains from 70KN), located in an abandoned hamlet of small stone houses. The restaurant has a large terrace with unobstructed views of the Adriatic islands and Brela below. It provides free transport from Brela and nearby towns.

RIDING THE RAILS TO MOSTAR

A great way to beat the crowds and do something different is to take a train from Ploče to Mostar in Bosnia and Hercegovina. The slow and huffy train leaves Ploče twice a day (33KN, 1½ hours), travelling through the gorgeous Dalmatian and Hercegovinian landscape, often tracing the upstream flow of the Neretva River. All Dubrovnik-bound buses that stop in Makarska pass Ploče (around 50KN). EU, US, Australian and Canadian citizens don't need visas to enter Bosnia and Hercegovina; other nationalities should check with their embassy.

Information

Berulia Travel (☎618 519; www.beruliatravel-brela.hr; Frankopanska 111) Finds private accommodation, changes money, books excursions and arranges airport transfers.

Tourist Office (☎618 455; www.brela.hr; Trg Alojzija Stepinca bb; ⏲8am-9pm Jun-Sep, 8am-3pm Mon-Fri, to noon Sat Oct-May) Provides a town map and a regional cycling map. Has an ATM outside.

Getting There & Away

All buses running between Makarska and Split stop at Brela, making it an easy day trip from either town. The bus stop (no left-luggage office) is behind Hotel Soline, a short walk downhill to Kneza Domagoja, the harbour street and the town centre.

BRAČ ISLAND

POP 14,434

Brač is famous for two things: its radiant white stone, from which Diocletian's Palace in Split and the White House in Washington, DC (oh, yes!) are made, and Zlatni Rat, the long pebbly beach at Bol that sticks out lasciviously into the Adriatic and adorns 90% of Croatia's tourism posters. It's the largest island in central Dalmatia, with two towns, several sleepy villages and a dramatic Mediterranean landscape of steep cliffs, inky waters and pine forests. The interior of the island is full of piles of rocks – the result of the back-breaking labour of women who, over hundreds of years, gathered the rocks in order to prepare the land for the cultivation of vineyards and olive, fig, almond and sour-cherry orchards.

The tough living conditions on the island meant that a lot of people moved to the mainland in search of work, leaving the interior almost deserted. Driving around and exploring Brač's stone villages is one of the loveliest experiences. The two main centres, Supetar and Bol, differ greatly from one another: Supetar has the appearance of a transit town, while Bol revels in its more exclusive appeal.

History

Remnants of a Neolithic settlement have been found in Kopačina cave near Supetar, but the first recorded inhabitants were the Illyrians, who built a fort in Škrip to protect against Greek invasion. The Romans arrived in 167 BC and promptly set to work exploiting the stone quarries near Škrip and building summer mansions around the island.

During the nearly four centuries of Venetian rule (1420–1797), the interior villages were devastated by plague and the inhabitants moved to the 'healthier' settlements along the coast, revitalising the towns of Supetar, Bol, Sumartin and Milna. After a brief period under Napoleonic rule, the island passed into Austrian hands. Wine cultivation expanded until the phylloxera epidemic at the turn of the 20th century ravaged the island's vines and people began leaving for North and South America. The island endured a reign of terror during WWII when German and Italian troops looted and burned villages, imprisoning and murdering their inhabitants. Although the tourism business took a hit in the mid-1990s, it has rebounded well.

 Getting There & Away

Air

Brač's **airport** (☎559 711; www.airport-brac.hr) is 14km northeast of Bol and 30km southeast of Supetar. There is one weekly flight from Zagreb

WORTH A TRIP

BRAČ'S QUIET ESCAPES

Sumartin is a quiet, pretty port with a few rocky beaches and little to do, but it makes a nice retreat from the busier tourist centres of Bol and Supetar. The bus station is in the centre of town, next to the ferry, and there are a number of *sobe* signs around the tiny town for those who decide to stay. Sumartin is the entry point on Brač if you're coming from Makarska.

The pretty village of **Dol** in the island's interior is one of the oldest settlements on Brač, a collection of well-preserved stone houses on a barren rock. A visit here offers a rare glance at Brač as it used to be, away from the tourist hubbub. You can have a fantastic homemade meal at the family-run **Konoba Toni** (www.toni-dol.info), a rustic tavern in a 300-year-old stone house.

For a quiet coastal getaway, head to **Pučišća** on the northern coast of Brač, a historic town overlooking Makarska Riviera and home to one of the island's best hotels, **Dešković Palace** (www.palaca-deskovic.com), a luxurious 15-room property in a 15th-century palazzo.

One of Brač's more interesting sites is the village of **Škrip**, the oldest settlement on the island, about 8km southeast of Supetar. Formerly a refuge of the ancient Illyrians, the fort was taken over by the Romans in the 2nd century BC, followed by inhabitants of Solin fleeing 7th-century barbarians and eventually early Slavs. Remains of the Illyrian wall are visible around the citadel in the southeastern corner. The most intact Roman monument on the island is the mausoleum at the base of Radojković's tower, a fortification built during the Venetian-Turkish wars.

The port of **Milna**, 20km southwest of Supetar, is the kind of lovely intact fishing village that in any other part of the world would have long ago been commandeered by package tourists. The 17th-century town is set at the edge of a deep natural harbour that was used by Emperor Diocletian on the way to Split. Paths and walks take you around the harbour, which is studded with coves and rocky beaches. Besides the picture-perfect setting, there's the 18th-century Church of Our Lady of the Annunciation, with a baroque front and early-18th-century altar paintings.

during the high season, but there's no transport from the airport to Supetar so you'll need to take a **taxi** (☎098 781 377), which costs about 300KN (150KN to Bol).

Boat

There are 14 daily car ferries between Split and Supetar in July and August (33/160KN per person/car, 50 minutes) and 12 daily in June and September (fewer in winter). The ferry drops you off in the centre of town, only steps from the bus station. Make bookings at **Jadrolinija** (☎631 357; www.jadrolinija.hr; Hrvatskih Velikana bb, Supetar), about 50m east of the harbour.

There's a Jadrolinija catamaran in summer between Split and Bol (40KN, one hour) that goes on to Jelsa on Hvar; buy your ticket in advance in Bol, as these can sell out fast in high season. There are also five daily summer car ferries between Makarska and Sumartin (33KN, one hour), reduced to four daily in June and September and two per day in winter. Note that you may have to wait an hour or two in Sumartin for a bus connection to Supetar. There's a daily fast passenger boat by **Krilo** (www.krilo.hr) that connects Split and Milna (18KN, 30 minutes).

Getting Around

Public transport to the island's highlights is sparse, so you may wish to have your own wheels if you want to see a few sites in a short time. You can hire cars from travel agencies on the island or bring them from the mainland (which is pricey due to ferry costs).

Supetar is the hub for bus transport around the island. There are several daily buses that connect Supetar with Bol (50 minutes) and with Sumartin (1½ hours). Note that the bus schedule is reduced on Sundays.

Supetar

POP 4082

Supetar is not a great beauty – it feels more like a transit town than a living place in itself. However, it's a great hub for transport and a short stroll around the town will reveal some nice stone streets and a pretty church and square. The pebbly beaches are an easy stroll from the town centre, making it a popular destination for families.

Supetar is easy to navigate since most offices, shops and travel agencies are on the main road that runs roughly east-west from the harbour. Called Porat at the harbour, the road becomes Hrvatskih Velikana in the east and Vlačica on to Put Vele Luke as it travels west. The bus station (no left-luggage office) is next to the Jadrolinija office.

Activities

Fun Dive Club DIVING

(☎098 13 07 384; www.fundiveclub.com) The best diving on the island is off the southwestern coast between Bol and Milna, making Bol a better base for divers. Still, you can book dives, take a course and rent equipment at this dive club at **Waterman Supetrus Resort Hotel** (www.watermanresorts.com), known to locals as Hotel Kaktus.

Beaches BEACH

There are five pebbly beaches on the coast. **Vrilo** beach is about 100m east of the town centre. Walking west, you'll come first to **Vlačica** then **Banj** beach, lined with pine trees. Next is **Bili Rat**, site of the water-sports centre, then if you cut across St Nikolaus Cape you come to **Vela Luka** beach, with soft pebbles on a peaceful bay.

Festivals & Events

The **Supetar Summer** festival lasts from mid-June through mid-September, when folk music, dances and classical concerts are presented several times a week in public spaces and churches. Tickets to festival events are usually free or cost very little. There are also frequent art exhibitions around town.

Sleeping

Most of the big hotels are in a tourist complex a few kilometres west of the port on Vela Luka bay. For a sprawling development of this kind, the landscaping is surprisingly pleasant, with pine trees, shrubbery and a nearby beach.

Travel agencies can find you good-quality rooms. Check www.supetar.hr for details of rooms and villas available.

Bračka Perla HOTEL €€€

(☎755 530; www.brackaperla.com; Put Vele Luke 53; d/ste 2360/2735KN; P ❄ @ 🛜 ≋) Supetar's latest offering is this exclusive little 'art hotel' with eight suites and three rooms, each painted by renowned artist Srećko Žitnik. The garden terrace is lovely, as are the sea vistas and the facilities, which include an open-air pool and a small wellness centre.

Hotel Amor HOTEL €€€

(☎606 606; www.velaris.hr; Put Vele Luke 10; s/d 885/1180KN; P ❄ @ 🛜 ≋) This upscale hotel features 50 rooms, all with balconies, decked out in yellows, olives and bright greens. The complex, surrounded by peaceful olive and pine woods and close to the beach, has a spa and a dive centre.

Pansion Palute GUESTHOUSE €
(☎631 541; palute@st.t-com.hr; Put Pašike 16; s/d 210/380KN; P ❄) This small, family-run *pansion* has clean and tidy rooms (most with balconies), wooden floors, TVs and a voluble proprietor. Outstanding homemade jam is served with breakfast.

Funky Donkey HOSTEL €
(☎630 937; www.brachostels.net; Polanda 20; dm 140-160KN, d 360KN; ⊙May-Aug; ❄@📶) This party hostel in the old town offers up dorms and doubles, free wi-fi, laundry service, a kitchen, a terrace with sea views and tours around the island, including cliff jumping.

Camping Supetar CAMPGROUND €
(☎091 19 40 246; per adult/site 22/30KN; ⊙Jun-Sep) A midsized autocamp about 300m east of town, with access to a small rocky beach.

Eating

Vinotoka SEAFOOD €
(Jobova 6; mains from 50KN) One of the best places in town, Vinotoka is decorated with marine-inspired pieces and has a glassed-in terrace and a wooden boat in the middle. The seafood is excellent, best accompanied by some local white. Try the tuna prosciutto.

Punta FISH €
(Punta 1; mains from 60KN) A well-located restaurant, with a beach terrace overlooking the sea. Choose from fish and seafood, dive into some meat or just have a pizza as you watch the waves and windsurfers.

Drinking & Entertainment

Thriller (Put Vele Luke 7) is an old favourite that recently changed owners; it's by the beach and near to the centre. Nearby, **Benny's Bar** (Put Vela Luke bb) and **Havana Club** (Put Vela Luke bb) are also popular.

Information

Atlas (☎631 105; Porat 10) Books excursions and private accommodation. Near the harbour.

Maestral (☎631 258; www.travel.maestral.hr; IG Kovačića 3; ⊙Jun-mid-Sep) Source of private accommodation.

Radeško (☎756 694; Put Barba Maškova 11) Finds private accommodation, books hotels and changes money.

Tourist Office (☎630 900; www.supetar.hr; Porat 1; ⊙8am-10pm mid-May–Sep, 8am-3.30pm Mon-Fri Oct-Dec, 8am-3.30pm Mon-Sat Jan–mid-May) Has a full array of brochures on the activities and sights in Supetar, as well as up-to-date bus and ferry timetables. A few steps east of the harbour.

Bol

POP 1958

The old town of Bol is an attractive place, with small stone houses and winding streets dotted with pink and purple geraniums. Bol's real highlight is Zlatni Rat, the seductive pebbly beach that 'leaks' into the Adriatic and draws crowds of swimmers and windsurfers in the summer months. A long coastal promenade, lined with pine trees, connects the beach with the old town, and along it are most of the town's hotels. It's a great, buzzing place in summer – one of Croatia's favourites and perennially popular.

The town centre is a pedestrian area that stretches east from the bus station. Sights in the old town are marked with interpretative panels, each explaining the cultural and historical heritage. Zlatni Rat beach is 2km west of town and in between are Borak and Potočine beaches. Behind them are several hotel complexes, including Hotel Borak, Elaphusa and Bretanide.

Sights

Zlatni Rat BEACH
Most people come to Bol to soak up the sun or windsurf at Zlatni Rat, which extends like a tongue into the sea for about 500m from the western end of town. It's a gorgeous beach made up of smooth white pebbles, and the shape of the tip is shuffled by the wind and waves. Pine trees provide shade and rocky cliffs rise sharply behind the beach, making the setting one of the loveliest in Dalmatia. To get there, follow the marble-paved seafront promenade, fringed with subtropical gardens. Note that the beach gets jam-packed in the high season.

Galerija Branislav Dešković GALLERY
(admission 10KN; ⊙10am-noon & 6-10pm Tue-Sun May-Nov) This gallery, inside a Renaissance-baroque townhouse right on the seafront, displays work by 20th-century Croatian artists, amounting to around 300 paintings and sculptures. A great place to pop in on a cloudy day.

Dragon's Cave CAVE
You can go by foot to Dragon's Cave, an extremely unusual set of reliefs believed to have been carved by an imaginative 15th-century friar. Carved angels, animals and a gaping dragon decorate the walls of this strange cave in a blend of Christian and Croat pagan symbols.

First walk 6km to Murvica; from there it's a one-hour walk. Note that the cave can only be visited by prior arrangement with a guide who has a key. He's best reached via the tourist office. It costs about 50KN per person to reach the cave from Murvica but there's a four-person minimum.

Activities

Bol is undoubtedly the **windsurfing** capital of Croatia and most of the action takes place at Potočine beach, west of town. Although the *maestral* (strong, steady westerly wind) blows from April to October, the best time to windsurf is at the end of May and the beginning of June, and at the end of July and the beginning of August. The wind generally reaches its peak in the early afternoon and then dies down at the end of the day. **Big Blue** (☎635 614; www.big-blue-sport.hr) is a large operation that rents windsurfing boards (per half-day 290KN) and offers beginners' courses (990KN). It also rents **mountain bikes** (per hr/day 40/120KN) and **kayaks** (per hr/day 50/180KN). It has three locations: inside a shop next to the tourist office on the seafront, on Borak beach and by Bretanide Hotel.

You can dive with another company confusingly also named **Big Blue** (☎306 222; www.big-blue-diving.hr; Hotel Borak, Zlatni Rat; dives from 200KN, with equipment rental 300KN). There are no wrecks but you can dive some coral reefs at 40m and a large cave; boats go out regularly during the high season.

You can rent boats from the **Nautic Center Bol stall** (☎635 367; www.nautic-center-bol.com; Potočine beach; per day from 400KN), which sits opposite the Bretanide Hotel during the day. In the evening you can find the stall at the harbour, where it moves to attract more customers. It also has lots of water sports activities such as wakeboarding, jet-skiing, waterskiing, tube riding and parasailing.

There are professional-quality clay tennis courts at the **Tennis Centre Potočine** (☎635 222; Zlatni Rat; per hr 100KN), along the road to Murvica. Rackets and balls can be rented.

If you fancy hiking, try the two-hour walk up to **Vidova Gora** (778m), the area's highest peak. There are also mountain-biking trails leading up. The local tourist office can give you info and basic maps.

Festivals & Events

The **Bol Summer Festival** is held from the middle of June through late September each year, with dancers and musicians from around the country performing in churches and open spaces. An annual event that takes place in late June, **Cultural Festival Imena** gathers writers, artists and musicians for a few days of exhibits, readings, concerts and happenings.

The patron saint of Bol is Our Lady of Carmel; on her **feast day** (5 August), there's a procession with residents dressed up in traditional costumes, as well as music and feasting on the streets.

Sleeping

There are few small hotels but several large tourist complexes, which, surprisingly, blend in well with the landscape. Several hotels are 'all-inclusive'. Reservations for most hotels are handled by **Blue Sun Hotels** (www.bluesunhotels.com).

Travel agencies can arrange private accommodation with private bathroom for around 150KN to 200KN per person. Two-person studio apartments cost around 350KN to 400KN in the high season; other sizes are available.

Campgrounds in Bol are small and familial. West of town and near the big hotels you'll find **Camp Kito** (☎635 551; www.camping-brac.com; Bračke Ceste bb; per adult/tent 60/22KN; ⏲mid-Apr–mid-Sep; P 📶), which is well kept and placed in a scenic spot.

TOP CHOICE **Villa Giardino** GUESTHOUSE €€€
(☎635 900; www.bol.hr/online/VillaGiardino.htm; Novi Put 2; s/d 635/850KN; P ❄ 📶) An iron gate opens onto a luxuriant garden at the end of which is this elegant white villa. Ten tastefully restored and spacious rooms are furnished with antiques; some overlook the garden while others have sea views. It's an oasis of peace, with a secluded garden out the back. It is cash only.

Funky Donkey HOSTEL €
(☎635 026; www.brachostels.net; Domovinskog Rata 62; dm 150-170KN, d 380KN; ⏲May-Sep; P @ 📶) Bol's best budget option, the new offshoot of Supetar's Funky Donkey sits a 10-minute walk from Zlatni Rat and a 10-minute walk to the town centre. It has four dorms and three doubles, plus three kitchens and a BBQ area.

Hotel Kaštil HOTEL €€
(☎635 995; www.kastil.hr; Frane Radića 1; s/d 540/800KN; P ❄ 📶) All 32 carpeted rooms have sea views in this central hotel in an old baroque townhouse. The decor is sparse but pleasant. Balconies adorn some of the units.

There's a lovely restaurant terrace, where hotel guests get 10% off the price of their meals.

Hotel Borak HOTEL €€€
(☎306 202; www.brachotelborak.com; Zlatni Rat; s/d 938/1230KN; P❄@🛜≋) Close to Zlatni Rat and sporting activities, this place lacks character thanks to its size and the socialist-style architecture. It is, however, a comfortable spot to relax after your windsurfing, mountain biking, kayaking, swimming...

Elaphusa HOTEL €€€
(☎306 200; www.hotelelaphusabrac.com; Put Zlatnog Rata bb; s/d 1024/1815KN; P❄@🛜≋) Enormous and glistening, four-star Elaphusa feels like the inside of a cruise ship. It's all smooth interiors, glass partitions, saltwater pools, slick rooms and every possible amenity, including a wellness centre. If you like glam and glitz, this (although quite soulless) is it.

Eating

Bol's restaurant scene is decent although unexciting. Expect plenty of fresh fish and seafood, and some attempts at creative cooking.

TOP CHOICE **Konoba Mali Raj** DALMATIAN €
(Iza Loze 5; mains from 50KN) Lovely little spot away from the tourist buzz, above the parking lot for Zlatni Rat, this al fresco tavern has a leafy garden with plenty of nooks and crannies to enjoy the delicious dishes such as sea anemone risotto, seafood skewers or monkfish in champagne sauce. It's cash only.

Taverna Riva DALMATIAN €€
(Frane Radića 5; mains from 70KN) This terrace right above the Riva is where locals go for a good meal. If you're feeling adventurous, try the *vitalac* (skewered lamb offal wrapped in lamb meat) or order ahead for the delicious lamb or octopus under *peka* (domed baking lid).

Ribarska Kućica SEAFOOD €
(Ante Starčevića bb; mains from 55KN; ⏰Jun-Nov) A lobster extravaganza is in order at this seaside restaurant, where you sit on the waterfront terrace or under straw sun umbrellas on a small pebble beach, gorging on well-prepared seafood. Service can be slow.

Konoba Dalmatino DALMATIAN €
(Frane Radića 14; mains from 65KN) This tavern offers good, informal dining in a setting of burnished wood, old photos and knick-knacks. The seafood and meat dishes are prepared simply but well.

Vagabundo SEAFOOD €€
(Ante Radića 36; mains from 80KN) Savour stellar fare at this fancy all-white terrace restaurant on the seafront. Lobster comes from Vagabundo's own tank. Try the speciality: paella vagabundo (with shellfish, chicken and chorizo).

Drinking & Entertainment

Varadero COCKTAIL BAR
(Frane Radića bb; ⏰May-Nov) At this open-air cocktail bar on the seafront you can sip coffee and fresh OJ under straw umbrellas during the day and return in the evening for fab cocktails, DJ music and lounging on wicker sofas and armchairs.

Marinero CAFE-BAR
(Rudina 46) A cult gathering spot for Bol locals, up the stairs from the seafront (follow the sign), with a leafy terrace on a square, live music on some nights and a diverse merry-making crowd.

Information

There are several ATMs in town, and many money changers in the port area.

Bol Tours (☎635 693; www.boltours.com; Vladimira Nazora 18) Books excursions, rents cars and finds private accommodation.

Interactiv (☎091 57 25 855; Rudina 6; per hr 30KN; ⏰May-Oct) A dozen fast computers and a call centre. Most cafes have wi-fi and there are several hotspots around town (for a fee).

DON'T MISS

TOP FIVE BEACHES OF CENTRAL DALMATIA

Zlatni Rat The famous beach finger that appears in nearly all of Croatia's tourist publicity (p227)

Brela A string of palm-fringed coves with ultrasoft pebbles (p224)

Pakleni Islands Rocky islands near Hvar with clothing-optional coves (p232)

Šolta Quiet, rocky coves not far from noisy Split (p215)

Stiniva Stunning and secluded pebble cove on Vis Island, flanked by high rocks (p238)

More (☎642 050; www.more-bol.com; Vladimira Nazora 28) Private accommodation, scooter rental, island tours and excursions.

Tourist Office (☎635 638; www.bol.hr; Porat Bolskih Pomoraca bb; ⊙8.30am-10pm Jul & Aug, 8.30am-2pm & 4-9pm May, Jun & Sep) Inside a Gothic 15th-century townhouse; a good source of information on town events and distributes plenty of brochures.

HVAR ISLAND

POP 10,948

Hvar is the number-one holder of Croatia's superlatives: it's the most luxurious island, the sunniest place in the country (2724 sunny hours each year) and, along with Dubrovnik, the most popular tourist destination. Hvar Town, the island's capital, is all about swanky hotels, elegant restaurants, trendy bars and clubs, posh yachties and a general sense that, if you care about seeing and being seen, this is the place to be. The coastal towns of Stari Grad and Jelsa, the cultural and historical centres of the island, are the more serene and discerning spots.

Hvar is also famed for the lilac lavender fields that dot its interior, as well as for other aromatic plants such as rosemary and heather. You'll find that some of the really deluxe hotels use skin-care products made out of these gorgeous-smelling herbs.

The interior of the island hides abandoned ancient hamlets, towering peaks and verdant, largely uncharted landscapes. It's worth exploring on a day trip, as is the southern end of the island, which has some of Hvar's most beautiful and isolated coves.

Getting There & Away

The local Jadrolinija car ferry from Split calls at Stari Grad (47KN, two hours) six times a day in summer. Jadrolinija also has three to five catamarans daily to Hvar Town (47KN, one hour) and two to Jelsa (40KN, 1½ hours). **Krilo** (www.krilo.hr), the fast passenger boat, travels once a day between Split and Hvar Town (45KN, one hour) in summer; it also goes on to Korčula (50KN, 1½ hours). You can buy tickets at Pelegrini Tours (p235) in Hvar.

There are at least 10 car ferries (fewer in the low season) running from Drvenik, on the mainland, to Sućuraj (16KN, 35 minutes) on the tip of Hvar Island. The **Jadrolinija agency** (☎741 132; www.jadrolinija.hr) is beside the landing in Stari Grad.

Connections to Italy are available in the summer season. Two Jadrolinija ferries a week (on Saturday and Sunday night) go from Stari Grad to Ancona in Italy. Blue Line also runs regular boats to Ancona from Hvar Town. Pelegrini Tours in Hvar sells these tickets.

In Hvar Town, **garderoba** (Left Luggage; per hr 20KN; ⊙7am-11pm) facilities are available in the public bathroom next to the bus station.

Getting Around

Buses meet most ferries that dock at Stari Grad and go to Hvar Town (27KN, 20 minutes) and Jelsa (32KN). There are 10 buses a day between Stari Grad and Hvar Town in summer, but services are reduced on Sunday and in the low season. A taxi costs from 300KN to 350KN. **Radio Taxi Tihi** (☎098 338 824) is cheaper if there are a number of passengers to fill up the minivan. It's easy to recognise, with a picture of Hvar painted on the side.

If you're driving from Stari Grad to Hvar Town, be aware that there are two routes: the scenic route, which is a narrow road winding through the interior mountains; and the direct route, which is a modern roadway (2960) that gets you to town rapidly.

Hvar Town

POP 3738

The island's hub and busiest destination, Hvar Town is estimated to draw around 20,000 people a day in the high season. It's odd that they can all fit in the small bay town, where 13th-century walls surround beautifully ornamented Gothic palaces and traffic-free marble streets, but fit they do. Visitors wander along the main square, explore the sights on the winding stone streets, swim on the numerous beaches or pop off to the Pakleni Islands to get into their birthday suits, but most of all they party at night.

There are several good restaurants here and a number of great hotels, but thanks to the island's appeal to well-heeled guests, the prices can be seriously inflated. Don't be put off if you're on a lower budget though, as private accommodation and a couple of hostels cater to a younger, more diverse crowd.

Sights

Don't organise your stay around the opening hours of the museums and churches, as they tend to be irregular. The hours given are for the summer season, which runs from June to September. In the low season, Hvar's highlights are open by appointment only.

Hvar is such a small, manageable town that it only recently got street names, but nobody really uses them. The main street is the long seaside promenade, dotted with small, rocky beaches, sights, hotels, bars and some restaurants. The town square is called Trg Svetog Stjepana and the bus stop is minutes away from here. On the northern slope above the square, and within the old ramparts, are the remains of several palaces that belonged to the Hvar aristocracy. From the bus station to the harbour, the town is closed to traffic.

St Stephen's Square CENTRAL SQUARE
(Trg Svetog Stjepana) The centre of town is this rectangular square, which was formed by filling in an inlet that once stretched out from the bay. At 4500 sq metres, it's one of the largest old squares in Dalmatia. The town first developed in the 13th century to the north of the square and later spread south in the 15th century. Notice the **well** at the square's northern end, built in 1520, with a wrought-iron grill dating from 1780.

Franciscan Monastery & Museum MONASTERY
(admission 25KN; ⌚9am-1pm & 5-7pm Mon-Sat) This 15th-century monastery overlooks a shady cove. The elegant **bell tower** was built in the 16th century by a well-known family of stonemasons from Korčula. The **Renaissance cloister** leads to a refectory containing lace, coins, nautical charts and valuable documents, such as an edition of *Ptolemy's Atlas,* printed in 1524. Your eye will immediately be struck by *The Last Supper,* an 8m by 2.5m work by the Venetian Matteo Ingoli dating from the end of the 16th century. The cypress in the **cloister garden** is said to be more than 300 years old. The adjoining church, named **Our Lady of Charity**, contains more fine paintings such as the three polyptychs created by Francesco da Santacroce in 1583, which represent the summit of this painter's work.

Fortica FORTRESS
(admission 25KN; ⌚8am-10pm Jun-Sep) The main town gate, northwest of the square, leads to a network of tiny streets with small palaces, churches and old houses. From there you can climb up through a park to the citadel built on the site of a medieval castle to defend the town from the Turks. The Venetians strengthened it in 1557 and then the Austrians renovated it in the 19th century by adding barracks. Inside is a tiny collection of ancient amphorae recovered from the seabed. The view over the harbour is magnificent, and there's a lovely cafe at the top.

Arsenal HISTORIC BUILDING
(Trg Svetog Stjepana) On the southern side of the square, the Arsenal was built in 1611 to replace a building destroyed by the Ottomans. Mentioned in Venetian documents as 'the most beautiful and the most useful building in the whole of Dalmatia', the Arsenal once served as a repair and refitting station for war galleons.

Renaissance Theatre HISTORIC BUILDING
(Trg Svetog Stjepana; admission 10KN; ⌚9am-9pm) Built in 1612, this theatre just upstairs from the Arsenal is reportedly the first theatre in Europe open to plebeians and aristocrats alike. It remained a regional cultural centre throughout the centuries. Plays were still staged here right up until 2008. Although much of the theatre is still under renovation, you can wander around the atmospheric interior and take in the faded frescoes and baroque loggias.

Cathedral of St Stephen CATHEDRAL
(Katedrala Svetog Stjepana; Trg Svetog Stjepana; ⌚30min before twice-daily Mass) The cathedral forms a stunning backdrop to the square. The bell tower rises four levels, each more elaborate than the last. The cathedral was built in the 16th and 17th centuries at the height of the Dalmatian Renaissance on the site of a cathedral destroyed by the Turks. Parts of the older cathedral are visible in the nave and in the carved 15th-century choir stalls.

Bishop's Treasury MUSEUM
(Riznica; admission 10KN; ⌚9am-1pm & 5-7pm Mon-Sat) Adjoining the Cathedral of St Stephen, the treasury houses silver vessels, embroidered Mass robes, numerous Madonnas, a couple of 13th-century icons and an elaborately carved sarcophagus.

Benedictine Monastery MONASTERY
(admission 10KN; ⌚9am-noon & 5-7pm Mon-Sat) Northwest of the main square, this monastery has a re-creation of a Renaissance house and a collection of lace painstakingly woven by the nuns from dried agave leaves.

Activities

There are several diving outfits in town, including **Marinesa Dive Centre** (☎091 51 57 229) and **Diving Centre Viking** (☎091 56 89 443; www.viking-diving.com). Both offer PADI certification courses and dives (from 250KN and up to 500KN for a full-day trip with two dives).

You can rent scooters at **Navigare** (☎718 721; www.renthvar.com; Trg Svetog Stjepana) for between 200KN and 250KN per day. They also rent cars (from 450KN per day) and boats (from 400KN per day).

PAKLENI ISLANDS

Most visitors to Hvar Town head to the Pakleni Islands (Pakleni Otoci), which got their name – 'Hell's Islands' in Croatian – from *paklina*, the resin that once coated boats and ships. This gorgeous chain of 21 wooded isles has crystal-clear seas, hidden beaches and deserted lagoons. Taxi boats leave regularly during the high season from in front of the Arsenal to the islands of **Jerolim** and **Stipanska** (35KN; 10-15min), which are popular naturist islands (although nudity is not mandatory). They continue on to **Ždrilca** and **Mlini** (40KN) and, further out, **Palmižana** (60KN), which has a pebble beach and the **Meneghello Place** (www.palmizana.hr), a beautiful boutique complex of villas and bungalows scattered among lush tropical gardens. Run by the artsy Meneghello family, the estate holds music recitals, and features two excellent restaurants and an art gallery. Also on Palmižana are two top restaurant-cum-hang-out spots, Toto and Laganini.

There are coves around the hotels Amfora and Dalmacija for swimming, as well as the fancy **Bonj Les Bains beach** run by Sunčani Hvar Hotels, with stone beach cabanas for open-air massages and expensive lounge chairs (650KN per day for two chairs).

A popular boat excursion (40KN, 20 minutes) is to **Mekićevica** bay on the south side of the island, where there's a great beachfront restaurant called **Robinson** (www.robinson-hvar.hr). Taxi boats also run to **Milna** (50KN; 30min). Also on the south side are other great beaches such as Zaraće, Dubovica, Lušišće and Sveta Nedelja/Ivan Dolac.

Contact **Hvar Adventure** (717 813; www.hvar-adventure.com; Obala bb) for adventure activities such as sailing (half-day 420KN), sea kayaking (half-day 350KN), cycling (half-day 500KN), hiking and rock climbing.

There are 120km of hiking trails and 96km of marked biking trails within easy access of Hvar Town. Maps are on sale from travel agencies and Tisak stores.

Tours

Don't miss the great off-road tour with **Secret Hvar** (717 615; www.secrethvar.com; Trg Svetog Stjepana 4a), which takes in hidden beauties of the island's interior, including abandoned villages, scenic canyons, ancient stone huts, endless fields of lavender and the island's tallest peak, **Sveti Nikola** (626m). It's worth every lipa of 600KN, which includes lunch in a traditional tavern and a stop on the beach. Secret Hvar also does wine tours (500KN, with snacks and samplings) and island tours (450KN).

Festivals & Events

Hvar's **Summer Festival**, which runs from late June to early September, includes classical concerts in the Franciscan monastery. **Lavender Festival** takes place in Velo Grablje village on the last weekend in June every year, with exhibits, concerts, wine tastings and a lavender fair – a fun local event.

Sleeping

As Hvar is one of the Adriatic's most popular destinations, don't expect many bargains. Most Hvar hotels are managed by **Sunčani Hvar Hotels** (www.suncanihvar.com) and many have undergone a total transformation.

Accommodation in Hvar is extremely tight in July and August, even though many houses have been renovated or constructed to accommodate the crush of tourism. Try the travel agencies for help. If you arrive without a reservation, you will be offered rooms at the ferry dock; there are also many *sobe* signs in town. If you rent a room or apartment from someone at a dock, make sure the house sports a blue *sobe* sign. Otherwise, they are renting illegally and you'll be unprotected in case of a problem. Get a business card if possible. It is amazingly easy to get lost in the warren of unnamed streets hanging over and around the old town and you may need to call the owner for help. Expect to pay anywhere from 150KN to 300KN per person for a room with a private bathroom in the town centre. Outside the high season you can negotiate a much better price.

Family-run private-apartment options are so numerous in Hvar that the choice can be overwhelming. Here are a few reliable, good-value apartments: **Apartments Ukić** (www.hvar-apartments-center.com), **Apartments Komazin** (www.croatia-hvar-apartments.com), **Apartments Ivanović** (www.ivanovic-hvar.com) and **Apartments Bracanović** (www.hvar-jagoda.com).

TOP CHOICE Hotel Croatia HOTEL €€€
(742 400; www.hotelcroatia.net; Majerovica bb; s/d 832/1110KN; P❄@) Only a few steps from the sea, this medium-sized, rambling 1930s building sits among gorgeous, peaceful gardens. The rooms – with a yellow, orange and lavender colour scheme – are simple and old-fashioned. Many (pricier ones) have balconies overlooking the gardens and the sea. There's a sauna, too.

Hotel Adriana HOTEL €€€
(750 200; www.suncanihvar.com; Fabrika bb; s/d 2343/2817KN; ❄@) This deluxe spa hotel is classified by the Leading Small Hotels of the World, which gives you some idea of the world of comfort you'll find here. All of the bright, swanky rooms overlook the sea and the medieval town. Facilities include the comprehensive Sensori Spa, a gorgeous rooftop pool next to the rooftop bar, a plush restaurant, 24-hour room service, excursions, you name it.

Hotel Riva HOTEL €€€
(750 100; www.suncanihvar.com; Riva bb; s/d 1390/2617KN; ❄@) The luxury veteran on Hvar's hotel scene, this 100-year-old hotel has 54 smallish rooms that play with blacks, reds and whites, with black-and-white posters of movie stars, and glass walls between the bedroom and bathroom. Rooms 115 and 215 are most spacious. The harbourfront location is perfect for watching the yachts glide up and away – hence it's known as a 'yacht harbour hotel'.

Hostel Marinero HOSTEL €
(091 17 41 601; Put Sv Marka 7; dm 200-240KN; ❄) Location is the highlight at this six-dorm hostel right off the seafront. Dorms are basic but clean. There is no shared kitchen but the restaurant downstairs is a good place to hang out. The hostel wristband gets you discounts and perks at spots around town. Be ready for some noise, as the Kiva Bar is right next door.

Hvar Out Hostel HOSTEL €
(717 375; hvarouthostel@gmail.com; Burak 23; dm 200-250KN; ❄@) By the same owners as Split Hostel Booze & Snooze, this party place, steps from the harbour in the maze of the old town, has seven well-equipped dorms, a small shared kitchen and a terrace on the top floor.

Aparthotel Pharia HOTEL €€€
(778 080; www.orvas-hotels.com; Put Podstina 1; s/d/apt 512/813/1009KN; P❄) This sparkling complex is only 50m from the sea in a quiet neighbourhood slightly west of the town centre, behind Hotel Croatia. All the rooms and apartments have balconies, some sea-facing. There are also four eight-person villas, each with a pool, and bikes for rent.

Luka's Lodge HOSTEL €
(742 118; www.lukalodgehvar.hostel.com; Šime Buzolića Tome 75; dm 140-180KN, d 340-440KN; ❄@) Friendly owner Luka really takes care of his guests at this homey hostel, a five-minute walk from town. All rooms come with fridges, some with balconies. There's a living room, two terraces, and a kitchen and laundry service. Upon request, Luka does pick-up from the ferry dock.

Villa Skansi HOSTEL €
(741 426; hostelvillaskansi1@gmail.com; Lučica bb; dm 150-200KN, d 400-500KN; ❄@) Popular hostel a short walk uphill from the seafront, with superclean dorms and doubles, fancy bathrooms, a great terrace with sea views, a bar and barbecue. There's a book exchange, laundry service, scooter, boat and bike rental, and booze cruises. Run by a friendly couple.

Hotel Podstine HOTEL €€€
(740 400; www.podstine.com; Put Podstina 11; s/d 2333/2592KN; P❄@) Just 2km southwest of the town centre on the secluded Podstine cove lies this family-run cheerful hotel with its own beach and a spa and wellness centre. The hotel has regular transfers to and from town, or you can rent a bike, scooter or motorboat. The cheapest rooms have no sea views.

Green Lizard HOSTEL €
(742 560; www.greenlizard.hr; Ulica Domovinskog Rata 13; dm/d 200/460KN; Apr-Oct; @) A friendly and cheerful budget option, a short walk from the ferry. Dorms are simple and clean, there's a communal kitchen and laundry service, and a few doubles are available (with private or shared facilities).

Camping Vira CAMPGROUND €
(741 803; www.campingvira.com; per adult/site 60/97KN; May–mid-Oct; P@) This four-star campground on a beautiful wooded bay 4km from town is one of the best in Dalmatia. There's a gorgeous beach, a lovely cafe and restaurant, and a volleyball court. The facilities are well kept and good quality.

Eating

Hvar's eating scene is good and relatively varied, though, as with the hotels, restaurants often target affluent diners. Make sure you try *hvarska gregada,* the island's traditional fish stew served in many restaurants. At most places, it must be ordered in advance. Note that many restaurants close between lunch and dinner.

Self-caterers can head to the supermarket next to the bus station or pick up fresh supplies at the vegetable market next door.

Konoba Menego DALMATIAN €€
(www.menego.hr; Groda bb; mains from 60KN) This rustic old house on the stairway towards Fortica is kept as simple and authentic as possible. As they say: no grill, no pizza, no Coca-Cola. The place is decked out in Hvar antiques, the staff wear traditional outfits, the service is informative and the marinated meats, cheeses and vegetables are prepared the old-fashioned Dalmatian way.

Divino MEDITERRANEAN €€€
(717 541; www.divino.com.hr; Put Križa 1; mains from 130KN; dinner only) The fabulous location and the island's best wine list are reason enough to splurge at this swank new restaurant. Add innovative food (think rack of lamb with crusted pistacchio) and dazzling views of the Pakleni Islands and you've got a winning formula for a special night out. Or have some sunset snacks and wine on the gorgeous terrace. Book ahead.

Zlatna Školjka MEDITERRANEAN €€
(098 16 88 797; Petra Hektorovića 8; mains from 100KN; dinner Sat & Sun) In a narrow alley packed with restaurants, this slow-food hideaway stands out for its creative fare conjured up by a local celebrity chef. A family-run affair, it has a stone interior and a terrace at the back. Innovative dishes include squid in wild orange sauce and an unbeatable *gregada* (fish stew) with lobster, sea snails and whatever first-class fish was caught that day.

Konoba Luviji DALMATIAN €€
(091 51 98 444; Jurja Novaka 6; mains from 50KN; dinner only) Food brought out of the wood oven at this tavern is simple, unfussy and tasty, although portions are modestly sized. Downstairs is the *konoba* where Dalmatian-style tapas are served, while the restaurant is upstairs on a small terrace, with old-town and harbour views.

Gariful SEAFOOD €€
(742 999; www.hvar-gariful.hr; Riva; mains from 95KN) This is the place to mingle with celebrities coming off their glitzy yachts parked right across the way, over some of Hvar's best-prepared fish and seafood. Prices match the clientele.

Nonica PASTRIES, CAKES €
(Burak 23; 8am-2pm & 5-11pm Mon-Sat, 8am-2pm Sun) Savour the best cakes in town, at this tiny storefront cafe right behind the Arsenal. Try the old-fashioned local biscuits such as *rafioli* and *forski koloc* and the Nonica tart with choco mousse and orange peel.

Luna INTERNATIONAL €€
(Petra Hektorovića 1; mains from 75KN) With its brightly painted walls and 'stairway to heaven' to the rooftop terrace, Luna is a slightly wacky place – a refreshing change from all those traditional and high-class Hvar restaurants. The menu is good, with dishes such as gnocchi with truffles.

Giaxa SEAFOOD €€
(www.giaxa.com; Petra Hektorovića 3; mains from 100KN) This top-end restaurant inside a 15th-century palazzo has a reputation as the place to be seen in Hvar. There is a lovely garden at the back. The food is excellent, with lobster being a popular choice.

Drinking & Entertainment

Hvar has some of the best nightlife on the Adriatic coast, mostly centred on the harbour. People come here to party hard, so expect plenty of action come nightfall.

Falko BEACH BAR
(8am-10pm mid-May–mid-Sep) A 20-minute walk from the town centre, past Hula-Hula and Hotel Amfora, brings you to this adorable hideaway in a pine forest just above the beach. A great unpretentious alternative to the flashy spots closer to town, it serves yummy sandwiches and salads (26KN to 45KN) from a hut, as well as its own limoncello and *rakija* (brandy; try *danderica,* made from a local berry). Think low-key artsy vibe, hammocks and a local crowd.

Carpe Diem LOUNGE BAR
(www.carpe-diem-hvar.com; Riva) Look no further – you have arrived at the mother of Croatia's coastal clubs. From a groggy breakfast to pricey late-night cocktails, there is no time of day when this swanky place is dull.

The house music spun by resident DJs is smooth, there are drinks aplenty, and the crowd is of the jet-setting kind. The **Carpe Diem Beach** on the island of Stipanska is the hottest place to party (from June to September), with daytime beach fun, a restaurant, a spa and all-night parties (100KN for boat transfers; admission is extra and varies depending on the DJ).

Hula-Hula BEACH BAR

(www.hulahulahvar.com) *The* spot to catch the sunset to the sound of techno and house music, Hula-Hula is known for its après-beach party (4pm to 9pm), where all of young, trendy Hvar seems to descend for sundowner cocktails.

Kiva Bar BAR

(www.kivabarhvar.com; Fabrika bb) A happening place in an alleyway behind Nautica. It's packed to the rafters most nights, with a DJ spinning old dance, pop and rock classics that really get the crowd going.

Nautica BAR

(Fabrika bb) With the latest cocktails and non-stop dance music – ranging from techno to hip hop – this disco-style bar is an obligatory stop on Hvar's night-crawl circuit.

Veneranda NIGHTCLUB

(admission 100-150KN; ⌚10pm-4am) A former fortress on the slope above the seafront, Veneranda is Hvar's only real nightclub, with a great sound system and late-night parties fuelled by famous DJs.

Shopping

Lavender, lavender and more lavender is sold in small bottles, large bottles or flasks, or made into sachets. Depending on the time of year, there will be anywhere from one to 50 stalls along the harbour selling the substance, its aroma saturating the air. Various herbal oils, potions, skin creams and salves are also hawked. Check out **Coral Shop** (www.coral-shop-hvar.com; Burak bb), a studio store run by a couple who handcrafts stunning jewellery out of silver, semiprecious stones and coral.

Information

Atlas Hvar (☎741 911; www.atlas-croatia.com) On the western side of the harbour, this travel agency finds private accommodation, rents bikes and boats, and books excursions to Vis, Bol and Dubrovnik.

Clinic (☎717 099; Biskupa Jurja Dubokovića 3) Medical clinic about 700m from the town centre, best for emergencies.

Del Primi (☎091 58 37 864; www.delprimi-hvar.com; Burak 23) Travel agency specialising in private accommodation. Also rents jet skis.

Fontana Tours (☎742 133; www.happyhvar.com; Riva 18) Finds private accommodation, runs excursions, books boat taxis around the island and handles rentals. It has a romantic and isolated two-person apartment on Palmižana (600KN per night).

Francesco (Burak bb; per hr 30KN; ⌚8.30am-midnight) Internet cafe and call centre right behind the post office. Left luggage (35KN per day) and laundry service (50KN per load).

Pelegrini Tours (☎742 743; www.pelegrini-hvar.hr; Riva bb) Private accommodation, boat tickets to Italy with Blue Line, excursions (its daily trips to the Pakleni Islands are popular) and bike, scooter and boat rental.

Post Office (Riva 19; ⌚7am-9pm Mon-Sat) Make phone calls here.

Tourist Office (☎741 059; www.tzhvar.hr; ⌚8am-2pm & 3-9pm Jul & Aug, 8am-2pm & 4-6pm Mon-Sat May, Jun, Sep & Oct, 8am-2pm Mon-Fri, 8am-noon Sat Nov-Apr) Right on Trg Svetog Stjepana.

Stari Grad

POP 2686

Stari Grad (Old Town), on the island's north coast, is a more quiet, cultured and altogether sober affair than its stylish and stunning sister. If you're not after pulsating nightlife and thousands of people crushing each other along the streets in the high season, head for Stari Grad and enjoy Hvar at a more leisurely pace.

Although most ferries connecting the island to the mainland list Stari Grad as their port of call, the town is actually a couple of kilometres northeast of the new ferry terminal. Stari Grad lies along a horseshoe-shaped bay, with the old quarter on the southern side of the horseshoe. The bus station (no left-luggage office) is at the foot of the bay. The northern side is taken up by residences, a small pine wood and the sprawling Helios hotel complex.

Sights

Tvrdalj FORTRESS

(Trg Tvrdalj; admission 10KN; ⌚10am-1pm & 6-9pm Jun-Sep) Tvrdalj is Petar Hektorović's 16th-century fortified castle. The leafy fish pond reflects the poet's love for fish and fishers. His poem *Fishing and Fishermen's Chat* (1555) paints an enticing portrait of his favourite pastime. The castle also contains quotes from the poet's work inscribed on the walls in Latin and Croatian.

Dominican Monastery MONASTERY
(Dominikanski Samostan; admission 10KN; 10am-1pm & 6-9pm Jun-Sep) This old Dominican monastery was founded in 1482, damaged by the Turks in 1571 and later fortified with a tower. In addition to the library and archaeological findings in the monastery museum, there is a 19th-century church with *The Interment of Christ,* attributed to Tintoretto, and two paintings by Gianbattista Crespi.

Sleeping & Eating

One of the agencies arranging private accommodation is **Hvar Touristik** (717 580; www.hvar-touristik.com; Jurja Škarpe 13), which will find doubles with private facilities for between 200KN and 400KN in July and August.

Hostel Sunce HOSTEL €
(092 10 65 152; www.hostelsunce.freshcreator.com; Zagrebačka 10; dm 110KN;) Stari Grad's only hostel has a great location in the old town and a variety of basic but pleasant rooms, from singles to dorms. There's a shared kitchen and dining room, and bike rental. The beach is a 10-minute walk away.

Helios HOTEL €€
(765 866; www.heliosfaros.hr; P) This large, rather soulless complex commandeers the northern wing of the town. Hotels include the three-star **Lavanda** (306 330; s/d 410/735KN) and the two-star **Arkada** (306 306; s/d 450/600KN), as well as **Studio Helios** (765 019; apt from 360KN) and **Trim Apartments** (765 019; 4-person apts 740KN).

Kamp Jurjevac CAMPGROUND €
(765 843; www.heliosfaros.hr; Njiva bb; per adult/tent 33/33KN; Jun-Sep) Near swimming coves off the harbour just east of the old town.

Antika DALMATIAN €
(Donja Kola 24; mains from 45KN) One of Hvar's loveliest restaurants and bars. It has three separate spaces in an ancient, rickety townhouse, tables lining the alleyway and an upstairs terrace that houses a bar. It's the place to hang out at night.

Eremitaž DALMATIAN €€
(Hrvatskih Branitelja; mains from 70KN) A 10-minute walk from town along the seafront towards Hotel Helios, this 15th-century hermitage has a stellar restaurant serving well-prepared Dalmatian staples and more creative dishes in an exposed stone interior and on the seafront terrace.

Shopping

Stari Grad has a small but growing art-gallery scene in the old town.

Little Horse and Baby Beuys GIFTS
(www.littlehorseandbabybeuys.com; Ante Starčevića 2) Supercool clothing for children (and adults), as well as shoes and paintings by the two sisters who own it.

Fantazam JEWELLERY
(www.fantazam.com; Ivana Gundulića 6) Bizarre and stunning jewellery.

Maya Con Dios ART
(Škvor 5) Marine-themed paintings.

Information

Tourist Office (765 763; www.stari-grad-faros.hr; Dr Franje Tuđmana 1; 8am-2pm & 3-9pm Mon-Sat, 9am-1pm & 5-9pm Sun Jun-Sep) Distributes a good local map.

Jelsa

POP 1600

Jelsa is a small town, port and resort 27km east of Hvar Town, surrounded by thick pine forests and high poplars. Although it lacks the Renaissance buildings of Hvar, the intimate streets and squares are pleasant and the town is within easy reach of swimming coves and sand beaches.

Jelsa is wrapped around a bay with several large hotels on each side; the old town sits at the foot of the harbour.

Activities include diving and boat outings. Find out more about the best nearby beaches, private accommodation (around 150KN per person) and hotels at the local **tourist office** (761 017; www.tzjelsa.hr; Riva bb; 8am-2pm & 3-10pm Mon-Sat, 10am-noon & 7-9pm Sun Jul & Aug, 8am-2pm & 3-9pm Mon-Sat May, Jun, Sep & Oct, 8am-1pm Mon-Sat Nov-Apr). A favourite for food is **Konoba Nono** (mains from 80KN), a charming family-run tavern that serves traditional island fare.

VIS ISLAND

POP 3483

Of all the Croatian islands, Vis is the most mysterious – even to locals. The furthest of the main central Dalmatian islands from the coast, Vis spent much of its recent history serving as a military base for the Yugoslav National Army, cut off from foreign visitors from the 1950s right up until 1989. The isolation preserved the island from development and drove much of the population to move elsewhere in search of work, leaving it underpopulated for many years.

As has happened with impoverished islands across the Mediterranean, Vis' lack of development has become its drawcard as a tourist destination. International and local travellers alike now flock to Vis, seeking authenticity, nature, gourmet delights and peace and quiet. Vis produces some of Croatia's best-known wines – *vugava* (white) and *plavac* (red) – and you'll see miles of vineyards across the island. You'll also taste some of the freshest seafood here, thanks to a still-thriving fishing tradition.

Vis is divided between two beautiful small towns at the foot of two large bays: Vis Town, in the northeast; and Komiža, in the southwest. There is friendly rivalry between the two – Vis Town is historically associated with the upper-class nobility while Komiža is proud of its working-class fishing heritage and pirate tales. The rugged coast around the island is dotted with gorgeous coves, caves and a couple of sand beaches. The island's remnants of antiquity, displayed in the Archaeological Museum and elsewhere around Vis Town, offer a fascinating insight into the complex character of this tiny island, which has become a destination for in-the-know travellers.

History

Inhabited first in Neolithic times, Vis Island was settled by the ancient Illyrians, who brought the Iron Age to Vis in the 1st millennium BC. In 390 BC a Greek colony was formed on the island, known then as Issa, from which the Greek ruler Dionysius the Elder controlled other Adriatic possessions. The island eventually became a powerful city state and established its own colonies on Korčula and at Trogir and Stobreč. Allying itself with Rome during the Illyrian wars, the island nonetheless lost its autonomy and became part of the Roman Empire in 47 BC. By the 10th century Vis had been settled by Slavic tribes and was sold to Venice along with other Dalmatian towns in 1420. Fleeing Dalmatian pirates, the population moved inland from the coast.

With the fall of the Venetian Empire in 1797, the island fell under the control of Austria, France, Great Britain, Austria again and then Italy during WWII, as the great powers fought for control of this strategic Adriatic outpost. Over the course of its history, it belonged to nine nations! Perhaps that explains why such a small island has no less than four distinct dialects.

Vis was an important military base for Tito's Partisans. Tito established his supreme headquarters in a cave on Hum Mountain, from where he coordinated military and diplomatic actions with Allied forces and allegedly made his legendary statement: 'We don't want what belongs to others, but we will not give up what belongs to us'.

Getting There & Around

Vis Town is best reached by car ferry from Split (50KN, 2½ hours, two to three daily) or by a fast passenger boat (26KN, 1¼ hours, one daily). Note that it's possible to visit on a day trip during the summer season, but irregular boat hours in low season make it impossible to visit Vis on a daily excursion.

The local **Jadrolinija office** (☎711 032; www.jadrolinija.hr; Šetalište Stare Isse; ⏲8.30am-7pm Mon-Fri, 9am-noon Sat) is in Vis Town. It opens one hour before boat departures.

The only bus transport on the island connects Vis Town with Komiža. The bus meets the Jadrolinija ferries at Vis Town. The connections are prompt in July and August, but you may have to wait in the low season.

Vis Town

POP 1660

On the northeast coast of the island, at the foot of a wide, horseshoe-shaped bay, lies the ancient town of Vis, the first settlement on the island. In only a short walk you can see the remains of a Greek cemetery, Roman baths and an English fortress. Ferry arrivals give spurts of activity to an otherwise peaceful town of coastal promenades, crumbling 17th-century townhouses and narrow alleyways twisting gently uphill from the seafront.

The town, on the southern slope of Gradina hill, is a merger of two settlements: 19th-century Luka on the northwestern part of the bay and medieval Kut in the southeast. The ferry ties up at Luka, from where a harbourside promenade runs

WORTH A TRIP

SWIM & EAT ON VIS

While there are **beaches** around Vis Town and Komiža, some of the island's best are a boat or scooter ride away. Several require downhill walking so bring comfortable shoes. The tourist offices and travel agencies can provide you with maps; many also organise transport.

The most unspoilt beaches are found on the south side of the island. **Stiniva** is Vis' most spectacular cove. Its very narrow rock entrance opens to a pebble beach flanked by rocks 35m high. Also worth a trip are **Srebrna** and **Milna**, as well as the sandy **Stončica** bay east of Vis, where you'll find a beachside tavern serving excellent barbecued lamb. Another great bay is **Rukavac**, with a gorgeous little beachside tavern and taxi boats ready to shuttle you to the island of Ravnik across the way, known for its Green Grotto (50KN), and the islet of Budikovac (100KN, with a visit to the cave).

For a special slow-food meal bordering on a performance, see if you can catch Senko Karuza, the local star poet, philosopher, bon vivant and chef, on a good day. He cooks up mean seafood meals at his house perched over **Mala Travna** bay. Call ahead on ☎099 35 25 803 to see if he's in the mood to have you over. If he is, you're in for a treat.

The interior of the island and its isolated coves are becoming a foodie's dream. In recent years a number of rural households have started offering local homemade food worth travelling for. These include **Golub** (☎098 96 50 327; mains from 50KN), in the hamlet of Podselje, 5km from Vis Town. Specialities include lamb and octopus under *peka* (domed baking lids) and all sorts of marinated and smoked fish, such as the tuna carpaccio. Don't miss the homemade grappas, which come in all flavours, from cactus to nettle and sage. **Konoba Pol Murvu** (☎091 56 71 990; mains from 50KN), in the village of Žena Glava, is known for its amazing tuna *pašticada*, a slow-cooked stew with wine and spices. **Roki's** (☎098 303 483; www.rokis.hr) in Plisko Polje is owned by a local winemaker, so the delicious smoked eel and under-*peka* fare can be washed down with some of the island's best *plavac* (red wine) or *vugava* (white wine). Many of these places will pick you up, often for free, and drop you back in town after the meal. The most recent addition to the island's culinary scene is **Kod Magića** (☎091 89 84 859; entire meal for 230KN), a 10-minute drive east of Vis Town. This family-run affair, smack in the middle of fields and vineyards, does homemade dishes using fresh local ingredients and serves great house wine. Don't skip its broad-bean stew with cuttlefish and *savur*, a Vis speciality with marinated sardines.

to Kut. Small beaches line this promenade, but the busiest town beach is on the west side of the harbour in front of Hotel Issa. Beyond it are nudist coves and a series of wild swimming spots. On the other side, past Kut and the British Naval Cemetery, is the popular pebble beach of Grandovac, which has a beach bar, a stretch of pebbles and a string of rocky beaches on either side.

Sights & Activities

Archaeological Museum MUSEUM

(Arheološki Muzej; Šetalište Viški Boj 12; admission 20KN; ⏲9am-1pm & 5-9pm Mon-Fri, to 1pm Sat Jun-Sep) In addition to extensive archaeological exhibitions, this museum also features a healthy ethnographic collection, including the low-down on the island's fishing, winemaking, shipbuilding and recent history. The 2nd floor has the largest collection of Hellenistic artefacts in Croatia, with Greek pottery, jewellery and sculpture, including an exquisite 4th-century bronze head of a Greek goddess. A leaflet gives an overview of the exhibits, the history of Vis and a useful map showing the locations of the ruins around town. From October to May, access is by appointment through the tourist office.

Island Exploring CYCLING

Scenic **coastal roads**, with their dramatic cliffs and hairpin turns, make it worth renting your own wheels for a day. You can hire mountain bikes (per hour/day 20/70KN), scooters (per three hours/day 120/180KN) and cars (per six hours/day 300/350KN) from Ionios (p240) and **Navigator** (☎717 786; www.navigator.hr; Šetalište Stare Isse 1). Note that most cars for rent on the island are beat-up old things, including the cool-looking cabrios.

Diving DIVING

Diving is excellent in the waters around Vis. Fish are plentiful and there's a **wreck** of an Italian ship dating from the 1866 naval battle between Austria and Italy. **ANMA** (☎091 521 3944; www.anma.hr) has extensive dive programmes; one-tank dives start from 220KN.

Tours

The handful of agencies in town offers tours, which are more or less identical. The most interesting is the tour of the island's **top-secret military sights** abandoned by the Yugoslav National Army in 1992. The trip takes in rocket shelters, bunkers, weapon storage spaces, submarine 'parking lots', Tito's Cave (which housed ex-Yugoslav president Tito during WWII) and nuclear shelters that served as communication headquarters for Yugoslavia's secret service. These sites occupy some of the island's most beautiful spots, only recently made accessible to the public. This tour is offered by **VisIt** (☎091 93 05 265; www.visit.hr; Šetalište Stare Isse 2; ⏰9am-1pm & 5-9.30pm) as well as **Vis Special** (☎711 524; www.vis-special.com; Šetalište Stare Isse 10), starting at 200KN for a two-hour jaunt.

Agencies in town also offer caving in the grottoes around the island, trekking, island tours with food and wine tasting, and boat trips to outer islands that take in the Blue Grotto, the Green Grotto and other great outlying spots.

Sleeping

There are no camping grounds in Vis Town and only a few hotels, but you should have no trouble finding **private lodging** (either rooms or apartments), which is the best way to go. Check www.info-vis.net. In summer, accommodation needs to be booked in advance. Navigator can find private accommodation. You'll pay around 250KN for a double with shared bathroom and 380KN for a double with a private bathroom and terrace. Apartments cost between 380KN and 500KN. The agency also has 14 **luxury seafront villas** (www.visvillas.com; villa 1900-2900KN) for two to 17 people.

Hotel San Giorgio HOTEL €€€
(☎711 362; www.hotelsangiorgiovis.com; Petra Hektorovića 2; s/d 758/1145KN; P❄📶) A gorgeous Italian-owned hotel in Kut, San Giorgio has 10 swish rooms and suites in two buildings. The rooms have wooden floors, great beds and all sorts of upscale perks. Some come with jacuzzis and sea-facing terraces. The restaurant serves creative Mediterranean cuisine, breakfast for nonguests and wine tastings each evening (150KN). Massages are available.

Villa Vis GUESTHOUSE €€
(☎098 94 87 490; www.villaviscroatia.com; Jakšina Ulica 11; s/d 600/750KN; ❄📶) Stylish option in Kut, with four colour-themed rooms, occasional yoga classes and a great location close to beaches and restaurants, all inside an old traditional townhouse with all-modern interiors. The place for hipsters who want style without the price tag.

Dionis B&B €€
(☎711 963; www.dionis.hr; Matije Gubca 1; s/d 430/504KN; ❄) Above the pizzeria with the same name, just off the seafront, is this renovated old stone house with eight rooms and one apartment. All units at the family-run B&B come with TVs and fridges; some have balconies. The triple room in the attic has a lovely terrace with mountain and town vistas.

Hotel Tamaris HOTEL €€€
(☎711 350; www.hotelsvis.com; Svetog Jurja 30; s/d 540/820KN; ❄📶) The best thing about this hotel is the location, in an attractive old building right on the seafront, about 100m southeast of the ferry dock. Its 25 smallish rooms are comfortable, with air-con, phone and TV. It's worth paying 30KN per person extra for a sea-view room and even getting half-board (lunch ends up costing you 15KN). The same hotel company manages **Hotel Issa** across the bay, which has 128 recently spiffed-up rooms with balconies.

Eating

Vis has some of Dalmatia's best restaurants, in the two small towns and the island's interior. There are a few local specialities: *viška pogača,* a flatbread with salted fish and onions, and *viški hib,* dried grated figs with aromatic herbs. Restaurants on the island serve excellent tuna prosciutto.

TOP CHOICE **Pojoda** SEAFOOD €€
(☎711 575; Don Cvjetka Marasovića 8; mains from 70KN) Croats in the know rave about this seafood restaurant with a leafy yard dotted with bamboo, orange and lemon trees. It surely does some mean tricks in its kitchen with fish (from 240KN per kilo), shellfish (260KN per kilo) and crustaceans (from 260KN per kilo). Try *orbiko,* its special dish with orzo, peas and shrimp. For dinner, reserve a table.

Kantun DALMATIAN €€
(Biskupa Mihe Pušića 17; mains from 70KN; ⏰dinner only) The small menu at this seafront tavern offers flavourful local fare made

with quality ingredients. The garden area is vine-covered and intimate, while the interior is a tasteful rustic space of exposed stone. Try the tuna prosciutto, and the artichokes with peas. The bill can be hefty.

Karijola PIZZERIA €
(Šetalište Viškog Boja 4; pizzas from 48KN) The island's best pizza, by the team that runs the namesake pizzeria in Zagreb. This thin-crust concoction comes with high-quality ingredients. The speciality pizza is Karijola, with tomato, garlic, mozzarella and prosciutto. Or try the surprisingly good sauceless white pizza.

Villa Kaliopa MEDITERRANEAN €€€
(☎091 27 11 755; Vladimira Nazora 32; mains from 120KN) In the exotic gardens of the 16th-century Gariboldi mansion, Villa Kaliopa is an upmarket restaurant full of yachting enthusiasts. Tall palm trees, bamboo and classical statuary provide the setting for a menu of Dalmatian specialities, which changes daily. It hosts occasional concerts and exhibits.

Val DALMATIAN €€
(Don Cvjetka Marasovića 1; mains from 70KN) Set in an old stone house, with a shady terrace overlooking the sea. The seasonal menu has an Italian twist; try the wild asparagus in spring, wild boar and mushrooms in winter, and lots of fish in summer. Don't miss the *pašta fazol* with fish.

Buffet Vis SEAFOOD €
(Svetog Jurja 35; mains from 40KN; ⏰closed Sat lunch) This is the cheapest place in town, right by the ferry dock next to Ionis Agency. It's tiny and unadorned, with a few tables outside. It's no frills but great value, with a local vibe and delicious seafood.

Drinking & Entertainment

Paradajz Lost BAR
(Pod Kulom 5) Vis Town's boho spot draws a crowd of artists, hippies and misfits to its cool stone courtyard that lies in the shadow of the tower, steps from the ferry landing in Luka. Pop into the adjacent gallery of a local art collective and listen to old records.

Lambik BAR
(Pod Ložu 2) Kut's best bar has al fresco seating in a lovely vine-covered stone passageway under an ancient colonnade and tables outside on a small square only steps from the seafront. Acoustic bands and singers perform on some nights.

Bejbi CAFE-BAR
(Pod Ložu 4) This cafe-bar in Kut is the place to sip coffee (between outings to the beach) during the day and have cocktails at night.

Summer Cinema CINEMA
(tickets 25KN) Look out for posters advertising the programme of the summer cinema, which sprouts on a terrace roughly halfway between Kut and Luka and attracts a mixed crowd of locals.

Information

You can change money at the bank, post office or any travel agency.

Vis has several wi-fi hotspots, including the Tamaris Bar at the Hotel Tamaris, which has free wi-fi and charges 40KN per hour for using the internet terminals.

Ionios Travel Agency (☎711 532; Svetog Jurja 37 & Pod Ložu 5) Finds private accommodation, changes money, rents cars, bikes and scooters, runs excursions and sells wi-fi vouchers (40KN for one day).

Post Office (Svetog Jurja 25; ⏰8am-8pm Mon-Fri, to 2pm Sat)

Tourist Office (☎717 017; www.tz-vis.hr; Šetalište Stare Isse 5; ⏰8am-2pm & 3-8pm Jun-Sep, 8am-2pm Mon-Fri Oct-May) Right next to the Jadrolinija ferry dock.

Komiža

POP 1519

On the west coast, at the foot of Hum mountain, Komiža is a captivating small town on a bay, with sand and pebble beaches at the eastern end. Komiža has die-hard fans among Croats, who swear by its somewhat bohemian, rough-around-the-edges ambience.

Narrow back streets lined with tawny 17th- and 18th-century townhouses twist uphill from the port, which has been used by fishers since at least the 12th century. East of town is a 17th-century church on the site of a Benedictine monastery, and at the end of the main wharf is a Renaissance citadel dating from 1585 known as the **Kaštel**. Inside is the **Fishing Museum** (admission 15KN; ⏰9-11am & 6-10pm Mon-Sat), which has exhibits of old dusty fishing equipment, plus a lovely rooftop terrace.

The bus from Vis Town stops at the edge of town next to the post office and a few blocks away from the citadel. Walking all the way around the harbour, past the Kaštel, you'll come to the municipal **tourist office** (☎713 455; www.tz-komiza.hr; Riva Svetog Mikule 2;

⏲9am-9pm Mon-Fri, 9am-noon & 6-9pm Sat, 3-9pm Sun Jul-Sep), which gives out very basic info.

Activities

Darlić & Darlić (☎713 760; www.darlic-travel.hr; Riva Svetog Mikule 13), just off the Riva as you're entering town from the bus stop, finds private accommodation from 300KN per double. It rents out scooters (300KN per day), mountain bikes (100KN per day), cabrio cars (400KN per day) and quads (400KN per day). It also has internet terminals (30KN per hour) and wireless access. Its taxi service costs 12KN per kilometre (about 150KN to Vis Town).

The town's most popular **beach**, fringed with pine trees, is right below Hotel Biševo, stretching to Gospa Gusarica church at the far end.

Tours

Darlić & Darlić runs a fun sunset tour to Hum, the island's highest point (150KN for two hours).

Alter Natura (☎717 239; www.alternatura.hr; Hrvatskih Mučenika 2) specialises in adventure tourism, including paragliding, trekking, kayaking and abseiling. It also offers excursions to the Blue Grotto, the islands of Brusnik, Sveti Andrija, Jabuka, Sušac and even the far-out Palagruža. It offers boat transfers to the island's best beaches, including Stiniva and Porat. It also does a guided military tour to Tito's underground tunnels and caves.

Sleeping & Eating

Most of the town action is along the Riva and around Škor, the small square right as you get to the seafront.

For daytime chill-out and late-night parties, head to Kamenica beach, which is home to the seasonal **Aquarius Club** (www.aquariuskomiza.com), hosting well-known DJs who spin anything from house to funk tunes.

Villa Nonna GUESTHOUSE €€

(☎713 500; www.villa-nonna.com; Ribarska 50; apt 630-825KN; ❄📶) This old townhouse has seven renovated apartments, each with wooden floors and a kitchen; some have balconies or patios. Next door is another gorgeous old house, **Casa Nono**, which can sleep six to nine people (from 1700KN to 2500KN per day), with a lovely garden.

Hotel Biševo HOTEL €€€

(☎713 279; www.hotel-bisevo.com.hr; Ribarska 72; s/d from 550/820KN; ❄@) Facilities here are modest and the decor reminiscent of the socialist era, but it's located right near the beach. Try for a renovated room (with fridge and TV) with a sea-facing balcony (60KN extra).

Bako SEAFOOD €€

(Gundulićeva 1; mains from 85KN; ⏲dinner only) The town's best restaurant, with a seaside terrace and excellent food – try the lobster *brodet* (seafood stew with polenta) or *komiška pogača* (fish-filled homemade bread). The cool stone interior contains a fish pond and a collection of Greek and Roman amphorae.

Konoba Jastožera SEAFOOD €€

(☎713 859; Gundulićeva 6; mains from 100KN) Scaly delicacies are served at this town classic where you sit on wooden planks over the water, amid old furniture and fishing paraphernalia. Lobster from a live tank is the speciality (from 700KN per kilogram) – grilled, gratin, boiled…you name it. Reserve ahead. Lunch only from mid-July through mid-August.

Komiža DALMATIAN €

(Riva 17; mains from 50KN) This nondescript seafront restaurant has been around forever, with its old-school naval theme, and waiters and simple down-home food, such as grilled sardines. Plus the views are lovely.

Biševo

The tiny islet of Biševo has little other than vineyards, pine trees and the spectacular **Blue Grotto** (Modra Špilja). Between 11am and noon the sun's rays pass through an underwater opening in this coastal cave to bathe the interior in an unearthly blue light. Beneath the crystal-blue water, rocks glimmer in silver and pink to a depth of 16m. The only catch is that the water can be too choppy for you to enter the cave outside the summer months or when the *jugo* (southern wind) is blowing. When the tourist season is at its peak in July and August, the cave can be woefully crowded and the line of boats waiting to get in discouragingly long. Outside of the high season, you may be able to swim here.

There's a regular boat from Komiža to Biševo (30KN per person) that leaves daily throughout July and August at 8am, returning at 4.30pm, or you can book an excursion through one of the travel agencies. Another option is to rent a boat from one of the agencies (admission 30KN). Many tours also offer excursions to the less-crowded **Green Grotto** (Zelena Špilja), located on the small island of Ravnik.

Dubrovnik & Southern Dalmatia

☎020

Includes »

Best Places to Eat

» LD (p269)
» Oyster & Sushi Bar Bota Šare (p256)
» Lucin Kantun (p256)
» Stermasi (p262)
» Konoba Komin (p269)
» Konoba Šiloko (p271)

Best Places to Stay

» Karmen Apartments (p253)
» Hotel Adriatic (p273)
» Hotel Korkyra (p271)

Why Go?

Dubrovnik is simply unique. It leaves many speechless: its beauty is bewitching, its setting sublime. Not that it's a secret, quite the contrary: thousands of visitors walk along its marble streets every day of the year, gazing, gasping and happily snapping away. But you'll find relaxing spots to escape the crowds, too.

The remarkable old town, ringed by mighty defensive walls, is the city's real highlight, acting as a kind of time capsule for some stunning baroque architecture.

Dubrovnik is also an ideal launching pad for expeditions to the region's lush islands and spectacular coastline: idyllic little Lokrum, lovely Korčula (famous for its excellent white wines and citadel), Mljet National Park, mountainous Pelješac Peninsula and gorgeous Trsteno Gardens.

When to Go

Dubrovnik

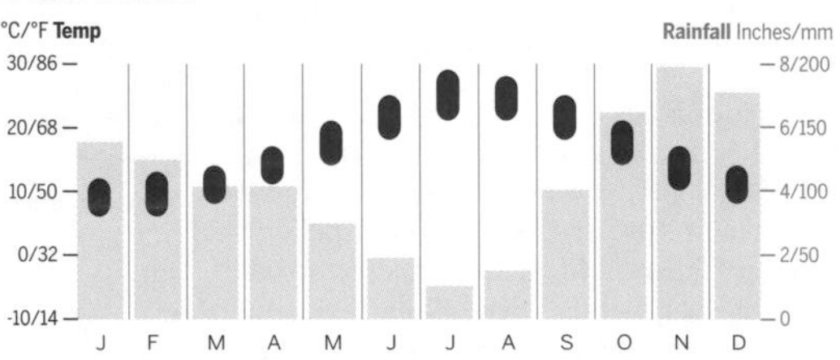

Mar or Apr Spectacular Easter processions through the medieval streets of Korčula.

July–Aug Sate your cultural appetite during Dubrovnik's prestigious Summer Festival.

Oct Sea temperatures are still warm enough for swimming along this coastline.

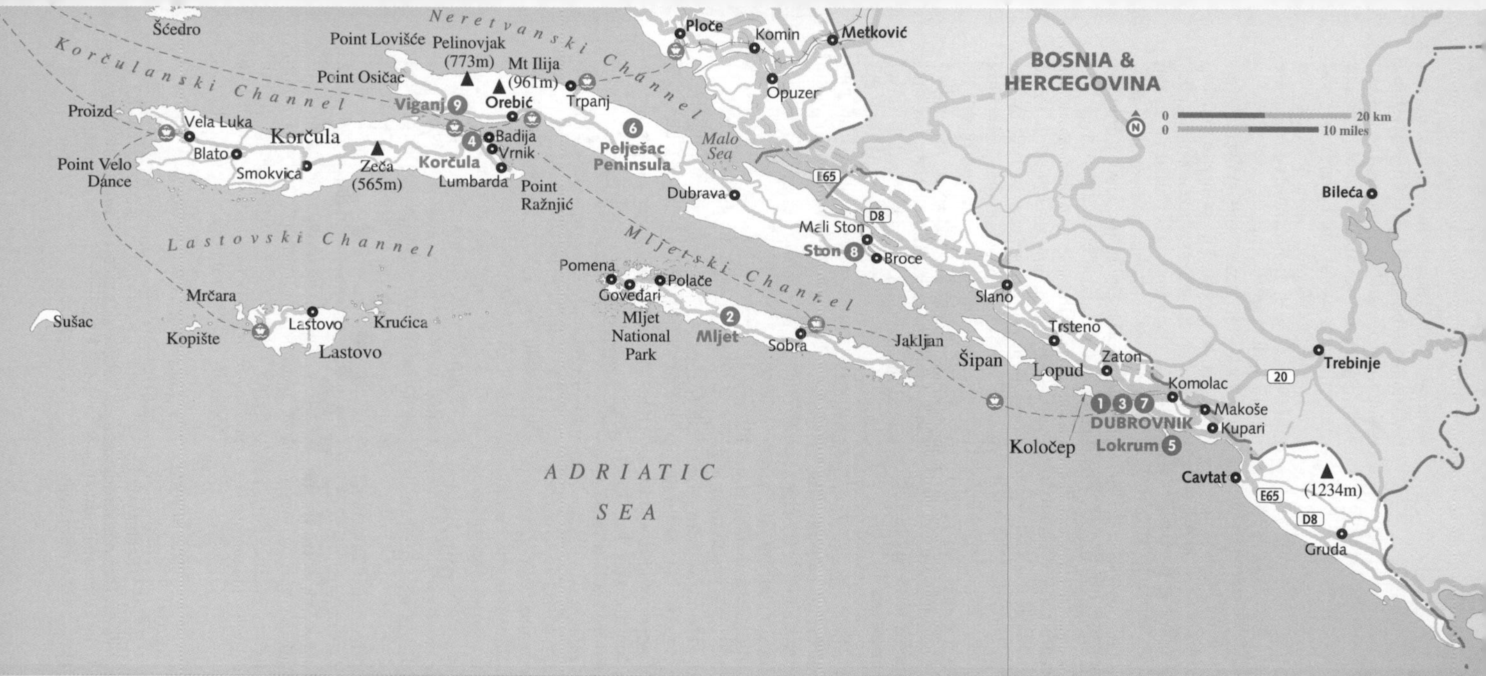

Dubrovnik & Southern Dalmatia Highlights

1 Revel in the most lovely and touristy of activities: seeing Dubrovnik from its **city walls** (p245)

2 Spend a few days on pristine, bucolic **Mljet** (p261), as close as Croatia gets to an island paradise

3 Visit the excellent **War Photo Limited** (p245) gallery in Dubrovnik and put Balkan history in perspective

4 Soak up the medieval atmosphere in the walled city of **Korčula** (p265)

5 Escape the crowds and explore the intriguing islet of **Lokrum** (p260)

6 Hike mountain trails up to the spine of the **Pelješac Peninsula** (p272)

7 Enjoy a sundowner from one of Dubrovnik's **Buža** (p257) bars

8 Dine on oysters in the fascinating old port of **Ston** (p273)

9 Skim across the Adriatic on a board from the windsurfing mecca of **Viganj** (p273)

DUBROVNIK

POP 29,995

Regardless of whether you are visiting Dubrovnik for the first time or the hundredth, the sense of awe and beauty when you set eyes on the Stradun never fades. Indeed it's hard to imagine anyone becoming jaded by the city's marble streets, baroque buildings and the endless shimmer of the Adriatic, or failing to be inspired by a walk along the ancient city walls that have protected this civilised, sophisticated republic for five centuries.

Although the shelling of Dubrovnik in 1991 horrified the world, the city has bounced back with characteristic vigour to enchant visitors again. Take the revamped cable car up to Mt Srđ. Marvel at the Mediterranean lifestyle and the interplay of light and stone. Trace the rise and fall of Dubrovnik in museums replete with art and artefacts. Exhaust yourself retracing history, then plunge into the azure sea.

History

The story of Dubrovnik begins with the 7th-century onslaught of the Slavs that wiped out the Roman city of Epidaurum (site of present-day Cavtat). Residents fled to the safest place they could find, which was a rocky islet (Ragusa) separated from the mainland by a narrow channel. Building walls was a matter of pressing urgency due to the threat of invasion; the city was well fortified by the 9th century when it resisted a Saracen siege for 15 months.

Meanwhile, another settlement emerged on the mainland, stretching from Zaton in the north to Cavtat in the south, and became known as Dubrovnik, named after the *dubrava* (holm oak) that carpeted the region. The two settlements merged in the 12th century, and the channel that separated them was filled in.

By the end of the 12th century Dubrovnik had become an important trading centre on the coast, providing a link between the Mediterranean and Balkan states.

Dubrovnik came under Venetian authority in 1205, finally breaking away from its control in 1358.

By the 15th century the Respublica Ragusina (Republic of Ragusa) had extended its borders to include the entire coastal belt from Ston to Cavtat, having previously acquired Lastovo Island, the Pelješac Peninsula and Mljet Island. It was now a force to be reckoned with. The city turned towards sea trade and established a fleet of its own ships, which were dispatched to Egypt, the Levant, Sicily, Spain, France and Istanbul. Through canny diplomacy the city maintained good relations with everyone – even the Ottoman Empire, to which Dubrovnik began paying tribute in the 16th century.

Centuries of peace and prosperity allowed art, science and literature to flourish, but most of the Renaissance art and architecture in Dubrovnik was destroyed in the earthquake of 1667, which killed 5000 people and left the city in ruins, with only the Sponza Palace and the Rector's Palace surviving. The earthquake also marked the beginning of the economic decline of the town.

The final coup de grâce was dealt by Napoleon whose troops entered Dubrovnik in 1808 and announced the end of the republic. The Vienna Congress of 1815 ceded Dubrovnik to Austria; though the city maintained its shipping, it succumbed to social disintegration. It remained a part of the Austro-Hungarian Empire until 1918 and then slowly began to develop its tourism industry.

Caught in the cross-hairs of the war that ravaged the former Yugoslavia, Dubrovnik was pummelled with some 2000 shells in 1991 and 1992, suffering considerable damage. All of the damaged buildings have now been restored.

Sights

Today Dubrovnik is the most prosperous, elegant and expensive city in Croatia. In many ways it still feels like a city state, isolated from the rest of the nation by geography and history. It's become such a tourism magnet that there's even talk about having to limit visitor numbers in the old town – when several cruise ships disgorge people at the same time, the main thoroughfares can get impossibly crowded.

Dubrovnik extends about 6km from north to south. The bulbous leafy promontory of Lapad in the northwest of the city contains many of the town's hotels. All the sights are in the old town, which is entirely closed to cars. Looming above the city is Mt Srđ, which is connected by cable car to Dubrovnik.

Pile Gate is the main entrance to the old town and the last stop for local buses from Lapad and the harbour of Gruž.

DUBROVNIK IN ...

Two Days

If you've only got a couple of days in Dubrovnik, start early and take a walk along the **City Walls**, seeing the old city on one side, and the endless expanse of the Adriatic on the other. Join the crowds at **Pile Gate**, and head on down the marvellous main street **Placa**, better known as the Stradun. Have coffee and cake at **Sugar & Spice**, and then check out the **Franciscan Monastery & Museum** and the **Dominican Monastery & Museum** before sitting down for a good lunch at **Lucin Kantun**. End the day with a swim and a cocktail at **Ploče Beach**. On the second day visit the marvellous **Rector's Palace** and the **Cathedral of the Assumption of the Virgin**. Make sure you find time to pop in to **Sponza Palace** before dining at the **Oyster & Sushi Bar Bota Šare** and drinking until the wee hours at **Buža bar**.

Four Days

With another couple of days to look around, get a boat to the paradisiacal islet of **Lokrum**, a mere hop away from Dubrovnik. Back in the city, enjoy live music at the **Troubadour bar**. With the beach and the sea beckoning, spend the fourth day exploring **Lapad** and its many beaches.

OLD TOWN

TOP CHOICE City Walls & Forts CITY WALLS

(Gradske Zidine; Map p250; adult/concession 70/30KN; ⌚9am-6.30pm Apr-Oct, 10am-3pm Nov-Mar) No visit to Dubrovnik would be complete without a leisurely walk around the spectacular city walls, the finest in the world and Dubrovnik's main claim to fame. Built between the 13th and 16th centuries, they are still intact today.

The first set of walls to enclose the city was built in the 13th century. In the middle of the 14th century the 1.5m-thick defences were fortified with 15 square forts. The threat of attacks from the Turks in the 15th century prompted the city to strengthen the existing forts and add new ones, so that the entire old town was contained within a stone barrier 2km long and up to 25m high. The walls are thicker on the land side – up to 6m – and range from 1.5m to 3m on the sea side. The round **Minčeta Tower** protects the northern edge of the city from land invasion, while the western end is protected from land and sea invasion by the detached **Lovrjenac Fort**. Pile Gate is protected by the **Bokar Tower**, and the **Revelin Fort** protects the eastern entrance.

The views over the town and sea are sublime, so be sure to take a walk around the walls – it will be the high point of your visit. The main entrance and ticket office to the walls is by the Pile Gate. You can also enter at the Ploče Gate in the east (a wise move at really busy times of day). The walls can only be walked clockwise.

Pile Gate CITY GATE

(Map p250) The natural starting point to any visit to Dubrovnik, this fabulous city gate was built in 1537. Crossing the drawbridge at the gate's entrance, imagine that this was once actually lifted every evening, the gate closed and the key handed to the prince. Notice the **statue of St Blaise**, the city's patron saint, set in a niche over the Renaissance arch. As you pass through the outer gate you come to an inner gate dating from 1460, and soon after you're struck by the gorgeous view of the main street, **Placa**, or as it's commonly known, Stradun, Dubrovnik's pedestrian promenade. It stretches right down to the end of the old town and at its eastern end it widens out into **Luža Square**, formerly used as a marketplace.

TOP CHOICE War Photo Limited PHOTOGRAPHIC GALLERY

(Map p250; ☎326 166; www.warphotoltd.com; Antuninska 6; admission 30KN; ⌚9am-9pm Jun-Sep, 9am-3pm Tue-Sat, to 1pm Sun May & Oct) An immensely powerful experience, this state-of-the-art photographic gallery has beautifully displayed and reproduced exhibitions curated by photojournalist Wade Goddard, who worked in the Balkans in the 1990s.

War Photo declares its intention to 'expose the myth of war...to let people see war as it is, raw, venal, frightening, by focusing

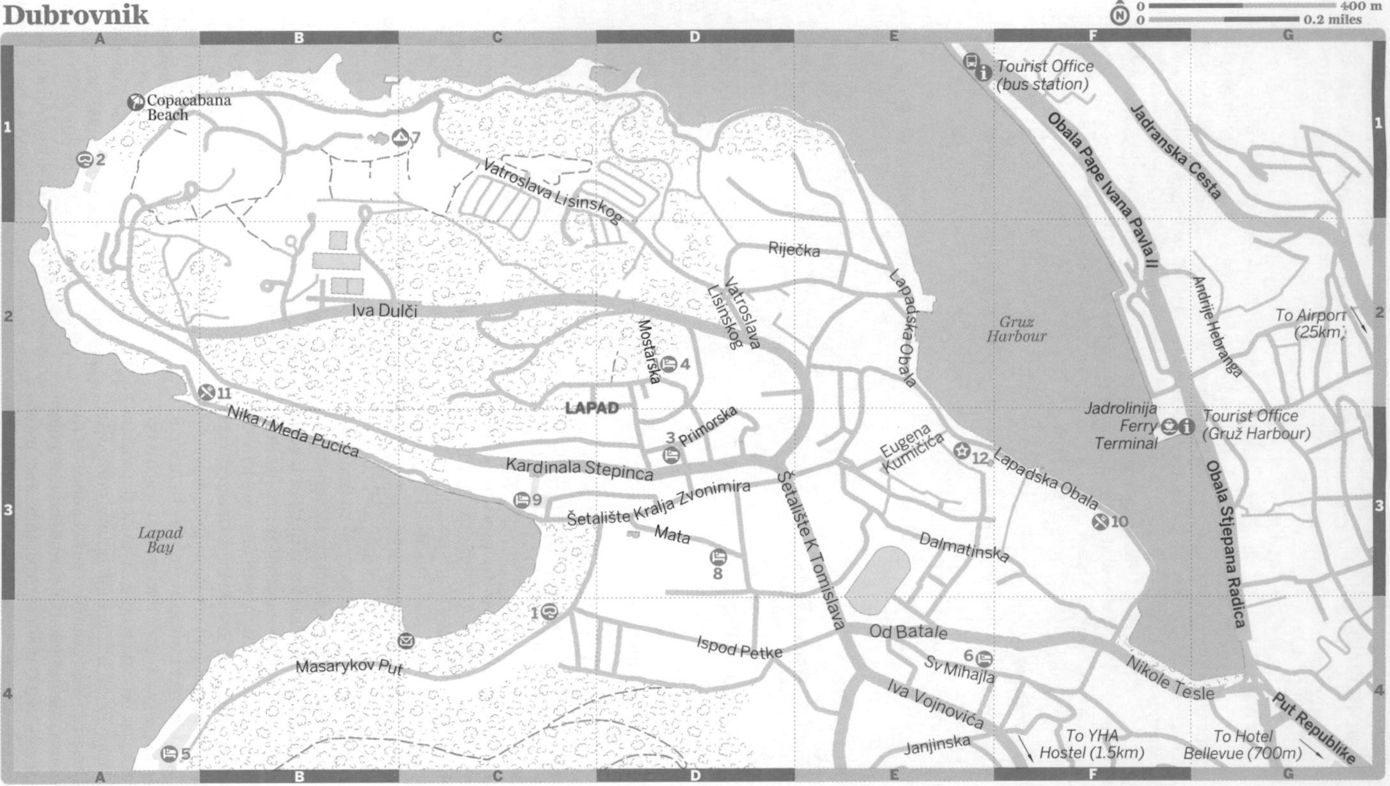
Dubrovnik
0 400 m
0 0.2 miles
Copacabana Beach
Tourist Office (bus station)
Obala Pape Ivana Pavla II
Jadranska Cesta
Vatroslava Lisinskog
Riječka
Lapadska Obala
Gruz Harbour
Andrije Hebranga
To Airport (25km)
Iva Dulči
Mostarska
LAPAD
Primorska
Nika i Meda Pucića
Kardinala Stepinca
Jadrolinija Ferry Terminal
Tourist Office (Gruž Harbour)
Eugena Kumičića
Šetalište Kralja Zvonimira
Šetalište K Tomislava
Mata
Dalmatinska
Obala Stjepana Radica
Lapad Bay
Od Batale
Ispod Petke
Masarykov Put
Sv Mihajla
Nikole Tesle
Iva Vojnovića
Put Republike
Janjinska
To YHA Hostel (1.5km)
To Hotel Bellevue (700m)

Dubrovnik

Activities, Courses & Tours
1 Blue Planet Diving ... C4
2 Navis Underwater Explorers ... A1

Sleeping
3 Begović Boarding House ... D3
4 Dubrovnik Backpackers Club ... D2
5 Dubrovnik Palace ... A4
6 Hotel Ivka ... E4
7 Solitudo ... C1
8 Vila Micika ... D3
9 Villa Wolff ... C3

Eating
10 Blidinje ... F3
11 Levanat ... B2

Entertainment
12 Open-Air Cinema (Lapad) ... E3

on how war inflicts injustices on innocents and combatants alike'. This it achieves with aplomb, as the consequences of conflict are revealed through imagery that's intensely emotive and compelling.

Recent exhibits have included 'Broken Lights of Yugoslavia' by Emmanuel Ortiz, the powerful 'Bosnians' by Paul Lowe, and 'Srebrenica' by Tarik Samarah. There's a permanent exhibition on the upper floor devoted to the war in Yugoslavia, with images from Ron Haviv and audiovisual displays. Note that War Photo closes from November to April.

Franciscan Monastery & Museum — MONASTERY

(Muzej Franjevačkog Samostana; Map p250; Placa 2; adult/concession 30/15KN; ⌚9am-6pm) Over the doorway of this monastery is a remarkable pietà sculpted by the local masters Petar and Leonard Andrijić in 1498. Unfortunately, the portal is all that remains of the richly decorated church, which was destroyed in the 1667 earthquake. Inside the monastery complex is a mid-14th-century **cloister**, one of the most beautiful late-Romanesque structures in Dalmatia. Notice how each capital over the incredibly slim dual columns is topped by a different figure, portraying human heads, animals and floral arrangements. Also enjoyable is the small square garden that's shaded by orange and palm trees.

Further inside you'll find the third-oldest functioning pharmacy in Europe, which has been in business since 1391 – it may have been the first pharmacy in Europe open to the general public. The small monastery museum has a collection of relics, liturgical objects including chalices, paintings, gold jewellery and pharmacy items such as laboratory gear and medical books. Ammunition remains that pierced the monastery walls during the 1990s war have been saved, too.

There's often a good exhibition of photographs or art on display here.

Dominican Monastery & Museum — MONASTERY

(Muzej Dominikanskog Samostana; Map p250; off Ulica Svetog Dominika 4; adult/concession 20/10KN; ⌚9am-6pm May-Oct, to 5pm Nov-Apr) This imposing structure is a real architectural highlight, built in a transitional Gothic-Renaissance style and containing a rich trove of paintings. Constructed around the same time as the city walls in the 14th century, the monastery's stark exterior resembles a fortress more than a religious complex. The interior contains a graceful 15th-century cloister constructed by local artisans after the designs of the Florentine architect Massa di Bartolomeo, and a large, single-naved church with an altarpiece by Vlaho Bukovac. The eastern wing contains the monastery's impressive art collection; notice the works of Nikola Božidarević, Dobrić Dobričević and Mihajlo Hamzić.

Rector's Palace — PALACE

(Map p250; Pred Dvorom 3; adult/concession 35/15KN, audioguide 30KN; ⌚9am-6pm May-Oct, to 4pm Nov-Apr) The Gothic-Renaissance Rector's Palace was built in the late 15th century and is adorned with outstanding sculptural ornamentation. It retains a striking compositional unity despite being rebuilt many times. Notice the finely carved capitals and the ornate staircase in the atrium, which is often used for concerts during the Summer Festival. Also in the atrium is a statue of Miho Pracat, who bequeathed his wealth to the Republic and was the only commoner in the 1000 years of the Republic's existence to be honoured with a statue (1638). We may assume that the bequest was considerable. The palace was built for the rector who governed Dubrovnik, and it contains the rector's office, his private chambers, public halls and administrative offices. Interestingly, the elected rector was not permitted to leave the building during his one-month term without the permission of the senate. Today the palace has been turned into a museum with artfully restored rooms, portraits, coats-of-arms and coins, evoking the glorious history of Dubrovnik.

Cathedral of the Assumption of the Virgin CATHEDRAL

(Stolna Crkva Velike Gospe; Map p250; Poljana M Držića; ⊙morning & late-afternoon Mass) Built on the site of a 7th-century basilica that was enlarged in the 12th century, the original Cathedral of the Assumption of the Virgin was supposedly the result of a gift from England's King Richard I, the Lionheart, who was saved from a shipwreck on the nearby island of Lokrum. Soon after the first cathedral was destroyed in the 1667 earthquake, work began on this new cathedral, which was finished in 1713 in a baroque style. The cathedral is notable for its fine altars, especially the altar of St John Nepomuk, made of violet marble. The cathedral **treasury** (Riznica; adult/concession 10/5KN; ⊙8am-5.30pm Mon-Sat, 11am-5.30pm Sun May-Oct, 10am-noon & 3-5pm Nov-Apr) contains relics of St Blaise as well as 138 gold and silver reliquaries largely made in the workshops of Dubrovnik's goldsmiths between the 11th and 17th centuries. Among a number of religious paintings, the most striking is the polyptych of the Assumption of the Virgin, made in the workshop of 16th-century Italian painter Titian.

Sponza Palace PALACE

(Map p250; Stradun) The 16th-century Sponza Palace was originally a customs house, then a minting house, a state treasury and a bank. Now it houses the **State Archives** (Državni Arhiv u Dubrovniku; admission 20KN; ⊙8am-3pm Mon-Fri, to 1pm Sat), which contain a priceless collection of manuscripts dating back nearly a thousand years. This superb structure is a mixture of Gothic and Renaissance styles beginning with an exquisite Renaissance portico resting on six columns. The 1st floor has late-Gothic windows and the 2nd-floor windows are in a Renaissance style, with an alcove containing a statue of St Vlaho. Also inside is the **Memorial Room of the Defenders of Dubrovnik** (⊙10am-10pm Mon-Fri, 8am-1pm Sat), a heartbreaking collection of portraits of young people who perished between 1991 and 1995.

St Ignatius Church CHURCH

(Crkva Svetog Ignacija; Map p250; Uz Jezuite; ⊙late-evening Mass) Built in the same style as the Cathedral of the Assumption of the Virgin and completed in 1725, the St Ignatius Church has frescos displaying scenes from the life of St Ignatius, founder of the Jesuit society. Abutting the church is the **Jesuit College**, located at the top of a broad flight of stairs leading down to the square Gundulićeva Poljana, where a bustling **morning market** is held. The monument in the centre of the square commemorates Dubrovnik's famous poet, Ivan Gundulić. Reliefs on the pedestal depict scenes from his epic poem, *Osman*.

St Blaise's Church CHURCH

(Crkva Svetog Vlahe; Luža Sq; ⊙morning & late-afternoon Mass Mon-Sat) Imposing church built in 1715 in a baroque style whose ornate exterior contrasts strongly with the sober residences surrounding it. The interior is notable for its marble altars and a 15th-century silver gilt statue of the city's patron, St Blaise, who is holding a scale model of pre-earthquake Dubrovnik.

Onofrio Fountain FOUNTAIN

(Map p250) One of Dubrovnik's most famous landmarks, Onofrio Fountain was built in 1438 as part of a water-supply system that involved bringing water from a well 12km away. Originally the fountain was adorned with sculpture, but it was heavily damaged in the 1667 earthquake and only 16 carved masks remain with water gushing from their mouths into a drainage pool.

Serbian Orthodox Church & Museum CHURCH, MUSEUM

(Muzej Pravoslavne Crkve; Map p250; Od Puča 8; adult/concession 10/5KN; ⊙9am-2pm Mon-Sat) Dating from 1877, the Serbian Orthodox Church & Museum has a fascinating collection of icons dating from the 15th to 19th centuries. In addition to portraits of the biblical family originating in Crete, Italy, Russia and Slovenia, there are several portraits by the illustrious Croatian painter Vlaho Bukovac. The church's icons were on loan in Belgrade for an exhibition at the time of research, but should be returned to the church by 2013.

Synagogue SYNAGOGUE

(Sinagoga; Map p250; Žudioska 5; admission 20KN; ⊙10am-8pm Mon-Fri May-Oct, to 3pm Nov-Apr) The oldest Sephardic and second-oldest synagogue in the Balkans dates back to the

15th century. Inside is a museum that exhibits religious relics and documentation on the local Jewish population.

St Saviour Church CHURCH
(Crkva Svetog Spasa; Map p250; Placa) Built between 1520 and 1528, this church was one of the few buildings to survive the earthquake of 1667. It's open for occasional exhibitions and candlelight concerts.

Ethnographic Museum MUSEUM
(Etnografski Muzej; Map p250; Od Rupa; adult/concession 40/20KN; ⌚9am-4pm Sun-Fri) Sitting in the 16th-century Rupe Granary, the Ethnographic Museum contains exhibits relating to agriculture and local customs.

Orlando Column MONUMENT
(Map p250; Luža Sq) The Orlando Column is a popular meeting place that used to be the spot where edicts, festivities and public verdicts were announced. Carved in 1417, the forearm of this medieval knight was the official linear measure of the Republic – the ell of Dubrovnik, which measures 51.1cm.

Maritime Museum MUSEUM
(Map p250; adult/concession 40/20KN; ⌚9am-6pm May-Sep, to 4pm Oct-Apr) Inside St John Fort, this museum traces the history of navigation in Dubrovnik with ship models, maritime objects and paintings.

EAST OF THE OLD TOWN

TOP CHOICE **Cable Car** CABLE CAR
(Map p250; www.dubrovnikcablecar.com; Petra Krešimira IV; adult/concession 87/50KN; ⌚9am-10pm Tue-Sun May-Oct, shorter hours rest of year) Dubrovnik's cable car whisks you from just north of the city walls up to Mt Srđ in under four minutes. At the end of the line there's a stupendous perspective of the city, from a lofty 405m down to the terracotta-tiled rooftops of the old town and the island of Lokrum, with the Adriatic and distant Elafiti Islands filling the horizon. Telescopes help you pick out details far, far below. There's a snack bar and a restaurant.

Homeland War Museum MUSEUM
(www.tzdubrovnik.hr; admission 20KN; ⌚8am-6pm daily Apr-Oct, 9am-4pm daily Nov-Mar) Dedicated to the 'Homeland War' – as the 1990s war is dubbed in Croatia – this is an interesting place for those who want to learn more about Dubrovnik's wartime history. Set inside a Napoleonic Fort and just above where the cable car drops you off, it displays the ammunition used to shell Dubrovnik and shows a detailed map of the damage wreaked on the city, as well as videos of the bombardment.

Museum of Modern Art MUSEUM
(Frana Supila 23; ⌚10am-7pm Tue-Sun) Features contemporary Croatian artists, particularly the local painter Vlaho Bukovac.

Activities

Swimming

There are several city beaches, but many take a boat to Lokrum Island or one of the Elafitis for more seclusion.

Banje Beach, around 600m east of the Ploče Gate, is the most popular city beach, though it's even more crowded now that a section has been roped off for the exclusive EastWest Club. Just southeast of here is **Sveti Jakov**, a good local beach that doesn't get rowdy and has showers, a bar and a restaurant. Buses 5 and 8 will get you there.

On the west side of the city, beaches past the Pile Gate include the pebbly **Šulići** and the rocky **Danče**. The nicest beach that's walkable from the old town is below Hotel Bellevue, where you'll find a lovely sheltered cove backed by high cliffs (which cast a shadow over its pebbled shore by late afternoon). It's fun watching kids high-dive into the sea here.

Lapad Bay is brimming with hotel beaches that you can use without a problem; try the bay by Hotel Kompas. A little further on is **Copacabana Beach** on Babin Kuk peninsula, a good shallow beach with a slide for kids. If you're a naturist, head down to **Cava**, signposted near Copacabana Beach.

In the old town, you can also swim below the two Buža bars, on the outside of the city walls. Steps help swimmers get in and out, and sunbathers can make use of cemented space between the rocks.

Diving, Kayaking & Rafting

There's some great diving around Dubrovnik.

Navis Underwater Explorers (Map p246; ☎099 35 02 773; www.navisdubrovnik.com; Copacabana Beach) offers recreational dives (including the wreck of the *Taranto*) and courses. **Blue Planet Diving** (Map p246; ☎091 89 90 973; www.blueplanet-diving.com; Masarykov Put 20, Hotel Dubrovnik Palace) offers the same services.

Dubrovnik Old Town

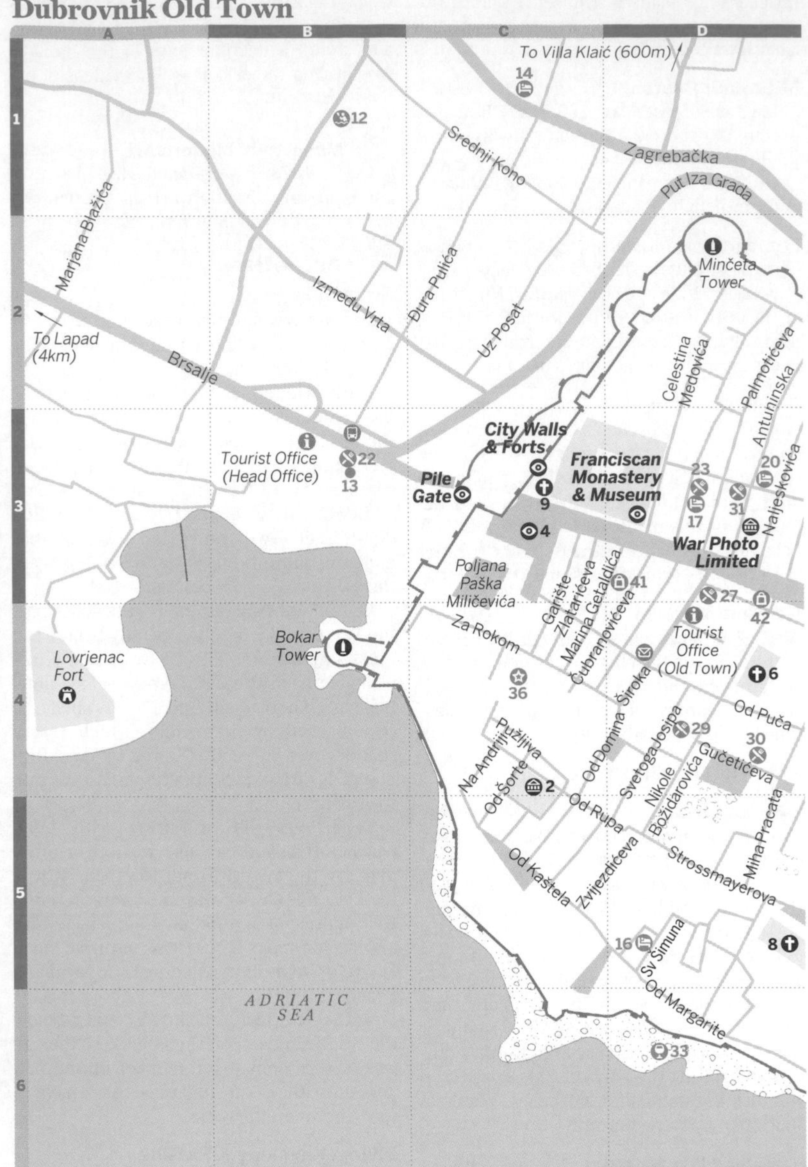

Contact **Adriatic Kayak Tours** (Map p250; ☎091 72 20 413; www.adriatickayaktours.com; Zrinsko Frankopanska 6) for kayak excursions (from a half-day paddle to a weeklong trip); it also offers white-water rafting on the Tara River in Montenegro.

Tours

Dubrovnik Walks WALKING

(Map p250; ☎095 80 64 526; www.dubrovnikwalks.com) Excellent guided walks in English. One-hour old-town tours (90KN) run daily at 10am and either 6pm (May, June, Septem-

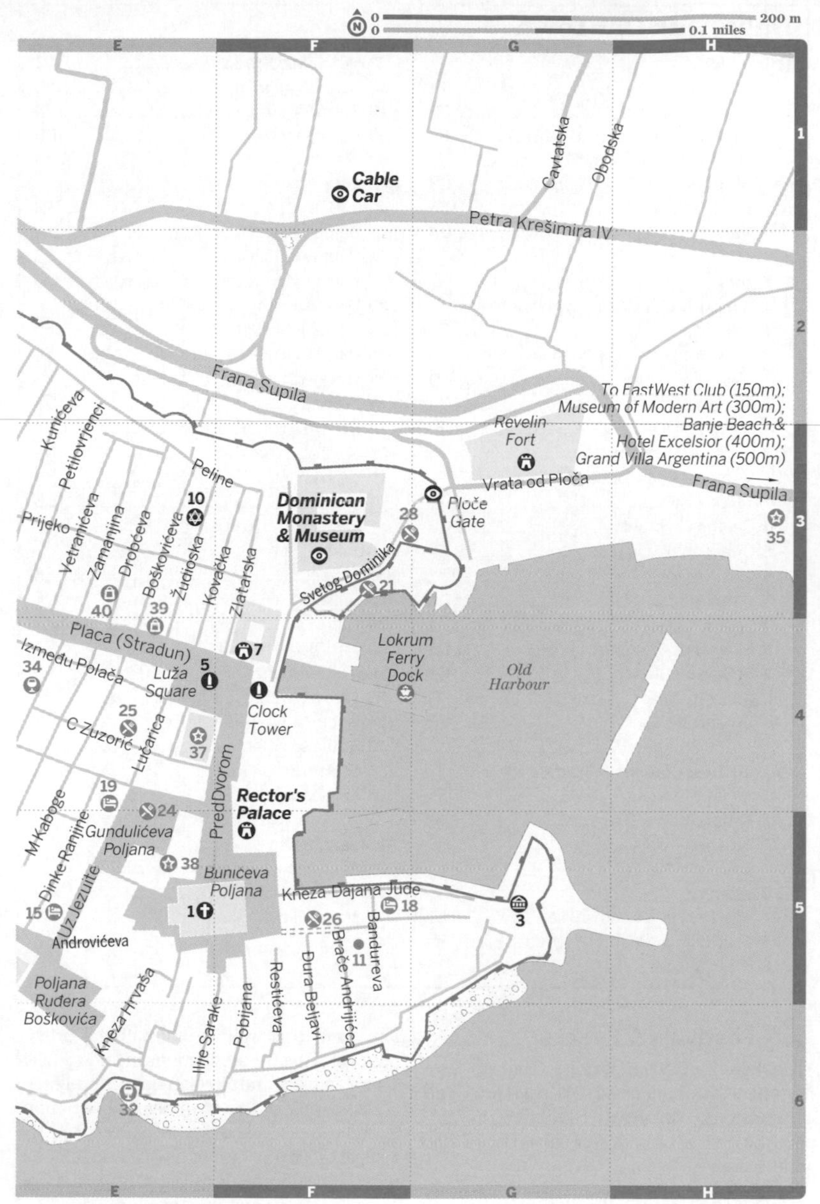

ber and October) or 7pm (July and August). It also offers 1½-hour walks of Dubrovnik's walls and forts (160KN) daily at 9.30am and 3.30pm (5.30pm July and August). The meeting place is the Fuego club just west of the Pile Gate. No reservation is necessary.

Adriatic Explore BUS, BOAT

(Map p250; ☎323 400; www.adriatic-explore.com; Bandureva 4) Day trips to Mostar and Montenegro (both 360KN) are very popular. Excursions to Korčula and Pelješac (390KN) are offered, too.

Dubrovnik Old Town

Top Sights
- Cable Car ... F1
- City Walls & Forts ... C3
- Dominican Monastery & Museum ... F3
- Franciscan Monastery & Museum ... D3
- Pile Gate ... C3
- Rector's Palace ... F5
- War Photo Limited ... D3

Sights
1 Cathedral of the Assumption of the Virgin ... E5
Cathedral of the Assumption of the Virgin Treasury ... (see 1)
2 Ethnographic Museum ... C4
Jesuit College ... (see 8)
3 Maritime Museum ... G5
Memorial Room of the Defenders of Dubrovnik ... (see 7)
4 Onofrio Fountain ... C3
5 Orlando Column ... E4
6 Serbian Orthodox Church & Museum ... D4
7 Sponza Palace ... F4
8 St Ignatius Church ... D5
9 St Saviour Church ... C3
State Archives ... (see 7)
10 Synagogue ... E3

Activities, Courses & Tours
11 Adriatic Explore ... F5
12 Adriatic Kayak Tours ... B1
13 Dubrovnik Walks ... B3

Sleeping
14 Apartments & Rooms Biličić ... C1
15 Apartments Amoret ... E5
16 Fresh Sheets ... D5
17 Hotel Stari Grad ... D3
18 Karmen Apartments ... F5
19 Pucić Palace ... E4
20 Rooms Vicelić ... D3

Eating
21 360° by Jeffrey Vella ... F3
Defne ... (see 19)
22 Dubravka 1836 ... B3
Konzum ... (see 24)
23 Lucin Kantun ... D3
24 Morning Market ... E5
25 Oliva Gourmet ... E4
26 Oyster & Sushi Bar Bota Šare ... F5
27 Proto ... D3
28 Revelin ... F3
29 Sugar & Spice ... D4
30 Taj Mahal ... D4
31 Wanda ... D3

Drinking
32 Buža ... E6
33 Buža II ... D6
34 Gaffe ... E4

Entertainment
35 Lazareti ... H3
36 Open-Air Cinema (Old Town) ... C4
37 St Blaise's Church ... E4
St Saviour Church ... (see 9)
38 Troubadur ... E5

Shopping
39 Algoritam ... E4
40 Lega-Lega ... E3
41 Magnolika ... D3
42 Uje ... D3

Festivals & Events

The **Feast of St Blaise** (3 February) is a city-wide bash marked by pageants and processions. **Carnival** festivities heralding the arrival of Lent in February are also celebrated.

Dubrovnik Summer Festival CULTURAL
(☎326 100; www.dubrovnik-festival.hr; tickets 50-300KN) The Dubrovnik Summer Festival is the most prestigious summer festival in Croatia. For five weeks in July and August a programme of theatre, concerts and dance is presented on open-air stages throughout the city. National artists and regional folklore groups, as well as international artists, perform. Theatre productions include Shakespearean plays and Greek tragedies and there are performances by chamber and symphonic orchestras. Tickets are available from the festival office on Placa or on-site one hour before the beginning of each performance. You can also reserve and buy them online.

Libertas Film Festival FILM
(www.libertasfilmfestival.com) Libertas Film Festival takes place between 29 June and 4 July, with films, documentaries and shorts being screened in the open air at old town venues.

DUBROVNIK: DESTRUCTION & RECONSTRUCTION

Many remember the TV footage of the shelling of Dubrovnik. Although now in the past, the memory of the city's year at war remains in the minds of locals – you'll see reminders of it on several plaques through the old town.

Shells struck 68% of the 824 buildings in the old town, leaving holes in two out of three tiled roofs. Building facades and the paving stones of streets and squares suffered 314 direct hits and there were 111 strikes on the great wall. Nine historic palaces were completely gutted by fire, while the Sponza Palace, Rector's Palace, St Blaise's Church, Franciscan Monastery and the carved fountains, Amerling and Onofrio, all sustained serious damage. The reconstruction bill was estimated at US$10 million. It was quickly decided that the repairs and rebuilding would be done with traditional techniques, using original materials whenever feasible.

Dubrovnik has since regained most of its original grandeur. The great town walls are once again intact, the gleaming marble streets are smoothly paved and famous monuments, such as the 15th-century Onofrio Fountain and the Clock Tower, have been lovingly restored. Damage to Sponza Palace, Rector's Palace, St Blaise's Church, the cathedral, and various 17th-century residences has been repaired with the help of an international brigade of specially trained stonemasons.

Park Orsula Music Festival MUSIC
(www.parkorsula.du-hr.net) There is a wonderful summer music festival at Park Orsula between mid-June and September featuring local musicians, from jazz to hip hop, traditional Dalmatian music and classical performances. The park is on a hill overlooking the city and the atmosphere is fantastic.

Sleeping

Dubrovnik is not a large city, but as it's such a big draw, accommodation is scattered all over the place. It's the most expensive city in the country – so expect to have to pay more for a room here. Lots of midrange hotels are in Lapad, 4km west of the centre; there's very little accommodation in the old town. As the bus system is good, it's not so bad to be located away from the centre. Book all accommodation well in advance, especially in the summer season.

If you're on a budget, you'll have little choice but to go for private accommodation: contact the recommended travel agencies or the tourist office for options. Beware the scramble of private owners at the bus station and ferry terminal. Some provide what they say they offer, others are scamming – try to pin down the location in advance if you want to be able to walk to the old town. Note that if you stay in unlicensed accommodation you are unprotected in case of a problem; all registered places should have a blue *sobe* (rooms available) sign. In high season, expect to pay from 300KN for a double room or from 500KN for an apartment.

OLD TOWN & AROUND

TOP CHOICE **Karmen Apartments** APARTMENTS €€
(Map p250; ☎098 619 282, 323 433; www.karmendu.com; Bandureva 1; apt 450-1200KN;) Run by Marc Van Bloemen, an Englishman who has lived in Dubrovnik for decades, these four inviting, homely apartments enjoy a great location a stone's throw from Ploče harbour. All have plenty of character and are individually styled with art, splashes of colour, tasteful furnishings and books to browse. Apartment 2 has a little balcony while Apartment 1 enjoys sublime port views. Marc and his mother look after their guests very well indeed. Book well ahead.

TOP CHOICE **Hotel Bellevue** HOTEL €€€
(☎330 000; www.hotel-bellevue.hr; Petra Čingrije 7; d from 1900KN; P@) Ignore the slightly dated tinted-glass frontage, this is a very classy hotel indeed. Positioned on a cliff overlooking the Adriatic, all rooms boast balconies that make the most of the inspirational views. Decor is modern, facilities are excellent, the staff is very switched-on and the restaurant, Vapor, is top-notch. Best of all there's a gem of a cove beach below, and the hotel's lift offers direct access. Fitness facilities are poor, but there's a nice spa. It's a 15-minute walk west of the Pile Gate.

TOP CHOICE **Fresh Sheets** HOSTEL €
(Map p250; ☎091 79 92 086; www.igotfresh.com; Sv Šimuna 15; dm/d 210/554KN; @) The only hostel in the old town is a classic

backpackers, warm and welcoming with a lively atmosphere. It's in a quiet location right by the city walls, close to Buža bar; it's a small hike, but worth it. Downstairs there's space for socialising and cold beers in the fridge. Upstairs there are two clean and simple eight-bed dorms with lockers and fans, a four-bed dorm and a cosy double with a sea view. Fresh Sheets is run by a super hospitable crew who organise imaginative outings, international dinners and other fun stuff.

Apartments Amoret APARTMENTS €€
(Map p250; ☎091 53 04 910; www.dubrovnik-amoret.com; Dinke Ranjine 5; apt 755-1423KN; ❄📶) Spread over three historic buildings in the heart of the old town, Amoret offers 11 high-quality renovated studio apartments, all with bathroom and wi-fi. Elegant decor, tasteful furniture, a dash of art and parquetry flooring feature throughout. Cooking facilities are kitchenette-style. Amoret 1 has a pleasant guests' terrace. No breakfast is offered.

Hotel Excelsior HOTEL €€€
(☎353 353; www.hotel-excelsior.hr; Frana Supila 12; s/d from 1640/1960KN; P❄@📶🏊) Dubrovnik's best address had an impressive €22 million renovation in 2008, and it wasn't in vain. There's a sense of occasion about this hotel, the haunt of royalty and Hollywood stars. Rooms and suites are simply wonderful, with modish furnishings, and many have remarkable views of the walled city. Its four restaurants offer everything from Slavonian paprika stews to sushi. Leisure facilities are top-notch (indoor and outdoor pools) and service is very polished indeed. It's a short stroll from the old town.

Apartments & Rooms Biličić RENTAL ROOMS €
(Map p250; ☎417 152; www.dubrovnik-online.com/apartments_bilicic; Privežna 2; r/apt 450/870KN; ❄) A highly atmospheric place to stay within walking distance of the old town (via some vertiginous steps). Offers bright, clean and pleasant rooms with a homely touch and TVs (though bathrooms are not en suite). There's a gorgeous garden with subtropical plants and quirky seating, and a guests' kitchen. Marija, the extremely hospitable and friendly owner, will pick you up from local transport terminals and offers advice about what to do in Dubrovnik.

Villa Klaić PRIVATE ACCOMMODATION €€
(☎411 144; Šumetska 11; s/d 288/492KN; P❄@🏊) In terms of service, five-star hotels could learn a lot from the owner, Milo Klaić, a worldly, hospitable character who takes a lot of trouble to make sure his guests are happy. Rooms are simple but comfortable (all with shower), and two have air-con. Free pick-ups are offered and there's a private outdoor swimming pool. The location is just off the main coast road, high above town, but free bus tickets are included (so if you can't face the hike, don't).

Hotel Stari Grad BOUTIQUE HOTEL €€€
(Map p250; ☎322 244; www.hotelstarigrad.com; Od Sigurate 4; s/d 1350/1800KN; ❄📶) This old-town hotel is all about location – it's very close to the Pile Gate and just off the Stradun. Its eight rooms are neat, attractive and smallish, but they're well presented and don't fall short on comfort. Staff are sweet and you'll enjoy the dramatic city views from the rooftop terrace. Note the hotel has many flights of stairs to negotiate (and no lift).

Pucić Palace HISTORIC HOTEL €€€
(Map p250; ☎326 222; www.thepucicpalace.com; Od Puča 1; s/d 2400/3900KN; ❄@📶) This is the only luxury hotel inside the city walls. Located in a converted aristocrat's mansion, it has a prime spot next to Luža Sq. Rooms are well furnished and boast high comfort levels (Egyptian cotton linen and antiques), though perhaps the design lacks a real 'wow' factor. It's classy and convenient, but the location commands a stratospheric price tag (which at least allows you complimentary access to a private beach nearby). Service standards could be improved.

Grand Villa Argentina HOTEL €€€
(☎440 555; www.gva.hr; Frana Supila 14; d from 1550KN; P❄@📶🏊) A kind of luxury city state, this five-star hotel has expanded its empire to include four luxury villas. All are grouped together a 10-minute walk east of the old town's Ploče Gate. Decor is a little chintzy with busily patterned bedspreads and swirling carpets, but all boast enviable views of the city walls and the comfort level can't be faulted. There are indoor and outdoor pools, and a wellness centre.

Rooms Vicelić RENTAL ROOMS €€
(Map p250; ☎098 97 90 843; www.roomsvicelic.hostel.com; Antuninska 9 & 10; r 585KN; ❄@📶) Quirky old-town place run by a friendly family with neat modern rooms, most of which have been recently renovated. All have a private bathroom (some are not en

suite though) and there are cooking facilities. Cash only.

YHA Hostel HOSTEL €
(☎423 241; dubrovnik@hfhs.hr; Vinka Sagrestana 3; dm 155KN; @) Its location is pretty good, in a quiet area 1km west of the old town, and this midsized hostel has decent, spacious if plain dorms (and one double). If you're allowed to choose a bed (rare), the best dorms are 31 and 32, which share a roof terrace. Rates include breakfast. Book ahead.

LAPAD

About 4km west of the old town, the leafy Lapad peninsula is a tranquil place to stay with a mix of residential and tourist neighbourhoods, including some package hotels. A walk along the coast past Hotel Kompas leads to lots of spots for sunbathing and swimming. Bus 6 runs between Pile Gate and Lapad.

Begović Boarding House PRIVATE ACCOMMODATION €
(Map p246; ☎435 191; www.begovic-boarding-house.com; Primorska 17; dm/r/apt 150/320/385KN; P @) A steep walk uphill from Lapad harbourfront, this is a very popular and welcoming family-run place where the English-speaking owners go to a lot of trouble to please their guests. Pine-trimmed rooms (with crisp linen) are smallish but very clean, and some open onto a wonderful communal garden with amazing views. A free pick-up is offered from the bus station or ferry terminal. Breakfast is extra, internet access is free and there's a kitchen. The family also organises excursions.

Hotel Ivka HOTEL €€
(Map p246; ☎362 600; www.hotel-ivka.com; Put Sv Mihajla 21; s/d 593/785KN; P ❄ @ ☜) Modern three-star hotel with pleasant, spacious rooms that have wooden floors (and most have a balcony) and free wi-fi. Comfort levels are high given the prices asked. It's closer to Lapad and the ferry terminal than the old town, but on a regular bus route.

Villa Wolff HOTEL €€€
(Map p246; ☎438 710; www.villa-wolff.hr; Nika i Meda Pucića 1; d/ste 1356/1569KN; P ❄ @ ☜) On a lovely seaside promenade, Wolff has six tasteful rooms, a verdant garden and very high service standards. Rates are a little steep, though.

Dubrovnik Backpackers Club HOSTEL €
(Map p246; ☎435 375; www.dubackpackers.com; Mostarska 2d; dm 120-170KN; @ ☜) Run by a very hospitable family, this sociable, popular backpackers has free internet, local calls, and tea/coffee, and shots of *rakija* (brandy) are gratis from time to time. You have to pay for your bed; it's extra for an en-suite dorm. There's a guests' kitchen and a balcony with bay views, and trips to Mostar are offered.

Vila Micika RENTAL ROOMS €€
(Map p246; ☎437 332; www.vilamicika.hr; Mata Vodapića; s/d/tr 210/420/637KN; P ❄ ☜) An attractive two-storey stone structure with seven simple rooms, all with a bathroom. It's about 300m from the shore and has a terrace for socialising. Good value, but you'll pay extra for breakfast, short stays and air-con (73KN per day).

Dubrovnik Palace HOTEL €€€
(Map p246; ☎430 000; www.dubrovnikpalace.hr; Masarykov Put 20; d from 1880KN; P ❄ @ ☜ ≋) Spilling down the side of a hill in Lapad, this large modern hotel has rooms with sweeping Adriatic views. Service is good and facilities are excellent: there's a spa, indoor/outdoor pools and a dive shop. It's right by the No 6 bus terminal; this bus runs until late to/from the old town.

Solitudo CAMPGROUND €
(Map p246; ☎448 200; www.camping-adriatic.com; per person/site 52/80KN; ⊙Apr-Nov) Just west of Lapad harbour, this site is about 5km from the old town and close to the beach. The shower blocks are bright and modern, and there's a cafe-bar.

Eating

There are a number of very average restaurants in Dubrovnik, so choose carefully. Prices here are the highest in Croatia.

OLD TOWN & AROUND

You have to choose carefully when dining out in the old town. Many places ride on the assumption that you're here just for a day (as many cruise passengers are) and that you won't be coming back. The two streets where average fodder is the norm are the Stradun and Prijeko; head to the back streets for more interesting restaurants.

There's a local **morning market** (Map p250; Gundulićeva Poljana; ⊙7am-1pm), which sells (pricey) fresh produce every morning; there's also a small **Konzum supermarket** (Map p250) on the same square.

TOP CHOICE **Oyster & Sushi Bar Bota Šare** SUSHI €€
(Map p250; ☎324 034; www.bota-sare.hr; Od Pustijerne bb; oysters/sushi from 12/15KN per piece) Not only is this place a treat for its offerings of fresh Ston oysters and the best sushi this side of Dalmatia, the setting is absolutely divine, with views of the Cathedral from its terrace tables. The family who runs this place also has branches in Split, Zagreb and Mali Ston, and they ensure all their fish and shellfish are caught daily. You can have oysters as they are or in a tempura sauce. Follow it up with the excellent sushi and sashimi. And it all goes wonderfully with a chilled Croatian white. The service is friendly and professional; highly recommended.

Lucin Kantun CROATIAN €€
(Map p250; ☎321 003; Od Sigurate bb; mains from 80KN) A modest-looking place with shabby-chic decor and a few pavement tables, but appearances are deceptive – this restaurant serves some of the most creative food in Dubrovnik. Virtually everything on the short meze-style menu is excellent, including amazing squid (stuffed with smoked ham and served with lemon and butter sauce), a lentil and shrimp creation, cheeses (including *paški sir*) and Dalmatian hams. Everything is freshly cooked from an open kitchen so you may have to wait a while at busy times.

Sugar & Spice PASTRIES & CAKES €
(Map p250; Sv Josipa 5; cakes from 8KN) A gorgeous little cafe/bakery whose owner is a master of cheesecake, carrot cake, banana pie and divine chocolate torte. She also makes her own jams and marmalades, and on a hot summer Dubrovnik day, her cool mint and lemon juice hits the spot. Everything has the cute vintage look of a granny's bakery. An original place in a sea of traditional patisseries.

Taj Mahal BOSNIAN, INTERNATIONAL €
(Map p250; www.tajmahaldubrovnik.com; Nikole Gučetićeva 2; mains from 40KN; 🖉) It's like an Aladdin's cave, with an interior loaded with Ottoman decorations and subdued lighting. Order the *džingis kan* (dried beef, beef sausage, peppers and spring onions with curdled milk) and get a taste of everything Bosnian, or feast on spicy *sudžukice* (beef sausage). Vegetarians will find plenty of choices including *aubergines alla edina* (eggplant stuffed with cheese). There are also three pavement tables.

Oliva Gourmet MEDITERRANEAN €€
(Map p250; ☎324 076; http://pizza-oliva.com; Cvijete Zuzorić 2; mains from 100KN) A lovely little place that has recently opened on a tiny street in the old town, with a terrace and a cute interior with vintage pieces adorning the traditional stone walls and colourful but tasteful modern furniture. The food is good, with an emphasis on keeping it simple and local. You'll be feasting on dishes such as king prawns in a pepper and tomato sauce, rosemary potatoes with roast lamb, and mussels in a white wine garlic and parsley sauce. The **Oliva Pizzeria**, next door, has good pizza.

Wanda ITALIAN €€
(Map p250; ☎098 94 49 317; www.wandarestaurant.com; Prijeko 8; mains from 70KN) Single-handedly saving the reputation of Prijeko restaurants, this is a very classy Italian place. Dishes include osso buco with saffron risotto and beautifully crafted pasta dishes. Eat from the fixed-priced tasting menus (150KN to 580KN) to see what the chefs are really capable of. You'll also find some great Croatian wines to sample.

Defne MEDITERRANEAN €€
(Map p250; ☎326 200; www.thepucicpalace.com; Od Puča 1; mains from 85KN) Enjoy old-town ambience at this fine restaurant in the Pućic Palace, which has a huge outdoor terrace and serves (mainly Eastern) Mediterranean cuisine. The cooking is accomplished and the setting is lovely.

360° by Jeffrey Vella MEDITERRANEAN €€€
(Map p250; ☎322 222; http://360dubrovnik.com; Ulica Svetog Dominika bb; mains from 170KN) Taken over by Maltese chef Jeffrey Vella, this is fine dining at its highest, with small, refined and flavour-bursting (and wallet-busting) parcels of creative Croatian food resting on your plate like jewels. The setting is unmatched, on top of the city walls with tables positioned so you can peer through the battlements over the harbour.

Dubravka 1836 INTERNATIONAL €
(Map p250; www.dubravka1836.hr; Brsalje 1; mains from 49KN) This place has arguably Dubrovnik's best dining terrace, right by the Pile Gate with stunning views over the walls and Adriatic. Though it draws quite a touristy clientele and the menu is international, locals still rate the fresh fish, risotto and salads, pizza and pasta. Prices are moderate given the location.

Revelin MEDITERRANEAN €€
(Map p250; www.revelinclub-dubrovnik.com; Ulica Svetog Dominika bb; mains from 65KN) This is a bar and restaurant on the terrace and a kicking nightclub inside. The wonderful terrace overlooking the harbour has a modern menu including good pastas and salads, fresh Adriatic fish and complex dishes such as beef tartufo (steak with cream and Istrian truffles).

Proto SEAFOOD €€
(Map p250; ☎323 234; www.esculap-teo.hr; Široka 1; mains from 80KN) This elegant place is recommended for fresh fish and seafood, with light sauces and bags of old-town atmosphere.

LAPAD

Lapad's main drag, Šetalište Kralja Tomislava, is completely packed with cafes, bars and restaurants.

TOP CHOICE **Levanat** CROATIAN €
(Map p246; ☎435 352; Nika i Meda Pucića 15; mains from 50KN) Levanat overlooks the sea from the forested hill between Lapad Bay and Babin Kuk. The cuisine is innovative: try the prawns with honey and sage. It's signposted from the main road and coastal footpath.

Blidinje GRILL €€
(Map p246; ☎358 794; Lapadska Obala 21; mains from 70KN) A locals' local that's perfect for a meat feast. Call first and order lamb or veal slow-cooked under hot coals, then turn up in a couple of hours and it'll be cooked to perfection.

Drinking

You won't go thirsty in Dubrovnik – the city has everything: swanky lounge bars, Irish pubs, boho bars on rock faces and lots and lots of Croatian-style cafe-bars. And that's just the old town.

TOP CHOICE **Buža** BAR
(Map p250; Ilije Sarake) Finding this isolated bar-on-a-cliff feels like a real discovery as you duck and dive around the city walls and finally see the entrance tunnel. Emerging by the sea, you find quite a scene with tasteful music (soul, funk) and a mellow crowd soaking up the vibes and views (and sunshine). Grab a cool drink, perch on a concrete platform and enjoy.

Buža II BAR
(Map p250; Crijevićeva 9) Just a notch more upmarket than the original Buža, this one is lower on the rocks and has a shaded terrace where you can snack on crisps, peanuts or a sandwich and lose a day quite happily, mesmerised by the Adriatic vistas.

EastWest Club COCKTAIL BAR
(www.ew-dubrovnik.com; Frana Supila bb) By day this upmarket outfit on Banje Beach rents out sun loungers and umbrellas and serves drinks to the bathers who come here to relax and rehydrate. Later on, the cocktail bar and restaurant come into their own and the in-crowd descends en masse.

Gaffe IRISH PUB
(Map p250; Miha Pracata bb) The busiest place in town (especially when there's football on), this huge pub has a homely interior and a long, covered side terrace. Check out the very cheap, homemade *marenda* (early lunch) option.

☆ Entertainment

TOP CHOICE **Lazareti** CULTURAL CENTRE
(Map p250; ☎324 633; www.lazareti.com; Frana Supila 8) Dubrovnik's best cultural centre, Lazareti hosts cinema nights, club nights, live music, gigs and pretty much all the best things in town.

Open-Air Cinema CINEMA
(Map p246; Kumičića, Lapad) In two locations, it's open nightly in July and August with screenings starting after sundown. There's an **old town branch** (Map p250; Za Rokom) at Za Rokom.

FREE **St Blaise's Church** FOLKLORE
(Map p250; Luža Sq) Open-air folklore shows are performed in front of the church at 11am on Sundays in May, June and September.

St Saviour Church CONCERTS
(Map p250; St Saviour Church, Placa) The Dubrovnik String Quartet gives concerts here throughout autumn on Monday nights.

Troubadur LIVE MUSIC
(Map p250; ☎412 154; Bunićeva Poljana 2) This corner bar looks pretty nondescript in the day, but on summer nights things get far more lively when there are live jazz concerts – often (though not always) featuring Marko, the owner, and his band.

WORTH A TRIP

CROSS-BORDER JAUNTS

Dubrovnik is an easy bus ride away from **Montenegro** and the gorgeous towns of Kotor, Herceg Novi and Budva. All three have wonderful historic centres, with curving marble streets and pretty architecture. If you really want to take your time and explore the region, you should hire a car, but you can also get there by public transport. Three daily buses run to Montenegro, passing Herceg Novi, Kotor and on to Budva (three hours). EU, US, Australian, New Zealand and Canadian citizens don't need a visa to enter Montenegro; other nationalities should check with their relevant embassy.

Buses also go to **Mostar**, giving you a chance to glance at Mostar's emblematic bridge and dip your toe into the world of Bosnia and Hercegovina. It's quite difficult to go for a day trip via public transport, but several tour companies, including Adriatic Explore and Atlas Travel Agency, organise day excursions (around 380KN) in private minibuses. These leave around 8am and travel via the incredibly pretty fortified village of Počitelj, arriving in Mostar around 11.30am. After a (typically very brief) guided tour you'll be left to your own devices until 3pm – which doesn't leave a lot of time to have lunch and explore the town. Mostar is still divided along Croat/Bosnian lines (with the river acting as border), but most of the historic sights are on the Bosnian side.

Shopping

Stradun is mostly lined with tacky souvenir shops; the best boutiques are down its side lanes.

Check out the morning market (p255) for local crafts and produce.

TOP CHOICE **Lega-Lega** DESIGN, GIFTS
(Map p250; www.lega-lega.com; Dropčeva 3; ⌚9am-7pm Mon-Sat) A hip place to shop for gifts with a difference – Lega-Lega is a Croatian design collective originating in the northern Croatian town of Osijek. Its fantastic t-shirt packaging – in a tetrapak-like box, stored in a 'fridge' – came second at the International Design Awards in LA in 2011. It's all simple and cool, and there's a wealth of notebooks, coasters, badges and other things to take home.

Uje FOOD
(Map p250; www.uje.hr; Placa 9; ⌚9am-9pm Mon-Sat, 9am-3pm Sun) The best place in town to stock up on quality Croatian produce, this is the Dubrovnik outlet for the Split-based designer deli. It specialises in Croatian olive oils – among the best is Brachia, from the island of Brač – and you can get some excellent jams (the lemon spread is divine), pickled capers, and local herbs and spices.

Magnolika ART, JEWELLERY
(Map p250; http://magnolika.com; Getaldićeva 7; ⌚10am-1pm & 6-8pm Tue-Fri, 10am-2pm Sat) A tiny space that sells art, design and jewellery by young Croatian designers. It's great for finding affordable, beautiful pieces to hang on your wall (or yourself).

Algoritam BOOKS
(Map p250; Placa 8; ⌚9am-8.30pm Mon-Fri, 9am-3pm Sat) A great bookshop with a wide range of English-language books, it comes up trumps when you run out of reading material. There's also a good variety of guides on Dubrovnik and Croatia.

Information

Internet Access

Netcafé (www.netcafe.hr; Prijeko 21; per hr 30KN) A place to chill, even if you're not surfing; has fast connections, CD burning, wi-fi, photo printing, scanning, and good drinks and coffee.

Medical Services

Hospital (☎431 777; Dr Roka Mišetića) A kilometre south of Lapad Bay.

Money

There are numerous ATMs in town, in Lapad and at the ferry terminal and bus station. Travel agencies and post offices will also exchange cash.

Post

Lapad Post Office & Telephone Centre (Šetalište Kralja Zvonimira 21)

Main Post Office (cnr Široka & Od Puča)

Tourist Information

Tourist Office (www.tzdubrovnik.hr; ⌚8am-8pm daily Jun-Sep, 8am-3pm Mon-Fri, 9am-2pm Sat Oct-May) bus station (☎417 581;

Obala Pape Ivana Pavla II 44a); Gruž Harbour (☎417 983; Obala Stjepana Radića 27); Head Office (☎020 312 011; Brsalje 5, west of the Pile Gate); Old Town (☎323 587; Široka 1) Maps, information and the indispensable *Dubrovnik Riviera* guide. The smart new head office that is under construction just west of the Pile Gate should open by the time you read this.

Travel Agencies

Atlas Travel Agency (www.atlas-croatia.com) Gruž Harbour (☎418 001; Obala Papa Ivana Pavla II 1, Gruž Harbour); Pile Gate (☎442 574; Sv Đurđa 1, Pile Gate) Organises excursions within Croatia and to Mostar and Montenegro. Also finds private accommodation.

Getting There & Away

Air

Flights (three daily) to and from Zagreb are operated by **Croatia Airlines** (☎01 66 76 555; www.croatiaairlines.hr). Fares vary between 270KN for promo fares and around 760KN for flexi-fares. Croatia Airlines also operates nonstop flights to Frankfurt and seasonal routes to cities including Rome, Paris and Amsterdam.

Dubrovnik airport is served by over 20 other airlines from across Europe. These include British Airways and EasyJet (both from London Gatwick, and the latter also from London Stansted), which both run flights all year round. FlyBe, Jet2 and Thompson Airways operate seasonal flights from the UK.

Boat

A twice-weekly **Jadrolinija** (☎418 000; www.jadrolinija.hr; Gruž Harbour) coastal ferry heads north to Korčula, Hvar, Split, Zadar and Rijeka. There's a local ferry that leaves Dubrovnik for Sobra on Mljet (60KN, 2½ hours) twice a week throughout the year; in summer there are also catamarans, which have a daily service to both Sobra and Polače (150KN, 1½ hours). Several daily ferries run year-round to the outlying Elafiti Islands of Koločep, Lopud and Šipan.

Ferries also go from Dubrovnik to Bari, in southern Italy; there are six per week in the summer season (300KN to 450KN, nine hours) and two in the winter months.

Jadroagent (☎419 000; Obala Stjepana Radića 32) offers ferry information and tickets.

Bus

Buses out of **Dubrovnik bus station** (☎060 305 070; Obala Pape Ivana Pavla II 44a) can be crowded, so book tickets ahead in summer.

Split–Dubrovnik buses pass briefly through Bosnian territory, so keep your passport handy for border-crossing points.

All bus schedules are detailed at www.libertasdubrovnik.hr. For those who need to store bags, there's a **garderoba** (1st hr 7KN, then per hr 2KN; ⏱4.30am-10pm) at the bus station.

Getting Around

To/From the Airport

Čilipi international airport (www.airport-dubrovnik.hr) is 24km southeast of Dubrovnik. Atlas buses (35KN) leave from the main bus station irregularly, supposedly two hours before Croatia Airlines domestic flights, but it's best to check the latest schedule at the Atlas office by the Pile Gate. These airport buses stop in Dubrovnik at Zagrebačka cesta, just north of the old town, en route out of the city (but not at the Pile Gate). Buses leave the airport for Dubrovnik bus station (via the Pile Gate in this direction) several times a day and are timed to coincide with arrivals; if your flight is late, there's usually still one waiting.

A taxi to the old town costs about 250KN.

BUSES FROM DUBROVNIK

DESTINATION	COST (KN)	DURATION	DAILY SERVICES
Korčula	105	3hr	2
Kotor	130	2½hr	2-3
Mostar	130	3hr	3
Orebić	95	2½hr	2
Plitvice	350	10hr	1
Rijeka	370-510	13hr	4-5
Sarajevo (Bosnia & Hercegovina)	230	5hr	2
Split	140	4½hr	19
Zadar	190-230	8hr	8
Zagreb	270	11hr	7-8

Bus

Dubrovnik has a superb bus service; buses run frequently and generally on time. The key tourist routes run until after 2am in summer, so if you're staying in Lapad, there's no need to rush home. The fare is 15KN if you buy from the driver and 12KN if you buy a ticket at a *tisak* (news-stand). Timetables are available at www.libertas dubrovnik.hr.

To get to the old town from the bus station, take buses 1a, 1b, 3 or 8. To get to Lapad, take bus 7.

From the Pile Gate, take bus 6 to get to Lapad, or bus 4 to the Hotel Dubrovnik Palace.

Car

The entire old town is a pedestrian area. Traffic is heavy at all times of year, particularly so in summer. The best-located **car park** (Ilijina glavica; per day 80KN; ⌚24hr) for the centre is a 10-minute walk above the Pile Gate. There are a few car-rental companies.

Budget Rent-a-Car (☎418 998; www.budget.hr; Obala Stjepana Radića 24) Branches in town and Dubrovnik airport.

Gulliver (☎313 313; www.gulliver.hr; Obala Stjepana Radića 31)

AROUND DUBROVNIK

Dubrovnik is an excellent base for day trips into the surrounding region. You can hop over to the Elafiti Islands for a day of peaceful sunbathing, head to the beautiful islands of Korčula and Mljet for some fine food and wine, and check out the heady smell of Trsteno Gardens. Cavtat is a quieter alternative to Dubrovnik, good for a lovely day's worth of sights, swimming and seafood.

Lokrum Island

A ferry shuttles roughly hourly in summer to lush Lokrum Island (40KN return, last boat back at 6pm), a Unesco-protected national park. It's a beautiful, forested place of holm oaks and black ash, pine and olive trees, and an ideal escape from urban Dubrovnik. Swimming is excellent, though beaches are rocky. The **nudist beach** (marked FKK) is a delight for naturists and very popular with the gay community. Check out the fine **botanical garden**, which has a cacti section with some giant agaves, and palms native to Brazil and South Africa. The ruined medieval **Benedictine monastery** is currently being renovated.

The attractive cafe-restaurant **Lacroma** (mains from 80KN) sells snacks, meals and ice cream; it's just above the harbour. Sometimes there's live guitar music here, too.

Note that no one can stay overnight and smoking is not permitted anywhere on the island.

Elafiti Islands

A day trip to one of the islands in this archipelago northwest of Dubrovnik makes a perfect escape from the summer crowds. The most popular islands are **Koločep**, **Lopud** and **Šipan**. One way to see all three islands in one day is to take one of the 'Three Islands & Fish Picnic' **tours** (250KN including drinks and lunch), offered by several operators that have desks at the Ploče Gate harbour. However, as these leave around 10am and return before 6pm, you don't get much more than a quick glimpse at each island.

Koločep is the nearest of the islands and is inhabited by a mere 150 people. There are several sand-and-pebble beaches, steep cliffs and sea caves, as well as centuries-old pine forests, olive groves and orchards filled with orange and lemon trees.

Car-free Lopud has a number of interesting churches and monasteries dating from the 16th century, when the inhabitants' seafaring exploits were legendary. Lopud village is composed of stone houses surrounded by exotic gardens. You can walk across the spine of the island to beautiful and sandy **Šunj beach**; here a little bar serves griddled sardines and other types of fish.

Šipan is the largest of the islands and was a favourite with the Dubrovnik aristocracy, who built houses here in the 15th century. The boat lands in **Šipanska Luka**, which has the remains of a Roman villa and a 15th-century Gothic duke's palace. Eat at **Kod Marka** (☎758 007; Šipanska Luka; mains from 50KN), where you'll have gloriously prepared seafood – try the Korčula-style fish stew.

ℹ Getting There & Around

The islands are accessible by the **Jadrolinija** (www.jadrolinija.hr) car ferry, which runs three times daily all year round, stopping at Koločep (17KN, 30 minutes), Lopud (20KN, 50 minutes) and Šipan (25KN, one hour). Prices drop a little in winter.

Mljet Island

POP 1232

Of all the Adriatic islands, Mljet (mil-yet) may be the most seductive. Much of the island is covered by forests and the rest is dotted with fields, vineyards and small villages. The northwestern half of the island forms **Mljet National Park**, where the lush vegetation, pine forests and spectacular saltwater lakes are exceptionally scenic. It's an unspoiled oasis of tranquillity that, according to legend, captivated Odysseus for seven years. We're sure he didn't regret a moment.

History

Ancient Greeks called the island 'Melita' or 'honey' for the many bees humming in the forests. It appears that Greek sailors came to the island for refuge against storms and to gather fresh water from the springs. At that time the island was populated by Illyrians, who erected hill forts and traded with the mainland. They were conquered by the Romans in 35 BC, who expanded the settlement around Polače by building a palace, baths and servants' quarters.

The island fell under the control of the Byzantine Empire in the 6th century and was later subjected to the 7th-century invasions of Slavs and Avars. After several centuries of regional rule from the mainland, Mljet was given to the Benedictine order in the 13th century, which constructed a monastery in the middle of Veliko Jezero. Dubrovnik formally annexed the island in 1410.

Although Mljet's fortunes were thereafter tied to those of Dubrovnik, the inhabitants maintained their traditional activities of farming, viticulture, husbandry and seafaring. All except seafaring remain key occupations today. The establishment of the national park in 1960 put Mljet on the map, but the island is anything but overrun and visitors are almost entirely drawn to the tourist enclave around Pomena. If you're searching for tranquillity, you won't have to look hard here.

Sights

The highlights of the island are **Malo Jezero** and **Veliko Jezero**, the two lakes on the island's western end connected by a channel. Veliko Jezero is connected with the sea by the Soline Canal, which makes the lakes subject to tidal flows.

In the middle of Veliko Jezero is an islet with a **Benedictine monastery**. The monastery was originally built in the 12th century but has been rebuilt several times, adding Renaissance and baroque features to the Romanesque structure. It contains the **Church of St Mary** (Crkva Svete Marije). In addition to building the monastery, the Benedictine monks deepened and widened the passage between the two lakes, taking advantage of the rush of sea water into the valley to build a **mill** at the entrance to Veliko Jezero. The monastery was abandoned in 1869 and the mill housed the government's forest-management offices for the island until 1941. It was then converted into a hotel, which was trashed during the 1990s war. Now it contains an atmospheric restaurant: Melita (p262).

There's a boat from Mali Most (about 1.5km from Pomena) on Malo Jezero that leaves for the island monastery every hour at 10 minutes past the hour. It's not possible to walk right around the larger lake as there's no bridge over the channel connecting the lakes to the sea. If you decide to swim it, keep in mind that the current can be strong.

Polače features a number of remains dating from the 1st to the 6th centuries. Most impressive is the **Roman palace**, probably from the 5th century. The floor plan was rectangular and on the front corners are two polygonal towers separated by a pier. On a hill over the town you can see the remains of a late-antique **fortification**, and northwest of the village are the remains of an early **Christian basilica** and a 5th-century **church**.

Activities

Renting a bicycle (25/110KN per hour/day) is an excellent way to explore the national park. Several places have bikes, including Hotel Odisej in Pomena. Be aware that Pomena and Polače are separated by a steep hill. The bike path along the lake is an easier and very scenic pedal, but it doesn't link the two towns. **Radulj Tours** (☎091 88 06 543) in Polače has open-top cars (280KN for five hours) plus scooters (190KN for five hours) for rent if you're feeling lazy, as does **Mini Brum** (☎745 084; www.rent-a-car-scooter-mljet.hr), which has a desk at Sobra, too.

You can rent a **paddle boat** and row over to the monastery, but be aware you'll need stamina.

The island offers some unusual opportunities for **diving**. There's a 3rd-century Roman wreck in relatively shallow water. The remains of the ship, including amphorae, have calcified over the centuries and this has protected it from pillaging. There's also a German torpedo boat from WWII and several walls to dive. Contact **Kronmar Diving** (☎744 022; Hotel Odisej).

Tours

Agencies in Dubrovnik and Korčula offer excursions to Mljet. Tours (around 390KN and 245KN, respectively) last from about 8.30am to 6pm and include the park entry fee.

Sleeping

The Polače tourist office arranges private accommodation (from around 250KN per double), but it's essential to make arrangements before peak season. You'll find more *sobe* signs around Pomena than Polače, and practically none at all in Sobra. Restaurants rent out rooms, too.

TOP CHOICE **Stermasi** APARTMENTS €€€
(☎098 93 90 362; www.stermasi.hr; Saplunara; apt 368-625KN; P❄) On the 'other' side of Mljet, these apartments are ideal for those wanting to enjoy the simple life and natural beauty of the island. All nine places are well presented, bright and modern, sleep two to four people, and either have a terrace or private balcony. Sandy beaches are on your doorstep, and the family owners couldn't be more helpful. Transport can be arranged. Guests get a 20% discount on meals at the amazing restaurant here.

Soline 6 ECOHOTEL €€
(☎744 024; www.soline6.com; Soline; d 598KN) Quite a concept and an undertaking, this very green place is the only accommodation within the national park. Everything has been built from recycled products, rainwater is reused and organic waste composted. Toilets are waterless and there's no electricity (as yet). If you're expecting a hippie commune, think again: the four studios are modern and clean, and each has a private bathroom, a balcony and a kitchen.

Camping Mungos CAMPGROUND €
(☎745 300; Babino Polje; per person 54KN; ⊙May-Sep) Close to the beach and the lovely grotto of Odysseus, this campground has a restaurant, currency exchange and a minimart.

Marina CAMPGROUND €
(☎745 071; Ropa; per person/site 25/47KN; ⊙Jun-Sep) A small campground in Ropa, about 1km from the park.

Eating

Pomena has the most choice, with a lovely strip of places right by the sea. Fish and seafood are very fresh and readily available, though not cheap. Kid and lamb are also popular, cooked 'under the bell' (from top and bottom under hot coals). A tip for boaters: you can moor at any of the restaurants for free if you eat there.

TOP CHOICE **Stermasi** DALMATIAN €€€
(☎098 93 90 362; www.stermasi.hr; Saplunara; mains 90-360KN) One of Dalmatia's top restaurants, Stermasi does everything very well indeed. Most importantly, the food is flavoursome, authentic and prepared with love and skill. House specialities include vegetables, octopus or kid cooked 'under the bell' (200/260/300KN, respectively) while wild boar with gnocchi (360KN) is almost enough for four. Or opt for a Mljet-style fish stew. The view from the terrace over the tiny islands of Saplunara bay is awesome.

Melita CROATIAN €€
(www.mljet-restoranmelita.com; St Mary's Island, Veliko Jezero; mains from 60KN) A more romantic (and touristy) spot can't be found on the island – this is the restaurant attached to the church on the little island in the middle of the big lake. Feast on fish, seafood and meat dishes, Mljet lobster, octopus, black risotto and local cheeses.

Triton GRILL €€
(☎745 131; Sršenovići 43, Babino Polje; mains from 70KN) Triston mainly focuses on meat, with veal and kid best cooked 'under the bell' – book ahead. And why not round off your meal with a wee nip of the owner's home-brewed spirit collection.

Information

The **tourist office** (☎744 186; www.mljet.hr; ⊙8am-1pm & 5-7pm Mon-Sat, 9am-noon Sun Jun-Sep, 8am-1pm Mon-Fri Oct-May) is in Polače and there's an ATM next door. You can buy a good walking map here and it has brochures, too. There's another ATM at the Hotel Odisej in Pomena.

Babino Polje, 18km east of Polače, is the island capital. It's home to another **tourist office**

MLJET: INS & OUTS

Sightseeing boats from Korčula arrive at Polače wharf in high season. The Dubrovnik catamarans travel to both Sobra and Polače in high season. Jadrolinija ferries use the port of Sobra close to the centre of the island. The entry point for **Mljet National Park** (www.mljet.hr; adult/concession 100/50KN) is between Pomena and Polače. Your ticket includes a bus and boat transfer to the Benedictine monastery. If you stay overnight on the island you only pay the park admission once.

(☎745 125; www.mljet.hr; ⊙9am-5pm Mon-Fri) and a post office.

Getting There & Around

Jadrolinija ferries stop only at Sobra (30KN, two hours) but the **G&V Line** (☎313 119; www.gv-line.hr; Vukovarska 34, Dubrovnik) catamaran goes to Sobra (40KN, one hour) and Polače (54KN, 1½ hours) in the summer months, leaving Dubrovnik's Gruž Harbour twice daily (9.15am and 7.10pm) and returning daily from Polače at 4.55pm, and twice daily from Sobra (6.15am and 5.35pm). You *cannot* reserve tickets in advance for this service; get to the harbour ticket office well in advance in high season to secure a seat (bicycles are not usually permitted either). In winter there's one daily catamaran. Tour boats from Korčula also run to Polače harbour in high season.

Infrequent buses connect Sobra and Polače.

Cavtat

POP 2021

Without Cavtat, there'd be no Dubrovnik. Well, at least not the Dubrovnik we know and love. The inhabitants of this (originally Greek) settlement fled from the Slavs and set up shop in Dubrovnik, establishing the city in 614. But Cavtat is interesting in itself. A lot more 'local' than Dubrovnik – read: not flooded by tourists on a daily basis – it has charm and grace. Wrapped around a very pretty harbour that's bordered by beaches and backed by a curtain of imposing hills, the setting is lovely.

History

Originally a Greek settlement called Epidaurus, Cavtat became a Roman colony around 228 BC and was later destroyed during the 7th-century Slavic invasions. Throughout most of the Middle Ages it was part of the Dubrovnik republic and shared the cultural and economic life of the capital city. Cavtat's most famous personality was the painter Vlaho Bukovac (1855–1922), one of the foremost exponents of Croatian modernism.

Sights

Cavtat has some intriguing sights. The former Rector's Palace – now the **Baltazar Bogišić Collection** (Obala Ante Starčevića 18; adult/concession 20/10KN; ⊙9am-1pm Mon-Sat) – houses the rich library belonging to 19th-century lawyer and historian Baltazar Bogišić, as well as lithographs and a small archaeological collection. One of the main draws is a painting by Vlaho Bukovac, depicting the Cavtat Carnival in the 19th century. Next door is the baroque **St Nicholas Church** (Crkva Svetog Nikole; admission 10KN; ⊙10am-1pm) with impressive wooden altars.

The **birth house of Vlaho Bukovac** (Rodna Kuća Vlahe Bukovca; Bukovca 5; admission 20KN; ⊙10am-1pm & 4-8pm Tue-Sat, 4-8pm Sun), Cavtat's most famous son, is at the northern end of Obala Ante Starčevića. The early-19th-century architecture provides a fitting backdrop to the mementos and paintings of Croatia's most renowned painter. Next door is the **Monastery of Our Lady of the Snow** (Samostan Snježne Gospe; Bukovca), which is worth a look for some notable early Renaissance paintings.

A path leads uphill from the monastery to the cemetery, which contains the **mausoleum** (admission 7KN; ⊙10am-noon & 5-7pm Jul & Aug) of the Račić family, built by Ivan Meštrović. The elaborate monument reflects the sculptor's preoccupation with religious and spiritual concerns.

Sleeping & Eating

For private accommodation try Atlas or one of the other travel agencies around the town centre.

You'll find the harbourfront is lined with cafes and restaurants for casual inexpensive dining.

TOP CHOICE **Castelletto** B&B €€

(☎478 246; www.dubrovnikexperience.com; Tiha bb; r 710KN; P❄@🛜🏊) This very well-run family-owned place has 13 spacious, immaculately presented rooms with tasteful modern furnishings in a converted villa. All have air-con and satellite TV and many have sweeping bay views. The location is peaceful, set well back from the harbour, which is a brisk 10-minute walk away via a pretty path. Staff are excellent; wi-fi and airport transfers are free.

Hotel Major RURAL INN €€€
(☎773 600; www.hrmajor.hr; Uskoplje bb; ste 910KN; P❄@📶🏊) A five-minute drive inland from Cavtat, this small rural hotel has five very spacious and good-value suite-sized rooms, all with air-con, heating, and sea or mountain views. Staff could not be more helpful and the restaurant (mains from 75KN) is also noteworthy – it has a huge terrace and a menu with a strong Dalmatian flavour.

Galija SEAFOOD €€
(www.galija.hr; Vuličelićeva 1; mains from 70KN) Long-established, very well-regarded restaurant with a great sea-facing terrace shaded by pines and an atmospheric interior of exposed stone walls. Start by tasting some of the Dalmatian-style entrées (including sea urchin soup). The main menu majors in fish and seafood – try the excellent sea platter (with oysters, mussels, shrimp and scampi).

ℹ Information

Antares (☎479 707; www.antarestravel.hr; Vlaha Paljetka 2) Books excursions and offers private accommodation.

Atlas Travel Agency (☎479 031; www.atlas-croatia.com; Trumbićev Put 2) Excursions and private accommodation.

Post Office (Kneza Domagoja 4; ⏰9am-6.30pm Mon-Sat) Near the bus station.

Tourist Office (☎479 025; www.tzcavtat-konavle.hr; Tiha 3; ⏰8am-7pm Jul & Aug, 8am-3.30pm Mon-Fri, 9am-noon Sat Sep-Jun) Very well stocked with leaflets and can provide a good colour map.

ℹ Getting There & Away

Bus 10 runs roughly hourly to Cavtat (20KN, 45 minutes) from Dubrovnik's bus station, the last buses return about midnight. Or you can take a boat (return 100KN, 12 daily June to September, three to five daily rest of year) from the Lokrum boat dock, near Ploče Gate.

Trsteno Gardens

Just 13km northwest of Dubrovnik, these wonderful gardens are well worth a visit. Trsteno came into its own during the 16th century when Dubrovnik's noblesse paid extra attention to the appearance of their gardens – Ivan Gučetić planted the first seeds here and started the trend.

Ivan Gučetić's descendants maintained the garden throughout the centuries, until the land was taken over by the (former Yugoslav and now Croatian) Academy of Sciences, which turned it into an **arboretum** (☎751 019; adult/concession 35/17KN; ⏰8am-7pm Jun-Sep, to 4pm Oct-May). The garden has a gorgeous Renaissance layout with a set of geometric shapes made with Mediterranean plants and bushes (lilac lavender, green rosemary, fuchsia, bougainvillea), while citrus orchards perfume the air. It's only partially landscaped, though – quite a bit of it is just wonderfully wild. There's a **maze** that children enjoy, a fine palm collection (including Chinese Windmill palms) and a gorgeous **pond** overlooked by a statue of Neptune and rich with white water lilies and dozens of bullfrogs. Don't miss the two **plane trees** at the entrance to Trsteno village – each is more than 400 years old and around 50m high.

The local campground, **Autocamp Trsteno** (☎751 060; www.trsteno.hr/camping.htm; per person/tent 26/20KN), is well equipped and has a nice bar. It's a five-minute walk down to the coast, where there are rocky coves.

To get to Trsteno, take any bus (30 minutes, 19 daily) bound for Split from Dubrovnik's bus station.

KORČULA ISLAND

POP 16,438

Korčula is rich in vineyards, olive groves, small villages and hamlets. The island's dense woods led the original Greek settlers to call the island Korkyra Melaina (Black Korčula). Its main settlement, Korčula Town, is a gorgeous grid of marble streets and impressive architecture. The steep southern coast is dotted with quiet coves and small beaches, while the flatter northern shore is rich in natural harbours. Tradition is alive and kicking on Korčula, with age-old religious ceremonies, folk music and dances still being performed to an ever-growing influx of tourists. Oenophiles will adore sampling its wine, especially the dessert wine made from the *grk* grape cultivated around Lumbarda.

Korčula is separated from the Pelješac Peninsula by a narrow channel. It's the sixth-largest Adriatic island, nearly 47km in length.

History

A Neolithic cave (Vela Špilja) located near Vela Luka, on the island's western end, points to the existence of a prehistoric settlement, but it was the Greeks who first began spreading over the island somewhere around the 6th century BC. Their most important settlement was in the area of today's Lumbarda around the 3rd century BC. Romans conquered Korčula in the 1st century, giving way to the Slavs in the 7th century. The island was conquered by Venice in AD 1000 and then passed under Hungarian rule. It was briefly part of the Republic of Dubrovnik before again falling to the Venetians in 1420, who remained until 1797. Under Venetian control the island became known for its stone, which was quarried and cut for export. Shipbuilding also flourished.

After the Napoleonic conquest of Dalmatia in 1797, Korčula's fortunes followed those of the region, which changed hands among the French, Austro-Hungarians and English before becoming a part of Yugoslavia in 1921. Today Korčula is one of Croatia's most prosperous islands, its historic capital drawing visitors in increasing numbers.

Getting There & Around

Boat

The island has two major entry ports – Korčula Town and Vela Luka. All the Jadrolinija ferries between Split and Dubrovnik stop in Korčula Town.

If you're travelling between Split and Korčula you have several options. There's a daily fast boat, the **Krilo** (www.krilo.hr), which runs from Split to Korčula (65KN, 2¾ hours) all year round, stopping at Hvar en route. Jadrolinija runs a passenger catamaran daily from June to September from Split to Vela Luka (70KN, two hours), stopping at Hvar and continuing on to Lastavo. There's also a regular afternoon car ferry between Split and Vela Luka (60KN, three hours) that stops at Hvar most days (although cars may not disembark at Hvar).

From the Pelješac Peninsula you'll find very regular boats link Orebić and Korčula. Passenger launches (20KN, 10 minutes, 13 daily June to September, at least five daily the rest of the year) sail to the heart of Korčula Town. Car ferries (22KN, 15 minutes, at least 14 daily all year round) also run this route, but use the deeper port of Dominče, 3km from Korčula Town. (As bus connections are poor and taxi fares are excessive – 80KN for a 3km journey – try to use the passenger launches if you're on foot.)

Bus

There are buses to Dubrovnik (95KN, three hours, one to three daily) and one to Zagreb (245KN, 11 hours). Book ahead in summer.

Korčula Town

POP 3135

Korčula Town is a stunner. Ringed by imposing defences, this coastal citadel is dripping in history, with marble streets rich in Renaissance and Gothic architecture. Its fascinating fishbone layout was cleverly designed for the comfort and safety of its inhabitants: western streets were built straight in order to open the city to the refreshing summer *maestral* (strong, steady westerly wind), while the eastern streets were curved to minimise the force of the winter *bura* (cold, northeasterly wind). The town cradles a harbour, overlooked by round defensive towers and a compact cluster of red-roofed houses.

There are rustling palms all around and several beaches are an easy walk away. This being a favourite family island, you'll need to get out of town to more remote beaches if you want some peace. Korčula Town is the best place to base yourself for day trips to Lumbarda, the islet of Badija, the town of Orebić on the Pelješac Peninsula and Mljet Island.

History

Although documents indicate that a walled town existed on this site in the 13th century, it wasn't until the 15th century that the current city was built. Construction coincided with the apogee of stone-carving skills on the island, lending the buildings and streets a distinctive style. In the 16th century masons added decorative flourishes such as ornate columns and coats-of-arms to building facades, which gave a Renaissance look to the original Gothic core. People began building houses south of the old town in the 17th and 18th centuries as the threat of invasion diminished and they no longer needed to protect themselves behind walls. The narrow streets and stone houses in the 'new' suburb attracted merchants and artisans, and this is still where you'll find most commercial activity.

Sights

City Defences CITY WALLS, TOWERS

Korčula's towers (and remaining city walls) look particularly striking when approached from the sea, their presence warning pirates

Korčula Town

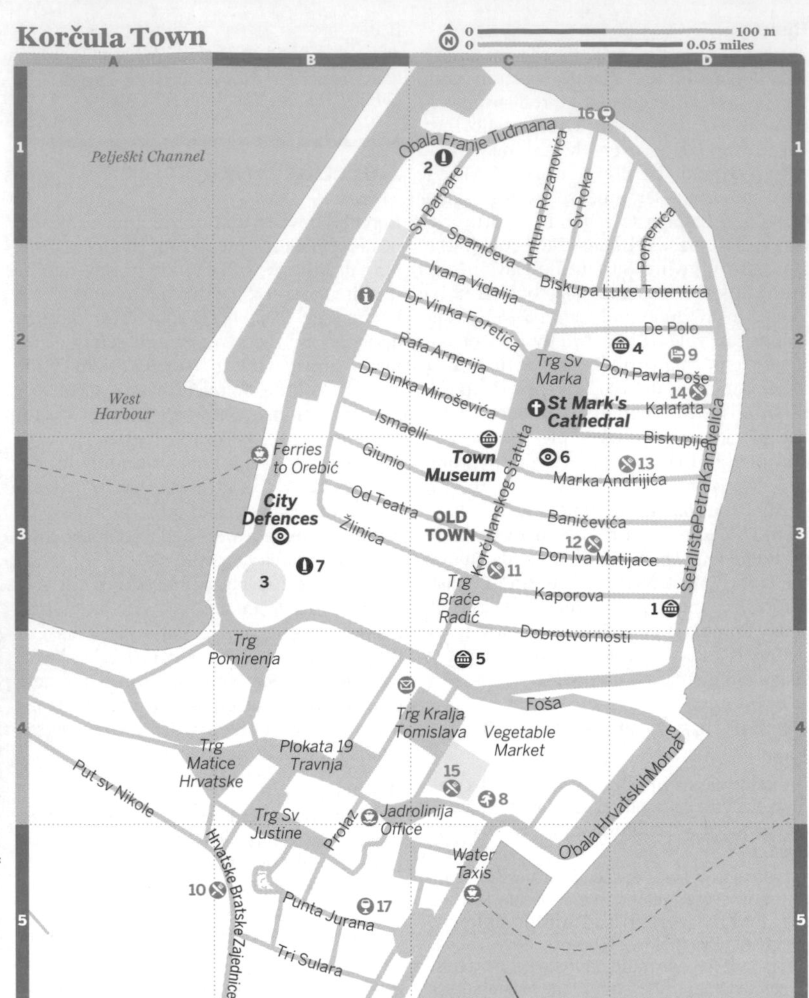

the town would be no pushover. Originally these defences would have been even more foreboding, forming a complete stone barrier against invaders that consisted of 12 towers and 20m-high walls.

From the western harbour the conical **Large Governor's Tower** (1483) and **Small Governor's Tower** (1449) protected the port, shipping and the Governor's Palace, which used to stand next to the town hall. Continuing clockwise around the edge of the old town peninsula, the **Tower of the West Sea Gate** has an inscription in Latin from 1592 stating that Korčula was founded after the fall of Troy. Next you'll come to the renovated **Kula Kanovelić Tower**, its semicircular profile topped with battlements, and then a smaller tower that has now been converted into, bizarrely, Cocktail Bar Massimo.

The entrance to the old city is through the **Veliki Revelin Tower** southern land gate. Built in the 14th century and later extended, this fortification is adorned with coats-of-arms of the Venetian doges and Korčulan governors. There was originally a wooden drawbridge here, but it was replaced in the 18th century by the wide stone steps that give a sense of grandeur to the entrance.

Korčula Town

Top Sights
City Defences ... B3
St Mark's Cathedral ... C2
Town Museum ... C3

Sights
1 Icon Museum ... D3
2 Kula Kanovelić Tower ... C1
3 Large Governor's Tower ... B3
4 Marco Polo Museum ... D2
5 Moreška Museum ... C4
6 Riznica Museum ... C3
7 Small Governor's Tower ... B3

Activities, Courses & Tours
8 Rent a Đir ... C4

Sleeping
9 Lešić Dimitri Palace ... D2

Eating
10 Cukarin ... B5
11 Gradski Podrum ... C3
12 Konoba Komin ... C3
13 Konoba Marinero ... D3
14 LD ... D2
15 Supermarket ... C4

Drinking
16 Cocktail Bar Massimo ... C1
17 Vinum Bonum ... B5

The best remaining part of the defence walls stretches west of here. The upper section of this tower is home to a small **museum** (admission 20KN; ⏲9am-9pm Jun-Sep, 10am-4pm May & Oct, closed rest of year) dedicated to the Moreška dance tradition; it has some costumes and old photos.

St Mark's Cathedral CATHEDRAL
(Katedrala Svetog Marka; Statuta 1214; ⏲9am-9pm Jul & Aug, Mass only Sep-Jun) Dominating Trg Svetog Marka (St Mark's Sq), the magnificent 15th-century St Mark's Cathedral was built from Korčula limestone in a Gothic-Renaissance style by Italian and local artisans. Over the solemn portal, the triangular gable cornice is decorated with a two-tailed mermaid, an elephant and other sculptures. The **bell tower** that rises from the cathedral over the town is topped by a balustrade and ornate cupola, beautifully carved by Korčulan Marko Andrijić. The facade was being cleaned at the time of research and should shine in all its glory upon completion.

Its interior has a wonderfully evocative ambience, the nave soars 30m in height and is lined with a twin colonnade of exposed limestone pillars. Look out for the ciborium, also carved by Andrijić, and behind it the altarpiece painting *Three Saints* by Tintoretto. Another painting attributed to Tintoretto or his workshop, *The Annunciation,* is on the baroque altar of St Anthony. Other noteworthy works include a bronze statue of St Blaise by Meštrović near the altar on the northern aisle and a painting by the Venetian artist Jacopo Bassano in the apse of the southern aisle. Check out the modern sculptures in the **baptistery** too, including a pietà by Ivan Meštrović.

Town Museum MUSEUM
(Gradski Muze; Statuta 1214; admission 25KN; ⏲9am-9pm Jun-Aug, 9am-1pm Mon-Sat Sep-May) Occupying the 16th-century Gabriellis Palace, this museum traces the history and culture of Korčula throughout the ages. It's not that well organised but there are some interesting curios to browse over its four floors – including a tablet recording Greek presence on the island in the 3rd century BC. The stone-carving collection follows the development of that craft with sculptures and stonemason tools, and shipbuilding exhibits display models of local boats. There's also an archaeology collection with prehistoric objects, and some examples of Korčulan traditional dress and art, furniture, textiles and portraits. Explanations are in English.

Before leaving the square, notice the elegantly ornamented **Arneri Palace** next door to the museum and extending west down the narrow street of the same name.

Marco Polo Museum MUSEUM
(De Polo; admission 20KN; ⏲9am-7pm Jun-Sep, 10am-4pm May & Oct) It's said that Marco Polo was born in Korčula in 1254, and though a lot of places claim to be his birthplace, there's reasonable evidence that it could be true. This small, claustrophobic museum is located in the skinny tower of the house that is supposed to have been his. Inside you'll find maps and charts relating to Polo's voyages, and portraits and busts of the great adventurer. But perhaps the real appeal of this building is the view. Climb the very steep steps for an eagle's-eye vista over the Korčula peninsula and Adriatic. Note that the access staircase can be a challenge, and there's a large gap in the railings, so those

with dodgy knees or young children may decide to skip the climb.

Riznica Museum ART COLLECTION
(Statuta 1214; admission 25KN; ⌚9am-7.30pm Mon-Sat May-Nov) Located in the 14th-century Abbey Palace, the Riznica Museum has an anteroom with a collection of icons and a hall of Dalmatian art with an excellent selection of 15th- and 16th-century Dalmatian paintings. The most outstanding work is the polyptych of *The Virgin* by Blaž Trogiranin. There are also liturgical items, jewellery, furniture and ancient documents relating to the history of Korčula.

Icon Museum MUSEUM
(Trg Svih Svetih; admission 15KN; ⌚10am-noon & 5-7pm Mon-Sat) The modest Icon Museum has a small collection of interesting Byzantine icons painted on wood on gold backgrounds, and 17th- and 18th-century ritual objects. Visitors are let into the beautiful old **All Saints' Church** (Crkva Svih Svetih) next door as a bonus. This 18th-century baroque church features a carved and painted 15th-century wood screen and a late-18th-century pietà, along with a wealth of local religious paintings.

Activities

There are some excellent bike and hiking trails around Korčula; pick up an island map from the tourist office or Kantun Tours (which rents out bikes for 100KN per day). Scooters (320KN for 24 hours) and boats (610KN per day) are available from **Rent a Đir** (☎711 908; www.korcula-rent.net; Biline 5). Be sure to visit the pretty town of Orebić, just over the water, which has a fine beach and good hiking trails.

In the summer season, water taxis offer trips to **Badija Island**, which has a 15th-century Franciscan monastery and a naturist beach.

Tours

Travel agencies can set you up on an island tour or a trip to Mljet and offer mountain biking (195KN), and sea-kayaking and snorkelling trips (220KN).

Festivals & Events

Holy Week celebrations are particularly elaborate in Korčula. Beginning on Palm Sunday, the entire week before Easter is devoted to ceremonies and processions organised by the local religious brotherhoods, whose members dress in traditional costumes. The townspeople sing medieval songs and hymns, Biblical events are reenacted and the city gates are blessed. The most solemn processions are on Good Friday when members of all brotherhoods parade through the streets. A schedule of events is available at the tourist office.

Sleeping

Korčula's hotel scene is on the bulky and resort side, but there are still decent hotels to be found. If you don't fancy staying in any of the big hotels, a more personal option is a guesthouse. Atlas Travel Agency (p270) arranges private rooms (from 250KN in high season).

There's one large and several small campgrounds. **Autocamp Kalac** (☎711 182; www.korculahotels.com; per person/site 54/48KN; ⌚May-Oct) is closest to the old town (a 30-minute walk away) and has an attractive site in a dense pine grove. It has tennis courts and fronts a slim beach but does get very crowded in summer.

About 10km west of town near Račišće are three small campgrounds that offer more privacy and access to uncrowded beaches. They are all open from June to mid-September and cost about 90KN per person, including a tent and car: **Kamp Oskorušica** (☎710 747); **Kamp Tri Žala** (☎721 244; trizala@vip.hr); and **Kamp Vrbovica** (☎721 311).

TOP CHOICE **Lešić Dimitri Palace** APARTMENTS €€€
(☎715 560; www.lesic-dimitri.com; Don Pavla Poše 1-6; apt 3363-9752KN; ❄📶) In a class of its own, this extraordinary place is exceptional in every way (including its rates). Spread over several town mansions, the six 'residences' have been finished to an impeccably high standard. All are named after Marco Polo's journeys, so you have a Chinese residence with a (slight) Asian flavour, while India subtly reflects the subcontinent. Every little detail – iPods, marble bathroom fittings, espresso machines – is immaculate, while original features including exposed beams, ancient stone walls and flagstones preserve the feeling that you're somewhere very special. Oh, and the restaurant is the best in town, too.

Villa DePolo APARTMENTS, RENTAL ROOMS €
(☎711 621; tereza.depolo@du.t-com.hr; Svetog Nikole bb; d 350KN; ❄📶) A great budget op-

tion, these small, simple but attractive modern rooms (and apartment) have muted colours and comfortable beds; one has a terrace with amazing views. The location is excellent, a short walk from both the old town and bus station. DePolo's layout is flexible so the units can accommodate two, four or six people. There's a surcharge in the summer for short stays.

Hotel Bon Repos RESORT €€
(☎726 800; www.korcula-hotels.com; d 596KN; P@≋) On the road to Lumbarda, this huge hotel has manicured grounds and a large pool overlooking a small beach. Rooms are in fair shape and represent decent value, and facilities are good, including tennis courts. There's a water-taxi service to Korčula Town, or it's a 30-minute walk.

Pansion Hajduk PANSION €
(☎711 267; olga.zec@du.t-com.hr; d from 440KN; ❄≋) It's a couple of kilometres from town on the road to Lumbarda, but you get a warm welcome, air-conditioned rooms with TVs and even a swimming pool. The in-house restaurant is also decent and there are a few swings for kids.

Ojdanić APARTMENTS €
(☎091 51 52 555; www.korcula-roko.com; apt from 430KN; ❄) A three-minute walk west of the old town along the harbour are two clean, very simple and inexpensive apartments. 'Ela' is studio-sized; 'Roko' could accommodate a family with two small children and has a terrace with great views of the mainland. Ratko, the owner, has a water taxi and offers fishing trips.

Eating

You can pick up picnic supplies and other basics at the supermarket.

TOP CHOICE **LD** MODERN MEDITERRANEAN €€
(☎715 560; www.lesic-dimitri.com; Don Pavla Poše 1-6; mains from 75KN) Korčula's finest restaurant is different from the rest in town, offering a modern, well-executed menu. Start with bite-sized crostini topped with delectable combinations of Med ingredients and move on to a spicy Slavonian sausage stew, sea bass, Pag lamb or smoked-tuna carpaccio. Allow the sommelier to select wines by the glass to accompany each course; there are many wonderful Croatian choices. The setting is also magnificent, with tables right above the water. There is a good-value fixed daily menu too.

TOP CHOICE **Konoba Komin** DALMATIAN €
(☎716 508; Don Iva Matijace; mains from 45KN) Highly atmospheric, this fine *konoba* (simple family-run establishment) looks almost medieval, with its *komin* (roaring fire), roasting meat, ancient stone walls and solid wooden tables. The menu is simple and delicious, with expertly cooked lamb, fish, mussels (in season), game and local wines available. Family-run and very welcoming, space is tight so book ahead.

Konoba Maslina DALMATIAN €
(Lumbarajska cesta bb; mains from 50KN) Everything you'd want from a rural *konoba*, this traditional place offers rustic character and really honest country cooking. Chef-patron Ivan will guide you through the menu and make suggestions: fresh fish, lamb and veal, and local ham and cheese feature strongly. It's about 3km out of town on the road to Lumbarda.

Konoba Marinero SEAFOOD €€
(Marka Andrijića; mains from 50KN) Friendly, marine-themed Marinero is family-run and cosy. The sons catch the fish and the parents prepare it according to a variety of traditional recipes.

Cukarin DELI €
(Hrvatske Bratske Zajednice; cakes from 10KN) Deli-style place that bakes amazing Korčulan creations such as *klajun* (walnut pastry) and *amareta* (round, rich cake with almonds). Also sells wine, jam and olive oil from the island.

Gradski Podrum CROATIAN €€
(Kaporova; mains from 70KN) Atmospheric old-town eatery and worth trying for its Korčula-style fish stew.

Drinking

Vinum Bonum WINE BAR
(Punta Jurana 66; ⊙11am-2pm & 6pm-midnight) Tucked away on a little pedestrianised lane just off the harbour, this casual place allows you to sample some of the island's best wines.

Dos Locos BAR
(Šetalište Frana Kršinića 14) Hangout for young Korčulans complete with R&B on the mix

MOREŠKA SWORD DANCES

One of the island's most colourful traditions is the Moreška sword dance, performed in Korčula since the 15th century. Although the dance is probably of Spanish origin, Korčula is now the only place it is performed. It tells the story of two kings – the White King (dressed in red) and the Black King – who fight for a princess abducted by the Black King. In the spoken introduction the princess declares her love for the White King, and the Black King refuses to relinquish her. The two armies draw swords and 'fight' in an intricate dance accompanied by a band. Enthusiastic townspeople perform the dance, which takes place outside the southern gate. Although traditionally performed only on Korčula's town day, 29 July, the dance now takes place at 9pm every Monday and Thursday evening between June and September. Tickets cost 100KN and can be purchased on the spot or from any travel agency.

Kumpanija dances in the villages of Pupnat, Smokvica, Blato and Čara make a fun night out, but you'll need your own transport to see them. These dances also involve a 'fight' between rival armies and culminate in the unfurling of a huge flag. They're accompanied by the *mišnice* (a local instrument like a bagpipe) and drums.

and music videos projected on the side of a building. It's just behind the bus station.

Cocktail Bar Massimo COCKTAIL BAR
(Šetalište Petra Kanavelića) This bar is lodged in a turret and accessible only by ladder; the drinks are brought up by pulley. Visit for views of the coast and cathedral, not the tacky cocktail list. No children.

 Information

There are several ATMs around town, including one at HVB Splitska Banka. You can also change money at the post office or at any of the travel agencies.

Atlas Travel Agency (☎711 231; atlas korcula@du.htnet.hr; Plokata 19 Travnja bb) Represents American Express, runs excursions and finds private accommodation.

Hospital (☎711 137; Kalac bb) About 1km past Hotel Marko Polo.

Kantun Tours (☎715 622; www.kantun-tours.com; Plokata 19 Travnja bb) Probably the best organised and largest agency, it offers private accommodation, lots of excursions, car hire and boat tickets. Also has internet access (25KN per hour) and luggage storage.

Post Office (Trg Kralja Tomislava)

Tourist Office (☎715 701; www.korcula.net; Obala Franje Tuđmana 4; ⌚8am-3pm & 5-8pm Mon-Sat, 9am-1pm Sun Jul & Aug, 8am-2pm Mon-Sat Sep-Jun) On the west harbour; an excellent source of information.

 Getting There & Away

There's a **Jadrolinija office** (☎715 410) about 25m down from the west harbour.

Lumbarda

Surrounded by vineyards and coves, Lumbarda is a laid-back village located around a harbour on the southeastern end of Korčula Island. The sandy soil is perfect for vineyards, and wine from the *grk* grape is Lumbarda's most famous product. In the 16th century, aristocrats from Korčula built summer houses around Lumbarda, and it remains a bucolic retreat from the more urbanised Korčula Town. The town beaches are small but sandy. A good beach (Plaza Pržina) is on the other side of the vineyards beyond the supermarket.

Sleeping & Eating

There are several small, inexpensive campgrounds up the hill from the bus stop.

Zure RURAL INN €€
(☎712 008; www.zure.hr; apt from 610KN; ⌚May-Nov; P❄@) A wonderful *agroturizam* run by a hospitable Croatian/German couple and their family in a quiet location. Zure consists of two modern apartments and a small house, all with terraces. *Grk* and *plavac mali* wines, cheese and dried ham are produced from the land; fresh fish and seafood (try the *buzara*, a sauce of tomatoes, white wine, onions and breadcrumbs) are served in the restaurant (mains from 70KN).

Pansion Marinka RURAL INN €
(☎712 007; marinka.milina-bire@du.t-com.hr; d 385KN; ⌚May-Nov) This is a working farm and vineyard with attractive, recently renovated accommodation (double rooms and

three apartments). The rural setting is lovely and within walking distance of the beach. The owners produce excellent wines, olive oil and cheese, and catch and smoke their own fish.

Hotel Borik HOTEL €€
(☎712 215; www.hotelborik.hr; d 720KN; P ❄ @ ☎) This hotel has 23 renovated, stylish modern rooms, all with clean lines, air-con and satellite TV (and a large annexe with a lot more). It's set back from the road on a small hill in the centre of town and has a lovely terrace. Bikes are available to hire.

Information

The **tourist office** (☎tel/fax 712 005; www.lumbarda.hr; ⊙8am-noon & 4-8pm mid-Jun–Aug, shorter hours rest of year) can help find accommodation.

Getting There & Away

In Korčula Town, water taxis wait around the eastern port for passengers to Lumbarda. Buses to Lumbarda (15KN, 15 minutes) run about hourly until midafternoon; no bus services on Sunday.

Vela Luka

Vela Luka, close to the western tip of Korčula, is a pretty little port set in a lovely natural harbour. There are coves for swimming but no beaches around town. Small boats can take you to the idyllic offshore islands of Proizd and Osjak.

Vela Luka is surrounded by hills covered with olive trees, and the production and marketing of Korčula's famous olive oil is vital to the local economy. Tourism and fishing are the other main employers.

Sights & Activities

Vela Luka's harbourfront is a pleasant place for a stroll, though sights are slim on the ground. You could take a look at the Neolithic **Vela Špilja** cave, which is spacious enough to make cave-dwelling seem like a viable accommodation option. Signs from town direct you there; it overlooks the town and harbour. The entrance is locked most of the year, but head to the tourist office and they'll give you the key. Inside there are information panels (in English and Croatian) that explain all.

There's also an **Olive Oil Museum** (admission 25KN; ⊙Jun-Sep), 2km east of Vela Luka on the main highway, which has some restored olive-oil presses and wicker gathering tools, plus fine oil for sale.

Gradina, 5km northwest of Vela Luka, is a lovely, peaceful bay very popular with yachties. There are no beaches here but there's decent swimming in very shallow water and a great restaurant. You'll need your own wheels to reach it.

Sleeping & Eating

The group **Hum Hotels** (www.humhotels.hr) has several options in the area.

TOP CHOICE **Hotel Korkyra** HOTEL €€
(☎601 000; www.hotel-korkyra.com; Obala 3; d/ste 754/1075KN; P ❄ ☎ ≋) The thorough refurb of this hotel has seriously upped accommodation standards in Vela Luka. The 58 rooms are finished to a very high standard, and have hip, contemporary decor and a modish bathroom. The theme continues in the reception areas, where you'll find seriously chic seating and lighting. There's a fitness room with bay views, a pool at the rear and a good restaurant. It's exceptional value.

Hotel Dalmacija HOTEL €€
(☎812 022; www.humhotels.hr; Obala bb; r 526KN) Small two-star hotel on the waterfront with 14 modern rooms that have cool Mediterranean colours and sea-facing balconies.

Camp Mindel CAMPGROUND €
(☎813 600; www.mindel.hr; per adult/tent 28/25KN; ⊙May-Sep) A compact, inexpensive site 5km west of town, ideal for country walks. There's no bus service here.

TOP CHOICE **Konoba Šiloko** SEAFOOD €
(Gradina; mains from 50KN) Right on Gradina bay, 5km northwest of town, this is a superb seafood restaurant, run by a welcoming family and very popular with boaters. Grilled fish, lobster fresh from the tank, black-cuttlefish risotto and mussels are just some of the tempting options. Pag cheese and Korčula lamb also feature. Tables overlook the sea and offshore islands.

Nautica INTERNATIONAL €
(Obala 2; mains from 35KN; ☎) A casual, attractive cafe-restaurant with a great harbourfront terrace. The inexpensive menu includes burritos, fish and salads, and the pizzas are the best in town.

WORTH A TRIP

IDYLLIC ISLANDS

For a total veg-out at the beach, nothing beats the offshore islands of **Proizd** and **Osjak**. The clear, blue water and white stones of Proizd are dazzling, while Osjak, the larger island, is known for its forest. Bring plenty of sunscreen as there is little shade. There are inexpensive eating options on both islands. Several small boats leave Vela Luka each morning in July and August and pick you up in the afternoon.

Information

Atlas Travel Agency (☎812 078; www.atlas-velaluka.com; Obala 3) On the quay; it finds accommodation and offers internet access (25KN per hour).

Tourist Office (☎tel/fax 813 619; www.tzvelaluka.hr; Ulica 41; ⌚8am-2pm & 5-8pm Mon-Fri, 9am-noon Sat Jun-Sep, 8am-2pm Mon-Fri Oct-May) Right on the waterfront, with helpful staff.

PELJEŠAC PENINSULA

The slender finger-like peninsula of Pelješac is coastal Croatia at its most relaxed. Blessed with a spine of craggy mountains, sweeping valleys and idyllic coves, it's a glorious place to visit. It has just one tiny resort.

Orebić

POP 1954

Orebić, on the southern coast of the Pelješac Peninsula, has the best beaches in southern Dalmatia – sandy coves bordered by groves of tamarisk and pine. Only 2.5km across the water from Korčula Town, it makes a perfect day trip or an alternative base. After lazing on the beach, you can take advantage of some excellent hiking up and around Mt Ilija (961m) or poke around a couple of churches and museums. Mt Ilija protects the town from harsh northern winds, allowing vegetation to flourish. The temperature is usually a few degrees warmer than Korčula; spring arrives early and summer leaves late.

History

Orebić and the Pelješac Peninsula became part of Dubrovnik in 1333 when it was purchased from Serbia. Until the 16th century the town was known as Trstenica (the name of its eastern bay) and was an important maritime centre. The name Orebić comes from a wealthy seafaring family, who, in 1658, built a citadel as a defence against the Turks. Many of the houses and exotic gardens developed by prosperous sea captains still grace the area. The height of Orebić seafaring occurred in the 18th and 19th centuries when it was the seat of one of the largest companies of the day: the Associazione Marittima di Sabioncello. With the decline of shipping, Orebić began to turn to tourism.

Sights & Activities

Both passenger launches and ferries from Korčula tie up just steps from the tourist office and bus stop. The main commercial street, Bana Josipa Jelačića, runs parallel to the harbourside.

Trstenica BEACH

There's a slim beach west of the dock, but the best beach is the long stretch at Trstenica about 700m east of the dock. A beautiful broad crescent of sand and fine shingle, it's fringed by mature trees and its sheltered waters are a near-Caribbean shade of turquoise.

Maritime Museum MUSEUM

(Obala Pomoraca; admission 15KN; ⌚10am-noon & 5-8pm Mon-Sat May-Oct, shorter hours in winter) Next to the tourist office, this museum is interesting enough for a peek. There are paintings of ships, boating memorabilia, navigational aids and prehistoric finds from archaeological excavations in nearby Majsan. Explanations are in English.

Walks HIKING

Orebić is great for hiking, so pick up the (free) map of the walking paths from the tourist office. A trail through pine woods leads from Hotel Bellevue to a 15th-century **Franciscan monastery** (admission 15KN; ⌚3-8pm Mon-Fri) on a ridge 152m above the sea. From their vantage point, Dubrovnik patrols could keep an eye on the Venetian ships moored on Korčula and notify the authorities of any suspicious movements. The village of **Karmen** near the monastery is the starting point for walks to picturesque upper villages and the more daring climb up **Mt Ilija**, the bare, grey massif that hangs over Orebić. The reward for climbers is a sweeping view of the entire coast. On a hill east of the monastery is the **Lady of**

Karmen Church (Gospa od Karmena), next to several huge cypresses, as well as a baroque **loggia** and the **ruins** of a duke's castle.

Sleeping & Eating

The tourist office and Orebić Tours find private rooms (from 170KN per person) as well as studios and apartments.

West of town are a handful of modern resort complexes run by **HTP Orebić** (www.orebic-htp.hr).

TOP CHOICE **Hotel Adriatic** BOUTIQUE HOTEL €€€
(☎714 488; www.hoteladriaticorebic.com; Šetalište Kneza Domagoja 8; r 1195-1307KN) A newly opened hotel at the end of Orebić's main drag, this is a converted sea captain's mansion with some of the most comfortable and beautiful rooms you'll find on Pelješac. The reception area may fail to impress with a slightly lacklustre atmosphere, but the rooms will delight with their exposed walls, lush wooden floors and fantastic, ample bathrooms. All have great sea views. A rich breakfast is served on the outside terrace that overlooks the Adriatic.

Hotel Indijan HOTEL €€€
(☎714 555; www.hotelindijan.hr; Škvar 2; s/d 787/1357KN; P❄@🛜≋) A relatively new and well-designed hotel with a contemporary feel throughout. All rooms are modern and well equipped, and some have balconies with great views over the Adriatic to Korčula. The heated pool is tiny but has a retractable glass roof so it's useable all year round. Service standards are high, and the hotel offers wine tours of the peninsula.

Glavna Plaža CAMPGROUND, APARTMENTS €
(☎713 399; www.glavnaplaza.com; Trstenica; camping per adult/site 29/22KN, apt 375-885KN; ⊙Apr-Sep) This small family-run campground overlooks long, sandy Trstenica beach and there are four simple apartments (two studios and one that can sleep six) with neutral colour schemes available as well. It's close to shops and cafes.

Dalmatino CROATIAN €
(Jelačića 47; mains from 40KN; 👪) Just west of the harbour, right on the seafront, this popular place has a pleasant atmosphere and tables shaded by pines. It's a good base to while away a few minutes if you're waiting for a boat, and it has a kids' play area. The menu includes squid (75KN), fish (per kg 290KN), shrimp, steak and pasta.

THE RIGHT KIND OF WIND

If you're into windsurfing, head over to **Viganj**, a village that sits close to the southwestern end of Pelješac, which has three schools and some of the best conditions in Croatia. The village is strung out along the coast, with few visitors except for those who are afflicted with windsurfing fever. **Antony-Boy** (☎719 077; www.antony-boy.com; per person/tent 39/39KN; @🛜), behind a pebble beach, is a good camping choice and has a windsurf school. Viganj is a low-key place but there are a couple of restaurants and one lively beach bar, **Karmela 2** (☎719 097; 🛜), which serves grub (July and August only), and has table football, a pool table and a great vibe in summer.

Information

Orebić Tours (☎713 367; www.orebic-tours.hr; Bana Josipa Jelačića 84a) Finds private accommodation, changes money and books excursions including wine tours and boat cruises.

Post Office (Trg Mimbeli bb) Next door to the tourist office.

Tourist Office (☎713 718; www.tz-orebic.com; Trg Mimbeli bb; ⊙8am-8pm Jul & Aug, 8am-2pm Mon-Fri Sep-Jun) Has a good hiking and biking map of the peninsula and plenty of brochures. Also finds private accommodation.

Getting There & Away

There are three or four daily ferries (seven in summer) from Ploče to Trpanj, which connect with a bus to Orebić. Korčula buses to Dubrovnik, Zagreb and Sarajevo stop at Orebić (on the harbourfront by the ferry port).

Ston & Mali Ston

POP 722

Ston and Mali Ston sit 59km northwest of Dubrovnik on an isthmus that connects the Pelješac Peninsula with the mainland. Formerly part of the Republic of Dubrovnik, Ston was and is an important salt-producing town. Its economic importance to Dubrovnik led, in 1333, to the construction of a 5.5km wall, one of the longest fortifications in Europe. Architects including Juraj Dalmatinac were involved in the design and construction, which included 40 towers and five forts. The walls are still standing, sheltering a cluster of medieval buildings in the town centre. Mali Ston, a little village and harbour situated 1km northeast of Ston, was built along with the wall as part of the defensive system. Both towns are major gastronomic destinations, turning out some of the best seafood dishes in Croatia – they're justly famed for oysters and mussels, farmed here since Roman times.

Sights & Activities

The major sight in Ston is the 14th-century **walls** (admission 30KN; 10am-dusk) that stretch from both towns far up the hill. They have been fully restored, and you can walk the ramparts for long stretches (the clear Pelješac air allows for fine views over the peninsula).

You could also drop by and see the **salt pans** (www.solanaston.hr; admission 15KN; 10am-6pm May-Oct) in Ston, which brought so much wealth and are still operational today. Salt is gathered between late July and September, and volunteers are needed to help out. It's a kind of working holiday; check the website for info.

There are no beaches in town but it's 4km or so to Prapratno, southwest of town, where there's a wonderful cove, camping and a pretty pebble beach. Watch out for sea urchins in the shallow water though.

Sleeping & Eating

Ostrea HISTORIC HOTEL €€€
(754 555; www.ostrea.hr; Mali Ston; s/d from 710/922KN; P ✱ @) A very attractive, historic stone structure with appealing green shutters. Staff are welcoming and professional and it's just steps from Mali Ston's pretty harbour. There are three classes of elegant rooms; all nine have polished timber floors and modern bathrooms, while the restaurant is one of the best in town (so half-board options are a good deal).

Camping Prapratno CAMPGROUND €
(754 000; www.duprimorje.hr; per adult/site 45/37KN;) This large campground is 4km southwest of Ston, right on Prapratno Bay. It has good facilities including tennis and basketball courts, a supermarket and restaurant.

Stagnum INTERNATIONAL €
(Imena Isusova 23, Ston; mains from 45KN; Apr-Oct) You'll be well looked after at this courtyard restaurant, which serves up generous, tasty portions of fresh mussels, steak, barbecued fish and risotto.

Kapetanova Kuća SEAFOOD €€
(754 452; Mali Ston; mains from 75KN) This is one of the most venerable seafood restaurants in the region. Dine on Ston oysters and mussels on the shady terrace.

Information

The **tourist office** (754 452; www.ston.hr; Peljestki put 1; 8am-8pm Jun-Sep, 8am-2pm & 4-7pm May & Oct, 8am-2pm Mon-Fri Nov-Apr) has brochures and bus timetables and can arrange private accommodation.

Getting There & Away

The bus stop is in the centre of Ston, near the tourist office and post office. Five daily buses go from Ston to Dubrovnik (60KN, 1½ hours), and one to Zagreb (245KN, nine hours).

Understand Croatia

population per sq km

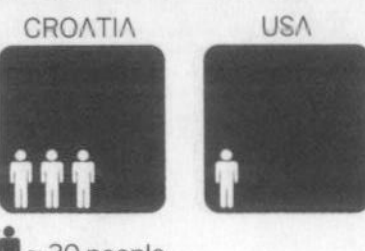

Croatia Today

Brand New to the EU

Precariously poised between the Balkans and Central Europe, Croatia has something of a love-hate affair with the outside world, including its next-door neighbours. Perhaps unsurprisingly, Croatia joining the EU in July 2013 opened a can of worms. Slovenia keeps nitpicking and complicating life for Croatia; and with Europe heaving under the debt crisis, Germany is displaying discomfort about extending the borders of the EU.

On home turf, things aren't simple either. In January 2012, about 44% of Croats turned up to vote in the referendum on the EU ascension and supported the joining by a margin of two to one. But attitudes towards the EU ascension remain divided, in no small part due to the European debt crisis. Younger generations are generally doubtful and anti-EU, despite the fact they have the most to gain. Older people lament the inevitable loss of industrial and agricultural independence. The divide aside, Croatia is slated to become the EU's 28th member state, which – on paper at least – will catapult it out of the Balkans and place it firmly in Central Europe. But the ascension is no big bang; Croatia's inner strife remains.

Political Drama & Discontent

Croatia harbours the love-hate relationship even with its own politicians, its political arena fuelled by constant drama. The pinnacle occurred in 2009, with the surprise resignation of then prime minister Ivo Sanader. In 2010 Sanader was arrested in Austria, in 2011 he was extradited to Croatia and later that year he was put on trial in Zagreb. The Sanader scandal remains the talk of the town; a fifth indictment on corruption charges was filed in September 2012.

Croatian politics took a major turn in the 2011 parliamentary election, when the SDP (Social Democratic Party) joined three other centre-left par-

Top Reads

» **Black Lamb and Grey Falcon** (Rebecca West) Recounts the writer's journeys through the Balkans in 1941.

» **Another Fool in the Balkans** (Tony White) White retraces Rebecca West's journey, juxtaposing the region's modern life with its political history.

» **Cafe Europa – Life After Communism** (Slavenka Drakulić) Wittily details the infiltration of Western culture in Eastern Europe.

On Yugoslavia

» **Croatia: a Nation Forged in War** (Marcus Tanner)

» **The Fall of Yugoslavia** (Misha Glenny)

» **The Death of Yugoslavia** (Laura Silber and Alan Little)

» **A Paper House** (Mark Thompson)

religious groups

(% of population)

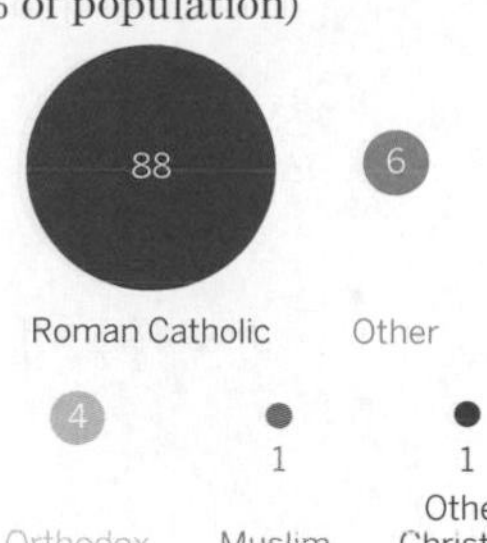

if Croatia were 100 people

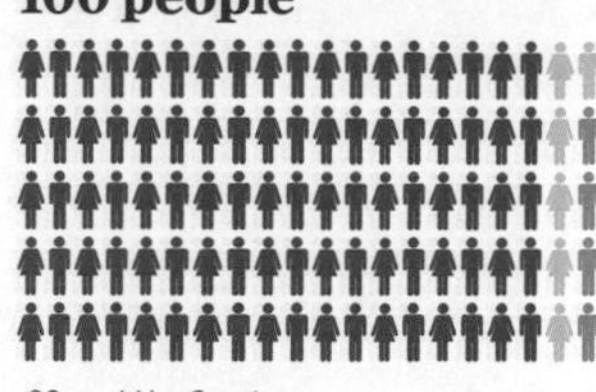

90 would be Croat
6 would be Other
4 would be Serb

ties to create the so-named Kukuriku coalition, an opposition bloc headed up by Zoran Milanović. Kukuriku won with an absolute majority, ousting HDZ (Croatian Democratic Union), which had been in government for 16 of the 20 years since Croatia became independent in 1991. Milanović took office as Croatia's prime minister in December 2011. But the slightly uplifted spirits quickly descended back into general discontent with politics, mainly due to the crisis and the unpopular austerity measures that ensued.

Population: 4,290,612

GDP per capita: €14,198 (2011)

Annual inflation: 2.3% (2011)

Unemployment: 17.8% (2011)

Literacy rate: 98.1%

Average monthly salary: 5441KN

Double-Dip Crisis

Croatia's economy has been in a shambles for several years, and the global downturn plus the EU crisis aren't helping. Unemployment is high, people's salaries are often months overdue, longstanding national companies are going bankrupt, pensions are ridiculously low and unemployment compensation isn't much better. Needless to say, from the point of view of the average Croat, life is tough and the global financial crisis has made itself clearly known. *Kriza* (crisis) is among the most uttered words in Croatia today; you'll hear it everywhere, all the time, like a mantra.

Despite the double-dip recession, Croatia stands as an emerging market of some promise. It is compensating for the drastic drop in foreign investments with rapid growth in tourism revenue. It has, in fact, become the fastest growing tourism market in the entire Mediterranean.

Kuna vs Euro

As a consequence of the Greek crisis, the EU is getting stricter with the criteria for the euro introduction for its new members. While there was talk of Croatia adopting the euro as early as 2014, this date is rumoured to be pushed back to 2020. The intention is for Croatia to build a solid, healthy economy before it enters the Eurozone.

» **Balkan Ghosts: A Journey through History** (Robert D Kaplan)

» **Europe's Backyard War** (Mark Almond)

Top Films

» **Occupation in 26 Pictures** (*Okupacija u 26 slika*; 1978) Lordan Zafranović

» **You Only Love Once** (*Samo jednom se ljubi*; 1981) Rajko Grlić

» **Cyclops** (*Kiklop*; 1982) Antun Vrdoljak

» **How the War on My Island Started** (*Kako je počeo rat na mom otoku*; 1997) Vinko Brešan

» **A Wonderful Night in Split** (*Ta divna splitska noć*; 2004) Arsen A Ostojić

» **Armin** (2006) Ognjen Sviličić

Recent Population Shifts

According to the most recent census (2011), Croatia has a population of roughly 4.3 million people, a decline from the prewar population of nearly five million. A discouraging economic outlook is largely responsible for a steady decline in Croatia's population, as educated young people leave in search of greater opportunities abroad. Then there was the still recent war of the 1990s, during which about 50% of the Serbian population departed; less than half have returned. The postindependence economic crunch that followed sparked a mass exodus of Croats; some 120,000 emigrated. That was balanced out by the roughly equal number of ethnic Croat refugees who arrived from Bosnia and Hercegovina and some 30,000 who came from the Vojvodina region of Serbia. These days, the recession-powered brain drain continues. It's not surprising: Croatia is right behind Spain and Greece when it comes to the unemployment rates of young educated under-thirties.

For up-to-date news on all things Croatian, in Croatia and abroad, check out www.croatiantimes.com.

The Serb population is highest in eastern Slavonia, which also includes a significant number of Hungarians and Czechs. Italians are concentrated in Istria, while Albanians, Bosniaks and Roma can be found in Zagreb, Istria and some Dalmatian towns. Some 3.5 million ethnic Croats live abroad, mainly in the USA, Germany, Australia, Canada and Argentina. Expats retain the right to vote in national elections, and many of those who do take a hard nationalistic line and tend to vote for right-wing parties.

Media

» TV networks: HRT (government-owned), Nova and RTL

» Newspapers: *Večernji List*, *Jutarnji List*, *24sata*

» Magazines: *Globus*, *24 Express*, *Gloria*

Don't Cross a Croat

» Don't refer to Croatia as Eastern Europe; Croats proudly think of themselves as part of Mitteleuropa.

» Dress modestly when visiting churches.

» Be sensitive when discussing the recent war.

» Wait to be invited to use a person's first name.

» Allow your host to pay the bill if you've been invited to a restaurant or bar.

History

Croatia has a long and torrid history, which has helped define the Croats and contributed much to the fabric of the country. For long periods, the Croats have been ruled by and have fought off others – Venetians, Ottomans, Hungarians, Habsburgs, the French, the Germans. The creation of Yugoslavia after WWII brought some semblance of unity to the south Slavic nations. Yet it didn't last long. After the death of Yugoslav leader Tito in 1980, Yugoslavia slowly disintegrated, and a brutal war ensued. Croatia declared its independence in 1991, yet it was not until the Dayton Peace Accords in December 1995 that Croatia started healing its war wounds. These days it's a country in transition, a young democracy with a recently elected president. Despite facing many hurdles, including widespread governmental corruption and elements of rabid nationalism, Croatia is slowly but steadily inching its way towards the EU. The joining date is mid-2013, finally placing Croatia inside Europe.

Croatia Before Christianity

Early Inhabitants

Around 30,000 years ago, Croatia was the haunt of Neanderthals, who lumbered through the hills of Slavonia. The Croatian Natural History Museum (p47) in Zagreb displays relics of this distant era, and the new Museum of the Krapina Neanderthal (p77) in Krapina offers a faithful picture of Neanderthal life.

By around 1000 BC, the Illyrians took centre stage in the area now comprised of Croatia, Serbia and Albania. The Illyrians had to contend with Greeks who established trading colonies on the Adriatic coast at Vis and elsewhere by the 4th century BC, and Celts who pushed down from the north.

The Adriatic is derived from the name of the ancient Illyrian tribe Ardeioi.

In 231 BC an uppity Illyrian, Queen Teuta, committed a fatal tactical error in seeking to conquer various Greek colonies. The put-upon Greeks asked the Romans for military support. The Romans pushed their way

TIMELINE

300 BC

Illyrian tribes achieve supremacy in the Balkans by founding city states – including Histri (the old name of Istria) and Liburnia – and establishing themselves as maritime powers in the Adriatic.

11 BC

The Roman province of Illyricum, covering present-day Dalmatia, is extended to the Danube after the defeat of Pannonian tribes. The new province takes in much of modern-day Croatia.

AD 257

Salona, the Roman capital, becomes the first diocese in Roman Dalmatia, thus creating a toehold for Catholicism in the region; within 30 years the Bishop of Salona has become pope.

into the region and by 168 BC they defeated Gentius, the last Illyrian king. And so, gradually, the Illyrians were Latinised.

The Romans & Diocletian's Dream

Croatia holds Eastern Europe's greatest Roman remnant – the spectacular, ramshackle and invaluable Diocletian's Palace (p197) in Split. Diocletian, who became emperor in AD 285, built and retired to his palace in Spalato (Split) in AD 305, but not before he attempted to simplify the unwieldy empire by dividing it into two administrative halves, thus sowing the seeds for the later division into the Eastern and Western Roman Empires. The Romans built a series of roads reaching to the Aegean and Black Seas and the Danube, facilitating trade and the expansion of Roman culture. The roads also accelerated the later spread of Christianity.

Dalmatian dogs are thought to be one of the oldest breeds, but there's no conclusive evidence that they originated in Dalmatia. Some experts believe the dogs may have been brought to Dalmatia by the Roma.

The last Roman leader to rule a united empire was Theodosius the Great, who adeptly staved off threats from the northern Visigoths. On Theodosius' death in AD 395, the empire was formally divided into eastern and western realms. The eastern half became the Byzantine Empire, which persisted until 1453. The Western Roman Empire fell in the 5th century, preceded by Visigoth, Hun and Lombard invasions.

Roman rule centred on the administrative headquarters of Salona (now Solin). Other important Roman towns included Jadera (Zadar), Parentium (Poreč) and Polensium (Pula). The amphitheatre (p99) at Pula remains an evocative reminder of the glory – or blood lust – of the Roman era.

Slavs Arrive

In the wake of the collapse of the Roman Empire, the Croats and other Slavic groups headed south from their original territory north of the Carpathians. Around the same time, the Avars (Eurasian nomads) were sallying around the Balkan fringes of the Byzantine Empire. The Avars ravaged the former Roman towns of Salona and Epidaurus, whose inhabitants took refuge in Spalato and Ragusa (Dubrovnik), respectively.

Best Roman Ruins

» Diocletian's Palace in Split, Central Dalmatia

» Salona in Solin, Southern Dalmatia

» Arena in Pula, Istria

By the middle of the 7th century, the Slavs in the Western Balkans had divided into two distinct groups. The Croats settled in Pannonia and Dalmatia, forming communities around the Dalmatian towns of Jadera, Aeona (Nin) and Tragurium (Trogir), while the Serbs settled the central Balkans. By the 8th century, the Dalmatian and Pannonian Croats had formed two powerful tribal entities, each led by a *knez* (duke).

395

After Theodosius the Great dies, the Roman Empire is split in two. Slovenia, Croatia and Bosnia fall into the Western Roman Empire, with Serbia, Kosovo and Macedonia in the Byzantine Empire.

614

Central Asian marauders, the Avars, sack Salona and Epidaurus. Some contend that the Croats followed in their wake; others that they were invited by Emperor Heraclius to fend off the Avars.

845–64

Trpimir establishes Croatia's first royal line. He fights and defeats the powerful Bulgarian state, and inflicts major defeats on the Byzantines. Croatian territory expands well into what is now Bosnia.

869

At the behest of Byzantium, Macedonian monks Methodius and Cyril create the Cyrillic alphabet, specifically with a view to speeding the spread of Christianity among the Slavic peoples.

Christianity & the Croat Kings

Charlemagne's Franks gradually encroached on Central Europe and in AD 800 they seized Dalmatia, baptising the previously pagan Croats en masse. After Charlemagne's death in AD 814, the Pannonian Croats revolted unsuccessfully against Frankish rule, without the support of the Dalmatian Croats, whose major coastal cities remained under the influence of the Byzantine Empire. The big breakthrough for the Croats happened when Branimir revolted against Byzantine control and won recognition from Pope John VIII. This brought them closer to the Vatican, and Catholicism became a defining feature of Croatian national identity.

Trpimir, who was *knez* from 845 to 864, is widely considered to have founded the first Croatian dynasty, but it was King Tomislav who first crowned himself king in 925, and united Pannonia and Dalmatia. His kingdom included virtually all of modern Croatia as well as parts of Bosnia and the coast of Montenegro.

But the glory days were not to last. During the 11th century, the Byzantines and the Venetians reimposed themselves on the Dalmatian coast, and new adversaries, the Hungarians, emerged in the north and advanced into Pannonia. Krešimir IV (r 1058–74) turned the tables and regained control of Dalmatia, but Croatia's rebound was only temporary and Krešimir was succeeded by Zvonimir and Stjepan, neither of whom produced an heir. The Hungarians, by stealth and outright invasion, terminated the era of the Croat kings at the end of the 11th century.

THE VENETIAN YOKE

For nearly 800 years the doges of Venice sought to control, colonise and exploit the Croatian coast. Coastal and island towns from Rovinj in the north to Korčula in the south still show a marked Venetian influence in architecture, cuisine and culture. However, as in Venice's other dominions, the period was not a happy time.

Venetian rule in Dalmatia and Istria was a record of virtually unbroken economic exploitation. The Venetians systematically denuded the landscape in order to provide timber for their ships. State monopolies set artificially low prices for olive oil, figs, wine, fish and salt, thus ensuring cheap commodities for Venetian buyers, while local merchants and producers were impoverished. Shipbuilding was effectively banned, since Venice tolerated no competition with its own ships. No roads or schools were built, and no investment was made in local industry.

910–28

Tomislav proclaims himself king while expanding territory at the expense of the Hungarians and defeating Bulgarian Tsar Simeon in modern Bosnia. Tomislav unites Pannonian and Dalmatian Croats.

1000

Venice capitalises on a lack of stability in Croatia to begin encroaching on the Dalmatian coast. So begins the tussle between Venice and other powers for control of Dalmatia.

1058–74

Soon after the 1054 split of the church into Orthodox and Catholic realms, the pope recognises Krešimir IV as king of Dalmatia and Croatia. This places Croatia within the Catholic sphere.

1091–1102

Hungarian King Ladislas, related to the late King Zvonimir, claims the Slavonian throne; his successor, Koloman, defeats the last Croatian king and cements Hungarian control of Croatia with the *Pacta conventa*.

Covetous Neighbours: Hungary vs Venice

In 1102 the Hungarian King Koloman imposed the *Pacta conventa*, ostensibly stating that Hungary and Croatia were separate entities under a single – Hungarian – monarchy. In practice, while Croatia maintained a *ban* (viceroy or governor) and a *sabor* (parliament), the Hungarians steadily marginalised the Croatian nobility. Under Hungarian rule, Pannonia became known as Slavonia, and the interior towns of Zagreb, Vukovar and Varaždin became thriving centres of trade and culture. In 1107, Koloman persuaded the Dalmatian nobility to bring the coast, long coveted by land-locked Hungarian kings, into his realm.

Upon Koloman's death in 1116, Venice launched new assaults on Biograd and the islands of Lošinj, Pag, Rab and Krk. Meanwhile, Zadar had grown to become the largest and most prosperous Dalmatian city and had successfully fended off two Venetian naval expeditions in the 1190s. But a vengeful Venetian doge in 1202 paid the soldiers of the Fourth Crusade to attack and sack Zadar; they did this before rumbling on to turn Constantinople on its ear.

The Mongolian juggernaut ravaged the Croatian interior in 1242, but not before King Bela IV of Hungary fled the onslaught and took refuge in Trogir. The Venetians used the chaos to consolidate their hold on Zadar, and, upon the death of King Bela in 1270, added Šibenik and Trogir to its possessions.

King Ludovic (Louis) I of Hungary (r 1342–82) re-established control over the country and even persuaded Venice to relinquish Dalmatia. But new conflicts emerged upon his death. The Croatian nobility rallied around Ladislas of Naples, who was crowned king in Zadar in 1403. Short of funds, Ladislas sold Zadar to Venice in 1409 for a paltry 100,000 ducats and renounced his rights to Dalmatia. In the early 15th century, Venice strengthened its grip on the Dalmatian coastline south from Zadar and remained in control until the Napoleonic invasion of 1797. Only the wily citizens of Ragusa managed to retain their independence.

The Ottoman Onslaught

Croatia had plenty to contend with as Venetians, Hungarians and others picked at the remnants of the original Croatian state, and yet another threat loomed from the east during the 14th century. The Ottoman Turks had emerged out of Anatolia in the early 1300s and rapidly swallowed up the Balkans.

The Serbs were rolled at Kosovo Polje in 1389, a hastily choreographed anti-Turkish crusade was garrotted in Hungary in 1396, and Bosnia was despatched in 1463. When the Croatian nobility finally faced up to the Ottomans in 1493 in Krbavsko Polje, they too were pummelled.

1242

The Mongols devastate the royal houses of Hungary and Croatia. The noble Šubić and Frankopan families step in to assume a degree of political and economic power that persists for centuries.

1300s

The Hungarian Anjou dynasty under Carl (Charles) and Louis (Ludovic) reasserts royal authority in Croatia and seeks to expel the Venetians who had taken Dalmatian territory.

1358

Ragusa (modern Dubrovnik) frees itself of Venice and becomes an independent city republic. It grows to become an advanced and liberal society, while cannily fending off Venetians and Ottomans.

» Statue of St Blaise (p245)

Despite a sudden show of unity among the remaining noble families, one city after another fell to the Ottoman sultans. The important bishopric at Zagreb heavily fortified the cathedral in Kaptol, which remained untouched, but the gateway town of Knin fell in 1521. Five years later, the Ottomans engaged the Hungarians in Mohács. Again the Turks won and annulled the might of the Hungarian army. The Turks threatened the Adriatic coast but never actually captured it, while Ragusa maintained its independence throughout the turmoil.

Turkish assaults on the Balkans caused massive havoc. Cities and towns were destroyed, people were enslaved and commandeered to the Ottoman war machine, and refugees scattered around the region.

Dubrovnik: A History by Robin Harris is a thoughtful and thorough look at the great city, investigating events, individuals and movements that have contributed to the architectural and cultural fabric of the 'pearl of the Adriatic'.

Enter the Habsburgs

With the Hungarians out of the picture, the Croats turned to the Austrians for protection. The Habsburg Empire, ruled from Vienna, duly absorbed a narrow strip of territory around Zagreb, Karlovac and Varaždin. The Habsburgs sought to build a buffer against the Ottomans, creating the Vojna Krajina (Military Frontier). In this region composed of a string of forts south of Zagreb, a standing army comprised largely of Vlachs and Serbs faced down the Ottomans.

Exactly a century after their defeat by the Ottomans, the Croats managed to turn the tables on the Turks. At Sisak in 1593 the Habsburg army, including Croat soldiers, finally inflicted a defeat on the Ottomans. In 1699 in Sremski Karlovci the Ottomans sued for peace for the first time, and the Turkish stranglehold on Central Europe was loosened.

THE REPUBLIC OF RAGUSA

While most of the Dalmatian coast struggled under Venetian rule, Ragusa (now Dubrovnik) led a charmed life, existing as a republic in its own right. A ruling class, abounding in business acumen and diplomatic skill, ensured that this minuscule city state punched well above its weight and played a significant role in the immediate region and beyond.

The Ragusans asked the pope for permission to trade with the Turks in 1371 and subsequently established trade centres throughout the Ottoman Empire. Burgeoning trade led to a flowering in the arts and sciences. The Ragusans, once described as 'mild and noble', were extremely liberal for the time, abolishing the slave trade in the 15th century. They were also scientifically advanced, establishing a system of quarantine in 1377.

However, the Ragusans had to maintain a perilous position sandwiched between Ottoman and Venetian interests. An earthquake in 1667 caused a great deal of damage, and Napoleon finally swallowed up the republic in 1808.

1409

Ladislas of Naples assumes the Croatian throne but is scared off by dynastic squabbling and sells Dalmatia to Venice for 100,000 ducats. Venetian control soon extends from Zadar to Ragusa.

1493

At Krbavsko Polje a joint Croatian-Hungarian army engages the Turks but is obliterated, leaving Croatia open to Turkish raids. The Turkish advance brings turmoil, as populations flee and famine ensues.

1526–27

The Battle of Mohács sees the Ottoman Turks annihilate the Hungarian nobility, ending Hungarian control of Croatia. Hungarian King Louis dies heirless, allowing the Austrian Habsburgs control.

1537–40

The Turks take Klis, the last Croatian bastion in Dalmatia. The Turkish advance continues to Sisak, just south of Zagreb. For reasons unknown, the Turks never push on to Zagreb.

The Habsburgs reclaimed Slavonia soon after, thus expanding the Krajina. This period saw a return to stability and advances in agricultural production, but Croatian culture and language languished.

Napoleon & the Illyrian Provinces

Habsburg support for the restoration of the French monarchy provoked Napoleon to invade Italian states in 1796. After conquering Venice in 1797 he agreed to transfer Dalmatia to Austria in the Treaty of Campo Formio in exchange for other concessions. The Croats' secret hopes that Dalmatia would be united with Slavonia were soon dashed, as the Habsburgs made it clear that the two territories would retain separate administrations.

Šibenik-born Faust Vrančić (1551–1617) made the first working parachute.

Austrian control of Dalmatia only lasted until Napoleon's 1805 victory over Austrian and Prussian forces at Austerlitz, which forced Austria to cede the Dalmatian coast to France. Ragusa quickly surrendered to French forces, which also swallowed up Kotor in Montenegro. Napoleon renamed his conquest the 'Illyrian provinces' and moved swiftly to reform the neglected territory. A tree-planting program was implemented to reforest the barren hills. Roads and hospitals were built and new crops introduced. Since almost the entire population was illiterate, the new government set up primary schools, high schools and a college at Zadar. Yet the French regime remained unpopular.

After Napoleon's Russian campaign and the fall of his empire, the 1815 Congress of Vienna recognised Austria's claims to Dalmatia and placed the rest of Croatia under the jurisdiction of Austria's Hungarian province. For the Dalmatians the new regime meant a return to the status quo, since the Austrians restored the former Italian elite to power, whereas the Hungarians imposed the Hungarian language and culture on the northern Croatian population.

Croatia Through History by Branka Magaš is a highly detailed doorstop of a history, focusing on pivotal events and clearly delineating the gradual development of Croatian national identity.

A South Slavic Consciousness

Traditionally, upper-class Dalmatians spoke Italian, and northern Croats spoke German or Hungarian, but flush with the Enlightenment fervour, Napoleon had sown the seeds of creating a south Slavic consciousness. This sense of a shared identity eventually manifested itself in an 'Illyrian' movement in the 1830s, which centred on the revival of the Croatian language. Napoleon's grand plan was to foster Serbian culture, too, but Serbia remained under Ottoman occupation.

The establishment of the first Illyrian newspaper in 1834, written in Zagreb dialect, prompted the Croatian *sabor* to call for the teaching of Slavic languages in schools.

Following the 1848 revolution in Paris, the Hungarians began to press for change within the Habsburg Empire. The Croats saw this as

1593

At Sisak, previously the Ottoman high-tide mark, the Habsburgs inflict the first major defeat on the Ottomans, thus prefiguring the long, slow Turkish retreat from Central Europe.

1671

A deputation led by Franjo Frankopan and Petar Zrinski, with the aim of ridding Croatia of Hungarian domination, is cut short. Both are hanged, their lands confiscated by the Habsburgs.

1699

At the Treaty of Karlovci, the Ottomans renounce all claims to Croatia. Venice and Hungary reclaim all freed lands over the next 20 years.

1780s

The Habsburgs begin a process of Germanisation, ordering all administration be conducted in German. This leads to rising nationalist feelings among the Habsburg's non-German subjects.

an opportunity to regain some control and unify Dalmatia, the Krajina and Slavonia. The Habsburgs paid lip service to Croatian sentiments and appointed Josip Jelačić *ban* of Croatia. Jelačić promptly called elections, claimed a mandate and declared war on Hungarian agitators in order to curry favour with the Habsburgs, but his demands for autonomy fell on deaf ears. Jelačić is immortalised in a martial pose in the heart of Zagreb.

Disillusionment spread after 1848 and was amplified after the birth of the Austro-Hungarian Dual Monarchy in 1867. The monarchy placed Croatia and Slavonia within the Hungarian administration, while Dalmatia remained within Austria. Whatever limited form of self-government the Croats enjoyed under the Habsburgs disappeared.

Dreams of Yugoslavia

The river of discontent forked into two streams that dominated the political landscape for the next century. The old 'Illyrian' movement became the National Party, dominated by Bishop Josif Juraj Strossmayer. Strossmayer believed that the Habsburgs and the Hungarians set out to emphasise the differences between Serbs and Croats, and that only through Jugoslavenstvo (literally, 'Southslavism' – or south Slavic unity) could the aspirations of both peoples be realised. Strossmayer supported the Serbian independence struggle in Serbia but favoured a Yugoslav (i.e. south Slavic) entity within the Austro-Hungarian Empire rather than complete independence.

By contrast, the Party of Rights, led by the militantly anti-Serb Ante Starčević, envisaged an independent Croatia made up of Slavonia, Dalmatia, the Krajina, Slovenia, Istria, and part of Bosnia and Hercegovina. At the time, the Eastern Orthodox Church was encouraging the Serbs to form a national identity based upon their religion. Until the 19th century, Orthodox inhabitants of Croatia identified themselves as Vlachs, Morlachs, Serbs, Orthodox or even Greeks. With the help of Starčević's attacks, the sense of a separate Serbian Orthodox identity within Croatia developed.

Under the 'divide and rule' theory, the Hungarian-appointed *ban* of Croatia blatantly favoured the Serbs and the Orthodox Church, but his strategy backfired. The first organised resistance formed in Dalmatia. Croats in Rijeka and Serbs in Zadar joined together in 1905 to demand the unification of Dalmatia and Slavonia, with a formal guarantee of Serbian equality as a nation. The spirit of unity mushroomed, and by 1906 Croat–Serb coalitions had taken over local government in Dalmatia and Slavonia, forming a serious threat to the Hungarian power structure.

Best Gothic Buildings

- » Cathedral of St Domnius in Split, Central Dalmatia
- » Cathedral of St Anastasia in Zadar, Northern Dalmatia
- » Cathedral of the Assumption of the Blessed Virgin Mary in Zagreb
- » Cathedral of St James in Šibenik, Northern Dalmatia

The Balkans, by noted historian Mark Mazower, is a highly readable short introduction to the region. It offers clearly discussed overviews of geography, culture and the broad historical sweep of the Balkans.

1797–1815

Napoleon brings the Venetian Republic to an end; Venetian dominions are initially given to the Habsburgs, but in 1806 Napoleon gains the Adriatic coast, which he dubs the 'Illyrian provinces'.

1830–50

The south Slavic consciousness is awakened, aiming to reverse the processes of Hungarianisation and Germanisation under the Habsburgs. An offshoot is the Croatian National Revival.

1867

The Habsburg throne devolves to become the Dual Monarchy of Austria-Hungary. Croatian territory is divided between them: Dalmatia is awarded to Austria, and Slavonia is under Hungarian control.

1905

Burgeoning Croatian national consciousness becomes visible in the Rijeka Resolution, which calls for increased democracy as well as the reunification of Dalmatia and Slavonia.

The Kingdom of Serbs, Croats & Slovenes

With the outbreak of WWI, Croatia's future was again up for grabs. Sensing that they would once again be pawns to the Great Powers, a Croatian delegation called the 'Yugoslav Committee' talked the Serbian government into establishing a parliamentary monarchy that would rule over the two countries. The Yugoslav Committee became the National Council of Slovenes, Croats and Serbs after the collapse of the Austro-Hungarian Empire in 1918. The council quickly negotiated the establishment of the Kingdom of Serbs, Croats and Slovenes to be based in Belgrade. Although many Croats were unclear about Serbian intentions, they were sure about Italian intentions, since Italy lost no time in seizing Pula, Rijeka and Zadar in November 1918. Effectively given a choice between throwing in their lot with Italy or Serbia, the Croats chose Serbia.

Problems with the kingdom began almost immediately. As under the Habsburgs, the Croats enjoyed scant autonomy. Currency reforms benefited Serbs at the expense of the Croats. A treaty between Yugoslavia and Italy gave Istria, Zadar and several islands to Italy. The new constitution abolished Croatia's *sabor* and centralised power in Belgrade, while new electoral districts severely under-represented the Croats.

Opposition to the new regime was led by the Croat Stjepan Radić, who favoured the idea of Yugoslavia but wished to transform it into a federal democracy. His alliance with the Serb Svetozar Pribićević proved profoundly threatening to the regime and Radić was assassinated in 1928. Exploiting fears of civil war, on 6 January 1929 King Aleksandar in Belgrade ended any hope of democratic change by proclaiming a royal dictatorship, abolishing political parties and suspending parliamentary government. Meanwhile, during the 1920s the Yugoslav Communist Party arose; Josip Broz Tito was to become leader in 1937.

CRAVAT

The neck tie is a descendant of the cravat, which originated in Croatia as part of military attire and was adopted by the French in the 17th century. The name 'cravat' is a corruption of Croat and Hrvat.

The Rise of Ustaše & WWII

One day after the proclamation of the royal dictatorship, a Bosnian Croat, Ante Pavelić, set up the Ustaše Croatian Liberation Movement in Zagreb, inspired by Mussolini. The stated aim was to establish an independent state, by force if necessary. Fearing arrest, he first fled to Sofia in Bulgaria and made contact with anti-Serbian Macedonian revolutionaries. He then moved on to Italy, where he established training camps for his organisation under Mussolini's benevolent eye. In 1934, he and the Macedonians assassinated King Aleksandar in Marseilles. Italy responded by closing down the training camps and imprisoning Pavelić and many of his followers.

When Germany invaded Yugoslavia on 6 April 1941, the exiled Ustaše were quickly installed by the Germans as well as the Italians, who

1908

Austria-Hungary takes control of Bosnia and Hercegovina, bringing the Slavic Muslims of the Balkans within its sphere of responsibility, thus creating the nucleus of the future Yugoslav federation.

1918

The Kingdom of Serbs, Croats and Slovenes is created after the break from Austria-Hungary. Serbian Prince Aleksander Karađorđević assumes the throne.

1920

Stjepan Radić establishes the Croatian Republican Peasant Party, which becomes the primary voice for Croatian interests in the face of Serb domination.

1941

Ante Pavelić proclaims the Independent State of Croatia (NDH), a Nazi puppet state. Ustaše begins prosecuting Serbs, Roma and Jews; the Serbs respond by forming the Četniks, who harass Croats.

hoped to see their own territorial aims in Dalmatia realised. Within days the Independent State of Croatia (NDH; Nezavisna Država Hrvatska), headed by Pavelić, issued a range of decrees designed to persecute and eliminate the regime's 'enemies', a thinly veiled reference to the Jews, Roma and Serbs. The majority of the Jewish population was rounded up and packed off to extermination camps between 1941 and 1945.

Serbs fared little better. The Ustaše programme explicitly called for 'one-third of Serbs killed, one-third expelled and one-third converted to Catholicism', an agenda that was carried out with appalling brutality. Villages conducted their own personal pogroms against Serbs and extermination camps were set up, most notoriously at Jasenovac (south of Zagreb), where Jews, Roma and antifascist Croats were killed. The exact number of Serb victims is uncertain and controversial. In all, it is estimated that around one in six Serbs was killed.

Ivan Vučetić (1858–1925), who developed dactyloscopy (fingerprint identification), was born on the island of Hvar in the Adriatic.

Tito & the Partisans

Not all Croats supported these policies, and some spoke out against them. The Ustaše regime drew most of its support from the Lika region, southwest of Zagreb, and western Hercegovina. Pavelić's agreement to cede a good part of Dalmatia to Italy was highly unpopular and the Ustaše had almost no support in that region.

Armed resistance to the regime took the form of Serbian 'Četnik' formations led by General Draža Mihailović. The Četniks began as an antifascist rebellion but soon retaliated against the Ustaše with in-kind massacres of Croats in eastern Croatia and Bosnia.

The most effective antifascist struggle was conducted by National Liberation Partisan units and their leader, Josip Broz, known as Tito. The Partisans, which had their roots in the outlawed Yugoslavian Communist Party, attracted long-suffering Yugoslav intellectuals, Croats disgusted with Četnik massacres, Serbs disgusted with Ustaše massacres, and antifascists of all kinds. The Partisans gained wide popular support with their early manifesto, which envisioned a postwar Yugoslavia based on a loose federation.

Although the Allies initially backed the Serbian Četniks, it became apparent that the Partisans were waging a far more focused and determined fight against the Nazis. With the diplomatic and military support of Churchill and other Allied powers, the Partisans controlled much of Croatia by 1943. They established functioning local governments in the territory they seized, which later eased their transition to power. On 20 October 1944, the Partisans entered Belgrade alongside the Red Army. When Germany surrendered in 1945, Pavelić and the Ustaše fled and the Partisans entered Zagreb.

1943

Tito's communist Partisans achieve military victories and build a popular antifascist front. They reclaim territory from retreating Italian brigades. The British and the USA lend military support.

1945–48

The Federal People's Republic of Yugoslavia is founded. Tito breaks with Stalin and steers a careful course between Eastern and Western blocs, and founds the nonaligned movement.

1960s

Croatian unrest about the centralisation of power in Belgrade builds. The use of Croatian money to support poorer provinces is resented, along with the over-representation of Serbs in government.

1971

In the 'Croatian Spring' Communist Party reformers, intellectuals, students and nationalists call for greater economic and constitutional autonomy for Croatia.

The remnants of the NDH army, desperate to avoid falling into the hands of the Partisans, attempted to cross into Austria. A small British contingent met the 50,000 troops and promised to intern them outside Yugoslavia. It was a trick. The troops were forced into trains that headed back into Yugoslavia, where the Partisans awaited them. The ensuing massacre claimed the lives of at least 30,000 men (although the exact number is in doubt) and left a permanent stain on the Yugoslav government.

For a quirky, or perhaps reverent, look at Tito, visit his home page: www.titoville.com. Enjoy pictures of him in statesman-like poses, scripts from his speeches, lists of his 'wives' and jokes about him.

The Birth of Yugoslavia

Tito's attempt to retain control of the Italian city of Trieste and parts of southern Austria faltered in the face of Allied opposition. Dalmatia and most of Istria did make a permanent part of postwar Yugoslavia. In creating the Federal People's Republic of Yugoslavia, Tito was determined to forge a state in which no ethnic group dominated the political landscape. Croatia became one of six republics – along with Macedonia, Serbia, Montenegro, Bosnia and Hercegovina, and Slovenia – in a tightly configured federation. However, Tito effected this delicate balance by creating a one-party state and rigorously stamping out all opposition.

During the 1960s, the concentration of power in Belgrade was an increasingly complicated issue as it became apparent that money from the more prosperous republics of Slovenia and Croatia was being distributed to the poorer autonomous province of Kosovo and the republic of Bosnia and Hercegovina. The problem seemed particularly blatant in Croatia, which saw money from its prosperous tourist business on the Adriatic coast flow into Belgrade. At the same time, Serbs in Croatia were overrepresented in the government, armed forces and police.

Misha Glenny's *The Balkans: Nationalism, War & the Great Powers, 1804–1999* explores the history of outside interference in the Balkans. His *The Fall of Yugoslavia* deciphers the complex politics, history and cultural flare-ups that led to the wars of the 1990s.

In Croatia the unrest reached a crescendo in the 'Croatian Spring' of 1971. Led by reformers within the Communist Party of Croatia, intellectuals and students called for a loosening of Croatia's ties to Yugoslavia. In addition to calls for greater economic autonomy and constitutional reform for Croatia, nationalistic elements manifested themselves too. Tito fought back, clamping down on the liberalisation that had gradually been gaining momentum in Yugoslavia. Serbs viewed the movement as the Ustaše reborn; in turn, jailed reformers blamed the Serbs for their troubles. The stage was set for the rise of nationalism and the war of the 1990s.

The Death of Yugoslavia

Tito left a shaky Yugoslavia upon his death in May 1980. With the economy in a parlous state, a presidency that rotated among the six republics could not compensate for the loss of Tito's steadying hand at the helm. The authority of the central government sank along with the economy, and long-suppressed mistrust among Yugoslavia's ethnic groups resurfaced.

1980

President Tito dies. There is a genuine outpouring of grief, and tributes are paid from around the world. Yugoslavia is left beset by inflation, unemployment and foreign debt.

1989

The communist system begins to collapse in Eastern Europe; Franjo Tuđman establishes Yugoslavia's first noncommunist party, the Croatian Democratic Union (HDZ). He's sworn in as president in 1990.

1991

The Croatian *sabor* (parliament) proclaims the independence of Croatia; Krajina Serbs declare independence from Croatia, with the support of Slobodan Milošević. War breaks out between Croats and Serbs.

1992

A first UN-brokered ceasefire takes effect temporarily. The EU recognises Croatian independence and Croatia is admitted into the UN. War breaks out in neighbouring Bosnia.

In 1989 repression of the Albanian majority in Serbia's Kosovo province sparked renewed fears of Serbian hegemony and precipitated the end of the Yugoslav Federation. With political changes sweeping Eastern Europe, Slovenia embarked on a course for independence. Many Croats felt the time had come for them to also achieve autonomy. In the Croatian elections of April 1990, Franjo Tuđman's Croatian Democratic Union (HDZ; Hrvatska Demokratska Zajednica) secured 40% of the vote, to the 30% won by the Communist Party, which retained the loyalty of the Serbian community as well as voters in Istria and Rijeka. On 22 December 1990, a new Croatian constitution changed the status of Serbs in Croatia from that of a 'constituent nation' to a national minority.

TITO

Josip Broz was born in Kumrovec in 1892 to a Croat father and a Slovene mother. When WWI broke out, Tito was drafted into the Austro-Hungarian army and was taken prisoner by the Russians. He escaped just before the 1917 revolution, became a communist and joined the Red Army. He returned to Croatia in 1920 and became a union organiser while working as a metalworker.

As secretary of the Zagreb committee of the outlawed Communist Party, he worked to unify the party and increase its membership. When the Nazis invaded in 1941, he adopted the name Tito and organised small bands of guerrillas, which formed the core of the Partisan movement. His successful campaigns attracted military support from the British and the Americans, but the Soviet Union, despite sharing his communist ideology, repeatedly rebuffed his requests for aid.

In 1945 he became prime minister of a reconstituted Yugoslavia. Although retaining a communist ideology, and remaining nominally loyal to Russia, Tito had an independent streak. In 1948 he fell out with Stalin and adopted a conciliatory policy towards the West.

Yugoslavia's rival nationalities were Tito's biggest headache, which he dealt with by suppressing all dissent and trying to ensure a rough equality of representation at the upper echelons of government. As a committed communist, he viewed ethnic disputes as unwelcome deviations from the pursuit of the common good.

Yet Tito was well aware of the ethnic tensions that simmered just below the surface in Yugoslavia. Preparations for his succession began in the early 1970s as he aimed to create a balance of power among the ethnic groups of Yugoslavia. He set up a collective presidency that was to rotate annually, but the system proved unworkable. Later events revealed how dependent Yugoslavia was on its wily, charismatic leader.

When Tito died in May 1980, his body was carried from Ljubljana (Slovenia) to Belgrade (Serbia). Thousands of mourners flocked the streets to pay respects to the man who had united a difficult country for 35 years. It was the last communal outpouring of emotion that Yugoslavia's fractious nationalities have been able to share.

1995

The 'Oluja' military campaign sees Croatian forces reclaim lost Croatian territory, expelling Serbs from Krajina. This leads to the Dayton Accords, bringing peace and establishing Croatia's borders.

1999

Croatia's first president, Franjo Tuđman, dies; elections the following January are won by a centrist coalition of anti-Tuđman parties, led by Ivica Račan (prime minister) and Stipe Mesić (president).

2003

The HDZ returns to power, having abandoned the nationalistic baggage it had borne under Tuđman. It has an agenda of economic reform and a goal of UN and NATO membership.

2005

War-crimes suspect Ante Gotovina is captured and handed to the International War Crimes Tribunal. The arrest of Gotovina is controversial in Croatia but regarded positively by the EU.

The constitution failed to guarantee minority rights and caused mass dismissals of Serbs from the public service. This stimulated Croatia's 600,000-strong ethnic Serb community to demand autonomy. In early 1991, Serb extremists within Croatia staged provocations in order to force federal military intervention. A May 1991 referendum (boycotted by the Serbs) produced a 93% vote in favour of Croatian independence. When Croatia declared independence on 25 June 1991, the Serbian enclave of Krajina proclaimed its independence from Croatia.

While the Croats are clearly related to other Slavic nations, the name by which they know themselves – Hrvat – is not a Slavic word. One theory posits that Hrvat is a Persian word, and the Croats are a Slavic tribe who were briefly ruled – and named – by a ruling cast of Persian-speaking Alans from Central Asia.

The War for Croatia

Under pressure from the EU, Croatia declared a three-month moratorium on its independence, but heavy fighting broke out in Krajina, Baranja and Slavonia. This initiated what Croats refer to as the Homeland War. The Yugoslav People's Army, dominated by Serbs, began to intervene in support of Serbian irregulars under the pretext of halting ethnic violence. When the Croatian government ordered a shutdown of federal military installations in the republic of Croatia, the Yugoslav navy blockaded the Adriatic coast and laid siege to the strategic town of Vukovar on the Danube. During the summer of 1991, a quarter of Croatia fell to Serb militias and the Serb-led Yugoslav People's Army.

In late 1991, the federal army and the Montenegrin militia moved against Dubrovnik, and the presidential palace in Zagreb was hit by rockets from Yugoslav jets in an apparent assassination attempt on President Tuđman. When the three-month moratorium ended, Croatia declared full independence. Soon after, Vukovar finally fell when the Yugoslav army moved in, in one of the more bloodthirsty acts in all of the Yugoslav wars. During six months of fighting in Croatia, 10,000 people died, hundreds of thousands fled and tens of thousands of homes were destroyed.

The UN Gets Involved

Beginning on 3 January 1992, a UN-brokered ceasefire generally held. The federal army was allowed to withdraw from its bases inside Croatia and tensions diminished. At the same time, the EU, succumbing to pressure from Germany, recognised Croatia. This was followed by US recognition, and in May 1992 Croatia was admitted to the UN.

The UN peace plan in Krajina was intended to bring about the disarming of local Serb paramilitary formations, the repatriation of refugees and the return of the region to Croatia. Instead, it only froze the existing situation and offered no permanent solution. In January 1993, the Croatian army suddenly launched an offensive in southern Krajina, pushing the Serbs back in some areas and recapturing strate-

2006

The European Commission publishes a report that demands more work of Croatia in the areas of corruption and discrimination against and intolerance of non-Croat citizens.

2007

The parliamentary elections in November result in the HDZ winning the most seats, but coalition partners are needed to form a majority.

2008

In January, the parliament approves the new coalition government headed up by prime minister Ivo Sanader. In April, Croatia is invited to join NATO at the summit in Bucharest.

2009

Slovenia threatens to block Croatia from joining the EU over an 18-year-old border dispute over the small bay of Piran in the Adriatic. In April, Croatia joins NATO.

gic points. The Krajina Serbs vowed never to accept rule from Zagreb and in June 1993 they voted overwhelmingly to join the Bosnian Serbs (and eventually Greater Serbia). The mass expulsion left only about 900 Croats in Krajina, out of an original population of 44,000. In early 2004, a comprehensive ceasefire substantially reduced the violence in the region. Demilitarised 'zones of separation' between the parties were established.

Troubles in Bosnia & Hercegovina

Meanwhile, neighbouring Bosnia and Hercegovina had been subjected to similar treatment at the hands of the Yugoslav army and Serbian paramilitaries. Initially, in the face of Serbian advances, Bosnia's Croats and Muslims had banded together but in 1993 the two sides fell out and began fighting each other. The Bosnian Croats, with tacit support from Zagreb, were responsible for several horrific events in Bosnia, including the destruction of the old bridge in Mostar. This conflagration was extinguished when the USA fostered the development of the Muslim-Croatian federation in 1994, as the world looked on in horror at the Serb siege of Sarajevo.

While these grim events unfolded in Bosnia and Hercegovina, the Croatian government quietly began procuring arms from abroad. On 1 May 1995, the Croatian army and police entered occupied western Slavonia, east of Zagreb, and seized control of the region within days. The Krajina Serbs responded by shelling Zagreb in an attack that left seven people dead and 130 wounded. As the Croatian military consolidated its hold in western Slavonia, some 15,000 Serbs fled the region despite assurances from the Croatian government that they were safe from retribution.

Belgrade's silence throughout the campaign showed that the Krajina Serbs had lost the support of their Serbian sponsors, encouraging Croats to forge ahead. On 4 August, the military launched an assault on the rebel Serb capital of Knin. The Serb army fled towards northern Bosnia, along with 150,000 civilians whose roots in the Krajina stretched back centuries. The military operation ended in days but was followed by months of terror, including widespread looting and burning of Serb villages.

The Dayton Peace Accords signed in Paris in December 1995 recognised Croatia's traditional borders and provided for the return of eastern Slavonia. The transition proceeded relatively smoothly, but the two populations still regard each other with suspicion and hostility.

Richard Holbrooke's *To End A War* recounts the events surrounding the Dayton Accords. As the American diplomat who prodded the warring parties to the negotiating table to hammer out a peace accord, Holbrooke was in a unique position to evaluate the personalities and politics of the region.

JOHN AND TINA REID / GETTY IMAGES ©

» Piran

July 2009

Ivo Sanader suddenly resigns as prime minister. His deputy, former journalist Jadranka Kosor, takes over as Croatia's first female prime minister.

2010

Ivo Josipović of the opposition Social Democratic Party of Croatia (SDP) is sworn in as the president of the country.

Postwar Croatia

A degree of stability returned to Croatia after the hostilities. A key provision of the agreement was the guarantee by the Croatian government to facilitate the return of Serbian refugees, and although the central government in Zagreb made the return of refugees a priority in accordance with the demands of the international community, its efforts have often been subverted by local authorities intent on maintaining the ethnic singularity of their regions.

On the political scene, Franjo Tuđman, the strong man of the war era, rapidly declined in popularity once the country was no longer under threat. His combination of authoritarianism and media control, resurrection of old NDH symbolism and leanings to the far right no longer appealed to the weary Croatian populace. By 1999 opposition parties united to work against Tuđman and the HDZ. Tuđman was hospitalised and died suddenly in late 1999. Planned elections were postponed until January 2000. Still, voters turned out in favour of a centre-left coalition, ousting the HDZ and voting the centrist Stipe Mesić into the presidency.

Move Towards Europe

The 2000 election results illustrated that Croatia had made a distinct turn towards the West and integration with modern Europe. The country gradually began welcoming foreign tourists again, and the economy opened up to international competition.

Croatia will be the second ex-Yugoslav country after Slovenia to join the EU, in the highly anticipated event in 2013.

Above all, the peaceful transition of power was interpreted by Europe as evidence of the maturity of Croatian democracy. The handover of General Ante Gotovina to the Hague in 2005 was the main condition for the beginning of Croatia's negotiations to join the EU. When the infamous fugitive was arrested in Spain, it seemed that Croatia was well on its way to joining the EU. In 2011 the Hague sentenced Gotovina and fellow ex-general Mladen Markač to 24 and 18 years in jail respectively (but liberated them in November 2012, after an appeal court ruling suggested there was no conspiracy to commit war crimes).

CORRUPTION, CRIME AND PUNISHMENT

The struggle against rife corruption came into the spotlight in late 2010, when Ivo Sanader – who had stepped down from serving a second term as prime minister in July 2009 without an explanation, becoming an MP – was charged with corruption and fled the country overnight. He denied fleeing but was arrested in Austria a few days later. He is the highest-profile politician in the country to be facing investigation, though two lower-ranking HDZ officials were sentenced for government corruption in 2011.

June 2010

Slovenia votes in a referendum regarding the border dispute with Croatia. The narrow majority of Slovenes supports the compromise resolution, clearing way for Croatia's entry into the EU.

DETLEV VAN RAVENSWAAY / GETTY IMAGES ©

» The twelve-star flag of Europe

2011

Landmark war crimes convictions are reached by the UN War Crimes Tribunal in the Hague against two senior Croatian generals – Ante Gotovina and Mladen Markac are found guilty of war crimes against Serbs.

The first of a number of hurdles that would thwart Croatia's entrance into the EU occurred in 2005. Slovenia's government declared an ecological zone in the Adriatic, prompting Croatia to call for international intervention to clear this border dispute. When the European Commission published a report in 2006 that stated Croatia needed to address corruption and discrimination against non-Croats, the journey towards the EU was seriously slowed down.

In the spring of 2008, Croatia was officially invited to join NATO at the summit in Bucharest; exactly a year later, it joined the alliance. In the meantime, 2008 was marked with a series of mafia-associated killings in Croatia, which forced the government to step up its fight against corruption and organised crime. It did so at least officially, since tougher action was a requirement of Croatia's application for EU membership. The border row with Slovenia didn't help matters either – in early 2009 Slovenia threatened to block its neighbour from joining the EU, but negotiations had resumed by October 2009 after international mediators addressed the disagreement.

Judicial reform was completed in accordance with the demands of the EU in 2011, marking the EU joining date for Croatia at 1 July 2013.

Clearly explaining centuries of complicated events, Marcus Tanner's *Croatia: A Nation Forged in War* sallies from the Roman era to President Tuđman, presenting in a lively, readable style the trials and tribulations of Croatian history.

December 2011

Croatia's EU accession negotiations are completed and accession treaty signed; the country is to become a full member on 1 July 2013.

November 2011

Former Prime Minister Ivo Sanader is tried on charges of corruption in one of the most scandalous political episodes in modern Croatia. The centre-left Social Democrats ousts the HDZ.

2012

A referendum on backing the joining of the EU shows Croats are in favour by a margin of two to one, though voter turnout is low at 44%.

November 2012

The Hague overturns 2011's ruling and sets Ante Gotovina and Mladen Markač free, ruling that there was no conspiracy to commit war crimes. The verdict was widely celebrated in Croatia, mned in Serbia.

Culture & People

Croatia's Split Personality

With its capital on the continent and the majority of its big cities on the coast, Croatia is torn between a more serious *mitteleuropean* mindset in Zagreb and northern Croatia (with meaty food, Austrian architecture and a strong interest in personal advancement over pleasure) and the coastal Mediterranean character, which is more laid-back and open. The Istrians, bilingual in Italian and Croatian, have a strong Italian influence, while the Dalmatians are generally a relaxed and easygoing bunch: many offices empty out at 3pm, allowing people to enjoy the long hours of sunlight on a beach or at an outdoor cafe.

Most people involved in the tourist industry speak German, English and Italian, though English is the most widely spoken language among the young. Croats can come across as uninterested and rude, even those working in the tourist sector, and too straightforward for some tastes. This is just the way they operate, so once you can get past that, you've made friends for life.

Nikola Tesla (1856–1943), the father of the radio and alternating electric current technology, was born in the village of Smiljan in Croatia. The Tesla unit for magnetic induction was named after him.

Croatia: West or East

The vast majority of Croats have a strong cultural identification with Western Europe and like to think of themselves as more Western than their 'Eastern' Bosnian and Serbian neighbours. Describing Croatia as part of Eastern Europe will not win you popularity among its people. The idea that Croatia is the last stop before the Ottoman East is prevalent in all segments of the population, though this idea is questionable when considering the recently overwhelming popularity of Serbian turbo folk in Croatia, a type of music frowned upon and avoided during the 1990s war. It seems that with the easing up of national tensions of the 1990s, the connecting Balkan elements are again being embraced in some parts of Croatia's society.

A Sporting Country

Football, tennis and skiing are enormously popular, and sporty Croatia has contributed a disproportionate number of world-class players in each sport. At London 2012, Croatia won no less than six medals – three golds, one silver and two bronzes.

Football

By far the most popular spectator sport in Croatia is football (soccer), which frequently serves as an outlet for Croatian patriotism and, occasionally, as a means to express political opposition. When Franjo Tuđman came to power he decided that the name of Zagreb's football club, Dinamo, was 'too communist', so he changed it to 'Croatia'. Waves of outrage followed the decision, led by angry young football fans who used the controversy to express their opposition to the regime. Even though the following government restored the original name, you will occasionally see *Dinamo volim te* (Dinamo I love you) graffiti in Zagreb. Dinamo's frequent rival is Hajduk of Split, named after ancient resisters to Roman rule. Hajduk and Dinamo supporters are infamous rivals, often causing brawls when the two teams meet.

The national team typically does well in championships. From their very first football match in 1940 till 2011, the team played 224 international matches and won 119 of those.

By far the biggest name in Croatian football, Davor Šuker scored 46 international goals by the end of his career, 45 of them for Croatia; he is the Croatian national team's all-time leading goal-scorer. Back in 2004, football great Pelé named him one of the top 125 greatest living footballers.

Be like the sporty locals and keep up with Croatian football by following the fortunes of Dinamo Zagreb at www.gnkdinamo.hr.

Basketball

The most popular sport after football, basketball is followed with some reverence. The teams of Split, Zadar and Zagreb's Cibona are known across Europe, though no one has yet repeated the star team of the 1980s, when players such as Dražen Petrović, Dino Rađa and Toni Kukoč formed Cibona and became European champions. For the thorough lowdown on Croatian basketball, go to www.kosarka.hr.

Tennis

'I don't know what's in the water in Croatia, but it seems like every player is over 7ft tall' – Andy Roddick.

Not quite. Yet Croatia is producing some mighty big players, in every sense of the word.

The 2001 victory of 6ft 4in Goran Ivanišević at Wimbledon provoked wild celebrations throughout the country, especially in his home town of Split. The charismatic serve-and-volley player was much loved for his engaging personality and on-court antics, and dominated the top 10 rankings during much of the 1990s. Injuries forced his retirement in 2004, but Croatia stayed on the court with a 2005 Davis Cup victory led by Ivan Ljubičić and Mario Ančić. Split-born Mario Ančić was dubbed 'Baby Goran' by Ivanišević himself but retired in 2011 due to an ongoing battle with illness. Ivo Karlović has made a name for himself in the world of tennis, while Marin Čilić is the rising tennis star of Croatia.

On the women's side, Zagreb-born Iva Majoli won the French Open in 1997 with an aggressive baseline game, but failed to follow up with other Grand Slam victories. She retired from tennis in 2004.

Tennis is more than a spectator sport in Croatia. The coast is amply endowed with clay courts. The biggest tournament in Croatia is the Umag Open in Istria, held in July.

GOLD

The celebrated Croatian high jumper Blanka Vlašić won her fourth consecutive gold medal at the World Championships in Doha in March 2010.

CROATS: NORMAL PEOPLE

Attitudes towards the 1990s 'Homeland War' or 'Patriotic War' vary by region. The destruction of Vukovar, the shelling of Dubrovnik and Osijek, and the ethnic cleansing of and by the Krajina Serbs have traumatised the surrounding regions. Comments questioning the assumption that Croats were wholly right and Serbs were wholly wrong are not likely to be appreciated. In other parts of the country, Croats are more open to a forthright discussion of the last decade's events.

The word 'normal' pops up frequently in Croats' conversations about themselves. 'We want to be a normal country', they might say. Croats will frequently make a distinction between rabid, flag-waving nationalists and 'normal people' who only wish to live in peace. This is among the reasons Croatia bowed to international pressure to turn over its war criminals.

Skiing

If Croatia had a national goddess it would be Janica Kostelić, the most accomplished skier to have emerged from Croatia. After winning the Alpine Skiing World Cup in 2001, Kostelić won three gold medals and a silver in the 2002 Winter Olympics – the first Winter Olympic medals ever for an athlete from Croatia. At the age of 20 she became the first female skier ever to win three gold medals at one Olympics. In 2002, Kostelić was plagued by a knee injury and the removal of her thyroid, but this didn't stop her from winning a gold medal in the women's combined and a silver in the Super-G at the 2006 Winter Olympics in Torino. In 2007, Kostelić announced her retirement from competitive racing.

Maybe it's in the genes. Brother Ivica Kostelić took the men's slalom World Cup title in 2002 and brought home a silver medal in the men's combined in Torino 2006. Since 2008, he has finished among the top six in the overall World Cup standings each season. He won the Alpine Ski World Cup in 2011, his most prestigious trophy so far.

Daily Life

Croats like the good life and take a lot of pride in showing off the latest fashions and mobile phones. Streets are tidy and clothes are stylish, featuring high fashion labels – the more prominent the label, the better. Even with a tight economy, people will cut out restaurant meals and films in order to afford a shopping trip to Italy or Austria for some new clothes.

Lounging in cafes and bars is an important part of life here, and you often wonder how the country's wheels are turning with so many people at leisure rather than work. But perhaps it's all that coffee that makes them work twice as fast once they're back in the office.

The cult of celebrity is extremely powerful in Croatia – the trashy tabloids are full of wannabe celebs and their latest shenanigans. Even the country's intellectuals, who wouldn't admit it publicly, are intimately involved with the private lives of A- and B-listers.

Family Matters

Most people own their homes, bought in the postcommunist years when previously state-owned homes were sold to the tenants for little money. These properties are passed down from grandparents, great-aunts and other relatives.

It's traditional and perfectly normal for children to live with their parents well into their adult life. The tradition extends particularly to sons, who often bring their wives to the family home where they'll continue to live – this is, however, mostly the case in rural and small-town areas.

A SLICE OF CROATIA TO BRING BACK HOME

The finest artisans' product from Croatia is the intricate lace from Pag Island, part of a centuries-old tradition that is still going strong. You can buy the pieces of lace directly from the women who make them.

Embroidered fabrics are featured in many souvenir shops. Croatian embroidery is distinguished by cheerful red geometric patterns set against a white background, which you'll see on tablecloths, pillowcases and blouses.

Lavender and other fragrant herbs made into scented sachets or oils make popular and inexpensive gifts. You can find them on most central Dalmatian islands, but especially on Hvar Island, which is known for its lavender fields.

Brač Island is known for its lustrous stone. Ashtrays, vases, candlestick holders and other small but heavy items carved from Brač stone are on sale throughout the island.

BROTHERHOOD & UNITY OR DUMB & DUMBER?

Turbo folk – a supercharged, techno version of Serbian folk music – is notoriously difficult to categorise as anything but itself. Widely listened to in Croatia, Serbia, Montenegro, Macedonia, and Bosnia and Hercegovina, it's a major contemporary unifying factor across former Yugoslavia. The undisputed queen of turbo folk is Svetlana 'Ceca' Ražnatović, widow of the Serbian Arkan, who was indicted by the UN for crimes against humanity. Ceca has produced numerous albums and performed at sell-out concerts at all the biggest stadiums across the region.

Turbo folk began and flourished under the Milošević regime and is widely associated with mafia types. Ceca herself was arrested (but later cleared of all charges) in connection with her ties to members of the Zemun clan, responsible for the murder of the Serbian prime minister Zoran Đinđić in 2003. Some *folkolekas* (clubs where turbo folk is played) have metal detectors at their entrances and, particularly in Bosnia and Hercegovina, are subject to occasional bomb attacks associated with 'unfinished business' among the local mafia members. The intellectual elite sees turbo folk as a sort of 'dumbing down' of the current generation, but its ever-growing popularity is an undeniable fact.

Family is very important to the Croats and extended-family links are strong and cherished.

Religion

According to the most recent census, 87.8% of the population identified itself as Catholic, 4.4% Orthodox, 1.3% Muslim, 0.3% Protestant, and 6.2% other and unknown. Croats are overwhelmingly Roman Catholic, while Serbs belong to the Eastern Orthodox Church, a division that has its roots in the fall of the Roman Empire. In fact, religion is the only factor separating the ethnically identical populations. In addition to various doctrinal differences, Orthodox Christians venerate icons, allow priests to marry and do not accept the authority of the pope.

It would be difficult to overstate the extent to which Catholicism shapes the Croatian national identity. The Croats pledged allegiance to Roman Catholicism as early as the 9th century and were rewarded with the right to conduct Mass and issue religious writings in the local language, which eventually became the Glagolitic script. The popes supported the early Croatian kings, who in turn built monasteries and churches to further promote Catholicism. Throughout the long centuries of Croatia's domination by foreign powers, Catholicism was the unifying element in forging a sense of nationhood.

Tragically, the profound faith that had animated Croatian nationalism was perverted into a murderous intolerance under the wartime Ustaše regime. The complicity of local parishes in 'cleansing' the population of Jews and Serbs prompted Tito to suppress religion – and, he hoped, nationalism – when he took power. Although religion was not officially forbidden, it was seen as 'politically incorrect' for ambitious Croats to attend Mass. Small wonder that the Vatican was the first entity to recognise an independent Croatia in 1991.

The Church enjoys a respected position in Croatia's cultural and political life, and Croatia is the subject of particular attention from the Vatican. The Church is also the most trusted institution in Croatia, rivalled only by the military.

Croats, both within Croatia and abroad, provide a stream of priests and nuns to replenish the ranks of Catholic clergy. Religious holidays are celebrated with fervour and Sunday Mass is strongly attended.

Equality in Croatia

Women face some hurdles in Croatia, although the situation is improving. Under Tito's brand of socialism, women were encouraged to become politically active and their representation in the Croatian *sabor* (parliament) increased to 18%. Currently 21% of the parliament is comprised of women.

More and more wives and mothers must work outside the home to make ends meet, but they still perform most household duties. Women are under-represented at the executive level.

For a thorough rundown of cultural events in Croatia, check out the informative www.culturenet.hr.

Women fare worse in traditional villages than in urban areas, and were hit harder economically than men after the Homeland War. Many of the factories that closed, especially in eastern Slavonia, had a high proportion of female workers.

Both domestic abuse and sexual harassment at work are quite common in Croatia and the legal system is not yet adequate for women to seek redress.

Although attitudes are slowly changing towards homosexuality, Croatia is an overwhelmingly Catholic country with highly conservative views of sexuality. Most homosexuals are highly closeted, fearing harassment if their sexual orientation were revealed.

The Cuisine

If thoughts of Croatian cuisine conjure images of greasy steaks with a side of boiled potatoes and sauerkraut, think again. While it still holds firm to its Eastern European roots and positively pleases meat-happy Balkan palates, Croatian food is a savoury smorgasbord of taste, echoing the varied cultures that have influenced the country over the course of its history. You'll find a sharp divide between the Italian-style cuisine along the coast and the flavours of Hungary, Austria and Turkey in the continental parts. From grilled sea bass smothered in olive oil in Dalmatia to a robust, paprika-heavy meat stew in Slavonia, there's something for every taste. Each area proudly touts its very own speciality, but regardless of the region you'll be surprised by the generally good food made from fresh, seasonal ingredients.

Istria and Kvarner have quickly shot to the top of the gourmet ladder but other places aren't lagging far behind. A new generation of chefs are updating traditional Croatian dishes and joining the cult of celebrity chefs – yes, this movement has even made it to Croatia! Wine and olive oil production have been revived, and there's now a network of signposted roads around the country celebrating these precious nectars.

For excellent reviews of restaurants all around Croatia and info about small producers, browse the excellent www.tasteofcroatia.org and download their app.

Foodie Culture

Although Croats are not overly experimental when it comes to food, they're particularly passionate about it. They'll spend hours discussing the quality of the lamb or the first-grade fish, and why it overshadows all food elsewhere. Foodie culture is on the rise here, inspired largely by the slow-food movement, which places emphasis on fresh, local and seasonal ingredients and the joy of slow-paced dining. Several restaurants around Croatia now offer slow food menus.

The price and quality of meals varies little in the midrange category, but if you're willing to splurge you can spend hours feasting on slow-food delicacies or savouring the innovative concoctions of up-and-coming young chefs. There is a limit to what the local crowd can afford to pay, so restaurants still cluster in the middle of the price spectrum – few are unbelievably cheap and few are exorbitantly expensive. Whatever your budget, it's hard to get a truly bad meal anywhere in Croatia. Another plus is that food is often paired with alfresco dining in warm weather.

COOKING COURSES

Cooking courses in Croatia are becoming increasingly popular but they don't come cheap. **Culinary Croatia** (www.culinary-croatia.com) is a great source of information, and offers a variety of cooking classes and culinary and wine tours, mainly in Dalmatia. Zagreb-based **Delicija 1001** (www.1001delicija.com) organises a variety of cooking courses and gourmet events. Istria-based **Eat Istria** (www.eatistria.com) offers cooking classes and wine tours around the peninsula.

Regional Staples & Specialities

Zagreb & Northwestern Croatia

Zagreb and northwestern Croatia favour the kind of hearty meat dishes you might find in Vienna. Juicy *pečenje* (spit-roasted and baked meat) features *janjetina* (lamb), *svinjetina* (pork) and *patka* (duck), often accompanied by *mlinci* (baked noodles) or *pečeni krumpir* (roast potatoes). Meat slow cooked under a *peka* (domed baking lid) is especially delicious, but needs to be ordered in advance at many restaurants. *Purica* (turkey) with *mlinci* is an institution on Zagreb and Zagorje menus, along with *zagrebački odrezak* (veal steak stuffed with ham and cheese, then crumbed and fried) – another calorie-laden speciality. Another mainstay is *sir i vrhnje* (fresh cottage cheese and cream), bought at local markets. For those with a sweet tooth, *palačinke* (thin pancakes) with various fillings and toppings are a common dessert.

OYSTERS

Research shows that the prized oysters in the Ston area on Pelješac Peninsula have been farmed since Roman times.

Slavonia

Spicier than the food of other regions, Slavonian cuisine uses liberal amounts of paprika and garlic. The Hungarian influence is most prevalent here: many typical dishes, such as *čobanac* (a meat stew), are in fact versions of *gulaš* (goulash). The nearby Drava River provides fresh fish, such as carp, pike and perch, which is stewed in a paprika sauce and served with noodles in a dish known as *fiš paprikaš*. Another speciality is *šaran u rašljama* (carp on a forked branch), roasted in its own oils over an open fire. The region's sausages are particularly renowned, especially *kulen,* a paprika-flavoured sausage cured over a period of nine months and usually served with cottage cheese, peppers, tomatoes and often *turšija* (pickled vegetables).

Kvarner & Dalmatia

Coastal cuisine in Kvarner and Dalmatia is typically Mediterranean, using a lot of olive oil, garlic, fresh fish and shellfish and herbs. Along the coast, look for lightly breaded and fried *lignje* (squid) as a main course; Adriatic squid is generally more expensive than squid from further afield. Meals often begin with a first course of pasta such as spaghetti or *rižoto* (risotto) topped with seafood. For a special appetiser, try *paški sir* (Pag cheese), a pungent hard cheese from the island of Pag. Dalmatian *brodet* (stewed mixed fish served with polenta; also known as *brodetto*) is another regional treat, but it's often only available in two-person portions. Dalmatian *pašticada* (beef stewed in wine and spices and served with gnocchi) appears on menus on the coast as well as in the interior. Lamb from Cres and Pag is deemed Croatia's best, as it's fed on fresh herbs, which makes the meat delicious.

Istria

Istrian cuisine has been attracting international foodies in recent years for its long gastronomic tradition, fresh ingredients and unique specialities. Typical dishes include *maneštra,* a thick vegetable-and-bean soup similar to minestrone, *fuži,* hand-rolled pasta often served with *tartufi* (truffles) or *divljač* (game meat), and *fritaja* (omelette often served with seasonal vegies, such as wild asparagus). Thin slices of dry-cured Istrian *pršut* (prosciutto) – also excellent in Dalmatia – are often on the appetiser list; it's expensive because of the long hours and personal attention involved in smoking the meat. Istrian olive oil is highly rated and has won awards. The tourist board has marked an olive oil route, along which you can visit local growers, tasting oils at the source. The best seasonal ingredients include white truffles, picked in autumn, and wild asparagus, harvested in spring.

The secret behind the pungent taste of *paški sir* (Pag cheese) is the diet of wild herbs on which the sheep feast.

Vegetarians & Vegans

A useful phrase is *Ja ne jedem meso* (I don't eat meat), but even then you may be served soup with bits of bacon swimming in it. That is slowly changing and vegetarians are making inroads in Croatia, but changes are mostly happening in the larger cities. Zagreb, Rijeka, Split and Dubrovnik now have vegetarian restaurants, and even standard restaurants in the big cities are beginning to offer vegetarian menus. Vegetarians may have a harder time in the north (Zagorje) and the east (Slavonia), where traditional fare has meat as its main focus. Specialities that don't use meat include *maneštra od bobića* (bean and fresh maize soup) and

THE OLIVE OIL BOOM OF ISTRIA

There's an olive tree on Veli Brijun in the Brijuni Islands proven to be 1600 years old. Early Greek and Roman manuscripts praised the quality of Istrian olive oil. Now there's a revival of this ancient agricultural activity, with 94 listed growers on the Istrian Peninsula and a network of signposted olive oil roads. In Istria, the plant is cultivated with special attention, and each tree given love and care. Several growers have received prestigious international awards and top marks for their fruity nectars, which is no small feat in the competitive world olive oil market.

Duilio Belić is a relative newbie on the scene. The son of a miner, he grew up in Raša and went on to become a successful Zagreb businessperson before starting an olive oil production. With his wife, Bosiljka, an agriculture specialist, he bought an old grove near Fažana a decade ago and started what has become a real hit among gourmets. He now has five olive groves in Istria, with a total of 5500 trees. Under the brand name Oleum Viride, they produce 11 single-variety extra-virgin olive oils, four of which are made of indigenous varietals – Buža, Istarska Bjelica, Rosulja and Vodnjanska Crnica. Their showcase oil is Selekcija Belić, a blend of six varieties with a flavour of vanilla and chicory.

Over a coffee at a Fažana cafe, Duilio reminds me of a simple fact most people forget: the olive is a fruit and olive oil is a fruit juice. Just as with wine, certain oils can be combined with certain dishes to enhance the flavours. Selekcija Belić, for example, is a great accompaniment to lamb and veal cooked under a *peka* (domed baking lid), or a wild-asparagus omelette. The highly prized Buža oil pairs wonderfully with raw fish and meat, as well as mushrooms and grilled vegetables. The golden-green Istarska Bjelica, with its scent of mown grass and a hint of radicchio, goes well with chocolate ice cream or a dark-chocolate hazelnut cake.

It's all sounding quite abstract to me so we move on to Vodnjanka, a restaurant in Vodnjan, where Duilio pulls out a box with a selection of his oils and orders a range of hors d'oeuvres. There, I learn to taste olive oil. A small sample is poured into a wine glass, which you warm up with your hand in order for the oil to reach body temperature. You then cover the glass with your hand to release the oil's natural aroma. Next, you place a small sip of the oil at the front of your mouth, mix it gently and then swallow in one go.

Such tastings have become a trend among Croatian foodies. Duilio organises the gatherings for his wider circle of friends and for groups of enthusiasts at his olive grove or his tasting room in Zagreb. His oils can also be sampled at Croatia's top restaurants: Bevanda (p141) in Opatija, Milan (p103) in Pula, Kukuriku (p137) in Rijeka, Foša (p175) in Zadar and Damir & Ornella (p120) in Novigrad.

I ask Duilio my last questions as we sample Vodnjanska Crnica in *maneštra* (vegetable-and-bean soup). I wonder what makes Istria such prime territory for growing olives. 'It's the microlocation,' Duilio says. 'Plus we harvest the olives early, unlike in Dalmatia, to preserve the natural antioxidants and nutrients. The oils may taste more bitter but they're also healthier.'

As we're parting ways, fascinated by the man's passion for olive oil, I wonder what made him enter this whole new world. 'It's simple – I love food, I love wine, I love all good things in life,' he replies. 'Olive oil is one of them.'

By Anja Mutić

juha od krumpira na zagorski način (Zagorje potato soup). Other options include *štrukli* (baked cheese dumplings) and *blitva* (Swiss chard boiled and often served with potatoes, olive oil and garlic). Along the coast you'll find plenty of pasta dishes and risotto with various vegetable toppings and delicious cheese. If fish and seafood are part of your diet, you'll eat royally nearly everywhere.

Drinks

Croatia is famous for its *rakija* (brandy), which comes in different flavours. The most commonly drunk are *loza* (grape brandy), *šljivovica* (plum brandy) and *travarica* (herbal brandy). Istrian grappa is particularly excellent, and ranges in flavour from *medica* (honey) to *biska* (mistletoe) and various berries. The island of Vis is famous for its delicious *rogačica* (carob brandy). It's customary to have a small glass of brandy before a meal. Other popular drinks include *vinjak* (cognac), maraschino (cherry liqueur made in Zadar), *prosecco* (sweet dessert wine) and *pelinkovac* (herbal liqueur).

On 1 April each year, the town of Ludbreg in the north of Croatia has wine instead of water flowing in its city fountain.

The two most popular types of Croatian *pivo* (beer) are Zagreb's Ožujsko, and Karlovačko from Karlovac. The small-distribution Velebitsko has a loyal following among in-the-know beer drinkers but only some bars and shops carry it, and they're mostly in continental Croatia. You'll want to practise saying *živjeli!* (cheers!).

Strongly brewed *kava* (espresso-style coffee), served in tiny cups, is popular throughout Croatia. You can have it diluted with milk (macchiato) or order a cappuccino. Although some places have decaf options this is considered somewhat sacrilegious, as Croats love their coffee. Herbal teas are widely available but regular tea *(čaj)* is apt to be too weak for aficionados. Tap water is drinkable.

Croatian-Style Celebrations

MARASCHINO

The Zadar sour-cherry liqueur maraschino was conjured up in the early 16th century by pharmacists working in Zadar's Dominican monastery.

Croats love to eat and will use any excuse to feast, so holidays and special celebrations such as weddings and christenings are party time for those who like food.

As in other Catholic countries, most Croats don't eat meat on Badnjak (Christmas Eve); instead they eat fish. In Dalmatia, the traditional Christmas Eve dish is *bakalar* (dried, salted cod). Christmas dinner may be roast suckling pig, turkey with *mlinci* or another meat. Also popular at Christmas is *sarma* (sauerkraut rolls stuffed with minced meat). Fresh Christmas Eve bread, also known as *badnji kruh,* is the centrepiece: it's made with honey, nuts and dried fruit. Another tradition is the Christmas braid, glazed dough made with nutmeg, raisins and almonds and shaped into a braid. It's often decorated with wheat and candles and left on the table until Epiphany (6 January), when it is cut and eaten. *Orahnjača* (walnut cake), *fritule* (fritters) and *makovnjača* (poppy-seed cake) are popular desserts at celebrations.

The most typical Easter dish is ham with boiled eggs, served with fresh vegies. *Pinca,* a type of hard bread, is another Easter tradition, especially in Dalmatia.

Where to Eat & Drink

A *restauracija* or *restoran* (restaurant) is at the top of the food chain, generally presenting a more formal dining experience and an elaborate wine list. A *gostionica* or *konoba* is usually a traditional family-run tavern – the produce may come from the family garden. A *pivnica* is more like a pub, with a wide choice of beer; sometimes hot dishes or sandwiches are available. A *kavana* is a cafe, where you can nurse your coffee for hours and, if you're lucky, have cakes and ice-cream. A *slastičarna* (pastry shop) serves ice cream, cakes, strudels and sometimes coffee, but

CROATIAN WINES

Wine from Croatia may be new to international consumers but *vino* has been an embedded part of the region's lifestyle for more than 25 centuries. Today the tradition is undergoing a renaissance in the hands of a new generation of winemakers with a focus on preserving indigenous varieties and revitalising ancestral estates. Quality is rising, exports are increasing and the wines are garnering global awards and winning the affections of worldly wine lovers thirsty for authentic stories and unique terroirs.

Croatia is roughly divided into four winemaking regions: Slavonia and Croatian Uplands in the continental zone with a cooler climate; and Istria, Kvarner and Dalmatia along the Adriatic with a Mediterranean climate. Within each lie multiple sub-regions (*vinogorje*), comprised of more than 300 geographically defined appellations.

White varieties such as *graševina*, *traminac*, pinot blanc, chardonnay and sauvignon blanc dominate the continental zone. Styles range from fruity, mildly aromatic, refreshing wines from cool northern areas to rich, savoury, age-worthy whites from warmer Slavonia, as well as luscious dessert (*predikatno*) wines. Kutjevo is a particular sweet spot for vine-growing with many wineries located within the hamlet. Look for bottles by Enjingi, Krauthaker, Kutjevo dd and Mihalj.

Ensconced in the pastoral hills of Međimurje, Plešivica and Zagorje, Croatian Uplands is a land of crisp, food-friendly whites (although pinot noir does well in spots). Beside *graševina* and native *škrlet*, international varieties like chardonnay, pinot blanc, pinot gris and sauvignon blanc thrive. For a regional sampler, check out wines from Bolfan, Korak and Tomac. For ice wine (*ledeno vino*), a coveted bottle of Bodren makes a delicious souvenir.

Crowning the northern Adriatic coast is Istria, home of *malvazija istarska*, a variety capable of award-winning wines with diverse profiles: lean and light to unctuous and sweet; crisp and unoaked to acacia wood-aged and orange wines. Benvenuti, Clai, Degrassi, Kozlović, Matošević, Piquentum and Trapan offer delightful examples. Istria also boasts a fiery signature red: *teran*. Look for Arman, Coronica, Geržinić, Roxanich and Terzolo.

Below Istria is Kvarner, home of *žlahtina*, a seafood-friendly white found in abundance on Krk. Katunar, Šipun and Toljanić are leading producers.

Going south the rugged beauty of Dalmatia, with its island vineyards (Hvar, Vis, Brač, Korčula), fosters a fascinating array of indigenous grape varieties that prosper in the Mediterranean climate, yielding full-bodied wines of rich character. Here *plavac mali*, scion of zinfandel (*crljenik kašteljanski*) and the obscure *dobričić*, is king of reds. Recommended labels include Korta Katarina, Miloš, Stina, Tomić and Zlatan Otok. FYI: wines labelled 'Dingač' are *plavac mali* from a specific vineyard on Pelješac that clings to a mountainside high above the sea. Production is tiny and good examples command premium prices. Benchmark bottlings include Bura, Kiridžija and Saints Hills. Other indigenous varieties worth seeking are Babić (red) and Pošip (white).

When planning a visit, keep in mind that most Croatian wineries are family-owned estates; not all have visitor-ready facilities. Below is a selection of recommended wineries with public tasting rooms. Appointments are highly recommended.

» **Slavonia** (p85)

» **Croatian Uplands** **Bolfan-Vinski Vrh** (www.bolfanvinskivrh.hr; Hraščina); **Cmrečnjak** (☎040-830-103; Štrigova); **Korak** (www.vino-korak.hr; Plešivica); **Tomac** (www.tomac.hr; Jastrebarsko); **Vuglec Breg** (p78).

» **Istria and Kvarner** **Cossetto** (www.cossetto.net; Kaštelir); **Degrassi** (www.degrassi.hr; Savudrija); **Geržinić** (www.gerzinic.com; Vižinada); **Kozlović** (www.kozlovic.hr; Momjan); **Matošević** (www.matosevic.com; Krunčići); **Toljanić-Gospoja** (www.gospoja.hr; Vrbnik, Krk); **Trapan** (www.trapan.hr; Šišan).

» **Dalmatia** **BIBICh** (☎022-775 597; Skradin); **Bire** (☎020-712 007; Lumbarda, Korčula); **Boškinac** (p186); **Carić** (www.vinohvar.hr; Hvar); **Grgić** (☎020-748 090; Trstenik, Pelješac); **Jako Vino** (www.stina-vino.hr; Bol, Brač); **Korta Katarina** (www.kortakatarinawinery.com; Orebić, Pelješac); **Matuško** (www.matusko-vina.hr; Potomje, Pelješac); **Tomić** (www.bastijana.hr; Jelsa, Hvar).

Cliff Rames is a Croatian-American sommelier and founder of Wines of Croatia (www.winesofcroatia.com).

QUICKIE SNACKS

For local fast food, you can snack on *ćevapčići* (small spicy meatballs of minced beef, lamb or pork), *pljeskavica* (an ex-Yugo version of a hamburger), *ražnjići* (small chunks of pork grilled on a skewer) or *burek* (pastry stuffed with ground meat, spinach or cheese). These are available at a variety of fast-food kiosks.

you usually have to gobble your food standing up or take it away. Self-service *samoposluživanje* (cafeterias) are good for a quick meal. Though the quality may vary, all you need to do is point to what you want.

There are 17,000 registered vine growers in Croatia, 2500 wines of controlled origin and 880 wineries.

If you're staying in hostels or at private accommodation, an elaborate breakfast might be difficult to arrange, and the easiest thing to do is to get coffee at a cafe and pastries from a bakery. Otherwise, you can buy some bread, cheese and milk at a supermarket and have a picnic. If you're staying in a hotel you'll be served a buffet breakfast that includes cornflakes, bread, yoghurt, a selection of cold meat, powdered 'juice' and cheese. More upmarket hotels have better buffets that include eggs, sausages and homemade pastries.

Fruit and vegetables from the market and a selection of cheese, bread and ham from a grocery store can make a healthy picnic lunch. If you ask nicely, the person behind the deli counter at supermarkets or grocery stores will usually make a *sir* (cheese) or *pršut* (prosciutto) sandwich and you only pay the regular price of the ingredients.

Habits & Customs

Throughout former Yugoslavia, the *doručak* (breakfast) of the people was *burek*. Modern Croats have opted for a lighter start to their day, usually just coffee and a pastry with some yoghurt and fresh fruit.

Restaurants open for *ručak* (lunch) around noon and usually serve continuously until midnight, which can be a major convenience if you're arriving in town at an odd hour or just feel like spending more time at the beach. Croats tend to eat either an earlier *marenda* or *gablec* (cheap, filling lunch) or a large, late lunch. *Večera* (dinner) is typically a much lighter affair, but most restaurants have adapted their schedules to the needs of tourists, who tend to load up at night. Few Croats can afford to eat out regularly; when they do, it's likely to be a large family outing on Saturday night or Sunday afternoon.

The salt extracted at the Pag and Ston saltpans is considered the cleanest in the entire Mediterranean region.

Croats are proud of their cuisine and vastly prefer it to all others (with the exception of Italian cuisine). Outside the main cities there are few restaurants serving international cuisine (mostly Chinese and Mexican) and few variations on the basic Croatian themes.

Architecture in Croatia

Dominko Blažević.

From prehistoric times on, due to its geostrategic position, the area of today's Croatia has been continuously inhabited and coveted by various conquerors, hence the country's wealth of diverse architectural monuments and ruins. Not to be missed are the cities of Dubrovnik, Korčula, Rovinj, Trogir, Zadar and Šibenik, and the Istrian hill towns all famous for their architectural beauty.

Dominko Blažević is an architecture writer from Croatia.

The Roman Era

The most stunning example of Roman architecture is the Diocletian's Palace (p197) in Split, built by the retiring emperor at the end of the 3rd century AD. On Unesco's world register of cultural monuments, this oversized villa is the best-preserved Roman emperor's palace in the world – it's been inhabited from the emperor's death in 316 AD until today. The aqueduct bringing water to the Palace still stands (and functions) at the outskirts of the city.

In the vicinity is Salona, today's Solin. This was a pre-Roman city (and the emperor's birthplace – hence the location of the palace) and, later on, both the administrative and commercial centre of the province. Its ruins include the remains of an amphitheatre.

Two more pre-Slavic examples, both in Istria, are worth seeing: the sizeable Roman Amphitheatre (p99) in Pula (Croatia's own coliseum), an arena from the 1st century AD, and the Early Christian Euphrasian Basilica (p114) in Poreč, from the 6th century AD, which has layers of older periods and buildings incorporated in its walls, and a precious mosaic in its apse.

Pre-Romanesque Churches

With the Slavs' arrival began the so-called Old Croatian, pre-Romanesque period. The best examples of its architecture are found along the Dalmatian coast, beginning with the impressive 9th-century Church of St Donat (p169) in Zadar, built on the Roman ruins. It has a round central structure, unique for late antiquity, and three semicircular apses. Two small churches in the area represent the jewels of this era as well: the 11th-century Holy Cross Church in Nin (with its cross-shaped plan, two apses and a dome above the centre point), and the postcard-perfect St Nicholas (Sv Nikola), just outside Nin. Not to be missed are the remains of circular pre-Romanesque churches that are still standing in Split (the Holy Trinity) and Trogir. Smaller churches on Šipan and Lopud, two islands near Dubrovnik, are built with cross-shaped ground plans, indicating the growing influence of Byzantine culture at the time.

The Cathedral of St Domnius (3rd and 4th centuries AD) in Split is the oldest – and smallest – cathedral building in the world, thanks to it being housed in the original Diocletian's mausoleum.

390 BC–c 400 AD

First Greeks then Romans arrive to eastern Adriatic shores, leaving in their wake extraordinary towns, buildings and infrastructure.

Early 4th Century

The Diocletian's Palace is completed. It still forms the core of today's Split.

9th Century

The church of St Donat is built in today's Zadar, in early Byzantine style.

11th–15th Centuries

Monumental Romanesque architecture followed by elegant Gothic style advances city development, structural innovations and increasingly elaborate detailing.

1431–1535

Cathedral of St James by Juraj Dalmatinac is built in Šibenik in Gothic Renaissance style.

17th & 18th Centuries

The golden age of Varaždin's baroque, as well as the major rebuilding period for earthquake-hit Dubrovnik.

19th Century

Classicist and historicist periods leave behind some of the most remarkable public buildings of today's Croatia.

1930s–1970s

During the Modernist period, Croatian architecture is in sync with the international style. The socialist period results in highly sophisticated and aesthetically mature examples of residential and civic architecture.

Croatia Goes Gothic

The Romanesque tradition of the Middle Ages persisted along the coast long after the Gothic style had swept the rest of Europe. In the 13th century the earliest examples of Gothic style were still combined with Romanesque forms. The most stunning work from this period is the portal of the Cathedral of St Lovro (p217) in Trogir, carved by the master artisan Radovan in 1240. Another Gothic masterpiece is the unusual portal of Split's Cathedral of St Domnius (p201), featuring 28 square reliefs by Andrija Buvina. Zadar has the Cathedral of St Anastasia (p171), built on the foundations of an old Christian basilica in the 12th and 13th centuries, and the St Grisogonus Church (p172), from 1175.

The Cathedral of the Assumption of the Blessed Virgin Mary (p45), formerly St Stephen's, in Zagreb was the first venture into the Gothic style in northern Croatia. Although reconstructed several times, the remnants of 13th-century murals are still visible in the sacristy.

The late-Gothic period was dominated by the builder and sculptor Juraj Dalmatinac, who was born in Zadar in the 15th century. His most outstanding work was Šibenik's Cathedral of St James (p189), which marked a transition from the Gothic to the Renaissance period. Dalmatinac constructed the church entirely of stone, and adorned its outer walls with a wreath of realistically carved portraits of local contemporaries. Another beauty from this period is the 15th-century St Mark's Cathedral (p267) in Korčula.

The Renaissance

The Renaissance flourished in Croatia, especially in then independent Ragusa (Dubrovnik). By the second half of the 15th century, Renaissance influences were appearing on late-Gothic structures. The Sponza Palace (p248), formerly the Customs House, is a fine example of this mixed style. By the mid-16th century, Renaissance features began to replace the Gothic style in the palaces and summer residences built in and around Ragusa by the wealthy nobility. Unfortunately, much was destroyed in the 1667 earthquake, so now Dubrovnik is known more for its mixed Gothic-Romanesque Franciscan Monastery (p247), the 15th-century Orlando Column (p249), the Onofrio Fountain (p248), the baroque St Blaise's Church (p248), the Jesuit St Ignatius Church (p248) and the Cathedral of the Assumption of the Virgin (p248).

Baroque Style

Northern Croatia is well known for the baroque style, which was introduced by Jesuit monks in the 17th century. The city of Varaždin was a regional capital in the 17th and 18th centuries, which, because of its location, enjoyed a steady interchange of artists, artisans and architects with northern Europe. The combination of wealth and creativity eventually led to Varaždin becoming Croatia's foremost city of baroque art. You'll notice

THE CROATIAN PLETER

The very first distinctively and uniquely Croatian design is *pleter* (plaited ornamentation), which appeared around AD 800 on the baptismal font of Duke Višeslav of Nin, in Nin's Church of the Holy Cross. *Pleter* appears frequently on church entrances and furniture from the early medieval (Old Croatian) period. Around the end of the 10th century, the latticework began to feature leaves and tendrils. The design is so linked with the country's culture that the late president Franjo Tuđman used it on posters during his first election campaign, to signal a return to traditional Croatian culture.

the style in the elaborately restored houses, churches and especially the impressive castle.

In Zagreb, fine examples of the baroque style are found in the Upper Town. Notice the Jesuit Church of St Catherine (p47) and the restored baroque mansion that is now the Croatian Museum of Naive Art (p45). Wealthy families built their baroque mansions around Zagreb, including at Brezovica, Miljana, Lobor and Bistra.

The Cathedral of St James in Šibenik (1431–1535) is the only Renaissance building in Europe constructed using the technique of mounting prefabricated stone elements.

Architecture Today

With its two architecture schools (one in Zagreb, and a newer one in Split), today's Croatia has a vibrant architecture scene that has been internationally recognised and repeatedly awarded. After the 1990s war, numerous open competitions were organised by both the state and private investors. Young architects in their 20s and 30s were suddenly given an opportunity to show their talents, bringing along a new spirit.

Some of the more important examples of this enthusiastic wave are the Gymnasium in Koprivnica by Studio UP, Hotel Lone (p109) in Rovinj by 3LHD,y and the Sea Organ (p169) in Zadar by Nikola Bašić, alongside many others.

The Natural Environment

The Lay of the Land

Croatia is shaped like a boomerang: from the Pannonian Plain of Slavonia between the Sava, Drava and Danube Rivers, across hilly central Croatia to the Istrian peninsula, then south through Dalmatia along the rugged Adriatic coast. The unusual geography makes it tricky to circle the country. If you're touring Croatia from Zagreb, you can either fly from Dubrovnik back to Zagreb to catch a flight out, double back by land through Split, or drive up through Bosnia and Hercegovina to enter Croatia from the east.

The narrow Croatian coastal belt at the foot of the Dinaric Alps is only about 600km long as the crow flies, but it's so indented that the actual length is 1778km. Most of the 'beaches' along the jagged coast consist of slabs of rock sprinkled with naturists. Don't come expecting to find sand, but the waters are sparkling clean, even around large towns.

There are 1244 islands and islets along the tectonically submerged Adriatic coastline, only 50 of them inhabited.

Croatia's offshore islands are astonishingly beautiful. The largest are Cres, Krk, Mali Lošinj, Pag and Rab in the north; Dugi Otok in the middle; and Brač, Hvar, Korčula, Mljet and Vis in the south.

Wildlife

Animals

Deer are plentiful in the dense forests of Risnjak National Park, as are brown bears, wild cats and *ris* (lynx), from which the park gets its name. Rarely, a wolf or wild boar may appear. Plitvice Lakes National Park, however, is an important refuge for wolves. A rare sea otter is also protected in Plitvice Lakes National Park, as well as in Krka National Park.

KARST CAVES & WATERFALLS

Croatia's most outstanding geological feature is the prevalent, highly porous limestone and dolomitic rock called karst. Stretching from Istria to Montenegro and covering large parts of the interior, karst is formed by the absorption of water into the surface limestone, which then corrodes and allows the water to seep into the harder layer underneath. Eventually the water forms underground streams, carving out fissures and caves before resurfacing, disappearing into another cave and eventually emptying into the sea. Caves and springs are common interior features of karstic landscapes, which explains Croatia's Pazin Chasm, Plitvice Lakes and the Krka waterfalls, as well as the Manita Peć cave in Paklenica. When the limestone collapses, a kind of basin (known as *polje*) is formed. These are then cultivated, despite the fact that this kind of field drains poorly and can easily turn into a temporary lake.

BIRDWATCHING

The griffon vulture, with a wingspan of 2.6m, has a permanent colony in Beli on Cres. Paklenica National Park is rich in peregrine falcons, goshawks, sparrow hawks, buzzards and owls. Krka National Park is an important migration route and winter habitat for marsh birds such as herons, wild duck, geese and cranes, as well as rare golden eagles and short-toed eagles. Kopački Rit Nature Park, near Osijek in eastern Croatia, is an extremely important bird refuge.

Two venomous snakes are endemic in Paklenica – the nose-horned viper and the European adder. The nonvenomous leopard snake, the four-lined snake, the grass snake and the snake lizard can be found in both Paklenica and Krka National Parks.

Plants

The country's richest plant life is found in the Velebit Range, part of the Dinaric Range, which provides the backdrop to the central Dalmatian coast. Botanists have counted around 2700 species and 78 endemic plants there, including the increasingly threatened edelweiss. Risnjak National Park is another good place to find edelweiss, along with black vanilla orchids, lilies and hairy alpenroses, which look a lot better than they sound. The dry Mediterranean climate along the coast is perfect for maquis, a low brush that flourishes all along the coast but especially on the island of Mljet. You'll also find oleander, jasmine and juniper trees along the coast, and lavender is cultivated on the island of Hvar. Mediterranean olive and fig trees are also abundant.

National Parks

When the Yugoslav federation collapsed, eight of its finest national parks ended up in Croatia. The national parks cover 1.097% of the country and have a total area of 961 sq km, of which 742 sq km is land and 219 sq km is water. Around 8% of Croatia is given over to its protected areas.

The temperature of the Adriatic Sea varies greatly: it rises from an average of 7°C (45°F) in December up to a balmy 23°C (73°F) in September.

National Parks on the Mainland

Risnjak National Park, southwest of Zagreb, is the most untouched forested park, partly because the climate at its higher altitudes is somewhat inhospitable, with an average temperature of 12.6°C in July. The winters are long and snowy but, when spring finally comes in late May or early June, everything blooms at once. The park has been kept deliberately free of tourist facilities, with the idea that only mountain lovers need venture this far. The main entrance point is the motel and information facility at Crni Lug.

The dramatically formed karstic gorges and cliffs make Paklenica National Park, along the Adriatic coast near Zadar, a rock-climbing favourite. Large grottoes and caves filled with stalactites and stalagmites make it an interesting park for cave explorers, and there are many kilometres of trails for hiking. Tourist facilities are well developed.

More rugged is the mountainous Northern Velebit National Park, a stunning patchwork of forests, peaks, ravines and ridges that backs northern Dalmatia and the Šibenik-Knin region.

The waterfalls of Plitvice Lakes National Park were formed by mosses that retain calcium carbonate as river water rushes through the karst. The park has been named a Unesco World Heritage Site and is easily accessible from either Zagreb or Zadar. The falls are at their watery best in spring.

REFUGE FOR YOUNG BEARS

In the village of Kuterevo in the northern Velebit Range lies the Kuterevo **refuge** (www.kuterevo-medvjedi.com.hr) for young bears. Founded in 2002, it protects young orphaned bears who are endangered due to traffic, hunting and poaching. In charge of the young orphaned bears is an association called Velebit Association Kuterevo (VUK), which works together with the villagers of Kuterevo. It has built a centre for baby and toddler bears.

From spring to late autumn, it's possible to visit the baby bears in the refuge, which attracts some 10,000 visitors per year. The website is in Croatian, but emails will be answered in English.

Krka National Park is an even more extensive series of lakes and waterfalls. The Zrmanja, Krka, Cetina and Neretva Rivers form waterfalls, but Manojlovac's power plant upstream can interfere somewhat with the flow, which can slow considerably around July and August. The main access point is in Skradinski Buk, with the largest cascade covering 800m.

National Parks on Croatia's Isles

The Kornati Islands consist of 140 sparsely vegetated islands, islets and reefs scattered over 300 sq km. The great indented form of the islands and extraordinary rock formations make them an Adriatic highlight. Unless you have your own boat, however, you'll need to join an organised tour from Zadar.

The northwestern half of the island of Mljet has been named a national park for its two highly indented saltwater lakes, which are surrounded by lush vegetation. Maquis shrubland is thicker and taller on Mljet than nearly anywhere else in the Mediterranean, which makes it a natural refuge for many animals.

The website of the Ministry of Environmental Protection (www.mzopu.hr) is the place to go for the latest news on Croatia's environment.

The Brijuni Islands are the most cultivated national park, as they were developed as a tourist resort in the late 19th century. They were the getaway paradise for Tito and now attract the glitterati and their yachts. Most of the animals and plants were introduced, but the islands are lovely. Access to the islands is restricted – you can only visit on an organised tour.

Environmental Issues

The lack of heavy industry in Croatia has had the happy effect of leaving its forests, coasts, rivers and air generally fresh and unpolluted. An increase in investment and development, however, brings forth problems and threats to the environment.

With the tourist boom, the demand for fresh fish and shellfish has risen exponentially. The production of farmed sea bass, sea bream and tuna (for export) is rising substantially, resulting in environmental pressure along the coast. Croatian tuna farms capture the young fish for fattening before they have a chance to reproduce and replenish the wild-fish population.

Coastal and island forests face particular problems. First logged by Venetians to build ships, then by local people desperate for fuel, the forests experienced centuries of neglect, which have left many island and coastal mountains barren. The dry summers and brisk *maestrals* (strong, steady westerly winds) also pose substantial fire hazards along the coast. In the last 20 years, fires have destroyed 7% of Croatia's forests.

The Arts

The arts are of major importance to the Croats, from the more traditional forms – classical music, theatre, dance and fine art – to modern styles such as pop, rock and electronic music, avant-garde and experimental theatre and dance, fashion and spoken word. Folk music and crafts are also very popular.

Literature

The Croatian language developed in the centuries following the great migration into Slavonia and Dalmatia. In order to convert the Slavs to Christianity, Greek missionaries Cyril and Methodius learned the language and Cyril put it into writing. This became known as Glagolitic script. The earliest known example is an 11th-century inscription in a Benedictine abbey on the island of Krk.

Award-winning writer Dubravka Ugrešić and four other female writers were accused of being 'witches' by a Croatian magazine for not wholeheartedly supporting the Croatian war for independence.

Poets & Playwrights

The first literary flowering in Croatia took place in Dalmatia, which was strongly influenced by the Italian Renaissance. The works of the scholar and poet Marko Marulić (1450–1524), from Split, are still venerated in Croatia. His play *Judita* was the first work produced by a Croatian writer in his native tongue. Ivan Gundulić's (1589–1638) epic poem *Osman* celebrated the Polish victory over the Turks in 1621, a victory that the author saw as heralding the destruction of the Ottoman rule. The plays of Marin Držić (1508–67), especially *Dundo Maroje,* express humanistic Renaissance ideals and are still performed, especially in Dubrovnik.

The most towering figure in the period after the 1990s war was the lyrical and sometimes satirical Vesna Parun. Although Parun was often harassed by the government for her 'decadent and bourgeois' poetry, her published work *Collected Poems* has reached a new generation, which finds solace in her vision of wartime folly.

Novelists

Croatia's towering literary figure is 20th-century novelist and playwright Miroslav Krleža (1893–1981). Always politically active, Krleža broke with Tito in 1967 over the writer's campaign for equality between the Serbian and Croatian literary languages. Depicting the concerns of a changing Yugoslavia, his most popular novels include *The Return of Philip Latinovicz* (1932), which has been translated into English, and *Banners* (1963–65), a multivolume saga about middle-class Croatian life at the turn of the 20th century.

Ivan Gundulić (1589–1638) from Ragusa (Dubrovnik) is widely considered to be the greatest Croatian poet.

Mention should also be made of Ivo Andrić (1892–1975), who won the 1961 Nobel Prize for Literature for his Bosnian historical trilogy *The Bridge on the Drina, Bosnian Story* and *Young Miss.* Born as a Catholic Croat in Bosnia, the writer used the Serbian dialect and lived in Belgrade, but identified himself as a Yugoslav.

Gold, Frankincense and Myrrh by Slobodan Novak, originally published in Yugoslavia in 1968, has been translated into English. The book is set on the island of Rab, where an elderly Madonna is dying, and her carer – the narrator – reminisces about life, love, the state, religion and memory. It's considered to be one of the pivotal works of 20th-century literature.

CONTEMPORARY WRITERS

Some contemporary writers have been strongly marked by the implications of Croatian independence. Alenka Mirković is a journalist who wrote a powerful memoir of the siege of Vukovar. Goran Tribuson uses the thriller genre to examine the changes in Croatian society after the war. In *Oblivion,* Pavao Pavličić uses a detective story to explore the problems of collective historical memory. American-based Josip Novakovich's work stems from nostalgia for his native Croatia. His most popular novel, *April Fool's Day* (2005), is an absurd and gritty account of the recent wars that gripped the region. Slavenka Drakulić is another worthy literary name, with books that are often politically and sociologically provocative, and always witty and intelligent. Look out for her excellent work, *Cafe Europa – Life After Communism* (1999).

Vedrana Rudan's novel *Night* (2004) perfectly illustrates the strong language and controversial antipatriarchal themes that are often ruffling feathers in the Croatian literary establishment.

Expat writer Dubravka Ugrešić has been a figure of controversy in Croatia and is acclaimed elsewhere. Now living in the Netherlands in self-imposed exile, she is best known for her novels *The Culture of Lies* (1998) and *The Ministry of Pain* (2006). Ugrešić also published *Nobody's Home* in 2007, a collection of stories and essays on travel across Europe and the USA, and the relationship between East and West.

Miljenko Jergović, born in Sarajevo but living in Croatia, is a witty, poignant writer whose *Sarajevo Marlboro* (1994) and *Mama Leone* (1999) powerfully describe the atmosphere in prewar Yugoslavia.

Cinema

Yugoslav cinema was dominated by Serbian directors, but Croatia had two important names to call its own: Krešo Golik (1922–98), who directed popular comedies such as *Plavi 9* (Blue 9; 1950) and *Tko pjeva zlo ne misli* (He Who Sings Never Means Harm; 1970); and Branko Bauer (b 1921), who directed thrillers, war dramas and adventure films. Croatia excelled at more experimental and 'intellectual' filmmaking (which wasn't necessarily very popular); prominent names include Branko Babaja, Zvonimir Berković, Lordan Zafranović and Vatroslav Mimica.

A great introduction to contemporary Croat writers is the collection of short stories *Croatian Nights* (2005), edited by Tony White, Borivoj Radaković and Matt Thorne. The excellent anthology of 19 short stories features both prominent Croat and British writers.

Franjo Tuđman's rule brought about a crisis in Croatian cinema, and the 1990s are considered to be the lowest point of Croatian filmmaking since WWII.

Some notable figures in more recent Croatian cinema are Vinko Brešan (b 1964) and Goran Rušinović (b 1968). Brešan's *Kako je počeo rat na mom otoku* (How the War Started on My Island; 1996) and *Maršal* (Marshal Tito's Spirit; 1999) were massively popular in Croatia. Rušinović's film *Mondo Bobo* (1997) is a stylish black-and-white crime drama inspired by the films of Jim Jarmusch and Shinya Tsukamoto, and was the first independent feature film made in Croatia.

Dalibor Matanić's *Fine mrtve djevojke* (Fine Dead Girls; 2002) was a popular thriller, while Rajko Grlić's *Karaula* (2006) recalled Yugoslav army days with much hilarity.

Music

Folk

Although Croatia has produced many fine classical musicians and composers, its most original musical contribution lies in its rich tradition of folk music. This music reflects a number of influences, many dating back to the Middle Ages when the Hungarians and the Venetians vied for control of the country. Franz Joseph Haydn (1732–1809) was born near a Croat enclave in Austria and his classical music pieces were strongly influenced by Croatian folk songs.

The instrument most often used in Croatian folk music is the *tamburica,* a three- or five-string mandolin that is plucked or strummed. Introduced by the Turks in the 17th century, the instrument rapidly gained a following in eastern Slavonia and came to be closely identified with Croatian national aspirations. *Tamburica* music continued to be played at weddings and local festivals during the Yugoslav period, too.

Vocal music followed the *klapa* tradition. Translated as 'group of people', *klapa* is an outgrowth of church-choir singing. The form is most popular in Dalmatia, particularly in Split, and can involve up to 10 voices singing in harmony about love, tragedy and loss. Traditionally the choirs were all-male, but now women are getting involved, although there are very few mixed choirs.

Another popular strain of folk music, which is strongly influenced by music from neighbouring Hungary, emanates from the region of Međimurje in northeastern Croatia. The predominant instrument is a *citura* (zither). The tunes are slow and melancholic, frequently revolving around themes of lost love. New artists have breathed life into this traditional genre, including Lidija Bajuk and Dunja Knebl, female singers who have done much to resuscitate the music and gained large followings in the process.

ROOTS MUSIC

For more about Croatian roots music, including the hot names on the contemporary scene, check out www.croatianrootsmusic.com.

Pop, Rock & the Rest

There's a wealth of home-grown talent in Croatia's pop and rock music scene. One of the most prominent bands is Hladno Pivo (Cold Beer), which plays energetic punky music with witty, politically charged lyrics. Then there's the indie rock band Pips, Chips & Videoclips, whose breakthrough single '*Dinamo ja te volim*' (Dinamo, I Love You) referred to Tuđman's attempts to rename Zagreb's football team, but whose music has generally been apolitical since. Vještice (The Witches) is a Zagreb-based band that mixes South African jive, folk music from Međimurje and punk rock.

The band Gustafi sings in the Istrian dialect and mixes Americana with local folk sounds, while the deliciously insane Let 3 from Rijeka is

RECOMMENDED FOLK RECORDINGS

» *Croatie: Music of Long Ago* is a good starting point as it covers the whole gamut of Croatian music.

» *Lijepa naša tamburaša* is a selection of Slavonian chants accompanied by *tamburica* (a three- or five-string mandolin).

» *Omiš 1967–75* is an overview of *klapa* (an outgrowth of church-choir singing) music.

» *Pripovid O Dalmaciji* is an excellent selection of *klapa* in which the influence of church-choral singing is especially clear.

FOLK DANCES

In dance, look for the *drmeš*, a kind of accelerated polka danced by couples in small groups. The *kolo*, a lively Slavic round dance in which men and women alternate in the circle, is accompanied by Roma-style violinists. In Dalmatia, the *poskočica* is also danced by couples creating various patterns.

Like the music, Croatian traditional dances are kept alive at local and national festivals. The best is the International Folklore Festival in Zagreb in July. If you can't make it to that, not to worry: music and folklore groups make a circuit in the summer, hitting most coastal and island towns at one point or another. Ask at a local tourist office for a current schedule.

CSARDAS BLUES

Watch out for music by Miroslav Evačić (www.miroslavevacic.com), which combines blues and Hungarian traditional elements into a fusion that he dubbed 'Csardas blues'.

(in)famous for its nutty tunes and live performances at which the band members often show up naked, with only a piece of cork up their backsides (yes, really). TBF (The Beat Fleet) is Split's answer to hip hop, using Split slang to talk about current issues, family troubles, heartbreak and happy times. Bosnian-born but Croatia-based hip-hop singer Edo Maajka is another witty voice.

The fusion of jazz and pop with folk tunes has been popular in Croatia for a while. Two of the more prominent names in this scene are the talented Tamara Obrovac from Istria, who sings in an ancient Istrian dialect that is no longer spoken, and Mojmir Novaković, formerly the singer of the popular band Legen.

The Croatian queen of pop is Severina, famous for her good looks and eventful personal life, which is widely covered by local celebrity and gossip magazines. Gibonni is another massively popular singer, and his major influence is Oliver Dragojević, a legendary singer of loveable schmaltz. All three (Severina, Gibonni and Dragojević) are from Split.

Afion is a progressive folk group from Zagreb that mixes traditional ethno songs from Croatia, Macedonia and Bosnia (also journeying into the sounds of Kosovo and Armenia) with jazzy undertones, world music influences and strong vocals in its acoustic performances.

If anything unifies the fractious former republics of Yugoslavia, it's music. Bosnian Goran Bregović teamed up with Serbian filmmaker Emir Kusturica for some remarkable scores and his music remains loved throughout the region.

Painting & Sculpture

The painter Vincent of Kastav was producing lovely church frescoes in Istria during the 15th century. The small church of St Maria near Beram contains his work, most notably the *Dance of Death*. Another notable Istrian painter of the 15th century is Ivan of Kastav, who has left frescoes throughout Istria, mostly in the Slovenian part.

Many artists born in Dalmatia were influenced by, and in turn influenced, Italian Renaissance style. The sculptors Lucijan Vranjanin and Frano Laurana, the miniaturist Julije Klović and the painter Andrija Medulić left Dalmatia while the region was under threat from the Ottomans in the 15th century and worked in Italy. Museums in London, Paris and Florence contain examples of their work, but few of their creations remain on display in Croatia.

Vlaho Bukovac (1855–1922) was the most notable Croatian painter in the late 19th century. After working in London and Paris, he came to Zagreb in 1892 and produced portraits and paintings on historical themes in a lively style. Early-20th-century painters of note include Miroslav Kraljević (1885–1913) and Josip Račić (1885–1908), but the most internationally recognised artist was the sculptor Ivan Meštrović (1883–1962), who created many masterpieces on Croatian themes. Antun Augustinčić (1900–79) was another internationally recognised sculptor, whose *Monument to Peace* is outside New York's UN building. A small museum of his work can be visited in the town of Klanjec, north of Zagreb.

Naive Art

Post-WWI artists experimented with abstract expressionism, but this period is best remembered for the naive art that began with the 1931 Zemlja (Soil) exhibition in Zagreb, which introduced the public to works by Ivan Generalić (1914–92) and other peasant painters. Committed to producing art that could be easily understood and appreciated by ordinary people, Generalić was joined by painters Franjo Mraz (1910–81) and Mirko Virius (1889–1943), and sculptor Petar Smajić (1910–85) in a campaign to gain acceptance and recognition for naive art.

Abstract Art

Abstract art infiltrated the postwar scene. The most celebrated modern Croatian painter is Edo Murtić (1921–2005), who drew inspiration from the countryside of Dalmatia and Istria. In 1959 a group of artists – Marijan Jevšovar (1922–88), Ivan Kožarić (b 1921) and Julije Knifer (1921–2004) – created the Gorgona group, which pushed the boundaries of abstract art. Đuro Pulitika (1922–2006), known for his colourful landscapes, was a well-regarded Dubrovnik painter, as were Antun Masle (1919–67) and Ivo Dulčić (1916–75).

Contemporary Art

The post-WWII trend towards avant-garde art has evolved into installation art, minimalism, conceptualism and video art. Contemporary Croatian artists worth seeing include Lovro Artuković (b 1959), whose highly realistic painting style is contrasted with surreal settings, and video artists Sanja Iveković (b 1949) and Dalibor Martinis (b 1947). The multimedia works of Andreja Kulunčić (b 1968), the installations of Sandra Sterle (b 1965) and the video art of Paris-based Renata Poljak (b 1974) are attracting international attention. The performances of Dubrovnik-born multimedia artist Slaven Tolj (b 1964), including his installations and video art, have received international acclaim. Lana Šlezić (b 1973) is a Toronto-based photographer whose excellent work is often shot in Croatia.

The most celebrated modern Croatian painter is Edo Murtić

The Gallery of Modern Art in Zagreb gives an excellent overview of the last 200 years of Croatian art. There's also a number of independent galleries in Zagreb featuring exhibitions by local artists.

Survival Guide

Accommodation

Budget accommodation includes campgrounds, hostels and some guesthouses, and costs up to 450KN for a double. Midrange accommodation costs 450KN to 800KN a double, while top end starts from 800KN and can go as high as 4000KN per double. For hotels, breakfast is often included.

Private accommodation is a lot more affordable in Croatia, and is often great value. If you don't mind forgoing hotel facilities, it's a great way to go.

Accommodation providers will handle travellers' registration with the local police, as required by Croatian authorities. To do this, they will need to take your passport away overnight.

Along the coast, accommodation is priced according to four seasons, which vary from place to place:

» November to March are the cheapest months. There may only be one or two hotels open in a coastal resort, but you'll get great rates.

» Generally, April, May and October are the next cheapest months.

» June and September are the shoulder season.

» In July and August you'll pay top price. The peak period runs from late July to mid- or late August. In these months you should make arrangements in advance.

» Note that many establishments add a 30% charge for stays shorter than three nights and include 'residence tax', which is around 7KN per person per day.

» Accommodation is generally cheaper in Dalmatia (except in Dubrovnik and Hvar) than in Kvarner or Istria.

BOOK YOUR STAY ONLINE

For more accommodation reviews by Lonely Planet authors, check out http://hotels.lonelyplanet.com. You'll find independent reviews, as well as recommendations on the best places to stay. Best of all, you can book online.

Booking Accommodation

» Once you know your itinerary it pays to start calling around to check prices and availability. Most receptionists speak English.

» It can be difficult to get a confirmed reservation without a deposit, particularly in the high season.

» Hotels are equipped to reserve accommodation using a credit-card number.

» Some guesthouses might require a SWIFT wire transfer (where your bank wires directly to their bank). Banks charge fees for the transaction, usually in the range of US$15 to US$30. The only way around it is to book online through an agency.

Camping

Nearly 100 campgrounds are scattered along the Croatian coast.

» Most operate from mid-April to mid-September only, although a few are open March to October.

» In spring and autumn, it's best to call ahead to make sure that the campground is open.

» Don't go by the opening and closing dates given by local tourist offices, in travel brochures or even this guide, as these can change.

PRICES FOR CAMPING

Many campgrounds in Istria are gigantic 'autocamps' with restaurants, shops and rows of caravans, but in Dalmatia they're smaller and often family owned.

» Prices listed here are per adult and site.

» Expect to pay up to 100KN for the site at some of the larger establishments.

» Most campgrounds charge from 40KN to 60KN per person per night.

» The tent charge is sometimes included in the price, but occasionally it's an extra 10KN to 15KN.

» The vehicle charge is sometimes included; it may be an extra 10KN to 50KN.

» Caravan sites cost about 30% more; electricity is not always included and may cost an extra 15KN per night.

» The residence tax costs about 7KN extra per person per night, depending on the season and the region.

TYPES OF CAMPS

Most grounds are still autocamps, although small, more family-owned campgrounds have popped up recently. If you want a more intimate environment, the town tourist office should be able to refer you to smaller campgrounds, but you may have to insist upon it.

» Naturist campgrounds (marked FKK) are among the best because their secluded locations ensure peace and quiet.

» 'Freelance' camping is officially prohibited.

» See www.camping.hr for camping information and links.

Hostels

The **Croatian YHA** (☎01-48 29 291; www.hfhs.hr; Savska 5/1, Zagreb) operates youth hostels in Rijeka, Dubrovnik, Pula, Punat, Zadar and Zagreb. Nonmembers pay an additional 10KN per person per day for a stamp on a welcome card; six stamps entitle you to membership. The Croatian YHA can also provide information about private youth hostels in Krk, Dubrovnik, Zadar and Zagreb.

» Most hostels are now open in winter but may not be staffed all day. It's wise to call in advance.

» Prices given here are for the high season in July and August; prices fall the rest of the year.

Hotels

» Formerly state-owned hotel complexes dating from the 1970s and 1980s are very similar to each other.

» Family-run *pansions* (guesthouses) offer excellent value and a more personal experience. Ask at the local tourist office as more *pansions* pop up each season.

» Double hotel rooms are a good size, and nearly all rooms in Croatian hotels have private bathrooms.

» The majority of hotels in Croatia are midrange: around 800KN for a double in high season along the coast; around 450KN in late spring or early autumn. At that price you can get a private bathroom, a telephone and sometimes a TV with a satellite hook-up.

» There is usually a surcharge for short stays (fewer than three or four nights) during the summer season along the coast and on the islands.

» Apartments are self-contained units that include equipped kitchens, a bed or beds, and a bathroom.

» Most hotels offer the option of half-board. In a 'tourist settlement' far from town, half-board may be the only dining possibility. Meals tend to centre on cheaper cuts of meat, although some hotels are starting to offer a vegetarian menu.

» The star-rating system for Croatian hotels is inconsistent and not very helpful.

Private Accommodation

The best value for money in Croatia is a private room or apartment, often within or attached to a local home – the equivalent of small private guesthouses in other countries. Not only is private accommodation cheaper than a hotel, the service is also likely to be friendlier and more efficient, and the food better.

Book private accommodation through travel agencies, by dealing directly with proprietors who meet you at the local bus or ferry station, or by knocking on the doors of houses with *sobe* or *zimmer* (rooms available) signs.

BOOKING THROUGH AN AGENCY

» Accommodation booked through an agency has been professionally vetted.

» Agencies can handle complaints (often in English) if things go wrong.

» Stays of fewer than four nights will attract an agency surcharge of at least 30%; some will insist on a seven-night minimum stay in the high season.

THINGS TO WATCH OUT FOR WITH PRIVATE RENTALS

» If you decide to go with proprietors (usually women) at the bus or ferry station, get an exact location or you could get stuck way out of town.

» Clarify whether the price is per person or per room.

» Avoid a surcharge by specifying the exact number of days you plan to stay and what time of day you plan to check out.

» If you land in a room or apartment without a blue *sobe* or *apartmani* sign outside, the proprietor is renting to you illegally (i.e. not paying residence tax). They will probably be reluctant to provide their full name or phone number and you'll have absolutely no recourse in case of a problem.

PRACTICALITIES

» **Newspapers and magazines** Widely read newspapers include *Večernji List*, *Jutarnji List*, *Slobodna Dalmacija* and the *Feral Tribune*. The most popular weekly is *Globus*.

» **Radio** The most popular radio station is Narodni Radio, which airs only Croatian music, followed by Antena Zagreb and Otvoreni Radio. Croatian Radio broadcasts news in English daily at 8.05pm on FM frequencies 88.9, 91.3 and 99.3.

» **Tipping** Bills include a service charge, but it's common to round up the bill.

» **Electricity** Electrical supply: 220V, 50Hz AC. The standard European round-pronged plug is used.

» **Weights and measures** Croatia uses the metric system.

» **TV and video** The video system is PAL.

KNOCKING-ON-DOORS APPROACH

» Houses with *sobe* or *zimmer* signs offer private accommodation.

» Start early in the day since proprietors may be out on errands in the afternoon.

» Leave your luggage in a *garderoba* (left-luggage office) before heading into town – you'll be more comfortable and in a better position to negotiate a price.

BARGAINING

» Don't hesitate to bargain, especially if you're staying for a week.

» In the high season along the coast it may be impossible to find a proprietor willing to rent you a room for one night only.

» Single rooms are scarce.

» Showers are always included but breakfast often isn't, so ask about the breakfast charge.

BOOKING HALF-BOARD

If possible, it may be worthwhile to take a half-board option and stay with a family. Most families on the coast have a garden, a vineyard and access to the sea. You could find yourself beginning your evenings with a homemade aperitif before progressing on to a garden-fresh salad, home-grown potatoes and grilled fresh fish, all washed down with your host's very own wine.

TYPES OF PRIVATE ACCOMMODATION

Travel agencies classify private accommodation according to a star system:

» **Three star** The most expensive; includes a private bathroom

» **Two star** The bathroom is shared with one other room

» **One star** The bathroom is shared with two other rooms or with the owner.

Studios with cooking facilities cost a little more than a double room, but self-catered meals are not cheap in Croatia. If you're travelling in a small group, it may be worthwhile to get an apartment. Under no circumstances will private accommodation include a telephone, but satellite TV is becoming common.

RATES & PRICING

Rates are usually fixed by the local tourist association and don't vary from agency to agency, though some agencies may not handle rooms in the cheapest category, and some only handle apartments. In legally rented accommodation there's often a 'registration tax' to register you with the police.

Any prices quoted here assume a four-night stay in high season. Prices fall greatly outside July and August.

Activities

Adriatic Croatia International Club (www.aci-club.hr) Manages 21 coastal marinas.

Association of Nautical Tourism (Udruženje Nautičkog Turizma; ☎051 209 147; www.croatiacharter.com; Bulevar Oslobođenja 23, Rijeka) Represents all Croatian marinas.

Cro Challenge (www.crochallenge.com) Extreme sports association.

Croatian Aeronautical Federation (www.caf.hr) Parachuting club.

Croatian Association of Diving Tourism (www.croprodive.info)

Croatian Diving Federation (www.diving-hrs.hr)

Croatian Mountaineering Association (www.plsavez.hr) Rock climbing, caving and hiking information.

Huck Finn (www.huck-finn.hr) Specialises in adventure travel and runs the gamut of adrenaline-lifting tours around Croatia: river and sea kayaking, rafting, canoeing, caving, cycling, fishing, hiking and sailing.

NGO Bicikl (www.bicikl.hr) Cycling information.

Outdoor (www.outdoor.hr) Adventure and incentive travel.

Pedala (www.pedala.com.hr) Cycling information.

Pro Diving Croatia (www.diving.hr)

Riverfree (www.riverfree.hr) Rafting and canoeing club.

Business Hours

Croats are early risers: by 7am there will be lots of people on the street and many places already open. Along the coast, life is more relaxed – shops and offices frequently close around noon for an afternoon break and reopen at about 4pm.

» Official office hours are from 8am to 4pm or 9am to 5pm Monday to Friday, and 8am to 1pm or 9am to 2pm Saturday.

» Banking hours are typically longer, from 8am or 9am to 7pm weekdays, and same as office hours on Saturday.

» Post offices are open 7.30am to 7pm on weekdays and 8am to noon on Saturday. They keep longer hours in coastal towns during the summer season.

» Many shops are open 8am to 8pm on weekdays and until 2pm or 3pm on Saturday. Shopping malls work longer hours.

» Supermarkets are open from 8am to 8pm Monday to Friday. On Saturday, some close at 2pm while others stay open until 8pm. Only some supermarkets are open on Sunday during the summer season.

» Restaurants are open long hours, often from noon to 11pm or midnight, and often close on Sunday out of peak season.

» Cafe hours are usually 8am to midnight, and bars open from 9am to midnight.

» In Zagreb and Split discos and nightclubs are open year-round, but many places along the coast are only open in summer. Cybercafes also open long hours – usually seven days a week.

» Coastal travel agencies open from 8am or 9am until 9pm or 10pm daily in high season, shortening their hours as the tourist season wanes. In continental Croatia, most agencies keep office hours.

Customs Regulations

» Travellers can bring their personal effects into the country, along with 1L of liquor, 1L of wine, 500g of coffee, 200 cigarettes and 50mL of perfume.

» Camping gear, boats and electronic equipment should be declared upon entering the country.

» There is no quarantine period for animals brought into the country, but you should have a recent vaccination certificate. Otherwise, the animal must be inspected by a local veterinarian, who may not be immediately available.

Discount Cards

Most museums, galleries, theatres and festivals in Croatia offer student discounts of up to 50%. For youth travel and the cards listed below, contact the travel section of **Croatian YHA** (☎01-48 29 291; www.hfhs.hr; Savska 5/1, Zagreb).

» An International Student Identity Card (ISIC) is the best international proof of student status.

» People under the age of 26 who are not students qualify for the International Youth Travel Card (IYTC).

» Croatia is a member of the **European Youth Card Association** (www.euro26.hr), which offers reductions in shops, restaurants and libraries in participating countries. The card can be used at around 1400 places of interest in Croatia.

Electricity

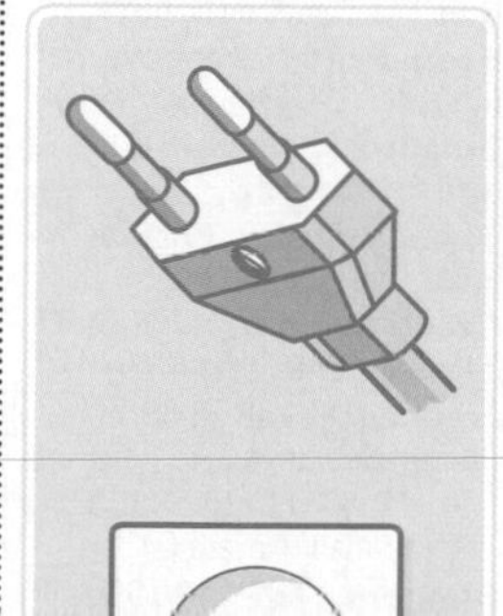

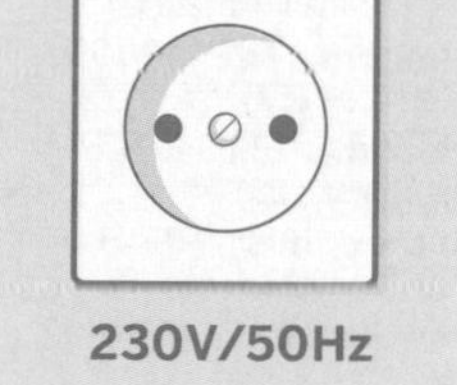

230V/50Hz

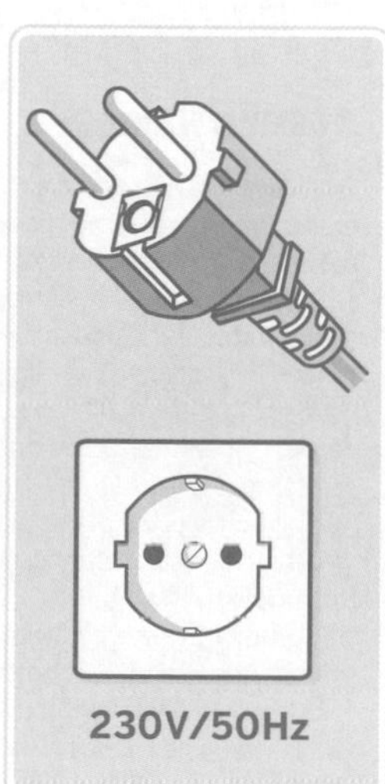

230V/50Hz

Embassies & Consulates in Zagreb

Albania (☎01-48 10 679; Jurišićeva 2a)
Australia (☎01-48 91 200; Nova Ves 11, Kaptol Centar)
Bosnia and Hercegovina (☎01-45 01 070; Torbarova 9)
Bulgaria (☎01-46 46 609; Nike Grškovića 31)
Canada (☎01-48 81 200; Prilaz Gjure Deželića 4)
Czech Republic (☎01-61 77 246; Radnička Cesta 47/6)
France (☎01-48 93 600; Andrije Hebranga 2)
Germany (☎01-61 58 100; Ulica Grada Vukovara 64)
Hungary (☎01-48 90 900; Pantovčak 257)
Ireland (☎01-63 10 025; Miramarska 23)
Netherlands (☎01-46 42 200; Medvešćak 56)
New Zealand (☎01-46 12 060; Vlaška 50a)
Poland (☎01-48 99 444; Krležin Gvozd 3)
Romania (☎01-46 77 550; Mlinarska 43)
Serbia (☎01-45 79 067; Pantovčak 245)
Slovakia (☎01-48 77 070; Prilaz Gjure Deželića 10)
Slovenia (☎01-63 11 000; Savska cesta 41/annex)
UK (☎01-60 09 100; I Lučića 4)
USA (☎01-66 12 200; Thomas Jefferson 2)

Food

For detailed information, see the Cuisine chapter (p299).

The following price ranges refer to a standard main course.

€	less than 70KN
€€	70KN to 120KN
€€€	more than 120KN

Gay & Lesbian Travellers

Homosexuality has been legal in Croatia since 1977 and it is tolerated, but not welcomed with open arms. Public displays of affection between same-sex couples may be met with hostility, especially outside the major cities.

» Exclusively gay clubs are a rarity outside Zagreb, but raves and many of the large discos attract a mixed crowd.

» On the coast, Rovinj, Hvar, Split and Dubrovnik are popular with gay male travellers, who often frequent naturist beaches.

» In Zagreb, the last Saturday in June is Gay Pride Zagreb day.

» Most Croatian websites devoted to the gay scene are in Croatian only, but a good starting point is http://travel.gay.hr.

» **LORI** (www.lori.hr) is a lesbian organisation based in Rijeka.

STREET NAMES

Particularly in Zagreb and Split, you may notice a discrepancy between the names used on maps and the names you'll actually see on the street.

In Croatian, street names can be rendered either in the nominative or possessive case. The difference is apparent in the name's ending. Thus, Ulica Ljudevita Gaja (street of Ljudevita Gaja) becomes Gajeva ulica (Gaja's Street). The latter is the one most commonly seen on the street sign and used in everyday conversation.

The same principle applies to a *trg* (square), which can be rendered as Trg Petra Preradovića or Preradovićev trg.

Some of the more common names are Trg Svetog Marka (Markov trg), Trg Josipa Jurja Strossmayera (Strossmayerov trg), Ulica Andrije Hebranga (Hebrangova), Ulica Pavla Radića (Radićeva), Ulica Augusta Šenoe (Šenoina), Ulica Nikole Tesle (Teslina) and Ulica Ivana Tkalčića (Tkalčićeva). Be aware also that Trg Nikole Šubića Zrinskog is almost always called Zrinjevac.

In an address the letters 'bb' following a street name (such as Placa bb) stand for *bez broja* (without number), which indicates that the building has no street number.

Health

Good health care is readily available in Croatia. Pharmacists can give valuable advice and sell over-the-counter medication for minor illnesses.

The standard of dental care is usually good, but it is sensible to have a dental check-up before a long trip.

Particular health issues:

» Tick-borne encephalitis, a serious brain infection, is spread by tick bites. Vaccination is advised for those in risk areas who are unable to avoid tick bites (such as campers and hikers). Two doses of vaccine will give a year's protection; three doses up to three years.

» Heat exhaustion is caused by excessive fluid loss and inadequate replacement of fluids and salt. Symptoms include headache, dizziness and tiredness.

» Dehydration is already happening by the time you feel thirsty – aim to drink sufficient water to produce pale, diluted urine. To treat heat exhaustion, replace lost fluids by drinking water and/or fruit juice, and cool the body with cold water and fans. Treat salt loss with salty fluids such as soup or Bovril, or add a little more table salt to foods than usual.

» Heatstroke is much more serious, resulting in irrational and hyperactive behaviour and eventually loss of consciousness, and death. Rapid cooling by spraying the body with water and fanning is ideal. Emergency fluid and electrolyte replacement by intravenous drip is recommended.

» Watch for sea urchins around rocky beaches. If you get some of their needles embedded in your skin, olive oil will help to loosen them. If they are not removed, they could become infected. As a precaution wear rubber shoes while walking on the rocks or bathing.

» To avoid getting bitten by snakes, do not walk barefoot or stick your hands into holes or cracks. Half of those bitten by venomous snakes are not actually injected with poison (envenomed). If bitten by a snake, do not panic. Immobilise the bitten limb with a splint (eg a stick) and apply a bandage over the site firmly, similar to a bandage over a sprain. Do not apply a tourniquet, or cut or suck the bite. Get medical help as soon as possible so that an antivenin can be administered if necessary.

Insurance

Worldwide travel insurance is available at www.lonelyplanet.com/travel_services. You can buy, extend and claim online any time – even when you're already on the road.

Internet Access

» Internet access at cybercafes costs around 30KN per hour.

» Local tourist offices should have the latest information on local internet access.

» In smaller towns, the tourist office may let you quickly check your email on their computer if you ask nicely.

» Public libraries usually have internet access, but their hours can be limited.

» Upmarket hotels are almost always equipped with wi-fi, as are business-geared hotels, although you may have to pay for access. Some private guesthouses also have wi-fi, though you shouldn't count on it.

Legal Matters

Although it is highly unlikely that you'll be hassled by the police, you should keep identification with you at all times as the police have the right to stop you and demand ID.

By international treaty, you have the right to notify your consular official if arrested. Consulates can normally refer you to English-speaking lawyers, although they will not pay for one.

Maps

Freytag & Berndt publishes a series of country, regional and city maps. Its 1:600,000 map of Croatia, Slovenia and Bosnia and Hercegovina is particularly useful if you're travelling in the region. Others include *Croatia, Slovenia* (1:800,000) by GeoCenter and *Hrvatska, Slovenija, Bosna i Hercegovina* (1:600,000) by Naklada Naprijed in Zagreb.

» Regional tourist offices often publish good regional driving maps.

» For cities other than Zagreb, Split, Zadar, Rijeka and Dubrovnik, there are few top-quality maps.

» Local tourist offices usually publish helpful maps.

Money

Croatia uses the kuna (KN). Commonly circulated banknotes come in denominations of 500, 200, 100, 50, 20, 10 and five kuna, bearing images of Croat heroes such as Stjepan Radić and Ban Josip Jelačić. Each kuna is divided into 100 lipa. You'll find silver-coloured 50- and 20-lipa coins, and bronze-coloured 10-lipa coins.

» The kuna has a fixed exchange rate tied to the euro. However, to amass hard currency, the government makes the kuna more expensive in summer when tourists visit.

» You'll get the best exchange rate from mid-September to mid-June. Otherwise, the rate varies little from year to year.

» International boat fares are priced in euros, not kuna, although you pay in kuna.

ATMs

Automatic teller machines (ATMs) are prevalent nearly everywhere in Croatia and can be a convenient way of changing money. Most are tied in with Cirrus, Plus, Diners Club and Maestro.

» Privredna Banka usually has ATMs for cash withdrawals using American Express cards.

» Most ATMs also allow you to withdraw money using a credit card; note that you pay interest on the amount immediately and are charged a withdrawal fee.

» All post offices will allow you to make a cash withdrawal on MasterCard or Cirrus, and a growing number work with Diners Club as well.

Changing Money

There are numerous places to change money in Croatia, all offering similar rates; ask at any travel agency for the location of the nearest exchange.

» Post offices change money and keep long hours.

» Most places deduct a commission of 1% to 1.5% to change cash, but some banks do not.

» Travellers cheques may be exchanged only in banks.

» Kuna can be converted into hard foreign currency only at a bank and only if you submit a receipt of a previous transaction.

» Hungarian currency (the forint) is difficult to change in Croatia.

» You can pay for a meal or small services in euros, but the rate is not as good.

» You can pay for most private accommodation in euros.

Credit Cards

Credit cards (Visa, Diners Club, MasterCard, American Express) are widely accepted in hotels but rarely accepted in any kind of private accommodation. Many smaller restaurants and shops do not accept credit cards.

Amex cardholders can contact Atlas travel agencies in Dubrovnik, Opatija, Poreč, Pula, Split, Zadar and Zagreb for the full range of Amex services. Privredna Banka is a chain of banks that handles services for Amex clients.

Following are the websites for Croatia's branches of the major credit-card companies: American Express (www.americanexpress.hr), Diners Club (www.diners.com.hr), Eurocard/MasterCard (www.zaba.hr) and Visa (www.splitskabanka.hr).

Taxes & Refunds

Travellers who spend more than 740KN in one shop are entitled to a refund of the value-added tax (VAT), which is equivalent to 22% of the purchase price. In order to claim the refund, the merchant must fill out the tax cheque (required form), which you must present to the customs office upon leaving the country. Mail a stamped copy to the shop within six months, which will then credit your credit card with the appropriate sum.

There is also a service called Global Refund System, which will give you your refund in cash at the airport or at participating post offices. Post offices in Zagreb, Osijek, Dubrovnik, Split, Rijeka, Pula and a few other towns participate in the system. For a complete list, see www.posta.hr.

Photography

» You can still find colour-print film produced by Kodak and Fuji in photo stores and tourist shops. It's fairly expensive in Croatia, so stock up ahead of time.

» The standard size for prints developed in Croatia is 9cm by 13cm.

» Digital-imaging techniques are available in Zagreb and other large cities, but few places develop APS film.

» One-hour developing is not widely available.

» Slide film is widely available in major cities and tourist centres, but can be scarce in out-of-the-way places.

» Military installations may not be photographed, and you may have a lot of angry naked people after you if you try to take pictures in a naturist resort.

Public Holidays

Croats take their holidays very seriously. Shops and museums are shut and boat services are reduced. On religious holidays, the churches are full; it can be a good time to check out the artwork in a church that is usually closed.

Croatian public holidays:

» **New Year's Day** 1 January

» **Epiphany** 6 January

» **Easter Monday** March/April

» **Labour Day** 1 May

» **Corpus Christi** 10 June

» **Day of Antifascist Resistance** 22 June; marks the outbreak of resistance in 1941

» **Statehood Day** 25 June

» **Homeland Thanksgiving Day** 5 August

» **Feast of the Assumption** 15 August

» **Independence Day** 8 October

» **All Saints' Day** 1 November

» **Christmas** 25 and 26 December

Safe Travel

Landmines

The former confrontation line between Croat and federal forces was heavily mined in the early 1990s, and over a million mines were laid in eastern Slavonia around Osijek, and in the hinterlands north of Zadar. The government has invested in de-mining operations, but it's a slow job. Mined areas are well signposted with skull-and-crossbones symbols and yellow tape, but don't wander off in sensitive regions before checking with a local. Never go poking around an obviously abandoned and ruined house.

Telephone

Area Codes

» To call Croatia from abroad, dial your international access code, then 385 (the country code for Croatia), then the area code (without the initial zero) and the local number.

» To call from region to region within Croatia, start with the area code (with the initial zero); drop it when dialling within the same code.

» Phone numbers with the prefix 060 are either free or charged at a premium rate, so watch out for the fine print.

» Phone numbers that begin with 09 are mobile phone numbers, which are billed at a much higher rate than regular numbers.

Mobile Phones

» If you have an unlocked 3G phone, you can buy a SIM card for about 50KN, which includes 20 minutes of connection time. You can choose from four network providers: **VIP** (www.vip.hr), **T-Mobile** (www.t-mobile.hr), **Tomato** (www.tomato.com.hr) and **Tele2** (www.tele2.hr).

» You can also buy a mobile and phonecard packet at any telecom shop from about 150KN.

» Mobile phone rental is not available in Croatia.

Phonecards

» You'll need a phonecard to use public telephones.

» Phonecards are sold according to *impulsi* (units); cards are available in 25 (15KN), 50 (30KN), 100 (50KN) and 200 (100KN) units. These can be purchased at any post office and most tobacco shops and newspaper kiosks.

» A call from Croatia using a phonecard will cost around 2KN per minute to the UK and Europe and 3.20KN to the USA or Australia.

» Local calls cost 0.26KN per minute from 7am to 7pm Monday to Saturday, and 0.14KN between 7pm and 7am Monday to Saturday, Sunday and public holidays.

» Many phone boxes are equipped with a button on the upper left with a flag symbol. Press the button for instructions in English.

» You can call from a post office without a phonecard.

» For local and national calls, the mark-up is negligible from cheaper hotels but significantly more from four-star establishments.

» Private accommodation never includes a private telephone, but you may be able to use the owner's for local calls.

Time

Croatia is on Central European Time (GMT/UTC plus one hour). Daylight saving comes into effect at the end of March, when clocks are turned forward an hour. At the end of September they're turned back an hour. Croatia uses the 24-hour clock.

Tourist Information

The **Croatian National Tourist Board** (www.croatia.hr) is a good source of information. Regional tourist offices supervise tourist development:

» **Dubrovnik-Neretva County** (www.visitdubrovnik.hr)

» **Istria County** (www.istra.hr)

» **Krapina-Zagorje County** (www.tzkzz.hr)

» **Osijek-Baranja County** (www.tzosbarzup.hr)

» **Primorje-Gorski Kotar (Kvarner) County** (www.kvarner.hr)

» **Šibenik-Knin County** (www.sibenikregion.com)

» **Split-Dalmatia County** (www.dalmatia.hr)

» **Zadar County** (www.zadar.hr)

» **Zagreb County** (www.tzzz.hr)

Municipal tourist offices have free brochures and good information on local events. Also try commercial travel agencies such as **Atlas Travel Agency** (www.atlas-croatia.com) and **Generalturist** (www.generalturist.com).

Travellers with Disabilities

More attention is being paid to the needs of people with disabilities in Croatia.

» Public toilets at bus stations, train stations, airports and large public venues are usually wheelchair accessible.

» Large hotels are wheelchair accessible, but very little private accommodation is.

» Bus and train stations in Zagreb, Zadar, Rijeka, Split and Dubrovnik are wheelchair accessible, but the local Jadrolinija ferries are not.

For further information: **Hrvatski Savez Udruga Tjelesnih Invalida** (☎01-48 12 004; www.hsuti.hr; Šoštarićeva 8, Zagreb).

Visas

Citizens of the EU, the USA, Canada, Australia, New Zealand, Israel, Ireland, Singapore and the UK do not need a visa for stays of up to 90 days. South Africans must apply for a 90-day visa in Pretoria. Contact any Croatian embassy, consulate or travel agency abroad for information.

If you want to stay in Croatia for longer than three months, the easiest thing to do is cross the border into Italy or Austria and return.

Croatian authorities require all foreigners to register with the local police when they arrive in a new area of the country, but this is a routine matter normally handled by the hotel, hostel, campground or agency securing your private accommodation.

If you're staying elsewhere (eg with relatives or friends), your host should take care of it for you.

Volunteering

For short-term volunteering programs, consider the **griffon vulture centre** (☎840 525; www.supovi.hr; Beli 4; adult/concession 50/25KN; ⏲9am-8pm, closed Nov-Mar) in Beli on Cres Island, the **Kuterevo refuge for young bears** (p310) in the Velebit Range, near Šibenik, and the **Lošinj Marine Education Centre** (www.blue-world.org; Kaštel 24; adult/concession 15/10KN; ⏲9am-1pm & 6-10pm Jul & Aug, 9am-1pm & 6-8pm Jun & Sep, 10am-4pm rest of year) on Lošinj Island.

Women Travellers

Women face no special danger in Croatia. There have been cases in large coastal cities of some lone women being harassed and followed, but this is not common.

Police will not always take reports of 'date rape' seriously. Be careful about being alone with an unfamiliar man.

Topless sunbathing is tolerated, but there are numerous nudist beaches.

Transport

GETTING THERE & AWAY

Getting to Croatia is becoming ever easier, especially if you're arriving in summer. Low-cost carriers have established routes to Croatia – you can now fly to Dubrovnik, Split, Zadar, Rijeka, Pula and Zagreb on a budget airline. A plethora of bus and ferry routes also shepherd holidaymakers to the coast. Flights, tours and rail tickets can be booked online at www.lonelyplanet.com/bookings.

Entering the Country

With an economy that depends heavily on tourism, Croatia has wisely kept red tape to a minimum for foreign visitors. The most serious hassle is likely to be long lines at immigration checkpoints.

Air

There are direct flights to Croatia from a variety of European cities; however, there are no nonstop flights from North America to Croatia.

There are several major airports in Croatia:

Dubrovnik (www.airport-dubrovnik.hr) Nonstop flights from Brussels, Cologne, Frankfurt, Hanover, London (Gatwick and Stansted), Manchester, Munich and Stuttgart.

Pula (www.airport-pula.com) Nonstop flights from London (Gatwick) and Manchester.

Rijeka (www.rijeka-airport.hr) Nonstop flights from Cologne and Stuttgart.

Split (www.split-airport.hr) Nonstop flights from Cologne, Frankfurt, London, Munich, Prague and Rome.

Zadar (www.zadar-airport.hr) Nonstop flights from Bari, Brussels, Dublin, London, Munich and more.

Zagreb (www.zagreb-airport.hr) Direct flights from all European capitals, plus Cologne, Hamburg and Stuttgart.

Boat

Regular boats connect Croatia with Italy.

Blue Line (www.blueline-ferries.com)

Commodore Cruises (www.commodore-cruises.hr)

Emilia Romagna Lines (www.emiliaromagnalines.it)

Jadrolinija (www.jadrolinija.hr)

SNAV (www.snav.com)

Split Tours (www.splittours.hr)

Ustica Lines (www.usticalines.it)

Venezia Lines (www.venezialines.com)

Land

Croatia has border crossings with Hungary, Slovenia, Bosnia and Hercegovina, Serbia and Montenegro.

Austria

BUS

Eurolines (www.eurolines.com) operates buses from Vienna to several destinations in Croatia.

» **Rijeka** €48, nine hours, two weekly

» **Split** €57, 11½ hours, two weekly

» **Zadar** €45, 8¼ hours, two weekly

» **Zagreb** €36, five to seven hours, two daily (one direct, the other via Varaždin)

TRAIN

There are two daily and two overnight trains between Vienna and Zagreb, via Slovenia and via Hungary. The price is between €50 and €60, and the journey takes between 5¾ and 6½ hours. In Zagreb, you can connect to other cities in Croatia.

Bosnia & Hercegovina

There are dozens of border crossings between Bosnia and Hercegovina and Croatia. Major destinations, such as Sarajevo, Mostar and Međugorje, are all accessible from Zagreb, Split, Osijek and Dubrovnik.

BUS

Buses run to Croatia from a number of destinations in Bosnia and Hercegovina.

TRAIN

Trains from Sarajevo service the following destinations:

» **Osijek** €21, six hours, daily

» **Ploče** (via Mostar and Banja Luka) €15, four hours, two daily

» **Zagreb** €35, 9½ hours, two daily

Germany

BUS

Bus services between the two countries are good, and fares are cheaper than the train.

All buses are handled by **Deutsche Touring GmbH** (www.deutsche-touring.de). There are no Deutsche Touring offices in Croatia, but numerous travel agencies and bus stations sell its tickets.

Scheduled departures to/from Germany:

» **Istria** To/from Frankfurt weekly; from Munich twice weekly.

» **Rijeka** To/from Berlin twice weekly.

» **Split** To/from Cologne, Dortmund, Frankfurt, Main, Mannheim, Munich, Nuremberg and Stuttgart daily; from Berlin (via Rijeka) twice a week.

» **Zagreb** To/from Cologne, Dortmund, Frankfurt, Main, Mannheim, Munich, Nuremberg and Stuttgart daily; from Berlin four times a week.

TRAIN

There are three trains daily from Munich to Zagreb (€43 to €91, 8½ to nine hours) via Salzburg and Ljubljana. Reservations are required southbound but not northbound.

Hungary

The main highway entry and exit points between Hungary and Croatia:

» **Donji Miholjac** Located 7km south of Harkány.

» **Gola** Located 23km east of Koprivnica.

» **Goričan** Between Nagykanizsa and Varaždin.

» **Terezino Polje** Opposite Barcs.

Donji Miholjac and Goričan are the most important.

TRAIN

There are three daily Zagreb–Budapest trains (€35 return, six to seven hours).

Italy

BUS

Trieste is well connected with the Istrian coast. Note that there are fewer buses on Sundays.

» **Dubrovnik** 420KN, 15 hours, one daily

» **Poreč** 75KN, two hours, three daily

» **Pula** 125KN, 2½ to 3¾ hours, six daily

» **Rijeka** 75KN, two hours, five daily

» **Rovinj** 93KN, three hours, two daily

» **Split** 284KN, 10½ hours, two daily

» **Zadar** 221KN, 7½ hours, one daily

There's also a bus from Padua that passes Venice, Trieste and Rovinj and ends up in Pula (245KN, six hours, Monday to Saturday).

CAR & MOTORCYCLE

Many insurance companies will not insure Italian rental cars for a trip into Croatia. Border officials know this and may refuse you entry unless permission to drive into Croatia is clearly marked on the insurance documents.

Most car-rental companies in Trieste and Venice are familiar with this requirement and will furnish you with the correct stamp. Otherwise, you must make specific inquiries.

TRAIN

Between Venice and Zagreb, there is one direct train at night (€25 to €43, 7½ hours) and several more that run through Ljubljana.

Montenegro

There are three daily buses from Kotor to Dubrovnik (110KN, 2½ hours), which start at Bar and stop at Herceg Novi.

Serbia

Border crossings abound, many off the main Zagreb–Belgrade highway.

BUS

There are five daily buses from Zagreb to Belgrade (220KN, six hours). At Bajakovo on the border, a Serbian bus takes you on to Belgrade.

TRAIN

Four daily trains connect Zagreb with Belgrade (169KN, 6½ hours).

CLIMATE CHANGE & TRAVEL

Every form of transport that relies on carbon-based fuel generates CO_2, the main cause of human-induced climate change. Modern travel is dependent on aeroplanes, which might use less fuel per kilometre per person than most cars but travel much greater distances. The altitude at which aircraft emit gases (including CO_2) and particles also contributes to their climate change impact. Many websites offer 'carbon calculators' that allow people to estimate the carbon emissions generated by their journey and, for those who wish to do so, to offset the impact of the greenhouse gases emitted with contributions to portfolios of climate-friendly initiatives throughout the world. Lonely Planet offsets the carbon footprint of all staff and author travel.

BUSES FROM BOSNIA & HERCEGOVINA

FROM	TO	COST (€)	DURATION	SERVICES
Međugorje	Dubrovnik	20	3hr	1 daily
Mostar	Dubrovnik	19	3hr	4 daily
Sarajevo	Dubrovnik	24	5hr	1 daily
Sarajevo	Rijeka	45	10hr	2 weekly
Sarajevo	Split (via Mostar)	28	7hr	2 daily
Sarajevo	Zagreb	29	8hr	3 daily

Slovenia

There are 26 border-crossing points between Slovenia and Croatia.

BUS

Slovenia is well connected with the Istrian coast. The following are serviced by buses from Ljubljana:

» **Rijeka** 185KN, 2½ hours, two daily

» **Rovinj** 185KN, four hours, three daily

» **Split** 320KN, 10 hours, one daily

There's also one bus each weekday that connects Rovinj with Koper (93KN, 2¾ hours), stopping at Poreč, Portorož and Piran.

TRAIN

Trains run to Croatia from Ljubljana:

» **Rijeka** 105KN, 2½ hours, two daily

» **Zagreb** 105KN to 172KN, 2½ hours, seven daily

GETTING AROUND

Air

Croatia Airlines (☎01-66 76 555; www.croatiaairlines.hr) is the only carrier for flights within Croatia. There are daily flights between Zagreb and Dubrovnik, Pula, Split and Zadar.

Note that all batteries must be removed from checked luggage when leaving from any airport in Croatia.

Bicycle

Cycling can be a great way to explore the islands. Relatively flat islands such as Pag and Mali Lošinj offer the most relaxed biking, but the winding, hilly roads on other islands offer spectacular views.

» Bicycles are easy to rent along the coast and on the islands.

» Some tourist offices, especially in the Kvarner and Istria regions, have maps of routes and can refer you to local bike-rental agencies.

» Cycling on the coast or the mainland requires caution: most roads are busy two-lane highways with no bicycle lanes.

» If you have some Croatian language skills, www.pedala.hr is a great reference for cycling routes around Croatia.

Boat

Jadrolinija Ferries

Jadrolinija operates an extensive network of car ferries and catamarans along the Adriatic coast. Ferries are a lot more comfortable than buses, though somewhat more expensive.

» **Frequency** Year-round. Services are less frequent in winter.

» **Reservations** Cabins should be booked a week ahead. Deck space is usually available on all sailings.

» **Tickets** You must buy tickets in advance at an agency or a Jadrolinija office. Tickets are not sold on board.

» **Cars** Check-in is two hours in advance in summer months.

» **Food** Somewhat mediocre fixed-price menus in on-board restaurants cost about 100KN; the cafeteria only offers ham-and-cheese sandwiches (30KN). Do as the Croats do: bring some food and drink on board with you.

Local Ferries

Local ferries connect the bigger offshore islands with each other and with the mainland, but you'll find many more ferries going from the mainland to the islands than from island to island.

» **Frequency** On most lines, service is less frequent between October and April. Extra passenger boats are added in the summer; these are usually faster, more comfortable and more expensive.

» **Reservations** On some shorter routes (eg Jablanac to Mišnjak), ferries run non-stop in summer and advance reservation is unnecessary.

» **Tickets** Buy at a Jadrolinija office or at a stall near the ferry (usually opens 30 minutes prior to departure).

There are no tickets sales on board. In summer, arrive one to two hours prior to departure, even if you've already bought your ticket.

» **Cars** Incur a charge, calculated according to the size of the car; this is often very pricey. Reserve as far in advance as possible. Check in several hours in advance.

» **Bicycles** Incur a small charge.

» **Food** There is no meal service; you can buy drinks and snacks on board. Most locals bring their own food.

Bus

» Bus services are excellent and relatively inexpensive.

» There are often a number of different companies handling each route, so prices can vary substantially.

» Luggage stowed in the baggage compartment under the bus costs extra (7KN to 10KN a piece, including insurance).

Bus Companies

The companies listed here are among the largest.

Autotrans (☎060 30 20 10; www.autotrans.hr) Based in Rijeka. Connections to Istria, Zagreb, Varaždin and Kvarner.

Brioni Pula (☎052 535 155; www.brioni.hr) Based in Pula. Connections to Istria, Padua, Split, Trieste and Zagreb.

Contus (☎023 317 062) Based in Zadar. Connections to Split and Zagreb.

Croatiabus (☎01-61 13 073; www.croatiabus.hr) Connects Zagreb with towns in Zagorje and Istria.

Samoborček (☎01-48 19 180; www.samoborcek.hr) Connects Zagreb with towns in Dalmatia.

Tickets & Schedules

» At large stations, bus tickets must be purchased at the office, not from drivers.

» Try to book ahead, especially in summer.

» Departure lists above the various windows at bus stations tell you which window sells tickets for your bus.

» On Croatian bus schedules, *vozi svaki dan* means 'every day' and *ne vozi nedjeljom i blagdanom* means 'no service Sunday and holidays'.

» Some buses travel overnight, saving you a night's accommodation. Don't expect to get much sleep, though, as the inside lights will be on and music might be blasting the whole night.

» Take care not to be left behind at meal or rest stops, which usually occur about every two hours.

Car & Motorcycle

Croatia's motorway connecting Zagreb with Split is only a few years old and makes some routes much faster. It is unknown when the 'autoroute' is expected to reach Dubrovnik. Zagreb and Rijeka are now connected by motorway, and an Istrian motorway has shortened the travel time to Italy considerably.

Although the new roads are in excellent condition, there are stretches where service stations and facilities are scarce.

Note that if you are using the motorway to go south towards Dubrovnik, the new road ends suddenly inland, some miles away from the town of Ploče, making the ensuing drive to the coast long and winding.

Car Hire

In order to rent a car

» You must be 21.

» You must have a valid driving licence.

» You must have a major credit card.

Independent local companies are often much cheaper than the international chains, but the big companies offer one-way rentals. Sometimes you can get a lower car-rental rate by booking the car from abroad, or by booking a fly-drive package.

Car Insurance

Third-party public liability insurance is included by law with car rentals, but make sure your quoted price includes full collision insurance, known as a collision damage waiver (CDW). Otherwise, your responsibility for damage done to the vehicle is usually determined as a percentage of the car's value, beginning at around 2000KN.

Driving Licences

Any valid driving licence is sufficient to drive legally and rent a car; an international driving licence is not necessary.

The **Hrvatski Autoklub** (HAK, Croatian Auto Club; ☎46 40 800; www.hak.hr; Avenija Dubrovnik 44) offers help and advice. To get help on the

ROAD DISTANCES (KM)

	Dubrovnik	Osijek	Rijeka	Split	Zadar	Zagreb
Dubrovnik	---					
Osijek	495	---				
Rijeka	601	459	---			
Split	216	494	345	---		
Zadar	340	566	224	139	---	
Zagreb	572	280	182	365	288	---

road, you can contact **HAK road assistance** (Vučna Služba; ☎987).

On the Road

» Petrol stations are generally open from 7am to 7pm, and often until 10pm in summer. Petrol is Eurosuper 95, Super 98, normal or diesel. See www.ina.hr for up-to-date fuel prices.

» You have to pay tolls on all motorways, to use the Učka tunnel between Rijeka and Istria, to use the bridge to Krk Island, and on the road from Rijeka to Delnice.

» For general news on Croatia's motorways and tolls, see www.hak.hr.

» The radio station HR2 broadcasts traffic reports in English every hour on the hour from July to early September.

Road Rules

» In Croatia you drive on the right, and use of seatbelts is mandatory.

» Unless otherwise posted, the speed limits for cars and motorcycles are as follows: 50km/h in built-up areas; 100km/h on main highways; 130km/h on motorways.

» On two-lane highways, it's illegal to pass long military convoys or a line of cars caught behind a slow-moving truck.

» It's illegal to drive with blood-alcohol content higher than 0.05%.

» You are required to drive with your headlights on even during the day.

Local Transport

The main form of local transport is bus (although Zagreb and Osijek also have rather well-developed tram systems).

» Buses in major cities such as Dubrovnik, Rijeka, Split and Zadar run about once every 20 minutes, less often on Sunday.

» A ride is usually 10KN to 15KN, with a small discount if you buy tickets at a *tisak* (news-stand).

» Small medieval towns along the coast are generally closed to traffic and have infrequent links to outlying suburbs.

» Bus transport within the islands is infrequent since most people have their own cars.

Tours

Atlas Travel Agency (www.atlas-croatia.com) Offers a wide variety of bus tours, fly-drive packages and excursions all around Croatia.

Huck Finn (www.huck-finn.hr) Specialises in adventure travel and runs the gamut of adrenaline-lifting tours around Croatia: river and sea kayaking, rafting, canoeing, caving, cycling, fishing, hiking and sailing.

Inselhüpfen (www.island-hopping.de) This German company combines boating and biking and takes an international crowd through southern Dalmatia, Istria or the Kvarner islands, stopping every day for a bike ride.

Katarina Line (www.katarina-line.hr) Offers week-long cruises from Opatija to Split, Mljet, Dubrovnik, Hvar, Brač, Korčula, Zadar and the Kornati Islands on an attractive wooden ship.

Southern Sea Ventures (www.southernseaventures.com) This Australia-based outfitter offers nine- to 16-day sea-kayaking trips in Croatia, including a gourmet kayaking tour.

Train

Trains are less frequent than buses but more comfortable. Note that delays are a regular occurrence on Croatian trains, sometimes for a matter of hours. For information about schedules, prices and services, contact **Croatian Railways** (Hrvatske Željeznice; ☎060 333 444; www.hznet.hr).

Zagreb is the hub for Croatia's less-than-extensive train system. No trains run along the coast and only a few coastal cities are connected with Zagreb. For travellers, the main lines of interest are the following:

» Zagreb–Osijek

» Zagreb–Rijeka–Pula (via Lupoglava, where passengers switch to a bus)

» Zagreb–Varaždin–Koprivnica

USEFUL TRAIN TERMS

Some terms you might encounter posted on timetables at train stations include the following:

» **brzi** – fast train

» **dolazak** – arrivals

» **polazak** – departures

» **ne vozi nedjeljom i blagdanom** – no service Sunday and holidays

» **poslovni** – business-class train

» **presjedanje** – change of trains

» **putnički** – economy-class/local train

» **rezerviranje mjesta obvezatno** – compulsory seat reservation

» **vozi svaki dan** – daily services

» Zagreb–Zadar–Šibenik–Split

Classes and costs:

» Domestic trains are either 'express' or 'passenger' (local).

» Express trains have 1st- and 2nd-class cars, plus smoking and nonsmoking areas.

» A reservation is advisable for express trains.

» Express trains are more expensive than passenger trains.

» Any prices quoted here are for unreserved 2nd-class seating.

» There are no couchettes on domestic services.

» There are sleeping cars on overnight trains between Zagreb and Split.

» Baggage is free on trains; most stations have left-luggage services charging around 15KN a piece per day.

» Travellers who hold a European InterRail pass can use it in Croatia for free travel. Those travelling only in Croatia are unlikely to do enough train travel to justify the cost.

Language

WANT MORE?

For in-depth language information and handy phrases, check out Lonely Planet's *Croatian Phrasebook*. You'll find it at **shop.lonelyplanet.com**, or you can buy Lonely Planet's iPhone phrasebooks at the Apple App Store.

Croatian belongs to the western group of the South Slavic language family. It's similar to other languages in this group, namely Serbian, Bosnian and Montenegrin.

Croatian pronunciation is not difficult – in the Croatian writing system every letter is pronounced and its sound does not vary from word to word. The sounds are pretty close to their English counterparts. Note that in our pronunciation guides n' is pronounced as the 'ny' in 'canyon', and zh as the 's' in 'pleasure'. Keeping these points in mind and reading our coloured pronunciation guides as though they were English, you'll be understood.

Word stress is also relatively easy in Croatian. In most cases the accent falls on the first vowel in the word – the last syllable of a word is never stressed in Croatian. The stressed syllable is indicated with italics in our pronunciation guides.

Some Croatian words have masculine and feminine forms, indicated after the relevant phrases in this chapter by 'm' and 'f'. Polite ('pol') and informal ('inf') alternatives are also shown for some phrases.

BASICS

Hello.	*Bog.*	bog
Goodbye.	*Zbogom.*	*zbo*·gom
Yes./No.	*Da./Ne.*	da/ne
Please.	*Molim.*	*mo*·leem
Thank you.	*Hvala.*	*hva*·la
You're welcome.	*Nema na čemu.*	*ne*·ma na *che*·moo
Excuse me.	*Oprostite.*	o·*pro*·stee·te
Sorry.	*Žao mi je.*	*zha*·o mee ye

How are you?
Kako ste/si? — *ka*·ko ste/see (pol/inf)

Fine. And you?
Dobro. — *do*·bro
A vi/ti? — a vee/tee (pol/inf)

My name is ...
Zovem se ... — *zo*·vem se ...

What's your name?
Kako se zovete/zoveš? — *ka*·ko se *zo*·ve·te/*zo*·vesh (pol/inf)

Do you speak (English)?
Govorite/Govoriš li (engleski)? — *go*·vo·ree·te/*go*·vo·reesh lee (*en*·gle·skee) (pol/inf)

I (don't) understand.
Ja (ne) razumijem. — ya (ne) ra·*zoo*·mee·yem

ACCOMMODATION

Do you have any rooms available?
Imate li slobodnih soba? — *ee*·ma·te lee *slo*·bod·neeh *so*·ba

Is breakfast included?
Da li je doručak uključen? — da lee ye *do*·roo·chak *ook*·lyoo·chen

How much is it (per night/per person)?
Koliko stoji (za noć/po osobi)? — ko·*lee*·ko *sto*·yee (za noch/po *o*·so·bee)

Do you have a ... room?	*Imate li ... sobu?*	*ee*·ma·te lee ... *so*·boo
single	*jednokrevetnu*	*yed*·no·kre·vet·noo
double	*dvokrevetnu*	*dvo*·kre·vet·noo

campsite	*kamp*	kamp
guest house	*privatni smještaj*	*pree*·vat·nee *smyesh*·tai
hotel	*hotel*	*ho*·tel
room	*soba*	*so*·ba
youth hostel	*prenoćište za mladež*	*pre*·no·cheesh·te za *mla*·dezh

air-con	*klima-uređaj*	*klee*·ma·*oo*·re·jai
bathroom	*kupaonica*	koo·pa·o·nee·tsa
bed	*krevet*	*kre*·vet
cot	*dječji krevet*	*dyech*·yee *kre*·vet
wi-fi	*bežični internet*	*be*·zheech·nee *een*·ter·net
window	*prozor*	*pro*·zor

DIRECTIONS

Where is ...?
Gdje je ...? gdye ye ...

What's the address?
Koja je adresa? *ko*·ya ye a·*dre*·sa

Can you show me (on the map)?
Možete li mi to pokazati (na karti)? *mo*·zhe·te lee mee to po·*ka*·za·tee (na *kar*·tee)

at the corner	*na uglu*	na *oo*·gloo
at the traffic lights	*na semaforu*	na *se*·ma·fo·roo
behind	*iza*	*ee*·za
in front of	*ispred*	*ees*·pred
far (from)	*daleko (od)*	*da*·le·ko (od)
left	*lijevo*	lee·*ye*·vo
near	*blizu*	*blee*·zoo
next to	*pored*	*po*·red
opposite	*nasuprot*	*na*·soo·prot
right	*desno*	*de*·sno
straight ahead	*ravno naprijed*	*rav*·no *na*·pree·yed

EATING & DRINKING

What would you recommend?
Što biste nam preporučili? shto *bee*·ste nam pre·po·*roo*·chee·lee

What's in that dish?
Od čega se sastoji ovo jelo? od *che*·ga se *sa*·sto·yee *o*·vo *ye*·lo

That was delicious!
To je bilo izvrsno! to ye *bee*·lo *eez*·vr·sno

Please bring the bill/check.
Molim vas donesite račun. *mo*·leem vas do·*ne*·see·te *ra*·choon

KEY PATTERNS

To get by in Croatian, mix and match these simple patterns with words of your choice:

When's (the next day trip)?
Kada je (idući dnevni izlet)? *ka*·da ye (*ee*·doo·chee *dnev*·nee *eez*·let)

Where's (a market)?
Gdje je (tržnica)? gdye ye (*trzh*·nee·tsa)

Where do I (buy a ticket)?
Gdje mogu (kupiti kartu)? gdye *mo*·goo (*koo*·pee·tee *kar*·too)

Do you have (any others)?
Imate li (kakve druge)? *ee*·ma·te lee (*kak*·ve *droo*·ge)

Is there (a blanket)?
Imate li (deku)? *ee*·ma·te lee (*de*·koo)

I'd like (that dish).
Želim (ono jelo). *zhe*·leem (*o*·no *ye*·lo)

I'd like to (hire a car).
Želio/Željela bih (iznajmiti automobil). *zhe*·lee·o/*zhe*·lye·la beeh (eez·*nai*·mee·tee a·oo·to·*mo*·beel) (m/f)

Can I (take a photograph of you)?
Mogu li (vas/te slikati)? *mo*·goo lee (vas/te *slee*·ka·tee) (pol/inf)

Could you please (help)?
Molim vas, možete li (mi pomoći)? *mo*·leem vas *mo*·zhe·te lee (mee *po*·mo·chee)

Do I have to (pay)?
Trebam li (platiti)? *tre*·bam lee (*pla*·tee·tee)

I'd like to reserve a table for ...	*Želim rezervirati stol za ...*	*zhe*·leem re·zer·*vee*·ra·tee stol za ...
(eight) o'clock	*(osam) sati*	(*o*·sam) *sa*·tee
(two) people	*(dvoje) ljudi*	(*dvo*·ye) *lyoo*·dee

I don't eat ...	*Ja ne jedem ...*	ya ne *ye*·dem ...
fish	*ribu*	*ree*·boo
nuts	*razne orahe*	*raz*·ne *o*·ra·he
poultry	*meso od peradi*	*me*·so od *pe*·ra·dee
red meat	*crveno meso*	*tsr*·ve·no *me*·so

Key Words

appetiser	*predjelo*	*pre*·dye·lo
baby food	*hrana za bebe*	*hra*·na za *be*·be
bar	*bar*	bar

Signs

Izlaz	Exit
Muškarci	Men
Otvoreno	Open
Ulaz	Entrance
Zabranjeno	Prohibited
Zahodi	Toilets
Zatvoreno	Closed
Žene	Women

bottle	*boca*	*bo*·tsa
bowl	*zdjela*	*zdye*·la
breakfast	*doručak*	*do*·roo·chak
cafe	*kafić/ kavana*	*ka*·feech/ ka·*va*·na
(too) cold	*(pre)hladno*	(pre·)*hlad*·no
dinner	*večera*	*ve*·che·ra
dish (food)	*jelo*	*ye*·lo
food	*hrana*	*hra*·na
fork	*viljuška*	*vee*·lyoosh·ka
glass	*čaša*	*cha*·sha
knife	*nož*	nozh
lunch	*ručak*	*roo*·chak
main course	*glavno jelo*	*glav*·no *ye*·lo
market	*tržnica*	*trzh*·nee·tsa
menu	*jelovnik*	ye·*lov*·neek
plate	*tanjur*	*ta*·nyoor
restaurant	*restoran*	re·*sto*·ran
spicy	*pikantno*	pee·*kant*·no
spoon	*žlica*	*zhlee*·tsa
with/without	*sa/bez*	sa/bez
vegetarian meal	*vegetarijanski obrok*	ve·ge·ta·*ree*·yan·skee *o*·brok

Meat & Fish

beef	*govedina*	*go*·ve·dee·na
chicken	*piletina*	*pee*·le·tee·na
fish	*riba*	*ree*·ba
lamb	*janjetina*	*ya*·nye·tee·na
pork	*svinjetina*	*svee*·nye·tee·na
veal	*teletina*	*te*·le·tee·na

Fruit & Vegetables

apple	*jabuka*	*ya*·boo·ka
apricot	*marelica*	ma·*re*·lee·tsa
(green) beans	*mahuna*	*ma*·hoo·na
cabbage	*kupus*	*koo*·poos
carrot	*mrkva*	*mrk*·va
corn	*kukuruz*	koo·*koo*·rooz
cherry	*trešnja*	*tresh*·nya
cucumber	*krastavac*	*kra*·sta·vats
fruit	*voće*	*vo*·che
grape	*grožđe*	*grozh*·je
lentils	*leća*	*le*·cha
lettuce/salad	*zelena salata*	ze·le·na sa·*la*·ta
mushroom	*gljiva*	*glyee*·va
nut	*orah*	*o*·rah
onion	*luk*	look
orange	*naranča*	*na*·ran·cha
peach	*breskva*	*bres*·kva
pear	*kruška*	*kroosh*·ka
peas	*grašak*	*gra*·shak
plum	*šljiva*	*shlyee*·va
potato	*krumpir*	*kroom*·peer
pumpkin	*bundeva*	*boon*·de·va
strawberry	*jagoda*	*ya*·go·da
tomato	*rajčica*	*rai*·chee·tsa
vegetable	*povrće*	*po*·vr·che
watermelon	*lubenica*	loo·*be*·nee·tsa

Other

bread	*kruh*	krooh
butter	*maslac*	*ma*·slats
cheese	*sir*	seer
egg	*jaje*	*ya*·ye
honey	*med*	med
jam	*džem*	jem
oil	*ulje*	*oo*·lye
pasta	*tjestenina*	tye·ste·*nee*·na
pepper	*papar*	*pa*·par
rice	*riža*	*ree*·zha
salt	*sol*	sol
sugar	*šećer*	*she*·cher
vinegar	*ocat*	*o*·tsat

Drinks

beer	*pivo*	*pee*·vo
coffee	*kava*	*ka*·va
juice	*sok*	sok
milk	*mlijeko*	mlee·*ye*·ko
(mineral) water	*(mineralna) voda*	(*mee*·ne·ral·na) *vo*·da
tea	*čaj*	chai
(red/white) wine	*(crno/bijelo) vino*	(*tsr*·no/*bye*·lo) *vee*·no

EMERGENCIES

Help!
Upomoć! oo·po·moch

I'm lost.
Izgubio/ Izgubila sam se. eez·goo·bee·o/ eez·goo·bee·la sam se (m/f)

Leave me alone!
Ostavite me na miru! o·sta·vee·te me na *mee*·roo

There's been an accident!
Desila se nezgoda! de·see·la se *nez*·go·da

Call a doctor!
Zovite liječnika! zo·vee·te lee·*yech*·nee·ka

Call the police!
Zovite policiju! zo·vee·te po·*lee*·tsee·yoo

I'm ill.
Ja sam bolestan/ bolesna. ya sam *bo*·le·stan/ *bo*·le·sna (m/f)

It hurts here.
Boli me ovdje. *bo*·lee me *ov*·dye

I'm allergic to ...
Ja sam alergičan/ alergična na ... ya sam a·*ler*·gee·chan/ a·*ler*·geech·na na ... (m/f)

SHOPPING & SERVICES

I'd like to buy ...
Želim kupiti ... zhe·leem *koo*·pee·tee ...

I'm just looking.
Ja samo razgledam. ya *sa*·mo *raz*·gle·dam

May I look at it?
Mogu li to pogledati? *mo*·goo lee to *po*·gle·da·tee

How much is it?
Koliko stoji? ko·*lee*·ko *sto*·yee

That's too expensive.
To je preskupo. to ye *pre*·skoo·po

Do you have something cheaper?
Imate li nešto jeftinije? ee·ma·te lee *nesh*·to yef·tee·nee·ye

There's a mistake in the bill.
Ima jedna greška na računu. ee·ma *yed*·na *gresh*·ka na ra·*choo*·noo

ATM	*bankovni automat*	*ban*·kov·nee a·oo·*to*·mat
credit card	*kreditna kartica*	*kre*·deet·na *kar*·tee·tsa
internet cafe	*internet kafić*	*een*·ter·net *ka*·feech

Question Words

How?	*Kako?*	*ka*·ko
What?	*Što?*	shto
When?	*Kada?*	*ka*·da
Where?	*Gdje?*	gdye
Who?	*Tko?*	tko
Why?	*Zašto?*	*za*·shto

post office	*poštanski ured*	*posh*·tan·skee *oo*·red
tourist office	*turistička agencija*	too·*ree*·steech·ka a·*gen*·tsee·ya

TIME & DATES

What time is it?
Koliko je sati? ko·*lee*·ko ye *sa*·tee

It's (10) o'clock.
(Deset) je sati. (*de*·set) ye *sa*·tee

Half past (10).
(Deset) i po. (*de*·set) ee po

morning	*jutro*	*yoo*·tro
afternoon	*poslijepodne*	*po*·slee·ye·*pod*·ne
evening	*večer*	*ve*·cher
yesterday	*jučer*	*yoo*·cher
today	*danas*	*da*·nas
tomorrow	*sutra*	*soo*·tra

Monday	*ponedjeljak*	po·*ne*·dye·lyak
Tuesday	*utorak*	*oo*·to·rak
Wednesday	*srijeda*	*sree*·ye·da
Thursday	*četvrtak*	chet·*vr*·tak
Friday	*petak*	*pe*·tak
Saturday	*subota*	*soo*·bo·ta
Sunday	*nedjelja*	*ne*·dye·lya

January	*siječanj*	see·*ye*·chan'
February	*veljača*	*ve*·lya·cha
March	*ožujak*	o·zhoo·yak
April	*travanj*	*tra*·van'
May	*svibanj*	*svee*·ban'
June	*lipanj*	*lee*·pan'
July	*srpanj*	*sr*·pan'
August	*kolovoz*	*ko*·lo·voz
September	*rujanj*	*roo*·yan'
October	*listopad*	*lee*·sto·pad
November	*studeni*	*stoo*·de·nee
December	*prosinac*	*pro*·see·nats

TRANSPORT

Public Transport

boat	*brod*	brod
bus	*autobus*	a·oo·*to*·boos
plane	*avion*	a·*vee*·on
train	*vlak*	vlak
tram	*tramvaj*	*tram*·vai

Numbers

1	*jedan*	*ye*·dan
2	*dva*	dva
3	*tri*	tree
4	*četiri*	*che*·tee·ree
5	*pet*	pet
6	*šest*	shest
7	*sedam*	*se*·dam
8	*osam*	*o*·sam
9	*devet*	*de*·vet
10	*deset*	*de*·set
20	*dvadeset*	*dva*·de·set
30	*trideset*	*tree*·de·set
40	*četrdeset*	che·tr·*de*·set
50	*pedeset*	pe·*de*·set
60	*šezdeset*	shez·*de*·set
70	*sedamdeset*	se·dam·*de*·set
80	*osamdeset*	o·sam·*de*·set
90	*devedeset*	de·ve·*de*·set
100	*sto*	sto
1000	*tisuću*	*tee*·soo·choo

I want to go to ...
Želim da idem u ... — *zhe*·leem da *ee*·dem oo ...

Does it stop at (Split)?
Da li staje u (Splitu)? — da lee *sta*·ye oo (*splee*·too)

What time does it leave?
U koliko sati kreće? — oo ko·*lee*·ko *sa*·tee *kre*·che

What time does it get to (Zagreb)?
U koliko sati stiže u (Zagreb)? — oo ko·*lee*·ko *sa*·tee *stee*·zhe oo (*zag*·reb)

Could you tell me when we get to (the Arena)?
Možete li mi reći kada stignemo kod (Arene)? — *mo*·zhe·te lee mee *re*·chee *ka*·da *steeg*·ne·mo kod (a·*re*·ne)

I'd like to get off at (Dubrovnik).
Želim izaći u (Dubrovniku). — *zhe*·leem ee·*za*·chee oo (*doob*·rov·nee·koo)

A ... ticket.	*Jednu ... kartu.*	*yed*·noo ... *kar*·too
1st-class	*prvorazrednu*	pr·vo·*raz*·red·noo
2nd-class	*drugorazrednu*	*droo*·go·*raz*·red·noo
one-way	*jednosmjernu*	*yed*·no·smyer·noo
return	*povratnu*	*po*·vrat·noo

the first	*prvi*	*pr*·vee
the last	*posljednji*	*pos*·lyed·nyee
the next	*sljedeći*	*slye*·de·chee

aisle seat	*sjedište do prolaza*	*sye*·deesh·te do *pro*·la·za
delayed	*u zakašnjenju*	oo za·kash·*nye*·nyoo
cancelled	*poništeno*	*po*·neesh·te·no
platform	*peron*	*pe*·ron
ticket office	*blagajna*	*bla*·gai·na
timetable	*red vožnje*	red *vozh*·nye
train station	*željeznička postaja*	*zhe*·lyez·neech·ka *pos*·ta·ya
window seat	*sjedište do prozora*	*sye*·deesh·te do *pro*·zo·ra

Driving & Cycling

I'd like to hire a ...	*Želim iznajmiti ...*	*zhe*·leem eez·*nai*·mee·tee ...
4WD	*džip*	jeep
bicycle	*bicikl*	bee·*tsee*·kl
car	*automobil*	a·oo·to·*mo*·beel
motorcycle	*motocikl*	mo·to·*tsee*·kl

bicycle pump	*pumpa za bicikl*	*poom*·pa za bee·*tsee*·kl
child seat	*sjedalo za dijete*	*sye*·da·lo za dee·*ye*·te
diesel	*dizel gorivo*	*dee*·zel *go*·ree·vo
helmet	*kaciga*	*ka*·tsee·ga
mechanic	*auto-mehaničar*	*a*·oo·to·me·*ha*·nee·char
petrol/gas	*benzin*	*ben*·zeen
service station	*benziska stanica*	*ben*·zeen·ska *sta*·nee·tsa

Is this the road to ...?
Je li ovo cesta za ...? — ye lee *o*·vo *tse*·sta za ...

(How long) Can I park here?
(Koliko dugo) Mogu ovdje parkirati? — (ko·*lee*·ko *doo*·go) *mo*·goo *ov*·dye par·*kee*·ra·tee

The car/motorbike has broken down (at Knin).
Automobil/ Motocikl se pokvario (u Kninu). — a·oo·to·*mo*·beel/ mo·to·*tsee*·kl se pok·*va*·ree·o (oo *knee*·noo)

I have a flat tyre.
Imam probušenu gumu. — ee·mam *pro*·boo·she·noo *goo*·moo

I've run out of petrol.
Nestalo mi je benzina. — *ne*·sta·lo mee ye ben·*zee*·na

I've lost the keys.
Izgubio/ Izgubila sam ključeve. — eez·*goo*·bee·o/ eez·*goo*·bee·la sam *klyoo*·che·ve (m/f)

GLOSSARY

(m) indicates masculine gender, (f) feminine gender and (pl) plural

amphora (s), **amphorae** (pl) – large, two-handled vase in which wine or water was kept

apse – altar area of a church

autocamps – gigantic campgrounds with restaurants, shops and row upon row of caravans

Avars – Eastern European people who waged war against Byzantium from the 6th to 9th centuries

ban – viceroy or governor

bb – in an address the letters 'bb' following a street name (such as Placa bb) stand for *bez broja* (without number), which indicates that the building has no street number

bura – cold northeasterly wind

cesta – road

crkva – church

fortica – fortress

galerija – gallery

garderoba – left-luggage office

Glagolitic – ancient Slavonic language put into writing by Greek missionaries Cyril and Methodius

gora – mountain

HDZ – Hrvatska Demokratska Zajednica; Croatian Democratic Union

Illyrians – ancient inhabitants of the Adriatic coast, defeated by the Romans in the 2nd century BC

karst – highly porous limestone and dolomitic rock

klapa – an outgrowth of church-choir singing

konoba – the traditional term for a small, intimate dining spot, often located in a cellar; now applies to a wide variety of restaurants; usually a simple, family-run establishment

knez – duke

maestral – strong, steady westerly wind

mali – small

maquis – dense growth of mostly evergreen shrubs and small trees

muzej – museum

nave – central part of a church flanked by two aisles

NDH – Nezavisna Država Hrvatska; Independent State of Croatia

obala – waterfront

otok (s), **otoci** (pl) – island

pansion – guesthouse

plaža – beach

polje – collapsed limestone area often under cultivation

put – path, trail

restoran – restaurant

rijeka – river

sabor – parliament

šetalište – walkway

sobe – rooms available

sveti – saint

svetog – saint (genitive case – ie of saint, as in the Church of St Joseph)

tamburica – a three- or five-string mandolin

tisak – news-stand

toplice – spa

trg – square

turbo folk – a techno version of Serbian folk music

ulica – street

uvala – bay

velik – large

vrh – summit, peak

zimmer – rooms available (a German word)

behind the scenes

SEND US YOUR FEEDBACK

We love to hear from travellers – your comments keep us on our toes and help make our books better. Our well-travelled team reads every word on what you loved or loathed about this book. Although we cannot reply individually to postal submissions, we always guarantee that your feedback goes straight to the appropriate authors, in time for the next edition. Each person who sends us information is thanked in the next edition – the most useful submissions are rewarded with a selection of digital PDF chapters.

Visit **lonelyplanet.com/contact** to submit your updates and suggestions or to ask for help. Our award-winning website also features inspirational travel stories, news and discussions.

Note: We may edit, reproduce and incorporate your comments in Lonely Planet products such as guidebooks, websites and digital products, so let us know if you don't want your comments reproduced or your name acknowledged. For a copy of our privacy policy visit lonelyplanet.com/privacy.

OUR READERS

Many thanks to the travellers who used the last edition and wrote to us with helpful hints, useful advice and interesting anecdotes:

Andrea Bartlett, Marlene Beard, Rolf Beckmann, Austin Bernhardt, Silvia Borelli, Nikki Buran, Pinar Caglayan Mcgivern, Albert Castell & Cristina Domínguez, Chere Chancey, Nt Cheung, Maris Cosmai, Jennifer Crawford, Josep Franch, Susan Gilchrist, Sharon Goodchild, Marc Grayson, Patrick Harris, Lara Insam, Anders Jeppsson, Dean Kenyon, George Kingston, Jasmina Krkić Poznić, Ilana Leppert, Catherine Macpherson, Martina Maggio, Ava Mandal, Sofia Mårtensson, Matt Mclennan, Aishling Middelburg, Desi Mier, Ivan Mikulic, Anke Moseler, Laurissa Mühlich, Callista Mulder, Roger Muller, Alex Nagtzaam, Luke Pearce, Rosie Pearce, Holger Peter, Michael Poesen, Marjory Powell, Douglas Press, Vanja Radovanović, Erhan Raif, Svenja Reiter, Stijepo Sanje, Jacques Schildknecht, Becky Shaw, Aida Simil, Adrijan Stermasi, Anton Stout, Finn Thilsted, Ciska Tillema, David Torrance, Jeanne Trojan, Nino Uremović, Roos Verhooren, Ian Winlaw and Carina Zingenberg.

AUTHOR THANKS

Anja Mutić

Hvala mama, for your home cooking and contagious laughter. *Obrigada,* Hoji, for being there before, during and after. A huge *hvala* to my friends in Croatia who gave me endless recommendations – this book wouldn't be the same without you. Special thanks go to Lidija in Zagreb and Mila in Split, as well as Viviana Vukelić, Petra Posilović and Dubravka Mičić at HTZ. Vesna, you're a fab coauthor! Finally, to the inspiring memory of my father who travels with me still.

Vesna Maric

Biggest thanks go to Rafael and Frida and my mother. Huge *hvalas* are due to the star crew in Rijeka: Mirna, Tomica and Eda. Massive thanks to Sanja and Jon, and beautiful Irian, in Dubrovnik. *Hvalas* to lovely Maja Gilja in Zagreb. Big thanks and always a pleasure to work with my coordinating author Anja Mutić, and a thanks to our commissioning editor Joanna Cooke for giving me the chance to work on this guide again.

THIS BOOK

This 7th edition of Lonely Planet's *Croatia* guidebook was researched and written by Anja Mutić and Vesna Maric. The previous edition was written by Anja Mutić and Iain Stewart, and the 5th edition was written by Anja Mutić and Vesna Maric with William Gourlay writing the History chapter. This guidebook was commissioned in Lonely Planet's London office, and produced by the following:

Commissioning Editors Joanna Cooke, James Smart

Coordinating Editors Susie Ashworth, Rebecca Currie

Coordinating Cartographer Julyon Philcox

Coordinating Layout Designer Jessica Rose

Managing Editor Sasha Baskett

Senior Editor Andi Jones

Managing Cartographers Alison Lyall, Anthony Phelan

Managing Layout Designer Chris Girdler

Assisting Editors Andrew Bain, Jessica Crouch, Gordon Farrer, Robyn Loughnane, Anne Mulvaney, Jenna Myers

Assisting Cartographer Rachel Imeson

Cover Research Naomi Parker

Internal Image Research Aude Vauconsant

Language Content Branislava Vladisavljevic

Thanks to Dan Austin, Kate Chapman, Ryan Evans, Jennifer Fernández, Larissa Frost, Tobias Gatineau, Jouve India, Asha Ioculari, Kate McDonell, Anna Metcalfe, Trent Paton, Raphael Richards, Averil Robertson, Fiona Siseman, Gerard Walker and Danny Williams.

ACKNOWLEDGMENTS

Climate map data adapted from Peel MC, Finlayson BL & McMahon TA (2007) 'Updated World Map of the Köppen Geiger Climate Classification', *Hydrology and Earth System Sciences*, 11, 163344.

Cover photograph: Dubrovnik. Johanna Huber/4Corners.

D

E

000 Map pages
000 Photo pages

000 Map pages
000 Photo pages

how to use this book

These symbols will help you find the listings you want:

- Sights
- Beaches
- Activities
- Courses
- Tours
- Festivals & Events
- Sleeping
- Eating
- Drinking
- Entertainment
- Shopping
- Information/ Transport

These symbols give you the vital information for each listing:

- Telephone Numbers
- Opening Hours
- Parking
- Nonsmoking
- Air-Conditioning
- Internet Access
- Wi-Fi Access
- Swimming Pool
- Vegetarian Selection
- English-Language Menu
- Family-Friendly
- Pet-Friendly
- Bus
- Ferry
- Metro
- Subway
- London Tube
- Tram
- Train

Reviews are organised by author preference.

Look out for these icons:

TOP CHOICE Our author's recommendation

FREE No payment required

A green or sustainable option

Our authors have nominated these places as demonstrating a strong commitment to sustainability – for example by supporting local communities and producers, operating in an environmentally friendly way, or supporting conservation projects.

Map Legend

Sights
- Beach
- Buddhist
- Castle
- Christian
- Hindu
- Islamic
- Jewish
- Monument
- Museum/Gallery
- Ruin
- Winery/Vineyard
- Zoo
- Other Sight

Activities, Courses & Tours
- Diving/Snorkelling
- Canoeing/Kayaking
- Skiing
- Surfing
- Swimming/Pool
- Walking
- Windsurfing
- Other Activity/ Course/Tour

Sleeping
- Sleeping
- Camping

Eating
- Eating

Drinking
- Drinking
- Cafe

Entertainment
- Entertainment

Shopping
- Shopping

Information
- Post Office
- Tourist Information

Transport
- Airport
- Border Crossing
- Bus
- Cable Car/ Funicular
- Cycling
- Ferry
- Monorail
- Parking
- S-Bahn
- Taxi
- Train/Railway
- Tram
- Tube Station
- U-Bahn
- Underground Train Station
- Other Transport

Routes
- Tollway
- Freeway
- Primary
- Secondary
- Tertiary
- Lane
- Unsealed Road
- Plaza/Mall
- Steps
- Tunnel
- Pedestrian Overpass
- Walking Tour
- Walking Tour Detour
- Path

Boundaries
- International
- State/Province
- Disputed
- Regional/Suburb
- Marine Park
- Cliff
- Wall

Population
- Capital (National)
- Capital (State/Province)
- City/Large Town
- Town/Village

Geographic
- Hut/Shelter
- Lighthouse
- Lookout
- Mountain/Volcano
- Oasis
- Park
- Pass
- Picnic Area
- Waterfall

Hydrography
- River/Creek
- Intermittent River
- Swamp/Mangrove
- Reef
- Canal
- Water
- Dry/Salt/ Intermittent Lake
- Glacier

Areas
- Beach/Desert
- Cemetery (Christian)
- Cemetery (Other)
- Park/Forest
- Sportsground
- Sight (Building)
- Top Sight (Building)

OUR STORY

A beat-up old car, a few dollars in the pocket and a sense of adventure. In 1972 that's all Tony and Maureen Wheeler needed for the trip of a lifetime – across Europe and Asia overland to Australia. It took several months, and at the end – broke but inspired – they sat at their kitchen table writing and stapling together their first travel guide, *Across Asia on the Cheap*. Within a week they'd sold 1500 copies. Lonely Planet was born.

Today, Lonely Planet has offices in Melbourne, London, Oakland and Delhi, with more than 600 staff and writers. We share Tony's belief that 'a great guidebook should do three things: inform, educate and amuse'.

OUR WRITERS

Anja Mutić

Coordinating Author, Zagreb, Zagorje, Slavonia, Istria, Split & Central Dalmatia It's been more than two decades since Anja left her native Croatia. The journey took her to several countries before she made New York City her base 13 years ago. But the roots are a'calling. She's been returning to Croatia frequently for work and play, intent on discovering a new place on every visit, be it a nature park, an offbeat town or a remote island. She's happy that Croatia's beauties are appreciated worldwide, but secretly longs for the time when you could head to Hvar and hear the sound of crickets instead of blasting music. Anja also wrote the Welcome to Croatia, 17 Top Experiences, Need to Know, What's New, If You Like, Month by Month, Itineraries, Regions at a Glance, Croatia Today, Culture & People and The Cuisine chapters.

Read more about Anja at: lonelyplanet.com/members/anjamutic

Vesna Maric

Kvarner, Northern Dalmatia, Dubrovnik & Southern Dalmatia Vesna was born in Mostar, Bosnia and Hercegovina, but has always cherished the Adriatic coast above all other places. Getting a chance to revisit her beloved Dubrovnik and Zadar, and discover the Kvarner coast and islands, has made her fall in love with Croatia all over again, despite the numerous sea urchins determined to make their way into her heels. For this edition, she particularly loved wandering the tiny streets of Rab Town, swimming off quiet coves on the islands of Lošinj and Cres, and tasting sushi in Dubrovnik, all with her two-year-old in tow. Vesna also wrote the Travel with Children, History, The Natural Environment, The Arts, Directory A–Z and Transport chapters.

Published by Lonely Planet Publications Pty Ltd
ABN 36 005 607 983
7th edition – April 2013
ISBN 978 1 74220 302 7

10 9 8 7 6 5 4 3 2 1
Printed in China